Full Stack Development with Microsoft Blazor

Building Web, Mobile, and Desktop Applications in .NET 8 and Beyond

Fourth Edition

Peter Himschoot

apress®

Full Stack Development with Microsoft Blazor: Building Web, Mobile, and Desktop Applications in .NET 8 and Beyond, Fourth Edition

Peter Himschoot
U2U-Developer and IT Training
Zellik, Belgium

ISBN-13 (pbk): 979-8-8688-1006-0 ISBN-13 (electronic): 979-8-8688-1007-7
https://doi.org/10.1007/979-8-8688-1007-7

Copyright © 2024 by Peter Himschoot

This work is subject to copyright. All rights are reserved by the Publisher, whether the whole or part of the material is concerned, specifically the rights of translation, reprinting, reuse of illustrations, recitation, broadcasting, reproduction on microfilms or in any other physical way, and transmission or information storage and retrieval, electronic adaptation, computer software, or by similar or dissimilar methodology now known or hereafter developed.

Trademarked names, logos, and images may appear in this book. Rather than use a trademark symbol with every occurrence of a trademarked name, logo, or image we use the names, logos, and images only in an editorial fashion and to the benefit of the trademark owner, with no intention of infringement of the trademark.

The use in this publication of trade names, trademarks, service marks, and similar terms, even if they are not identified as such, is not to be taken as an expression of opinion as to whether or not they are subject to proprietary rights.

While the advice and information in this book are believed to be true and accurate at the date of publication, neither the authors nor the editors nor the publisher can accept any legal responsibility for any errors or omissions that may be made. The publisher makes no warranty, express or implied, with respect to the material contained herein.

Managing Director, Apress Media LLC: Welmoed Spahr
Acquisitions Editor: Shaul Elson
Development Editor: Laura Berendson
Editorial Assistant: Gryffin Winkler

Cover designed by eStudioCalamar

Distributed to the book trade worldwide by Springer Science+Business Media New York, 1 New York Plaza, Suite 4600, New York, NY 10004-1562, USA. Phone 1-800-SPRINGER, fax (201) 348-4505, e-mail orders-ny@springer-sbm.com, or visit www.springeronline.com. Apress Media, LLC is a California LLC and the sole member (owner) is Springer Science + Business Media Finance Inc (SSBM Finance Inc). SSBM Finance Inc is a **Delaware** corporation.

For information on translations, please e-mail booktranslations@springernature.com; for reprint, paperback, or audio rights, please e-mail bookpermissions@springernature.com.

Apress titles may be purchased in bulk for academic, corporate, or promotional use. eBook versions and licenses are also available for most titles. For more information, reference our Print and eBook Bulk Sales web page at http://www.apress.com/bulk-sales.

Any source code or other supplementary material referenced by the author in this book is available to readers on GitHub. For more detailed information, please visit https://www.apress.com/gp/services/source-code.

If disposing of this product, please recycle the paper

Table of Contents

About the Author xix

Introduction xxi

Chapter 1: Introduction to Blazor 1

    A Tale of Two Wars 1

        The First Browser War 1

        The Second Browser War 3

    Introducing WebAssembly 3

        Which Browsers Support WebAssembly? 6

        WebAssembly and Mono 6

    Interacting with the Browser with Blazor 7

        Blazor Static Website 7

        Blazor WebAssembly 7

        Blazor Server 9

        Blazor Server vs. Blazor WebAssembly 11

        Blazor Auto Rendering 12

    Your First Blazor Project 12

        Installing Blazor Prerequisites 12

        Understanding the Blazor Templates for VS/Code 16

        Running the Generated Project 20

    Examining the Project's Parts 21

        Dependency Injection and Middleware 22

        Required JavaScript 23

        Project Structure 24

        Layout Components 24

TABLE OF CONTENTS

Debugging Blazor 26
    Debugging with Visual Studio 26
    Debugging with Visual Studio Code 28
Developing with Hot Reload 29
    Hot Reload with .NET CLI 30
    Hot Reload with Visual Studio 30
The Blazor Bootstrap Process 31
    Blazor WASM 31
The Blazor Server Bootstrap Process 34
Nullable Reference Types 36
    An Apology 36
    Using Null in C# 36
    Using References 39
    The Null Forgiving Operator 40
    Required Properties 41
    Nullable Reference Types and .NET Libraries 41
Summary 42

Chapter 2: Components and Structure for Blazor Applications 43

A Quick Look at Razor 43
    Using @ 44
    Control Structures 44
    Razor Comments 45
    Razor Directives 45
    Directive Attributes 45
What Is a Blazor Component? 46
    Examining the Generated Code 47
Building a Simple Alert Component with Razor 50
    Create a New Component with Visual Studio 50
    Create a New Component with Code 51
    Implement the Alert Component 51

EditorRequired	53
Components and Namespaces	54
Separating View and View Model	56
Create a DismissibleAlert Component	56
Styling Components	58
CSS Isolation	58
Child Components and CSS Isolation	60
Logging for Components	60
Logging with Blazor Server	62
Logging with Blazor WebAssembly	62
Logging in Program.cs	64
Summary	64

Chapter 3: Data Binding 65

One-Way Data Binding	65
One-Way Data Binding Syntax	66
Attribute Binding	67
Conditional Attributes	68
Event Handling and Data Binding	69
Event Binding Syntax	69
Event Arguments	70
Using C# Lambda Functions	71
Two-Way Data Binding	71
Two-Way Data Binding Syntax	71
Two-Way Explicit Binding	73
Binding to Other Events: @bind-value:{event}	74
Preventing Default Actions	75
Stopping Event Propagation	77
Formatting Dates	79
Change Detection	79
Updating the UI Using StateHasChanged	81
Understanding Parent–Child Communication	82

TABLE OF CONTENTS

    One-Way Data Binding Between Components 82

    Add a Delay Component 84

    Use Two-Way Component to Component Data Binding 87

    Add Support for Two-Way Data Binding 87

    Fixing the Delay Component 90

Data Binding Side Effects 92

Referring to a Child Component 95

The PizzaPlace Single-Page Application 96

    Creating the PizzaPlace Project 96

    Adding Shared Classes to Represent the Data 97

    Building the UI to Show the Menu 99

    The Menu Component 101

    Debugging Tip 105

    The Shopping Basket Component 106

Summary 110

Chapter 4: Forms and Validation 111

HTML Forms 111

Blazor Forms 113

Blazor Validation 120

    Using DataAnnotations 120

    Showing Validation Feedback 122

    Customizing the Validation Feedback 124

Custom Validation 126

Using Fluent Validation 133

    DataAnnotations, Fluent or Custom Validation? 135

Disabling the Submit Button 135

Entering the PizzaPlace Customer 137

    Add the Customer Class 138

    Implement the CustomerEntry Component 139

    Add Fluent Validation 142

TABLE OF CONTENTS

    Adding Two-Way Data Binding 144

    Notifying the Parent Component 145

  Summary.. 147

Chapter 5: Services and Dependency Injection 149

  What Is Dependency Inversion?... 149

    Understanding Dependency Inversion 150

    Using the Dependency Inversion Principle 151

  Adding Dependency Injection... 153

    Use an Inversion-of-Control Container 154

    Constructor Dependency Injection... 154

    Property Dependency Injection.. 155

  Configuring Dependency Injection 156

    Singleton Dependencies.. 158

    Transient Dependencies 159

    Scoped Dependencies 160

  Understanding Blazor Dependency Lifetime 160

    Blazor WebAssembly Experiment 162

    Blazor Server Experiment.. 165

    Using OwningComponentBase 167

    The Result of the Experiment 169

  Dependency Injection with .NET 8 and 9 170

    .NET 8 Keyed Services... 170

    .NET 9 Constructor Injection 172

  Building Pizza Services.. 172

    Adding the MenuService and IMenuService Abstraction............................ 173

    Ordering Pizzas with a Service 177

  Summary... 179

Chapter 6: Component Life Cycle Hooks 181

  Life Cycle Overview.. 181

    Constructor 184

    IDisposable 184

vii

TABLE OF CONTENTS

SetParametersAsync 184

OnParametersSet and OnParametersSetAsync 185

OnInitialized and OnInitializedAsync 189

ShouldRender 190

OnAfterRender and OnAfterRenderAsync 193

IDisposable 194

A Word on Asynchronous Methods 195

Summary 196

Chapter 7: Advanced Components 197

Communicating with Cascading Parameters 197

Use the CascadingValue Component 198

Resolving Ambiguities with Multiple Values 201

Fixed Cascading Values 203

Root-Level Cascading Values 204

Using Templated Components 205

Create the Grid Templated Component 205

Use the Grid Templated Component 207

Specify the Type Parameter's Type Explicitly 211

Using Generic Type Constraints 211

Razor Templates 212

Wig-Pig Syntax 214

Using Blazor Error Boundaries 217

Virtualization 222

Display a Large Number of Rows 222

Use the Virtualize Component 227

Add Paging 228

Attribute Splatting 232

Referring to a Component 233

Component Reuse and PizzaPlace 235

TABLE OF CONTENTS

Add the PizzaItem Component 235
Create the ItemList Templated Component 237
Summary 240

Chapter 8: Component Libraries 241
Building a Component Library 241
Create the Component Library Project 241
Add Components to the Library 242
Refer to the Library from Your Project 243
Using the Library Components 244
Static Resources in a Component Library 245
Summary 247

Chapter 9: Built-In Components 249
Public Component Libraries 249
Microsoft FluentUI 249
MudBlazor 251
Blazor Bootstrap 252
Blazorise 253
Telerik UI for Blazor 254
Others 254
PageTitle, HeadContent, and HeadOutlet 254
PageTitle 256
HeadContent and HeadOutlet 257
Dynamic Components 258
Uploading Files with InputFile 268
Add the InputFile Component 268
Implement the Server UploadService 272
Implement the WASM UploadService 275
QuickGrid 277
The Starter Project 277
Add a Simple QuickGrid 279

ix

TABLE OF CONTENTS

  Sort Columns 281

  Use Template Columns 282

  Add Filtered Columns 286

  Fix Layout 289

  Add Pagination 290

  Use Virtualization 291

 Summary 291

Chapter 10: Routing 293

 What Is a Single-Page Application? 293

  Single-Page Applications 294

 Layout Components 294

  Using Blazor Layout Components 294

  Configure the Default Layout Component 296

  Selecting a Layout Component 297

  Nesting Layouts 299

  The NavMenu Component 300

 Blazor Routing 303

  Installing the Router 303

  FocusOnNavigate 304

  Setting the Route Template 304

  Route Constraints 306

  Catch-All Route Parameters 306

  Routing and Component Libraries 307

 Redirecting to Other Pages 308

 Navigation Interception 310

 Understanding the Base Tag 312

 Constant-Based Routing 312

 Lazy Loading with Routing 313

  Lazy Loading Component Libraries 313

  Marking an Assembly for Lazy Loading 315

  Dynamically Loading an Assembly 316

x

TABLE OF CONTENTS

Lazy Loading and Dependency Injection 318

Adding Another Page to PizzaPlace 321

Summary 330

Chapter 11: Blazor Render Modes 331

Server-Side Rendering 331

    Examine a SSR Project 331

    Enhanced Navigation 335

    Streaming Rendering 338

    SSR and Forms 340

Interactive Server 341

    Examine a Blazor Server Web App 342

    Render Modes 345

    Setting the Render Mode 345

Interactive WebAssembly 347

    Examine a Blazor WASM Web App 348

Interactive Auto 350

    Examine a Blazor Server Auto Web App 350

    Using a Component with Difference Render Modes 353

Detecting the Current Render Mode 354

    Using RenderModeProvider 358

    Detecting RenderMode in .NET 9 360

Prerendering 361

    Disabling Prerendering 361

    Supporting Prerendering 362

State Persistence 364

    Using PersistentComponentState 364

Summary 367

Chapter 12: JavaScript Interoperability 369

Calling JavaScript from C# 369

    Providing a Glue Function 369

    Using IJSRuntime to Call the Glue Function 370

xi

TABLE OF CONTENTS

    Storing Data in the Browser with Interop 370

    Use OnAfterRenderAsync 374

Passing a Reference to JavaScript 375

Calling .NET Methods from JavaScript 379

    Adding a Glue Function Taking a .NET Instance 379

Using Services for Interop 381

    Building the LocalStorage Service 382

    Setting Focus to an Input Element 386

Dynamically Loading JavaScript with Modules 387

    Using JavaScript Modules 387

    Loading the Module into a Blazor Service 388

Adding a Map to PizzaPlace 390

    Choosing the Map JavaScript Library 390

    Adding the Leaflet Library 390

    Building the Leaflet Map Razor Library 391

    Registering with the Map Provider 394

    Creating the Map Component 395

    Consuming the Map Component 396

    Adding Markers to the Map 398

Summary 401

Chapter 13: Testing Components with BUnit 403

Where Can We Find Bugs? 403

    Requirements 404

    Coding 404

    Integration 405

    Beta-Testing 405

    Post-release 406

Why Should We Use Unit Tests? 406

    What Makes a Good Unit Test? 406

TABLE OF CONTENTS

Unit Testing Blazor Components 407
- Adding a Unit Test Project 407
- Adding bUnit to the Test Project 408

Write Your First Unit Test 409
- Writing Good Unit Test Methods 409
- Running Your Tests 410
- Making Your Test Pass 411

Facts and Theories 412
- Checking Your Sanity 413

Write bUnit Tests with C# 415
- Understanding bUnit 415
- Testing Component Interaction 419
- Passing Parameters to Our Component 421
- Testing Two-Way Data Binding and Events 425
- Testing Components That Use RenderFragment 427
- Using Cascading Parameters 435

Using NSubstitute to Create Fake Implementations 437
- Injecting Dependencies with bUnit 437
- Replacing Dependencies with Fake Objects 440
- Using Stubs 441
- Using Mocks 443
- Building Stubs and Mocks with NSubstitute 447

Writing bUnit Tests in Razor 449
- The First Razor Test 450

Handling Asynchronous Re-renders 453

Configuring Semantic Compare 456
- Why Do We Need Semantic Compare? 456
- Customizing Semantic Compare 457

Summary 459

xiii

TABLE OF CONTENTS

Chapter 14: Communication 461

Examining the Server Project 461
The Server Project 461
Adding a WebAPI Endpoint 463
The Client Project 464
The WeatherForecast Class 464
The Weather Component 465
Retrieving Data from the Server 466
Understanding the HttpClient Class 467
Emulating a Slow Network in Chrome or Edge 469
The HttpClientJsonExtensions Methods 470
GetFromJsonAsync 470
PostAsJsonAsync and PutAsJsonAsync 472
Customizing Serialization with JsonSerializerOptions 473
Using IHttpClientFactory 474
Why Use IHttpClientFactory? 474
Enhancing PizzaPlace 478
Enabling Blazor WebAssembly 478
Talking to the Server 482
Disable Prerendering 487
Showing a Loading Screen 488
Summary 491

Chapter 15: Building Real-Time Applications with Blazor and SignalR 493

What Is SignalR? 493
How Does SignalR Work? 493
Building a WhiteBoard Application 494
Creating the WhiteBoard Solution 494
Implementing the Mouse Handling Logic 498
Painting the Segments on the Board 499
Adding a SignalR Hub on the Server 502
Implementing the BoardHub Class 502

    Configuring the Server 504

  Implementing the SignalR Client... 505

    Making the SignalR Hub Connection 505

    Notifying the Hub From the Client 506

    Cleaning Up the Hub Connection 507

  Summary... 508

Chapter 16: Efficient Communication with gRPC 509

  What Is gRPC?.. 509

    Pros and Cons of RPC... 509

    Understanding gRPC... 510

    Protocol Buffers... 510

  Describing Your Network Interchange with Proto Files.. 510

    Installing the gRPC Tooling 511

    Adding the Service Contract.. 513

    Implementing gRPC on the Server 516

    Implementing the Service 516

    Adding gRPC.. 518

  Building a gRPC Client in Blazor 519

    Creating the ForecastGrpcService 520

    Enabling gRPC on the Client 521

  Comparing REST with gRPC... 523

  Summary... 526

Chapter 17: Deploying Your Blazor Application 527

  Deploy Standalone Blazor WebAssembly 527

    Hosting on GitHub... 527

    Creating a Simple Website.. 529

    Deploying a Simple Site in GitHub 530

    Deploying a Blazor WASM Project 531

    Fix the Base Tag 531

    Publish the Project 532

TABLE OF CONTENTS

    Disabling Jekyll 536

    Fixing GitHub 404s 537

    Production Download Size.. 537

    Alternatives for GitHub 539

Ahead-of-Time Compilation 539

Deploying Hosted Applications.. 540

    Understanding the Deployment Models 540

    Deploying to Microsoft Azure... 541

    Creating the Publishing Profile 541

    Selecting Publishing Options... 545

    Publishing the Application 547

Summary... 548

Chapter 18: Security with OpenId Connect... 549

Representing the User 549

    Using Claims-Based Security 549

    Understanding Token Serialization 551

    Representing Claims In .NET 553

OpenId Connect... 553

    Understanding OpenId Connect Hybrid Flow 554

Identity Providers 555

    Implementing the Identity Provider with IdentityServer..................................... 555

Understanding User Consent 563

Protecting a Blazor Server Application with Hybrid Flow....................................... 564

    Adding OpenId Connect to Blazor Server... 565

    Implementing Authorization in Blazor Server 567

    Using AuthorizeView.. 577

    Adding and Removing Claims.. 578

    Enabling Role-Based Security 581

Accessing a Secured API... 584

    Using an Access Token 585

    Register the API Project with the Identity Provider... 588

xvi

Adding JWT Bearer Token Middleware	590
Enabling the Bearer Token in the Client	591
Using Policy-Based Access Control	597
Summary	601

Chapter 19: Securing Blazor WebAssembly 603

Authorization Code Flow with PKCE	603
Understanding PKCE	604
Registering the WASM Client Application	605
Creating and Examining the Application	605
Registering the Client Application	608
Implementing Authentication	609
Customizing the Login Experience	611
Understanding the Login Process	613
Accessing a Protected API	614
Fetching Forecasts from WeatherAPI	615
Using the AuthorizationMessageHandler	617
Adding Client-Side Authorization	619
Using Role-Based Security	620
Creating the Claims Component	620
Enabling RBAC	622
Promoting the Role Claim	624
Using Policy-Based Access Control	626
Updating Scopes	626
Adding Policies	627
Summary	629

Chapter 20: Securing Blazor Auto 631

The Challenge	631
The Blazor Server Project	631
PersistingAuthenticationStateProvider	632
The Blazor WASM Project	635

xvii

TABLE OF CONTENTS

Invoking Services with Auto 636
    Using an Internal Service 637
    Using an External Service 638

Backend for Frontend 638
    BFF on the Server 639
    BFF on the WASM Side 641

Summary 642

Chapter 21: Blazor State Management 643

Examining Component State 643
    What Not to Store 644
    Local Storage 644
    URL 649
    Using Protected Browser Storage 650

The Redux Pattern 652
    The Big Picture 652
    The Application Store 653
    Actions 653
    Reducers 654
    Views 654

Using Fluxor 654
    Creating the Store 654
    Using the Store in Our Blazor Application 656
    Implementing the Reducer 658

Redux Effects 659
    Adding the First Action 660
    Implement the WeatherService 662
    Add the Second Action and Effect 663

Summary 665

Index 667

About the Author

Peter Himschoot works as a lead trainer, an architect, and a strategist at U2U. He has a wide interest in software development that includes applications for the Web, Windows, and mobile devices. He has trained thousands of developers, is a regular speaker at international conferences, and has been involved in many web and mobile development projects as a software architect. He has been a Microsoft Regional Director (from 2003 to 2019) and cofounded the Belgian Visual Studio User Group (VISUG) in 2006, which is a group of trusted advisors to developer and IT professional audiences and to Microsoft.

Introduction

Full Stack Web Development with C#

Building modern single-page application websites today typically means writing JavaScript on the client and C# on the server when you are using the Microsoft development stack. But with Blazor, you can build everything using C# and reuse the knowledge and experience you gained with .NET. Porting existing C# applications like WinForms to the Web does not involve translating some of your logic to JavaScript; you can again reuse most of this code, resulting in less testing and bugs. With today's Blazor, you can build server-side web applications that mainly show static information, but also fully interactive web apps that previously required JavaScript. And all with C#!

Is This Book for You?

This book assumes you know C#, and you have some experience writing applications with it. Since this is also about web development, basic knowledge about HTML, CSS, and JavaScript is also required. Completing this book will allow you to build professional applications with Blazor, including mastery of some harder topics like authentication. You will see learning Blazor is fun!

Practical Development

I wrote this book with practice in mind, so sit down next to your computer and follow along with the examples; the best way to learn is to just do things with Blazor. I did my best to make the code samples easy to read, but this means breaking lines of code to fit nicely on the page. When in doubt, you can always consult the included code, which you can download from the book's product page, located at www.apress.com/ 979-8-8688-1006-0. You can find last-minute additions and errata at https://github.com/PeterHimschoot/microsoft-blazor-book-4, including every sample and exercise using the latest version of .NET.

CHAPTER 1

Introduction to Blazor

I was attending the Microsoft Most Valued Professionals and Regional Directors summit 2018 where we were introduced to Blazor for the first time by Steve Sanderson and Daniel Roth. And I must admit, I was super excited about Blazor! Blazor is a framework that allows you to build all kinds of applications, including single-page applications, using C# and allows you to run any standard .NET library in the browser. Before Blazor, your options for building a SPA were Angular, React, and Vue.js (and others) using JavaScript or one of the other higher-level languages like TypeScript (which get transpiled into JavaScript anyway). In this introduction, we will look at how browsers are now capable of running .NET assemblies in the browser using SignalR, WebAssembly, and Blazor.

A Tale of Two Wars

Think about it. The browser is one of the primary applications on your computer. You use it every day. Companies who build browsers know that very well and are bidding for you to use their browser. At the beginning of mainstream Internet, everyone was using Netscape, and Microsoft wanted a share of the market, so in 1995 they built Internet Explorer 1.0, released as part of Windows 95 Plus! pack.

The First Browser War

Newer versions were released rapidly, and browsers started to add new features such as `<blink>` and `<marquee>` elements. This was the beginning of the first browser war, giving people (especially designers) headaches because some developers were building pages with blinking marquee controls 😉. But developers were also getting sore heads because of incompatibilities between browsers. The first browser war was about having more HTML capabilities than the competition.

CHAPTER 1   INTRODUCTION TO BLAZOR

But all of this is now behind us with the introduction of HTML5 and modern browsers like Google Chrome, Brave, Microsoft Edge, Firefox, Safari, and Opera. HTML5 not only defines a series of standard HTML elements but also rules on how these should render, making it a lot easier to build a website that looks the same in all modern browsers. Then, in 1995 Brendan Eich wrote a little programming language known as ECMAScript. It was quickly dubbed JavaScript because its syntax was very similar to Java. I will be using the JavaScript name here because that is what most people call it. Fun fact: It was initially called Mocha, later changed to LiveScript, and was written in 10 days. (What!?)

> **Note**   JavaScript and Java are not related. Java and JavaScript have as much in common as ham and hamster (I don't know who formulated this first, but I love this phrasing).

Little did Mr. Eich know how this language would impact the modern web and even desktop application development. In 1995, Jesse James Garett wrote a white paper called Ajax (Asynchronous JavaScript and XML), describing a set of technologies where JavaScript is used to load data from the server and that data is used to update the browser's HTML. This avoids full-page reloads and allows for client-side web applications, which are applications written in JavaScript that run completely in the browser. One of the first companies to apply Ajax was Microsoft when they built Outlook Web Access (OWA) in 1995. OWA is a web application almost identical to the Outlook desktop application proving the power of Ajax. Soon, other Ajax applications started to appear, with Google Maps stuck in my memory as one of the other keystone applications. Google Maps would download maps asynchronously and, with some simple mouse interactions, allowed you to zoom and pan the map. Before Google Maps, the server would do the map rendering, and a browser displayed the map like any other image by downloading a bitmap from a server.

Building an Ajax website was a major undertaking that only big companies like Microsoft and Google could afford. This soon changed with the introduction of JavaScript libraries like jQuery and knockout.js (Knockout was also written by Steve Sanderson, the author of Blazor!). Today we build rich web apps with Angular, React, and Vue.js. All of them are using JavaScript, or higher-level languages like TypeScript.

CHAPTER 1 INTRODUCTION TO BLAZOR

Transpiling will take one language and convert it into another language. This is very popular with TypeScript which gives you a modern high-level typed language. You need JavaScript to run it in a browser, so TypeScript gets "transpiled" into JavaScript.

The Second Browser War

This brings us back to JavaScript and the second browser war. JavaScript performance is paramount in modern browsers. Chrome, Edge, Firefox, Safari, and Opera are all competing with one another, trying to convince users that their browser is the fastest with cool-sounding names for their JavaScript engine like V8 and Chakra. These engines use the latest optimization tricks like JIT compilation where JavaScript gets converted into native code as illustrated by Figure 1-1.

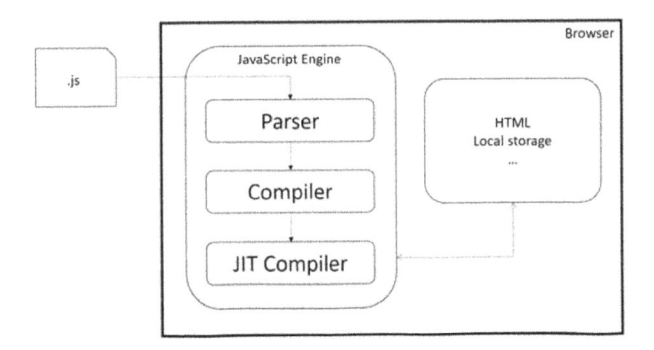

Figure 1-1. *The JavaScript execution process*

This process takes a lot of effort because JavaScript needs to be downloaded into the browser, then it gets parsed, then compiled into bytecode and then Just-In-Time converted into native code. So how can we make this process even faster?

The second browser war was all about JavaScript performance, but they have all reached the limits of optimization. Read on for the next war.

Introducing WebAssembly

WebAssembly allows you to take the parsing and compiling to the server, before your users even open their browser. With WebAssembly, you compile your code in a format called WASM (an abbreviation of WebASseMbly), which gets downloaded by the browser where it gets Just-In-Time compiled into native code (your hardware's machine code) as in Figure 1-2.

3

CHAPTER 1 INTRODUCTION TO BLAZOR

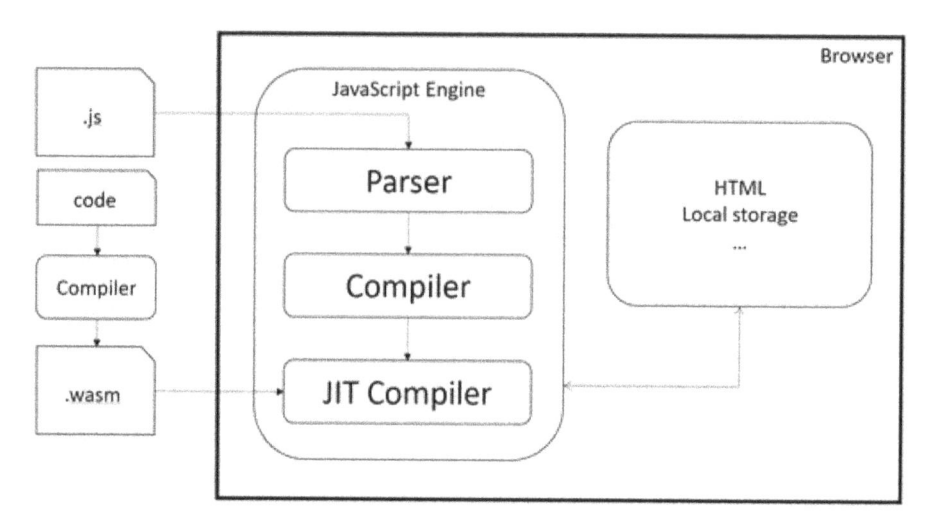

Figure 1-2. *The WebAssembly execution process*

Open your browser and open `https://earth.google.com`. This should take you to the Google Earth app written in WebAssembly as shown in Figure 1-3.

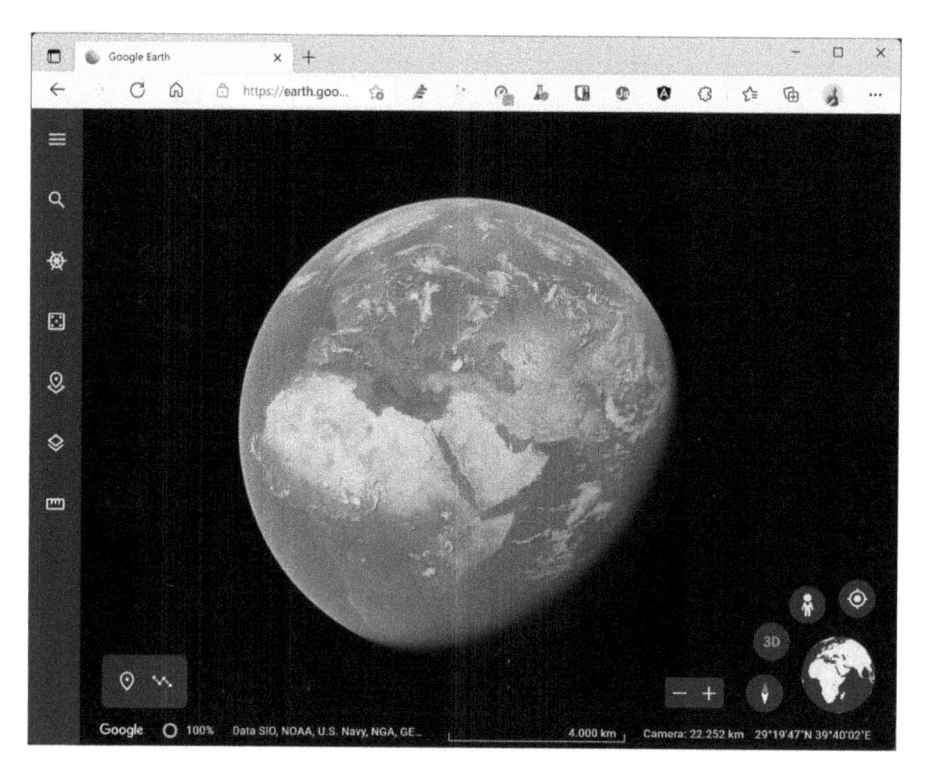

Figure 1-3. *Google Earth in WebAssembly*

4

CHAPTER 1   INTRODUCTION TO BLAZOR

Play around with this a little bit, and you will see that this application has excellent performance, but the initial load takes a fair amount of time because it needs to download the whole WASM application's code.

What is WebAssembly? From the official site webassembly.org:

> *WebAssembly (abbreviated Wasm) is a binary instruction format for a stack-based virtual machine. Wasm is designed as a portable target for compilation of high-level languages like C/C++/Rust, enabling deployment on the web for client and server applications.*

So WebAssembly is a new binary format optimized for browser execution; it is NOT JavaScript. It uses a stack-based virtual machine, just like .NET does. There are compilers for languages like C++ and Rust which compile to WASM. Some people have compiled C++ applications to WASM, allowing to run them in the browser. There is even a Windows 2000 operating system compiled to WASM so you can play minesweeper as shown in Figure 1-4!

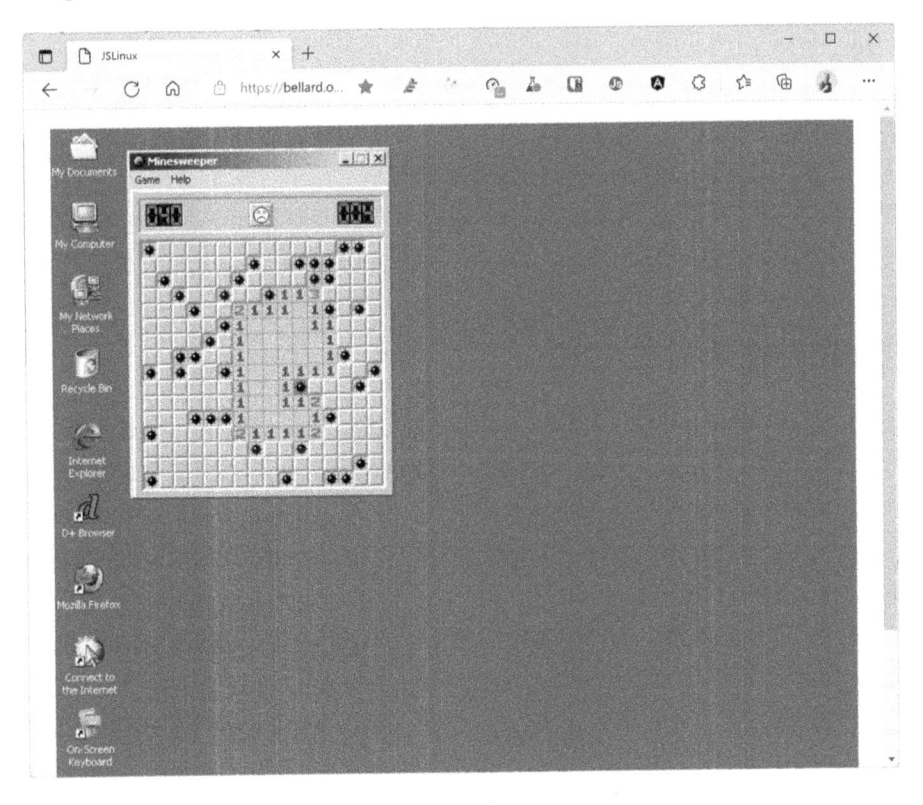

Figure 1-4. Windows 2000 running in the browser

Which Browsers Support WebAssembly?

WebAssembly is supported by all major browsers: Chrome, Edge, Safari, Opera, and Firefox, including their mobile versions. You can verify support yourself by visiting `https://caniuse.com/?search=WASM` as shown in Figure 1-5.

Chrome	Edge	Safari	Firefox	Opera	IE
			2-46		
4-50	12-14		47-51	10-37	
51-56	15	3.1-10.1	52	38-43	
57-124	16-123	11-17.4	53-125	44-108	6-10
125	124	17.5	126	109	11
126-128		17.6-TP	127-129		

Figure 1-5. *WebAssembly support*

As WebAssembly will become more and more important, we will see other browsers follow suit but don't expect Internet Explorer to support WASM.

WebAssembly and Mono

Mono is an open source implementation of the .NET CLI specification, meaning that Mono is a platform for running .NET assemblies. Mono is used in .NET MAUI (formerly Xamarin) for building mobile applications that run on the Windows, Android, and iOS mobile operating systems. You can also use it to build applications for MacOS, Linux, Tizen, and others. Mono also allows you to run .NET on Linux (its original purpose) and is written in C++. This last part is important because we saw that you can compile C++ to WebAssembly. So, what happened is that the Mono team decided to try to compile Mono to WebAssembly, which they did successfully. There are two approaches. One is where you take your .NET code, and you compile it together with the Mono runtime into one big WASM application. However, this approach takes a lot of time because you need to take several steps to compile everything into WASM, not so practical for day-to-day development. The other approach takes the Mono runtime, compiles it into WASM, and this runs in the browser where it will execute .NET Intermediate Language just like normal .NET does. The big advantage is that you can simply run .NET assemblies without having to compile them first into WASM.

This is the approach currently taken by Blazor. In the beginning, Blazor used the Mono runtime, but they have now built their own .NET Core runtime for WebAssembly. The disadvantage of this approach is that it needs to download the runtime AND a lot of .NET assemblies. Don't worry too much about the size of this download; when you deploy it in production, you can shrink it down to around 1-2 MB. This can be done by using tree shaking algorithms which remove all unused code from assemblies. We will look at this in the deployment chapter.

Interacting with the Browser with Blazor

Blazor gives you different models for building websites. You can start by building websites that have no interactivity and just return static content. This website would run all its code on the server, just like ASP.NET Core MVC, no WASM required. Later you can add pages that have interactivity using Blazor Server, or use Blazor WebAssembly, or both.

Blazor Static Website

You can build websites with no interactivity (meaning that the only interactivity you get is the one provided by your browser, such as clicking hyperlinks and form submit buttons) using ASP.NET Core MVC or Razor Pages. Now, with Blazor you can also build these static sites, using Blazor components, with one major advantage. Blazor components can stand on their own and are reusable. If you are familiar with ASP.NET MVC, you know that each page rendered by MVC uses code which runs in a `Controller`, and the HTML is rendered using a `View`. With Blazor this logic sits in a single Blazor component; thus, it is easier to reuse and very similar in building.

Blazor WebAssembly

WebAssembly with the .NET runtime allows you to run .NET code in the browser. Microsoft used this to build Blazor. Blazor uses the popular ASP.NET MVC approach for building applications that run in the browser. With Blazor WebAssembly, you build

CHAPTER 1 INTRODUCTION TO BLAZOR

Razor files which execute inside the browser to dynamically build a web page. With Blazor, you don't need JavaScript to build a web app which is good news for thousands of .NET developers who want to continue using C# (or F#). To use some browser features, you will still need JavaScript, and we will discuss this in the JavaScript Interoperability chapter.

Let's start with a simple Razor file in Listing 1-1 which you can find when you create a new Blazor project (which we will do further on in this chapter, no need to type anything yet).

Note Each code sample has been formatted for readability, sometimes splitting lines where this is not necessary and using less indentation. I leave it to you how you decide to format your code.

Listing 1-1. The Counter razor file

```
@page "/counter"

<PageTitle>Counter</PageTitle>

<h1>Counter</h1>

<p role="status">Current count: @currentCount</p>

<button class="btn btn-primary" @onclick="IncrementCount">
  Click me
</button>

@code {
  private int currentCount = 0;

  private void IncrementCount()
  {
    currentCount++;
  }
}
```

This file gets compiled into a .NET class (you'll find out in the components chapter in this book) which is then executed by the Blazor engine. The result of this execution is a tree-like structure called the render tree. The render tree is then sent to JavaScript which updates the DOM to reflect the render tree (creating, updating, and removing HTML elements and attributes).

Listing 1-1 will result in `<h1>`, `<p>` (with the contents set to the value of currentCount) and `<button>` HTML elements. When you interact with the page, for example, when you click the button, this will trigger the button's click event which will invoke the `IncrementCount` method from Listing 1-1. The render tree is then regenerated, and any changes are sent again to JavaScript which will update the DOM. This process is illustrated in Figure 1-6.

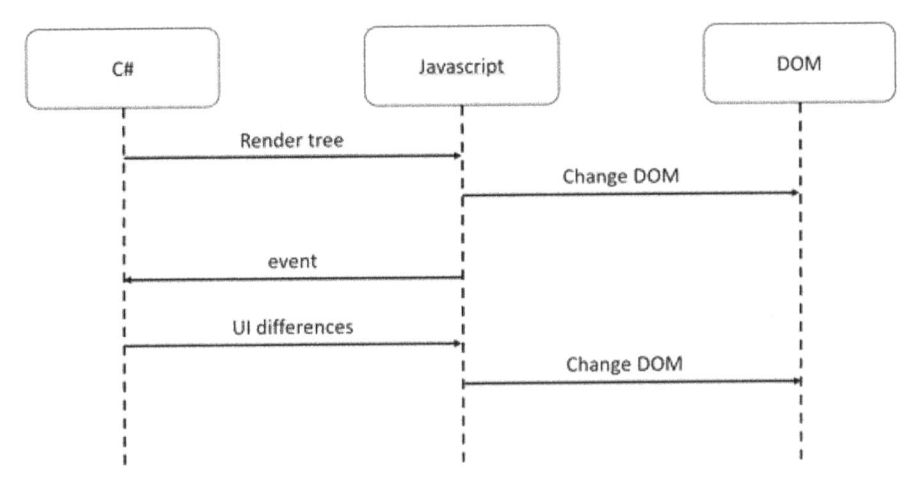

Figure 1-6. The Blazor WebAssembly DOM generation process

This model is very flexible. You can build standalone single-page applications, just like Angular or React which run completely inside the browser. It allows you to build progressive web apps, and your app can be embedded in desktop applications, for example, using Electron. Electron is an open source framework developed by GitHub that allows for the creation of desktop applications using web technologies such as HTML, CSS, and JavaScript. Visual Studio Code is JavaScript running inside Electron, giving you a desktop application.

Blazor Server

On August 7, 2018, ASP.NET community standup Daniel Roth introduced a new execution model for Blazor now called Blazor Server. In this model, your Blazor site is running on the server resulting in a way smaller download for the browser.

CHAPTER 1　INTRODUCTION TO BLAZOR

We just saw that Blazor WebAssembly builds a render tree using the .NET runtime running in the browser which then gets sent to JavaScript to update the DOM. With Blazor Server, the render tree is built on the server using regular .NET and then gets serialized to the browser using SignalR (SignalR enables developers to add real-time web functionality to their applications. Real-time web functionality is the ability to have server-side code push content to connected clients instantly as it becomes available, rather than having the server wait for a client to request new data. We will look at SignalR in its own chapter). JavaScript in the browser then deserializes the render tree to update the DOM. Pretty like the Blazor WebAssembly model.

When you interact with the site, events get serialized back to the server which then executes the .NET code, updating the render tree and the changes get serialized back to the browser. I've illustrated this process in Figure 1-7. The big difference is that there is no need to send the .NET runtime and your Blazor assemblies to the browser. And the programming model stays the same! You can switch Blazor Server-side and Blazor WebAssembly with just a couple of small changes to your code. Or with the new Web App model, you can start running on the server, download the Blazor runtime in the background into the browser, and then continue running your Blazor application in the browser.

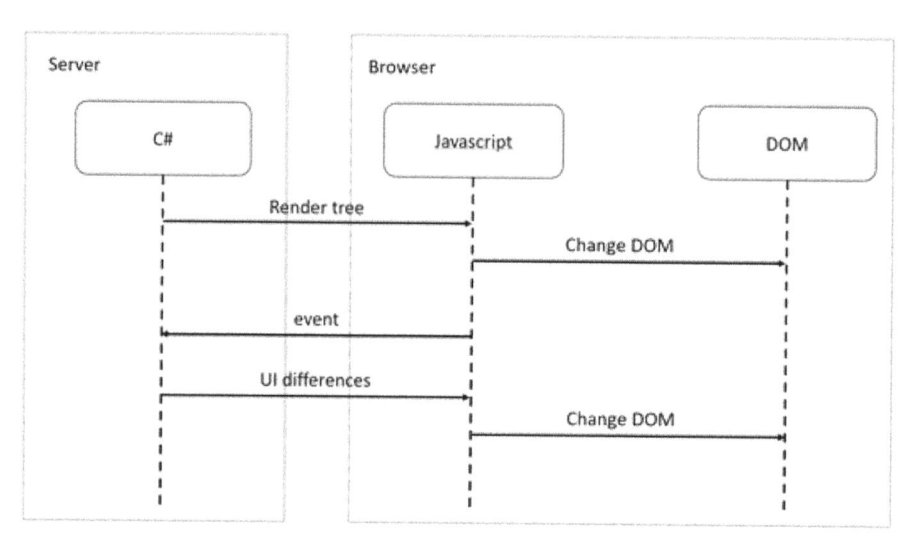

Figure 1-7.　Blazor Server runtime model

Blazor Server vs. Blazor WebAssembly

The Blazor Server model has a couple of benefits, but also some drawbacks. Let's discuss these here so you can decide which model fits your application's needs.

- Smaller downloads: With Blazor Server, your application does not need to download dotnet.wasm (the .NET runtime) nor all your .NET assemblies. The browser downloads a small JavaScript library which sets up the SignalR connection to the server. This means that the application will start a lot faster, especially on slower connections.

- Development process: Blazor WebAssembly does not support all modern debugging capabilities, resulting in added logging. Because your .NET code is running on the server, you can use the regular .NET debugger with all its advanced features. You could start building your Blazor application using the server-side model, and when it is finished, switch to the client-side model by making a small change to your code.

- .NET APIs: Because you are running your .NET code on the server, you can use all the .NET APIs you would use with regular ASP.NET Core MVC applications, for example, accessing the database directly. Do note that doing this will stop you from quickly converting it into a client-side application. You can limit this by writing service classes and using dependency injection to inject different implementations depending on the environment your components are hosted in.

- Online only: Running the Blazor application on the server does mean that your users will always need access to the server. And if the connection drops between the browser and server, your user could lose some work because the application will stop functioning. Blazor will try to reconnect to the server without losing any data, so most of the time users will not lose any work done.

- Server scalability: All your .NET code runs on the server so if you have thousands of clients, your server(s) will have to handle all the work. Not only that, Blazor uses a state-full model which will require you to keep track of every user's state on the server. So your server will need more resources than with Blazor WebAssembly which can use a stateless model.

Blazor Auto Rendering

With .NET 8 comes a new application model for Blazor, the Blazor Web App solution. In this model, your application will start running as a Blazor Server application, and while the user is using your application, the WebAssembly runtime will download, and once everything is downloaded, the browser will start using Blazor WebAssembly. Talk about the best of both worlds! This, however, comes at a cost; your application must be built in a certain way to support transitioning from server to WebAssembly. We will look at this in the Render Modes and Communication chapters.

Your First Blazor Project

Getting hands-on is the best way to learn. You will first install the prerequisites to developing with Blazor. Then you will create your first Blazor project, run the project to see it work, and finally inspect the different aspects of the project to get a "lay of the land" view for how Blazor applications are developed.

Note I learned an important lesson from the first edition of this book: never underestimate the speed at which Microsoft innovates! All code samples in the first edition of *Blazor Revealed* became invalid quite rapidly. I do not expect this to happen again with this edition since it is based on the Release to Manufacture (RTM) version of Blazor. If something does not work, simply consult the sources that come with this book. I will keep these up to date. Promise!

The source code for this book is available on GitHub via the book's product page, located at www.apress.com/ISBN.

Installing Blazor Prerequisites

Working with Blazor requires you to install some prerequisites, so in this section, you will install what is needed to get going.

Using the .NET CLR

Blazor runs on top of ASP.NET Core, optionally providing the web server for your project which will serve the client files that run in the browser and run any server-side APIs that your Blazor project needs. .NET Core is Microsoft's cross-platform solution for working with .NET on Windows, Linux, and macOS.

You can find the installation files at https://www.microsoft.com/download. Look for the latest version of the .NET Core SDK. Follow the installation instructions, and install it on your machine, using Windows, OSX, or Linux.

> **Note** This book was written using .NET 8, which at the time of writing was the long-term release (LTS) version. Every sample should still work with version 9.

Verify the installation when the installer is done by opening a new command prompt and typing the following command:

```
dotnet --version
```

Output should indicate that you installed the correct version. The version number should be at least 8.0. On my machine I get:

```
8.0.303
```

Should the command's output show an older version, you will need to download and install a more recent version of .NET Core SDK. These can run side-by-side so you will not break other .NET Core projects doing this.

Using Visual Studio

For people using Windows, Visual Studio (from now on I will refer to Visual Studio as VS) is one of the integrated development environments (IDE) we will use throughout this book. If you are using macOS or Linux, you can use Visual Studio Code (or Rider from JetBrains which I will not discuss). With any of these, you can edit your code, compile it, and run it all from the same application. And the code samples are also the same.

If you want to use Visual Studio, download the latest version of Visual Studio from https://www.visualstudio.com/downloads/. There is the free community version which should work for all samples.

CHAPTER 1　INTRODUCTION TO BLAZOR

Run the installer and make sure that you install the ASP.NET and web development role as shown in Figure 1-8.

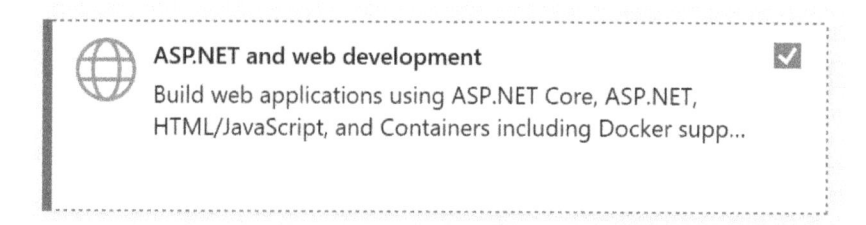

Figure 1-8. *The Visual Studio Installer Workloads selection*

After installation, run Visual Studio from the Start menu. Then open the help menu and select About Microsoft Visual Studio. The About Microsoft Visual Studio dialog window should specify at least version 17.9.0 as illustrated by Figure 1-9.

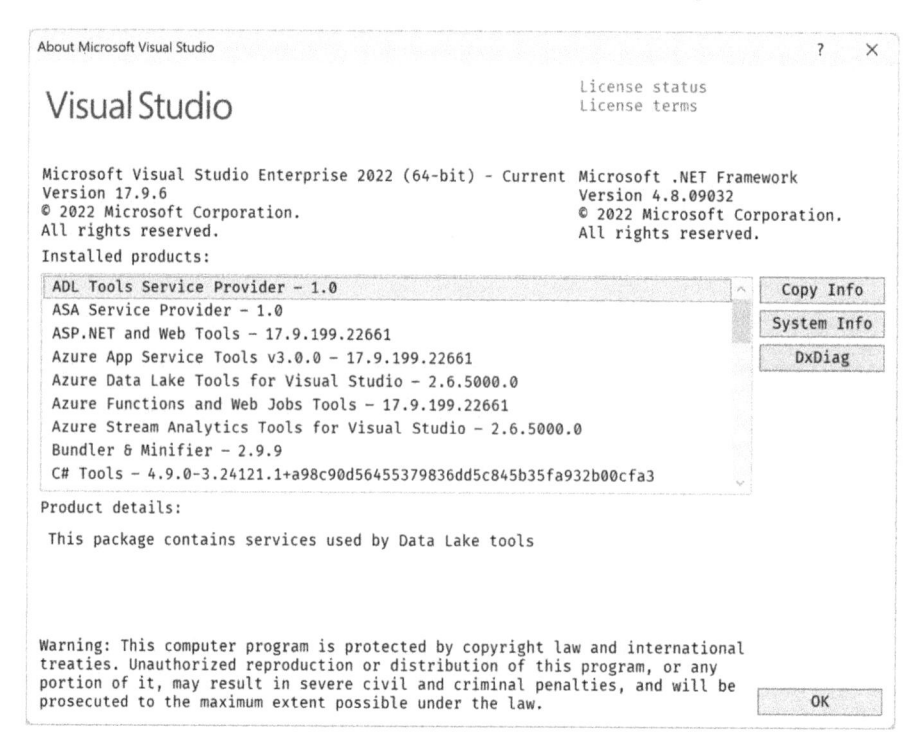

Figure 1-9. *Verify the version of Visual Studio*

CHAPTER 1 INTRODUCTION TO BLAZOR

Using Visual Studio Code

Visual Studio Code (VSC) is a free, modern, cross-platform development environment with an integrated editor, git source control, and debugger. The environment has a huge range of extensions available allowing you to use all kinds of languages and tools directly from VSC. So, if you don't have access to (because you're running a non-Windows operating system or you don't want to use) Visual Studio, use VSC.

Install VSC from `https://code.visualstudio.com/download`. Install using the defaults.

After installation, you should install a couple of extensions for Code, especially the C# extension. Start Code, and on the left side, select the extensions tab as shown in Figure 1-10.

Figure 1-10. Visual Studio Code Extensions tab

You can search for extensions, so start with C# Dev Kit which is the first extension from Figure 1-11. This extension will give you IntelliSense and debugging for the C# programming language and .NET assemblies. You will probably get a newer version listed so take the latest.

Click install.

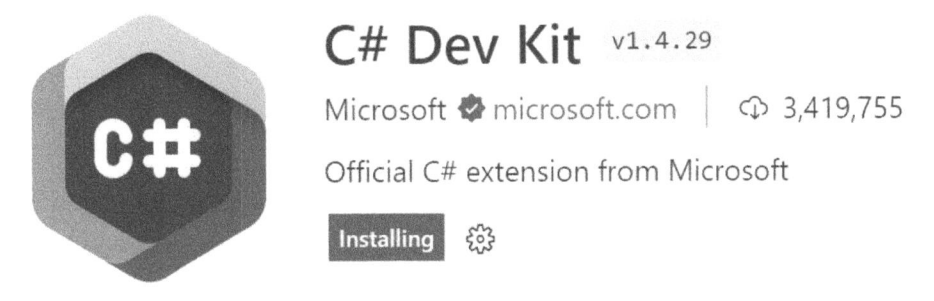

Figure 1-11. C# for Visual Studio Code

15

PowerShell

In this book, I will provide you with PowerShell scripts to quickly create the projects we will build. Please consult `https://learn.microsoft.com/powershell/scripting/install/installing-powershell` on installing the latest PowerShell for your machine.

Understanding the Blazor Templates for VS/Code

Throughout this book, we will create several different Blazor projects. With ASP.NET Core, we can use the Command Line Interface (CLI) to create all kinds of projects, including Blazor WebAssembly, Blazor Server, and Blazor Web Apps.

> **Note** I will provide you with PowerShell scripts to quickly create the different projects we will build in this book. Of course, you can always create these using VS(C).

Let us begin by looking at the installed templates; you can list all installed templates using the following CLI command. You can execute this from a command prompt, or from the VSC Terminal.

```
dotnet new list
```

You will see four columns. The first shows the template's description, the second column displays the name, the third lists the languages for which the template is available, and the last shows the tags, a kind of group name for the template. Among those listed are the following of interest:

```
Template Name                         Short Name
-------------------------------       ------------------
Blazor Server App                     blazorserver
Blazor Web App                        blazor
Blazor WebAssembly Standalone App     blazorwasm
```

With Blazor projects, you have a couple of choices. You can create a stand-alone Blazor WebAssembly project (using the `blazorwasm` template) that does not need server-side code. This kind of project known as Blazor WebAssembly has the advantage that you can simply deploy it to any web server which will function as a file server, allowing browsers to download your site just like any other (pure client) site. We will look at deployment in a later chapter.

The second option is to run all Blazor code on the server (using the `blazorserver` template). In this case, the browser will use a SignalR connection to receive UI updates from the server and to send user interaction back to the server for processing.

The third option is to run as a Blazor Web App (the `blazor` template). This template gives you a lot of options, you can build your project as a static website, use Blazor Server interactivity, or using Blazor WebAssembly interactivity, and start with Blazor Server, and when the WebAssembly resources have been downloaded into the browser, continue running as Blazor WebAssembly.

In this book, we will use the third option (Blazor Web App) most of the time, but the concepts you will learn in this book are the same for all three options (except things like security).

Generating Your Project with Visual Studio

Start Visual Studio and select Create a new project.

Type Blazor in the search box, and select the "Blazor Web App" project template as illustrated by Figure 1-12.

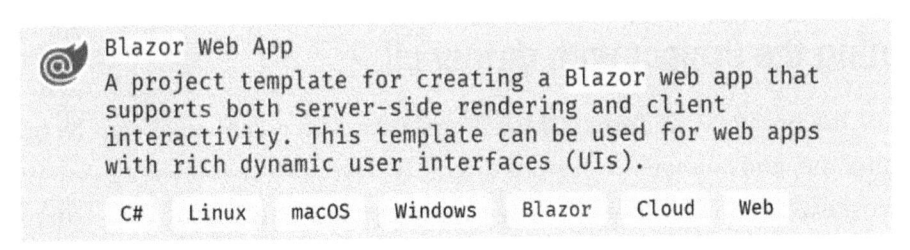

```
Blazor Web App
A project template for creating a Blazor web app that
supports both server-side rendering and client
interactivity. This template can be used for web apps
with rich dynamic user interfaces (UIs).
    C#    Linux    macOS    Windows    Blazor    Cloud    Web
```

Figure 1-12. *Visual Studio New Project dialog*

Click Next.

Name your project BlazorApp.Intro, choose the location where the project should be generated, and click Next.

On the next screen, you can select the framework to use. Choose the latest version (at time of writing that is .NET 8.0), leave Authentication Type set to None, choose Server as the Interactive render mode, choose Global as the Interactivity location, and then click Create. An example is shown in Figure 1-13.

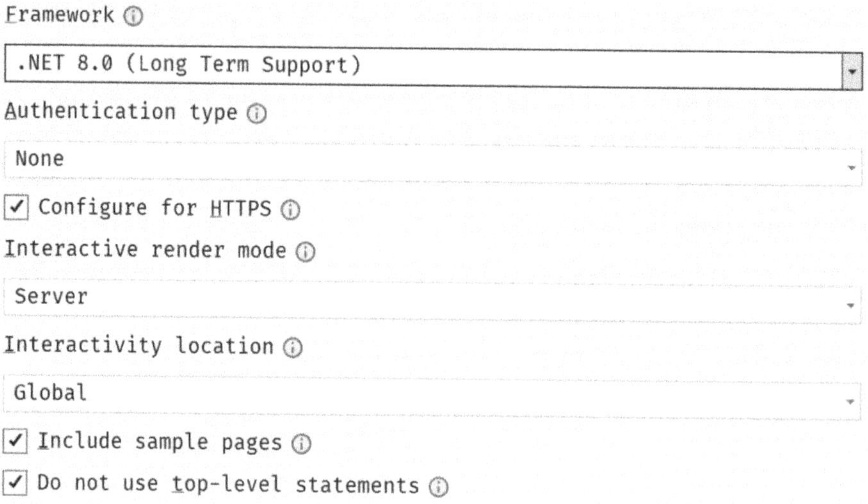

CHAPTER 1   INTRODUCTION TO BLAZOR

Figure 1-13. *New ASP.NET Core web application*

Wait for Visual Studio to complete. Then build and run your solution by pressing F5. After a little while, the browser will open and display the Blazor application.

Generating the Project with dotnet cli

To generate the project with dotnet CLI, which works on any machine, start by opening a command line, and change the current directory to wherever you want to create the project. Now execute the following commands to create a new Blazor Web App project, which uses Blazor Server interactivity.

```
$ProjectName = "BlazorApp.Intro"
mkdir $ProjectName
cd $ProjectName
dotnet new sln -n $ProjectName
mkdir src
cd src
dotnet new blazor -n $ProjectName --all-interactive --interactivity Server
cd ..
dotnet sln add src\$ProjectName
dotnet build
```

CHAPTER 1 INTRODUCTION TO BLAZOR

First, we define the project name as a variable; we create a new folder for our project. Inside this folder, a .sln is created with a src folder for the projects. Inside this folder, we create the Blazor project, which gets the same name as the solution (just convention).

The dotnet is the command line, taking the new instruction, with the template being blazor. The --interactivity Server option will choose Blazor Server, and the --all-interactive will make this the default. Finally, we add the project to the solution and build it.

This should build without any errors.

Now we can run the project from the command line using

```
cd .\src\BlazorApp.Intro
dotnet run
```

This will show you some output, including the URL of the Blazor application:

```
Building...
info: Microsoft.Hosting.Lifetime[14]
      Now listening on: https://localhost:7209
info: Microsoft.Hosting.Lifetime[14]
      Now listening on: http://localhost:5249
info: Microsoft.Hosting.Lifetime[0]
      Application started. Press Ctrl+C to shut down.
info: Microsoft.Hosting.Lifetime[0]
      Hosting environment: Development
info: Microsoft.Hosting.Lifetime[0]
      Content root path: C:\Code\GitHub\microsoft-blazor-book-4\Ch01\BlazorApp.Intro\src\BlazorApp.Intro
```

Open your browser on the address shown on the third line, and you are ready to play!

Note In this sample output, I got `https://localhost:7209`, but on your machine, expect another port number so use that one!

19

CHAPTER 1 INTRODUCTION TO BLAZOR

Running Blazor with Visual Studio Code

For Visual Studio Code, I am going to refer you to the Microsoft online documentation at `https://learn.microsoft.com/aspnet/core/blazor/tooling?view=aspnetcore-8.0&pivots=vsc`. Select the Blazor Web App template.

Running the Generated Project

Press F5 or Ctrl-F5 (no debugger) to run (this should work for both VS and VSC). Your (default) browser should open and display the home page as shown in Figure 1-14.

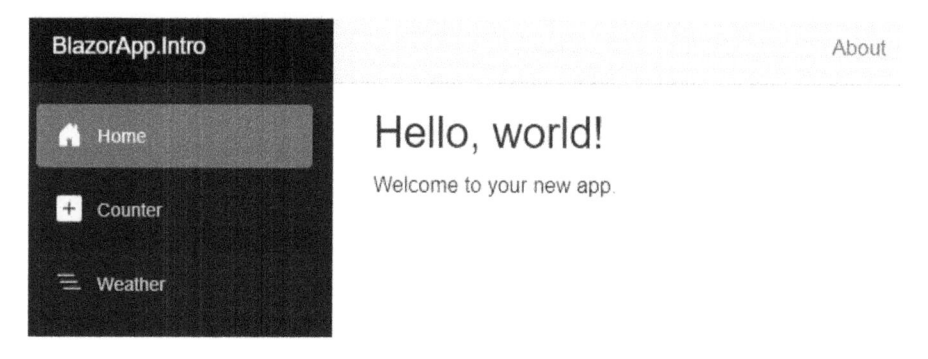

Figure 1-14. Your first application – Home Screen

This generated single-page application (SPA) has on the left side a navigation menu allowing you to jump between different pages. On the right side, you will see the selected component; in Figure 1-14, it shows the Home component. And in the top right corner, there is an About link to `https://learn.microsoft.com/aspnet/core/`, which is the official ASP.NET and Blazor documentation website.

The Home page shows the mandatory "Hello, world!" demo. In the navigation menu, click the Counter link. Doing so opens a simple screen with a number and a button as illustrated by Figure 1-15. Clicking the button will increase the counter. Try it!

CHAPTER 1   INTRODUCTION TO BLAZOR

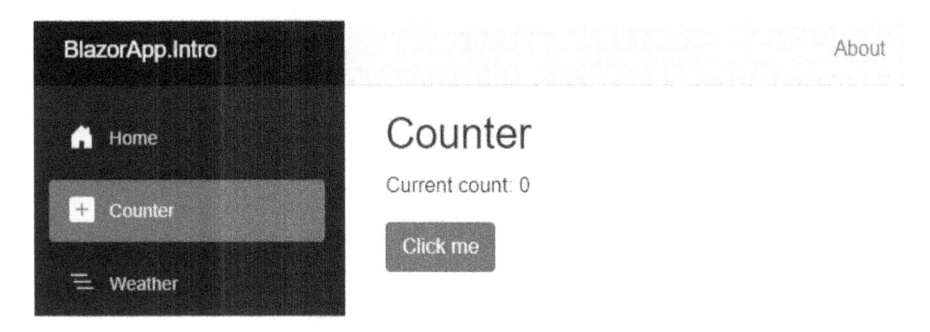

Figure 1-15. *Your first application – Counter screen*

In the navigation menu, click the Weather link. Here you can watch a (random and fake) weather forecast as shown in Figure 1-16. This forecast is generated on the server when asked by the client.

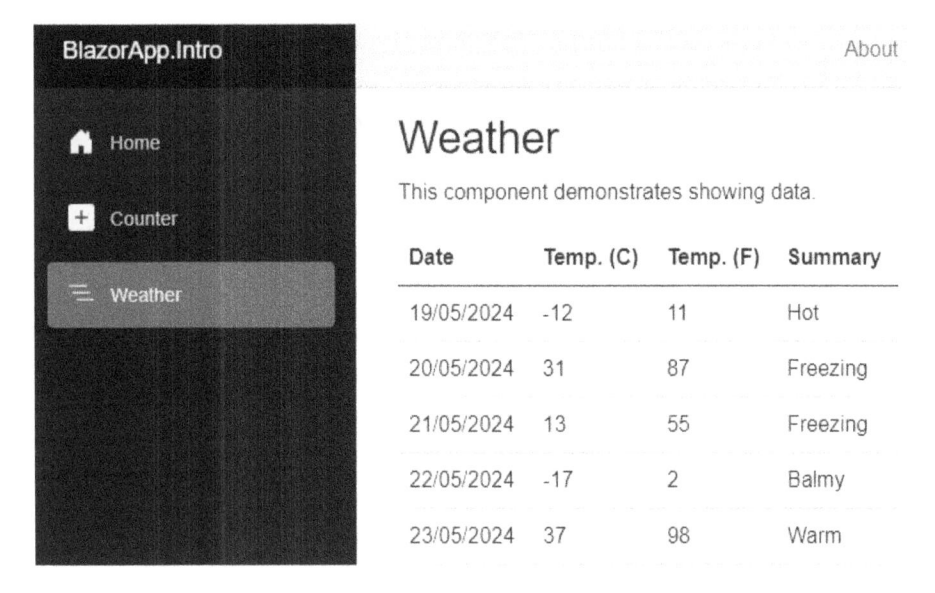

Figure 1-16. *Your first application – fetch data screen*

Examining the Project's Parts

Now being able to play with these pages is all nice, but let us have a look at how all this works. Web applications are a bunch of files that get downloaded by the browser from a server. It is the server's job to provide the files to the browser upon request. There is a whole range of existing servers to choose from, for example, Internet Information

CHAPTER 1   INTRODUCTION TO BLAZOR

Services (IIS) on Windows or Apache on Linux. ASP.NET Core has a built-in server known as Kestrel which you can then run on Windows, Linux, or OSX. This is the preferred option to use during development, because Kestrel is just a console application that acts as a web server which makes it very easy and fast to spin up with our application during debugging sessions.

Dependency Injection and Middleware

The topic of this book is Blazor, so we're not going to discuss all the details of the server project that got generated (Microsoft has very good documentation on .NET Core at https://learn.microsoft.com/aspnet/core), but I do want to show you an important thing. Look for Program.cs. In Listing 1-2, the `AddRazorComponents` method installs the dependencies required for Blazor, and the `AddInteractiveServerComponents` allows for Blazor Server. There is a similar method for Blazor WebAssembly dependencies.

Listing 1-2. Configuring dependency injection for Blazor

```
// Add services to the container.
builder.Services.AddRazorComponents()
    .AddInteractiveServerComponents();
```

Look at Listing 1-3. At the end of the "Program" class Blazor Middleware is installed, with support for Blazor Server. Again, there is a similar method for Blazor WebAssembly.

Listing 1-3. Adding Blazor Middleware

```
app.MapRazorComponents<App>()
    .AddInteractiveServerRenderMode();
```

Middleware objects are little .NET components that each have a clear responsibility. When you type in a URL, the browser sends a HTTP(S) request to the server, which then passes it on to the middleware components in the listed order. Some of these will take the request and return a response; some of them take the response and do something with it. For example, the `UseStaticFiles` method will check if the URL matches a file from the wwwroot folder, and if it exists will return the file's contents.

Required JavaScript

See the App class in Listing 1-4. This class is a Blazor component that is the root component. At the end of the component, you will see "blazor.web.js" which is required in Blazor, except for pure static websites. This JavaScript enables interactivity for your application.

Listing 1-4. The App component

```
<!DOCTYPE html>
<html lang="en">

<head>
    <meta charset="utf-8" />
    <meta name="viewport" content="width=device-width, initial-scale=1.0" />
    <base href="/" />
    <link rel="stylesheet" href="bootstrap/bootstrap.min.css" />
    <link rel="stylesheet" href="app.css" />
    <link rel="stylesheet" href="BlazorApp.Intro.styles.css" />
    <link rel="icon" type="image/png" href="favicon.png" />
    <HeadOutlet @rendermode="InteractiveServer" />
</head>

<body>
    <Routes @rendermode="InteractiveServer" />
    <script src="_framework/blazor.web.js"></script>
</body>

</html>
```

Note The templates for Blazor Web App, Blazor Server, and Blazor WebAssembly use different JavaScript files and a slightly different startup process.

CHAPTER 1 INTRODUCTION TO BLAZOR

Project Structure

Let us look at the project's structure, as illustrated by Figure 1-17.

```
▲ + 🌐 BlazorApp.Intro
  ▷   ⊛ Connected Services
  ▷   🗗 Dependencies
  ▷ 🔒 Properties
  ▷ 🔒 ⊕ wwwroot
  ▷ 🔒 📁 Components
  ▷ + {} appsettings.json
  ▷ + C# Program.cs
```

Figure 1-17. *The project's structure*

- The wwwroot folder contains resources that are downloaded by your program, things like CSS, JavaScript, images, etc.

- The appsettings.json file contains configuration settings.

- The Components folder as its name implies is used for your components. You have already seen three components, the Home component which renders as the Home page, the Counter component which shows a counter, and the Weather component displaying fake weather forecasts. Blazor is all about building components! There are two subfolders: Layout for layout components and Pages for routed components. All of these are components!

Layout Components

Look at Figure 1-14, Figure 1-15, and Figure 1-16. All have the same menu. This menu is shared among all our Blazor components and is known as a layout component. We will discuss layout components in the Routing chapter. The default layout can be found in the Components/Layout/MainLayout component, listed in Listing 1-5.

Listing 1-5. The MainLayout component

```
@inherits LayoutComponentBase

<div class="page">
  <div class="sidebar">
    <NavMenu />
  </div>

  <main>
    <div class="top-row px-4">
      <a href="https://learn.microsoft.com/aspnet/core/" target="_blank">About</a>
    </div>

    <article class="content px-4">
      @Body
    </article>
  </main>
</div>

<div id="blazor-error-ui">
  An unhandled error has occurred.
  <a href="" class="reload">Reload</a>
  <a class="dismiss"> ✕ </a>
</div>
```

This component contains a `<div>` HTML element with two nested `<div>`s. The first nested `<div>` with class `sidebar` contains a single Blazor component: `NavMenu`. This is where your navigation menu gets defined. The sidebar will display a menu, allowing you to navigate between `Home`, `Counter`, and `Weather` components. We will look in more detail at navigation and routing in the Routing chapter.

> **Note** Razor contains a mix of HTML tags and Razor components. At first this can be confusing, but since Razor components are classes, and classes should start with a capital letter, they are easy to recognize!

CHAPTER 1 INTRODUCTION TO BLAZOR

The next nested `<div>` with class `main` has two parts. The first is the About link you see on every page. The second part contains the `@Body`; this is where the selected page will be shown. For example, when you click on the Counter link in the navigation menu, the `@Body` will be replaced with the `Counter` component.

This is all for now, but the rest of the book will explain each part as we go along.

Debugging Blazor

Of course, while building your Blazor app, you will encounter unexpected behavior from time to time. Debugging Blazor Server can be done just like any .NET project using Visual Studio or Code. But with Blazor WebAssembly, your code will be running in the browser. You will be happy to learn that the VS/VSC debugger works with Blazor, although limited. You can put breakpoints in your code, step through your code, and observe variables holding simple types like `bool`, `int`, and `string`. You also will need to use Chrome or Edge, each Chromium-based browser. FireFox is also supported.

Debugging with Visual Studio

To enable debugging with Visual Studio, open the Properties/launchSettings.json file from the project you will use as your startup project. The launchSettings.json file is used to configure how your application is launched during development. This file is found in the Properties folder of your project and contains settings that determine how the application runs, such as the environment variables, command-line arguments, and the launch URL.

You will need to set the `inspectUri` property here, like in Listing 1-6 (the template normally will configure this for you). This property enables the IDE to detect that this is a Blazor WebAssembly app and instructs the script debugging infrastructure to connect to the browser through the Blazor's debugging proxy.

Listing 1-6. The launchSettings.json file for Debugging (excerpt)

```
{
  "$schema": "http://json.schemastore.org/launchsettings.json",
  "iisSettings": {
    "windowsAuthentication": false,
    "anonymousAuthentication": true,
```

```json
    "iisExpress": {
      "applicationUrl": "http://localhost:47786",
      "sslPort": 44335
    }
  },
  "profiles": {
    "http": {
      "commandName": "Project",
      "dotnetRunMessages": true,
      "launchBrowser": true,
      "applicationUrl": "http://localhost:5249",
      "environmentVariables": {
        "ASPNETCORE_ENVIRONMENT": "Development"
      }
    },
    "https": {
      "commandName": "Project",
      "dotnetRunMessages": true,
      "launchBrowser": true,
      "applicationUrl": "https://localhost:7209;http://localhost:5249",
      "environmentVariables": {
        "ASPNETCORE_ENVIRONMENT": "Development"
      }
    },
    "IIS Express": {
      "commandName": "IISExpress",
      "launchBrowser": true,
      "environmentVariables": {
        "ASPNETCORE_ENVIRONMENT": "Development"
      }
    }
  }
}
```

CHAPTER 1　INTRODUCTION TO BLAZOR

Now run your application in VS with the debugger by pressing F5. Be patient while your Blazor site starts to run. Now you can put a breakpoint in your code, for example, on the IncrementCount method of the Counter component as in Figure 1-18, line 17. Simply click the gray area left of your code (also known as the gutter), and a red dot will appear, indicating that the debugger will stop at this code.

```
14      private void IncrementCount()
15      {
16          currentCount++;
17      }
18  }
19
```

Figure 1-18. *Setting a breakpoint in the IncrementCount method*

Go back to your Blazor application and click the Counter's Click Me button. The debugger should stop on the IncrementCount method. You can now examine the content of simple variables in the Locals window, like in Figure 1-19.

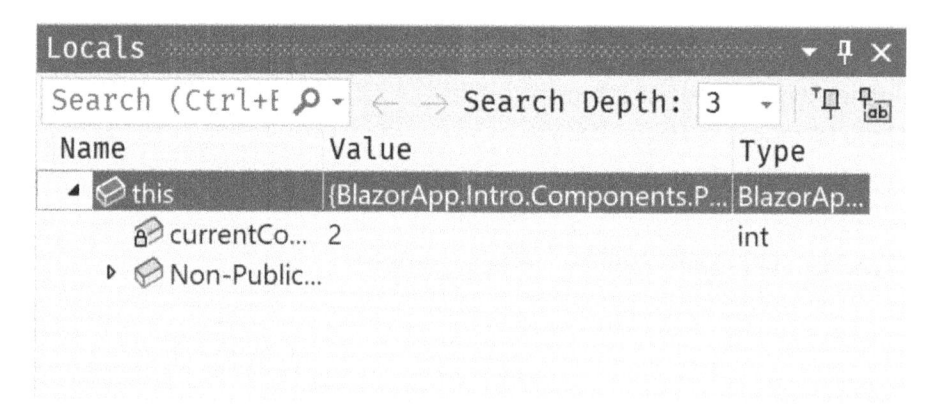

Figure 1-19. *Using the Locals Debugger Window to inspect simple variables*

Debugging with Visual Studio Code

Start VSC. Open the folder containing the solution file. Also ensure launchSettings.json from Listing 1-6 is set up correctly like Visual Studio (this is independent of your IDE).

Now run your application in VSC with the debugger by pressing F5. Be patient while your Blazor site starts to run. Now you can put a breakpoint in your code, for example, on the IncrementCount method of the Counter component as in Figure 1-20, line 16.

Simply click the area left to your code (also known as the gutter), and a red dot will appear, indicating that the debugger will stop at this code.

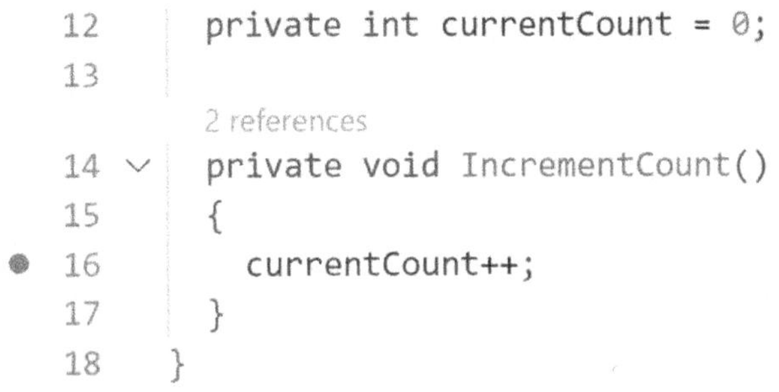

```
12      private int currentCount = 0;
13
        2 references
14  ∨   private void IncrementCount()
15      {
●16         currentCount++;
17      }
18  }
```

Figure 1-20. Adding a breakpoint in VSC

Go back to your Blazor application, and click the `Counter`'s Click Me button. The debugger should stop on the `IncrementCount` method. You can now examine the content of simple variables in the Locals window, like in Figure 1-21.

```
∨ VARIABLES
  ∨ Locals
    ∨ this: {BlazorApp.Intro.C...
        currentCount [int]: 2
      > Non-Public members


∨ WATCH
    currentCount: 2
```

Figure 1-21. Inspecting variables in VSC

Developing with Hot Reload

With .NET Core 6.0 and later, Microsoft introduces a nice feature called hot reload. This allows you to make changes to your code and markup while your application is running. As soon as you make the change, your application will update (hot reloads), even keeping the existing state of the application.

CHAPTER 1   INTRODUCTION TO BLAZOR

Hot Reload with .NET CLI

Let us start using Hot Reload using the command line interface. Open a command prompt and change the directory to the "BlazorApp.Intro" project and run:

dotnet watch

This should start the project, and the browser should also open with your application.

dotnet watch 🔥 Hot reload enabled. For a list of supported edits, see https://aka.ms/dotnet/hot-reload.
  💡 Press "Ctrl + R" to restart.

Open the Counter component, and increment the counter a couple of times. Now make a change to the Counter component, for example, Listing 1-7. Save.

Listing 1-7. A simple change

```
private void IncrementCount()
{
  currentCount+=3;
}
```

As soon as you make the change, the browser will update itself, keeping the current count!

Clicking the Increment button will now add 3 to the counter.

If you want to restart again, go back to the command line and press Ctrl-Shift-R.

Hot Reload with Visual Studio

Open the solution in Visual Studio and run the application. Hot reload is normally enabled by default, and Visual Studio has some settings that allow you to tweak hot reload, as shown in Figure 1-22. Settings is where you can enable hot reload.

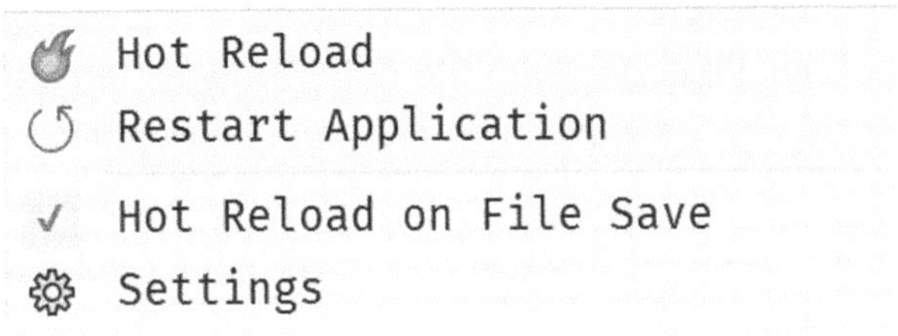

```
🔥  Hot Reload
 ↻  Restart Application
 ✓  Hot Reload on File Save
 ⚙  Settings
```

Figure 1-22. Hot Reload

The Blazor Bootstrap Process

In this section, we will look at the bootstrap process for both Blazor WebAssembly and Blazor Server. We will also look at the network traffic to get a better understanding of both application models.

Blazor WASM

Create a new Blazor WebAssembly Standalone application, either using VS(C) or this PowerShell script (I like to run this from Windows terminal, which is a free download from the Microsoft Store):

```
$ProjectName = "BlazorApp.WebAssembly"
mkdir $ProjectName
cd $ProjectName
dotnet new sln -n $ProjectName
mkdir src
cd src
dotnet new blazorwasm -n $ProjectName
cd ..
dotnet sln add src\$ProjectName
dotnet build
```

Run the Blazor application. Open the browser's developer tools (most browsers will open the developer tools when you press F12; otherwise, you can always search on how to enable the developer tools in your browser. The search phrase "Finding Your Browser's Developer Console" found me a web site on how to enable developer tools in the browser). We will have a look at what happens at the network layer.

CHAPTER 1 INTRODUCTION TO BLAZOR

> **Note** In all screenshots, I will be using the Edge browser which is very similar to Chrome. If you prefer to use another browser, go right ahead!

First open the browser debugger's Application tab, and press the Clear site data button as in Figure 1-23. This will clear the browser's cache and will give you a better view of what happens when someone visits a Blazor WebAssembly application for the first time.

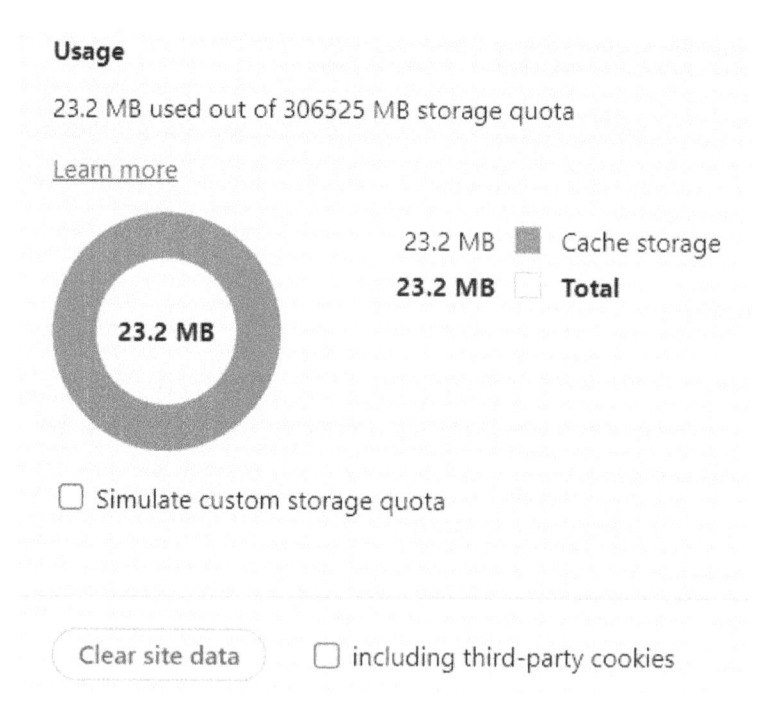

Figure 1-23. Clearing the browser's storage

Now open the browser debugger's Network tab. Refresh your browser (empty cache and hard refresh) to see what gets downloaded from the server as in Figure 1-24. First, you will see localhost being downloaded, which in turn downloads bootstrap.min.css and app.css, and then blazor.webassembly.js. A little lower you will see that blazor.boot.js gets downloaded, which in turn will download dotnet.native.wasm. This is the .NET Core runtime compiled to run on WebAssembly!

32

CHAPTER 1   INTRODUCTION TO BLAZOR

```
Name
→  localhost
   bootstrap.min.css
   app.css
   BlazorApp.WebAssembly.styles.css
→  blazor.webassembly.js
   dotnet.js
   favicon.png
   blazor.boot.json
   dotnet.runtime.8.0.5.gongq8hbow.js
   dotnet.native.8.0.5.ew1vqrwwsw.js
→  dotnet.native.wasm
```

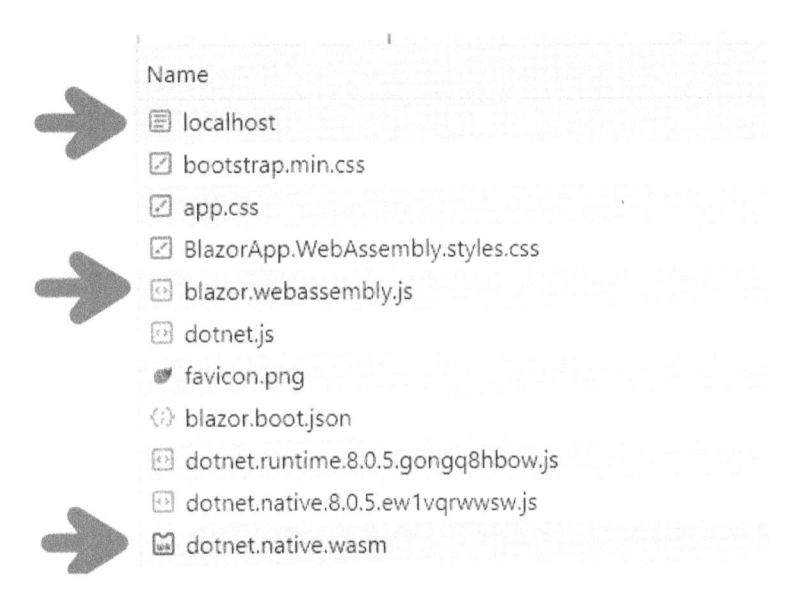

Figure 1-24. *Examining the bootstrap process using the network log*

Now that the .NET runtime is running, you will see (scroll down?) that BlazorApp.WebAssembly.wasm gets downloaded, followed by all its dependencies, including mscorlib.wasm and System.wasm.

Note   The list of rows here might become long and go out of view; if you can't find this, try scrolling down until you see these files.

These files contain the .NET libraries containing classes such as `string` used to execute all kinds of things, and they are the same libraries you use on the server. This is very powerful because you can re-use existing .NET libraries in Blazor you or others built before!

At the bottom of the network tab, you will see the total download size as in Figure 1-25. Almost 10 MB (in development, production will be a lot less)! This is because we are using an empty cache; the next download will show a lot less as shown in Figure 1-26 because now Blazor can retrieve most of the files from the cache. We will look at reducing the full download size for production applications in the deployment chapter.

33

CHAPTER 1 INTRODUCTION TO BLAZOR

```
208 requests   9.4 MB transferred   23.8 MB resources   Finish: 3.76 s
```

Figure 1-25. *Total download size with empty cache*

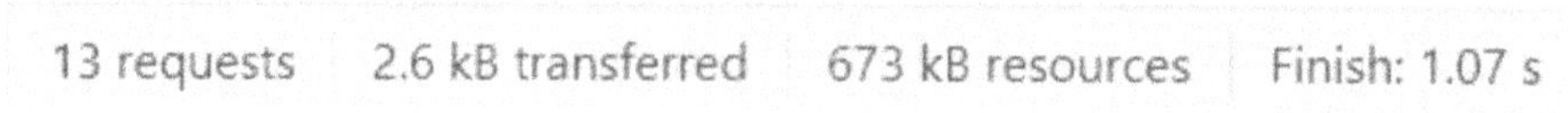

```
13 requests   2.6 kB transferred   673 kB resources   Finish: 1.07 s
```

Figure 1-26. *Total download size with filled cache*

Let us now compare this with Blazor Server.

The Blazor Server Bootstrap Process

Let's look at the bootstrapping process of a Blazor Server project.

Create a new project using VS(C), and create a new Blazor Server project named BlazorApp.Server. Or open a command line, and run the following command which will create a new Blazor Server project and solution.

```
$ProjectName = "BlazorApp.Server"
mkdir $ProjectName
cd $ProjectName
dotnet new sln -n $ProjectName
mkdir src
cd src
dotnet new blazorserver -n $ProjectName
cd ..
dotnet sln add src\$ProjectName
```

Now we can build and run this application. Open it with Visual Studio (Code) and hit F5.

Should you get an error like the following line, it means another project is still running. Stop that project first and retry.

```
Failed to bind to address https://127.0.0.1:5001: address already in use
```

CHAPTER 1   INTRODUCTION TO BLAZOR

The Blazor application should be shown. Now open the browser's debugger on the network tab, disable the cache (on the network tab you have a checkbox to disable the cache), and make your page refresh. Now compare what gets downloaded as in Figure 1-27. As you can see, the total download size is a lot smaller, resulting in your page getting loaded faster. You can also see that a WebSocket is opened between server and browser, allowing the Blazor runtime to exchange UI changes and events.

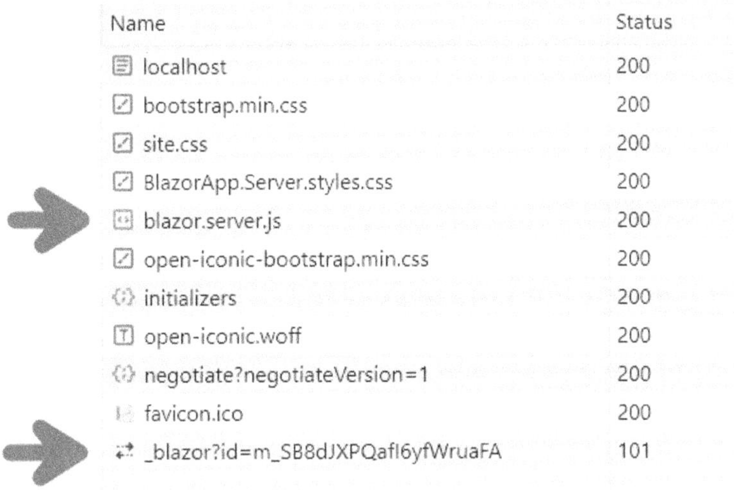

Name	Status
localhost	200
bootstrap.min.css	200
site.css	200
BlazorApp.Server.styles.css	200
blazor.server.js	200
open-iconic-bootstrap.min.css	200
initializers	200
open-iconic.woff	200
negotiate?negotiateVersion=1	200
favicon.ico	200
_blazor?id=m_SB8dJXPQafl6yfWruaFA	101

Figure 1-27. *Looking at server-side Blazor network activity*

Now click the Counter link in the navigation menu, and select the WebSocket link in the network debugger tab. Each time you click, you will see a couple of SignalR messages appear as in Figure 1-28. These binary messages are all tiny because only changes are transmitted this way. For example, when you click the Increment button in the `Counter` component, the browser only needs to update the number in the browser.

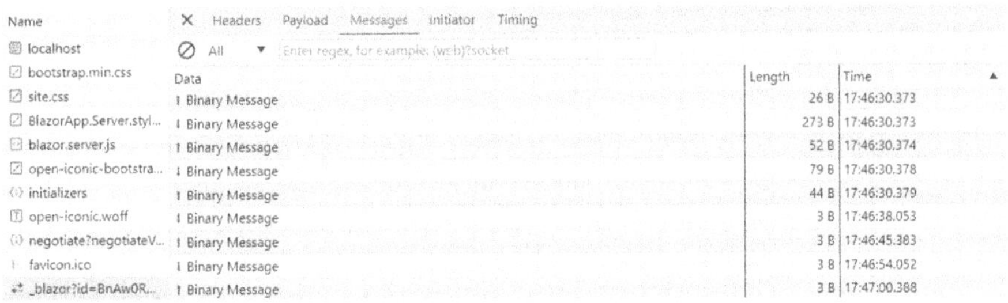

Figure 1-28. *The SignalR messages*

35

Nullable Reference Types

Throughout this book, I will be using modern C# with some of the latest features. But there is one C# feature I want to discuss right now. Every developer, from time to time, will encounter a `NullReferenceException`, which is a real bug because you can always avoid it. What if the compiler can help you with this, and warn you about a possible `NullReferenceException`? This is what nullable reference types are all about.

An Apology

Who invented the `null` reference? Tony Hoare did, and he apologized in 2009 and denoted this as his billion-dollar mistake:

> *I call it my billion-dollar mistake. It was the invention of the null reference in 1965. At that time, I was designing the first comprehensive type system for references in an object-oriented language (ALGOL W). My goal was to ensure that all use of references should be absolutely safe, with checking performed automatically by the compiler. But I couldn't resist the temptation to put in a null reference, simply because it was so easy to implement. This has led to innumerable errors, vulnerabilities, and system crashes, which have probably caused a billion dollars of pain and damage in the last forty years.*

Many object-oriented programming languages still use the `null` reference, and C# is no exception. Some languages even treated `null` differently. For example, in Objective-C when a pointer is `null`, the compiler would not invoke a method on it. And it would do this silently! Of course you would not get a `NullReferenceException`, but it did skip an important piece of functionality.

Using Null in C#

Let us start with the basics. In .NET there are two different kinds of types: reference types and value types. A reference type uses a reference to point to an object, and a value type holds the value of an object. Because of this, value types cannot be `null`. But in databases, you can have a column holding a number (a value type) which can be null. So how do you represent this in C#? For this we can denote a nullable value type by adding a question mark after the type, for example, in Listing 1-8.

Listing 1-8. A nullable value type

```
int? i = null;
```

Now in C# we can tell the compiler to treat reference types in the same way, meaning that we will get a warning if we assign a null value to a reference type, except when we add a question mark after the type. Listing 1-9 shows both examples.

Listing 1-9. Nullable reference types

```
// No warning

string? canBeNull = null;

// Warning:

// Converting null literal or possible null value to non-nullable type

string cannotBeNull = null;
```

Of course this would break every existing C# application out there, so we need to enable this in our project properties. You can do this in Visual Studio using your project properties as shown in Figure 1-29.

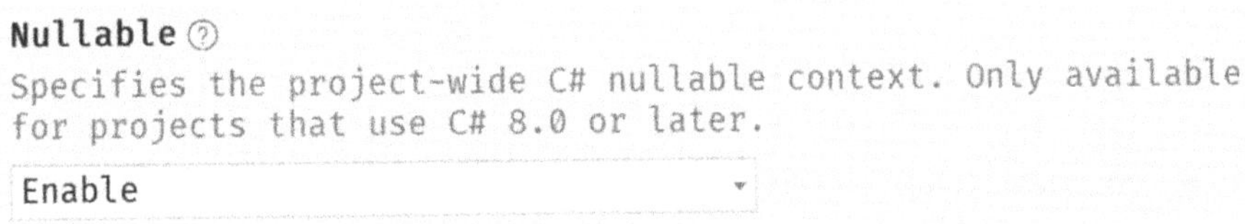

Nullable ⓘ
Specifies the project-wide C# nullable context. Only available for projects that use C# 8.0 or later.
Enable

Figure 1-29. Setting the Nullable compiler option

You can also do this directly in your project as shown in Listing 1-10.

Listing 1-10. Enabling Nullable reference types in the project file

```xml
<Project Sdk="Microsoft.NET.Sdk.Web">

  <PropertyGroup>
    <TargetFramework>net8.0</TargetFramework>
    <Nullable>enable</Nullable>
```

```
    <ImplicitUsings>enable</ImplicitUsings>
  </PropertyGroup>
</Project>
```

This causes the compiler to set a nullable flag for every field, property, and method that is of (or returns) a reference type. You can inspect this flag in VS by hovering over it as shown in Figure 1-30.

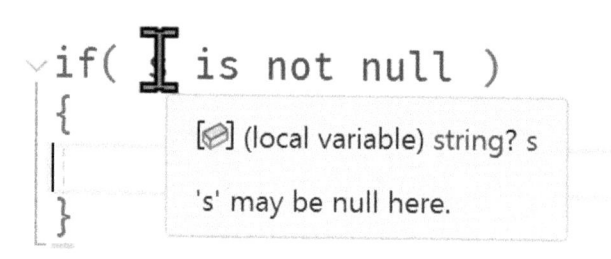

```
if( I is not null )
{
     [icon] (local variable) string? s
|
     's' may be null here.
}
```

Figure 1-30. Inspecting the Nullable flag

The compiler then uses that flag to issue warnings if you attempt to use a nullable reference type, for example, by getting the length of the string. Figure 1-31 will display a warning because the reference can be null.

```
len = s.Length;   ⚠ CS8602: Dereference of a possibly null reference.
```

Figure 1-31. Possible null reference

However, if we nest this in a condition as in Figure 1-32 where we check against `null`, the compiler will no longer issue a warning.

```
if( s is not null )
{
    len = s.Length;
}
```

Figure 1-32. No possible null reference

The whole idea of nullable reference types is to make the compiler do the analysis and to issue a warning when we can have a possible null being used which would result in a `NullReferenceException`.

Using References

In C# we can declare a class with an example in Listing 1-11. But when you do this with nullable reference types enabled, you will get compiler warnings. Why? Because you can create a new instance of a `Person` with a `null` `FirstName` and/or `null` `LastName`. So again, the compiler will warn about this.

Listing 1-11. A Person class

```csharp
public class Person
{
  public string FirstName { get; set; } // warning
  public string LastName { get; set; } // warning
}
```

There are a couple of ways we can make the compiler stop issuing warnings. We can use a constructor as in Listing 1-12. Now we cannot create a `Person` instance with a `null` property. Should someone call this constructor with a `null` argument, the compiler will again issue a warning.

Listing 1-12. Using a constructor

```csharp
public class Person
{
  public Person(string firstName, string lastName)
  {
    FirstName = firstName;
    LastName = lastName;
  }
  public string FirstName { get; set; } // warning
  public string LastName { get; set; } // warning
}
```

CHAPTER 1 INTRODUCTION TO BLAZOR

Sometimes you simply cannot use a constructor to silence the compiler. For example, you might want to use this `Person` class with Entity Framework Core. In this case, you could make `FirstName` and `LastName` nullable as in Listing 1-13.

Listing 1-13. Person with nullable name

```
public class Person
{
  public string? FirstName { get; set; } // warning
  public string? LastName { get; set; } // warning
}
```

However, this does not mimic real life. There is another technique we can use.

The Null Forgiving Operator

Sometimes you just know that a nullable reference is not `null`, and you want to tell the compiler about this. For this we can use the null forgiving operator by appending the nullable reference with an exclamation mark as in Figure 1-33. This sets the nullable flag to `false`, and the compiler is happy.

```
len = s!.Length;
```

Figure 1-33. *The null forgiving operator*

We can even use this to have a `null` value with the nullable flag set to false! What?! Let us look at the `Person` class again. When we want to use this class with a library such as Entity Framework Core, and we trust this library to always provide us with non-null values, we can silence the compiler as in Listing 1-14. This looks weird. Here we assign the `default!` value, whose nullable flag is set to false so the compiler does not give us warnings.

Listing 1-14. Using the null forgiving operator with types

```
public class Person
{
  public string FirstName { get; set; } = default!;
```

```
  public string LastName { get; set; } = default!;
}
```

Required Properties

Modern C# has the `required` modifier for properties. This tells the compiler to give errors for code that would create a Person without setting the required properties. For example, look at Listing 1-15.

Listing 1-15. Using required properties

```
public class Person
{
  public required string FirstName { get; set; }
  public required string LastName { get; set; }
}
```

No more warnings! This is exactly the technique we will use to create Blazor components that have reference properties who we cannot initialize using a constructor.

Of course, with `string` properties, we can also assign them an empty string instead of `null` as in Listing 1-16. But for other reference types, this is not always possible.

Listing 1-16. The Person class

```
public class Person
{
  public string FirstName { get; set; } = string.Empty;
  public string LastName { get; set; } = string.Empty;
}
```

Nullable Reference Types and .NET Libraries

Microsoft has gone through a lot of effort to make all their libraries support nullable reference types. I want you to realize that this is all compiler meta-data, so you can use the new libraries supporting nullable reference types with older projects; the compiler will simply ignore this meta-data. You can also use libraries that do not support this meta-data, but you will need to use the null forgiving operator with a lot of methods. But do yourself a favor; get to use nullable reference types, and your code will be shipped with a lot less bugs! If you want to learn more, the Microsoft documentation is at `https://learn.microsoft.com/dotnet/csharp/nullable-references`.

Summary

In this chapter, we looked at the history of the browser wars and how this resulted in the creation of WebAssembly. The .NET runtime allows you to run .NET assemblies, and because it can now also run on WebAssembly, we can now run .NET assemblies in the browser! All of this resulted in the creation of Blazor, where you build razor files containing .NET code which update the browser's DOM, giving us the ability to build single-page applications in .NET, instead of JavaScript.

First, we installed the prerequisites needed for developing and running Blazor applications. We then created our first Blazor Web App project. Similar projects will be used throughout this book to explain all the Blazor concepts you need to know about.

Finally, we looked at using nullable reference types and how this can help writing better code with less bugs.

CHAPTER 2

Components and Structure for Blazor Applications

In modern web development, we build applications by constructing them from components, which typically are again built from smaller components. A Blazor component is a self-contained chunk of user interface. Blazor components are classes built from Razor and C# with one specific purpose (also known as Single Responsibility Principle) and are easier to understand, debug, and maintain. And of course, you can re-use the same component in different pages, which can be a huge advantage.

In this chapter, we will explore how to build Blazor components, and we will look at lots of additional features of components in the following chapters.

A Quick Look at Razor

Blazor is the combination of Browser + Razor (with a lot of artistic freedom). So, to understand Blazor, we need to understand browsers and the Razor language. I will assume you understand what a browser is since the Internet has been very popular for over more than a few decades. But Razor (as a computer language) might not be that clear (yet). Razor is a markup syntax that allows you to embed code in an HTML template. Razor can be used to dynamically generate HTML, but you can also use it to generate code and other formats. For example, at the company I work for, we generate emails using Razor.

Razor made its first appearance in ASP.NET MVC. In ASP.NET Core MVC, Razor is executed at the server-side to generate HTML which is sent to the browser. But in Blazor, this code can also be executed inside your browser (with Blazor WebAssembly) and will

CHAPTER 2   COMPONENTS AND STRUCTURE FOR BLAZOR APPLICATIONS

dynamically update the web page without having to go back to the server. The whole Razor language can be found at https://learn.microsoft.com/aspnet/core/mvc/views/razor.

Using @

Inside an HTML Razor file, you will find HTML syntax, and you switch to C# using the @ symbol. For example, `<div>@System.DateTime.Now.ToLongDateString()</div>` would render the current date inside a `<div>` element by evaluating the expression following the @ symbol. The expression following the @ symbol cannot contain spaces, except when using the `await` keyword. If you need to use spaces inside an expression, wrap the expression in parenthesis, for example, `<p>@(DateTime.Now - new DateTime(1967, 12, Day))</p>`.

There is an exception though: the @ symbol in an email address inside HTML attributes and content like the following `<a href="mailto:peter@u2u.be">peter@u2u.be</a>` will be ignored.

If you want to render some plain text inside a C# construct like a look you can use @:. For example:

```
@for(int i = 0; i < 5; i++)
{
  <br/>
  @:Number @i
}
```

And if you need to display an @ symbol, you can escape it with another @, for example, `<p>@@</p>`.

Control Structures

You can use if statements in Razor; you do have to prepend the if with a @, so you should use `@if`. Same thing goes for other control structures, such as `@switch`, `@for`, `@foreach`, `@while`, and `@do while`.

Razor Comments

Razor uses @* Some comment *@ for comments.

Razor Directives

Razor directives are represented by specific keywords after the @ symbol. Directives change the way the Razor file will generate into a .NET class. We will discuss many of these directives in further content of this book.

- The @namespace directive changes the namespace of the generated class.
- The @attribute directive adds the given attribute to the generated class, for example, @attribute [Authorize] will add the [Authorize] to the class. Some directives will generate a specific attribute.
- The @page "/counter" is used by Blazor routing and will generate the Route attribute as in the following: @attribute [Route("/counter")]. Better use the @page directive.
- You can change the base class using @inherits BaseClass.
- Use the @implements syntax to implement an interface, for example, @implements IDisposable.
- The @inject directive is used by dependency injection. For example, @inject SomeDependency dep will use dependency injection to inject an instance of the SomeDependency class as the dep property.
- The @using directive adds the namespace just like the C# using statement.

Directive Attributes

Directive attributes are Razor defined attributes which change the way an element is parsed or behaved.

- Use @bind for data binding. Look at the Data Binding chapter.
- @formname is used to assign a name to a form element. More about this in the Forms chapter.

- Events use the @on{EVENT} syntax, for example, @onclick. There are also the @on{EVENT}:preventDefault and @on{EVENT}:stopPropagation directive attributes. This is discussed in the Data Binding chapter.

- @ref creates a reference to a component. Look at the advanced components chapter.

- @key changes the way components re-render. Again this is discussed in the advanced components chapter.

- @attributes is used for rendering non-declared attributes. See advanced components.

What Is a Blazor Component?

To put it in a simple manner, each .razor file in Blazor is a component. It's that simple! A .razor file in Blazor contains markup and has code in the @code section. And components can be built by adding other components and HTML markup as children.

A component is a self-contained, re-usable bit of user interface that may contain logic to handle user interaction. Some components might just display some data, and others can handle complex user interactions. You can use these components in Blazor and MVC applications; you can nest components in other components and publish them as a component library so we can share the same components among different projects.

Any class that derives from the ComponentBase class becomes a Blazor component; a little later, we will build an example of this. When you use a .razor file, the generated class will also derive from ComponentBase.

Open a PowerShell command line (I like to use Terminal), and run the following commands:

```
$ProjectName = "BlazorApp.ComponentsIntro"
mkdir $ProjectName
cd $ProjectName
dotnet new sln -n $ProjectName
mkdir src
cd src
```

```
dotnet new blazor -n $ProjectName --all-interactive --interactivity Server
cd ..
dotnet sln add src\$ProjectName
```

This will create a standard Blazor WebApp solution and project.

Open the .sln file using Visual Studio (Code).

Examine the Components/Pages/Counter.razor file as in Listing 2-1.

Listing 2-1. The Counter component

```
@page "/counter"

<PageTitle>Counter</PageTitle>

<h1>Counter</h1>

<p role="status">Current count: @currentCount</p>

<button class="btn btn-primary" @onclick="IncrementCount">Click me</button>

@code {
  private int currentCount = 0;

  private void IncrementCount()
  {
    currentCount++;
  }
}
```

This Razor file will be converted into a class with the same name as the .razor file, in this case into the `Counter` class. This is done through a modern C# Roslyn compiler feature known as a source generator. Let us look at the generated code. Why? This will help you understand how Razor components get compiled and can also help you with debugging, even fixing some compiler errors.

Examining the Generated Code

Add the `EmitCompilerGeneratedFiles` to the project file as in Listing 2-2.

CHAPTER 2   COMPONENTS AND STRUCTURE FOR BLAZOR APPLICATIONS

Listing 2-2. Modifying the project file

```
<Project Sdk="Microsoft.NET.Sdk.Web">

  <PropertyGroup>
    <TargetFramework>net8.0</TargetFramework>
    <Nullable>enable</Nullable>
    <ImplicitUsings>enable</ImplicitUsings>
    <EmitCompilerGeneratedFiles>true</EmitCompilerGeneratedFiles>
  </PropertyGroup>

</Project>
```

This will make the source generator emit the generated code into a file (something it does not do by default to speed up compilation, the compiler just keeps the source code in memory). Open the project's obj folder (which is a subfolder of your project), and go deeper (Debug/netx.0/generated/…) until you find the Components_Pages_Counter_razor.g.cs file. This contains the generated code (cleaned up a bit for easier reading in Listing 2-3).

Listing 2-3. The generated code after cleanup

```
[RouteAttribute("/counter")]
public partial class Counter : ComponentBase
{
  // Generated from the markup section

  protected override void BuildRenderTree(
    RenderTreeBuilder __builder)
  {
    __builder.OpenComponent<PageTitle>(0);
    __builder.AddAttribute(1, "ChildContent",
    (RenderFragment)((__builder2) =>
    {
      __builder2.AddContent(2, "Counter");
    }
    ));
    __builder.CloseComponent();
    __builder.AddMarkupContent(3, "\r\n\r\n");
```

```
__builder.AddMarkupContent(4, "<h1>Counter</h1>\r\n\r\n");
__builder.OpenElement(5, "p");
__builder.AddAttribute(6, "role", "status");
__builder.AddContent(7, "Current count: ");
__builder.AddContent(8, currentCount);
__builder.CloseElement();
__builder.AddMarkupContent(9, "\r\n\r\n");
__builder.OpenElement(10, "button");
__builder.AddAttribute(11, "class", "btn btn-primary");
__builder.AddAttribute(12, "onclick",
  EventCallback.Factory.Create<MouseEventArgs>(
  this, IncrementCount
));
__builder.AddContent(13, "Click me");
__builder.CloseElement();
}

// Copied from the @code section

private int currentCount = 0;

private void IncrementCount()
{
  currentCount++;
}
}
```

Look at the listing for the Counter.razor file. Because the file is named Counter.razor, the class's name becomes Counter. When a class is generated, we make it a `partial` class, which you can see in the second line of the generated code.

The first line contains a @page directive, which gets generated as the RouteAttribute. We will look at the @page directive in the Routing chapter.

Now examine the markup between the @page and @code directive. This gets generated as the BuildRenderTree method, which kind of copies each line of markup into one or more __builder methods.

CHAPTER 2 COMPONENTS AND STRUCTURE FOR BLAZOR APPLICATIONS

Finally, the @code directive contents are copied into the generated code.

Note You can examine the generated code for any Razor component.

Building a Simple Alert Component with Razor

Let us build our own Blazor component that will show a simple alert. Alerts are used to draw the attention of the user to some message, for example, a warning.

Create a New Component with Visual Studio

Open the BlazorApp.ComponentsIntro solution.

Right-click the Pages folder and select Add ➤ Razor Component. The Add New Item window should open as in Figure 2-1.

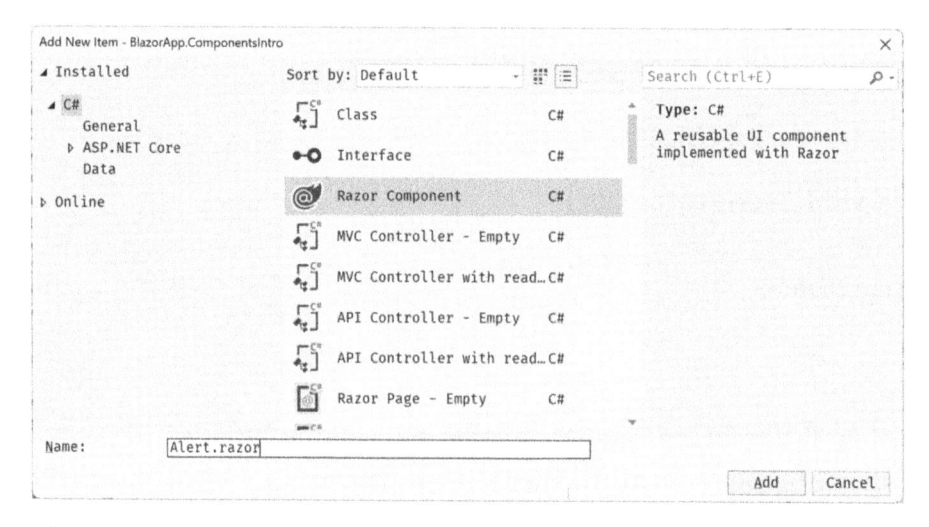

Figure 2-1. The Add New Item window

Select Razor Component and name it Alert.razor. Click Add.

CHAPTER 2   COMPONENTS AND STRUCTURE FOR BLAZOR APPLICATIONS

Create a New Component with Code

Open the BlazorApp.ComponentsIntro solution.

Right-click the Pages folder and select New File. Name it Alert.razor. Unlike Visual Studio, this will not generate any code in this file. There are extensions available for creating Blazor components. I will let you explore which one you like best (e.g., https://visualstudiomagazine.com/articles/2020/04/08/vs-code-blazor.aspx).

Implement the Alert Component

Remove all existing content from Alert.razor and replace it with Listing 2-4. Let us have a look at this component.

Listing 2-4. The Alert component

```
@if (Show)
{
  <div class="alert alert-secondary mt-4" role="alert">
    @ChildContent
  </div>
}

@code {

  [Parameter]
  public bool Show { get; set; }

  [Parameter]
  public RenderFragment ChildContent { get; set; } = default!;
}
```

The first line in the Alert component uses an @if conditional to hide or show its inner content. This is a common technique if you want to conditionally display content. So, if the Show public property (parameter) is false, the whole component is not shown. This allows us to "hide" the component until needed. With Razor, when the condition for the @if is false, it does not generate any of the markup which is in the true part of the @if. In the example from Listing 2-4, this means there is no <div> generated if Show is false. The Weather component also uses an @if to either show a loading message when there are no forecasts yet or show the forecasts.

CHAPTER 2   COMPONENTS AND STRUCTURE FOR BLAZOR APPLICATIONS

If you want to pass some object to a component, you need to add a public property, and add the [Parameter] attribute to it as in Listing 2-4. Here we have a bool parameter named Show.

Our Alert component will show some content in a <div> element as an alert (using bootstrap styles), so how do we pass this content to the Alert component? Inside the @if, there is a <div> element with @ChildContent as its child. You use @ChildContent if you want to access the nested element in the Alert component, as you'll see when we use the Alert component in Listing 2-4.

Blazor dictates that this parameter should be named ChildContent, and it needs to be of type RenderFragment because this is the way the Blazor engine passes it (we will look at this later in this and other chapters).

> **Note** The default Blazor templates use bootstrap 5.1 for styling. Bootstrap (https://getbootstrap.com) is a very popular CSS framework, originally built for Twitter, giving easy layout for web pages. However, Blazor does not require you to use Bootstrap, so you can use whatever styling you prefer. In that case, you would have to update all the Razor files in the solution using the other styles, just like in regular web development. In this book, we will use Bootstrap, simply because it is there.

Let us now add the Alert component to the Home page. Complete the Alert and add a button as in Listing 2-5.

Listing 2-5. Using our Alert component in Home.razor

```
@page "/"

<PageTitle>Home</PageTitle>

<h1>Hello, world!</h1>

Welcome to your new app.

<Alert Show="@ShowAlert">
  <span class="oi oi-check mr-2" aria-hidden="true"></span>
  <strong>Blazor is soo cool!</strong>
</Alert>
```

CHAPTER 2 COMPONENTS AND STRUCTURE FOR BLAZOR APPLICATIONS

```
<button @onclick="ToggleAlert" class="btn btn-success">Toggle</button>

@code {
  public bool ShowAlert { get; set; } = true;
  public void ToggleAlert() => ShowAlert = !ShowAlert;
}
```

As you start to type, Visual Studio and Code are smart enough to provide you with IntelliSense, as illustrated in Figure 2-2, for the Alert component and its parameters!

Figure 2-2. Visual Studio IntelliSense support for custom Blazor components

Inside the `<Alert>` tag, there is a `<strong>` element displaying a simple message. These will be set as the ChildContent property of the Alert component.

Build and run your project. When you click the `<button>`, it calls the ToggleAlert method which will hide and show the Alert as in Figure 2-3.

Figure 2-3. Our simple Alert component before clicking the Toggle button

EditorRequired

The Alert component has two parameters. What happens when you don't supply a value of the Show parameter? This will default to false, so the Alert component never gets shown. Can we avoid this?

The EditorRequired attribute makes a parameter mandatory, so if it is not set, then the compiler issues a warning. So, fix the Alert component as in Listing 2-6.

Listing 2-6. Using the EditorRequired attribute

```
[Parameter]
[EditorRequired]
public bool Show { get; set; }

[EditorRequired]
[Parameter]
public RenderFragment ChildContent { get; set; } = default!;
```

Components and Namespaces

What about namespaces and Blazor components? Start by adding a new Entities folder to the Blazor.ComponentsIntro project, and in it add a new class Employee as in Listing 2-7.

Listing 2-7. The Employee class

```
public class Employee
{
  public required string FirstName { get; set; }
  public required string LastName { get; set; }
}
```

Now add a new Blazor component to the Pages folder, and name it EmployeeList. razor as in Listing 2-8.

Listing 2-8. The EmployeeList component

```
<h3>EmployeeList</h3>

@code {
  private List<Employee> _employees = [];
}
```

However, when typing, you will see that it does not know about the Employee type! Normally, when you write this in a .cs file, you would add a using statement to the top of this class. You can do the same with Razor, except you need to use the @using syntax as in Listing 2-9.

Listing 2-9. *@using*

```
@using BlazorApp.ComponentsIntro.Entities
<h3>EmployeeList</h3>
```

Now you can complete the component as in Listing 2-10.

Listing 2-10. *The complete EmployeeList component*

```
@using BlazorApp.ComponentsIntro.Entities

<h3>EmployeeList</h3>

@code {
  private List<Employee> _employees = [
    new Employee { FirstName = "John", LastName = "Laplace" },
    new Employee { FirstName = "Mary", LastName = "Laplace" }
    ];
}
```

You can also add the @using statement to the _Imports.razor file, which will apply the @using to all components in the same directory and sub-directories.

Normally your component will also receive the namespace created from the folder structure in your project. You can change the namespace for your component(s) by applying the @namespace directive.

For example, the EmployeeList component will now use the BlazorApp.ComponentsIntro.Employees namespace as in Listing 2-11.

Listing 2-11. *The EmployeeList with a different namespace*

```
@namespace BlazorApp.ComponentsIntro.Employees

@using BlazorApp.ComponentsIntro.Entities

<h3>EmployeeList</h3>

@code {
  private List<Employee> _employees = [
    new Employee { FirstName = "John", LastName = "Laplace" },
    new Employee { FirstName = "Mary", LastName = "Laplace" }
    ];
}
```

Separating View and View Model

You might not like this mixing of markup (view) and code (view model). If you like, you can use two separate files, one for the view using Razor and another for the view model using C#. The view will display the data from the view model, and event handlers in the view will invoke methods from the view model.

Some people prefer this way of working because it's more like the MVVM pattern.

We have seen that each Blazor Razor file gets generated into a C# partial class. If you want to separate the code from the Razor file, put the code in a partial class with the same name as the component. The C# compiler will merge code from both files into a single class. Let's try this!

Create a DismissibleAlert Component

If you haven't done so yet, open the BlazorApp.ComponentsIntro solution.

Add a new Razor Component and name it DismissibleAlert.razor. Also, add a new C# class, and call the file DismissibleAlert.razor.cs. So now we have two files, the Razor which will generate to the `DismissableAlert partial` class and another C# file with a `partial DismissibleAlert` class. These will be joined into one single class by the C# compiler.

A `DismissibleAlert` is an alert with a little x-button, which the user can click to dismiss the alert. It is quite like the previous `Alert` component. Replace the markup in the Razor file with Listing 2-12.

Listing 2-12. The markup for Dismissible.razor

```
@if (Show)
{
  <div class="alert alert-warning alert-dismissible fade show"
       role="alert">
    @ChildContent
    <button type="button"
            class="btn-close" data-bs-dismiss="alert"
            aria-label="Close"></button>
  </div>
}
```

Listing 2-16. Using CSS isolation

```
h1 {
  color: blue;
}
```

Don't forget to remove the rules from app.css and run. Now only the Counter's `<h1>` will be blue!

How does this work? Use your browser's debugger to inspect the `<h1>` element in the Counter component as in Listing 2-17.

Listing 2-17. The header element of the Counter component

```
<h1 b-4hl9v4ydge="" tabindex="-1">Counter</h1>
```

Do you see the weird named attribute (also known as the scope identifier)? This uses a rule defined by the third link from Listing 2-18.

Listing 2-18. A CSS selector with scope identifier

```
/* _content/BlazorApp.ComponentsIntro/Components/Pages/Counter.razor.rz.scp.css */
h1[b-4hl9v4ydge] {
  color: blue;
}
```

This BlazorApp.ComponentsIntro.styles.css file gets dynamically generated when you build your application. This file bundles all scoped CSS files from your project into one.

Note You can find this file under {PROJECT}\obj\{CONFIG}\{VERSION}\scopedcss\projectbundle.

Your application will download this file using a stylesheet link. This link to the bundle follows the following convention:

```
<link href="{ASSEMBLY NAME}.styles.css" rel="stylesheet">
```

Child Components and CSS Isolation

You can have the style applied to child components. Let us look at an example: add a new file named Home.razor.css next to the Home component. Replace its contents with Listing 2-19.

Listing 2-19. Using ::deep

```
::deep {
  color: red;
}
```

When you run the component, you will also see that the `<Alert>` component's text color is also red, because of the ::deep modifier.

The ::deep pseudo-element selects elements that are descendants of an element's generated scope identifier.

Logging for Components

When running Blazor applications, you might want to add logging. Good for us is that Blazor uses the same logging framework as ASP.NET Core, and logging to the Console is enabled by default.

> **Note** You can also use Console.WriteLine to write to the console, but the built-in logging allows you to easily filter logging messages.

Start by creating a new Blazor Web application.

```
Set-Variable -Name "ProjectName" -Value "BlazorApp.Logging"
mkdir $ProjectName
cd $ProjectName
dotnet new sln -n $ProjectName
mkdir src
dotnet new blazor -n $ProjectName -o src -int Auto
dotnet sln add .\src\BlazorApp.Logging\
dotnet sln add .\src\BlazorApp.Logging.Client\
```

CHAPTER 2 COMPONENTS AND STRUCTURE FOR BLAZOR APPLICATIONS

This project supports both Blazor Server and Blazor WebAssembly.

Open the Home component and update it as in Listing 2-20.

Listing 2-20. The Home component with logging

```
@page "/"
@inject ILogger<Home> _logger;

@rendermode InteractiveServer
@* @rendermode InteractiveWebAssembly *@

<PageTitle>Logging</PageTitle>

<h1>Logging</h1>

<div>Click these buttons to see some logging.</div>

<button class="btn btn-info" @onclick="LogDebug">Debug</button>
<button class="btn btn-secondary" @onclick="LogInformation">Info</button>
<button class="btn btn-warning" @onclick="LogWarning">Warning</button>
<button class="btn btn-danger" @onclick="LogError">Error</button>
<button class="btn btn-dark" @onclick="LogCritical">Critical</button>
<button class="btn btn-primary" @onclick="LogConsole">Console</button>

@code {
    private void LogDebug() => _logger.LogDebug("Hmmmm...");
    private void LogInformation() => _logger.LogInformation("Hi there!");
    private void LogWarning() => _logger.LogWarning("Some warning");
    private void LogError() => _logger.LogError("Some error");
    private void LogCritical() => _logger.LogCritical("Aaahhhh!");
    private void LogConsole() => Console.WriteLine("This works too!");
}
```

This Home component takes an instance of ILogger<Home> through dependency injection. There are buttons, each for a different LogLevel. Currently we will run this using Blazor Server, hence the @rendermode InteractiveServer. We will cover render modes in the Render Modes chapter, so ignore this for the moment. We need this for the example to work.

Logging with Blazor Server

When will logging write a message? That depends on the `LogLevel` set for the logger. Let us look at an example.

When you run this application, I want you to watch the server's Console window (remember that I asked you to run the examples in Kestrel, which is a console application so the output will appear in the console). When you click on the Warning button, you should see a log message appear:

```
warn: BlazorApp.Logging.Client.Pages.Home[0]
      Some warning
```

However, clicking the Debug button will do nothing. That is because by default the `LogLevel.Trace` is disabled (the default is `Information`. You can enable this in Blazor server by editing the appsettings.json file from the BlazorApp.Logging project as in Listing 2-21.

Listing 2-21. The Blazor Server appsettings.json file

```
{
  "Logging": {
    "LogLevel": {
      "Default": "Information",
      "Microsoft.AspNetCore": "Warning",
      "BlazorApp.Logging.Client.Pages.Home": "Trace" // ADD!
    }
  },
  "AllowedHosts": "*"
}
```

Clicking the Debug button will now emit a message.

Logging with Blazor WebAssembly

Update the `rendermode` of the `Home` component as in Listing 2-22.

Listing 2-22. Updating the rendermode

```
...
@* @rendermode InteractiveServer *@
@rendermode InteractiveWebAssembly
...
```

Clicking the buttons will now emit log messages, but now you need to look inside the browser's Console as shown in Figure 2-4!

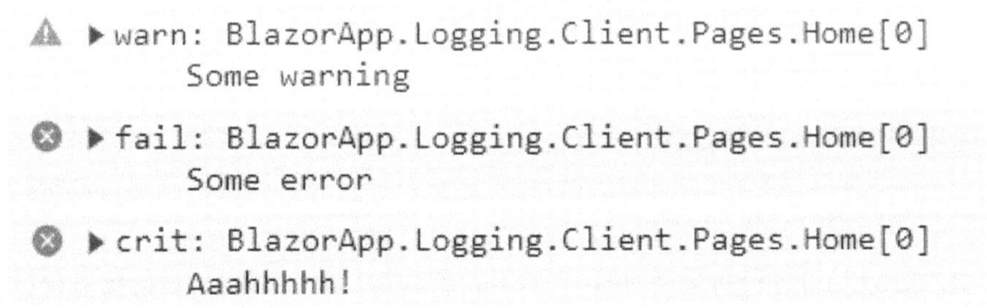

```
⚠ ▶ warn: BlazorApp.Logging.Client.Pages.Home[0]
       Some warning
❌ ▶ fail: BlazorApp.Logging.Client.Pages.Home[0]
       Some error
❌ ▶ crit: BlazorApp.Logging.Client.Pages.Home[0]
       Aaahhhhh!
```

Figure 2-4. Logging output

Again, clicking the Debug button will not emit any message, and if you update the LogLevel in the appconfig.json file (which lives in the wwwroot folder for Blazor WebAssembly), this will still not log any messages. That is because with Blazor WebAssembly, the minimum log level cannot go below Information by default. You can change this if you like in Program.cs as in Listing 2-23.

Listing 2-23. Lowering the minimum log level

```
WebAssemblyHostBuilder builder = WebAssemblyHostBuilder.
CreateDefault(args);

// Enable this to get all logging messages
#if DEBUG
builder.Logging.SetMinimumLevel(LogLevel.Trace);
#endif
```

Please wrap this with conditional compilation because this will generate a lot of logging!

Logging in Program.cs

You can also log some information in Program.cs. However, this requires a slight change in running the host. Update your Client's Program.cs as in Listing 2-24.

Listing 2-24. Logging in Program.cs

```
WebAssemblyHost host = builder.Build();

ILogger<Program> logger = host.Services
                .GetRequiredService<ILoggerFactory>()
                .CreateLogger<Program>();

logger.LogInformation("Logged after the app is built in the Program file.");

await host.RunAsync();
```

To use logging in the Program class, you need to Build the host first, and then you can retrieve the ILoggerFactory which you then use to create a ILogger<Program>.

Summary

In this chapter, we covered the basics of building Blazor components. A Blazor component is just another class inherited from ComponentBase, written with Razor and/or C#. Blazor components can receive data of any type from the parent component using a [Parameter], and they can be nested using a parameter of type RenderFragment named ChildContent. You can put the markup and code in a single file, or you can separate them into two files, one using Razor and the other C#. Components can use CSS isolation for styling. Finally, we looked at logging for Blazor. Time to build us some Blazor components in the next chapter.

CHAPTER 3

Data Binding

Imagine an application that needs to display data to the user and capture changes made by that user to save the modified data. One way you could build an application like this is to, once you got the data, iterate over each item of data. For example, for every member of a list, you would generate the same repeating element, and then inside that element, you would generate textboxes, drop-downs, and other UI elements that present data. Later, after the user has made some changes, you would iterate over your generated elements, and for every element, you would inspect the child elements to see if their data was changed. If so, you copy the data back into your objects that will be used for saving that data.

This is an error-prone process and a lot of work if you want to do this with something like jQuery (jQuery is a very popular JavaScript framework which allows you to manipulate the browser's _Document Object Model_ (_DOM_)).

Modern frameworks like Angular and React have become popular because they simplify this process greatly through _data binding_. With data binding, most of this work for generating UI and copying data back into objects is done by the framework.

One-Way Data Binding

One-way data binding is where data flows from the component to the DOM, or vice-versa, but only in one direction. Data binding from the component to the DOM is where some data, like the customer's name, needs to be displayed. Data binding from the DOM to the component is where a DOM event takes place, like the user clicking a button, and we want some code to run.

There is also the concept of two-way data binding, where we want the property of an instance to be kept in sync with the property of an `<input>` element or Blazor component. Editing the element updates its value, which then automatically updates the value of the instance, and vice-versa. This also works between Blazor components.

CHAPTER 3   DATA BINDING

One-Way Data Binding Syntax

Again, we will use a hands-on approach, so create a new Blazor Server application to experiment with data binding:

```
$ProjectName = "BlazorApp.DataBinding"
mkdir $ProjectName
cd $ProjectName
dotnet new sln -n $ProjectName
mkdir src
cd src
dotnet new blazor -n $ProjectName --all-interactive --interactivity Server
cd ..
dotnet sln add src\$ProjectName
```

This will generate some sample components, including the Counter component from Listing 3-1.

Listing 3-1. Examining one-way data binding with Counter.razor

```
@page "/counter"

<PageTitle>Counter</PageTitle>

<h1>Counter</h1>

<p role="status">Current count: @currentCount</p>

<button class="btn btn-primary" @onclick="IncrementCount">Click me</button>

@code {
  private int currentCount = 0;

  private void IncrementCount()
  {
    currentCount++;
  }
}
```

On this component, you get a simple counter, which you can increment by clicking the button as illustrated by Figure 3-1.

CHAPTER 3   DATA BINDING

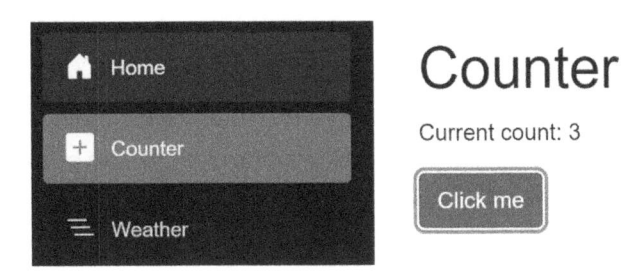

Figure 3-1. The Counter page

Let's look at the workings of this component. The `currentCount` field is defined in the @code section in Counter.razor. This is not a field that can be set from outside, so there is no need for the [Parameter] attribute and we can keep it `private`.

To display the value of the counter in razor, we use the `@currentCount` razor syntax as shown in Listing 3-2.

Listing 3-2. Data binding from the component to the DOM

```
<p role="status">Current count: @currentCount</p>
```

Any time you click the button, the Blazor runtime sees that `currentCount` may have been updated, and it will automatically update the DOM with the latest value of `currentCount`.

Attribute Binding

You can also use this same syntax to bind the value of an HTML attribute.

Add a scoped css file named Counter.razor.css with content from Listing 3-3.

Listing 3-3. Some simple styles

```
.red-background {
  background: red;
  color: white;
}
.yellow-background {
  background: yellow;
  color: black;
}
```

67

Wrap the currentCount in an <span> as in Listing 3-4. Here we also add a BackgroundColor conversion method, which takes some value (in this case currentCount) and converts it into another value (in this case the name of a css class). Every time you change the value of currentCount by clicking the button, it changes the currentCount's background color.

Listing 3-4. Binding a HTML attribute

```
@page "/counter"

<PageTitle>Counter</PageTitle>

<h1>Counter</h1>

<p role="status"><span class="@BackgroundColor">@currentCount</span></p>

<button class="btn btn-primary" @onclick="IncrementCount">Click me</button>

@code {
  private int currentCount = 0;

  private void IncrementCount()
  {
    currentCount++;
  }

  private string BackgroundColor
    => (currentCount % 2 == 0) ? "red-background" : "yellow-background";
}
```

One-way data binding can be used to supply a value in a component's HTML.

Conditional Attributes

Sometimes you can control the browser by adding some attributes to DOM elements. For example, in Listing 3-5, to disable a button, you can simply use the `disabled` attribute.

Listing 3-5. Disabling a button using the disabled attribute

```
<button disabled>Disabled Button</button>
```

With Blazor, you can data bind an attribute to a Boolean expression (e.g., a field, property, or method of type `bool`), and Blazor will hide the attribute if the expression evaluates to `false` (or `null`) and will show the attribute if it evaluates to `true`.

Go back to the Counter.razor, and update the button with the `disabled` attribute from Listing 3-6.

Listing 3-6. Disabling the Click Me button

```
<button class="btn btn-primary"
  disabled="@(currentCount >= 10)"
  @onclick="IncrementCount">Click me</button>
```

Try it. Clicking the button until the `currentCount` becomes 10 will disable the button by adding the `disabled` attribute to the button. As soon as `currentCount` falls below 10, the button will become enabled again (except there is no way you can do this for the moment).

Event Handling and Data Binding

We update `currentCount` using the `IncrementCount()` method from Listing 3-1. This method gets called by clicking the "Click Me" button. This again is a one-way data binding, but in the other direction, from the button to your component. You are not data binding to data, but to a method, which gets invoked when an event takes place. So in our example, when you click the button, the Blazor runtime invokes the `IncrementCount` method. Blazor allows you to react to DOM events (like the DOM's click event) this way, instead of using JavaScript. You can also build your own components that have events, where you can use the same syntax to react to them. This is discussed later in this chapter.

Event Binding Syntax

Look at Listing 3-7. Now we are using the `@on{EVENT}` syntax (where `{EVENT}` is a placeholder for the event name, such as `click`, `input`, `mouseenter`).

Listing 3-7. Data binding from the DOM to the component

```
<button class="btn btn-primary" @onclick="IncrementCount">
  Click me
</button>
```

In this case, we want to bind to the button's click DOM-event, so we use the @onclick attribute on the button element, and we pass it the name of the method we want to call.

Clicking the button will trigger the DOM's click event, which then will call the IncrementCount method, which will cause the UI to be updated with the new value of the currentCount field. Whenever the user interacts with the site, for example, by clicking a button, Blazor assumes that the event will have some side effect because a method gets called, so it will update the UI with the latest values. The UI updates because there was an event handled by the Blazor runtime. Simply calling a method will not cause Blazor to update the UI. We will discuss this later in this chapter.

Event Arguments

In regular .NET, event handlers of type EventHandler can find out more information about the event using the sender and EventArgs arguments. In Blazor, event handlers don't follow the strict event pattern from .NET. The event handler method does not require any arguments, but you can declare the event handler method to take an argument of a type derived from EventArgs, for example, MouseEventArgs, as shown in Listing 3-8. Here we are using the MouseEventArgs instance to see if the Ctrl-key is being pressed, and if so, to decrement the currentCount field. If you were simply interested in any key press, you could ignore or leave out the MouseEventArgs.

Each event uses a specific kind of EventArgs, so please refer to online documentation at https://docs.microsoft.com/aspnet/core/blazor/components/event-handling for more information about a specific event.

Listing 3-8. A Blazor event handler taking arguments

```
private void IncrementCount(MouseEventArgs e)
{
  if (e.CtrlKey)
  {
    currentCount--;
  }
  else
  {
    currentCount++;
  }
}
```

Using C# Lambda Functions

Data binding to an event does not always require you to write a method. You can also use C# lambda function syntax with an example shown in Listing 3-9.

Listing 3-9. Event data binding with lambda syntax

```
<button class="btn btn-primary"
        disabled="@(currentCount >= 10)"
        @onclick="() => currentCount++">
  Click me
</button>
```

Two-Way Data Binding

Sometimes you want to display some data to the user, and you want to allow the user to make changes to this data. This is common in data-entry forms. Here we will explore Blazor's two-way data binding syntax.

Two-Way Data Binding Syntax

With two-way data binding, we will have the DOM update whenever the component changes, but the component will also update because of modifications in the DOM. The simplest example is with an `<input>` HTML element.

Let's try something. Modify Counter.razor by adding an increment field and an `<input>` element using the `@bind` attribute as shown in Listing 3-10. Also modify the `IncrementCount` method to use the `increment` field when you click the button.

Listing 3-10. Adding an increment and an input

```
@page "/counter"

<PageTitle>Counter</PageTitle>
<h1>Counter</h1>
<p role="status"><span class="@BackgroundColor">
  @currentCount
</span></p>
```

```
<p><input type="number" @bind-value="@increment" /></p>
<button class="btn btn-primary"
        disabled="@(currentCount >= 10)"
        @onclick="IncrementCount">
  Click me
</button>

@code {
  private int currentCount = 0;
  private int increment = 1;

  private void IncrementCount(MouseEventArgs e)
  {
    if (e.CtrlKey)
    {
      currentCount -= increment;
    }
    else
    {
      currentCount += increment;
    }
  }

  private string BackgroundColor
    => (currentCount % 2 == 0) ? "red-background"
                               : "yellow-background";
}
```

Build and run.

Change the value of the input, for example, 3. You should now be able to increment the currentCount with other values as in Figure 3-2.

CHAPTER 3 DATA BINDING

Counter

5

[2]

[Click me]

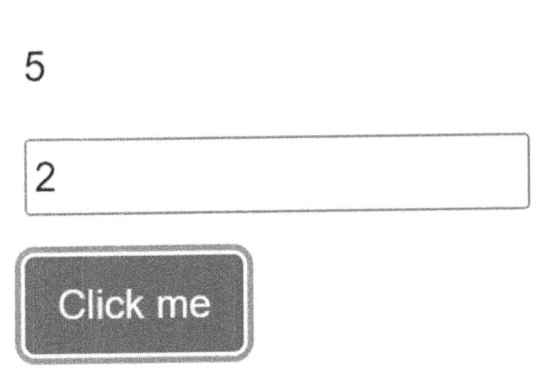

Figure 3-2. Adding an increment with two-way data binding

Look at the `<input>` element you just added, repeated here in Listing 3-11.

Listing 3-11. Two-way data binding with the @bind syntax

```
<p><input type="number" @bind-value="@increment" /></p>
```

The `@bind-value` syntax will "bind" the `value` property (attribute) of the input element to the `increment` field of the `Counter` component. If the user changes the value of the input, it will automatically change the value of the increment field, and vice-versa.

Note The input's `value` is the default property used during two-way data binding, so `@bind-value` and `@bind` mean the same thing when you data bind to an `<input>` element.

Two-Way Explicit Binding

Here we are using the `@bind-value` syntax which is the equivalent of two different one-way bindings as shown in Listing 3-12.

1. One-way data binding `value="@increment"` to set the input's `value` property to the `increment` variable.

73

2. When the user modifies the contents of the input element, the change event @onchange will trigger and will set the increment variable to the input's value increment = int.Parse($"{e.Value}").

When one side changes, the other will be updated.

Listing 3-12. Data binding in both directions

```
<p>
  <input type="number"
         value="@increment"
         @onchange="@((ChangeEventArgs e) => increment = int.Parse($"{e.
         Value}"))" />
</p>
```

This alternative syntax is very verbose and not that handy to use. Using @bind-value is way more practical. However, don't forget about this technique; using the more verbose syntax can sometimes be a more elegant solution!

Binding to Other Events: @bind-value:{event}

Blazor will update the value in two-way data binding when the DOM's onchange event occurs. This means that the increment field of the Counter component will be updated when the user changes the focus to another element, for example, the button. But maybe this is too late for you. Let's look at how you can change the event that triggers data binding.

Add a second <input> by copying the line from Listing 3-12. Run this example, and change the value of one <input> by typing a number into it (don't use the increment/decrement buttons that browsers add for number inputs). The other input's value will not update immediately. Clicking the other input will update it. This is because we're using the onchange event, which triggers when the <input> loses focus! If you want data binding to occur immediately, you can bind to the oninput event by using the explicit @bind:{EVENT} syntax. The oninput event triggers after each change in the <input>. Update the second <input> element to match Listing 3-13. Typing in the second input will update the first input after each keystroke.

Listing 3-13. Explicit binding to events

```html
html
<p>
  <input type="number"
         @bind-value="@increment" @bind-value:event="oninput" />
</p>
```

Preventing Default Actions

In Blazor you can react to events, and the browser will also react to these. For example, when you press a key with the focus on an `<input>` element, the browser will react by adding the keystroke to the `<input>`.

But what if you don't want the browser to behave as normal? Let's say you want to allow the user to increment and decrement an input's value simply by pressing "+" or "-". In JavaScript you would use the `preventDefault()` method. Blazor allows you to do the same, but without you writing JavaScript! Change the `<input>` from Listing 3-11 to react to the keypress event as in Listing 3-14 and Listing 3-15.

Listing 3-14. Handling keypress events

```
<p>
 <input type="number" @bind="@increment"
        @onkeypress="KeyHandler" />
</p>
```

Listing 3-15. The KeyHandler method

```
private void KeyHandler(KeyboardEventArgs e)
{
  if (e.Key == "+")
  {
    increment += 1;
  }
  else if (e.Key == "-")
```

```
    {
      increment -= 1;
    }
  }
}
```

Build and run.

Pressing "+" and "-" will increment and decrement the value in the input, but you will also see any key you just pressed added to the <input> html element because this is the default behavior for an input. To stop this default behavior, we can add @{EVENT}:preventDefault like in Listing 3-16. Here we use a bool field shouldPreventDefault (set to true) to stop the default behavior of the <input>, but you can use any Boolean expression.

Listing 3-16. Stopping the default behavior of the input

```
<p>
  <input type="number" @bind="@increment"
    @onkeypress="KeyHandler"
    @onkeypress:preventDefault="@shouldPreventDefault"/>
</p>

// add this next to the KeyHandler method
private bool shouldPreventDefault = true;
private void KeyHandler(KeyboardEventArgs e)
```

Build and run again. Now pressing "+" will increment the input's value as expected.

You can also leave out the value for preventDefault, and then it will always prevent the default action as in Listing 3-17.

Listing 3-17. Shorter notation

```
<p>
  <input type="number" @bind="@increment"
         @onkeypress="KeyHandler"
         @onkeypress:preventDefault />
</p>
```

Stopping Event Propagation

In a browser, events propagate to the parent element, then to that parent element's parent, etc. Again, generally this is desirable, but not always.

Let's look at an example. Start by adding two nested `<div>` elements to the `Counter` component which each handle the `@onmousemove` event as in Listing 3-18. Just keep the rest of the component.

Listing 3-18. Event propagation example

```
<h1>Stop Propagation</h1>

<div class="background"
     @onmousemove="OuterMouseMove">
  <p>@outerPos</p>
  <div class="foreground"
       @onmousemove="InnerMouseMove" >
    <p>@innerPos</p>
  </div>
</div>
```

Also add code from Listing 3-19. These event handlers simply show the mouse position in the element.

Listing 3-19. The event handlers

```
private string outerPos = "Move mouse";
private void OuterMouseMove(MouseEventArgs e)
{
  outerPos = $"Mouse last at {e.ClientX}x{e.ClientY}";
}
private string innerPos = "";
private void InnerMouseMove(MouseEventArgs e)
{
  innerPos = $"Mouse last at {e.ClientX}x{e.ClientY}";
}
```

CHAPTER 3   DATA BINDING

Also add to Counter.razor.css some more styles from Listing 3-20.

Listing 3-20. The Counter styles

```css
.background {
  width: 400px;
  height: 400px;
  background-color: yellow;
}
.foreground {
  width: 250px;
  height: 250px;
  background-color:aqua;
  margin: 50px
}
```

Build and run.

Move the mouse pointer around in the yellow square. Now do the same for the green rectangle. However, moving the mouse in the green square also updates the yellow one! This is because the `mousemove` event (and others) get sent to the element where the event occurs, but also to its parent element, all the way up to the root element!

If you want to avoid this, you can stop this propagation by adding the `{EVENT}:stopPropagation` attribute. Add it to the inner square as in Listing 3-21. From now on moving the mouse in the inner square does not update the outer square.

Listing 3-21. Stopping the event from propagating to the parent

```html
<h1>Stop Propagation</h1>

<div class="background" @onmousemove="OuterMouseMove">
  <p>@outerPos</p>
  <div class="foreground" @onmousemove="InnerMouseMove"
                          @onmousemove:stopPropagation>
    <p>@innerPos</p>
  </div>
</div>
```

If you want to be able to turn this on and off from code, assign a bool expression to this attribute, just like `preventDefault`.

Formatting Dates

Data binding to a `DateTime` value can be formatted with the `@bind-value:format` directive attribute as shown in Listing 3-22. If you need to format the date depending on the user's language and culture, keep on reading. This is discussed in the chapter on multicultural applications.

Listing 3-22. Formatting a date

```
<p>
  <input @bind="@Today" @bind:format="yyyy-MM-dd" />
</p>

@Today.ToLongDateString()

@code {
  private DateTime Today { get; set; } = DateTime.Now;
}
```

Currently, `DateTime` values are the only ones supporting the `@bind-value:format` attribute.

Change Detection

The Blazor runtime will update the DOM whenever it thinks changes have been made to your data. One example is when an event executes some of your code, it assumes you've modified some values as a side effect and renders the UI. However, Blazor is not always capable of detecting all changes, and in this case, you will have to tell Blazor to apply the changes to the DOM. A typical example is with background threads, so let us look at an example of this.

Open Counter.razor and add another button that will automatically increment the counter when pressed as in Listing 3-23.

CHAPTER 3 DATA BINDING

Listing 3-23. Demonstrating change detection

```
@* Add this after the Click me button *@
<button class="btn btn-primary" @onclick="AutoIncrement">Auto</button>
```

Add the `AutoIncrement` method from Listing 3-24 to the bottom of the @code section.

Listing 3-24. The AutoIncrement method

```
private void AutoIncrement()
{
  Timer timer = new(
  callback: (_) =>
  {
    // Changes need to be done on the correct thread!
    this.InvokeAsync(() =>
    {
      Console.WriteLine("++");
      IncrementCount(new MouseEventArgs());
    });
  },
  state: null,
  dueTime: TimeSpan.FromSeconds(1),
  period: TimeSpan.FromSeconds(1));
}
```

The `AutoIncrement` method uses a .NET `System.Threading.Timer` instance to increment the `currentCount` every second. A timer instance will run on a background thread, executing the callback delegate at intervals (just like `setInterval` with JavaScript).

You might find the lambda function argument in the `Timer`'s constructor a little strange. I use an underscore when I need to name an argument that is not used in the body of the lambda function. Call it anything you want, for example, `ignore`, it does not matter. I simply like to use underscore because then I don't have to think of a good name for the argument. C# 7 made this official, it is called _discards_, and you can find more at `https://docs.microsoft.com/dotnet/csharp/discards`.

Another thing I need to explain. Just like many other technologies, invoking logic that might update the UI needs to be done on a specific `SynchronizationContext`.

CHAPTER 3 DATA BINDING

Each Blazor component has an `InvokeAsync` method that takes a delegate and invokes it on the correct `SynchronizationContext`. Here we use it to invoke the `IncrementCount` method.

Run this page. Clicking the "Auto Increment" button will start the timer, but the `currentCount` will not update on the screen. Why? Try clicking the "Increment" button. The `currentCount` has been updated, so it is a UI problem. If you open the server's console, you will see a ++ appear every second, so the timer works! That's because I've added a `Console.Writeline`, which sends the output to the console. Sometimes an easy way to see if things are working.

Updating the UI Using StateHasChanged

Blazor will re-render the page whenever an event occurs. It will also re-render the page in case of asynchronous operations. However, some changes cannot be detected automatically. In this case, because we are making some changes on a background thread, you need to tell Blazor to update the page by calling the `StateHasChanged` method which every Blazor component inherits from its base class.

Go back to the `AutoIncrement` method and add a call to `StateHasChanged` as in Listing 3-25. `StateHasChanged` tells Blazor that some state has changed (Who would have thought!) and that it needs to re-render the page.

Listing 3-25. Adding StateHasChanged

```
private void AutoIncrement()
{
  Timer timer = new(
  callback: (_) =>
  {
    // Changes need to be done on the correct thread!
    this.InvokeAsync(() =>
    {
      Console.WriteLine("++");
      IncrementCount(new MouseEventArgs());
      StateHasChanged(); // Tell Blazor that changes were made
    });
  },
```

81

```
    state: null,
    dueTime: TimeSpan.FromSeconds(1),
    period: TimeSpan.FromSeconds(1));
}
```

Run again. Now pressing "Auto Increment" will work.

As you can see, sometimes we will need to tell Blazor manually to update the DOM. In general, the Blazor runtime will detect when to update the UI. When the user interacts with your application, events get triggered which will make change detection happen. When an async method completes, change detection will occur. It is only when we go outside the Blazor runtime, for example, using a .NET `Timer`, that we need to trigger change detection ourselves.

Understanding Parent–Child Communication

Parent and child components typically communicate through data binding. When a parent component wants to pass a value to a child component, we can use data binding to set the value of the child's parameter. And when the parent wants to be notified when something happens in the child component (an event), the parent can pass a callback method to the child, which the child invokes to notify the parent. And we can use both to set up two-way data binding. In this section, we will discuss data binding between components.

One-Way Data Binding Between Components

Start by copying the `DismissibleAlert` component from the previous chapter, repeated here in Listing 3-26 and Listing 3-27.

Listing 3-26. The DismissibleAlert component's razor

```
@if (Show)
{
  <div class="alert alert-warning alert-dismissible fade show"
  role="alert">
    @ChildContent
    <button type="button" class="btn-close" data-bs-dismiss="alert"
```

        aria-label="Close" @onclick="Dismiss">
    </button>
  </div>
}

Listing 3-27. The DismissibleAlert component's code

```
using Microsoft.AspNetCore.Components;

namespace BlazorApp.DataBinding.Components.Pages;

public partial class DismissibleAlert
{
  [Parameter]
  public bool Show { get; set; }

  [Parameter]
  public RenderFragment ChildContent { get; set; } = default!;

  public void Dismiss()
  => Show = false;
}
```

Now add this component to the Home component as in Listing 3-28, where we are using our DismissibleAlert component, which communicates with the parent component through the parent's ShowAlert property. Clicking the Toggle button will hide and show the alert. Each time we click the Toggle button, the value of ShowAlert changes, and the DismissibleAlert updates according to the value of its Show parameter which is data bound to the parent's ShowAlert property.

Note Notice that clicking the DismissibleAlert's close button does not work. We will fix this in the next section on two-way data binding.

CHAPTER 3 DATA BINDING

Listing 3-28. Using DismissibleAlert

```
@page "/"

<PageTitle>Home</PageTitle>
<h1>Hello, world!</h1>

Welcome to your new app.

<DismissibleAlert Show="@ShowAlert">
  <strong>Blazor is soo cool!</strong>
</DismissibleAlert>

<button @onclick="ToggleAlert" class="btn btn-success">Toggle</button>

@code {
  public bool ShowAlert { get; set; } = true;
  public void ToggleAlert() => ShowAlert = !ShowAlert;
}
```

Add a Delay Component

Here I want to show you that you can also build Blazor components that do not render, and simply provide a service. We will add a `Delay` component to automatically execute some logic after a certain amount of time has expired.

Start by adding a new class called `Delay` to the `Components` folder as shown in Listing 3-29. The `Delay` component will not have any visual part, so we don't even need a .razor file to build the view.

A Blazor component is a class that inherits the `ComponentBase` class. Since we want to use the `Delay` class as a Blazor component, we need to inherit from `ComponentBase`.

Listing 3-29. The Delay component

```
using Microsoft.AspNetCore.Components;

namespace BlazorApp.DataBinding.Com3ponents;

public class Delay : ComponentBase, IDisposable
{
  [Parameter]
```

```csharp
  public double TimeInSeconds { get; set; }

  [Parameter]
  public Action Tick { get; set; } = default!;

  private Timer timer = default!;

  protected override void OnInitialized()
  {
    timer = new(
      callback: (_) => InvokeAsync(() => Tick?.Invoke()),
      state: null,
      dueTime: TimeSpan.FromSeconds(TimeInSeconds),
      period: Timeout.InfiniteTimeSpan);
  }

  public void Dispose() => timer.Dispose();
}
```

This Delay component will invoke a delegate (Tick) after a certain number of seconds (TimeInSeconds) have expired. The Tick parameter is of type Action, which is one of the built-in delegate types of .NET. An Action is simply a method returning a void with no parameters. There are other generic Action types, such as Action<T>, which is a method returning void with one parameter of type T. This allows the parent component to set the Action, so the child will execute the Action (in this case after TimeInSeconds has expired).

Now add the Delay component to the Home page as in Listing 3-30. With this change, the Delay component will invoke the ToggleAlert method after 5 seconds.

Listing 3-30. Adding the Delay component to dismiss the alert

```razor
@page "/"

<PageTitle>Home</PageTitle>

<h1>Hello, world!</h1>

Welcome to your new app.

<DismissibleAlert Show="@ShowAlert">
  <strong>Blazor is soo cool!</strong>
```

CHAPTER 3   DATA BINDING

```
</DismissibleAlert>

<button @onclick="ToggleAlert" class="btn btn-success">Toggle</button>

@* Add the Delay component *@
<Delay TimeInSeconds="5" Tick="ToggleAlert" />

@code {
  public bool ShowAlert { get; set; } = true;

  public void ToggleAlert() => ShowAlert = !ShowAlert;
}
```

Run the application and wait at least 5 seconds. The alert does not hide! Why?!

Look at the markup, which is in Listing 3-30, for `DismissibleAlert`. It shows the component based on the Show parameter, and this parameter gets set through data binding. Does the `ToggleAlert` method get called?

Modify the `ToggleAlert` method as in Listing 3-31.

Listing 3-31. Adding some logging to ToggleAlert

```
public void ToggleAlert() {
  Console.WriteLine($"Toggle {ShowAlert}");
  ShowAlert = !ShowAlert;
}
```

Run the Blazor website again, and immediately open the Console. After a little while (5 seconds), you should see the `Console.WriteLine` output appear. So the `ToggleAlert` method does get called!

Think about this. We invoke a method asynchronously using a `System.Threading.Timer`. When the timer fires, we set the Home component's `ShowAlert` property to `false`. But we still need to update the UI because change detection does not get triggered.

Note   This is very important! The Blazor runtime updates the UI automatically when an event triggers, like the button click. The Blazor runtime also updates the UI for its own asynchronous methods, but not for other asynchronous methods like `Timer`.

Time to fix our application. Add a call to StateHasChanged in the ToggleAlert method as in Listing 3-32.

Listing 3-32. Adding StateHasChanged to Update the UI

```
public void ToggleAlert() {
  Console.WriteLine($"Toggle {ShowAlert}");
  ShowAlert = !ShowAlert;
  this.StateHasChanged();
}
```

Run again, wait and after 5 seconds the alert disappears!

So, we are trying to dismiss the alert automatically when the Timer ends. One way to reach this goal is by making the client re-render itself by calling StateHasChanged.

To be honest, I don't like this solution to our problem. Because a child component calls the ToggleAlert method, we manually need to call StateHasChanged. Is there no better way? And we haven't even solved another problem. When the user dismissed the alert before the Delay triggered the Tick method, it should reappear after 5 seconds because it will set ShowAlert back to true!

We will fix both problems, but first, we need to understand two-way data binding between components.

Use Two-Way Component to Component Data Binding

When the user clicks the DismissibleAlert component's close button, it sets its own Show property to false, as intended. The problem is that the parent Home component's ShowAlert stays true. Changing the value of the DismissibleAlert's local Show property will not update the Home component's ShowAlert property. What we need is two-way data binding between components, and Blazor has that.

Add Support for Two-Way Data Binding

With two-way data binding, changing the value of the Show parameter will update the value of the parent's ShowAlert property, and vice-versa.

You can use the @bind-{NameOfProperty} syntax to data bind any property of a child component. The @bind syntax we have already seen is shorthand for the @bind-value syntax. This will use two-way data binding. Update the Home page to use two-way data binding as in Listing 3-33. Also comment out the Delay component.

Listing 3-33. Using two-way data binding

```
<DismissibleAlert @bind-Show="@ShowAlert">
  <strong>Blazor is soo cool!</strong>
</DismissibleAlert>

@* Comment the Delay component *@
@* <Delay TimeInSeconds="5" Tick="ToggleAlert" /> *@
```

Run the website. However, you will not see any valid page. The Blazor runtime encountered a problem. You can discover the problem by opening the Console. You will see a bunch of messages, one of which is stating:

```
System.InvalidOperationException: Object of type 'BlazorApp.DataBinding.
Components.Pages.DismissibleAlert' does not have a property matching the
name 'ShowChanged'.
```

Parameters that support two-way data binding need a way to tell the parent that the parameter has changed. The child component uses a delegate for that, so the parent component through the Blazor runtime can install its own change handler (just like an event) when the property has changed. This change handler will then update the parent component's data bound property. The child component is responsible for invoking the {PARAMETERNAME}Changed delegate when the property changes.

Open the DismissibleAlert class and its implementation to match Listing 3-34. There are two changes.

Listing 3-34. The DismissibleAlert class with two-way binding support

```
using Microsoft.AspNetCore.Components;

namespace BlazorApp.DataBinding.Components.Pages;

public partial class DismissibleAlert
{
  [Parameter]
  public bool Show { get; set; }
```

```csharp
[Parameter]
public required EventCallback<bool> ShowChanged { get; set; }

[Parameter]
public RenderFragment ChildContent { get; set; } = default!;

private async Task UpdateShow(bool value)
{
  if (value != Show)
  {
    await ShowChanged.InvokeAsync(value);
  }
}

public async Task Dismiss()
  => await UpdateShow(false);
}
```

First, we add an extra parameter which should be called {PARAMETERNAME}Changed of type EventCallback<{PARAMETERTYPE}>. For example, the property is named Show of type bool, so we add ShowChanged of type EventCallback<bool>. EventCallback<T> is a special type used in Blazor for implementing two-way data binding and is very similar to Action<T>. Through this parameter, the Blazor runtime can install its own handler to be notified when the Show parameter changes.

The second change is the extra private method named UpdateShow which triggers the ShowChanged delegate with the new value. This will update the parent's property, which will pass down the new value as the parameter, thus updating it (indirectly). You should always use the UpdateShow method to update the two-way data bound Show property!

Note This implementation of two-way data binding is somewhat different from the previous editions of my book. The older one still works, but I think this new technique is better.

Now, when the DismissibleAlert Show parameter changes, Blazor will update the parent's ShowAlert property because we are using two-way data binding. Because we are using the special EventCallback<T> type, we don't need to take care of calling StateHasChanged on the parent; EventCallback<T> takes care of that! Neat!

CHAPTER 3 DATA BINDING

> **Note** The `UpdateShow` method checks if the value has changed. Only trigger a Changed `EventCallback` when there is an actual change. This will avoid a possible endless loop of Changed handling.

Fixing the Delay Component

We still need to fix the problem when the `Delay` fires, and that is that the parent still needs to invoke `StateHasChanged` when the `Tick` gets called. Start by uncommenting the `Delay` component in the `Home` component, and remove the `StateHasChanged` from the `ToggleAlert` method as in Listing 3-35.

Listing 3-35. Update the UI when ShowAlert changes the value

```
@page "/"

<PageTitle>Home</PageTitle>

<h1>Hello, world!</h1>

Welcome to your new app.

<DismissibleAlert @bind-Show="@ShowAlert">
  <strong>Blazor is soo cool!</strong>
</DismissibleAlert>

<button @onclick="ToggleAlert" class="btn btn-success">Toggle</button>

<Delay TimeInSeconds="5" Tick="ToggleAlert" />

@code {
  public bool ShowAlert { get; set; } = true;

  public void ToggleAlert() {
    Console.WriteLine($"Toggle {ShowAlert}");
    ShowAlert = !ShowAlert;
  }
}
```

CHAPTER 3 DATA BINDING

Replace the Tick parameter's type with EventCallback, and update the callback argument of the Timer as in Listing 3-36. Since the InvokeAsync method of the EventCallback type is asynchronous, we need to sprinkle a couple of async and await keywords too. Also worth noting is that EventCallback is a value type, so there is no need to check for null.

Listing 3-36. Using EventCallback for the Delay component

```
using Microsoft.AspNetCore.Components;

namespace BlazorApp.DataBinding.Components;

public class Delay : ComponentBase, IDisposable
{
  [Parameter]
  public double TimeInSeconds { get; set; }

  [Parameter]
  public EventCallback Tick { get; set; } = default!;

  private Timer timer = default!;

  protected override void OnInitialized()
  {
    timer = new(
      callback: async (_)
        => await InvokeAsync(async ()
          => await Tick.InvokeAsync()),
      state: null,
      dueTime: TimeSpan.FromSeconds(TimeInSeconds),
      period: Timeout.InfiniteTimeSpan);
  }

  public void Dispose() => timer.Dispose();
}
```

Run. Wait 5 seconds.

The DismissibleAlert should automatically hide as illustrated by Figures 3-3 and 3-4.

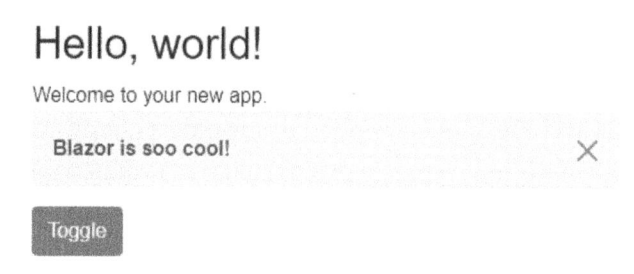

Figure 3-3. The Alert being shown

Figure 3-4. The Alert automatically hides after 5 seconds

Should your project still not update, you can debug a Blazor project by adding breakpoints or using logging or some `Console.WriteLine` statements. These will appear in the Console window.

In general, you should prefer `EventCallback` and/or `EventCallback<T>` over normal delegates for parent–child communication, such as events and two-way data binding. There are rare exceptions to the rule (e.g., the fact that `EventCallback` triggers component re-rendering might be a problem, and then using a delegate can be the solution).

Data Binding Side Effects

What if you want data binding to cause some side effects? For example, when someone types in a search box you want to look up something asynchronously. Each time two-way data binding completes updating the value, you can register an asynchronous method. Do this using the `@bind:after="{SOMEASYNCMETHOD}"` syntax.

Note Do NOT use the property setter to invoke asynchronous methods! This will block your component from rendering, and your component will not be interactive while the async method is running.

This is best illustrated with a simple example: Replace the Home component's content with Listing 3-37.

Listing 3-37. Invoking an asynchronous method after data binding

```
@page "/"

<PageTitle>Home</PageTitle>

<h1>Hello, world!</h1>

Welcome to your new app.

<input @bind="searchText" @bind:after="PerformSearch"/>

<br/>

@if (searchResult is not "")
{
  <p>Search found: @searchResult</p>
}

@code {

  private string searchText = string.Empty;
  private string searchResult = string.Empty;

  private async Task PerformSearch()
  {
    await Task.Delay(TimeSpan.FromSeconds(2));
    searchResult = $"Found result for {searchText}";
  }
}
```

This example uses a simple async method that simply returns a new string. In real life this could run a database query or make a REST call.

Hit Run. Type something in the text box. When you tab out of the textbox, after a slight delay, you will see the result being displayed.

If you like, you can take full control over two-way data binding. You can register a value for the binding (the getter), and an async method for the setter. In this case you use

CHAPTER 3   DATA BINDING

the @bind:get="@{SOMEVALUE}" and @bind:set="{SOMEASYNCMETHOD}. Continuing with the previous example, let's say you want to clear the result before performing the search.

Update the Home component as in Listing 3-38.

Listing 3-38. Using an explicit getter and setter

```
@page "/"

<PageTitle>Home</PageTitle>

<h1>Hello, world!</h1>

Welcome to your new app.

<input @bind:get="searchText"
       @bind:set="ClearResult"/>

<br/>

@if (searchResult is not "")
{
  <p>Search found: @searchResult</p>
}

@code {

  private string searchText = string.Empty;
  private string searchResult = string.Empty;

  private async Task PerformSearch()
  {
    await Task.Delay(TimeSpan.FromSeconds(2));
    searchResult = $"Found result for {searchText}";
  }

  private async Task ClearResult(string value) {
    searchText = value;
    searchResult = string.Empty;
    await PerformSearch();
  }
}
```

CHAPTER 3 DATA BINDING

Run the example. Type something in the textbox. Tab out of the textbox, and after 2 seconds you should see some search result. Type some more in the textbox. Tab out. You should see the result clear, and after 2 seconds a new result will appear.

Referring to a Child Component

Generally, you should prefer data binding to have components communicate with one another. This way one component does not need to know anything about another component, except the data bindings. It also makes the Blazor runtime take care of updating components with changes.

However, you can also directly interact with a _child component_. Let's look at an example: we want the dismissible alert to disappear by calling its Dismiss method. Update your code to match Listing 3-39, where we use the @ref syntax to place a reference to the DismissibleAlert component in the _dismissibleAlert field. Please make sure that field is of the component's type. Also add a button to invoke the Home component's Dismiss method.

Listing 3-39. Referring to a child component

```
@page "/"

<PageTitle>Home</PageTitle>

<h1>Hello, world!</h1>

Welcome to your new app.

<DismissibleAlert @bind-Show="@ShowAlert"
  @ref="_dismissibleAlert">
  <strong>Blazor is soo cool!</strong>
</DismissibleAlert>

<button @onclick="ToggleAlert" class="btn btn-success">Toggle</button>
<button @onclick="Dismiss" class="btn btn-success">Dismiss</button>

<Delay TimeInSeconds="5" Tick="ToggleAlert" />

@code {
  public bool ShowAlert { get; set; } = true;
```

```csharp
  public void ToggleAlert() {
    Console.WriteLine($"Toggle {ShowAlert}");
    ShowAlert = !ShowAlert;
  }

  private DismissibleAlert _dismissibleAlert = default!;

  private async Task Dismiss()
  {
    await _dismissibleAlert.Dismiss();
  }
}
```

The PizzaPlace Single-Page Application

Let us apply this newfound knowledge and build a nice Pizza ordering website. Throughout the rest of this book, we will enhance this site with all kinds of features.

Creating the PizzaPlace Project

Create a new Blazor WebApp project named BlazorApp.PizzaPlace, using the dotnet cli. We will create a new Blazor Server project:

```
$ProjectName = "BlazorApp.PizzaPlace"
mkdir $ProjectName
cd $ProjectName
dotnet new sln -n $ProjectName
mkdir src
cd src
dotnet new blazor -n $ProjectName --all-interactive --interactivity Server
dotnet new classlib -o "$ProjectName.Shared"
cd ..
dotnet sln add "src\$ProjectName"
dotnet sln add "src\$ProjectName.Shared"
```

This PowerShell script also creates a BlazorApp.PizzaPlace.Shared class library project; this is for holding entity classes such as the `Pizza` class. This is to allow you to migrate code to different Blazor projects later.

Out of the box, Blazor uses the popular Bootstrap 5 layout framework (https://getbootstrap.com/). Expect to see bootstrap CSS classes in the code samples. However, you can use any other layout framework, because Blazor uses standard HTML and CSS. This book is about Blazor, not fancy layouts, so we're not going to spend a lot of time choosing nice colors and making the site look great. Focus!

Adding Shared Classes to Represent the Data

We need a couple of classes to represent business entities, and we will add all of these to the BlazorApp.PizzaPlace.Shared class library project.

What do we need? Since we will build a site around pizzas, creating a class to represent this makes sense.

Start with classes representing a `Pizza` and how spicy it is as in Listing 3-40 and Listing 3-41.

Listing 3-40. The Spiciness class

```
namespace BlazorApp.PizzaPlace.Shared;

public enum Spiciness
{
  None,
  Spicy,
  Hot
}
```

Listing 3-41. The Pizza class

```
namespace BlazorApp.PizzaPlace.Shared;

public class Pizza
{
  public required int Id { get; init; }
  public required string Name { get; init; }
```

CHAPTER 3   DATA BINDING

```
  public required decimal Price { get; init; }
  public required Spiciness Spiciness { get; init; }
}
```

Hoping to sell lots of pizzas, we also need something to represent the customer's shopping basket. Add a new class named ShoppingBasket with code from Listing 3-42.

Listing 3-42. The ShoppingBasket class

```
namespace BlazorApp.PizzaPlace.Shared;

public class ShoppingBasket
{
  public List<int> Orders { get; } = [];
  public void Add(int pizzaId)
    => Orders.Add(pizzaId);
  public void RemoveAt(int pos)
    => Orders.RemoveAt(pos);
}
```

Please note that we just keep the pizza id in the Orders collection. This is a developer's choice; you could also keep references to the Pizza instances.

Finally, we need some class to keep all our data in one handy place. By convention, this is named the State class, with Listing 3-43.

Listing 3-43. The State class

```
namespace BlazorApp.PizzaPlace.Shared;

public class State
{
  public Pizza[] Pizzas { get; set; } = [];
  public ShoppingBasket Basket { get; } = new();
  public decimal TotalPrice
    => Basket.Orders.Sum(id => GetPizza(id)!.Price);
  public Pizza? GetPizza(int id)
    => Pizzas.SingleOrDefault(pizza => pizza.Id == id);
}
```

CHAPTER 3 DATA BINDING

> **Note** In the next chapter on using forms, we will also add a `Customer` class.

There is another good reason to put all these classes into the BlazorApp.PizzaPlace. Shared project. There is limited debugging for Blazor. By putting these classes into the BlazorApp.PizzaPlace.Shared project, we can apply unit testing best practices on the shared classes because it is a regular .NET project, and even use the Visual Studio debugger to examine weird behavior. The Shared project can also be used by other projects, for example, a Windows or MAUI client!

Building the UI to Show the Menu

With these classes in place to represent the data, the next step is to build the user interface that shows the menu. We will start by displaying the menu to the user, and then we will enhance the UI to allow the user to order one or more pizzas.

The problem of displaying the menu is twofold: First, you need to display a list of data. The menu can be thought of as a list, like any other list. Secondly, in our application, we'll need to convert the spiciness choices from their numeric values into URLs leading to the icons used to indicate different levels of hotness.

Start by adding a project reference to the BlazorApp.PizzaPlace.Shared project as in Listing 3-44 so we can use the shared classes.

Listing 3-44. The Blazor project

```xml
<Project Sdk="Microsoft.NET.Sdk.Web">

  <PropertyGroup>
    <TargetFramework>net8.0</TargetFramework>
    <Nullable>enable</Nullable>
    <ImplicitUsings>enable</ImplicitUsings>
  </PropertyGroup>

  <ItemGroup>
    <ProjectReference Include="..\BlazorApp.PizzaPlace.Shared\BlazorApp.PizzaPlace.Shared.csproj" />
  </ItemGroup>

</Project>
```

CHAPTER 3   DATA BINDING

> **Note** Did you know that with Visual Studio you can drag the BlazorApp.PizzaPlace. Shared project to the BlazorApp.PizzaPlace to create a project reference?

Add a @using statement for the BlazorApp.PizzaPlace.Shared namespace to the _Imports.razor file; this way we don't need to @using statements all over the place. Refer to Listing 3-45 when in doubt.

Listing 3-45. The Imports.razor file

```
@using System.Net.Http
@using System.Net.Http.Json
@using Microsoft.AspNetCore.Components.Forms
@using Microsoft.AspNetCore.Components.Routing
@using Microsoft.AspNetCore.Components.Web
@using static Microsoft.AspNetCore.Components.Web.RenderMode
@using Microsoft.AspNetCore.Components.Web.Virtualization
@using Microsoft.JSInterop
@using BlazorApp.PizzaPlace
@using BlazorApp.PizzaPlace.Components
@using BlazorApp.PizzaPlace.Shared
```

Open Home.razor. Add the @code section to hold our restaurant's (limited) menu with code from Listing 3-46 by initializing the State instance.

Listing 3-46. Initializing our application's menu

```
@page "/"

<PageTitle>The PizzaPlace</PageTitle>

<h1>Hello, world!</h1>

Welcome to your new app.

@code {
  private State State { get; set; } = new()
    {
      Pizzas = [
```

100

```
      new Pizza {
        Id = 1,
        Name = "Pepperoni",
        Price = 8.99M,
        Spiciness = Spiciness.Spicy },
      new Pizza {
        Id = 2,
        Name = "Margherita",
        Price = 7.99M,
        Spiciness = Spiciness.None },
      new Pizza {
        Id = 3,
        Name = "Diavola",
        Price = 9.99M,
        Spiciness = Spiciness.Hot }
    ]
  };
  private void AddPizzaToBasket(Pizza pizza)
  {
    State.Basket.Add(pizza.Id);
  }
}
```

The Menu Component

Add a new razor component file named Menu.razor to your project under the Components folder.

Add a new `Pizzas` parameter to this component in the `@code` section as shown in Listing 3-47. We are adding the `[Parameter]` attribute, and the `[EditorRequired]` attribute since we do need a list of Pizzas for this component to work (this makes the parameter required).

CHAPTER 3　DATA BINDING

Listing 3-47. Starting the Menu component

```
[Parameter]
[EditorRequired]
public Pizza[] Pizzas { get; set; } = [];
}
```

Add a @foreach loop in the markup of the Menu component as in Listing 3-48.

Listing 3-48. Iterating over the list of pizzas

```
<h1>Our selection of pizzas</h1>

@foreach (Pizza pizza in Pizzas)
{
  <div class="row">
    <div class="col">
      @pizza.Name
    </div>
    <div class="col text-right">
      @($"{pizza.Price:0.00}")
    </div>
    <div class="col"></div>
    <div class="col">
      <img src="@SpicinessImage(pizza.Spiciness)"
           alt="@pizza.Spiciness" />
    </div>
    <div class="col">
      <button class="btn btn-success pl-4 pr-4"
              @onclick=@(async () => await Selected.InvokeAsync(pizza))>
        Add
      </button>
    </div>
  </div>
}
```

102

CHAPTER 3　DATA BINDING

What we are doing here is iterating over each pizza in the menu and generating a row with 4 columns, one for the name, price, spiciness, and finally one for the order button. There are still some compiler errors which we will fix next.

We still have a little problem. We need to convert the spiciness value to a URL, which is done by the `SpicinessImage` method as shown in Listing 3-49. Add this method to the @code area of the Menu.razor file.

Listing 3-49. Converting a value with a converter function

```
[Parameter]
[EditorRequired]
public Pizza[] Pizzas { get; set; } = [];

private string SpicinessImage(Spiciness spiciness)
=> $"images/{spiciness.ToString().ToLower()}.png";
```

This converter function simply converts the name of the enumeration's value from Listing 3-40 into the URL of an image file which can be found in the Blazor project's images folder as shown in Figure 3-5. Add this folder (which can be found in this book's download) to the wwwroot folder.

Figure 3-5. *The content of the images folder*

We also want to notify the parent component when the user clicks on the Add button. How can we do this? We will add a parameter to the Menu component that will be used to notify the parent about selected pizzas. Start by adding the Selected parameter of type EventCallback<Pizza> as in Listing 3-50.

Listing 3-50. Adding the selected callback parameter

```
[Parameter]
[EditorRequired]
public Pizza[] Pizzas { get; set; } = [];

private string SpicinessImage(Spiciness spiciness)
```

103

CHAPTER 3   DATA BINDING

```
=> $"images/{spiciness.ToString().ToLower()}.png";

[Parameter]
public EventCallback<Pizza> Selected { get; set; }
```

Go back to the Home component and replace its markup with Listing 3-51.

Listing 3-51. The Home component with the Menu

```
@page "/"

<PageTitle>The PizzaPlace</PageTitle>

<Menu Pizzas="@State.Pizzas" Selected="AddPizzaToBasket" />
```

What is happening here? We pass two parameters to the Menu component; the first is the list of Pizzas we want the component to display; consider this an input for the Menu component. The second parameter is a method to call when the user selects a Pizza from the list. Here we pass the AddPizzaToBasket method, which adds the Pizza to the order, so the Menu component will indirectly call this method when the user clicks Add. Thanks to the EventCallback<T> type, there is no need to call StateHasChanged. Had we used an Action<T> or Func<T>, the UI would not update, and you would need to call StateHasChanged whenever you receive events from a child component!

Run your application. You should see a list of pizzas as in Figure 3-6.

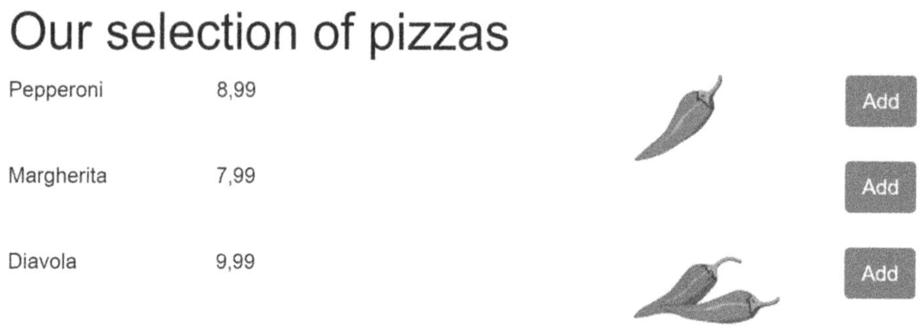

Figure 3-6. *The PizzaPlace application showing the menu*

Click the Add button. Nothing happens? You can put a breakpoint in the AddPizzaToBasket method, and you will see the breakpoint being hit. We just need a component to display the order!

CHAPTER 3　DATA BINDING

Debugging Tip

Even with modern debuggers, you want to see the `State` object because it contains details as you are interacting with the application. For this, we'll use a simple trick by displaying the `State` on our page, so you can review it at any time.

Start by adding a new static class named `DebuggingExtensions` to the BlazorApp.PizzaPlace.Shared library project as in Listing 3-52.

Listing 3-52. The DebuggingExtensions class

```csharp
using System.Text.Json;

namespace BlazorApp.PizzaPlace.Shared;

public static class DebuggingExtensions
{
  private static readonly JsonSerializerOptions options =
    new()
    {
      WriteIndented = true
    };

  public static string ToJson(this object obj)
  => JsonSerializer.Serialize(obj, options);
}
```

And at the bottom of Home.razor, add a simple paragraph as in Listing 3-53.

Listing 3-53. Showing State

```razor
<Menu Pizzas="@State.Pizzas" Selected="AddPizzaToBasket" />

<p>@State.ToJson()</p>

@code {
```

Run your project. As you interact with the page, you'll see `State` changes with an example shown in Figure 3-7.

105

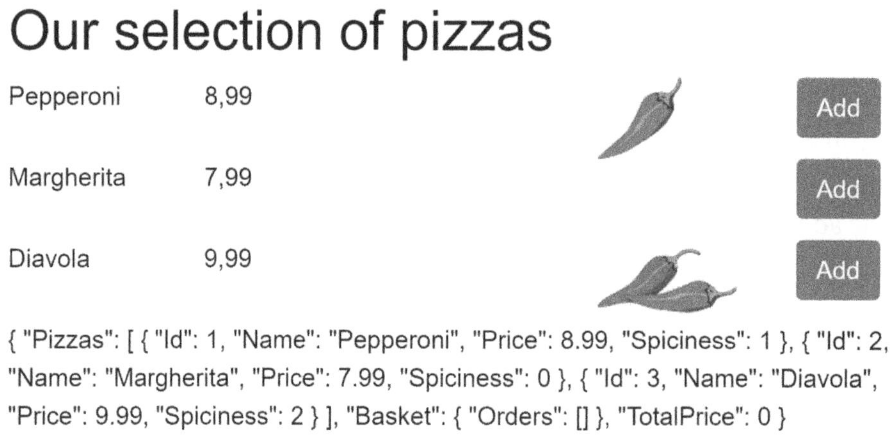

CHAPTER 3   DATA BINDING

Our selection of pizzas

Pepperoni	8,99		Add
Margherita	7,99		Add
Diavola	9,99		Add

{ "Pizzas": [{ "Id": 1, "Name": "Pepperoni", "Price": 8.99, "Spiciness": 1 }, { "Id": 2, "Name": "Margherita", "Price": 7.99, "Spiciness": 0 }, { "Id": 3, "Name": "Diavola", "Price": 9.99, "Spiciness": 2 }], "Basket": { "Orders": [] }, "TotalPrice": 0 }

Figure 3-7. *Watching State changes*

It should be obvious that we remove this debugging feature when the page is ready ☺. For example, you could add an #if DEBUG inside the ToJson method to only make it work outside release builds.

The Shopping Basket Component

The next thing on the menu is displaying the shopping basket. We are going to use a feature from C# called _tuples_. I will explain tuples in a moment.

Add a new Razor component to the Components folder, and name it Basket. In the @code section, add a new parameter for State as in Listing 3-54.

Listing 3-54. *Shopping Basket needs State*

```
[Parameter]
[EditorRequired]
public required State State { get; set; }
```

In our UI we need to know the position in the list of a pizza, because we will remove a pizza from a certain position.

Again, in the @code section, add a GetPizzas method to retrieve a list of pizzas together with the position as shown in Listing 3-55.

Listing 3-55. Retrieving a list of pizzas with position using ValueTuples

```
private IEnumerable<(Pizza? pizza, int pos)> GetPizzas()
    => State.Basket.Orders.Select((id, pos) => (State.GetPizza(id), pos));
```

Most of this stuff is very similar, but now we are iterating over a list of ValueTuples (keep reading, a very handy new feature in C# https://learn.microsoft.com/dotnet/csharp/tuples).

Tuples are very similar to anonymous types from C# in that they let you store and return intermediate multi-part results without you having to build a helper class.

Let's look at this code of the GetPizzas method in a little more detail. We are using LINQ's Select to iterate over the list of orders (which contain pizza ids). Examine the lambda function used in the Select:

```
(id, pos) => (State.GetPizza(id), pos)
```

The LINQ Select method has two overloads, and we're using the overload taking an element from the collection (id) and the position in the collection (pos). We use these to create ValueTuples. Each tuple represents a pizza from the basket and its position in the basket! We could have done the same, creating a little helper class with the pizza and position, but this is now done for us! And it is efficacious, using less memory than a class because it is a value type!

Time to add the UI. Update the Basket component's markup as in Listing 3-56.

Listing 3-56. The Basket component's markup

```
@if (State.Basket.Orders.Any())
{
  <h1 class="">Your current order</h1>

  @foreach (var (pizza, pos) in GetPizzas())
  {
    <div class="row mb-2">
      <div class="col">
        @pizza!.Name
      </div>
      <div class="col text-right">
        @($"{pizza.Price:0.00}")
      </div>
```

```
            <div class="col"></div>
            <div class="col"></div>
            <div class="col">
              <button class="btn btn-danger"
                      @onclick="@(async ()
                      => await RemoveFromBasket(pos))">
                Remove
              </button>
            </div>
          </div>
        }
        <div class="row">
          <div class="col"></div>
          <div class="col"><hr /></div>
          <div class="col"> </div>
          <div class="col"> </div>
        </div>
        <div class="row">
          <div class="col"> Total:</div>
          <div class="col text-right font-weight-bold">
            @($"{State.TotalPrice:0.00}")
          </div>
          <div class="col"> </div>
          <div class="col"> </div>
          <div class="col"> </div>
        </div>
      }
```

First we check if the order is not empty using `@if (State.Basket.Orders.Any())`. If so, we iterate over the `ValueTuples` of the `GetPizzas` method. Again, we use four columns for each order item. The first column displays the pizza's name, the second the pizza's price, the third column is just white space, while the fourth column displays a Delete button.

CHAPTER 3 DATA BINDING

The pizza is used to display its name and price, while the position is used in the Delete button. This button invokes the RemoveFromBasket method from Listing 3-57.

Listing 3-57. The RemoveFromBasket method

```
private async ValueTask RemoveFromBasket(int pos)
{
  State.Basket.RemoveAt(pos);
  await StateChanged.InvokeAsync(State);
}
```

We want the Home component's State to update when the Basket component changes it. We could use a callback to notify the parent, but using two-way data binding makes more sense.

Add the StateChanged EventCallback<State> property from Listing 3-58.

Listing 3-58. Implementing two-way data binding

```
[Parameter]
public required EventCallback<State> StateChanged { get; set; }
```

When should we notify the parent that State has changed? When we remove an item from the basket, so update the RemoveFromBasket method as in Listing 3-59.

Listing 3-59. Notifying the parent with two-way data binding

```
private async ValueTask RemoveFromBasket(int pos)
{
  State.Basket.RemoveAt(pos);
  await StateChanged.InvokeAsync(State);
}
```

At the bottom of the shopping basket, the total order amount is shown. This is calculated by the State class using the TotalPrice method from Listing 3-43. Please note the use of the null-forgiving operator (!) because I am assuming that the ShoppingBasket will always contain valid pizza ids.

Add the Basket component to the Home component as in Listing 3-60.

CHAPTER 3   DATA BINDING

Listing 3-60. Using the Basket component

```
<PageTitle>The PizzaPlace</PageTitle>

<Menu Pizzas="@State.Pizzas" Selected="AddPizzaToBasket" />

<Basket @bind-State="@State"/>

<p>@State.ToJson()</p>
```

Run the application and order some pizzas. You should see your current order like Figure 3-8.

Our selection of pizzas

Pepperoni	8,99		Add
Margherita	7,99		Add
Diavola	9,99		Add

Your current order

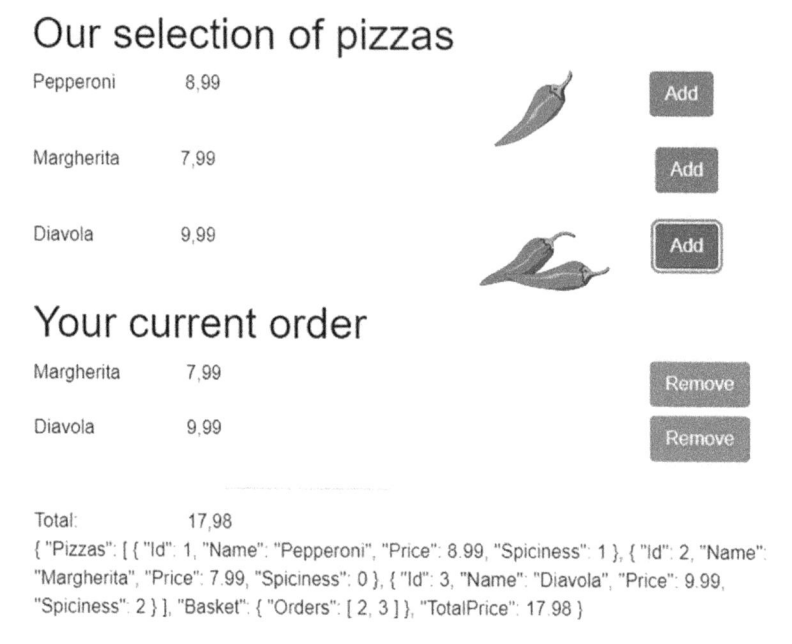

| Margherita | 7,99 | Remove |
| Diavola | 9,99 | Remove |

Total: 17,98
{ "Pizzas": [{ "Id": 1, "Name": "Pepperoni", "Price": 8.99, "Spiciness": 1 }, { "Id": 2, "Name": "Margherita", "Price": 7.99, "Spiciness": 0 }, { "Id": 3, "Name": "Diavola", "Price": 9.99, "Spiciness": 2 }], "Basket": { "Orders": [2, 3] }, "TotalPrice": 17.98 }

Figure 3-8. *Your shopping basket with a couple of pizzas*

Summary

In this chapter, we looked at data binding in Blazor. We started with one-way data binding where we can embed the value of a property or a field in the UI using the @ syntax. We then looked at event binding where you bind an element's event to a method using the @on{EVENT}="@SomeEventHandlerMethod" syntax. Blazor also has support for two-way data binding where we can update the UI with the value of a property and vice-versa using the @bind="SomeProperty" syntax. Finally, we looked at how we can implement components to support data binding using the EventCallback<T> type.

CHAPTER 4

Forms and Validation

HTML Forms

In the beginning, HTML was just about displaying articles. But as the Internet caught on, people wanted to use it for selling products, and then the customer needed to type their details, right?

So, the `<form>` and all kinds of `<input>` HTML elements were introduced.
In Listing 4-1, you can find an example of using these elements (not using Blazor yet!).

Listing 4-1. An example form

```
<!DOCTYPE html>
<html>
<head>
  <title>Sample Form</title>
</head>
<body>

<h2>Sample HTML Form</h2>

<form action="submit_form" method="post">
  <label for="name">Name:</label>
  <input type="text" id="name" name="name"><br><br>

  <label for="email">Email:</label>
  <input type="email" id="email" name="email"><br><br>

  <label for="password">Password:</label>
  <input type="password" id="password" name="password"><br><br>

  <label for="message">Message:</label>
```

CHAPTER 4 FORMS AND VALIDATION

```
    <textarea id="message" name="message"></textarea><br><br>

    <label for="country">Country:</label>
    <select id="country" name="country">
        <option value="us">United States</option>
        <option value="ca">Canada</option>
        <option value="uk">United Kingdom</option>
    </select><br><br>

    <label>
      <input type="checkbox" name="subscribe" value="newsletter">
      Subscribe to newsletter
    </label><br><br>

    <label>
      <input type="radio" name="gender" value="male">
      Male
    </label>
    <label>
      <input type="radio" name="gender" value="female">
      Female
    </label><br><br>

    <input type="submit" value="Submit">
</form>

</body>
</html>
```

- The `<form>` HTML element groups a bunch of `<label>` and `<input>` elements. When the user fills in the inputs and presses the Submit button, the values of the inputs get sent back to the server using the `method` and `action` URL. So, in this example, the content will be POSTed back to the `submit_form` URL. A server there can then process the details.

- The `<input type="text">` is used for single-line text input. It is important that you give an `<input>` a unique value for the `name` attribute, since this is the key of the value that will be sent to the server.

- The `<input type="email">` is just a single-line text input but expecting an email address. This allows your browser to give extra support, for example, on your mobile, it will use a keyboard layout more suitable for entering an email.

- The `<input type="password">` is for passwords, but the contents will be hidden by replacing the characters with, for example, a "•".

- The `<textarea>` input is used for multi-line input.

- The `<select>` will display as a drop-down list, with each `<option>` a different value to choose from.

- The `<input type="checkbox">` allows the user to select an option. Each checkbox should have a unique name, and its value will be boolean.

- The `<input type="radio">` allows the user to select one option from a set of values. Here each radio button has the same name attribute, which defines the set, and this will choose the value of the radio button (in the example male or female).

- The `<input type="submit">` will render as a button, and when clicked, this will trigger the forms action and send the name=value pairs back to the server's URL (action).

This works for Blazor too, but there is more.

Blazor Forms

Let us learn things again by building a sample application. Create a new Blazor Server application by running this PowerShell script:

```
$ProjectName = "BlazorApp.UsingForms"
mkdir $ProjectName
cd $ProjectName
dotnet new sln -n $ProjectName
mkdir src
cd src
```

CHAPTER 4 FORMS AND VALIDATION

```
dotnet new blazor -n $ProjectName --all-interactive --interactivity Server
cd ..
dotnet sln add src\$ProjectName
```

Add the Countries class as in Listing 4-2.

Listing 4-2. Some Countries

```
namespace BlazorApp.UsingForms;

public static class Countries
{
  public static Dictionary<string, string> All { get; } = new()
  {
    ["us"] = "United States",
    ["ca"] = "Canada",
    ["uk"] = "United Kingdom",
    ["be"] = "Belgium"
  };
}
```

We also need some genders, as in Listing 4-3. Keeping it short for our example.

Listing 4-3. Some Genders

```
namespace BlazorApp.UsingForms;

public enum Gender
{
  Female, Male
}
```

Add a Member class, which is like the data from Listing 4-1. Code is in Listing 4-4.

Listing 4-4. The Member class

```
namespace BlazorApp.UsingForms;

public class Member
{
  public required string Name { get; set; }
```

```csharp
    public required string Email { get; set; }
    public required string Password { get; set; }
    public string Message { get; set; } = string.Empty;
    public required string Country { get; set; }
    public bool Subscriber { get; set; }
    public Gender Gender { get;set; }
}
```

Remember the `DebuggingExtensions` we wrote in the previous chapter? Copy this class in this project and change the namespace of the `DebuggingExtensions` class to this project's namespace.

Now we are ready to build a Blazor component using a form. Add a new component named `MemberForm` to the Components folder, as in Listing 4-5.

Listing 4-5. Beginning the MemberForm

```razor
<h3>Forms with Blazor Components</h3>

<EditForm FormName="member-form"
          OnValidSubmit="Submit"
          Model="@Member" >

  <div class="form-group mb-0">
    <button type="submit" class="btn btn-primary">
      Submit
    </button>
  </div>
</EditForm>

@code {

  [Parameter]
  [EditorRequired]
  public required Member Member { get; set; }
```

CHAPTER 4   FORMS AND VALIDATION

```
  public void Submit()
  {
    Console.WriteLine(Member.ToJson());
  }
}
```

The `MemberForm` takes a `Member` as a parameter, and the `Submit` method will print the `Member` to the console. Our `MemberForm` uses the built-in `EditForm`, which takes a `FormName` parameter, which is a unique identifier for the form, a `Model` and an `OnValidSumbit` method. `EditForm` also supports an `OnInvalidSubmit` method, but we don't need that here.

Note   Blazor now requires each form to have a unique FormName!

Add a new `InputText` to the form as in Listing 4-6. Here we are using bootstrap styling so there are some `<div>`s involved. `InputText` is straightforward, using two-way data binding.

Listing 4-6. Adding our first InputText

```
<div class="form-group row mb-1">
  <label class="col-sm-3 col-form-label"
         for="Name">Name:</label>
  <div class="col-sm-9">
    <InputText class="form-control"
               @bind-Value="Member.Name" />
  </div>
</div>
```

Add another `InputText` for the `Email` property as in Listing 4-7. Almost identical, except that we add an additional `type="email"` attribute to set the type of the input.

Listing 4-7. The InputText for Email

```
<div class="form-group row mb-1">
  <label class="col-sm-3 col-form-label"
         for="Email">Email:</label>
```

CHAPTER 4   FORMS AND VALIDATION

```
  <div class="col-sm-9">
    <InputText type="email" class="form-control"
               formnovalidate
               @bind-Value="Member.Email" />
  </div>
</div>
```

The InputText for Password is similar; see Listing 4-8.

Listing 4-8. The InputText for Password

```
<div class="form-group row mb-1">
  <label class="col-sm-3 col-form-label"
         for="Password">Password:</label>
  <div class="col-sm-9">
    <InputText type="password" class="form-control"
               @bind-Value="Member.Password" />
  </div>
</div>
```

Now add an InputTextArea for the Message as in Listing 4-9.

Listing 4-9. Using an InputTextArea

```
<div class="form-group row mb-1">
  <label class="col-sm-3 col-form-label"
         for="Message">Message:</label>
  <div class="col-sm-9">
    <InputTextArea class="form-control"
                   @bind-Value="Member.Message" />
  </div>
</div>
```

To give the user a selection for countries, use an InputSelect as in Listing 4-10. We do need to generate the option elements ourselves, using a @foreach. Each option has a value which is used to set the Country property and a user-friendly display.

117

CHAPTER 4　FORMS AND VALIDATION

Listing 4-10. Using an InputSelect

```
<div class="form-group row mb-1">
  <label class="col-sm-3 col-form-label"
         for="Country">Country:</label>
  <div class="col-sm-9">
    <InputSelect class="form-control"
                 @bind-Value="Member.Country">
      @foreach (var country in Countries.All)
      {
        <option value="@country.Key">
          @country.Value
        </option>
      }
    </InputSelect>
  </div>
</div>
```

Using an `InputCheckbox` is similar to using an `InputText` since we only have one possible bool value to bind to. Refer to Listing 4-11.

Listing 4-11. Checking the InputCheckbox

```
<div class="form-group row mb-1">
  <label class="col-sm-3 col-form-label"
         for="Subscriber">Subscribe:</label>
  <div class="col-sm-9">
    <InputCheckbox class="form-check-input"
                   @bind-Value="Member.Subscriber" />
  </div>
</div>
```

With radio buttons, we need to group them into an `InputRadioGroup` and add an `InputRadio` for each option. Add Listing 4-12 to the form. Since we are using an enum to hold the choices, we iterate over each value of the enum. Should we decide to add more options, we don't need to update this component. Nice!

Listing 4-12. Adding Radio Buttons

```
<div class="form-group row mb-1">
  <label class="col-sm-3 col-form-label"
         for="Gender">Gender:</label>
  <div class="col-sm-9">
    <InputRadioGroup Name="Gender"
                     @bind-Value="Member.Gender">
      @foreach (Gender gender in Enum.GetValues<Gender>())
      {
        <InputRadio class="form-check-input"
                    Name="Gender"
                    Value="@gender" />
        <label class="form-check-label">@gender</label>
      }
    </InputRadioGroup>
  </div>
</div>
```

Build and run. You should be able to enter the details for a member, with an example shown in Figure 4-1. However, if you leave the required password textbox empty, it still works! We need to add some validation. And what is that weird green border which appears? Read on.

CHAPTER 4 FORMS AND VALIDATION

Forms with Blazor Components

Name:	Peter
Email:	peter@mail.be
Password:	•••••
Message:	I ♥ Blazor! I hope you love it too!
Country:	Belgium
Subscribe:	☑
Gender:	○ Female ● Male

Submit

Figure 4-1. *Entering the details of a Member*

Blazor Validation

To err is human, to forgive divine.

Let us add validation to this component. First, I need you to realize that there are many ways in which we could validate the data. In ASP.NET MVC, you can use the System.ComponentModel.DataAnnotations namespace, which contains attributes to describe the entity's constraints. You could also use the popular FluentValidation library or build your own custom validation.

Using DataAnnotations

Classes like Member should be validated using business rules because business has the best knowledge about the validity of an entity's properties. With data annotations, you add attributes to your entity's properties, indicating what kind of validation is required.

Open the Member class to add validation attributes as shown in Listing 4-13. There are many choices for validation, for example, Required, CreditCard, Range, EmailAddress, MaxLength, MinLength, Phone, etc. Each of these attributes can take arguments, and an important one is the ErrorMessage to show a user, helping the user enter the correct value.

Listing 4-13. Adding validation using Data Annotations

```
using System.ComponentModel.DataAnnotations;

namespace BlazorApp.UsingForms;

public class Member
{
  public const string EmailRegEx =
    "^[a-zA-Z0-9._%+-]+@[a-zA-Z0-9.-]+\\.[a-zA-Z]{2,}$";

  [Required(ErrorMessage = "Name is mandatory")]
  [StringLength(100, ErrorMessage =
    "Name cannot be longer that 100 characters")]
  public required string Name { get; set; }

  [Required(ErrorMessage = "Email is mandatory")]
  [RegularExpression(EmailRegEx, ErrorMessage =
    "This is not a valid e-mail address")]
  public required string Email { get; set; }

  [Required(ErrorMessage = "Password is mandatory")]
  [StringLength(maximumLength: 100,
    MinimumLength = 14,
    ErrorMessage =
    "Passwords should be at least 14 long, an no more that 100")]
  public required string Password { get; set; }

  public string Message { get; set; } = string.Empty;

  public required string Country { get; set; }

  public bool Subscriber { get; set; }

  public Gender Gender { get; set; }
}
```

The Member class also uses a regular expression for the email address.

Chapter 4   Forms and Validation

> **Note** While this regex covers most common email formats, it might not capture every valid email address according to the full specifications of RFC 5322, which defines the syntax for email addresses. However, this regex should suffice for most practical purposes

Adding these attributes is not enough. We need to tell our component to use these attributes, these data annotations for validation. This is easy. There is the DataAnnotationsValidator component for that. Update your MemberForm by adding it to the EditForm component as in Listing 4-14.

Listing 4-14. Adding DataAnnotationsValidator

```
<EditForm FormName="member-form"
          OnValidSubmit="Submit"
          Model="@Member" >

  <DataAnnotationsValidator />
```

Showing Validation Feedback

Entering values in the MemberForm will trigger validation, but we don't have a way to display the error messages from validation. How can we do this? Blazor comes with two built-in validation components, the ValidationsSummary and ValidationMessage components:

- The ValidationsSummary shows you a list of validation errors.
- The ValidationMessage shows only errors for one property of the model.

Update the MemberForm component by adding ValidationMessage components for Name, Email, Password, and Message as shown in Listing 4-15. The For parameter takes a lambda which is used to retrieve the name of the property being validated.

Listing 4-15. Adding ValidationMessage

```
<div class="form-group row mb-1">
  <label class="col-sm-3 col-form-label"
         for="Name">Name:</label>
```

```
  <div class="col-sm-9">
    <InputText class="form-control"
               @bind-Value="Member.Name" />
    <ValidationMessage For="@(() => Member.Name)" />
  </div>
</div>
...
<div class="form-group row mb-1">
  <label class="col-sm-3 col-form-label"
         for="Email">Email:</label>
  <div class="col-sm-9">
    <InputText type="email" class="form-control"
               formnovalidate
               @bind-Value="Member.Email" />
    <ValidationMessage For="@(() => Member.Email)" />
  </div>
</div>
...
<div class="form-group row mb-1">
  <label class="col-sm-3 col-form-label"
         for="Password">Password:</label>
  <div class="col-sm-9">
    <InputText type="password" class="form-control"
               @bind-Value="Member.Password" />
    <ValidationMessage For="@(() => Member.Password)" />
  </div>
</div>
...
<div class="form-group row mb-1">
  <label class="col-sm-3 col-form-label"
         for="Message">Message:</label>
  <div class="col-sm-9">
    <InputTextArea class="form-control"
                   @bind-Value="Member.Message" />
```

CHAPTER 4　FORMS AND VALIDATION

```
    <ValidationMessage For="@(() => Member.Message)" />
  </div>
</div>
```

Editing the form with some mistakes will result in the error message being shown, for example, look at Figure 4-2.

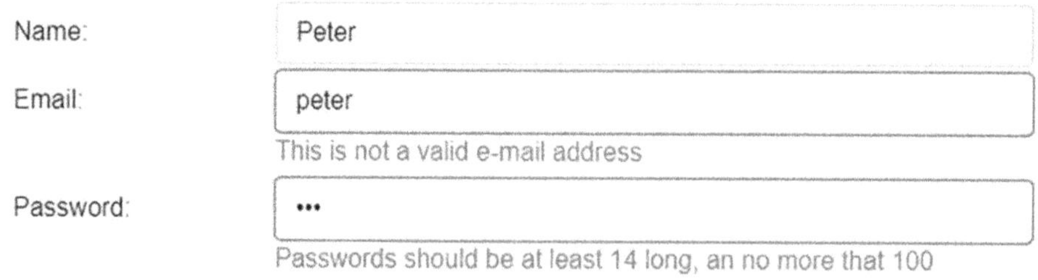

Figure 4-2. Showing validation messages

If you like, add the `ValidationsSummary` to the top, displaying all error messages in a list as showing in Figure 4-3.

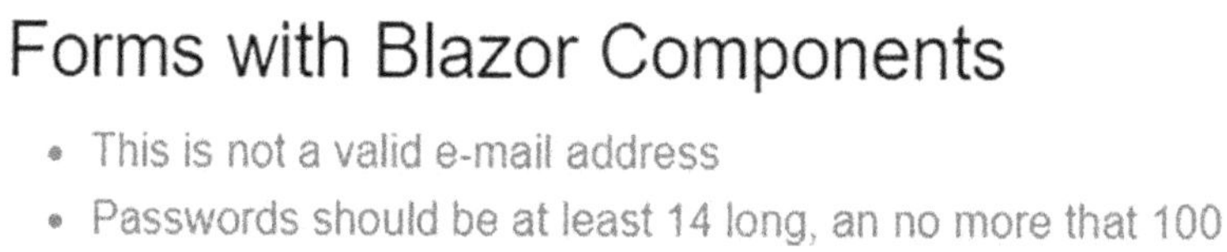

Figure 4-3. ValidationsSummary

Blazor validation also adds some styles and by default; this will put a red border around inputs with validation errors. Note that the Submit button does not invoke the `Submit` method if there are validation errors.

Customizing the Validation Feedback

When you enter a value in an `InputText` element (or one of the other input components), Blazor validation gives you feedback about the validity of the value by adding certain CSS classes. Let us have a look at how this is implemented. Run the BlazorApp.UsingForms project, right-click the Email input, and then select Inspect from the browser's menu.

Initially, an untouched input will have the `valid` class, as in Listing 4-16 (the other class comes from the class attribute in Listing 4-15).

124

Listing 4-16. Validation uses the valid CSS class.

```
<input class="form-control valid" ...>
```

When you make a valid change to an input, the modified class is added as in Listing 4-17.

Listing 4-17. Validation adds the modified class after a change

```
<input class="form-control modified valid" ...>
```

With an invalid input, you get the invalid class, as in Listing 4-18.

Listing 4-18. Bad input uses the invalid css class.

```
<input class="form-control modified invalid" ...>
```

Finally, validation messages get the validation-message CSS class, as in Listing 4-19.

Listing 4-19. Validation messages use the validation-message class.

```
<div class="validation-message">Name is mandatory</div>
```

Out of the box, Blazor uses following CSS styling for validation, as shown in Listing 4-20. You can find these CSS rules in wwwroot/app.css. Simply put, these add a green outline to an input if it has valid modifications, and a red outline when the input has an invalid value.

Listing 4-20. Blazor's built-in CSS validation rules

```
.valid.modified:not([type=checkbox]) {
  outline: 1px solid #26b050;
}

.invalid {
  outline: 1px solid #e50000;
}

.validation-message {
  color: #e50000;
}
```

So, if you want to customize how your feedback looks like, you customize these CSS rules. For example, you can use the following CSS from Listing 4-21 to make validation look like Figure 4-4.

Listing 4-21. Some custom CSS rules to change validation feedback

```
.valid.modified:not([type=checkbox]):not([type=radio]) {
  /*outline: 1px solid #26b050;*/
  border-left: 5px solid #42A948; /* green */
}

.invalid {
  /*outline: 1px solid #e50000;*/
  border-left: 5px solid #a94442; /* red */
}

.validation-message {
  /*color: #e50000;*/
  color: #a94442;
}
```

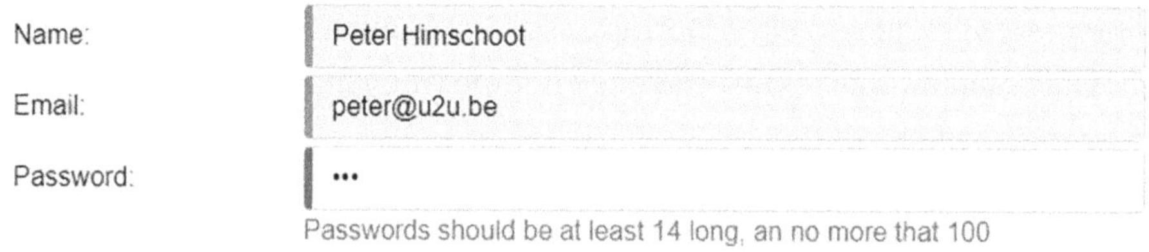

Name:	Peter Himschoot
Email:	peter@u2u.be
Password:	•••

Passwords should be at least 14 long, an no more that 100

Figure 4-4. *Customized validation feedback*

Custom Validation

Can I build my own validation? Yes, you can! First, we need to understand `EditContext`. This type is used to track modifications to the model, including validation and validation errors.

Start by making a copy of the `MemberForm` component, naming it `MemberFormEditContext`. Replace the `Model` parameter of the `EditForm` with the `EditContext` parameter as in Listing 4-22.

Listing 4-22. Using EditContext

```
<h3>Custom Validation With EditContext</h3>

<EditForm EditContext="@editContext"
          FormName="member-form"
          OnValidSubmit="Submit">
  @* No changes inside the EditForm *@
</EditForm>

@code {

  [Parameter]
  [EditorRequired]
  public required Member Member { get; set; }

  private EditContext? editContext;
  private ValidationMessageStore? messageStore;

  protected override void OnInitialized()
  {
    editContext = new(Member); // Member has already been set
    editContext.OnValidationRequested +=
      HandleValidationRequested;
    messageStore = new(editContext);
  }

  private void HandleValidationRequested(object? sender,
    ValidationRequestedEventArgs e)
  {
    messageStore?.Clear();
    if (Member.Name is not string { Length: > 0 })
    {
      messageStore?.Add(() => Member.Name,
        "Name is mandatory");
    }
    else if (Member.Name is not string  { Length: < 100 })
    {
```

```
      messageStore?.Add(() => Member.Name,
        "Name cannot be longer that 100 characters");
    }
  }
  public void Submit()
  {
    Console.WriteLine(Member.ToJson());
  }
}
```

Inside the component, we override the `OnInitialized` method (which we discuss in the chapter on Lifecycle Hooks) to initialize the `editContext` field, and we implement the `OnValidationRequested` event, which gets triggered when the user submits the form. We also initialize the `messageStore` which stores the validation errors.

An `EditForm` component requires an `EditContext`, and you can have it created implicitly through the `Model` parameter, or you can create it manually as this component does. Each time you make a change to an input, the `OnFieldChanged` event triggers (which we will use a little later), and each time the whole model needs to be validated, the `OnValidationRequested` event triggers. In the case of the `MemberFormEditContext`, we implement this event in the `HandleValidationRequested` method to validate the `Member` instance and add any validation errors to the `messageStore`.

Replace the `MemberForm` with the `MemberFormEditContext` component and run. Validation works! Of course, this example is just to illustrate how you could implement custom validation.

Let us look at custom validation for real. I don't think it is a good idea to let the component do the validation; this should be done with another class. So let us create a `MemberCustomValidator` which we can add to the form just like the `DataAnnotationsValidator`. A validator is just another component. Start by adding a new generic class `CustomValidator`, with its implementation shown in Listing 4-23.

Listing 4-23. The CustomValidator class

```
using Microsoft.AspNetCore.Components;
using Microsoft.AspNetCore.Components.Forms;

namespace BlazorApp.UsingForms.Components;
```

```csharp
public abstract class CustomValidator<T> : ComponentBase
{
  [CascadingParameter]
  public required EditContext EditContext { get; set; }

  protected override void OnInitialized()
  {
    if (EditContext is null)
    {
      throw new InvalidOperationException(
        "The CustomValidator needs to be nested in an EditForm");
    }

    ValidationMessageStore store = new(EditContext);

    EditContext.OnValidationRequested += (sender, e) =>
    {
      store?.Clear();
      foreach (string field in Fields)
      {
        Action<T, ValidationMessageStore> validator =
          GetFieldValidator(field);
        validator((T)EditContext.Model, store!);
      }
    };

    EditContext.OnFieldChanged += (sender, e) =>
    {
      store?.Clear();
      Action<T, ValidationMessageStore> validator =
        GetFieldValidator(e.FieldIdentifier.FieldName);
      validator((T)EditContext.Model, store!);
    };
  }
  protected abstract IEnumerable<string> Fields { get; }
```

```
  protected abstract Action<T, ValidationMessageStore>
    GetFieldValidator(string field);
}
```

The `CustomValidator<T>` class allows you to implement custom validation for any class, not just `Member`. That is why it has a generic parameter: T. It does work like the `DataAnnotationsValidator`. First, we ask the `EditForm` for its `EditContext`, using a cascading parameter. This technique is discussed in the advanced component chapter. Then we implement both the `OnFieldChanged` and `OnValidationRequested` events. The `OnFieldChanged` event gets passed the name of the property we need to validate. The `OnValidationRequested` event should validate all properties. How the `OnFieldChanged` event needs to be validated is implemented by a derived class, and that is why we have an abstract method `GetFieldValidator`.

Let us look at an example of a derived class, the one that will validate the `Member` class. Add a new class named `MemberCustomValidatior`, implemented in Listing 4-24.

Listing 4-24. The MemberCustomValidator

```
using Microsoft.AspNetCore.Components.Forms;
using System.Text.RegularExpressions;

namespace BlazorApp.UsingForms.Components;

public partial class MemberCustomValidator : CustomValidator<Member>
{
  public const string EmailRegExPattern =
    "^[a-zA-Z0-9._%+-]+@[a-zA-Z0-9.-]+\\.[a-zA-Z]{2,}$";

  [GeneratedRegex(EmailRegExPattern)]
  public static partial Regex EmailRegEx();

  protected override IEnumerable<string> Fields { get; } =
    [nameof(Member.Name), nameof(Member.Email)];

  protected override Action<Member, ValidationMessageStore>
    GetFieldValidator(string field)
  {
    return field switch
    {
```

```
      nameof(Member.Name) => ValidateName,
      nameof(Member.Email) => ValidateEmail,
      _ => (_, _) => { }
    };
}
private void ValidateName(Member member,
                          ValidationMessageStore store)
{
    if (member.Name is not string { Length: > 0 })
    {
      store?.Add(() => member.Name,
        "Name is mandatory");
    }
    else if (member.Name is not string { Length: < 100 })
    {
      store?.Add(() => member.Name,
        "Name cannot be longer that 100 characters");
    }
}
private void ValidateEmail(Member member,
  ValidationMessageStore store)
{
    if (member.Email is not string { Length: > 0 })
    {
      store?.Add(() => member.Email,
        "Email is mandatory");
    }
    else
    if (!EmailRegEx().IsMatch(member.Email))
    {
      store?.Add(() => member.Email,
        "This is not a valid e-mail address");
    }
  }
}
```

Focus on the `GetFieldValidator` method first. This method gets passed the name of the property to validate, and it should return a method that does so (using an `Action` delegate). My implementation uses a switch expression (https://learn.microsoft.com/en-us/dotnet/csharp/language-reference/operators/switch-expression) and returns a method to validate the property.

The `ValidateEmail` method gets passed the model to validate (here an instance of `Member`), and the store to add validation errors into. First, we check if `Email` is not empty, and since I like pattern matching style, I am checking to see if the `Email` matches an object with a `Length` property larger than 0. Next, I use a regular expression to validate the email.

> **Note** Concerning regular expressions, I use a source generator which generates the code for the regular expression at compile time. Previously, this was done at runtime, but the source generated regular expression is about 30% faster.

What about the `OnValidationRequested` event? The derived class needs to override the `Fields` property, returning the names of all fields that need validation. The `CustomValidator` uses this list of fields to iterate and validate each field.

Create a copy of the `MemberForm` naming it `MemberFormCustom`, and replace the `DataAnnotationsValidator` with the `MemberCustomValidator` as in Listing 4-25.

Listing 4-25. Using the MemberCustomValidator

```
<h3>Custom Validation</h3>

<EditForm FormName="member-form"
          OnValidSubmit="Submit"
          Model="@Member" >

    <MemberCustomValidator/>
```

Run. You will see that validation works for both `Name` and `Email`. `Password` is left as an exercise for the reader.

Using Fluent Validation

There is another option. There is a very popular NuGet package named FluentValidation which is quite powerful and easy to use. That is a win-win for me, so let us examine how we can use this package in Blazor.

To use FluentValidation, we need to add the Blazored.FluentValidation package first, so do this either using Visual Studio or the CLI (run this in the project's folder):

dotnet add package Blazored.FluentValidation

With FluentValidation, you create a validator class that contains the rules about an entity, written in the "Fluent" style. Add a new class named FluentMemberValidator with code from Listing 4-26.

Listing 4-26. The FluentMemberValidator

```
using FluentValidation;
using System.Text.RegularExpressions;

namespace BlazorApp.UsingForms;

public partial class FluentMemberValidator : AbstractValidator<Member>
{
  public const string EmailRegExPattern = "^[a-zA-Z0-9._%+-]+@[a-zA-Z0-9.-]+\\.[a-zA-Z]{2,}$";

  [GeneratedRegex(EmailRegExPattern)]
  public static partial Regex EmailRegEx();

  public FluentMemberValidator()
  {
    _ = RuleFor(member => member.Name)
      .Must(name => name is string { Length: > 0 })
      .WithMessage("Name is mandatory")
      .Must(name => name is string { Length: < 100 })
      .WithMessage("Name cannot be longer that 100 characters");

    _ = RuleFor(member => member.Email)
      .Must(email => email is string { Length: > 0 })
```

CHAPTER 4 FORMS AND VALIDATION

```
        .WithMessage("Email is mandatory");

    _ = When(member => member.Email is { Length: > 0 }, () =>
    {
        _ = RuleFor(member => member.Email)
            .Must(email => EmailRegEx().IsMatch(email))
            .WithMessage("This is not a valid e-mail address");
    });
  }
}
```

This class needs to inherit from the `AbstractValidator<Member>` base class and add the rules in the constructor. Rules can be described in the `RuleFor` method. You can also have conditional rules, for example, When email is not empty, it needs to match a regular expression.

Copy the `MemberForm` component, and name the copy `MemberFormFluent`. Replace the validator with `FluentValidationValidator` as in Listing 4-27.

Listing 4-27. Using FluentValidationValidator

```
<FluentValidationValidator Validator="validator" />
```

Add a field to the @code section of type `FluentMemberValidator` as in Listing 4-28.

Listing 4-28. Using the FluentMemberValidator

```
@code {
  [Parameter]
  [EditorRequired]
  public required Member Member { get; set; }

  private FluentMemberValidator validator = new();

  public void Submit()
  {
    Console.WriteLine(Member.ToJson());
  }
}
```

CHAPTER 4 FORMS AND VALIDATION

Inside the Home component, use the MemberFormFluent as in Listing 4-29.

Listing 4-29. Validating with FluentValidation

```
@page "/"

<PageTitle>Home</PageTitle>

<MemberFormFluent Member="@Member" />

@code {
  private Member Member { get; set; } = new Member
    {
      Name = "Peter",
      Email = string.Empty,
      Password = string.Empty,
      Country = "be",
      Message = "I ♡ Blazor!",
      Gender = Gender.Male,
      Subscriber = true
    };
}
```

Run.

DataAnnotations, Fluent or Custom Validation?

Which one is best? Choose whichever works for you. Data annotations are simple, and that is both good and bad. Data Annotations do not allow for more complex rules and use reflection. If you have complex rules, custom or fluent validation is better. You can express quite complex rules with fluent validation and reuse them from outside Blazor, since this also works for ASP.NET MVC or other applications.

Disabling the Submit Button

What if you need to disable the Submit button as long as there are fields that do not pass validation? To make this work, we do need to make some more changes. Remember

135

CHAPTER 4 FORMS AND VALIDATION

EditContext and the OnFieldChanged event? The EditContext class has another method: Validate which returns a bool with the result of validation.

Copy MemberFormFluent, and name it MemberFormSubmit. Add an EditContext and a bool as shown in Listing 4-30. This logic will set the formValid field with the result of validation.

Listing 4-30. Adding support for disabling the Submit button

```
[Parameter]
[EditorRequired]
public required Member Member { get; set; }

private FluentMemberValidator validator = new();
private EditContext editContext = default!;
private bool formValid = false;

protected override void OnInitialized()
{
  editContext = new(Member); // Member has been set already
  editContext.OnFieldChanged += (_, _) =>
  {
    formValid = editContext.Validate();
    StateHasChanged();
  };
}

public void Submit()
{
  Console.WriteLine(Member.ToJson());
}
```

To disable the button, we add the disabled attribute to the Submit button as in Listing 4-31.

Listing 4-31. Disabling the Submit button

```
<div class="form-group mb-0">
  <button type="submit" class="btn btn-primary"
    disabled="@(!formValid)">
```

```
    Submit
  </button>
</div>
```

Finally, we need to replace the `Model` parameter with the `EditContext` parameter for the `EditForm`, illustrated by Listing 4-32.

Listing 4-32. Using EditContext

```
<EditForm FormName="member-form"
          OnValidSubmit="Submit"
          EditContext="@editContext">
```

Replace the `MemberFormFluent` with `MemberFormButton` in the `Home` component.

Run. When you have validation errors, the button will be disabled. Once you fix them, the button will be enabled.

In Listing 4-30, we initialize the `formValid` field to `false`, which will disable the button initially. Should you want validation to run, and set the `formValid` according to the validation's result, you can call the validator explicitly as shown in Listing 4-33.

Listing 4-33. Perform explicit validation.

```
protected override void OnInitialized()
{
  editContext = new(Member); // Member has been set already
  editContext.OnFieldChanged += (_, _) =>
  {
    formValid = editContext.Validate();
    StateHasChanged();
  };

  formValid = validator.Validate(Member).IsValid;
}
```

Entering the PizzaPlace Customer

Here we will add some more functionality to the PizzaPlace application we built in the previous chapter. You can continue from there.

CHAPTER 4 FORMS AND VALIDATION

Add the Customer Class

Add a new class named Customer to the shared project, as in Listing 4-34.

Listing 4-34. The Customer class

```
namespace BlazorApp.PizzaPlace.Shared;

public class Customer
{
  public int Id { get; set; }

  public required string Name { get; set; }

  public required string Street { get; set; }

  public required string City { get; set; }

  public required string ZipCode { get; set; }
}
```

We should also add a Customer property to the State class, as in Listing 4-35.

Listing 4-35. Adding Customer to State

```
namespace BlazorApp.PizzaPlace.Shared;

public class State
{
  public Pizza[] Pizzas { get; set; } = [];
  public ShoppingBasket Basket { get; } = new();

  public Customer Customer { get; set; } = new()
  {
    Id = 0,
    Name = string.Empty,
    Street = string.Empty,
    City = string.Empty,
    ZipCode = string.Empty
  };
```

```
    public decimal TotalPrice
    => Basket.Orders.Sum(id => GetPizza(id)!.Price);

    public Pizza? GetPizza(int id)
    => Pizzas.SingleOrDefault(pizza => pizza.Id == id);
}
```

Time to build the `CustomerEntry` component.

Implement the CustomerEntry Component

Add a new razor component named `CustomerEntry`. This will use an `EditForm` to allow entry of the `Customer` information. Let us gradually build this component.

Our `CustomerEntry` component will have a `Title`, which we will pass from the parent. Start with Listing 4-36.

Listing 4-36. Beginning the CustomerEntry component

```
<h1 class="mt-2 mb-2">@Title</h1>

@code {
  [Parameter]
  [EditorRequired]
  public string Title { get; set; } = default!;
}
```

Add the `CustomerEntry` after the `Basket` component from Listing 4-37.

Listing 4-37. Using the CustomerEntry component

```
<PageTitle>The PizzaPlace</PageTitle>
<Menu Pizzas="@State.Pizzas" Selected="AddPizzaToBasket" />
<Basket @bind-State="@State"/>
<CustomerEntry Title="Please enter your details below"/>
```

Add a required `Customer` parameter to this component. We will disable the "Place Order" button in case of validation errors, so add an `EditContext` and `bool` field. We also need the `ValidSubmit` method. Look at Listing 4-38 for details.

CHAPTER 4   FORMS AND VALIDATION

Listing 4-38. Adding parameters to the CustomerEntry component

```
[Parameter]
[EditorRequired]
public string Title { get; set; } = default!;

[Parameter]
[EditorRequired]
public required Customer Customer { get; set; }

private EditContext editContext = default!;
private bool formValid = false;

protected override void OnInitialized()
{
  editContext = new(Customer);
  editContext.OnFieldChanged += (_, _) =>
  {
    formValid = editContext.Validate();
    StateHasChanged();
  };
}

public async Task ValidSubmit()
{

}
```

Pass the State its Customer to the CustomerEntry component; see Listing 4-39.

Listing 4-39. The Home component

```
<CustomerEntry Title="Please enter your details below"
    Customer="@State.Customer"/>
```

Add the EditForm and inputs for our customer from Listing 4-40. You might want to copy this from the provided files; this is not typing training. Note that the "Place Order" button will be disabled should there be validation errors.

Listing 4-40. Adding the EditForm

```
<EditForm FormName="CustomerEntry"
          EditContext="@editContext"
          OnValidSubmit="ValidSubmit">

  <fieldset>
    <div class="row mb-2">
      <label class="col-2" for="name">Name:</label>
      <InputText class="form-control col-6"
        @bind-Value="@Customer.Name" />
    </div>
    <div class="row mb-2">
      <div class="col-6 offset-2" >
        <ValidationMessage For="@(() => Customer.Name)" />
      </div>
    </div>
    <div class="row mb-2">
      <label class="col-2" for="street">Street:</label>
      <InputText class="form-control col-6"
        @bind-Value="@Customer.Street" />
    </div>
    <div class="row mb-2">
      <div class="col-6 offset-2">
        <ValidationMessage For="@(() => Customer.Street)" />
      </div>
    </div>
    <div class="row mb-2">
      <label class="col-2" for="city">City:</label>
      <InputText class="form-control col-6"
        @bind-Value="@Customer.City" />
    </div>
    <div class="row mb-2">
      <div class="col-6 offset-2">
        <ValidationMessage For="@(() => Customer.City)" />
      </div>
    </div>
```

CHAPTER 4   FORMS AND VALIDATION

```
      <div class="row mb-2">
        <label class="col-2" for="city">ZipCode:</label>
        <InputText class="form-control col-6"
          @bind-Value="@Customer.ZipCode" />
      </div>
      <div class="row mb-2">
        <div class="col-6 offset-2">
          <ValidationMessage For="@(() => Customer.ZipCode)" />
        </div>
      </div>
      <div class="row mb-2">
        <button class="btn btn-primary"
                disabled="@(!formValid)">
          Place Order
        </button>
      </div>
    </fieldset>
</EditForm>
```

You can run the application and see the form. However, we need to add some validation.

Add Fluent Validation

Add the FluentValidation NuGet package to the BlazorApp.PizzaPlace.Shared project, either by using Visual Studio or by running this command in the project's folder:

```
dotnet add package FluentValidation
```

Add a new folder to the BlazorApp.PizzaPlace.Shared project named Validation. Inside it add a new class named CustomerFluentValidator. This will validate a customer, and its code is in Listing 4-41.

Listing 4-41. The CustomerFluentValidator class

```
using FluentValidation;
using System.Text.RegularExpressions;
```

```csharp
namespace BlazorApp.PizzaPlace.Shared.Validation;

public partial class CustomerFluentValidator
  : AbstractValidator<Customer>
{
  [GeneratedRegex("^[1-9]\\d{3}$",
    RegexOptions.CultureInvariant | RegexOptions.IgnoreCase)]
  public static partial Regex _zipcode();

  public CustomerFluentValidator()
  {
    _ = RuleFor(cust => cust.Name)
      .Must(name => name is { Length: > 0 })
      .WithMessage("Please provide a name");

    _ = RuleFor(cust => cust.Street)
      .Must(street => street is { Length: > 0 })
      .WithMessage("Please provide a street with house number.");

    _ = RuleFor(cust => cust.City)
      .Must(city => city is { Length: > 0 })
      .WithMessage("Please provide a city");

    _ = RuleFor(cust => cust.ZipCode)
      .Must(zipcode => zipcode is { Length: > 0 })
      .WithMessage("Please provide a zip code");

    _ = RuleFor(cust => cust.ZipCode)
      .Must(zipcode => _zipcode().IsMatch(zipcode))
      .WithMessage("Zipcode is between 1000 and 9999");
  }
}
```

Add the Blazored.FluentValidation package to the Blazor project, for example, using this command:

```
dotnet add package Blazored.FluentValidation
```

Add the `CustomerFluentValidator` to the `CustomerEntry` component as a field, shown in Listing 4-42.

CHAPTER 4　FORMS AND VALIDATION

Listing 4-42. Adding the CustomerFluentValidator

```
private EditContext editContext = default!;
private bool formValid = false;
private CustomerFluentValidator validator = new();
```

Add the `FluentValidationValidator` inside the `EditForm`, as shown in Listing 4-43.

Listing 4-43. Adding the FluentValidationValidator

```
@using BlazorApp.PizzaPlace.Shared.Validation
@using Blazored.FluentValidation
<h1 class="mt-2 mb-2">@Title</h1>

<EditForm FormName="CustomerEntry"
          EditContext="@editContext"
          OnValidSubmit="ValidSubmit">

  <FluentValidationValidator/>
```

Run the PizzaPlace application. Enter some customer's details. Once all fields are valid, you can click on the Place Order button.

Look at the JSON output we added as a debugging aid. The customer does not get updated!? We need to add two-way data binding and a way to notify the Home component.

Adding Two-Way Data Binding

When the "Place Order" button gets clicked, we want to parent component (in this case the Home component) to see the changes and be notified about the click. We will send changes back to the parent using two-way data binding, and we will have a callback action that the parent component can pass to the CustomerEntry component.

Add a new parameter named CustomerChanged, of type EventCallback<Customer>. This class is discussed in the data binding chapter should you need a refresher. Invoke

CHAPTER 4 FORMS AND VALIDATION

the `CustomerChanged` in the `ValidSubmit` method as in Listing 4-44, which gets called when the user clicks the "Place Order" button.

Listing 4-44. Notifying the parent component

```
[Parameter]
[EditorRequired]
public required Customer Customer { get; set; }

[Parameter]
public EventCallback<Customer> CustomerChanged { get; set; }

public async Task ValidSubmit()
{
    await CustomerChanged.InvokeAsync();
}
```

And don't forget to update the Home component to use two-way data binding as in Listing 4-45.

Listing 4-45. Using two-way data binding

```
<CustomerEntry Title="Please enter your details below"
   @bind-Customer="@State.Customer"/>
```

Notifying the Parent Component

Finally, we need a way to notify the parent that the user has clicked the "Place Order" button. Let us add a parameter called `OrderPlaced` of type `EventCallback`.

Hmm. Thinking about this, maybe we should have a `SubmitTitle` parameter to make this component more reusable? In other places, we could call this button "Save," or something else. And instead of calling the `EventCallback OrderPlaced`, we could name it `SubmitClicked`?

Make it so. Add two parameters to the `CustomerEntry` component as in Listing 4-46.

Listing 4-46. Updating the CustomerEntry with an EventCallback and SubmitTitle

```
[Parameter]
```

145

CHAPTER 4 FORMS AND VALIDATION

```
[EditorRequired]
public required string SubmitTitle { get; set; }

[Parameter]
[EditorRequired]
public required EventCallback SubmitClicked { get; set; }
```

Update the button with the `SubmitTitle` as in Listing 4-47.

Listing 4-47. Updating the Submit button

```
<div class="row mb-2">
  <button class="btn btn-primary"
          disabled="@(!formValid)">
    @SubmitTitle
  </button>
</div>
```

When the form gets submitted, the `EditForm` calls the `ValidSubmit` method, and here we invoke the `SubmitClicked` `EventCallback` as in Listing 4-48.

Listing 4-48. Invoking the SubmitClicked EventCallback

```
public async Task ValidSubmit()
{
  await CustomerChanged.InvokeAsync(Customer);
  await SubmitClicked.InvokeAsync();
}
```

Finally, we update the `Home` component to pass the `Submit` parameters as in Listing 4-49.

Listing 4-49. Implementing the Home component

```
@page "/"

<PageTitle>The PizzaPlace</PageTitle>

<Menu Pizzas="@State.Pizzas" Selected="AddPizzaToBasket" />

<Basket @bind-State="@State"/>
```

```
<CustomerEntry Title="Please enter your details below"
    @bind-Customer="@State.Customer"
    SubmitTitle="Place Order"
    SubmitClicked="SubmitClicked"/>

<p>@State.ToJson()</p>

@code {
  ...
  private void SubmitClicked()
  {
    Console.WriteLine("Order has been placed");
  }
}
```

Run your application. You should be able to order some pizzas. Look in the Console window to see if the order has been placed after clicking the "Place Order" button.

This concludes this part of PizzaPlace!

Summary

In this chapter, we discussed data entry using forms. Blazor has a range of Input components that allow the user to enter all kinds of details. We also had a look at validation, including the built-in and custom validation techniques. And we saw how we can disable a "submit" button if there are validation errors. We are not finished with Blazor Forms; we will look some more at using Forms in the chapter on building static websites.

CHAPTER 5

Services and Dependency Injection

Dependency Inversion is one of the basic principles of good _Object-Oriented Design_. The big enabler is _Dependency Injection_. In this chapter, we will discuss dependency inversion and injection and why it is a fundamental part of Blazer. We will illustrate this by building a _Service_ that encapsulates where the data gets retrieved and stored.

What Is Dependency Inversion?

Currently, our PizzaPlace app retrieves its data from hard-coded sample data. But in a real-life situation, this data will probably be stored in a _database_ on the server. Retrieving and storing this data could be done in the component itself, but this is a bad idea. Why? Because technology changes quite often, and different customers for your application might want to use their specific technology, requiring you to update your app for every customer.

Instead, we will put this logic into a _Service object_. A Service object's role is to encapsulate specific business rules, or how data is communicated between the client and the server. A Service object is also a lot easier to test since we can write _unit tests_ that run on their own, without requiring a user to interact with the application for testing.

But first, let's talk about the dependency inversion principle and how dependency injection allows us to apply this principle.

CHAPTER 5　SERVICES AND DEPENDENCY INJECTION

Understanding Dependency Inversion

Imagine a `ProductList` component that uses a `ProductsService` service class, and the component creates the service using the new operator, as in Listing 5-1 (no need to type).

Listing 5-1. A component using a ProductsService

```
@using Dependency.Inversion.Shared
@foreach (var product in productsService.GetProducts())
{
  <div>@product.Name</div>
  <div>@product.Description</div>
  <div>@product.Price</div>
}
@code {
  private ProductsService productsService =
    new ProductsService();
}
```

This component is now completely dependent on the `ProductsService`! This is known as _tight-coupling_; see Figure 5-1.

```
┌─────────────┐          ┌──────────────────┐
│ ProductList │─────────▶│ ProductsService  │
└─────────────┘          └──────────────────┘
```

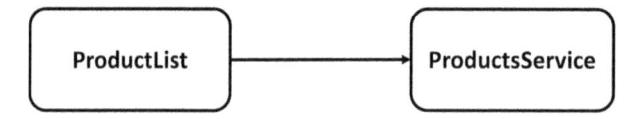

Figure 5-1. *Tight-coupling*

Now you want to test the `ProductList` component, and `ProductsService` requires a server on the network to talk to. In this case, you will need to set up a server just to run the test. And if the server is not ready yet (the developer in charge of the server hasn't come around to it), you cannot test your component! Or you are using the `ProductsService` in several places in your location, and you need to replace it with another class. Now you will need to find every use of the `ProductsService` and replace the class. What a maintenance nightmare!

Using the Dependency Inversion Principle

The _Dependency Inversion_ principle states

    A. High-level modules should not depend on low-level modules. Both should depend on abstractions.

    B. Abstractions should not depend on details. Details should depend on abstractions.

What this means is that the ProductsList component (the higher-level module) should not directly depend on the ProductsService (the lower-level module). Instead, it should rely on an _abstraction_. Using C# terminology: It should rely on an _interface_ describing what a ProductsService should be able to do, not a class describing how it should work.

The IProductsService interface would look like Listing 5-2.

Listing 5-2. The abstraction as described in an interface

```
public interface IProductsService
{
  IEnumerable<Product> GetProducts();
}
```

And we change the ProductsList component to rely on this abstraction, as in Listing 5-3. Please note that we still need to assign an instance to the productService variable.

Listing 5-3. The ProductList component using the IProductsService interface

```
@using Dependency.Inversion.Shared
@foreach (var product in productsService.GetProducts())
{
  <div>@product.Name</div>
  <div>@product.Description</div>
  <div>@product.Price</div>
}

@code
{
  private IProductsService productsService;
}
```

CHAPTER 5　SERVICES AND DEPENDENCY INJECTION

Now the `ProductList` component (the high-level module from above) only relies on the `IProductsService` interface, an abstraction. And the abstraction does not reveal how we will implement the `GetProducts` method.

Of course, now we make the `ProductsService` (which is the low-level module) implement the `IProductsService` interface as in Listing 5-4.

Listing 5-4. The ProductsService implementing the IProductsService interface

```
public class ProductsService : IProductsService
{
  public IEnumerable<Product> GetProducts()
    => ...
}
```

If you want to test the `ProductList` component implemented using dependency inversion, you build a hard-coded version of the `IProductsService` and run the test without needing a server, for example, in Listing 5-5. We will discuss some of these techniques for testing in the BUnit chapter.

Listing 5-5. A hard-coded IProductsService used for testing

```
public class HardCodedProductsService : IProductsService
{
  public IEnumerable<Product> GetProducts()
  {
    yield return new Product
    {
      Name = "Isabelle's Homemade Marmelade",
      Description = "...",
      Price = 1.99M
    };

    yield return new Product
    {
      Name = "Liesbeth's Applecake",
```

```
      Description = "...",
      Price = 3.99M
    };
  }
}
```

If you are using the `IProductsService` interface in different places in your application (instead of the `ProductsService` class), all you need to do to replace its implementation is to build another class that implements the `IProductsService` interface and tell your application to use the other class!

By applying the _Dependency Inversion Principle_ (see Figure 5-2), we gained a lot more flexibility.

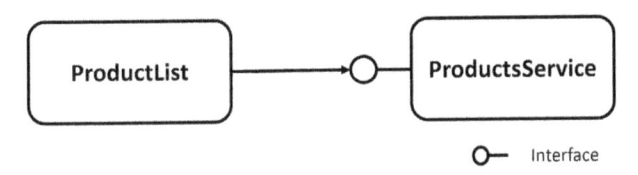

Figure 5-2. *Loosely coupled objects through dependency inversion*

Adding Dependency Injection

If you were to run this application, you would get a `NullReferenceException`. Why? Because the `ProductsList` component from Listing 5-3 still needs an instance of a class implementing `IProductsService`! We could pass the `ProductsService` in the constructor of the `ProductList` component, for example, in Listing 5-6.

Listing 5-6. Passing the ProductsService in the constructor

```
new ProductList(new ProductsService())
```

But if the `ProductsService` also depends on another class, it quickly becomes like Listing 5-7. This is of course not a practical way of working! Because of that, we will use an Inversion-of-Control Container (I didn't invent this name!).

Listing 5-7. Creating a deep chain of dependencies manually

```
new ProductList( new ProductsService(new Dependency()))
```

CHAPTER 5 SERVICES AND DEPENDENCY INJECTION

Use an Inversion-of-Control Container

An _Inversion-of-Control Container_ (IoCC) is just another object, which specializes in creating objects for you. You simply ask it to create for you an instance of a type, and it will take care of creating any dependencies it requires.

It is a little bit like in a movie where a surgeon, in the middle of an operation, needs a scalpel. The surgeon in the movie holds out his (or her) hand and asks for "Scalpel number 5!" The nurse (the Inversion-of-Control container) who is assisting, simply hands the surgeon the scalpel. The surgeon doesn't care where the scalpel comes from, or how it was built.

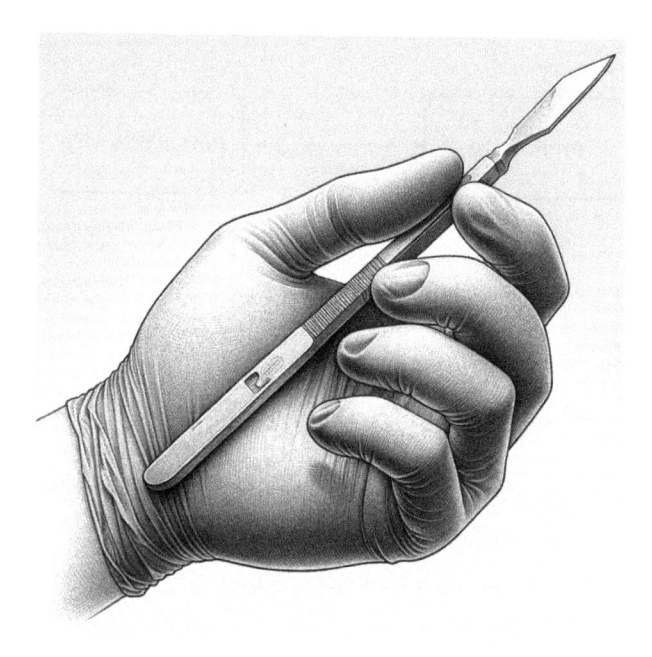

Figure 5-3. *A surgeon holding a scalpel*

So, how can the IoCC know which dependencies your component needs? There are a couple of ways, heavily depending on the IoCC.

Constructor Dependency Injection

Classes that need a dependency can simply state their dependencies in their constructor. The IoCC will examine the constructor and instantiate the dependencies before calling the constructor. And if these dependencies have their own dependencies, then the IoCC will also build them! For example, if the ProductsService has a constructor that takes an argument of type Dependency, as in Listing 5-8, then the IoCC will create an instance of type Dependency and will then call the ProductsService's constructor with that instance. The ProductsService constructor then stores a reference to the dependency in some field. Should the ProductsService's constructor take multiple arguments, then the IoCC will pass an instance for each argument. Constructor injection is normally used for required dependencies.

Listing 5-8. The ProductsService's constructor with arguments

```
public class ProductsService
{
  private readonly Dependency dep;

  public ProductsService(Dependency dep)
  {
    this.dep = dep;
  }
}
```

Property Dependency Injection

If the class that the IoCC needs to build has properties that indicate a dependency, then these properties are filled in by the IoCC. The way a property does that depends on the IoCC (in .NET there are a couple of different IoCC frameworks; some of these use an attribute on the property), but in Blazor you can have the IoCC inject an instance with the @inject directive in your razor file, for example, the second line of code in Listing 5-9.

Listing 5-9. Injecting a dependency with the @inject directive

```
@using Dependency.Inversion.Shared

@inject IProductsService productsService

@foreach (var product in productsService.GetProducts())
{
  <div>@product.Name</div>
```

```
    <div>@product.Description</div>
    <div>@product.Price</div>
}

@code
{ }
```

If you're using code separation, you can add a property to your class and apply the [Inject] attribute as in Listing 5-10. Since this listing uses nullable reference types, we need to assign a default! to remove the compiler warning (or make it required). Or you can also use the required modifier.

Listing 5-10. Using the Inject attribute for property injection

```
public partial class ProductList
{
  [Inject]
  public IProductsService ProductsService { get; set; }
    = default!;
}
```

You can then use this property directly in your razor file, as in Listing 5-11.

Listing 5-11. Using the ProductsService property that was dependency injected

```
@foreach (var product in productsService.GetProducts())
{
  <div>@product.Name</div>
  <div>@product.Description</div>
  <div>@product.Price</div>
}
```

Configuring Dependency Injection

There is one more thing we need to discuss. When your dependency is a class, then the IoCC can easily know that it needs to create an instance of the class with the class's constructor. But if your dependency is an interface, which it generally needs to be if you are applying the principle of Dependency Inversion, then which class does it use to create the instance? Without your help, it cannot know.

CHAPTER 5   SERVICES AND DEPENDENCY INJECTION

An IoCC has a mapping between interfaces and classes, and it is your job to configure this mapping. You configure the mapping in your Blazor project's `Program` class, as in Listing 5-12.

Listing 5-12. The Program class

```
using BlazorApp.DependencyInjection.Intro.Components;
using BlazorApp.DependencyInjection.Intro.Services;

WebApplicationBuilder builder = WebApplication.CreateBuilder(args);
builder.Services.AddRazorComponents()
    .AddInteractiveServerComponents();

builder.Services
        .AddSingleton<IProductsService, HardCodedProductsService>();

WebApplication app = builder.Build();
if (!app.Environment.IsDevelopment())
{
  _ = app.UseExceptionHandler("/Error", createScopeForErrors: true);
  _ = app.UseHsts();
}
app.UseHttpsRedirection();
app.UseStaticFiles();
app.UseAntiforgery();
app.MapRazorComponents<App>()
    .AddInteractiveServerRenderMode();
app.Run();
```

The `Program` class creates a `WebApplicationBuilder` instance, which has a property `Services` of type `IServiceCollection`. It is this `IServiceCollection` we need to configure. If you are familiar with ASP.NET Core, this is the same configuration.

To configure the mapping for the IoCC, you use extension methods on the `IServiceCollection` instance. Which extension method you call depends on the lifetime you want to give the dependency. There are three options for the lifetime of an instance which we will discuss next.

> **Note** The lifetime of instances is different for Blazor WebAssembly and Blazor Server. It is even different from the lifetime you know from ASP.NET Core!

Singleton Dependencies

Singleton classes are classes that only have one instance (in the application's scope). These are typically used to manage some global state. For example, you could have a class that keeps track of how many times people have clicked on a certain product. Having multiple instances of this class would complicate things because they will have to start communicating with each other to keep track of the clicks. Singleton classes can also be classes that don't have any state, that only have behavior (utility classes such as one that does conversions between imperial and metric units). In this case, you could have multiple instances, but this is just wasteful and will make the garbage collector work harder.

You configure dependency injection to reuse the same instance all the time with the `AddSingleton` extension method, for example, Listing 5-13. Every time the IoCC needs an instance of the `IProductsService` interface, it will use the same instance of the `ProductService` class.

Listing 5-13. Adding a singleton to dependency injection

```
builder.Services
    .AddSingleton<IProductsService, ProductsService>();
```

There is an overload available (Listing 5-14) that allows you to create the singleton instance yourself, and then tell IoCC to use that instance, giving you more control over the creation of the singleton instance.

Listing 5-14. Create the singleton yourself

```
ProductsService productsService = new ProductsService();
builder.Services
    .AddSingleton<IProductsService>(productsService);
```

In case your class does not have an interface, you can also use Listing 5-15.

Listing 5-15. Adding a singleton to dependency injection

```
builder.Services
       .AddSingleton<ProductsService>();
```

Why not use static methods instead of singletons you say? Static methods and properties are very hard to replace with fake implementations during testing (have you ever tried to test a method that uses a date with `DateTime.Now`, and you want to test it with February 29 of some quantum leap year?). During testing, you can easily replace the real class with a fake class because it implements an interface! In .NET 8, Microsoft introduced the `TimeProvider` class to make unit testing the `DateTime` a lot more practical!

Now about the difference between Blazor WebAssembly and Blazor Server. In Blazor WebAssembly, your application is running in a browser's tab. You can even have multiple copies of the same Blazor application running in different tabs of your browser (even different browsers). Each tab will have its own singleton instance, in the memory of that browser tab. So, you cannot use singletons to share state between tabs with Blazor WASM. And when you refresh the tab, the application will re-initialize with a new instance for the singleton.

With Blazor Server, the application is running on the server. So here the singleton is shared among every user running the Blazor application on the same server! But even here your application can be hosted with several servers, and each server will have its own singleton!

Transient Dependencies

Transient means short lived. In .NET there are a lot of objects which are short lived, which might not even survive beyond a single method call. For example, when you are concatenating a couple of strings, the intermediate strings are thrown away almost instantly after being created. Using transient objects makes a lot of sense when you don't want to be affected by the previous state of an object. Instead, you start with a fresh slate by creating a new instance.

When you configure dependency injection to use a transient lifetime for a class, each time an instance is needed by the IoCC, it will create a fresh instance.

You configure dependency injection to use transient instances with the `AddTransient` extension method, as in Listing 5-16.

CHAPTER 5   SERVICES AND DEPENDENCY INJECTION

Listing 5-16. Adding a transient class to dependency injection

```
builder.Services
      .AddTransient<IProductsService, ProductsService>();
```

However, in Blazor we are working client-side, and in that case, the UI stays put for the entire interaction. This means that you will have components that only have one created instance and only one instance of the dependency. You might think in that case transient, and singleton will do the same thing. But there can be another component that needs the same type of dependency. If you are using a singleton, then both components will share the same instance of the dependency, while transient each gets a unique instance! You should be aware of this.

Scoped Dependencies

When you configure dependency injection to use a _scoped_ dependency, the IoCC will re-use the same instance per scope but uses new instances between different scopes. But what does a scope mean?

Again, there is a difference between Blazor WASM and Blazor Server. In Blazor WASM, the scope is the application (running in the browser) itself. With Blazor WASM, a scoped instance will have the same lifetime as a singleton.

Blazor Server uses a _circuit_ which is the SignalR connection to keep track of a single user's application (somewhat like a session). This circuit spans across HTTP requests but not across the SignalR connection used with Blazor Server.

You configure the dependency to use scoped lifetime with the `AddScoped` extension method as in Listing 5-17.

Listing 5-17. Registering a class to use scoped lifetime

```
builder.Services
      .AddScoped<IProductsService, ProductsService>();
```

Understanding Blazor Dependency Lifetime

Let's look at the lifetime of the dependency injected dependencies in Blazor. For this, I have written a demo app (BlazorApp.DependencyInjection.Comparison) which you can find in the included sources for this book.

CHAPTER 5 SERVICES AND DEPENDENCY INJECTION

The source code for this book is available on GitHub via the book's product page, located at www.apress.com/ISBN.

I started by building three services, each one with a different lifetime (determined through the configuration of dependency injection). For example, see Listing 5-18. Every time an instance gets created, it gets assigned a GUID. By displaying the instance's GUID, it becomes easy to see which instance gets replaced with a new instance. These classes also implement IDisposable, so we can see when they get disposed by looking in the browser's debugger Console.

Listing 5-18. One of the dependencies used for the experiment

```
using BlazorApp.DependencyInjection.Comparison.Client.Services;

namespace BlazorApp.DependencyInjection.Comparison.Services;

public class SRSingletonService : ISingletonService, IDisposable
{
  public Guid Guid { get; set; } = Guid.NewGuid();

  public void Dispose()
  => Console.WriteLine("SRSingletonService Disposed");
}
```

Then I added these three services to the service collection, as in Listing 5-19 (Blazor Wasm) and Listing 5-20 (Blazor Server).

Listing 5-19. Adding the dependencies for Blazor Wasm (excerpt)

```
builder.Services
       .AddSingleton<ISingletonService, WASMSingletonService>()
       .AddTransient<ITransientService, WASMTransientService>()
       .AddScoped<IScopedService, WASMScopedService>();
```

Listing 5-20. Adding the dependencies for Blazor Server (excerpt)

```
builder.Services
       .AddSingleton<ISingletonService, SRSingletonService>()
       .AddTransient<ITransientService, SRTransientService>()
       .AddScoped<IScopedService, SRScopedService>();
```

CHAPTER 5   SERVICES AND DEPENDENCY INJECTION

And finally, I consume these services in the SRUsingServices and WASMUsingServices component from Listing 5-21. This will display GUIDs for each dependency.

Listing 5-21. The component consuming the dependencies

```
@rendermode Interactive Server

@inject ISingletonService singletonService
@inject ITransientService transientService
@inject IScopedService scopedService

<h3>Interactive Server</h3>

<div>
  <h1>Singleton</h1>
  Guid: @singletonService.Guid
  <h1>Transient</h1>
  Guid: @transientService.Guid
  <h1>Scoped</h1>
  Guid: @scopedService.Guid
</div>

@code { }
```

Blazor WebAssembly Experiment

Run the BlazorApp.DependencyInjection.Comparison project, which will start both Blazor Server and WebAssembly. On the left is Blazor Server, and on the right Blazor WebAssembly. We get Figure 5-4 on the first page (your GUIDs will be different). Switching to the Counter page and back shows Figure 5-5.

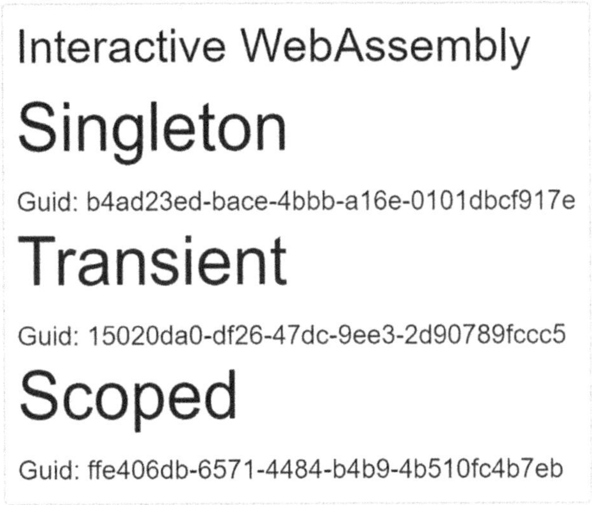

CHAPTER 5   SERVICES AND DEPENDENCY INJECTION

> **Interactive WebAssembly**
>
> **Singleton**
>
> Guid: b4ad23ed-bace-4bbb-a16e-0101dbcf917e
>
> **Transient**
>
> Guid: 15020da0-df26-47dc-9ee3-2d90789fccc5
>
> **Scoped**
>
> Guid: ffe406db-6571-4484-b4b9-4b510fc4b7eb

Figure 5-4. *Displaying client-side Blazor dependencies*

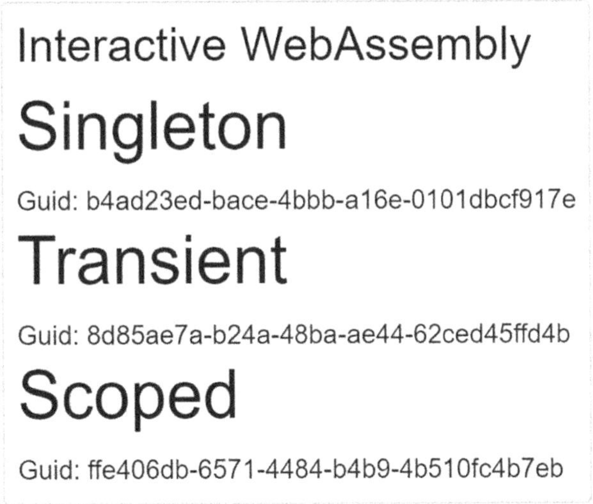

> **Interactive WebAssembly**
>
> **Singleton**
>
> Guid: b4ad23ed-bace-4bbb-a16e-0101dbcf917e
>
> **Transient**
>
> Guid: 8d85ae7a-b24a-48ba-ae44-62ced45ffd4b
>
> **Scoped**
>
> Guid: ffe406db-6571-4484-b4b9-4b510fc4b7eb

Figure 5-5. *The dependencies from the other page*

Each time the WASMUsingServices component gets created, it will ask dependency injection for instances of the ISingletonService, ITransientService, and IScopedService. The WASMSingletonService instance gets reused all the time because we see the same GUID. The WASMTransientService instance gets replaced each time (because each time we get a different GUID). We also see the same instance for the

163

CHAPTER 5   SERVICES AND DEPENDENCY INJECTION

WASMScopedService. In Blazor WebAssembly, scoped instances are scoped by default to the browser's tab (the application); they behave like singletons, so there is no difference.

And what if we open another tab? Since we have a fresh copy of the Blazor application running in the other tab, we get a new instance for the singleton, and because the scope is the connection, we get another instance of the scoped instance. If you expected to see the same instance for the singleton in both tabs, please remember that here each tab holds another copy of the Blazor application.

When do our instances get disposed? Both the singleton and scoped instance will live as long as your application is running, so these are not disposed. But what about the transient instance? If you really need to have a transient instance disposed when the component gets disposed, you need to implement the IDisposable interface as in Listing 5-22 on the component and call Dispose on the transient instance yourself! Or use OwningComponentBase (later).

Listing 5-22. Implementing IDisposable on a component

```
@implements IDisposable

@inject ISingletonService singletonService
@inject ITransientService transientService
@inject IScopedService scopedService

<h3>Interactive WebAssembly</h3>

<div>
  <h1>Singleton</h1>
  Guid: @singletonService.Guid
  <h1>Transient</h1>
  Guid: @transientService.Guid
  <h1>Scoped</h1>
  Guid: @scopedService.Guid
</div>

@code {
```

CHAPTER 5　SERVICES AND DEPENDENCY INJECTION

```
    public void Dispose()
    {
       (transientService as IDisposable)?.Dispose();
    }
}
```

Blazor Server Experiment

Now run the BlazorApp.DependencyInjection.Comparison project again. Your browser should open the Home page, showing the Blazor Server as in Figure 5-6. Select the Counter page and go back to the Home page to see Figure 5-7 (again you will have different GUIDs).

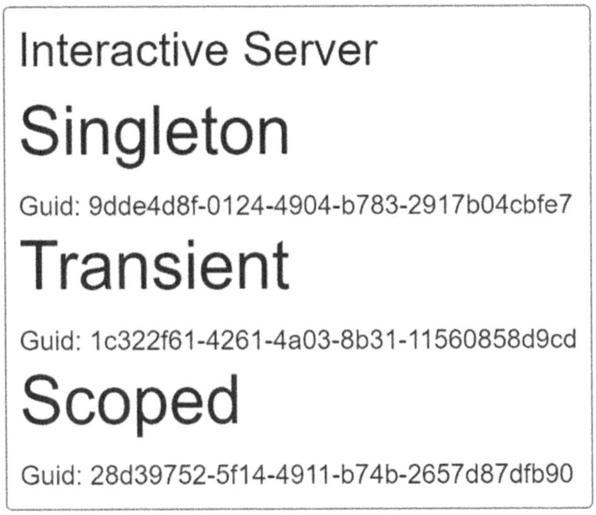

> Interactive Server
>
> **Singleton**
>
> Guid: 9dde4d8f-0124-4904-b783-2917b04cbfe7
>
> **Transient**
>
> Guid: 1c322f61-4261-4a03-8b31-11560858d9cd
>
> **Scoped**
>
> Guid: 28d39752-5f14-4911-b74b-2657d87dfb90

Figure 5-6. *Displaying server-side dependencies*

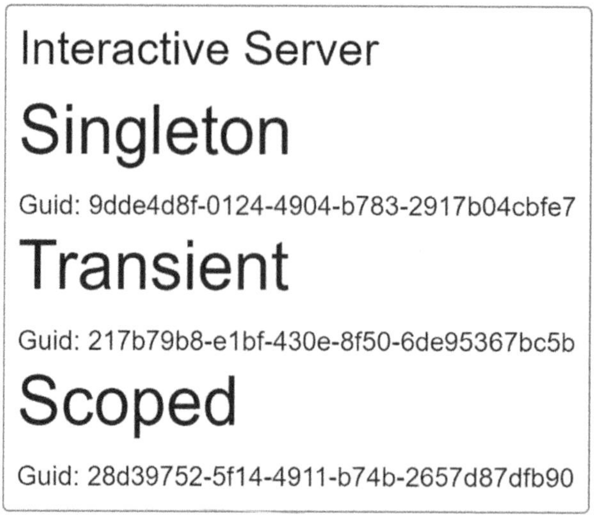

CHAPTER 5   SERVICES AND DEPENDENCY INJECTION

> Interactive Server
>
> **Singleton**
>
> Guid: 9dde4d8f-0124-4904-b783-2917b04cbfe7
>
> **Transient**
>
> Guid: 217b79b8-e1bf-430e-8f50-6de95367bc5b
>
> **Scoped**
>
> Guid: 28d39752-5f14-4911-b74b-2657d87dfb90

Figure 5-7. *After clicking on the other link*

Here we see a similar behavior like the one we saw for Blazor WASM. But don't get fooled. This is not the same, and we can see that by opening another tab. You should see the same GUID for the singleton instance as in Figure 5-8. Now we are running on the server, and the server will have one instance of singleton for all users. Open the page in another browser; again you will see the same GUID.

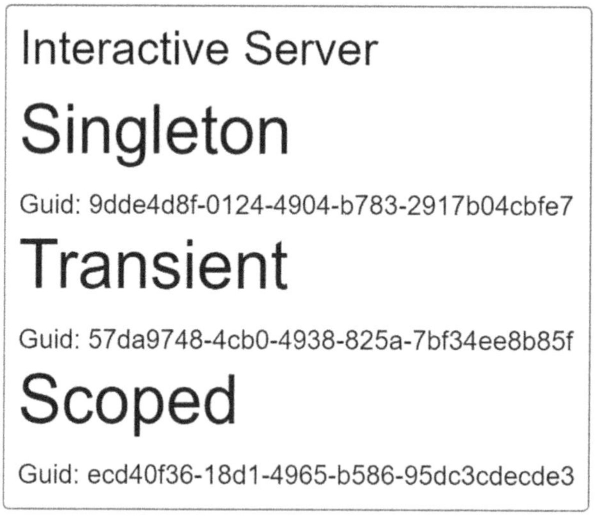

> Interactive Server
>
> **Singleton**
>
> Guid: 9dde4d8f-0124-4904-b783-2917b04cbfe7
>
> **Transient**
>
> Guid: 57da9748-4cb0-4938-825a-7bf34ee8b85f
>
> **Scoped**
>
> Guid: ecd40f36-18d1-4965-b586-95dc3cdecde3

Figure 5-8. *Opening another tab with server-side on the Home page*

Using OwningComponentBase

What if you need a service instance that belongs to your component and you want this instance to be disposed automatically when the component gets disposed? You can make your component create its own scope by deriving from the `OwningComponentBase` class. Look at Listing 5-23 which is the `WASMUsingOwnedScopedServices` which you can find in the provided project. Here we inherit from `OwningComponentBase`. Instead of using regular dependency injection, the `OwningComponentBase` class has the `ScopedServices` property which is an `IServiceProvider`. Any scoped instances should be created through the `ScopedServices`' `GetService` or `GetRequiredService` method. These instances now belong to the component's scope and will automatically be disposed when the component is disposed.

Listing 5-23. A component deriving from OwningComponentBase

```
@rendermode InteractiveWebAssembly

@inherits OwningComponentBase

@inject ISingletonService singletonService
@inject ITransientService transientService
@inject IScopedService scopedService

<h3>OwningComponentBase</h3>

<div>
  <h1>Scoped</h1>
  Guid: @scopedService.Guid
  <h1>Owning</h1>
  Guid: @someService.Guid
</div>

@code {
  private IScopedService someService = default!;

  protected override void OnInitialized()
  {
    base.OnInitialized();
    someService = ScopedServices.GetRequiredService<IScopedService>();
  }
}
```

CHAPTER 5 SERVICES AND DEPENDENCY INJECTION

If you only need one scoped instance, you can also use the generic OwningComponentBase<T> base class, which has a Service property of type T which will hold the scoped instance of type T. Listing 5-24 shows an example of this. You can still use the ScopedServices property if you need to create additional scoped instances.

Listing 5-24. Using generic OwningComponentBase

```
@rendermode InteractiveWebAssembly

@inherits OwningComponentBase<IScopedService>

@inject ISingletonService singletonService
@inject ITransientService transientService
@inject IScopedService scopedService

<h3>OwningComponentBase&lt;T&gt;</h3>

<div>
  <h1>Scoped</h1>
  Guid: @scopedService.Guid
  <h1>Owning</h1>
  Guid: @Service.Guid
</div>

@code {

  // Service property inherited from OwningComponentBase<T>

  protected override void OnInitialized()
  {
    base.OnInitialized();
  }
}
```

Now add both these components to the Home component as in Listing 5-25. Both components for Blazor Server and Blazor WebAssembly as used.

Listing 5-25. Updating Home

```
<div class="d-flex">
  <div class="flex-column m-1 p-2 border border-primary rounded">
    <SRUsingServices />
  </div>
  <div class="flex-column m-1 p-2 border border-warning rounded">
    <WASMUsingServices />
  </div>
</div>
<div class="d-flex">
  <div class="flex-column m-1 p-2 border border-success rounded">
    <WASMUsingOwnedScopedServices />
  </div>
  <div class="flex-column m-1 p-2 border border-danger rounded">
    <WASMUsingOwnedScopedServices2 />
  </div>
</div>
```

Run your project and make sure you have the Console open. Now click the Counter component. The Console should show the ScopedService instances being disposed. Also note that each time the WASMUsingOwnedScopedServices and WASMUsingOwnedScopedServices2 get instantiated, they receive a new instance of the WASMScopedService.

Note Don't implement IDisposable on components deriving from OwningComponentBase because this will cease the automatic disposal of the scoped instances!

The Result of the Experiment

Now the experiment is complete, let us draw some conclusions about the lifetime of the injected dependencies. Every time an instance gets created, it gets a new GUID. This makes it easy to see if a new instance gets created or the same instance gets reused.

CHAPTER 5   SERVICES AND DEPENDENCY INJECTION

Transient lifetime is easy. Transient lifetime means you get a new instance every time. This is the same for both Blazor WASM and Blazor Server.

Singleton lifetime means that in Blazor WASM you get one instance for the entire duration of the application. If you really need to share in instance between all the users and tabs, you need to put this on the server and access it through calls to the server. But with Blazor Server, everyone uses the same instance. Please make sure you don't put any user's information in a singleton because this will bleed to other users (bad!).

Scoped lifetime with Blazor WASM means the same as singleton lifetime. But with Blazor Server, we need to be careful. Blazor Server uses a SignalR connection (called a circuit) between the browser and the server, and scoped instances are linked to the circuit. You can derive from the `OwningComponentBase` class if you need scoped behavior for a specific component.

For both Blazor WASM and Blazor Server, if you need to have the same instance, no matter which tab the user is using, you cannot rely on dependency injection to do this for you. You will need to do some state handling yourself! More about this in the chapter about Blazor State Management.

Dependency Injection with .NET 8 and 9

Let us look at some of the new things added to .NET 8 and 9.

.NET 8 Keyed Services

With keyed services, you can inject dependencies using a key, instead of using a type. Imagine there are more than one implementation of the `IGreeter` interface (Listing 5-26).

Listing 5-26. The IGreeter interface with implementations

```
public interface IGreeter
{
  string Message();
}

public class FrenchGreeter : IGreeter
{
```

```
  public string Message() => "Bonjour!";
}
public class EnglishGreeter : IGreeter
{
  public string Message() => "Hello!";
}
```

Then you need to register your dependencies using the AddKeyed methods, providing a key, with an example in Listing 5-27.

Listing 5-27. Using Keyed Services

```cs
builder.Services
      .AddKeyedSingleton<IGreeter, FrenchGreeter>(
         serviceKey: "French")
      .AddKeyedSingleton<IGreeter, EnglishGreeter>(
         serviceKey: "English");
```

You can then request different versions of the same IGreeter interface using the [Inject(Key = SOMEKEY)] syntax. For example, look at Listing 5-28.

Listing 5-28. Using IGreeter implementations

```
<h3>Using Keyed Services</h3>

<div>@FrenchGreeter.Message()</div>

<div>@EnglishGreeter.Message()</div>

@code {

  [Inject(Key = "French")]
  public required IGreeter FrenchGreeter { get; set; }

  [Inject(Key = "English")]
  public required IGreeter EnglishGreeter { get; set; }
}
```

.NET 9 Constructor Injection

Blazor components do not support constructor injection, until .NET 9. When you use a component, the Blazor runtime requires a parameter less constructor. Otherwise, you will see this error:

```
MissingMethodException: Cannot dynamically create an instance of
type 'BlazorApp.DependencyInjection.Comparison.Client.Components.
ComponentWithConstructor'. Reason: No parameterless constructor defined.
```

This changes in .NET 9. Then you can build a component and inject dependencies using the constructor.

Building Pizza Services

Let's go back to our BlazorApp.PizzaPlace project and introduce it to some services. I can think of at least two services, one to retrieve the menu and one to place the order when the user clicks the Order button. For the moment these services will be very simple, but later we will use these to setup communication with a database.

Start by reviewing the Home component, which is Listing 5-29 with the markup left out for conciseness.

Listing 5-29. The Home component

```
private State State { get; set; } = new()
  {
    Pizzas = [
      new Pizza {
        Id = 1,
        Name = "Pepperoni",
        Price = 8.99M,
        Spiciness = Spiciness.Spicy },
      new Pizza {
        Id = 2,
        Name = "Margherita",
        Price = 7.99M,
        Spiciness = Spiciness.None },
      new Pizza {
```

```
        Id = 3,
        Name = "Diavola",
        Price = 9.99M,
        Spiciness = Spiciness.Hot }
    ]
  };
private void AddPizzaToBasket(Pizza pizza)
{
  State.Basket.Add(pizza.Id);
}

private void SubmitClicked()
{
  Console.WriteLine("Order has been placed");
}
```

Pay special attention to the `State` property. Instead of hard coding it, we will initialize the `State.Pizzas` property from the `MenuService` service (which we will build next), and we will use dependency injection to pass the service.

Adding the MenuService and IMenuService Abstraction

Add a new interface `IMenuService` to the shared project and complete it as in Listing 5-30.

Listing 5-30. The IMenuService interface

```
namespace BlazorApp.PizzaPlace.Shared;

public interface IMenuService
{
  ValueTask<Pizza[]> GetMenu();
}
```

This interface allows us the retrieve a menu. Note that the `GetMenu` method returns a `ValueTask<Pizza[]>`; that is because we expect the service to retrieve our menu from a server (we will build this in the following chapters), and we want the method to support an asynchronous call.

CHAPTER 5 SERVICES AND DEPENDENCY INJECTION

Let's elaborate on this. First update the Home component's OnInitializedAsync method (don't forget the @inject at the top) as in Listing 5-31. This is an asynchronous method using the async keyword in its declaration.

> **Note** Never call asynchronous services in your Blazor component's constructor; always use OnInitializedAsync or OnParametersSetAsync. More on this in the next chapter.

Inside the OnInitializedAsync method, we call the GetMenu method using the await keyword which requires GetMenu to return a Task<Pizza[]> or ValueTask<Pizza[]>. But why a ValueTask<T>, and not Task<T>? Because I don't know how someone will implement the GetMenu method. They may do this synchronously, for example, by retrieving it from a cache, and then using a Task<T> is more expensive than a ValueTask<T>. Also, the ValueTask<T> is a value type, meaning that this one does not end up on the heap in the synchronous case. If you want to learn more about this, Apress has an excellent book about all of this called *Pro .NET Memory Management: For Better Code, Performance, and Scalability*.

Listing 5-31. Using the IMenuService

```
@page "/"

@inject IMenuService MenuService

<PageTitle>The PizzaPlace</PageTitle>

<Menu Pizzas="@State.Pizzas" Selected="AddPizzaToBasket" />

<Basket @bind-State="@State"/>

<CustomerEntry Title="Please enter your details below"
   @bind-Customer="@State.Customer"
   SubmitTitle="Place Order"
   SubmitClicked="SubmitClicked"/>

<p>@State.ToJson()</p>

@code {
```

```csharp
    private State State { get; set; } = new();

    protected override async Task OnInitializedAsync()
    {
        State.Pizzas = await MenuService.GetMenu();
    }

    private void AddPizzaToBasket(Pizza pizza)
    {
        State.Basket.Add(pizza.Id);
    }

    private void SubmitClicked()
    {
        Console.WriteLine("Order has been placed");
    }
}
```

We are not ready to run this application yet because we still have to configure dependency injection. But run it anyway! When you get an error, look at the console. You should see the following error:

```
Cannot provide a value for property 'MenuService' on type 'BlazorApp.
PizzaPlace.Components.Pages.Home'. There is no registered service of type
'BlazorApp.PizzaPlace.Shared.IMenuService'.
```

Dependency injection could not provide an instance for IMenuService. Of course it can't! We have not implemented this interface yet.

Add a new HardCodedMenuService class to the shared project, as in Listing 5-32. The GetMenu method returns a new ValueTask<Pizza[]> containing three different kinds of pizza.

Listing 5-32. The HardCodedMenuService class

```csharp
namespace BlazorApp.PizzaPlace.Shared.Services;

public class HardCodedMenuService : IMenuService
{
    public ValueTask<Pizza[]> GetMenu()
    {
```

CHAPTER 5   SERVICES AND DEPENDENCY INJECTION

```
    Pizza[] pizzas = [
      new Pizza {
        Id = 1,
        Name = "Pepperoni",
        Price = 8.99M,
        Spiciness = Spiciness.Spicy
      },
      new Pizza {
        Id = 2,
        Name = "Margherita",
        Price = 7.99M,
        Spiciness = Spiciness.None
      },
      new Pizza
      {
        Id = 3,
        Name = "Diavola",
        Price = 9.99M,
        Spiciness = Spiciness.Hot
      }
    ];
    return ValueTask.FromResult(pizzas);
  }
}
```

Now we are ready to use the IMenuService in our Home component. Open Program.cs. We'll use a transient object as stated in Listing 5-33.

Listing 5-33. Configuring dependency injection for the MenuService

```
using BlazorApp.PizzaPlace.Components;
using BlazorApp.PizzaPlace.Shared;
using BlazorApp.PizzaPlace.Shared.Services;

WebApplicationBuilder builder = WebApplication.CreateBuilder(args);

// Add services to the container.
builder.Services.AddRazorComponents()
```

```
        .AddInteractiveServerComponents();
builder.Services
        .AddTransient<IMenuService, HardCodedMenuService>();

WebApplication app = builder.Build();

// Configure the HTTP request pipeline.
if (!app.Environment.IsDevelopment())
{
    app.UseExceptionHandler("/Error",
      createScopeForErrors: true);
    app.UseHsts();
}

app.UseHttpsRedirection();

app.UseStaticFiles();
app.UseAntiforgery();

app.MapRazorComponents<App>()
   .AddInteractiveServerRenderMode();

app.Run();
```

Run your Blazor project. Everything should still work! In the next chapters, we will replace this with a service to retrieve everything from a database on the server.

Ordering Pizzas with a Service

When the user makes a selection of pizzas and fulfills the customer information, we want to send the order to the server, so they can warm up the oven and send some nice pizzas to the customer's address. Start by adding an `IOrderService` interface to the shared project as in Listing 5-34.

Listing 5-34. The IOrderService abstraction as a C# interface

```
namespace BlazorApp.PizzaPlace.Shared;

public interface IOrderService
```

```
{
  ValueTask PlaceOrder(Customer customer, ShoppingBasket basket);
}
```

To place an order, we just send the basket to the server. In a later chapter, we will build the actual server-side code to place an order; for now, we will use a fake implementation that simply writes the order to the console. Add a class called `ConsoleOrderService` to the shared project as in Listing 5-35.

Listing 5-35. The ConsoleOrderService

```
namespace BlazorApp.PizzaPlace.Shared.Services;

public class ConsoleOrderService : IOrderService
{
  public ValueTask PlaceOrder(Customer customer, ShoppingBasket basket)
  {
    Console.WriteLine($"Placing order for {customer.Name}");
    return new ValueTask();
  }
}
```

The `PlaceOrder` method simply writes the basket to the console. However, this method implements the asynchronous pattern from .NET, so we need to return a new `ValueTask` instance.

Inject the `IOrderService` into the Home component as in Listing 5-36.

Listing 5-36. Injecting the IOrderService

```
@page "/"

@inject IMenuService MenuService
@inject IOrderService OrderService

<PageTitle>The PizzaPlace</PageTitle>
```

And use the order service when the user clicks on the order button by replacing the implementation of the `PlaceOrder` method in the Home component. Since the `OrderService` returns a `ValueTask` (same with `Task`), we need to invoke it using the `await` syntax, as in Listing 5-37.

CHAPTER 5   SERVICES AND DEPENDENCY INJECTION

Listing 5-37. The asynchronous PlaceOrder method

```
private async Task SubmitClicked()
{
    await OrderService.PlaceOrder(State.Customer, State.Basket);
}
```

As the final step, configure dependency injection. Again, we will make the `IOrderService` transient as in Listing 5-38.

Listing 5-38. Configuring dependency injection for the OrderService

```
builder.Services
       .AddTransient<IMenuService, HardCodedMenuService>()
       .AddTransient<IOrderService, ConsoleOrderService>();
```

Think about this. How hard will it be to replace the implementation of one of the services? There is only one place that says which class we will be using, and that is in `Program`. In a later chapter, we will build the code needed to store the menu and the orders, and in the chapter after that, we will replace these services with the real deal!

Build and run your project again; open the Console. Order some pizzas and click on the order button. You should see some feedback being written to the Console.

Summary

In this chapter, we discussed dependency inversion, which is a best practice for building easily maintainable and testable object-oriented applications. We also saw that dependency injection makes it very easy to create objects with dependencies, especially objects that use dependency inversion. Then we looked at the dependency injection that comes with Blazor.

When you configure dependency injection, you need to be careful with the lifetime of your instances, so let's repeat that:

   Transient objects are always different; a new instance is provided to every component and every service.

   Scoped objects are the same for a user's connection, but different across different users and connections. You can derive from the OwningComponentBase class if you need scoped behavior for a specific component.

   Singleton objects are the same for every object and every request, but still have a different lifetime between Blazor WebAssembly and Blazor Server.

CHAPTER 6

Component Life Cycle Hooks

A Blazor component has a life cycle just like any other .NET object. A component is born, goes through a couple of changes, and then dies. A Blazor component has _life cycle methods_ you can override to capture the life cycle of the component. In this chapter, we will look at these life cycle hooks because it's very important to understand them well. Putting code in the wrong life cycle hook will likely break your component.

> **Note** You should also remember that each life cycle method gets called at least once for every component. Even a component with no parameters will see methods like `SetParametersAsync` and `OnParametersSetAsync` called at least once.

Life Cycle Overview

Let us start with the big picture. I have created a `LifeCycleDemo` component from Listing 6-1 to experiment with (find it in the provided sources). We will make some changes to get through the explanation of a component's life cycle (and its children). If you would like to run the demo, you will have to comment/uncomment sections of the code to match.

Listing 6-1 also shows how you can implement an interface in a component using the `@implements` syntax.

Chapter 6   Component Life Cycle Hooks

Listing 6-1. The LifeCycleDemo class

```
@page "/life-cycle"
@implements IDisposable

<h3>Life Cycle Demo</h3>

@code {
  public LifeCycleDemo()
  {
    Console.Clear();
    Console.WriteLine("Inside LifeCycle constructor");
  }

  public override Task SetParametersAsync(
    ParameterView parameters)
  {
    Console.WriteLine("Inside LifeCycle SetParametersAsync");
    return base.SetParametersAsync(parameters);
  }

  protected override async Task OnParametersSetAsync()
  {
    Console.WriteLine($"Inside LifeCycle OnParametersSetAsync");
    await Task.CompletedTask;
  }

  protected override async Task OnInitializedAsync()
  {
    Console.WriteLine($"Begin LifeCycle OnParametersSetAsync");
    await Task.CompletedTask;
  }

  protected override Task OnAfterRenderAsync(bool firstRender)
  {
    Console.WriteLine(
      $"LifeCycle Demo Rendered - FirstRender = {firstRender}");
    return Task.CompletedTask;
  }
```

```
  public void Dispose()
  {
    Console.WriteLine("Inside LifeCycle Dispose");
  }
}
```

Running the application and navigating to the component will show this in the Console:

```
Inside LifeCycle constructor
Inside LifeCycle SetParametersAsync
Begin LifeCycle OnInitializedAsync
Inside LifeCycle OnParametersSetAsync
LifeCycle Demo Rendered - FirstRender = True
```

Figure 6-1 shows this life cycle overview.

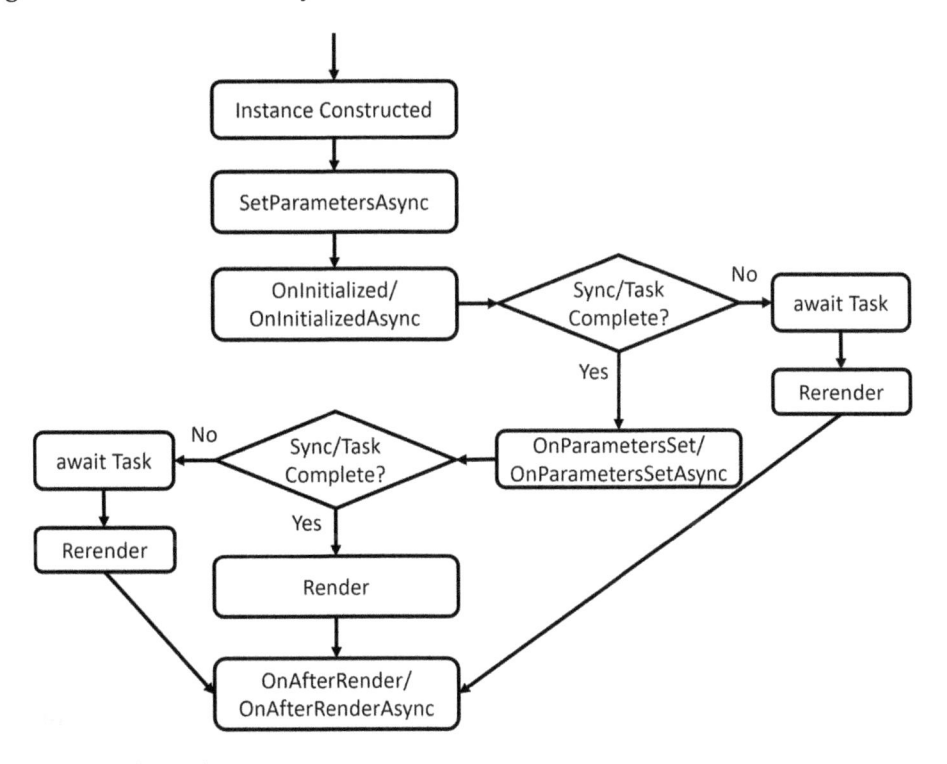

Figure 6-1. Life cycle overview

Constructor

As you can see, the component's constructor gets invoked first. But because properties and child components have not been initialized, it is better to place initialization logic in another method.

IDisposable

When you navigate away from this component, the component is disposed as shown in the console (when you actually implement the `IDisposable` interface). This is the place to cleanup your component in a controlled way.

Inside LifeCycle Dispose

SetParametersAsync

If you need to execute some code before the parameters are set, you can override the `SetParametersAsync` method. The default implementation of the `SetParametersAsync` method will set each `[Parameter]` and `[CascadingParameter]` that has a value in the `ParameterView` argument. Other parameters (that don't have a value in `ParameterView`) are left unchanged.

You can find the parameters in the `ParameterView` argument which behaves like a dictionary. Let's look at an example in Listing 6-2. This example uses the `SetParametersAsync` method to inspect the parameters, looking for a "Counter" parameter. If this parameter is even, we update `CurrentCount`; otherwise, we don't do anything. Also note that we call the base method passing the `ParameterView.Empty` object, ignoring additional parameters (of which there are none).

There is one snag: when you don't call the base method, the UI doesn't update, so you should always call `base.SetParametersAsync(ParameterView.Empty)` if you want the component to update (the base method indirectly calls `StateHasChanged`).

Listing 6-2. Overriding SetParametersAsync in CounterWithParameter

```
<p role="status">Current count: @CurrentCount</p>

@code {
  [Parameter]
```

```
  [EditorRequired]
  public required int CurrentCount { get; set; }

  public override Task SetParametersAsync(ParameterView parameters)
  {
    if (parameters.TryGetValue(nameof(CurrentCount), out int cc))
    {
      if (cc % 2 == 0)
      {
        CurrentCount = cc;
      }
    }
    return base.SetParametersAsync(ParameterView.Empty);
  }
}
```

OnParametersSet and OnParametersSetAsync

When you need one or more parameters to lookup data after a change to the parameters, you use OnParametersSet or OnParametersSetAsync. Every time data binding updates one or more of your parameters, these methods get called again, so they are ideal for calculated properties, filtering, etc. For example, you could have a DepartmentSelector component that allows the user to select a department from a company, and another EmployeeList component that takes the selected department as a parameter. The EmployeeList component can then fetch the employees for that department in its OnParametersSetAsync method.

Use OnParametersSet (Listing 6-3) if you are only calling synchronous methods

Listing 6-3. The OnParametersSet method

```
[Parameter]
[EditorRequired]
public int DepartmentId { get; set; }

[Inject]
public required IDepartmentService DepartmentService { get; set; }

private IEnumerable<string>? _employees = null;
```

CHAPTER 6　COMPONENT LIFE CYCLE HOOKS

```
protected override void OnParametersSet()
{
  _employees = DepartmentService.GetEmployees(DepartmentId);
}
```

Use `OnParametersSetAsync` (Listing 6-4) if you need to call asynchronous methods. For example, retrieving values from a database that depend on a parameter value should be done in an asynchronous way. In general, any use of methods that take longer than 60 milliseconds should be done asynchronously.

Listing 6-4. *The OnParametersSetAsync method*

```
protected override async Task OnParametersSetAsync()
{
  _employees = await DepartmentService.GetEmployeesAsync(DepartmentId);
}
```

In a Blazor application, the `OnParametersSet(Async)` method can get called multiple times during a component's life cycle due to several reasons. Here are some common scenarios that can cause this behavior:

- Initial render and subsequent parameter changes:
  When a component is first rendered, `OnParametersSet(Async)` is called to initialize the component with its parameters. If the parameters change after the initial render (due to parent component updates, parameter bindings, or other state changes), `OnParameters(Async)` will be called again to handle the updated parameters.

- State has changed:
  Blazor uses a mechanism to track changes in state and re-renders components as needed. If a state change triggers a re-render of the parent component, it might also cause `OnParametersSet(Async)` to be called again in the child components.

- Parameter binding:
  When parameters are bound to properties of a parent component or service, any changes to those bound properties will trigger OnParametersSet(Async). This can happen if the parent component itself is re-rendered or its state changes, causing it to re-pass parameters to child components.

Example Scenario

Consider the following example where a parent component (Listing 6-5) passes a parameter to a child component (Listing 6-6).

Listing 6-5. The ParentComponent

```
@page "/parent"

<h3>Parent Component</h3>
<button @onclick="() => counter++">Increment Counter</button>

<ChildComponent Counter="counter" />

@code {
  private int counter = 0;

  protected override void OnInitialized()
  {
    // Simulate a state change after the initial render
    Task.Delay(1000).ContinueWith(_ =>
    {
      counter++;
      InvokeAsync(StateHasChanged);
    });
  }
}
```

CHAPTER 6   COMPONENT LIFE CYCLE HOOKS

Listing 6-6. The ChildComponent

```
<h3>Child Component</h3>
<p>Counter: @Counter</p>

@code {
  [Parameter]
  public int Counter { get; set; }

  protected override async Task OnParametersSetAsync()
  {
    Console.WriteLine($"OnParametersSetAsync - Counter updated:
    {Counter}");
    await base.OnParametersSetAsync();
  }
}
```

Explanation

- Initial render: When the parent component is first rendered, `OnParametersSetAsync` is called in the child component with the initial `Counter`.

- State change: After the simulated delay in `OnInitialized`, the `counter` value in the parent component is incremented, triggering a re-render of the parent component. This, in turn, updates the `Counter` parameter in the child component, causing `OnParametersSetAsync` to be called again.

Debugging Multiple Calls

To understand why `OnParametersSetAsync` is called multiple times in your specific scenario, you can add logging or debugging statements to track when and why the method is being triggered. Check the following:

- Parent component re-renders: Ensure the parent component isn't re-rendering more often than expected, causing its children to re-render.

- State changes: Track any state changes that might be causing re-renders.
- Parameter changes: Verify if and why the parameters being passed to the child component are changing.

OnParametersSetAsync can be called multiple times due to initial rendering, parameter changes, and parent component re-renders. By understanding these triggers and examining your component's life cycle, you can identify why this method is being called multiple times in your application and adjust your logic accordingly.

OnInitialized and OnInitializedAsync

When your component has been created and the parameters have been set, the OnInitialized and OnInitializedAsync methods are called. Implement one of these methods if you want to do some one-time extra initialization after the component has been created, for example, fetching some data from a server like the Weather component from the project. The OnInitialized/OnInitializedAsync methods are _only called once_, right after the creation of the component.

Use OnInitialized for _synchronous_ code as in Listing 6-7. Here we execute synchronous code like fetching the current DateTime.

Listing 6-7. The OnInitialized life cycle hook

```
private DateTime _createdDate;

protected override void OnInitialized()
{
  _createdDate = DateTime.Now;
}
```

Use OnInitializedAsync (Listing 6-8) to call _asynchronous_ methods, for example, making asynchronous REST calls (we will look at making REST calls in further chapters).

Listing 6-8. The OnInitializedAsync life cycle hook

```
protected override async Task OnInitializedAsync()
{
  forecasts = await Http.GetFromJsonAsync<WeatherForecast[]>
                  ("sample-data/weather.json");
}
```

I do find it important to mention that the `OnInitializedAsync` method causes the component to be rendered after returning from the first `await` statement and again at the end of the method. If your `OnInitializedAsync` method has multiple `awaits`, these will not cause rendering, unless you add additional `StateHasChanged` invocations.

ShouldRender

The `ShouldRender` method returns a `bool` value, indicating if the component should be re-rendered. Do realize that the first render ignores this `ShouldRender` method, so a component will render at least once. The default implementation always returns true. You want to override this method to stop the component from re-rendering. `ShouldRender` allows you to optimize the rendering of child components, simply by telling the parent that the child component does not need any rendering.

Create a new component named `CounterWithShouldRender` as in Listing 6-9. This component is very similar to `Counter`, but it also displays the number of times it has been rendered.

Listing 6-9. The CounterWithShouldRender component

```
<h1>Counter</h1>

<p role="status">Current count: @CurrentCount</p>
<p role="status">Rendered: @renderCount</p>
<p role="status">Shared: @Shared</p>

<button class="btn btn-primary" @onclick="IncrementCount">Click me</button>

@code {

  [Parameter]
  public int Shared { get; set; }

  private int prevCount;
  private int currentCount;
  private int renderCount;

  public int CurrentCount
  {
    get
```

CHAPTER 6　COMPONENT LIFE CYCLE HOOKS

```
    {
      renderCount += 1;
      return currentCount;
    }
    set
    {
      currentCount = value;
    }
  }
  private void IncrementCount()
  {
    currentCount++;
  }
}
```

Add this component to the Home component from Listing 6-10.

Listing 6-10. The Home component

```
@page "/"

<PageTitle>Home</PageTitle>

<h1>Hello, world!</h1>

<CounterWithShouldRender Shared="@renderCount" />
<CounterWithShouldRender Shared="@renderCount" />

<button class="btn btn-primary" @onclick="()=>renderCount++">
  @renderCount
</button>

@code {
  private int counter = 0;
  private int renderCount = 0;
}
```

Running this will show two components, each with their own count and render count. Clicking the "Click Me" button will render only that child component.

191

CHAPTER 6   COMPONENT LIFE CYCLE HOOKS

However, clicking the parent's button (the one with the number inside) will render the parent and the child components, although there is nothing changed in them!

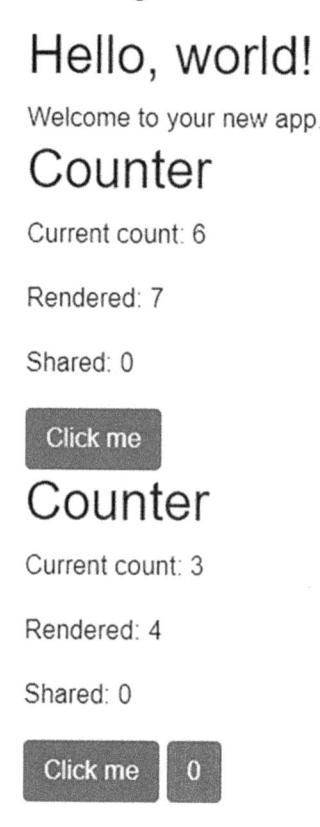

Figure 6-2. Running without ShouldRender

Let us add some optimization. Implement the ShouldRender method on the CounterWithShouldRender component as in Listing 6-11. This method checks if currentCount has been modified. If not, it returns false which will prevent this component from rendering.

Listing 6-11. Implementing ShouldRender for CounterWithShouldRender

```
protected override bool ShouldRender()
{
  // This component should only render when currentCount is changed
  bool shouldRender = prevCount != currentCount;
  prevCount = currentCount;
  return shouldRender;
}
```

Run the application again. Clicking the parent's button will not cause rendering of the child components since each implement `ShouldRender` correctly as shown in Figure 6-3.

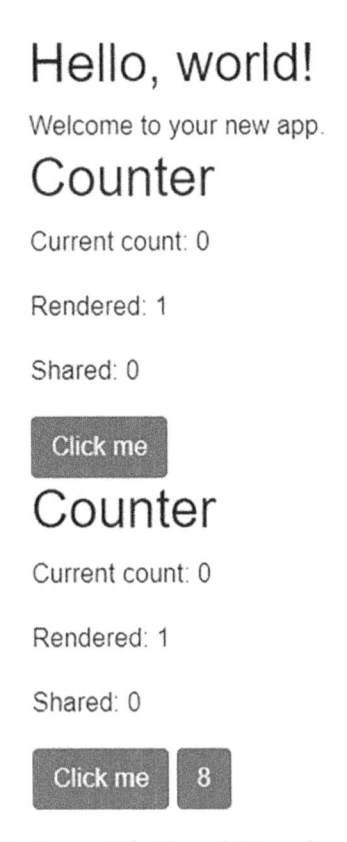

Figure 6-3. Optimized rendering with ShouldRender

OnAfterRender and OnAfterRenderAsync

The `OnAfterRender` and `OnAfterRenderAsync` methods are called after Blazor has completely rendered the component. This means that the browser's DOM has been updated with changes made to your Blazor component. Use these methods to invoke JavaScript code that needs access to elements from the DOM (which we will cover in the JavaScript chapter). This method takes a Boolean `firstRender` argument, which allows you to attach JavaScript event handlers only once.

CHAPTER 6   COMPONENT LIFE CYCLE HOOKS

> **Note** Avoid calling StateHasChanged in this method, as it can cause an infinite loop.

Use `OnAfterRender` shown in Listing 6-12 to call synchronous methods, for example, to call JavaScript methods that return a value.

Listing 6-12. The OnAfterRender life cycle hook

```
protected override void OnAfterRender(bool firstRender)
{
}
```

Use `OnAfterRenderAsync` as shown in Listing 6-13 to call asynchronous methods, for example, JavaScript methods that return promises or observables.

Listing 6-13. The OnAfterRenderAsync life cycle hook

```
protected override Task OnAfterRenderAsync(bool firstRender)
{
}
```

IDisposable

If you need to run some _cleanup_ code when your component is removed from the UI, implement the IDisposable/IAsyncDisposable interface. You can implement this interface in razor using the `@implements` syntax, for example, in Listing 6-14. Normally you put the `@implements` at the top of the .razor file, but if you use code separation, you can also declare it on the partial class (just like any other interface on a class with C#).

> **Note** Most of the time dependency injection will take care of calling the `Dispose` method of your component's dependencies, so generally, you won't need to implement `IDisposable/IAsyncDisposable` if you only need to dispose of your dependencies.

The `IDisposable` interface requires you to implement a `Dispose` method as in Listing 6-14.

Listing 6-14. Implementing the Dispose method

```
@implements IDisposable

public void Dispose()
{
  // Cleanup code here
}
```

Implementing IAsyncEnumerable is similar, allowing for async cleanup code as in Listing 6-15. The IAsyncEnumerable interface was added in .NET 8. Because many classes do not support this interface yet, it is a good practice, when implementing the IAsyncDisposable interface, to implement the IDisposable interface too.

Note The Blazor runtime will only invoke the DisposeAsync method when present if you implement both interfaces!

Listing 6-15. Implementing the DisposeAsync method

```
@implements IAsyncDisposable

public async ValueTask DisposeAsync()
{
  // Async cleanup code here
}
```

A Word on Asynchronous Methods

When the Blazor runtime calls asynchronous methods like OnInitializedAsync and OnParametersSetAsync, it does an await on this method and will also render the component. The only exception to this is the OnAfterRenderAsync method, which will not trigger a render (otherwise, this will cause an infinite render loop).

This is the reason you should always check variables that get initialized in an asynchronous method for null values. A nice example of this is the Weather component as in Listing 6-16. The forecasts field gets initialized in the OnInitializedAsync method, so until this method completes, the forecast field is null. This means that we should check this field for null values.

CHAPTER 6 COMPONENT LIFE CYCLE HOOKS

Listing 6-16. Initializing forecasts

```
@page "/weather"

<PageTitle>Weather</PageTitle>

<h1>Weather</h1>

<p>This component demonstrates showing data.</p>

@if (forecasts == null)
{
  <p><em>Loading...</em></p>
}
else
{
  ...
}

@code {
  private WeatherForecast[]? forecasts;

  protected override async Task OnInitializedAsync()
  {
    await forecasts = ...
  }
}
```

Summary

In this chapter, we looked at the life cycle methods which allow you to intercept points in the lifetime of a Blazor component by overriding them. Each of these methods will be called at least once.

CHAPTER 7

Advanced Components

In Chapter 2, we looked at building components for Blazor. But we are not done yet. There is still a lot more we need to discuss about components. We will start with cascading parameters. One of the things we really need to look at is templated components and razor templates. Then we will look at error boundaries, virtualization, and attribute splatting and how we can refer to a child component from code.

Communicating with Cascading Parameters

When a higher-level component wants to pass data to an immediate child, life is easy. Simply use data binding to pass the value to a child component using a parameter. But when a higher-level component needs to share some data with a deeper nested component, passing data using data binding requires each intermediate component to expose that data through a parameter and pass it down to the next level. Not only is this inconvenient when you have several levels of components, but who says that you are in control of these components? Blazor solves this problem with cascading values and parameters. Let us look at an example which you can find in the provided sources.

Listing 7-1 shows the `CounterData` class, which is the object we want to share between different components at different levels. This class has a `Count` property and a `CountChanged` callback `Action<int>?` which is used to notify others about changes (similar to the `INotifyPropertyChanged` interface which you might already know).

Listing 7-1. The CounterData class

```
namespace BlazorApp.CascadingParameters.State;

public class CounterData
{ // Or use INotifyPropertyChanged interface
  private int count;
  public int Count
```

CHAPTER 7 ADVANCED COMPONENTS

```
  {
    get => this.count;
    set
    {
      if (value != this.count)
      {
        this.count = value;
        CountChanged?.Invoke(this.count);
      }
    }
  }
  public Action<int>? CountChanged { get; set; }
}
```

Use the CascadingValue Component

Listing 7-2 shows the GrandMother component, which creates an instance of the CounterData class and passes it down to its children using the built-in CascadingValue component. The CascadingValue component "wraps" a subtree of the component hierarchy and supplies a single value to all components within the subtree. Any component which is part of the ChildContent will now be able to access the CounterData instance from GrandMother. The GrandMother component also registers for the CountChanged callback in case any other component changes the Count so it can use StateHasChanged to cause it to render, showing the current value of the Count property.

Listing 7-2. The GrandMother component

```
<div>
  <h3>GrandMother</h3>
  <span role="status">Counter: @data.Count</span>

  <CascadingValue Value="@this.data">
    @ChildContent
  </CascadingValue>

  <span>@someCounter</span>
```

```
  <button @onclick="Increment" class="btn btn-success">Inc</button>
</div>

@code {
  public CounterData data = new CounterData { Count = 10 };

  private void Increment()
  {
    someCounter += 1;
  }

  protected override void OnInitialized()
  {
    this.data.CountChanged += (newCount) =>
      this.StateHasChanged();
  }

  [Parameter]
  public RenderFragment ChildContent { get; set; } = default!;
}
```

Listing 7-3 shows the GrandChild component, which has a property named gmData (grand mother data) with the CascadingParameter attribute. This attribute will make the Blazor runtime look up the chain of components until it finds a CascadingValue with Value of type CounterData. Cascading values are bound to cascading parameters by type. If none is found, the gmData property will be null.

Listing 7-3. The GrandChild component

```
<div>
  <h3>GrandChild</h3>
  <button @onclick="Increment" class="btn btn-success">Inc</button>
</div>

@code {
  [CascadingParameter]
  public CounterData gmData { get; set; } = default!;

  private void Increment()
```

CHAPTER 7   ADVANCED COMPONENTS

```
    {
        gmData.Count += 1;
    }
}
```

Let us use these components together as in Listing 7-4. This component has two child components, one is a direct `GrandChild` component (which we will build after this), and another is a `GrandChild` component wrapped in a `SomeComponent` component. This last component knows nothing about `CounterData` or `GrandMother`. Still, the `GrandMother` component will be able to pass its cascading value to the `GrandChild` component. Both `GrandMother` and `GrandChild`(ren) now share the same instance of `CounterData`.

Listing 7-4. The Home component

```
@page "/"

<PageTitle>Cascading Parameters</PageTitle>

<GrandMother>
    <SomeComponent>
        <GrandChild />
    </SomeComponent>
    <GrandChild />
</GrandMother>
```

When you click the "Inc" button of `GrandChild`, the `CounterData`'s `Count` property increments. The `GrandMother` components want to display this value every time it gets incremented, so `CounterData` notifies the `GrandMother` of changes. The `GrandMother` component subscribes to these changes and calls `StateHasChanged` to update itself. How the shared object handles this notification is up to you, for example, `CounterData` uses a delegate. You could also use `INotifyPropertyChanged` interface which is built-into .NET. If you're not familiar with this interface, it is used in a lot of .NET applications to notify interested parties that a property has changed. For example, WPF heavily relies on this interface. If you would like to learn more, any good book on WPF will explain this, or you can find more information at https://docs.microsoft.com/dotnet/api/system.componentmodel.inotifypropertychanged.

CHAPTER 7   ADVANCED COMPONENTS

Note Just like parameters, components taking a cascading parameter will be re-rendered when the value of the parameter changes.

Resolving Ambiguities with Multiple Values

What if there are several components exposing the same type of cascading value? In this case, you can name the cascading value. For example, Listing 7-5 adds the someCounter field and wraps the CascadingValue with another (this way multiple cascading values can be passed down). But there is a difference. The outer CascadingValue has a Name property which allows a child to "pick" just this value.

Listing 7-5. Using a named cascading value

```
<div>
  <h3>GrandMother</h3>
  <span role="status">Counter: @data.Count</span>

  <CascadingValue Value="@someCounter" Name="Jefke">
    <CascadingValue Value="@this.data">
      @ChildContent
    </CascadingValue>
  </CascadingValue>

  <span>@someCounter</span>

  <button @onclick="Increment" class="btn btn-success">Inc</button>

</div>

@code {
  public CounterData data = new CounterData { Count = 10 };

  public int someCounter = 5;

  private void Increment()
  {
    someCounter += 1;
  }
```

CHAPTER 7   ADVANCED COMPONENTS

```
  protected override void OnInitialized()
  {
    this.data.CountChanged += (newCount) =>
      this.StateHasChanged();
  }

  [Parameter]
  public RenderFragment ChildContent { get; set; } = default!;
}
```

Listing 7-6 shows the source for the `SomeComponent` component. This component has a property using the `CascadingParameter` attribute, but now with the `Name` set (here I used the name "Jefke" to honor my cat 😊).

Listing 7-6. Consuming a named cascading property

```
<div>
  @ChildContent
</div>

<span>@SomeCounter</span>

@code {
  [Parameter]
  public RenderFragment ChildContent { get; set; } = default!;

  [CascadingParameter(Name ="Jefke")]
  public int SomeCounter { get; set; }
}
```

The final result is shown in Figure 7-1.

CHAPTER 7   ADVANCED COMPONENTS

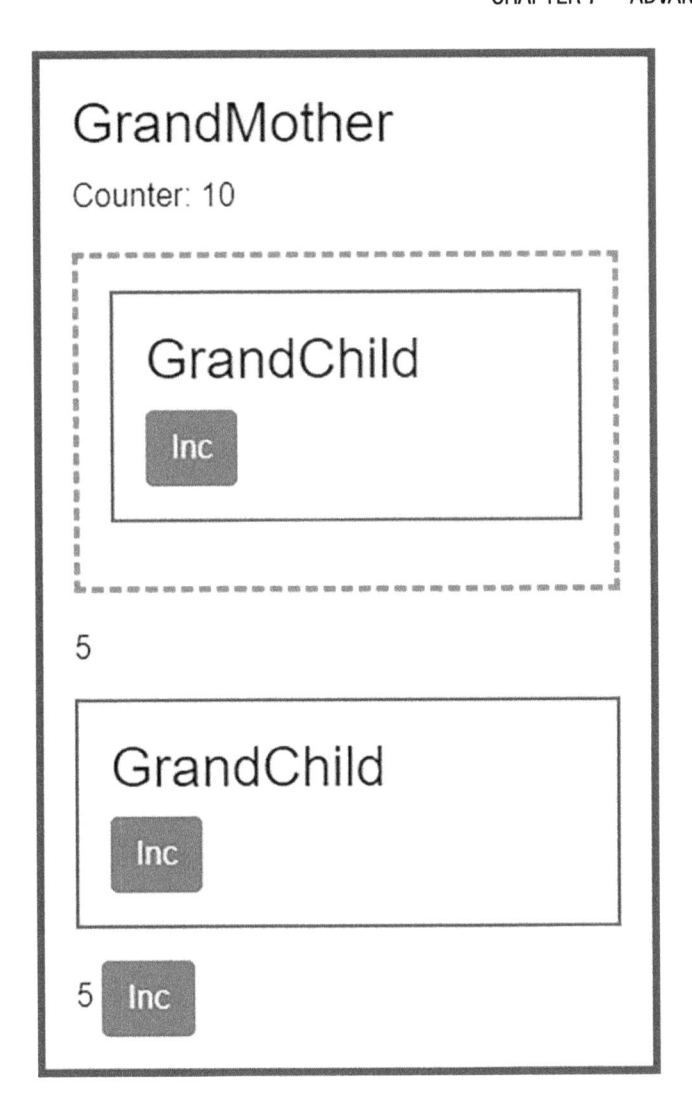

```
GrandMother
Counter: 10
┌─────────────────────────────────┐
│                                 │
│   ┌─────────────────────────┐   │
│   │ GrandChild              │   │
│   │                         │   │
│   │  ┌─────┐                │   │
│   │  │ Inc │                │   │
│   │  └─────┘                │   │
│   └─────────────────────────┘   │
└─────────────────────────────────┘
5

┌─────────────────────────────────┐
│ GrandChild                      │
│                                 │
│  ┌─────┐                        │
│  │ Inc │                        │
│  └─────┘                        │
└─────────────────────────────────┘

   ┌─────┐
 5 │ Inc │
   └─────┘
```

Figure 7-1. Using cascading values

Fixed Cascading Values

What happens when the cascading value changes? In that case any component which receives the cascading value will subscribe to change notifications. Each subscription does add some overhead, so it is best to disable these notifications by setting the Fixed property to true, with an example in Listing 7-7.

203

Listing 7-7. Fixing the cascading value

```
<CascadingValue Value="@this.data" IsFixed="true">
```

Root-Level Cascading Values

Can you register a cascading value to the whole component hierarchy to access it? This is known as a root-level cascading value, and you register this using the AddCascadingValue method with examples shown in Listing 7-8.

Listing 7-8. Registering root-level cascading values

```
// Add services to the container.
builder.Services
        .AddRazorComponents()
        .AddInteractiveServerComponents();

// Add a root-level cascading value
builder.Services.AddCascadingValue(
  _ => new UserInfo { UserName = "Jefke" });

// Add a root-level named cascading value
builder.Services.AddCascadingValue("Named",
  _ => new UserInfo { UserName = "Peter" });

// Add a root-level non-fixed cascading value
builder.Services.AddCascadingValue("Fixed",
  _ =>
  {
    UserInfo ui = new() { UserName = "Peter" };
    CascadingValueSource<UserInfo> source =
      new(ui, isFixed: false);
    return source;
  });
```

Using this value is done again using the CascadingParameter attribute, with an example shown in Listing 7-9.

Listing 7-9. Using a root-level cascading value

```
@page "/root-level"

<h3>Root Level Cascading Value</h3>

<div>User Name : @UserInfo.UserName</div>

@code {

  [CascadingParameter]
  public required UserInfo UserInfo { get; set; }
}
```

Using Templated Components

Components are Blazor's building block for reuse. In C# generics are heavily used for reuse; just think about all the collections like List<T> you use with generics. Would it not be cool if Blazor had something like generic components? Yes, Blazor does!

Blazor supports _templated components_ where you can specify one or more UI templates as parameters, making templated components even more reusable! For example, your application could be using grids all over the place. You can now build a templated component for a grid taking the type used in the grid as a parameter (very much like you can build a generic type in .NET) and specify the UI used for each item separately! Let's look at an example.

Create the Grid Templated Component

Create a new Blazor Web App, select global server interactivity project, and call it BlazorApp.Components.Templated. For your convenience, here is the powershell script to create everything:

```
$ProjectName = "BlazorApp.Components.Templated"
mkdir $ProjectName
cd $ProjectName
dotnet new sln -n $ProjectName
mkdir src
```

CHAPTER 7   ADVANCED COMPONENTS

```
cd src
dotnet new blazor -n $ProjectName --all-interactive --interactivity Server
cd ..
dotnet sln add src\$ProjectName
```

Now add a new razor component to the project's Components folder and name it Grid as in Listing 7-10.

This is a templated component because it states the TItem as a _type parameter_ using the @typeparam TItem syntax in the razor file. This will generate a partial class named Grid<TItem>. This is a _generic type_ stated in C#. Compare this with class List<T> where T is a type parameter (I prefer to use TItem here instead of just T). You can have as many type parameters as you like, simply list each type parameter using the @typeparam syntax, but for this Grid<TITem> component, we only need one.

Listing 7-10. The templated grid component

```
@typeparam TItem

<table class="table">
  <thead>
    <tr>@Header</tr>
  </thead>
  <tbody>
    @foreach (var item in Items)
    {
      <tr>@Row(item)</tr>
    }
  </tbody>
  @if (Footer is not null)
  {
    <tfoot>
      <tr>@Footer</tr>
    </tfoot>
  }
</table>

@code {
```

206

```
    [Parameter]
    [EditorRequired]
    public required RenderFragment Header { get; set; }

    [Parameter]
    [EditorRequired]
    public required RenderFragment<TItem> Row { get; set; }

    [Parameter]
    public RenderFragment? Footer { get; set; }

    [Parameter]
    public IReadOnlyList<TItem> Items { get; set; } = default!;
}
```

The `Grid` component has four parameters. The `Header` and `Footer` parameters are of type `RenderFragment` which represents some markup (HTML, Blazor components) which we can specify when we use the `Grid` component (we will look at an example right after explaining the `Grid` component further). Look for the `<thead>` element in Listing 7-10 in the `Grid` component. Here we use the `@Header` razor syntax telling the `Grid` component to put the markup for the `Header` parameter here. Same thing for the `Footer`.

Note Think of a RenderFragment as a piece of the render tree.

The `Row` parameter is of type `RenderFragment<TItem>` which is a generic version of `RenderFragment`. In this case, you can specify markup with access to the `TItem` instance allowing you access to properties and methods of the `TItem`. The `Items` parameter here is an `IReadOnlyList<TItem>` which can be data-bound to any class with the `IReadOnlyList<TItem>` interface, for example, a `List<T>`. Look for the `<tbody>` element in Listing 7-10. We iterate over all the items (of type `TItem`) of the `IReadOnlyList<TItem>` using a `foreach` loop, and we use the `@Row(item)` razor syntax to apply the `Row` parameter, passing the current item as an argument.

Use the Grid Templated Component

Now let's look at an example of using the `Grid` templated component. Open the `Weather` component. Replace the `<table>` with the `Grid` component as in Listing 7-11.

CHAPTER 7   ADVANCED COMPONENTS

> **Note** The Weather component uses a couple of things such as @page which we will discuss in later chapters, so bear with the example.

The `Weather` component uses the `Grid` component specifying the `Items` parameter as the `forecasts` array of `WeatherForecast` instances. Look again at the type of `Items` in the `Grid` component: `IReadOnlyList<TItem>`. The compiler is smart enough to infer from this that the `Grid`'s type parameter (`TItem`) is the `WeatherForecast` type. I love type inference!

Listing 7-11. Using the Grid templated component in the Weather component

```
@page "/weather"

<PageTitle>Weather</PageTitle>

<h1>Weather</h1>

<p>This component demonstrates showing data.</p>

@if (forecasts == null)
{
  <p><em>Loading...</em></p>
}
else
{
  <Grid Items="forecasts">
    <Header>
    <th>Date</th>
    <th>Temp. (C)</th>
    <th>Temp. (F)</th>
    <th>Summary</th>
    </Header>
    <Row>
      <td>@context.Date</td>
      <td>@context.TemperatureC</td>
      <td>@context.TemperatureF</td>
      <td>@context.Summary</td>
```

```
    </Row>
    <Footer>
    <td colspan="4">Spring is in the air!</td>
    </Footer>
  </Grid>
}

@code {

  private WeatherForecast[]? forecasts;

  string[] summaries = ["Freezing", "Bracing", "Chilly", "Cool", "Mild",
  "Warm", "Balmy", "Hot", "Sweltering", "Scorching"];

  protected override async Task OnInitializedAsync()
  {
    // Simulate asynchronous loading to demonstrate a loading indicator
    await Task.Delay(500);

    var startDate = DateOnly.FromDateTime(DateTime.Now);
    forecasts = Enumerable.Range(1, 5)
      .Select(index => new WeatherForecast
      {
        Date = startDate.AddDays(index),
        TemperatureC = Random.Shared.Next(-20, 55),
        Summary = summaries[Random.Shared.Next(summaries.Length)]
      }).ToArray();
  }
}
```

Now look at the Header parameter of the Grid component in Listing 7-11. This syntax will bind whatever is inside the <Header> element to the Grid's Header parameter which is of type RenderFragment. In this example, we specify some HTML table headers (<th>). The grid will put these inside the table row (<tr>) element from Listing 7-10. The Footer parameter is similar.

Examine the Row parameter in Listing 7-11. Inside the <Row> element, we want to use the current item from the iteration in Listing 7-10. But how should we access the current item? By default, Blazor will pass the item as the context argument (of type TItem), so you would access the date of the forecast instance as @context.Date.

CHAPTER 7 ADVANCED COMPONENTS

You can override the name of the argument as shown in Listing 7-12. This is what we do with the Context parameter (provided by Blazor) using `<Row Context="forecast">`. Now the item from the iteration can be accessed using the forecast argument. Can you guess what the output of the Grid will be?

Listing 7-12. Overriding the Context argument

```
<Grid Items="forecasts">
  <Header>
  <th>Date</th>
  <th>Temp. (C)</th>
  <th>Temp. (F)</th>
  <th>Summary</th>
  </Header>
  <Row Context="forecast">
    <td>@forecast.Date</td>
    <td>@forecast.TemperatureC</td>
    <td>@forecast.TemperatureF</td>
    <td>@forecast.Summary</td>
  </Row>
  <Footer>
  <td colspan="4">Spring is in the air!</td>
  </Footer>
</Grid>
```

Run your solution and select the Weather link from the navigation menu. Admire your new templated component as in Figure 7-2.

CHAPTER 7 ADVANCED COMPONENTS

Weather

This component demonstrates showing data.

Date	Temp. (C)	Temp. (F)	Summary
05/06/2024	43	109	Warm
06/06/2024	1	33	Mild
07/06/2024	3	37	Warm
08/06/2024	25	76	Balmy
09/06/2024	9	48	Mild

Figure 7-2. Showing forecasts with the Grid templated component

Now we have a reusable `Grid` component that we can use to show any list of items passing the list to the `Items` parameters and specifying what should be shown in the `Header`, `Row`, and `Footer` parameters! But there is more!

Specify the Type Parameter's Type Explicitly

Normally the compiler can infer the type of the `TItem` type parameter, but if this does not work as you expect, you can specify the type explicitly. Please note that this is the name of the type parameter, same as `List<TItem>`. You can use any name that makes sense. Simply specify the type of your type parameter by specifying it as `TItem` (the name of the type parameter used in the templated component) when you use the component as in Listing 7-13.

Listing 7-13. Explicitly specifying the type parameter

```
<Grid Items="forecasts" TItem="WeatherForecast">
```

Using Generic Type Constraints

With C# generics, you can specify constraints on a generic type using the `where` syntax. Listing 7-14 shows an example using plain C#. A constraint states that whatever type will be used for T should implement the `IDisposable` interface. You can learn more about it at https://docs.microsoft.com/dotnet/csharp/programming-guide/generics/constraints-on-type-parameters.

CHAPTER 7   ADVANCED COMPONENTS

Listing 7-14. Generics using a constraint

```
public class DisposableList<T> where T : IDisposable
```

We can do the same for templated components. For example, we could state that `TItem` should implement `IDisposable` for the `Grid` templated component as shown in Listing 7-15.

Listing 7-15. Using constraints with a templated component

```
@typeparam TItem where TItem : IDisposable
```

Razor Templates

In templated components, you can have parameters of type `RenderFragment`, which can then be given a value using markup. You can also give a `RenderFragment` or `RenderFragment<TItem>` a value using a razor template.

A _Razor Template_ is a way to define a UI snippet, for example, `@<span>Hello!</span>`, which you can then pass into a `RenderFragment`. A razor template generally uses the `@<element>...</element>` syntax. In the example's case, we specify a `RenderFragment` without any arguments, for example to use in the `Grid`'s `Header` parameter. But if you need to pass an argument to the `RenderFragment<TItem>`, you create a razor template using a syntax that looks a lot like a lambda function.

Think of a razor template as special C# syntax for creating a `RenderFragment`.

Let's look at an example. Start by adding a new component called `ListView` as in Listing 7-16. This will show an unordered list of items (of type `TItem`) using `<ul>` and `<li>` HTML elements.

Listing 7-16. The template ListView component's code

```
@typeparam TItem

<ul>
  @foreach (var item in Items)
  {
    <li>
      @ItemTemplate(item)
    </li>
  }
```

212

```
</ul>
@code {
  [Parameter]
  [EditorRequired]
  public required RenderFragment<TItem> ItemTemplate { get; set; }

  [Parameter]
  [EditorRequired]
  public required IReadOnlyList<TItem> Items { get; set; }
}
```

Now add the ListView to the Weather component as in Listing 7-17 (I have left out most of the unchanged parts). The ItemTemplate parameter now uses the forecastTemplate RenderFragment which is specified in the @code section. Look at the forecastTemplate in Listing 7-17. This uses a syntax very similar to a C# lambda function taking the forecast as an argument and returns a RenderFragment<TItem> using the (forecast) => @@forecast.Summary Razor syntax.

In the ListView component's ItemTemplate we simply invoke the template as if it was a lambda function. So, you could say that a razor template is like an invokable function returning a RenderFragment!

Listing 7-17. Using the ListView component with a RenderFragment

```
<ListView Items="forecasts">
  <ItemTemplate>
    @forecastTemplate(context)
  </ItemTemplate>
</ListView>

@code {

  private RenderFragment<WeatherForecast> forecastTemplate =
    (forecast) =>@<span>@forecast.Summary</span>;

}
```

Razor templates can also be used as light-weight components; we will talk about this later in the performance chapter.

Wig-Pig Syntax

Let's go wild: can we have a RenderFragment<RenderFragment>? Currently our ListView<TItem> is using an <ul> to wrap the items, but what if the user of the ListView<TItem> wants to use an <ol>, or something different? A RenderFragment<RenderFragment> would allow us to wrap another RenderFragment.

Looking at Listing 7-16, this means that we want to be able to replace the outer (<ul>) markup with a template, loop over the items, and use another template to render each item.

Create a new component called PWListView as in Listing 7-18 (kind of enhanced version of ListView). Note that in Listing 7-18 the ListTemplate parameter is of type RenderFragment<RenderFragment>. Why would we want this? Because we want to use the ListTemplate as a wrapper around another RenderFragment, so RenderFragment<RenderFragment> makes sense!

Listing 7-18. The PWListView component

```
@typeparam TItem

@ListTemplate(
  @:@{
    foreach(var item in Items)
    {
    @ItemTemplate(item)
    }
  })
@code {
  [Parameter]
  [EditorRequired]
  public required RenderFragment<RenderFragment> ListTemplate
    { get; set; }

  [Parameter]
  [EditorRequired]
  public required RenderFragment<TItem> ItemTemplate
    { get; set; }

  [Parameter]
  [EditorRequired]
  public required IReadOnlyList<TItem> Items
    { get; set; }
}
```

What do we want? We want the ListTemplate to wrap the foreach loop which then calls the ItemTemplate for each TItem in the Items list. We need to pass a RenderFragment to it that will contain the foreach loop. But how can we do this in our component?

Let me introduce you to the _Pig-Wig syntax_: @:@{. It is called that because it looks like a grumpy pig with a wig (not my invention!).

Inside our PWListView component, we will invoke the ListTemplate as in Listing 7-18, line 4, which uses the pig-wig syntax passing a RenderFragment that loops over each item and calls the ItemTemplate. The pig-wig syntax consists of two parts. The @: part tells razor to switch to C# mode, and the @{ tells the C# compiler to create a razor template.

CHAPTER 7   ADVANCED COMPONENTS

Time to use the `PWListView` component as in Listing 7-19. Copy the `Weather` component and replace with Listing 7-19. Since the `ListTemplate` parameter takes a `RenderFragment` as an argument, we call the context (called `innerTemplate`) here, wrapped in the markup for the list. This will execute the foreach loop which will call the `ItemTemplate`. So as the consumer of a `PWListView` component, you provide the `ListTemplate`, but also call the `innerTemplate` to allow the `PWListView` component to render its pig-wig template. Phew.

Listing 7-19. Using the PWListView component

```
@page "/weather-piggywig"

<PageTitle>Weather</PageTitle>

<h1>Weather with PiggyWig</h1>

<p>This component demonstrates showing data.</p>

@if (forecasts is null)
{
  <p><em>Loading...</em></p>
}
else
{
  <div class="summaries">
    <PWListView Items="forecasts">
      <ListTemplate Context="innerTemplate">
        <ol>
          @innerTemplate
        </ol>
      </ListTemplate>
      <ItemTemplate Context="forecast">
        <li>@forecast.Summary</li>
      </ItemTemplate>
    </PWListView>
  </div>
}
```

```
@code {
  private WeatherForecast[]? forecasts;

  string[] summaries = ["Freezing", "Bracing", "Chilly", "Cool", "Mild",
  "Warm", "Balmy", "Hot", "Sweltering", "Scorching"];

  protected override async Task OnInitializedAsync()
  {
    await Task.Delay(500);

    var startDate = DateOnly.FromDateTime(DateTime.Now);
    forecasts = Enumerable.Range(1, 5)
      .Select(index => new WeatherForecast
      {
        Date = startDate.AddDays(index),
        TemperatureC = Random.Shared.Next(-20, 55),
        Summary = summaries[Random.Shared.Next(summaries.Length)]
      }).ToArray();
  }
}
```

Using Blazor Error Boundaries

With reusable components like templated components, you allow the user of your component to inject their own logic. But what if that logic is flawed and starts throwing exceptions?

Blazor error boundaries allow you to handle exceptions within your component and to provide some nice UI indicating the problem, without the exception taking the rest of the page down with it. The ErrorBoundary component wraps around some UI containing one or more child components. When the wrapped UI does not throw an exception, it is simply rendered. When the wrapped UI throws an exception, it renders an error UI, which is customizable.

Note You can use the ErrorBoundary component anywhere, not just in templated components!

CHAPTER 7   ADVANCED COMPONENTS

Let us use an example: start by creating a copy of the WeatherForecast class to throw an exception when it is too cold as in Listing 7-20.

Listing 7-20. Emulating some flawed logic

```
public class BelgianWeatherForecast
{
  public DateOnly Date { get; set; }
  public int TemperatureC { get; set; }
  public string? Summary { get; set; }
  public int TemperatureF
  => (TemperatureC > 0)
    ? 32 + (int)(TemperatureC / 0.5556)
    : throw new Exception("Too cold!");
}
```

Copy the Weather component to the new BelgianWeather component as in Listing 7-21.

Listing 7-21. Using the flawed logic in a component

```
@page "/weather-belgian"

<PageTitle>Weather</PageTitle>

...

@code {
  ...
  protected override async Task OnInitializedAsync()
  {
    await Task.Delay(500);

    var startDate = DateOnly.FromDateTime(DateTime.Now);
    forecasts = Enumerable.Range(1, 5).Select(index
      => new BelgianWeatherForecast
      {
        Date = startDate.AddDays(index),
```

```
            TemperatureC = Random.Shared.Next(-20, 55),
            Summary = summaries[Random.Shared.Next(summaries.Length)]
        }).ToArray();
    }
}
```

Running the application and choosing the `BelgianWeather` component will most of the time crash the whole page (you might get lucky (?) when there is no forecast with cold temperature). Not a nice user experience.

Update the `Grid` templated component to use the `ErrorBoundary` component as in Listing 7-22. To protect any place where you want to display an error UI if the inner element throws an exception, wrap it with an `ErrorBoundary`.

Listing 7-22. Using an ErrorBoundary

```
@typeparam TItem

<table class="table">
  <thead>
    <tr>@Header</tr>
  </thead>
  <tbody>
    @foreach (var item in Items)
    {
      <ErrorBoundary>
        <tr>@Row(item)</tr>
      </ErrorBoundary>
    }
  </tbody>
  @if (Footer is not null)
  {
    <tfoot>
      <tr>@Footer</tr>
    </tfoot>
  }
</table>
```

CHAPTER 7　ADVANCED COMPONENTS

Running the application and choosing the `BelgianWeather` component will now result in errors being shown as in Figure 7-3.

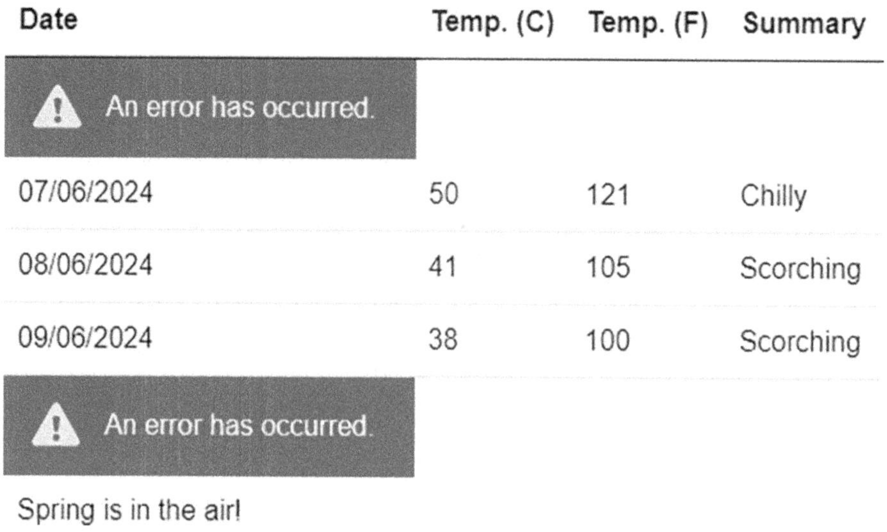

Date	Temp. (C)	Temp. (F)	Summary
⚠ An error has occurred.			
07/06/2024	50	121	Chilly
08/06/2024	41	105	Scorching
09/06/2024	38	100	Scorching
⚠ An error has occurred.			

Spring is in the air!

Figure 7-3. *Using the ErrorBoundary*

By default, the `ErrorBoundary`'s error UI uses an empty `<div>` with the `blazor-error-boundary` CSS class. You can customize this CSS class to change the error UI for the whole application.

You can also customize the error UI of a specific `ErrorBoundary` component using its `ErrorContent` parameter, with an example shown in Listing 7-23 and Figure 7-4.

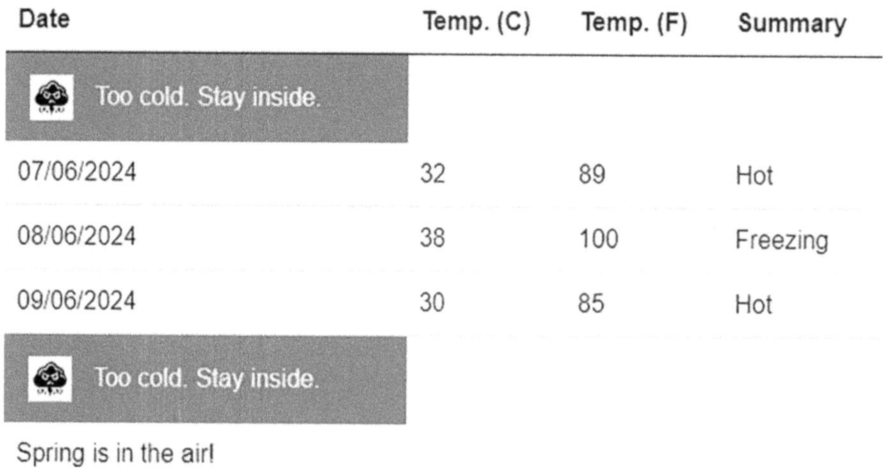

Date	Temp. (C)	Temp. (F)	Summary
🥶 Too cold. Stay inside.			
07/06/2024	32	89	Hot
08/06/2024	38	100	Freezing
09/06/2024	30	85	Hot
🥶 Too cold. Stay inside.			

Spring is in the air!

Figure 7-4. *Customizing the ErrorBoundary*

220

CHAPTER 7 ADVANCED COMPONENTS

Listing 7-23. Customizing an ErrorBoundary

```css
/* Custom style for weather */

tbody .blazor-error-boundary {
  background: url(data:image/png;base64,iVBORw...) no-repeat 1rem/1.8rem,
  #818589;
  padding: 1rem 1rem 1rem 3.7rem;
  color: white;
}

  tbody .blazor-error-boundary::after {
    content: "Too cold. Stay inside."
  }
```

Or if you like, you can set the `ErrorContent` parameter of the `ErrorBoundary` as shown in Listing 7-24 and Figure 7-5. The custom CSS is shown in Listing 7-25.

Listing 7-24. Customizing ErrorBoundary with ErrorContent

```
<ErrorBoundary>
  <ChildContent>
    <tr>@Row(item)</tr>
  </ChildContent>
  <ErrorContent>
    <tr>
      <td class="errorContent">
        <p class="errorContent"> ☁ Too cold. Stay inside!</p>
      </td>
      <td class="errorContent"></td>
      <td class="errorContent"></td>
      <td class="errorContent"></td>
    </tr>
  </ErrorContent>
</ErrorBoundary>
```

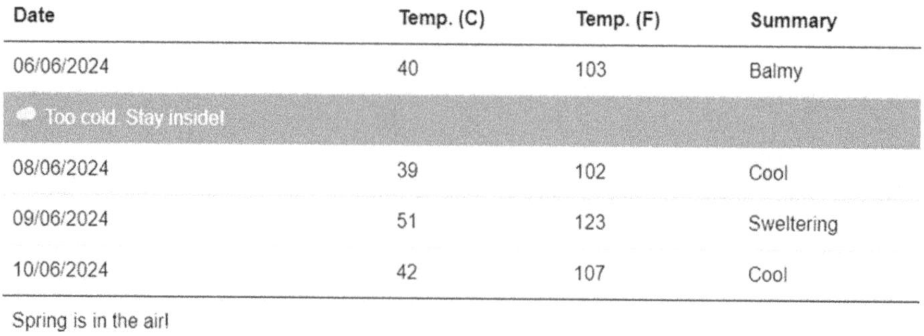

Date	Temp. (C)	Temp. (F)	Summary
06/06/2024	40	103	Balmy
Too cold. Stay inside!			
08/06/2024	39	102	Cool
09/06/2024	51	123	Sweltering
10/06/2024	42	107	Cool

Spring is in the air!

Figure 7-5. *Customized ErrorBoundary with ErrorContent*

Listing 7-25. The ErrorContent's CSS

```
p.errorContent {
  color: white;
  display: table-cell;
}

td.errorContent {
  padding-top: 8px;
  padding-bottom: 8px;
  background-color: darkgray;
}
```

Virtualization

Sometimes you need to display a lot of data, maybe thousands of rows. If you are going to use a simple `foreach` loop to create the UI for each row, you will get a noticeable delay between loading the data and the rendering of the data, because the Blazor runtime will have to create the UI for each row. Here we will look at the built-in virtualization which will only render visible rows.

Display a Large Number of Rows

If you like, the provided sources contain the complete solution, but maybe you like to type along, and for that you can create the project with this powershell script:

CHAPTER 7 ADVANCED COMPONENTS

```
$ProjectName = "BlazorApp.Components.Virtualization"
mkdir $ProjectName
cd $ProjectName
dotnet new sln -n $ProjectName
mkdir src
cd src
dotnet new blazor -n $ProjectName --all-interactive --interactivity Server
cd ..
dotnet sln add src\$ProjectName
```

Let us start by building the class for the data and a class that will generate a large number of instances of this data.

Add a new Data folder to the project and add the Measurement class from Listing 7-26. You can also copy this class from the book's sources to save some typing.

Listing 7-26. The Measurement class

```
public class Measurement
{
  public required int Row { get; init; }
  public required Guid Guid { get; init; }
  public required double Min { get; init; }
  public required double Avg { get; init; }
  public required double Max { get; init; }
}
```

Create a Services folder, and add the MeasurementService class from Listing 7-27 to it. The MeasurementService class has a single GetMeasurements method that returns many rows. You can change the nrOfRows constant to play with the number of rows. So why does the GetMeasurements method return a ValueTask<T>? Because this allows me later to change my mind and call some asynchronous methods, for example, to retrieve the data using a REST call. Think of ValueTask<T> as the union of T and Task<T>, giving the choice whether to implement a method synchronously or asynchronously. You can learn more about ValueTask<T> at https://devblogs.microsoft.com/dotnet/understanding-the-whys-whats-and-whens-of-valuetask.

223

CHAPTER 7   ADVANCED COMPONENTS

Listing 7-27. The MeasurementService class

```
using BlazorApp.Components.Virtualization.Data;

namespace BlazorApp.Components.Virtualization.Services;

public class MeasurementsService
{
  public ValueTask<List<Measurement>> GetMeasurements()
  {
    const int nrOfRows = 1000;
    List<Measurement> result = new ();
    for (int i = 0; i < nrOfRows; i += 1)
    {
      result.Add(new Measurement()
      {
        Row = i,
        Guid = Guid.NewGuid(),
        Min = Random.Shared.Next(0, 100),
        Avg = Random.Shared.Next(100, 300),
        Max = Random.Shared.Next(300, 400),
      });
    }
    return ValueTask.FromResult(result);
  }
}
```

Add a razor component called `NonVirtualizedMeasurements` from Listing 7-28 to the Components folder. Again, you can copy this from the provided sources. This component looks a lot like the `Weather` component where we fetch the data, and then iterate over it with a `foreach` loop. The `NonVirtualizedMeasurements` component also has some logic to display the amount of time it took to render the component using the .NET `Stopwatch` class. This class has a `Start` and `Stop` method and will measure the amount of time between them.

Listing 7-28. NonVirtualizedMeasurements component displaying many rows

```
@using BlazorApp.Components.Virtualization.Data
@using System.Diagnostics
@using BlazorApp.Components.Virtualization.Services

@if (measurements is null)
{
  <p><em>Loading...</em></p>
}
else
{
  <table class="table">
    <thead>
      <tr>
        <th>#</th>
        <th>Guid</th>
        <th>Min</th>
        <th>Avg</th>
        <th>Max</th>
      </tr>
    </thead>
    <tbody>
      @foreach (Measurement measurement in measurements)
      {
        <tr>
          <td>@measurement.Row</td>
          <td>@measurement.Guid.ToString()</td>
          <td>@measurement.Min</td>
          <td>@measurement.Avg</td>
          <td>@measurement.Max</td>
        </tr>
      }
    </tbody>
  </table>
}
```

CHAPTER 7 ADVANCED COMPONENTS

```
@code {
  private List<Measurement>? measurements;
  private Stopwatch timer = new Stopwatch();

  protected override async Task OnInitializedAsync()
  {
    MeasurementsService measurementService = new ();
    measurements = await measurementService.GetMeasurements();
    timer.Start();
  }

  protected override void OnAfterRender(bool firstRender)
  {
    timer.Stop();
    Console.WriteLine($"Full rendering took {timer.
    ElapsedMilliseconds} ms.");
  }
}
```

To complete this part of the demo, add the NonVirtualizedMeasurements component to your Home component as in Listing 7-29.

Listing 7-29. Using the NonVirtualMeasurements component

```
@page "/"

<PageTitle>Home</PageTitle>

<NonVirtualizedMeasurements/>
```

Build and run the application. Depending on the speed of your computer, you will see a noticeable delay while Blazor is building the UI (you might even run out of memory or crash the browser!). We can also look at the console to see how long it took to render. On my machine, I got the following output:

```
Full rendering took 148 ms.
```

Which is not so bad thinking about the number of rows being created.

CHAPTER 7   ADVANCED COMPONENTS

Now let us examine how much HTML got generated. Right-click a row in the list and select "Inspect". Your browser's debugging tools should open. Now look at the number of `<tr>` elements that got generated! One for each measurement, while the user is only seeing about 20 to 30 rows. What a waste!

Use the Virtualize Component

So how can we lighten the load? Blazor has a `Virtualize` component just for this! The `Virtualize` component will only create the UI for visible rows, and depending on the height of your screen, the rendered rows in this demo should be about 20 rows. Way better than 1000 rows! When you scroll, the `Virtualize` component will then dynamically render the new rows which become visible. There are some limits to this. First, all rows should have the same height; otherwise, the `Virtualize` component cannot calculate which row to render without rendering all other preceding rows. You should only use this component when there are many rows which are not visible. Time to see this in action.

Copy-paste the NonVirtualizedMeasurements.razor file, and name it VirtualizedMeasurements.razor. Replace the `foreach` loop as in Listing 7-30. The `Virtualize` component is a templated component that receives its items through the `Items` parameter and uses the `Virtualize.ItemContent` parameter to render each item. Think of `<ItemContent>` as the body of a `foreach`-loop.

Listing 7-30. Replace the foreach with the Virtualize component

```
<tbody>
  <Virtualize Items="@measurements" Context="measurement">
    <ItemContent>
      <tr>
        <td>@measurement.Row</td>
        <td>@measurement.Guid.ToString()</td>
        <td>@measurement.Min</td>
        <td>@measurement.Avg</td>
        <td>@measurement.Max</td>
      </tr>
    </ItemContent>
  </Virtualize>
</tbody>
```

227

CHAPTER 7   ADVANCED COMPONENTS

Replace the NonVirtualMeasurements component in Home component with the VirtualizedMeasurements component.

Build and run. Now the UI renders almost instantly, and when I look in the console I see:

`Full rendering took 32 ms.`

This is way faster! Try scrolling. It scrolls smoothly! With the Virtualize component, you get a lot of features with almost no work. But that is not all of it!

Add Paging

There is more we can do. Our component is loading all the data from the service, while we are only displaying a tiny fraction of rows. With the Virtualize component, we can change the service, so it only returns rows that are being displayed. We do this by setting the ItemsProvider parameter on the Virtualize component, which is an asynchronous delegate taking an ItemsProviderRequest and returns an ItemsProviderResult<T>.

Let us change our measurements to do this. First implement the GetMeasurementsPage method in the MeasurementsService class as in Listing 7-31. This method returns a tuple containing the segment of rows and the total number of rows (all of them, not just the segment size). It also simulates a 50ms delay, like accessing data from a database.

Listing 7-31. Adding paging to the MeasurementsService

```
public async ValueTask<(List<Measurement>, int)> GetMeasurementsPage
(int from, int count, CancellationToken cancellationToken)
{
  const int maxMeasurements = 1000;
  // Start Add delay to emulate database access
  const int delay = 50;
  await Task.Delay(delay, cancellationToken);
  // End Add delay
  var result = new List<Measurement>();
  var rnd = new Random();
  count = Math.Max(0, Math.Min(count, maxMeasurements - from));
  for (int i = 0; i < count; i += 1)
```

CHAPTER 7 ADVANCED COMPONENTS

```
  {
    result.Add(new Measurement()
    {
      Row = i,
      Guid = Guid.NewGuid(),
      Min = rnd.Next(0, 100),
      Avg = rnd.Next(100, 300),
      Max = from + i //rnd.Next(300, 400),
    });
  }
  return (result, maxMeasurements);
}
```

Copy-paste the VirtualMeasurements component and name it PagedVirtualMeasurements. Update the Virtualize component with the ItemsProvider parameter as in Listing 7-32. Now the Virtualize component will ask the LoadMeasurements method to fetch several rows. Of course, it must do an estimate on how many rows fit on the screen, and that is why I also provide the ItemSize parameter.

The ItemsProvider is an async method taking an ItemsProviderRequest which has three properties, a StartIndex, a Count, and a CancellationToken. We use these properties to call the GetMeasurementPage method which returns a collection of rows and the total number of rows. This is then returned as an ItemsProviderResult.

Listing 7-32. Using the ItemsProvider

```
@using BlazorApp.Components.Virtualization.Data
@using System.Diagnostics
@using BlazorApp.Components.Virtualization.Services

<table class="table">
  <thead>
    <tr>
      <th>#</th>
      <th>Guid</th>
      <th>Min</th>
      <th>Avg</th>
      <th>Max</th>
```

CHAPTER 7   ADVANCED COMPONENTS

```
    </tr>
  </thead>
  <tbody>
    <Virtualize
      ItemsProvider="@LoadMeasurements"
      Context="measurement"
      ItemSize="41">
      <ItemContent>
        <tr>
          <td>@measurement.Row</td>
          <td>@measurement.Guid.ToString()</td>
          <td>@measurement.Min</td>
          <td>@measurement.Avg</td>
          <td>@measurement.Max</td>
        </tr>
      </ItemContent>
    </Virtualize>
  </tbody>
</table>

@code {
  private Stopwatch timer = new Stopwatch();
  MeasurementsService measurementService = new();

  private async ValueTask<ItemsProviderResult<Measurement>>
    LoadMeasurements(ItemsProviderRequest request)
  {
    Console.WriteLine($"{request.StartIndex}-{request.Count}");
    var (measurements, totalItemCount) =
      await measurementService.GetMeasurementsPage
      (request.StartIndex,
       request.Count,
       request.CancellationToken);
    return new ItemsProviderResult<Measurement>
      (measurements, totalItemCount);
  }
```

```
  protected override async Task OnInitializedAsync()
  {
    timer.Start();
  }

  protected override void OnAfterRender(bool firstRender)
  {
    timer.Stop();
    Console.WriteLine($"Full rendering took {timer.
    ElapsedMilliseconds} ms.");
  }
}
```

Replace the `VirtualizedMeasurements` component with the `PagedVirtualizedMeasurements` component in Home component. Now we are ready to run. Again, the experience is pretty smooth. The UI renders instantaneously, and scrolling is very fast.

Run this and start scrolling. Because of the delay, the Virtualize component might not have the row to render, so there is a `Placeholder` parameter shown in Listing 7-33 which is displayed in its place. Of course, the moment the row is loaded, it gets replaced with the `ItemContent`.

Listing 7-33. Using a PlaceHolder

```
<Virtualize
  ItemsProvider="@LoadMeasurements"
  Context="measurement"
  ItemSize="41">
  <ItemContent>
    <tr>
      <td>@measurement.Row</td>
      <td>@measurement.Guid.ToString()</td>
      <td>@measurement.Min</td>
      <td>@measurement.Avg</td>
      <td>@measurement.Max</td>
    </tr>
  </ItemContent>
  <Placeholder>
```

```
    <tr><td colspan="4">Loading...</td></tr>
  </Placeholder>
</Virtualize>
```

Attribute Splatting

What if you want to build a wrapper component around an HTML element, for example, an `<input>` element. This element supports a whole range of HTML attributes. Do we need to add a parameter for each possible HTML attribute? And what about future changes to this HTML element? Blazor supports attribute splatting, which allows you to capture attributes into a dictionary and use these for rendering the component. Let us look at an example.

One approach would be to have a parameter for each possible HTML attribute, as shown in Listing 7-34. Here I only implement four attributes, but there are a lot more HTML attributes for an `<input>` element. Implementing each possible combination is down-right impractical!

Listing 7-34. Using parameters

```
<input type="@Type" class="@Class"
       placeholder="@PlaceHolder" disabled="@Disabled" />
@code {
  [Parameter]
  public string PlaceHolder { get; set; } = string.Empty;

  [Parameter]
  public string Class { get; set; } = string.Empty;

  [Parameter]
  public string Type { get; set; } = string.Empty;

  [Parameter]
  public bool Disabled { get; set; }
}
```

You can also tell the Blazor runtime to put each attribute which does not map to one of the parameters of the Blazor component in a dictionary. You can then use the dictionary to render as attributes, for example, in Listing 7-35.

Listing 7-35. Using attribute splatting

```
<input @attributes="@Attributes" />

@code {
  [Parameter(CaptureUnmatchedValues =true)]
  public Dictionary<string,object>? Attributes { get; set; }
}
```

You can then use the component with additional attributes like Listing 7-36.

Listing 7-36. Applying attributes with attribute splatting

```
<MyInput type="email" class="form-control" placeholder="E-mail"/>
```

This will render as the following HTML:

```
<input type="email" class="form-control" placeholder="E-mail">
```

Referring to a Component

Sometimes you want to set a property directly on a component (without using data binding) or invoke a method directly on a component. In this case you need a reference to that component, so you can use it from code.

Look at the Message component in Listing 7-37. This component has two methods: Show and Hide. When the Show method gets called, it displays a message, guess what Hide does.

Listing 7-37. The Message component

```
@if (show)
{
  <div class="alert alert-primary" role="alert">
    @Text
  </div>
}

@code {
  private bool show = false;
```

CHAPTER 7   ADVANCED COMPONENTS

```
  [Parameter]
  [EditorRequired]
  public string Text { get; set; } = string.Empty;

  public void Show()
  {
    show = true;
    StateHasChanged();
  }

  public void Hide()
  {
    show = false;
    StateHasChanged();
  }
}
```

In Listing 7-38, I use the Message component, and I capture a reference to this component using the @ref syntax. This allows the Home component to directly invoke Show and Hide.

Listing 7-38. Using the Message component

```
@page "/"

<PageTitle>Home</PageTitle>

<Message Text="Now you see me..." @ref="message" />

<button class="btn btn-success" @onclick="ShowMessage">Show</button>
<button class="btn btn-danger" @onclick="HideMessage">Hide</button>

@code {
  private Message message = default!;

  private void ShowMessage() => message.Show();
  private void HideMessage() => message.Hide();
}
```

CHAPTER 7   ADVANCED COMPONENTS

Running this and clicking the "Show" button will show the message as illustrated by Figure 7-6.

Figure 7-6. After clicking show

Component Reuse and PizzaPlace

In previous chapters, we built a couple of components for the PizzaPlace application. There was an opportunity to have more reuse, and we are going to take that here. We will build a templated component for showing lists of pizza and then reuse it to show the menu and the shopping basket. Open the PizzaPlace solution from previous chapter (or the sources that come with this book).

Add the PizzaItem Component

Examine the body of the foreach loop inside Menu and Basket. Do these look similar? We can bring these together in a PizzaItem component, shown in Listing 7-39. This component takes a Pizza as a parameter, with a ButtonText and ButtonAction parameter for the button, since this is different for Menu and Basket.

Listing 7-39. The PizzaItem component

```
<div class="row">
  <div class="col">
    @Pizza.Name
  </div>
  <div class="col text-right">
    @($"{Pizza.Price:0.00}")
  </div>
  <div class="col"></div>
  <div class="col">
    <img src="@SpicinessImage(Pizza.Spiciness)"
         alt="@Pizza.Spiciness" />
```

235

CHAPTER 7   ADVANCED COMPONENTS

```
    </div>
    <div class="col">
      <button class="btn btn-success pl-4 pr-4"
              @onclick=@(async ()
        => await ButtonAction.InvokeAsync(Pizza))>
        @ButtonText
      </button>
    </div>
</div>

@code {
  [Parameter]
  [EditorRequired]
  public required Pizza Pizza { get; set; }

  [Parameter]
  [EditorRequired]
  public required string ButtonText { get; set; }

  [Parameter]
  public EventCallback<Pizza> ButtonAction { get; set; }

  private string SpicinessImage(Spiciness spiciness)
    => $"images/{spiciness.ToString().ToLower()}.png";
}
```

We can now use `PizzaItem` to simplify the `Menu` and `Basket` components as in Listing 7-40 and Listing 7-41.

Listing 7-40. Using PizzaItem with menu

```
<h1>Our selection of pizzas</h1>

@foreach (Pizza pizza in Pizzas)
{
  <PizzaItem Pizza="@pizza" ButtonText="Add" ButtonAction="@Selected"/>
}
```

Listing 7-41. Using PizzaItem with Basket

```
@if (State.Basket.Orders.Any())
{
  <h1 class="">Your current order</h1>

  @foreach (var (pizza, pos) in GetPizzas())
  {
    <PizzaItem Pizza="@pizza" ButtonText="Remove"
      ButtonAction="@(async () => await RemoveFromBasket(pos))"/>
  }

  <div class="row">
    <div class="col"></div>
    <div class="col"><hr /></div>
    <div class="col"> </div>
    <div class="col"> </div>
  </div>

  <div class="row">
    <div class="col"> Total:</div>
    <div class="col text-right font-weight-bold">
      @($"{State.TotalPrice:0.00}") </div>
    <div class="col"> </div>
    <div class="col"> </div>
    <div class="col"> </div>
  </div>
}
```

Run the application. It should still work!

Create the ItemList Templated Component

Both Menu and Basket iterate over a list, so there is an opportunity here for reuse. Create a new component called ItemList from Listing 7-42. Here we have a Header and Footer of type RenderFragment? and a mandatory Row parameter of type RenderFragment<TItem>. The Header and Footer parameters are optional, and that is why we use an @if. There is also the Items parameter of type IEnumerable<TItem>,

CHAPTER 7 ADVANCED COMPONENTS

and this parameter allows the compiler to infer the type of TItem when we assign it a collection. We iterate over this parameter using a @foreach, and we call the Row RenderFragment.

Listing 7-42. The ItemList component

```
@typeparam TItem

@if (Header is not null)
{
  @Header
}
@foreach (TItem item in Items)
{
  @Row(item)
}
@if (Footer is not null)
{
  @Footer
}
@code {
  [Parameter]
  public RenderFragment? Header { get; set; }

  [Parameter]
  [EditorRequired]
  public required RenderFragment<TItem> Row { get; set; };

  [Parameter]
  public RenderFragment? Footer { get; set; }

  [Parameter]
  [EditorRequired]
  public required IEnumerable<TItem> Items { get; set; };
}
```

Now that we have this templated component, we can use it for both the Menu and Basket components.

CHAPTER 7   ADVANCED COMPONENTS

Update the markup for the Menu component as in Listing 7-43.

Listing 7-43. The Menu component using the ItemList

```
<ItemList>
  <Header>
    <h1>Our selection of pizzas</h1>
  </Header>
  <Row>
    @foreach (Pizza pizza in Pizzas)
    {
      <PizzaItem Pizza="@pizza" ButtonText="Add"
        ButtonAction="@Selected" />
    }
  </Row>
</ItemList>
```

And replace the Basket markup with Listing 7-44.

Listing 7-44. The Basket component using the ItemList

```
@if (State.Basket.Orders.Any())
{
  <ItemList>
    <Header>
      <h1 class="">Your current order</h1>
    </Header>
    <Row>
      @foreach (var (pizza, pos) in GetPizzas())
      {
        <PizzaItem Pizza="@pizza" ButtonText="Remove"
                   ButtonAction="@(async ()
          => await RemoveFromBasket(pos))" />
      }
    </Row>
    <Footer>
      <div class="row">
```

```
            <div class="col"></div>
            <div class="col"><hr /></div>
            <div class="col"> </div>
            <div class="col"> </div>
          </div>

          <div class="row">
            <div class="col"> Total:</div>
            <div class="col text-right font-weight-bold">
              @($"{State.TotalPrice:0.00}") </div>
            <div class="col"> </div>
            <div class="col"> </div>
            <div class="col"> </div>
          </div>
        </Footer>
      </ItemList>
    }
```

Now we have enhanced our PizzaPlace application by adding a templated component which we reuse for both the `Menu` and `Basket` components. Compile and run. The PizzaPlace application should work as before.

Summary

In this chapter, we saw that cascading parameters and values are a very nice way of sharing data between components in a hierarchy. In Blazor, you can build templated components, which resemble generic classes. These templated components can be parameterized to render different UIs, which makes them quite reusable! We discussed razor templates, which allow us to write markup in C# and had a look at the weird Piggy-Wig syntax. We can limit errors by wrapping them into an error boundary, and how we can display large lists of data using virtualization. We discussed attribute splatting and how a component can reference a child component.

We applied this knowledge by building a simple templated component for showing lists of pizzas which we need in several places.

In the next chapter, we will see how you can expose your components as a component library.

CHAPTER 8

Component Libraries

Building a Component Library

Components should be reusable. But you don't want to reuse a component between projects by copy-pasting the component between them. In this case, it is much better to build a _component library_, and as you will see, this is not hard at all! By putting your Blazor components into a component library, you can include it into different Blazor projects, use it both for Client-Side Blazor and Server-Side Blazor, and even publish it as a _NuGet_ package!

What we will do now is to move our templated component to a component library, and then we will use this library in our Blazor project.

Create the Component Library Project

Depending on your development environment, creating a component library is different. We will look at using Visual Studio and the dotnet cli (which is development environment agnostic, so this works no matter your choice of IDE).

The provided sources come with the BlazorApp.Components.ComponentLibraries solution, which is a copy of the previous chapter's demo.

With Visual Studio, right-click this solution, and select Add New Project. Look for the Razor Class Library project template as in Figure 8-1.

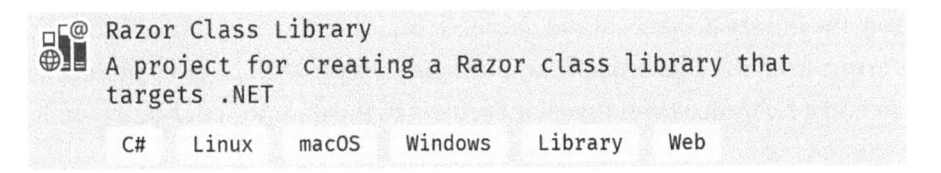

> Razor Class Library
> A project for creating a Razor class library that targets .NET
>
> C#   Linux   macOS   Windows   Library   Web

Figure 8-1. Add a new component library project

© Peter Himschoot 2024
P. Himschoot, *Full Stack Development with Microsoft Blazor*, https://doi.org/10.1007/979-8-8688-1007-7_8

CHAPTER 8   COMPONENT LIBRARIES

Click Next. Name this project BlazorApp.Components.MyComponentLibrary, select the "src" next to your other solution, and click Next. In the next screen, click Create.

With dotnet cli, open a command prompt or use the integrated terminal from Visual Studio Code. Change the current directory to the "src" directory. Type in the following command:

```
dotnet new razorclasslib -n BlazorApp.Components.MyComponentLibrary
```

The `dotnet new` command will create a new project based on the `razorclasslib` template. If you want the project to be created in a subdirectory, you can specify it using the "-o <<subdirectory>>" parameter.

Executing this command should show you output like:

```
The template "Razor Class Library" was created successfully.
```

Change to the solution's directory. Add it to your solution by typing in the next command (with "<<path-to>>" a place holder for you to replace):

```
dotnet sln add src/BlazorApp.Components.MyComponentLibraryv
```

Open the BlazorApp.Components.MyComponentLibrary project. This component library project comes with some sample files. There is the Component1 component, the ExampleJsInterop C# class, and inside the wwwroot folder there is a background.png and exampleInterop.js file. Remove all of these; we don't need them here.

Add Components to the Library

Previously, we built a couple of templated components. Some of these are very reusable, so we will move them to our library project. Start with "Grid."

Move (you can use Shift+Drag-and-Drop) the Grid.razor file from your BlazorApp.Components.ComponentLibraries project to the BlazorApp.Components. MyComponentLibrary project.

Do the same for the "`ListView`" and "`PWListView`" components.

Building the library project should succeed. Building the solution will still get compiler errors from the BlazorApp.Components.ComponentLibraries project because we need to add a reference from the client project to the component library, which we will fix in the next part.

242

CHAPTER 8 COMPONENT LIBRARIES

Refer to the Library from Your Project

Now that our library is ready, we are going to use it in our project. The way the library works means we can also use it in other projects (just like any other library project in .NET). Hey, you could even make it into a NuGet package (if you want more information, look at https://docs.microsoft.com/dotnet/core/deploying/creating-nuget-packages, and let the rest of the world enjoy your work!).

To use our component library in a project, we have two options:

Using Visual Studio, start by right-clicking the client project, and select Add ➤ Project Reference. Make sure you check BlazorApp.Components.MyComponentLibrary, and click OK. Blazor Component Libraries are just another kind of library/assembly.

Note You can also drag the library project onto the main project to create a project reference!

Using the project file (e.g., with Visual Studio Code), open the BlazorApp.Components.ComponentLibraries.csproj file and add the "`<ProjectReference>`" element to it as in Listing 8-1.

Listing 8-1. Add a reference to another project

```
<Project Sdk="Microsoft.NET.Sdk.Web">
  <PropertyGroup>
    <TargetFramework>net8.0</TargetFramework>
    <Nullable>enable</Nullable>
    <ImplicitUsings>enable</ImplicitUsings>
  </PropertyGroup>
  <ItemGroup>
    <ProjectReference Include="..\BlazorApp.Components.MyComponentLibrary\
    BlazorApp.Components.MyComponentLibrary.csproj" />
  </ItemGroup>
</Project>
```

CHAPTER 8   COMPONENT LIBRARIES

Using the Library Components

Now that you have added the reference to the component library, you can use these components like any other component, except that these components live in another namespace. Just like in C#, you can use the fully qualified name to refer to a component like in Listing 8-2.

Listing 8-2. Using the fully qualified component name

```
<BlazorApp.Components.MyComponentLibrary.Grid Items="forecasts">
    ...
</BlazorApp.Components.MyComponentLibrary.Grid>
```

And like in C#, you can add a "@using" statement so you can use the component's name as in Listing 8-3. Add @using statements to the top of the razor file.

Listing 8-3. Add a @using statement in razor

```
@page "/weather"
@using BlazorApp.Components.MyComponentLibrary
```

With razor, you can add the "@using" statement to the _Imports.razor_ file as in Listing 8-4 which will enable you to use the namespace in all the .razor files which are in the same directory or subdirectory. The easiest way to think about this is that Blazor will copy the contents of the Imports.razor file to the top of every .razor file in that directory and sub-directory. Just like C# "global using."

Listing 8-4. Add a @using to _Imports.razor

```
@using System.Net.Http
@using System.Net.Http.Json
@using Microsoft.AspNetCore.Components.Forms
@using Microsoft.AspNetCore.Components.Routing
@using Microsoft.AspNetCore.Components.Web
@using static Microsoft.AspNetCore.Components.Web.RenderMode
@using Microsoft.AspNetCore.Components.Web.Virtualization
@using Microsoft.JSInterop
```

CHAPTER 8   COMPONENT LIBRARIES

```
@using BlazorApp.Components.ComponentLibraries
@using BlazorApp.Components.ComponentLibraries.Components

@using BlazorApp.Components.MyComponentLibrary
```

Your solution should compile now and run just like before.

Why did we move our components into a component library? To make the components in the component library reusable for other projects. Simply add a reference to the library, and its components can be used!

Static Resources in a Component Library

Maybe you want to use an image (or some other static file like CSS or JavaScript) in your component library. The Blazor runtime requires you to put static resources in the project's wwwroot folder. If you want static resources in your application instead of the library, you should put these resources in the wwwroot folder of the application's project. For both cases, you need to put these in the wwwroot folder; the only difference is that for library projects you need to use a different URL.

I downloaded an image of a cloud from https://openclipart.org and copied it into the wwwroot folder (any image will do). The cloud image is shown in Figure 8-2.

Figure 8-2. Cloud.png

You can then refer to this static resource using a URL that uses the content path to the resource. If your resource is in the Blazor application's project, the path starts at the wwwroot folder, but for library projects the URL should start with "_content/{LibraryProjectName}" and refers to the wwwroot folder from your library project. For example, to refer to the cloud.png file in the Components.Library project, open Home.razor and add the image from Listing 8-5.

245

CHAPTER 8   COMPONENT LIBRARIES

Listing 8-5. Referring to a static resource in a component library

```
@page "/"

<PageTitle>Home</PageTitle>

<h1>Hello, world!</h1>

Welcome to your new app.

<div>
  <img src="_content/BlazorApp.Components.MyComponentLibrary/cloud.png" />
</div>
```

Run. You should see the cloud image, as shown in Figure 8-3.

Figure 8-3. *Referring to a static resource in a component Library*

You can also refer to this static content inside the component library from your main project using the same URL. For example, add a new Blazor component named Cloud to the component library, as shown in Listing 8-6.

Listing 8-6. A simple "Cloud" component

```
<div>
  <img src="_content/BlazorApp.Components.MyComponentLibrary/cloud.png" />
</div>
```

You can now add this component to the "Home" component, as shown in Listing 8-7.

Listing 8-7. Using the Cloud component

```
@page "/"

<PageTitle>Home</PageTitle>

<h1>Hello, world!</h1>

Welcome to your new app.

<Cloud/>
```

Summary

In this (very short) chapter, we discussed component libraries. We can build component libraries to maximize reuse of our components and to expose static resources such as images, JavaScript, and others. In the next chapter, we will look at some public Blazor component libraries.

CHAPTER 9

Built-In Components

You don't have to build everything from scratch. There are existing component libraries that can help you quickly build robust and visually appealing Blazor applications by providing a wide range of pre-built components and utilities. Blazor itself comes with a range of built-in components, so we will look at some of them here. More specific components will be reviewed in other chapters.

Public Component Libraries

A lot of people have been building excellent component libraries, some applying common styles like bootstrap, material design, and so on. Some libraries expose specialized components which wrap the `<canvas>` element, draw maps, etc. Some of these libraries are available completely for free; some others have a paying version.

> **Note** In no way do I want to list all available component libraries, nor give any preference to a specific library. Just want to give you an idea about the ecosystem out there.

Microsoft FluentUI

Microsoft Fluent UI (https://developer.microsoft.com/en-us/fluentui#/) is a collection of UX frameworks and libraries designed to create consistent, high-quality, and accessible user interfaces across Microsoft's products and services. It is part of Microsoft's Fluent Design System, which aims to provide a coherent design language for both web and desktop applications.

FluentUI provides us with many components, for example, the `Counter` component with FluentUI components such as `FluentButton` is shown in Listing 9-1.

CHAPTER 9   BUILT-IN COMPONENTS

Listing 9-1. Counter using FluentUI

```
@page "/counter"

<PageTitle>Counter</PageTitle>

<h1>Counter</h1>

<div role="status" style="padding-bottom: 1em;">
  Current count:
  <FluentBadge Appearance="Appearance.Neutral">
    @currentCount
  </FluentBadge>
</div>

<FluentButton Appearance="Appearance.Accent" @onclick="IncrementCount">
  Click me
</FluentButton>

@code {
  private int currentCount = 0;

  private void IncrementCount()
  {
    currentCount++;
  }
}
```

Figure 9-1 shows what some of these components look like.

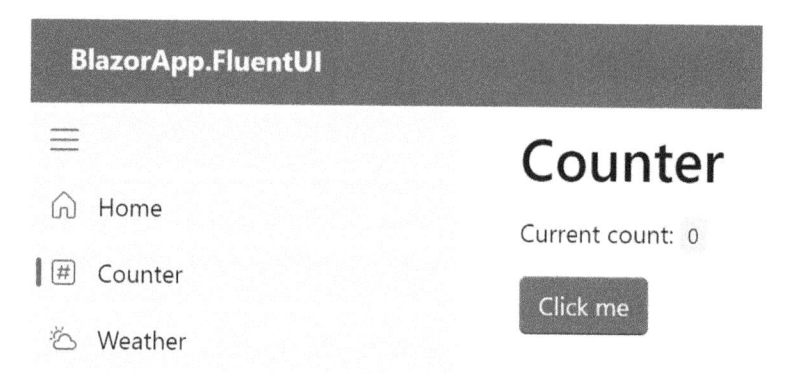

Figure 9-1. *Some FluentUI components*

250

MudBlazor

MudBlazor (https://mudblazor.com/) is a Blazor component library that provides a comprehensive set of UI components following Google's Material Design principles. It aims to offer developers a modern and consistent design experience with easy-to-use and highly customizable components for building responsive web applications. MudBlazor is open source and features extensive documentation and community support, making it accessible for developers to integrate into their projects. Counter using MudBlazor is shown in Listing 9-2.

Listing 9-2. Counter using MudBlazor

```
@page "/counter"

<PageTitle>Counter</PageTitle>

<MudText Typo="Typo.h3" GutterBottom="true">
  Counter
</MudText>
<MudText Class="mb-4">
  Current count: @currentCount
</MudText>
<MudButton Color="Color.Primary" Variant="Variant.Filled"
           @onclick="IncrementCount">
  Click me
</MudButton>

@code {
  private int currentCount = 0;

  private void IncrementCount()
  {
    currentCount++;
  }
}
```

An example of some components is shown in Figure 9-2.

CHAPTER 9   BUILT-IN COMPONENTS

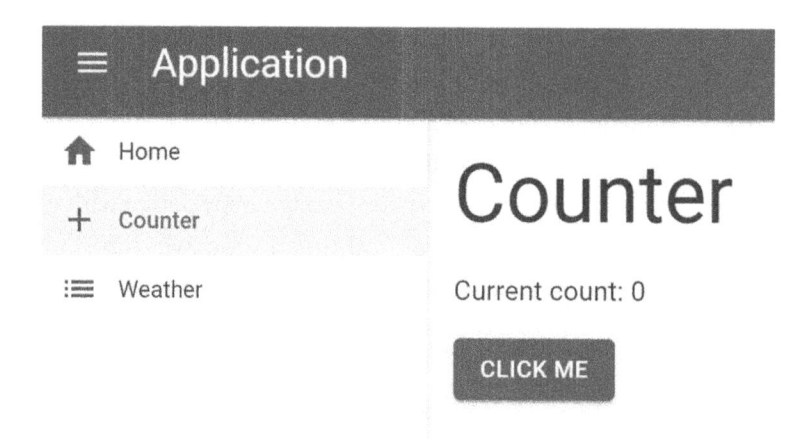

Figure 9-2. Some MudBlazor components

Blazor Bootstrap

Blazor Bootstrap (https://demos.blazorbootstrap.com/) provides a set of pre-built UI components that are styled using Bootstrap. These components include buttons, forms, modals, alerts, and other common UI elements. A Grid is shown in Listing 9-3.

Listing 9-3. Using Blazor Bootstrap's Grid component

```
<Grid Data="@forecasts"
      Class="table table-hover table-bordered table-striped"
      AllowSorting="true">
  <GridColumn TItem="WeatherForecast" HeaderText="Date"
    PropertyName="Date"
    SortKeySelector="item => item.Date">
    @context.Date
  </GridColumn>
  <GridColumn TItem="WeatherForecast" HeaderText="Temp. (C)"
    PropertyName="Name"
    SortKeySelector="item => item.TemperatureC">
    @context.TemperatureC
  </GridColumn>
  <GridColumn TItem="WeatherForecast" HeaderText="Temp. (C)"
    PropertyName="DOJ"
    SortKeySelector="item => item.TemperatureF">
```

```
      @context.TemperatureF
    </GridColumn>
    <GridColumn TItem="WeatherForecast" HeaderText="Designation"
      PropertyName="Designation"
      SortKeySelector="item => item.Summary">
      @context.Summary
    </GridColumn>
</Grid>
```

Weather looks like Figure 9-3 using Blazor Bootstrap.

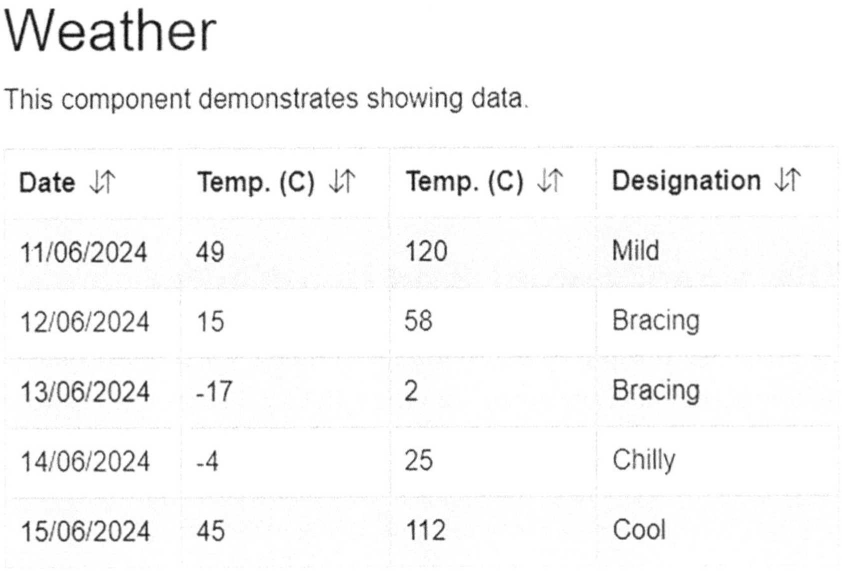

Weather

This component demonstrates showing data.

Date ↕	Temp. (C) ↕	Temp. (C) ↕	Designation ↕
11/06/2024	49	120	Mild
12/06/2024	15	58	Bracing
13/06/2024	-17	2	Bracing
14/06/2024	-4	25	Chilly
15/06/2024	45	112	Cool

Figure 9-3. Weather using Grid Blazor Bootstrap

Blazorise

Blazorise (https://blazorise.com/) is a versatile component library for Blazor, providing a wide range of customizable UI components that integrate seamlessly with popular CSS frameworks like Bootstrap, Bulma, and Material. It aims to simplify the development of responsive and modern web applications using C# and .NET by offering ready-to-use components with consistent design principles. Blazorise is open source, well-documented, and supported by an active community, making it an accessible choice for Blazor developers.

CHAPTER 9   BUILT-IN COMPONENTS

Telerik UI for Blazor

Telerik Blazor (https://www.telerik.com/blazor-ui) is a professional-grade UI component library specifically designed for Blazor, offering a comprehensive suite of highly customizable and performant components for building sophisticated web applications. It provides features such as advanced data grids, charts, forms, and more, all adhering to Telerik's high-quality standards and designed to integrate seamlessly with Blazor's framework. Telerik Blazor also includes robust documentation, dedicated support, and regular updates, making it a reliable choice for enterprise-level development.

Others

Others I did not mention yet: Ant Blazor, Radzen Blazor Components, SyncFusion Blazor UI Components, DevExpression Blazor Components, etc.

PageTitle, HeadContent, and HeadOutlet

Each web page consists of the `<head>` and `<body>` elements. For now, we have been looking at rendering the `<body>` element's content. But what about the `<head>` element?

For example, Listing 9-4 shows the `App` component of a Blazor Web App project. The `<head>` element of the provided HTML contains metadata and links to external resources that are essential for the proper functioning and styling of the web page.

Listing 9-4. The App component

```
<!DOCTYPE html>
<html lang="en">

<head>
  <meta charset="utf-8" />
  <meta name="viewport" content="width=device-width, initial-scale=1.0" />
  <base href="/" />
  <link rel="stylesheet" href="bootstrap/bootstrap.min.css" />
  <link rel="stylesheet" href="app.css" />
```

CHAPTER 9 BUILT-IN COMPONENTS

```
    <link rel="stylesheet" href="BlazorApp.Headers.styles.css" />
    <link rel="icon" type="image/png" href="favicon.png" />
    <HeadOutlet @rendermode="InteractiveServer" />
</head>

<body>
    <Routes @rendermode="InteractiveServer" />
    <script src="_framework/blazor.web.js"></script>
</body>

</html>
```

Here's a detailed explanation of each element within the `<head>` section:

`<meta charset="utf-8" />`

- This specifies the character encoding for the HTML document as UTF-8, which is a widely used encoding that covers almost all characters and symbols in the world.

`<meta name="viewport" content="width=device-width, initial-scale=1.0" />`

- This meta tag is essential for responsive web design. It sets the viewport to match the device's width and sets the initial zoom level to 1.0. This ensures the page scales correctly on all devices, including mobile phones and tablets.

`<base href="/" />`

- The `<base>` tag sets a base URL for all relative URLs in the document. Here, it sets the base URL to the root of the domain. This means any relative links will be resolved relative to the root URL. More about this in the Routing chapter.

`<link rel="stylesheet" href="bootstrap/bootstrap.min.css" />`

- This link element includes an external CSS file for Bootstrap, a popular front-end framework that provides pre-styled components and a responsive grid system. The provided Blazor templates use Bootstrap CSS by default, but you can switch to any CSS you like.

  ```
  <link rel="stylesheet" href="app.css" />
  ```

- This link element includes a custom CSS file (app.css) which contains styles specific to this web application.

  ```
  <link rel="stylesheet" href="BlazorApp.Headers.styles.css" />
  ```

- This link element includes another custom CSS file (BlazorApp.Headers.styles.css), which is dynamically generated from the component's isolated CSS styles. More on this can be found in the component's chapter.

  ```
  <link rel="icon" type="image/png" href="favicon.png" />
  ```

- This specifies the icon that appears in the browser tab. The type="image/png" specifies the type of the icon file, and href="favicon.png" is the path to the icon file. The icon itself can be found in the wwwroot folder.

  ```
  <HeadOutlet @rendermode="InteractiveServer" />
  ```

- This tag is specific to Blazor. The HeadOutlet component is used to manage the content of the <head> element dynamically. The @rendermode="InteractiveServer" attribute specifies that the content will be rendered interactively on the server. More on this in this chapter, and the RenderModes chapter.

PageTitle

Open the Home component from the provided BlazorApp.Headers solution, shown in Listing 9-5. On the third line, you can see the <PageTitle> built-in component, which will set the <title> element in the <head> section of the rendered HTML page. The Counter component uses the same <PageTitle> component but with different content.

Listing 9-5. The Home component using the PageTitle component

```
@page "/"

<PageTitle>Home</PageTitle>

<h1>Hello, world!</h1>

Welcome to your new app.
```

Run the demo project. You will see that the `<head>` element now contains the `<title>` element, which is used to set the title of the browser's tab, as shown in Figure 9-4.

@ Home

Figure 9-4. The browser's tab showing the title

HeadContent and HeadOutlet

If you need to set additional elements in the `<head>` element of the rendered page, you can use the built-in `<HeadContent>` component.

Let's say you need to set some additional metadata on the Counter page. Listing 9-6 shows the use of the `<HeadContent>` component. This will set an additional `<meta>` element in the page. Where does this end up? Listing 9-4 contains the `<HeadOutlet>` and whatever you put in `<HeadContent>` gets rendered inside `<HeadOutlet>`.

Listing 9-6. Using the HeadContent

```
@page "/counter"

<PageTitle>Counter</PageTitle>

<h1>Counter</h1>

<p role="status">Current count: @currentCount</p>

<button class="btn btn-primary" @onclick="IncrementCount">Click me</button>

<HeadContent>
  <meta name="description" content="@CounterTitle">
</HeadContent>
```

257

CHAPTER 9 BUILT-IN COMPONENTS

```
@code {
  private int currentCount = 0;

  private string CounterTitle => $"Counter {currentCount}";

    private void IncrementCount()
    {
        currentCount++;
    }
}
```

Dynamic Components

Sometimes you might not know the component which you need to render a UI. Maybe you need to wait for the user to make a choice, and then you display the component, depending on the user's choice. How would you do that? You could use an elaborate `if` statement for each choice, but this will become a maintenance nightmare soon! However, Blazor now has the `DynamicComponent` component that makes it easy to select a component at run-time. Imagine you want to open a pet hotel, so people need to be able to register their pet(s). Initially you will board cats and dogs, but in the long run you might want to board other animals.

Create a new Blazor Web App project named BlazorApp.PetHotel. Here is the PowerShell script:

```
$ProjectName = "BlazorApp.PetHotel"
mkdir $ProjectName
cd $ProjectName
dotnet new sln -n $ProjectName
mkdir src
cd src
dotnet new blazor -n $ProjectName --all-interactive --interactivity Server
cd ..
dotnet sln add src\$ProjectName
```

Create a Data folder in the project and add the `AnimalKind` enumeration from Listing 9-7.

Listing 9-7. An AnimalKind enumeration

```
namespace BlazorApp.PetHotel.Data;

public enum AnimalKind
{
  Unknown,
  Dog,
  Cat
}
```

Next you add classes from Listing 9-8 for each kind of Animal, using inheritance to make it easier to reuse some of the properties.

Listing 9-8. Different kinds of animals

```
namespace BlazorApp.PetHotel.Data;

public class Animal
{
  public string Name { get; set; } = string.Empty;
}

public class Cat : Animal
{
  public bool Scratches { get; set; }
}

public class Dog : Animal
{
  public bool IsAGoodDog { get; set; }
}
```

You also need some components, one for each kind of animal. Let us start with the base component for Animal which is in Listing 9-9. Yes, you can also use inheritance with Blazor components if they somehow inherit from ComponentBase!

CHAPTER 9   BUILT-IN COMPONENTS

Listing 9-9. The base AnimalComponent

```
using Microsoft.AspNetCore.Components;

namespace BlazorApp.PetHotel.Components;

public class AnimalComponent : ComponentBase
{
  [Parameter]
  public EventCallback ValidSubmit { get; set; }
}
```

Now we derive from this the `CatComponent` as in Listing 9-10. All of this should be familiar by now, except that in the markup you will see the syntax to inherit from another component: the `@inherits AnimalComponent` tells the compiler to derive from `AnimalComponent` instead of `ComponentBase`. I also added images of a happy dog and cat to the wwwroot/images folder.

Listing 9-10. The CatComponent code

```
@inherits AnimalComponent
@using BlazorApp.PetHotel.Data

<img src="images/Cat.png"/>

<EditForm Model="@Instance"
          OnValidSubmit="@ValidSubmit"
          FormName="cat-form">

  <DataAnnotationsValidator />

  <fieldset>
    <div class="row mb-2">
      <label class="col-2" for="name">Name:</label>
      <InputText class="form-control col-6"
                 @bind-Value="@Instance.Name" />
    </div>
    <div class="row mb-2">
      <div class="col-6 offset-2">
        <ValidationMessage For="@(() => Instance.Name)" />
```

```
      </div>
    </div>
    <div class="row mb-2">
      <label class="col-2 form-check-label"
         for="scratches">Scratches</label>
      <div class="col-1 pl-0 w-auto">
        <InputCheckbox class="form-check-input col-6"
                    @bind-Value="@Instance.Scratches" />
      </div>
    </div>
    <div class="row mb-2">
      <div class="col-2">
        <button class="btn btn-success">Save</button>
      </div>
    </div>
  </fieldset>
</EditForm>

@code {
  [Parameter]
  public Cat Instance { get; set; } = default!;
}
```

In a very similar fashion (meaning you can copy-paste most of this), we have the DogComponent in Listing 9-11.

Listing 9-11. The DogComponent

```
@inherits AnimalComponent
@using BlazorApp.PetHotel.Data

<img src="images/Dog.png" />

<EditForm Model="@Instance"
          OnValidSubmit="@ValidSubmit">

  <DataAnnotationsValidator />

  <fieldset>
```

```
    <div class="row mb-2">
      <label class="col-2" for="name">Name:</label>
      <InputText class="form-control col-3"
                 @bind-Value="@Instance.Name" />
    </div>
    <div class="row mb-2">
      <div class="col-6 offset-2">
        <ValidationMessage For="@(() => Instance.Name)" />
      </div>
    </div>
    <div class="row mb-2">
      <label class="col-2 form-check-label"
             for="scratches">Is a good dog</label>
      <div class="col-1 pl-0 w-auto">
        <InputCheckbox class="form-check-input col-2"
                       @bind-Value="@Instance.IsAGoodDog" />
      </div>
    </div>
    <div class="row mb-2">
      <div class="col-2">
        <button class="btn btn-success">Save</button>
      </div>
    </div>
  </fieldset>
</EditForm>

@code {
  [Parameter]
  public Dog Instance { get; set; } = default!;
}
```

Now add a new component called `AnimalSelector` as in Listing 9-12. This is the component where we will use the `DynamicComponent`. Why? Because we will ask the user to select a kind of animal, and then we will display the component that matches that animal.

Listing 9-12. The AnimalSelector component

```
@using BlazorApp.PetHotel.Data

<div class="row">
  <div class="col-2">
    Please select:
  </div>
  <div class="col-6 pl-0 pr-0">
    <select class="form-control"
      @onchange="@((ChangeEventArgs e)
        => AnimalSelected(e.Value))">
      @foreach (AnimalKind kind in
        Enum.GetValues(typeof(AnimalKind)))
      {
        <option value="@kind">@kind.ToString()</option>
      }
    </select>
  </div>
</div>

@code {
  ComponentMetadata? Metadata;

  private void AnimalSelected(object? value)
  {
    string? val = value?.ToString();
    if (Enum.TryParse<AnimalKind>(val, out AnimalKind kind))
    {
      Metadata = kind.ToMetadata();
    }
  }
}
```

What does ComponentMetadata from Listing 9-13 contain? It contains a Type property (yes, of type Type) and a Parameters property of type Dictionary<string,object>.

These are used by DynamicComponent to select a Component to display (e.g., when Type is CatComponent, the DynamicComponent will replace itself with the CatComponent).

CHAPTER 9   BUILT-IN COMPONENTS

Now `CatComponent` has a `[Parameter]` property (called `Instance`), so `DynamicComponent` needs to provide this parameter. The `ComponentMetadata`'s `Parameters` dictionary will contain a key called `Instance`, with the value set for the `Instance` parameter.

Listing 9-13. The ComponentMetaData class

```
namespace BlazorApp.PetHotel.Data;

public class ComponentMetadata
{
  public ComponentMetadata(Type type,
    Dictionary<string, object> parameters)
  {
    Type = type;
    Parameters = parameters;
  }

  public Type Type { get; set; }

  public Dictionary<string, object> Parameters { get; }
}
```

One more thing to complete this example: Look at the `AnimalSelected` method from Listing 9-12. How do we convert the `AnimalKind` to a `ComponentMetadata` instance? For this I have an `ToMetadata` extension method in class `AnimalMetadata` from Listing 9-14. This method uses the new C# pattern matching `switch-expression` statement which is ideal for this kind of thing (https://learn.microsoft.com/en-us/dotnet/csharp/language-reference/operators/switch-expression). Here we switch on the `AnimalKind` value. If it is a `Dog`, we return the `ComponentMetadata` for a dog, similar for a `Cat`, and for all the rest (using the _ discard syntax), we return a `null` value.

Listing 9-14. The AnimalMetaData class

```
using BlazorApp.PetHotel.Components;
using Microsoft.AspNetCore.Components;

namespace BlazorApp.PetHotel.Data;

public static class AnimalMetadata
```

```
{
  private static Dictionary<string, object> ToParameters(
    this object instance)
    => new Dictionary<string, object>
      {
        [nameof(DynamicComponent.Instance)] = instance
      };

  public static ComponentMetadata? ToMetadata(this AnimalKind animal)
    => animal switch
    {
      AnimalKind.Dog => new ComponentMetadata(
        typeof(DogComponent),
        new Dog().ToParameters()
      ),
      AnimalKind.Cat => new ComponentMetadata(
        typeof(CatComponent),
        new Cat().ToParameters()
      ),
      _ => null
    };
}
```

To complete the `AnimalSelector` component, we will look at the value of the `Metadata` property (in Listing 9-12) and use a `DynamicComponent` to select the appropriate component for the selected animal and set its parameters as in Listing 9-15.

Listing 9-15. Completing the AnimalSelector component

```
@using BlazorApp.PetHotel.Data

<div class="row">
  <div class="col-2">
    Please select:
  </div>
  <div class="col-6 pl-0 pr-0">
    <select class="form-control"
```

CHAPTER 9   BUILT-IN COMPONENTS

```
      @onchange="@((ChangeEventArgs e)
        => AnimalSelected(e.Value))">
      @foreach (AnimalKind kind in
        Enum.GetValues(typeof(AnimalKind)))
      {
        <option value="@kind">@kind.ToString()</option>
      }
    </select>
  </div>
</div>

@if (Metadata is not null)
{
  <div class="mt-2">
    <DynamicComponent
      Type="@Metadata.Type"
      Parameters="@Metadata.Parameters" />
  </div>
}

@code {
  ComponentMetadata? Metadata;

  private void AnimalSelected(object? value)
  {
    string? val = value?.ToString();
    if (Enum.TryParse<AnimalKind>(val, out AnimalKind kind))
    {
      Metadata = kind.ToMetadata();
    }
  }
}
```

Add the `AnimalSelector` to your Home component (as in Listing 9-16).

CHAPTER 9 BUILT-IN COMPONENTS

Listing 9-16. The Index component with AnimalSelector

```
@page "/"

<PageTitle>Pet Hotel</PageTitle>

<h1>What kind of pet?</h1>

<AnimalSelector />
```

Run the application. Now when you select a dog, the appropriate editor is shown as in Figure 9-5.

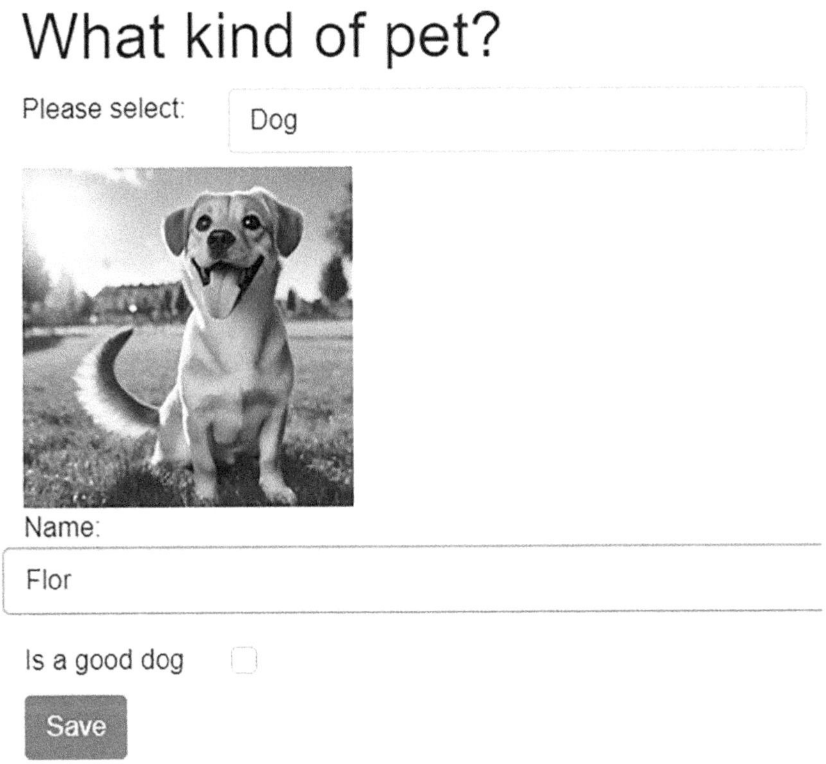

Figure 9-5. *The AnimalSelector after selecting a dog*

267

Uploading Files with InputFile

In the Forms chapter, we looked at all kinds of input components, but there is one more. The built-in <InputFile> component allows the uploading of files into the browser. It will render an <input> element of type file. When the user clicks the component, a file open dialog is displayed, where the user can select one or more files, after which the component's OnChange event triggers.

Let us look at an example, either use the provided files, or create your own Web App project using the following PowerShell script:

```
$ProjectName = "BlazorApp.UploadingFiles"
mkdir $ProjectName
cd $ProjectName
dotnet new sln -n $ProjectName
dotnet new globaljson
mkdir src
dotnet new blazor -n $ProjectName -o src -int Auto
dotnet sln add ".\src\$ProjectName\"
dotnet sln add ".\src\$ProjectName.Client\"
```

This will generate a solution with two projects, one for rendering the component on the server and one for rendering the component in the browser using WASM. The Client project in this case will hold components which can render using Server rendering, but also using WASM rendering (and auto rendering). More on this in the RenderModes chapter.

Add the InputFile Component

Add the UploadFiles razor component to the Client project, as in Listing 9-17. This component uses the <InputFile> component and allows you to upload multiple files. The actual processing of the files is done through a service with the IUploadService interface, which we will add next.

Listing 9-17. The UploadFiles component

```
<InputFile OnChange="@LoadFiles" multiple />

@LoadingStatus()

@if (loadedFiles.Any())
{
  <ul>
    @foreach (var file in loadedFiles)
    {
      <li>
        <ul>
          <li>Name: @file.Name</li>
          <li>Last modified: @file.LastModified.ToString()</li>
          <li>Size (bytes): @file.Size</li>
          <li>Content type: @file.ContentType</li>
        </ul>
      </li>
    }
  </ul>
}

@code
{
  [Inject]
  public required IUploadService UploadService { get; set; }

  private bool isLoading = false;
  private bool loadingComplete = false;

  private List<IBrowserFile> loadedFiles = [];

  private RenderFragment LoadingStatus()
  => (isLoading, loadingComplete) switch
  {
    (true, false) => @<div class="loading-container"><div class="loading-bar">
    </div><p class="loading-text">Uploading files...</p></div>,
```

CHAPTER 9 BUILT-IN COMPONENTS

```
    (true, true) => @<div class="loading-container"><div class="loaded-
    bar"></div><p class="loading-text">Loading complete...</p></div>,
    _ =>@<p></p>
};

private async void LoadFiles(InputFileChangeEventArgs e)
{
    isLoading = true;
    loadingComplete = false;
    // Emulate a bit slow network
    await Task.Delay(5000);
    loadedFiles = await UploadService.LoadFilesAsync(e);
    loadingComplete = true;
    StateHasChanged();
    }
}
```

The UploadFiles component also uses some styles from Listing 19-18 bis, so add these in the UploadFiles.razor.css file by copying this file from the provided sources.

Listing 19-18. bis. The UploadFiles component's style

```
.loading-container {
  width: 30em;
  height: 30px;
  background-color: #f0f0f0;
  position: relative;
  overflow: hidden;
  margin-top: 1em;
  margin-bottom: 1em;
}
.loading-text {
  position: absolute;
  top: 0;
  left: 0;
  width: 100%;
  height: 100%;
```

```css
  display: flex;
  align-items: center;
  justify-content: center;
  font-size: 18px;
  color: white;
  z-index: 1;
}

.loading-bar {
  position: absolute;
  top: 0;
  left: 0;
  height: 100%;
  width: 0;
  background-color: #007bff;
  animation: load 2s linear infinite;
  z-index: 0;
}

.loaded-bar {
  position: absolute;
  top: 0;
  left: 0;
  height: 100%;
  width: 100%;
  background-color: #007bff;
  animation: pulse 5s infinite;
  z-index: 0;
}

@keyframes pulse {
  0% {
    background-color: #007bff;
  }

  50% {
    background-color: #66b2ff;
  }
```

```
      100% {
        background-color: #007bff;
      }
    }
    @keyframes load {
      to {
        width: 100%;
      }
    }
```

Implement the Server UploadService

Now we need something to process the files, and for this we will need two implementations, one running on the server where we can access the file system, and one for running in the browser. Add a new IUploadService interface to the Client projects as shown in Listing 9-19. This way the IUploadService interface is known to both projects.

Listing 9-19. The IUploadService interface

```
using Microsoft.AspNetCore.Components.Forms;

namespace BlazorApp.UploadingFiles.Client;

public interface IUploadService
{
    ValueTask<List<IBrowserFile>> LoadFilesAsync(InputFileChangeEventArgs e);
}
```

The InputFileChangeEventArgs gives access to the files as IBrowserFile instances, with details about each file. Let us use these files.

In the Server project (BlazorApp.UploadingFiles), add a new Services folder and add the ServerUploadService class to it from Listing 9-20. The LoadFilesAsync method takes the InputFileChangeEventArgs instance and iterates over the files.

CHAPTER 9 BUILT-IN COMPONENTS

Listing 9-20. The Server UploadService

```
using BlazorApp.UploadingFiles.Client;
using Microsoft.AspNetCore.Components.Forms;

namespace BlazorApp.UploadingFiles.Services;

public class ServerUploadService : IUploadService
{
  private const int maxAllowedFiles = 10;
  private const int maxFileSize = 10_000_000;
  private readonly IWebHostEnvironment _environment;
  private readonly ILogger<ServerUploadService> _logger;

  public ServerUploadService(IWebHostEnvironment environment,
    ILogger<ServerUploadService> logger)
  {
    _environment = environment;
    _logger = logger;
  }

  public async ValueTask<List<IBrowserFile>>
    LoadFilesAsync(InputFileChangeEventArgs e)
  {
    List<IBrowserFile> loadedFiles = [];

    foreach (IBrowserFile file in e.GetMultipleFiles(maxAllowedFiles))
    {
      try
      {
        loadedFiles.Add(file);

        string trustedFileNameForFileStorage = Path.GetRandomFileName();
        string path = Path.Combine(_environment.ContentRootPath,
            _environment.EnvironmentName, "Uploads",
            trustedFileNameForFileStorage);

        await using FileStream fs = new(path, FileMode.Create);
        await file.OpenReadStream(maxFileSize).CopyToAsync(fs);
      }
```

273

CHAPTER 9   BUILT-IN COMPONENTS

```
      catch (Exception ex)
      {
        _logger.LogError("File: {Filename} Error: {Error}", file.Name,
          ex.Message);
      }
    }
    return loadedFiles;
  }
}
```

Add this as a dependency injected Singleton to the Server project:

```
builder.Services
  .AddSingleton<IUploadService, ServerUploadService>();
```

You will also need to add a .gitkeep file to the new Development/Uploads folder, which you also need to create. The .gitkeep file tells git source control to keep the folder.

Before running, one more thing. Add the `FileUpload` component to the Home component as in Listing 9-21: this uses the `rendermode` directive to tell Blazor that this component needs to run on the server.

Listing 9-21. Using the UploadFiles component

```
@page "/"

<PageTitle>Home</PageTitle>

<h1>Upload some files</h1>

<UploadFiles @rendermode="InteractiveServer" />
```

Now run. You should be able to upload some files to the server, as shown in Figure 9-6.

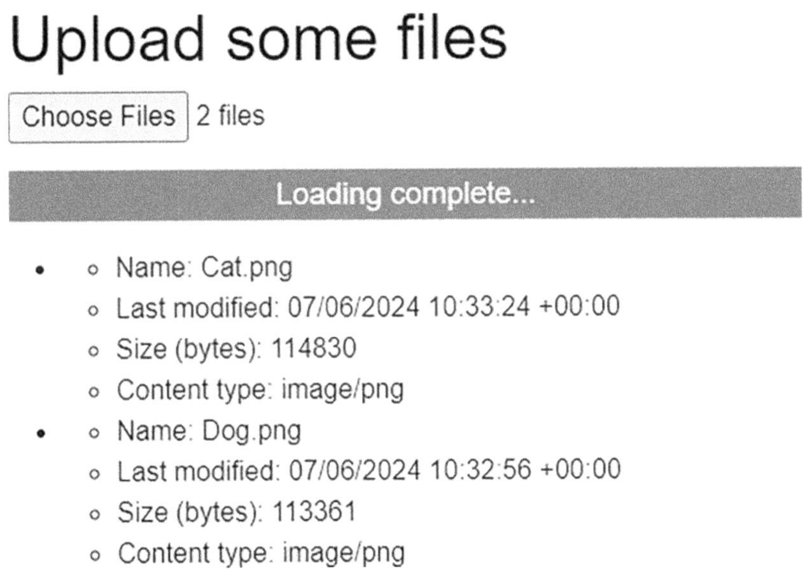

CHAPTER 9 BUILT-IN COMPONENTS

Upload some files

Choose Files | 2 files

Loading complete...

- - Name: Cat.png
  - Last modified: 07/06/2024 10:33:24 +00:00
  - Size (bytes): 114830
  - Content type: image/png
- - Name: Dog.png
  - Last modified: 07/06/2024 10:32:56 +00:00
  - Size (bytes): 113361
  - Content type: image/png

Figure 9-6. The FileUpload in action

Note There are limits to the size of the files allowed to be uploaded!

Implement the WASM UploadService

We can also upload files to a Blazor application running WASM. In this case, we cannot access the local filesystem, but we can still do useful things!

Add a new Services folder to the Client project, and inside add the WASMUploadService class from Listing 9-22. This service here only creates a list of uploaded files; in a real situation, you could process these files, for example, red-eye removal, spell-checking, build your own AI like ChatGPT, etc. Also update dependency injection like Listing 9-23.

Listing 9-22. The WASMUploadService class

```
using Microsoft.AspNetCore.Components.Forms;

namespace BlazorApp.UploadingFiles.Client.Services;

public class WASMUploadService : IUploadService
```

CHAPTER 9   BUILT-IN COMPONENTS

```csharp
{
  private const int maxAllowedFiles = 10;
  private const int maxFileSize = 10_000_000;
  private readonly ILogger<WASMUploadService> _logger;

  public WASMUploadService
    (ILogger<WASMUploadService> logger)
  {
    _logger = logger;
  }

  public ValueTask<List<IBrowserFile>> LoadFilesAsync
    (InputFileChangeEventArgs e)
  {
    List<IBrowserFile> loadedFiles = [];
    foreach (var file in e.GetMultipleFiles(maxAllowedFiles))
    {
      try
      {
        loadedFiles.Add(file);
      }
      catch (Exception ex)
      {
        _logger.LogError("File: {FileName} Error: {Error}",
            file.Name, ex.Message);
      }
    }
    return ValueTask.FromResult(loadedFiles);
  }
}
```

Listing 9-23. Using dependency injection

```csharp
using BlazorApp.UploadingFiles.Client;
using BlazorApp.UploadingFiles.Client.Services;
using Microsoft.AspNetCore.Components.WebAssembly.Hosting;
```

CHAPTER 9 BUILT-IN COMPONENTS

```
var builder = WebAssemblyHostBuilder.CreateDefault(args);

// Add this line
builder.Services.AddSingleton<IUploadService, WASMUploadService>();

await builder.Build().RunAsync();
```

Update the Home component to use WebAssembly, as in Listing 9-24.

Listing 9-24. Switching to WebAssembly

```
<UploadFiles @rendermode="InteractiveWebAssembly" />
```

Run. You get a similar experience.

QuickGrid

Most of the Blazor Component Libraries like MudBlazor have a grid component to show data as a table (like Excel). ASP.NET Blazor also comes with one of these: QuickGrid.

QuickGrid makes it simple to bind to data and gives us filtering, sorting, and paging with minimal effort.

Let us build a Blazor Web App with some data and QuickGrid. The provided sources contain a starter solution and project, so get a copy.

The Starter Project

The Starter project contains the Employee class from Listing 9-25. Here I use records since these types are used to serialize and deserialize JSON received from a REST service.

Listing 9-25. The Employee record and its parts

```
namespace BlazorApp.QuickGridDemo.Entities;

public record class Name(string Title, string First, string Last);

public record class Picture(string Large, string Medium, string Thumbnail);

public record class Dob(DateTime Date, int Age);

public record class Employee(Name Name, Dob Dob, Picture Picture);
```

CHAPTER 9 BUILT-IN COMPONENTS

There is also an EmployeeService with a GetEmployees method as shown in Listing 9-26. We will discuss communication with REST services in the Communication chapter.

Listing 9-26. The EmployeeService

```
using BlazorApp.QuickGridDemo.Entities;

namespace BlazorApp.QuickGridDemo.Services;

public class EmployeeService
{
  private readonly IHttpClientFactory _clientFactory;
  private readonly ILogger<EmployeeService> _logger;

  public EmployeeService(IHttpClientFactory clientFactory,
    ILogger<EmployeeService> logger)
  {
    _clientFactory = clientFactory;
    _logger = logger;
  }

  public async Task<IEnumerable<Employee>> GetEmployees(
    int? results, int? page = null)
  {
    HttpClient httpClient =
      _clientFactory.CreateClient(nameof(EmployeeService));

    string queryString = "?seed=u2u";
    if (results.HasValue)
    {
      queryString = $"{queryString}&results={results.Value}";
    }
    if (page.HasValue)
    {
      queryString = $"{queryString}&page={page.Value}";
    }
    RandomUserResult? result =
```

```
    await httpClient.GetFromJsonAsync<RandomUserResult>(queryString);
  return result!.Results;
  }
}
```

Open the Home component and inject this service into it as in Listing 9-27.

Listing 9-27. Injecting the EmployeeService in the Home component

```
[Inject]
public required EmployeeService EmployeeService { get; set; }
```

Override the OnInitializedAsync method on the Home component to load the employees from Listing 9-28. This uses a free Internet service randomuser.me which generates random user data.

Listing 9-28. Fetching the Employees from the service

```
private IQueryable<Employee>? employees = null;

protected override async Task OnInitializedAsync()
{
  employees = (await EmployeeService.GetEmployees(100)).AsQueryable();
}
```

QuickGrid requires the data to be presented as an IQueryable<T>.

Add a Simple QuickGrid

Now we have everything in place to load several sample employees, and we can use QuickGrid to show a simple list.

The QuickGrid component lives in the Microsoft.AspNetCore.Components. QuickGrid NuGet package, so install it in the project. Add a QuickGrid component to the Home component with four columns as shown in Listing 9-29 which shows the complete Home component.

- The QuickGrid component has an Items property which is of type IQuerable<TGridItem>. Set this property to the collection of items you want displayed. The collection could be, for example, an Entity Framework Core query, of a list of items wrapped as an IQueryable.

CHAPTER 9   BUILT-IN COMPONENTS

- QuickGrid has two kinds of columns: `PropertyColumn` and `TemplateColumn`. You can also build your own kind of column; simply derive it from `ColumnBase`.

- `PropertyColumn` displays the value of the property, specified by the `Property` parameter. You pass the property using a lambda expression, for example, `<PropertyColumn Property="@(item => item.Title)" />`. The `Title` of the column is derived from the name of the property. You can also specify a `Format`, which is the format string passed to the `IFormattable` interface.

- `TemplateColumn` will be discussed further on in this chapter.

Listing 9-29. Using QuickGrid with PropertyColumn

```
@page "/"
@using BlazorApp.QuickGridDemo.Entities
@using BlazorApp.QuickGridDemo.Services
@using Microsoft.AspNetCore.Components.QuickGrid

<PageTitle>Using QuickGrid</PageTitle>

<h1>Hello colleagues!</h1>

@if (employees is null)
{
  <div><Loading /></div>
}
else
{
  <!-- Add a simple quickgrid -->
  <QuickGrid Items="@employees">
    <PropertyColumn Property="@(p => p.Name.Title)" />
    <PropertyColumn Property="@(p => p.Name.First)" />
    <PropertyColumn Property="@(p => p.Name.Last)" />
    <PropertyColumn Property="@(p => p.Dob.Date)" Format="yyyy-MM-dd" />
  </QuickGrid>
}
```

```
@code {

  [Inject]
  public required EmployeeService EmployeeService { get; set; }

  private IQueryable<Employee>? employees = null;

  protected override async Task OnInitializedAsync()
  {
    employees = (await EmployeeService.GetEmployees(100)).AsQueryable();
  }
}
```

This uses a Loading component which displays some loading UI (thanks to https://tobiasahlin.com/spinkit which contains a nice bunch of spinners).

Run. You should see a list of employees, with an example shown in Figure 9-7.

Hello colleagues!

Title	First	Last	Date
Monsieur	Rocco	Michel	1974-04-16
Ms	Buse	Köylüoğlu	1968-03-25
Mr	Hette	Van der Snoek	1950-02-06
Ms	Phoebe	Holland	1993-12-09
Mrs	Gopika	Kaur	1998-07-29
Mr	Matias	Remes	1970-04-23
Miss	Natalia	Zamora	1968-01-14

Figure 9-7. A simple list of Employees using QuickGrid

Sort Columns

QuickGrid allows you to easily sort columns. Let us add some.

Update the QuickGrid by making the columns sortable through setting the Sortable and optional InitialSortDirection parameter of PropertyColumn as shown in Listing 9-30.

Listing 9-30. Making columns sortable

```
<!-- Enable sorting -->
<QuickGrid Items="@_employees">
  <PropertyColumn Property="@(p => p.Name.Title)" />
  <PropertyColumn Property="@(p => p.Name.First)"
                  Sortable="true"
                  InitialSortDirection="SortDirection.Ascending" />
  <PropertyColumn Property="@(p => p.Name.Last)"
                  Sortable="true" />
  <PropertyColumn Property="@(p => p.Dob.Date)"
                  Format="yyyy-MM-dd"
                  Sortable="true" />
</QuickGrid>
```

Run. You can now sort the columns as shown in Figure 9-8.

Hello colleagues!

Title	First ⋀	Last	Date
Mrs	Aada	Ojala	1971-03-06
Mr	Aiden	Edwards	1972-08-13
Mr	Aleksi	Elo	1970-04-15
Miss	Alex	Lawson	1990-09-12
Ms	Alicja	Haakonsen	1987-11-29
Mrs	Amber	Wood	1962-02-05

Figure 9-8. *Sorting by first name*

Use Template Columns

Our employee data also comes with image URLs. So, let's display each employee's image.

For this we need to use a `TemplateColumn`, which uses a `RenderFragment` to render the cell's content. Since it cannot infer the `Title`, you need to supply this as well.

`TemplateColumn` has additional parameters:

- `Align`: To align the column `Align.Left/Center /Start/End`.

CHAPTER 9   BUILT-IN COMPONENTS

- **Class**: To set the CSS class on the header and body cells.
- **ColumnOptions**: Again a RenderFragment that gets displayed when the user clicks on the "column options" button.
- **HeaderTemplate**: A RenderFragment to set the header's content. In this case, you are also responsible for setting the sort indicator, and you need to call the grid's SortByColumnAsync method if the header is clicked.
- **InitialSortDirection**: The default sort direction, choose between SortDirection.Ascending, SortDirection.Descending, and SortDirection.Auto.
- **IsDefaultSortColumn**: Should QuickGrid sort by this column by default.
- **PlaceHolderTemplate**: A RenderFragment to be used while data is loading. This only applies to virtualized grids.
- **Sortable**: Indicate with true or false if the column should support sorting. The default value of this property depends on the column type and options.

Add a template column with a title and centered image as in Listing 9-31.

Listing 9-31. Displaying a picture in a TemplateColumn

```
<!-- Add a picture column using template column -->
<QuickGrid Items="@_employees">
  ...
  <PropertyColumn Property="@(p => p.Dob.Date)"
                  Format="yyyy-MM-dd"
                  Sortable="true" />
  <TemplateColumn Title="Picture" Align="Align.Left">
    <img class="picture" src="@context.Picture.Thumbnail" />
  </TemplateColumn>
</QuickGrid>
```

You can give the user the option to show or hide certain columns simply by using @if, for example, see Listing 9-32.

283

Listing 9-32. Using checkboxes to show or hire columns

```
@page "/"
@using BlazorApp.QuickGridDemo.Entities
@using BlazorApp.QuickGridDemo.Services
@using Microsoft.AspNetCore.Components.QuickGrid

<PageTitle>Using QuickGrid</PageTitle>

<h1>Hello colleagues!</h1>

@if (employees is null)
{
  <div><Loading /></div>
}
else
{
  <!-- Let the user decide which columns to see -->
  <p>
    Show:
    <label><input type="checkbox" @bind="showBirthdate" /> Birth
    date</label>
    <label><input type="checkbox" @bind="showPicture" /> Picture</label>
  </p>

  <!-- Add a picture column using template column -->
  <QuickGrid Items="@employees">
    <PropertyColumn Property="@(p => p.Name.Title)" />
    <PropertyColumn Property="@(p => p.Name.First)"
                    Sortable="true"
                    InitialSortDirection="SortDirection.Ascending" />
    <PropertyColumn Property="@(p => p.Name.Last)"
                    Sortable="true" />
    @if (showBirthdate)
    {
      <PropertyColumn Property="@(p => p.Dob.Date)"
      Format="yyyy-MM-dd"
      Sortable="true" />
```

```
    }
    @if (showPicture)
    {
      <TemplateColumn Title="Picture" Align="Align.Center" >
        <img class="picture" src="@context.Picture.Thumbnail" />
      </TemplateColumn>
    }
  </QuickGrid>
}

@code {
  [Inject]
  public required EmployeeService EmployeeService { get; set; }

  private IQueryable<Employee>? employees = null;
  private bool showBirthdate = true;
  private bool showPicture = true;

  protected override async Task OnInitializedAsync()
  {
    employees = (await EmployeeService.GetEmployees(100)).AsQueryable();
  }
}
```

This also requires some CSS, as in Listing 9-33.

Listing 9-33. The Home component's CSS

```
img.picture {
  border: 8px solid #006bb7;
  border-radius: 8px;
}

label{
  gap: 0.5rem;
  border: 1px solid #aaa;
  padding: 0.3rem 0.75rem;
  margin-left: 0.5rem;
  border-radius: 0.5rem;
```

```
display: inline-flex;
align-items: center;
background: rgba(0,0,0,0.04);
cursor: pointer;
}
```

The result should look like Figure 9-9.

Hello colleagues!

Show: ☑ Birth date   ☑ Picture

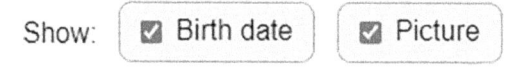

Figure 9-9. *Showing and hiding columns*

Add Filtered Columns

`QuickGrid` requires you to set up your own user interface and logic for filtering. It does allow you to place the filter UI using the `ColumnOptions` parameter.

We want to add filtering on first name and on age. Let us start with first name. Add a field that will contain the filter, as shown in Listing 9-34.

Listing 9-34. Adding a name filter

```
[Inject]
public required EmployeeService EmployeeService { get; set; }

private IQueryable<Employee>? employees = null;
private bool showBirthdate = true;
private bool showPicture = true;
// Add this for filtering
private string nameFilter = string.Empty;

protected override async Task OnInitializedAsync()
{
  employees = (await EmployeeService.GetEmployees(100)).AsQueryable();
}
```

Add a `ColumnOptions` to the first name column to display a search box as in Listing 9-35.

Listing 9-35. Adding ColumnOptions

```
<PropertyColumn Property="@(p => p.Name.First)"
                Sortable="true">
  <ColumnOptions>
    <div class="search-box">
      <input type="search" autofocus @bind="nameFilter"
        @bind:event="oninput" placeholder="filter..." />
    </div>
  </ColumnOptions>
</PropertyColumn>
```

We also need a `FilteredEmployees` property as in Listing 9-36 which takes the filter.

Listing 9-36. Adding the FilteredEmployees property

```
private IQueryable<Employee> FilteredEmployees
{
  get
  {
    IQueryable<Employee> result = employees!;
    if (nameFilter is { Length: > 0 })
    {
      result = result.Where(e => e.Name.First
        .Contains(nameFilter, StringComparison.CurrentCultureIgnoreCase));
    }
    return result;
  }
}
```

Update the `QuickGrid` component to use the `FilteredEmployees` as in Listing 9-37.

Listing 9-37. Make QuickGrid use the FilteredEmployees.

```
<QuickGrid Items="@FilteredEmployees">
```

You can now filter on first name, as illustrated by Figure 9-10.

Chapter 9 Built-in Components

Hello colleagues!

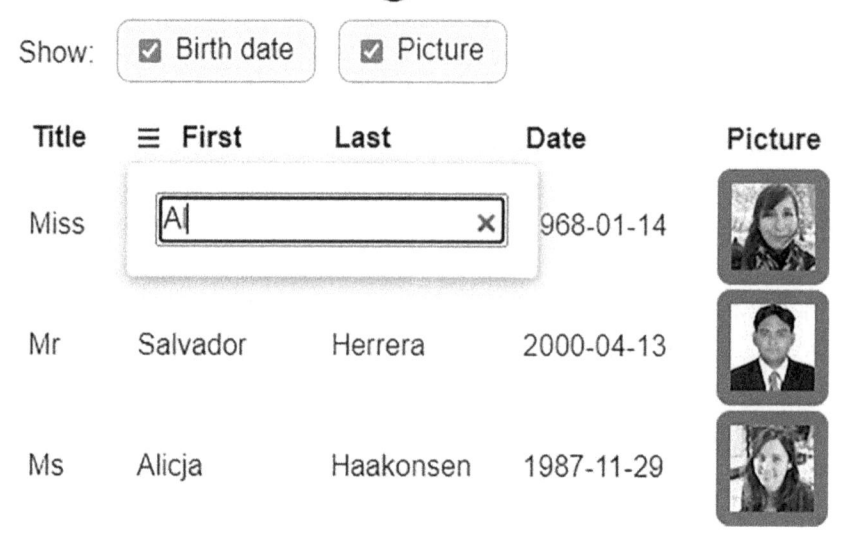

Figure 9-10. Filtering on first name

Add more `ColumnOptions`, but now for the Age column, as shown in Listing 9-38.

Listing 9-38. Additional filtering on age

```
<PropertyColumn Property="@(p => p.Dob.Date)"
  Format="yyyy-MM-dd"
  Sortable="true" >
  <ColumnOptions>
    <p>
      Min: <input type="range" @bind="minAgeFilter"
                  @bind:event="oninput" min="20" max="30" />
      <span class="inline-block w-10">@minAgeFilter</span>
    </p>
    <p>
      Max: <input type="range" @bind="maxAgeFilter"
                  @bind:event="oninput" min="30" max="100" />
      <span class="inline-block w-10">@maxAgeFilter</span>
    </p>
  </ColumnOptions>
</PropertyColumn>
```

Implement the filter by changing the FilteredEmployees as shown in Listing 9-39.

Listing 9-39. Filter by age.

```
private int minAgeFilter = 20;
private int maxAgeFilter = 100;

...

IQueryable<Employee> result = _employees!
  .Where(e => e.Dob.Age >= minAgeFilter
     && e.Dob.Age <= maxAgeFilter);
```

Run. You can filter by name and/or age.

Fix Layout

When you move the sliders, you will see your UI jumping back and forth. Let us fix this. Start by wrapping the QuickGrid in a <div>, and add a Class parameter to First and Last columns; see Listing 9-40 for details.

Listing 9-40. Adding class parameters

```
<div>
  <QuickGrid Items="@FilteredEmployees">
    <PropertyColumn Property="@(p => p.Name.Title)" />
    <PropertyColumn Property="@(p => p.Name.First)"
                    Sortable="true" Class="first-name"
                    InitialSortDirection=
                       "SortDirection.Ascending">
        ...
    </PropertyColumn>
    <PropertyColumn Property="@(p => p.Name.Last)"
                    Sortable="true" Class="last-name" />
    ...
  </QuickGrid>
</div>
```

We need to add more styles to the Home.razor.css file, as in Listing 9-41.

CHAPTER 9   BUILT-IN COMPONENTS

Listing 9-41. Using CSS to set table and column width

```
...
::deep table {
  min-width: 100%;
}
::deep th.first-name {
  width: 14rem;
}
::deep th.last-name {
  width: 20rem;
}
```

Note the use of ::deep. This will make the CSS rule apply to any child of the Home component.

Run. The table will now take the full width of the browser.

Add Pagination

Let us add some pagination to QuickGrid. As you will see, this is really simple.

Add a PaginationState to the Home component, as shown in Listing 9-42.

Listing 9-42. Adding a PaginationState

```
[Inject]
public required EmployeeService EmployeeService { get; set; }
PaginationState pagination = new PaginationState { ItemsPerPage = 10 };
```

Set the Pagination parameter of QuickGrid and the Paginator component below QuickGrid as per Listing 9-43.

Listing 9-43. Adding the Paginator

```
<QuickGrid Items="@FilteredEmployees" Pagination="@pagination">
...
<Paginator State="@pagination" />
```

Run to see the pagination at work!

Use Virtualization

Remember the `Virtualize` component from the Advanced Components chapter? You can also set the `ItemsProvider` just like the `Virtualize`.

Summary

In this chapter, we looked at what kind of components are out there. First, we looked at existing component libraries which give you a rich choice of common UI controls. Then we looked at components which come out of the box such as the `InputFile` component. Finally, we looked at QuickGrid, which makes displaying data as a grid a breeze.

CHAPTER 10

Routing

Blazor is a .NET framework you use for building _single-page applications_ (SPA), just like you can use popular JavaScript frameworks such as Angular, React, and VueJs. But what is a _SPA_? In this chapter, you will use routing to jump between different sections of a SPA and send data between different components.

What Is a Single-Page Application?

At the beginning of the Web, there were only static pages. A _static page_ is an HTML file somewhere on the server that gets sent back to the browser upon request. Here the server is really nothing but a file server, returning HTML pages to the browser. The browser renders HTML. The only interaction with the browser then was that you could click on a link (the anchor <a> HTML element) to get another page from the server.

Later came the rise of dynamic pages. When a browser requests a _dynamic page_, the server runs a program to build the HTML in memory and sends the HTML back to the browser (this HTML never gets stored to disk; of course, the server can store the generated HTML in its cache for fast retrieval later, also known as _Output Caching_). Dynamic pages are flexible in the way that the same code can generate thousands of different pages by retrieving data from a database and using it to construct the page. Lots of commercial websites like amazon.com use this. But there is still a usability problem. Every time your user clicks on a link, the server must generate the next page from scratch and send it to the browser for rendering. This results in a noticeable wait period, and of course the browser re-renders the whole page.

In 1995, _Brendan Eich_ invented _JavaScript_ (today known as ECMAScript) to allow simple interactions in the browser. Web pages started to use JavaScript to retrieve parts of the page when the user interacts with the UI. One of the first examples of this technique was Microsoft's _Outlook Web Application_. This web application looks and feels like Outlook, a desktop application, with support for all user interactions you expect

CHAPTER 10 ROUTING

from a desktop application. Google's Gmail is another example. They are now known as single-page applications. SPAs contain sections of the web page that are replaced at runtime depending on the user's interaction. If you click an email, the main section of the page is replaced by the email's view. If you click your inbox, the main section gets replaced by a list of emails, etc.

Single-Page Applications

A SPA is a web application that replaces certain parts of the UI without reloading the complete page. SPAs use JavaScript to implement this manipulation of the browser's control tree, also known as the Document Object Model (DOM), and most of them consist of a fixed UI and a placeholder element where the contents are overwritten depending on where the user clicks. One of the main advantages of using a SPA is that you can make a SPA state full. This means that you can keep information loaded by the application in memory, just like when you build a desktop application. You will look at an example of a SPA, built with Blazor, in this chapter.

Layout Components

Let's start with the fixed part of a SPA. Every web application contains UI elements that you can find on every page, such as a header, footer, copyright, menu, etc. Copy-pasting these elements to every page would be a lot of work and would require updating every page if one of these elements needed to change. Developers don't like to do that, so every framework for building web sites has had a solution for this. For example, ASP.NET WebForms uses master pages; ASP.NET MVC has layout pages. Blazor also has a mechanism for this called _layout components_.

Using Blazor Layout Components

Layout components are Blazor components. Anything you can do with a regular component you can do with a layout component, like dependency injection, data binding, and nesting other components. The only difference is that they must inherit from the `LayoutComponentBase` class.

The `LayoutComponentBase` class adds a Body parameter to `ComponentBase` as in Listing 10-1. `LayoutComponentBase` class inherits from the `ComponentBase` class. This is why you can do the same things as with normal components.

Listing 10-1. The LayoutComponentBase class (simplified)

```
public abstract class LayoutComponentBase : ComponentBase
{
  [Parameter]
  public RenderFragment? Body { get; set; }
}
```

Let's look at an example of a layout component. Open the BlazorApp.UsingLayouts solution from the code provided with this chapter. Now, look at the MainLayout component in the components/layout folder, which you'll find in Listing 10-2.

Listing 10-2. The MainLayout component

```
@inherits LayoutComponentBase

<div class="page">
  <div class="sidebar">
    <NavMenu />
  </div>

  <main>
    <div class="top-row px-4">
      <a href="https://learn.microsoft.com/aspnet/core/"
        target="_blank">About</a>
    </div>

    <article class="content px-4">
      @Body
    </article>
  </main>
</div>

<div id="blazor-error-ui">
  An unhandled error has occurred.
```

```
    <a href="" class="reload">Reload</a>
    <a class="dismiss">🗙</a>
</div>
```

On the first line, the `MainLayout` component declares that it inherits from `LayoutComponentBase`. Then you see a sidebar `<div>` and `<main>` element, with the `<article>` element data binding to the inherited Body property. Any component that uses this layout component will end up where the @Body property is, so inside the `<div class="content px-4">`. The last `<div>` with id `blazor-error-ui` is used to display errors, for example, when you have an uncaught exception.

In Figure 10-1, you can see the sidebar on the left side (containing links to the different components of this single-page application), and the main area on the right side with the @Body emphasized with a black rectangle (which I added to the figure). Clicking the Home, Counter, or Weather link in the sidebar will replace the Body parameter with the selected component, updating the UI without reloading the whole page.

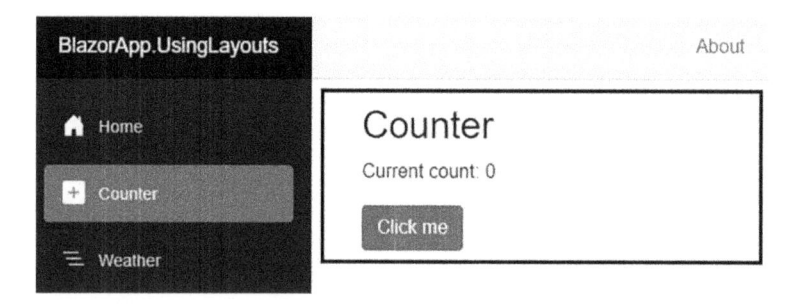

Figure 10-1. The MainLayout component

You can find the CSS style used by this layout component in the MainLayout.razor.css file.

Configure the Default Layout Component

So how does a component know which layout component to use? A component can change the layout component for itself, and an application can set a default layout component which will be used for all components that do not explicitly set their layout. Let us start with the application. Open the Routes.razor file as in Listing 10-3. The first thing to notice here is the `RouteView` component, which has a `DefaultLayout` property of type Type. This is where the default layout for this application is set. Any component selected by this RouteView component will use the MainLayout by default. And for Blazor WebAssembly (so not shown here), should no suitable component be found to display, the Routes component uses a LayoutView to display an error message. Again this LayoutView uses the MainLayout, but of course you can change this to any layout you like.

Listing 10-3. The Routes component

```
<Router AppAssembly="typeof(Program).Assembly">
  <Found Context="routeData">
    <RouteView
      RouteData="routeData"
      DefaultLayout="typeof(Layout.MainLayout)" />
    <FocusOnNavigate
      RouteData="routeData"
      Selector="h1" />
  </Found>
</Router>
```

Internally the RouteView component uses the LayoutView component to select the appropriate layout component. LayoutView allows you to change the layout component for any part of your component.

Selecting a Layout Component

Every component can select which layout to use by stating the name of the layout component with the @layout razor directive. For example, start by copying the MainLayout.razor file to MainLayoutRight.razor (this should also make a copy of the CSS file). This will generate a new layout component called MainLayoutRight, inferred from the file name (you might need to rebuild the project to force this). Inside the CSS file for this component change both flex-direction properties to their reverse counterpart as shown in Listing 10-4.

CHAPTER 10   ROUTING

Listing 10-4. A second layout component

```
.page {
  position: relative;
  display: flex;
  flex-direction: column-reverse; /* CHANGE */
}
@media (min-width: 641px) {
  .page {
    flex-direction: row-reverse; /* CHANGE */
}
```

Now open the Counter component and add a @layout razor directive as in Listing 10-5, line 3.

Listing 10-5. Choosing a different layout with @layout

```
@page "/counter"
@using BlazorApp.UsingLayouts.Components.Layout
@layout MainLayoutRight

<PageTitle>Counter</PageTitle>

<h1>Counter</h1>

<p role="status">Current count: @currentCount</p>

<button class="btn btn-primary" @onclick="IncrementCount">Click me</button>

@code {
    private int currentCount = 0;

    private void IncrementCount()
    {
        currentCount++;
    }
}
```

Run the application and watch the layout change as you alternate between Home and Counter.

> **Note** You can also use the `LayoutAttribute` if you're building your component completely in code.

Most components will use the same layout. Instead of copying the same @layout razor directive to every page, you can also add an _Imports.razor file to the same folder as your components. Open the Pages folder and add a new _Imports.razor file. Replace its content with Listing 10-6.

Listing 10-6. _Imports.razor

```
@using BlazorApp.UsingLayouts.Components.Layout
@layout MainLayoutRight
```

Any component in this folder (or sub-folder) that does not explicitly declare a @layout component will use the `MainLayoutRight` layout component.

Nesting Layouts

Layout components can also be nested. You could define the `MainLayout` to contain all the UI that is shared between all components, and then define a nested layout to be used by a subset of these components. For example, add a new Razor View called NestedLayout.razor to the Layout folder and replace its contents with Listing 10-7.

Listing 10-7. A simple nested layout

```
@inherits LayoutComponentBase

@layout MainLayout

<div class="paper">
  @Body
</div>
```

To build a nested layout, you `@inherit` from `LayoutComponentBase` and set its `@layout` to another layout, for example, `MainLayout`. Our nested layout uses a paper class, so add a NestedLayout.razor.css file next to the component and add Listing 10-8.

CHAPTER 10 ROUTING

Listing 10-8. The NestedLayout component's style

```
.paper {
  background-image: url("images/paper.jpg");
  padding: 1em;
}
```

This style uses the paper.jpg background from the images folder.

Now add a @layout directive to the _Imports.razer file within the Pages folder as in Listing 10-9.

Listing 10-9. Nested layout

```
@using BlazorApp.UsingLayouts.Components.Layout
@layout NestedLayout
```

Run your application; now you have the Home component inside the nested layout which is inside the main layout, as shown in Figure 10-2.

Figure 10-2. *The Home component using the nested layout*

The NavMenu Component

Review the `MainLayout` component from Listing 10-2. On the fourth line, you will see the NavMenu component. This component contains the links to navigate between components. This component comes with the template, feel free to change this component, or use another component for navigation. We will use this component here to explore some of the concepts. Look for the `NavMenu` component in the Layout folder, which is repeated in Listing 10-10.

Listing 10-10. The NavMenu component

```
<div class="top-row ps-3 navbar navbar-dark">
  <div class="container-fluid">
    <a class="navbar-brand" href="">BlazorApp.UsingLayouts</a>
  </div>
</div>

<input type="checkbox"
  title="Navigation menu" class="navbar-toggler" />

<div class="nav-scrollable"
  onclick="document.querySelector('.navbar-toggler').click()">
  <nav class="flex-column">
    <div class="nav-item px-3">
      <NavLink class="nav-link" href=""
        Match="NavLinkMatch.All">
        <span class="bi bi-house-door-fill-nav-menu"
        aria-hidden="true"></span> Home
      </NavLink>
    </div>

    <div class="nav-item px-3">
      <NavLink class="nav-link" href="counter"
        Match="NavLinkMatch.Prefix"> @* Added *@
        <span class="bi bi-plus-square-fill-nav-menu"
        aria-hidden="true"></span> Counter
      </NavLink>
    </div>

    <div class="nav-item px-3">
      <NavLink class="nav-link" href="weather">
        <span class="bi bi-list-nested-nav-menu"
        aria-hidden="true"></span> Weather
      </NavLink>
    </div>
  </nav>
</div>
```

CHAPTER 10 ROUTING

The first part of Listing 10-10 contains a checkbox disguised as a toggle button which allows you to hide and show the navigation menu. This button is only visible on displays with a narrow width (e.g., mobile displays). If you want to look at it, run your application and make the browser width smaller until you see the _hamburger button_ in the top right corner, as in Figure 10-3. Click the button to show the navigation menu and click it again to hide the menu again.

Figure 10-3. *Your application on a narrow display shows the toggle button*

The remaining markup contains the navigation menu, which consists of `NavLink` components. Let's look at the `NavLink` component.

The `NavLink` component is a specialized version of an anchor element `<a/>` used for creating navigation links, also known as hyperlinks. When the browser's URI matches the `href` property of the `NavLink`, it applies a CSS style (the `active` CSS class if you want to customize it) to itself to let you know it is the current route. This is a great way to let the user know which part of your site they are seeing. For example, look at Listing 10-11.

Listing 10-11. The Counter Route's NavLink

```
<NavLink class="nav-link" href="counter"
  Match="NavLinkMatch.Prefix"> @* Added *@
  <span class="bi bi-plus-square-fill-nav-menu"
  aria-hidden="true"></span> Counter
</NavLink>
```

When the browser's URI starts with /counter (ignoring things like query strings), this `NavLink` will apply the `active` style. Let's look at another one in Listing 10-12.

302

Listing 10-12. The Default Route's NavLink

```
<NavLink class="nav-link" href=""
  Match="NavLinkMatch.All">
  <span class="bi bi-house-door-fill-nav-menu"
  aria-hidden="true"></span> Home
</NavLink>
```

When the browser's URI is empty (except for the site's URL), the NavLink from Listing 10-11 will be active. But here you have a special case. Normally NavLink components only match the prefix of the URI. For example, /counter matches the NavLink from Listing 10-10. But with an empty URI, this would match everything! This is why in the special case of an empty URI, you need to tell the NavLink to match the whole URI. You do this with the Match parameter, which by default is set to NavLinkMatch.Prefix, illustrated explicitly in Listing 10-10. If you want to match the whole URI, use NavLinkMatch.All as in Listing 10-12.

Blazor Routing

Single-page applications use routing to select which component gets picked to fill in the layout component's Body parameter. Routing is the process of matching the browser's URI to a collection of _route templates_ and is used to select the component to be shown on screen. That is why every page component in a Blazor SPA uses a @page directive to define the route template to tell the router which component to pick.

Installing the Router

When you create a Blazor solution from scratch, the router is already installed, but let's have a look at how this is done. Open Routes.razor. This Routes component only has one component, the Router component, as shown in Listing 10-13.

Listing 10-13. The Routes component containing the Router

```
@using BlazorApp.UsingLayouts.Components.Layout

<Router AppAssembly="typeof(Program).Assembly">
  <Found Context="routeData">
    <RouteView
      RouteData="routeData"
```

```
        DefaultLayout="typeof(Layout.MainLayout)" />
    <FocusOnNavigate
        RouteData="routeData" Selector="h1" />
    </Found>
</Router>
```

The Router component is a component with two templates. The Found template is used for known routes, and the NotFound is shown when the URI does not match any of the known routes (but not used anymore for Blazor Web Apps, use ASP.NET middleware to handle requests with routes which do not match any of the routes). You can replace the contents of the last to show a nice error page to the user.

The Found template uses a RouteView component which will render the selected component with its layout (or default layout). When the Router component gets instantiated, it will search its AppAssembly parameter for all components that have the RouteAttribute (the @page razor directive gets compiled into a RouteAttribute) and pick the component that matches the current browser's URI. For example, the Counter component has the @page "/counter" razor directive, and when the URL in the browser matches /counter, it will display the Counter component in the MainLayout component.

Note Two components using the same route will result in an error.

FocusOnNavigate

Some people like to use a screen reader; a screen reader tool announces the current page verbally. But what should it announce? Normally this would be the <h1> element, and you can set the default using the FocusOnNavigate component. This will set the focus on the Selector element, which is then used by the screen reader.

Setting the Route Template

The RouteView component from Blazor examines the browser's URI and searches for a component's route template to match. But how do you set a component's route template? Open the counter component shown in Listing 10-5. At the top of this file is the @page "/counter" razor directive. It defines the route template. A route template is a string matching a URI, and that can contain parameters, which you can then use in your component. The leading / is mandatory.

You can change what gets displayed in the component by passing parameters in the route. You could pass the id of a product, look up the product's details with the id, and use it to display the product's details. Let's look at an example. Change the Counter component to look like Listing 10-14 by adding another route template which will set the CurrentCount parameter. This listing illustrates a couple of things. First, you can have multiple @page razor directives, so the /counter and /counter/55 will both route to the Counter component. The second @page directive will set the CurrentCount parameter property from routing, and the name of the parameter is case-insensitive in the @page directive. Of course, parameters need to be encased in curly brackets so the router can identify it.

If you are building your components as pure C# components, apply the RouteAttribute to your class with the route template as an argument. This is what the @page directive gets compiled into.

Listing 10-14. Defining a Route Template with a parameter

```
@page "/counter"
@page "/counter/{CurrentCount:int?}"

@using BlazorApp.UsingLayouts.Components.Layout
@layout MainLayoutRight

<PageTitle>Counter</PageTitle>

<h1>Counter</h1>

<p role="status">Current count: @CurrentCount</p>

<button class="btn btn-primary" @onclick="IncrementCount">Click me</button>

@code {

  [Parameter]
  public int CurrentCount { get; set; }

  private void IncrementCount()
  {
    CurrentCount++;
  }
}
```

Route Constraints

Just like routes in ASP.NET MVC Core, you can use _route constraints_ to limit the type of parameter to match. For example, if you were to use the /counter/Blazor URI, the route template would not match because the parameter does not hold an integer value and the router would not find any component to match.

Constraints are even mandatory if you're not using string typed parameters; otherwise, the router does not cast the parameter to the proper type. You specify the constraint by appending it using a colon, for example, `@page "/counter/{currentCount:int}"`.

You can also make the parameter optional, by appending a question mark after the constraint as shown in Listing 10-14.

A list of other routing constraints can be found in Table 10-1. Each of these maps to the corresponding .NET type. Not all ASP.NET route constraints are supported.

Table 10-1. Routing constraints

Constrai	Example	Example Matches
bool	{active:bool}	true, FALSE
datetime	{dob:datetime}	2016-12-31, 2016-12-31 7:32pm
decimal	{price:decimal}	49.99, -1,000.01
double	{weight:double}	1.234, -1,001.01e8
float	{weight:float}	1.234, -1,001.01e8
guid	{id:guid}	CD2C1638-1638-72D5-1638...
int	{id:int}	123456789, -123456789
long	{ticks:long}	123456789, -123456789

Catch-All Route Parameters

You can also have a parameter which takes the remainder of the URL, for example, allowing you to pass a path to some directory. This parameter is always of type string and can only be the last segment, for example:

`@page "/catch-all/{*directory}"`

Routing and Component Libraries

What about page components that sit in a component library? Normally the Router will only scan the page components from the one AppAssembly, which is your current project. The demo .sln for this chapter also has a component library project, containing the `MemberForm` component. This component uses the `@page "/member"` route template. However, navigating to this page will not work, unless you tell the router component about it. The easiest way to accomplish this is by passing a collection of additional assemblies to scan using the `Router`'s `AdditionalAssemblies` parameter, as shown in Listing 10-15. The router will now also look in the component library project for components with a route template, for example, with the `@page` directive.

Listing 10-15. Using AdditionalAssemblies

```
@using System.Reflection
@using BlazorApp.UsingLayouts.Components.Layout
@using BlazorApp.UsingLayouts.Components.Pages
@using BlazorApp.UsingLayouts.Lib.Components

<Router AppAssembly="typeof(Program).Assembly"
  AdditionalAssemblies="@additionalAssemblies">
  <Found Context="routeData">
    <RouteView
      RouteData="routeData"
      DefaultLayout="typeof(Layout.MainLayout)" />
    <FocusOnNavigate
      RouteData="routeData" Selector="h1" />
  </Found>
  <NotFound>
    <LayoutView Layout="typeof(ErrorLayout)">
      Nothing here...
    </LayoutView>
  </NotFound>
</Router>
```

```
@code {
  private Assembly[] additionalAssemblies = [
    typeof(MemberForm).Assembly
    ];
}
```

With Blazor Server Side Rendering (SSR), you need to register your additional assemblies in another way. Then you call `AddAdditionalAssembles` where you register the App (or another root) component.

```
app.MapRazorComponents<App>()
  .AddAdditionalAssemblies([typeof(MemberForm).Assembly]);
```

Redirecting to Other Pages

How do you navigate to another component using routing? You have three choices: use a standard anchor element, use the `NavLink` component, and use code. Let's start with the normal anchor tag.

Using an anchor (the `<a/>` HTML element) is effortless if you use a relative `href`. For example, add Listing 10-16 below the button of Listing 10-14.

Listing 10-16. Navigation using an anchor tag

```
<a class="btn btn-primary" href="/">Home</a>
```

This link has been styled as a button using Bootstrap 5. Run your application and navigate to the `Counter` component. Click the Home button to navigate to the Home component whose route template matches "/".

The `NavLink` component uses an underlying anchor, so its usage is similar. The only difference is that a `NavLink` component applies the active class when it matches the route. Generally, you only use a `NavLink` in the `NavMenu` component, but you are free to use it instead of anchors.

Navigating in code is also possible, but you will need an instance of the `NavigationManager` class through dependency injection. This instance allows you to examine the page's URI and has a helpful `NavigateTo` method. This method takes a string that will become the browser's new URI.

CHAPTER 10   ROUTING

    Let's try an example. Modify the Counter component to look like Listing 10-17. You tell dependency injection with the @inject razor directive to give you an instance of NavigationManager and put it in the navigationManager field. The NavigationManager is one of the types that Blazor provides out of the box through dependency injection. Then you add a button that calls the StartFrom50 method when clicked. This method uses the NavigationManager to navigate to another URI by calling the NavigateTo method.

Listing 10-17. Using the NavigationManager

```
@page "/counter"
@page "/counter/{CurrentCount:int?}"

@inject NavigationManager navigationManager

@using BlazorApp.UsingLayouts.Components.Layout
@layout MainLayoutRight

<PageTitle>Counter</PageTitle>

<h1>Counter</h1>

<p role="status">Current count: @CurrentCount</p>

<button class="btn btn-primary" @onclick="IncrementCount">
  Click me
</button>

<a class="btn btn-primary" href="/">Home</a>

<button class="btn btn-primary" @onclick="StartFrom50">
  Start from 50
</button>

@code {

  [Parameter]
  public int CurrentCount { get; set; }

  private void IncrementCount()
  {
```

309

CHAPTER 10 ROUTING

```
    CurrentCount++;
  }
  private void StartFrom50()
  {
    navigationManager.NavigateTo("/counter/50");
  }
}
```

Run your application and click the "Start from 50" button. You should navigate to /counter/50.

Navigation Interception

Sometimes a user might navigate to another page in the same site, or to another page in a different site. But when the user was making a series of changes, he or she might lose a lot of work. Using the `NavigationLock` component, you can intercept navigation and ask the user to confirm the navigation.

The demo application contains a `MemberForm` with an excerpt in Listing 10-18, where you can enter user information. It also sports the `NavigationLock` component with two parameters set:

- `ConfirmExternalNavigation`: Will prompt the user to prevent or continue the navigation. This uses the `beforeunload` javascript event if you like to learn more.

- `OnBeforeInternalNavigation`: Calls the method when there are internal navigation events. This allows your logic to decide to continue with the navigation.

Listing 10-18. *Using NavigationLock to intercept navigation events*

```
@inject NavigationManager navigationManager
@inject IJSRuntime jsRuntime

<h3>Add Member</h3>

<NavigationLock ConfirmExternalNavigation="true"
```

```
                OnBeforeInternalNavigation="OnBeforeInternalNavigation" />
<EditForm EditContext="@editContext"
          FormName="member-form"
          OnValidSubmit="Submit">
```

The `OnBeforeInternalNavigation` method can be found in Listing 10-19. This method gets triggered for internal navigation, and you can call the `PreventNavigation` method to cancel the navigation. This implementation checks whether the user has made changes to the form by checking `editContext.IsModified`.

Listing 10-19. OnBeforeInternalNavigation

```
private async Task OnBeforeInternalNavigation(
  LocationChangingContext context)
{
  if (editContext!.IsModified())
  {
    bool isConfirmed = await jsRuntime
      .InvokeAsync<bool>("confirm",
      "Are you sure you want to throw away your changes?");
    if (!isConfirmed)
    {
      context.PreventNavigation();
    }
  }
}
```

When the user submits the form, we also need to ensure that `editContext.IsModified()` returns false, so we need to call `editContext.MarkAsUnmodified` as in Listing 10-20.

Listing 10-20. Clearing editContext

```
public void Submit()
{
  editContext.MarkAsUnmodified();
}
```

CHAPTER 10   ROUTING

Understanding the Base Tag

Please don't use absolute URIs when navigating. Why? Because when you deploy your application on the Internet, the base URI will change. Instead, Blazor uses the `<base/>` HTML element, and all relative URIs will be combined with this `<base/>` tag. Where is the `<base/>` tag? You set it in the `<head>` element, so with a Blazor Web App, you can find this in the App component. With Blazor WebAssembly, find it in the wwwroot folder of your Blazor project as index.html. If you are using Blazor Server, the `<base/>` tag can be found in _Host.cshtml.

When you deploy in production, all you need to do is to update the base tag. For example, you might deploy your application to `https://online.u2u.be/selfassessment`. In this case, you would update the base element to `<base href="/selfassessment" />`. So why do you need to do this? If you deploy to `https://online.u2u.be/selfassement`, the counter component's URI becomes `https://online.u2u.be/selfassessment/counter`. Routing will ignore the base URI so it will match the counter as expected. You only need to specify the base URI once.

You can also access the base URI (with a trailing slash) using the `NavigationManager.BaseUri` property. This can be useful for passing absolute URIs, for example, to certain JavaScript libraries. We will discuss JavaScript interoperability in the following chapter.

Constant-Based Routing

You might not like using string literals in the `@page` directive. Instead, you can use string constants, but then you need to specify this using the `@attribute` directive and the `RouteAttribute` as shown in Listing 10-21.

Listing 10-21. Using string constants

```
@attribute [Route(Constants.Weather)]

public static class Constants
{
  public const string Weather = "/Weather";
}
```

Lazy Loading with Routing

Some components in your Blazor application might not be used frequently. But even then, Blazor will need to load these components into the browser before running your application. For large applications, this can mean that your application will take even longer to load. However, with Blazor we can load components the moment we need them. This is called lazy loading.

> **Note** This only makes sense when running your components in the browser using WASM!

Lazy Loading Component Libraries

Lazy loading works by moving your infrequently used components into one or more component libraries, and then download the library when you need them. We discussed building component libraries in the component chapters. But let us start with a project, move these components and their dependencies into libraries, and then lazy-load them. In the book's download, you should find a solution called BlazorApp.LazyLoading. If you like, you can also create this from scratch using the following powershell script:

```
$ProjectName = "BlazorApp.LazyLoading"
mkdir $ProjectName
cd $ProjectName
dotnet new sln -n $ProjectName
mkdir src
cd src
dotnet new blazorwasm -n $ProjectName
cd ..
dotnet sln add src\$ProjectName
```

Open it. This project should look familiar. You should be able to build and run this application. Now, for the sake of the example, assume that the Counter and Weather components are components we want to lazy load.

Let us start with the Counter component. Create a Razor Class Library project called BlazorApp.LazyLoadedComponents. Move the Counter component to this

CHAPTER 10 ROUTING

library. Now add a project reference to this library in the client project, and add a @using directive to Imports.razor.

Build and run your solution. Click the Counter link. Hmm. No Counter has been found. Why?

When the Router component gets initialized, it searches the assembly from its AppAssembly parameter for components that have a @page razor directive. Before we moved the Counter component to the razor library, the Counter was part of this assembly. But now we have moved it to the razor library. So, we need to tell the Router component to search this library for routable components. We can easily do this by setting the Router's AdditionalAssemblies parameter. Open App.razor and update it as in Listing 10-22. Here we set the AdditionalAssemblies parameter to a List<Assembly>, which contains the Assembly for the Counter component. Now the application should show the Counter component!

Listing 10-22. Using AdditionalAssemblies

```
@using System.Reflection
<Router
  AppAssembly="@typeof(App).Assembly"
  AdditionalAssemblies="@additionalAssemblies">
  <Found Context="routeData">
    <RouteView RouteData="@routeData" DefaultLayout=
    "@typeof(MainLayout)" />
    <FocusOnNavigate RouteData="@routeData" Selector="h1" />
  </Found>
  <NotFound>
    <PageTitle>Not found</PageTitle>
    <LayoutView Layout="@typeof(MainLayout)">
      <p role="alert">Sorry, there's nothing at this address.</p>
    </LayoutView>
  </NotFound>
</Router>

@code {
  List<Assembly> additionalAssemblies = [typeof(Counter).Assembly];
}
```

CHAPTER 10 ROUTING

We moved the Counter component to a razor library, but we still load the Counter component when the application is loaded. Time to enable lazy loading for the razor library.

First, we will tell the runtime not to load the assembly automatically, and then we will load it when needed.

Marking an Assembly for Lazy Loading

Open the client project file using the editor, and add the BlazorWebAssemblyLazyLoad element as in Listing 10-23. This tells the runtime not to load the BlazorApp.LazyLoadedComponents.wasm automatically.

There are two parts to the Include property. The name of the component library assembly and the extension. In .NET 6, Blazor uses the ".dll" extension, but because some firewalls block files using this extension, .NET 8 uses the webcil packaging format which uses the ".wasm" extension. Webcil files use a standard webassembly wrapper around the ".dll" which is not blocked by firewalls.

Listing 10-23. Turning on lazy loading

```
<Project Sdk="Microsoft.NET.Sdk.BlazorWebAssembly">
  <PropertyGroup>
    <TargetFramework>net8.0</TargetFramework>
    <Nullable>enable</Nullable>
    <ImplicitUsings>enable</ImplicitUsings>
  </PropertyGroup>
  <ItemGroup>
    ...
  </ItemGroup>
  <ItemGroup>
    <BlazorWebAssemblyLazyLoad
      Include="BlazorApp.LazyLoadedComponents.wasm"/>
  </ItemGroup>
</Project>
```

If you try to run the application, you will get a runtime error. When the application starts, the router tries to scan all assemblies for @page directives. But we just told Blazor

CHAPTER 10　ROUTING

WebAssembly not to load the component library! You can remove the error by removing the initial assembly from `additionalAssemblies` as shown in Listing 10-24.

Listing 10-24. Getting rid of the runtime error

```
List<Assembly> additionalAssemblies = []; // [typeof(Counter).Assembly];
```

Dynamically Loading an Assembly

Now we need to load this assembly when needed. When do we load this assembly? When we navigate to a component that needs components from this assembly. How do we know we are navigating? The Router component has an event for this called `OnNavigateAsync`, and we will use it to detect when we navigate to a component that uses a lazy loaded component. Then we will download the assembly using the `LazyAssemblyLoader` so it is ready for use.

Update App.razor as in Listing 10-25. First we get an instance of the `LazyAssemblyLoader` using dependency injection. Then we implement the `OnNavigateAsync` event using the `NavigateAsync` method. This method receives a `NavigationContext` instance, and we check the `Path` if we are navigating to the `Counter` component. If so, we load the assembly for the `Counter` component (BlazorApp. LazyLoadedComponents.wasm), and we add it to the `additionalAssemblies` collection, so the `Router` component can scan it for route templates.

Listing 10-25. Loading an assembly when needed

```
@using System.Reflection
@using Microsoft.AspNetCore.Components.WebAssembly.Services

@inject LazyAssemblyLoader lazyAssemblyLoader

<Router
  AppAssembly="@typeof(App).Assembly"
  AdditionalAssemblies="@additionalAssemblies"
  OnNavigateAsync="NavigateAsync">
  <Found Context="routeData">
    <RouteView RouteData="@routeData" DefaultLayout=
    "@typeof(MainLayout)" />
    <FocusOnNavigate RouteData="@routeData" Selector="h1" />
```

```
    </Found>
    <NotFound>
      <PageTitle>Not found</PageTitle>
      <LayoutView Layout="@typeof(MainLayout)">
        <p role="alert">Sorry, there's nothing at this address.</p>
      </LayoutView>
    </NotFound>
</Router>

@code {
  List<Assembly> additionalAssemblies = [];

  private async Task NavigateAsync(NavigationContext context)
  {
    if(context.Path.ToLower() == "counter")
    {
      var assemblies = await lazyAssemblyLoader
        .LoadAssembliesAsync(["BlazorApp.LazyLoadedComponents.wasm"]);
      additionalAssemblies.AddRange(assemblies);
    }
  }
}
```

Build and run the application. It should start, and when we click Counter, the browser will download it, and then render it.

What if we are on a slow network? Maybe we want to show some loading UI, while the assembly downloads? The Router has a Navigating RenderFragment which it shows while loading. So update the App.razor file again as in Listing 10-26, adding the Navigating UI.

Listing 10-26. Showing a navigating UI

```
<Router AppAssembly="@typeof(App).Assembly"
        AdditionalAssemblies="@additionalAssemblies"
        OnNavigateAsync="NavigateAsync">
  <Found Context="routeData">
    <RouteView RouteData="@routeData" DefaultLayout=
    "@typeof(MainLayout)" />
```

```
    <FocusOnNavigate RouteData="@routeData" Selector="h1" />
  </Found>
  <NotFound>
    <PageTitle>Not found</PageTitle>
    <LayoutView Layout="@typeof(MainLayout)">
      <p role="alert">Sorry, there's nothing at this address.</p>
    </LayoutView>
  </NotFound>
  <Navigating>
    Loading additional components...
  </Navigating>
</Router>
```

Lazy Loading and Dependency Injection

Let us now try to lazy load the Weather component. This component uses an IWeatherService instance, implemented by the WeatherService class (the one in the Blazor project). We will move both into the component library.

Start moving the Weather component, IWeatherService interface, and WeatherService and WeatherForecast classes to the component library.

Your library project should compile now.

Update the OnNavigate method from App.razor to check for the weather URI as in Listing 10-27.

Listing 10-27. The OnNavigate method for Weather

```
List<string> lazyLoadedRoutes = ["counter", "weather"];

private async Task NavigateAsync(NavigationContext context)
{
  if (lazyLoadedRoutes.Contains(context.Path.ToLower()))
  {
    var assemblies = await lazyAssemblyLoader
      .LoadAssembliesAsync(["BlazorApp.LazyLoadedComponents.wasm"]);
    additionalAssemblies.AddRange(assemblies);
  }
}
```

After fixing a couple of namespaces in C#, the project should build. But running will fail. Why? In Program.cs, you are adding the WeatherService class from the lazy loaded library, but that has not been loaded (because you told the runtime not to load it).

Maybe we could postpone registering the WeatherService with dependency injection? Sorry, that will not work. After initialization, dependency injection becomes immutable so you cannot add dependencies later. Of course, we could keep the WeatherService in the Blazor client project, but let us pretend it is worth our while to lazy load it. Time to introduce a little abstraction layer. We will use a factory method to create the dependency, and we will use dependency injection to inject the factory method. This will require a couple of changes.

> **Note** A factory is a class that has a method that will create an instance of some class, hiding the creation process. For example, a factory could create an instance, where the class of the instance depends on some business rule. Of course, all instances returned should have some common base class or interface. IServiceProvider used by dependency injection is also a factory, but we cannot use it here because it does not know about the existence of the WeatherService. Use your favorite search engine and search "Factory Pattern in C#" to learn more about this.

Both the component library and Blazor client application will need to share the factory interface, so create a new class library project named BlazorApp.LazyLoadedServices.

Move the IWeatherService interface to this class library. Now we will add an additional layer between the Weather component and the WeatherService. Create an interface named IWeatherServiceFactory from Listing 10-28 in the class library project.

Listing 10-28. The IWeatherServiceFactory interface

```
namespace BlazorApp.LazyLoadedServices.Services;

public interface IWeatherServiceFactory
{
    IWeatherService Create();
}
```

CHAPTER 10 ROUTING

Update the Weather component to use the IWeatherServiceFactory to create the IWeatherService instance as in Listing 10-29.

Listing 10-29. Update the Weather component

```
@page "/weather"
@using BlazorApp.LazyLoadedServices.Services
@using BlazorApp.LazyLoading
@using BlazorApp.LazyLoading.Services
@inject IWeatherServiceFactory weatherServiceFactory

...

@code {
  private WeatherForecast[]? forecasts;

  protected override async Task OnInitializedAsync()
  {
    IWeatherService weatherService = weatherServiceFactory.Create();
    forecasts = await weatherService.GetForecastsAsync();
  }
}
```

The Weather component now has a dependency on the IWeatherServiceFactory which is not lazy loaded, so we only need to replace dependency injection to use the WeatherServiceFactory as in Listing 10-30.

Listing 10-30. Program.cs

```
using BlazorApp.LazyLoadedServices.Services;
using BlazorApp.LazyLoading;
using Microsoft.AspNetCore.Components.Web;
using Microsoft.AspNetCore.Components.WebAssembly.Hosting;

WebAssemblyHostBuilder builder = WebAssemblyHostBuilder.CreateDefault(args);
builder.RootComponents.Add<App>("#app");
builder.RootComponents.Add<HeadOutlet>("head::after");
```

```
builder.Services.AddScoped(sp => new HttpClient { BaseAddress = new
Uri(builder.HostEnvironment.BaseAddress) });

//builder.Services.AddScoped<IWeatherService, WeatherService>();
builder.Services.AddScoped<IWeatherServiceFactory,
WeatherServiceFactory>();

await builder.Build().RunAsync();
```

Finally, we will implement the IWeatherServiceFactory interface in the client project as in Listing 10-31 to create the actual WeatherService. Because we only need the WeatherService implementation when we use the factory, this will work because the library containing the WeatherService will be loaded through lazy loading. However, the WeatherService has its own dependencies, so we will request these in the factory and pass them to the actual service. The factory is a tiny class, and when the actual service with its dependencies is large, this technique becomes interesting.

Listing 10-31. Implementing the IWeatherServiceFactory

```
using BlazorApp.LazyLoading.Services;

namespace BlazorApp.LazyLoadedServices.Services;

public class WeatherServiceFactory
{
  private readonly HttpClient _http;

  public WeatherServiceFactory(HttpClient http)
  => _http = http;

  public IWeatherService Create()
  => new WeatherService(_http);
}
```

Adding Another Page to PizzaPlace

Let us add a details page to the PizzaPlace application. This will allow the customer to check the ingredients and nutritional information about pizzas.

CHAPTER 10   ROUTING

When you navigate between different Blazor components with routing, you will probably encounter the need to send information from one component to another. One way to accomplish this is by setting a parameter in the destination component by passing it in the URI. For example, you could navigate to /pizzadetail/5 to tell the destination component to display information about the pizza with id 5. The destination component can then use a service to load the information about pizza #5 and then display this information. But in Blazor there are other ways to pass information from one component to another. If both components share a common parent component, we can use data binding. Otherwise, we can use a _State_ class (most developers call this State, but this is just a convention, and you can call it anything you want; State just makes sense) and then use dependency injection to give every component the same instance of this class. This single State class contains the information that components need. We have seen this before in the chapter on dependency injection: this is known as the _Singleton Pattern_. Our PizzaPlace application is already using a State class, so it should not be too much work to use this pattern.

> **Note**   You can also implement State using a cascading parameter.

Start by opening the Pizza Place solution. Open the Home component from the Pages folder (in the BlazorApp.PizzaPlace project) and look for the private State property. Enable dependency injection for this property as in Listing 10-32.

Listing 10-32. Using dependency injection to get the state singleton instance

```
[Inject]
public required State State { get; set; }
```

Now configure dependency injection in Program.cs to inject the State instance as a singleton, as in Listing 10-33. Careful! To have a single instance per user, which lifetime should we use in Blazor? That would be scoped!

Listing 10-33. Configuring dependency injection for the state singleton

```
using BlazorApp.PizzaPlace.Components;
using BlazorApp.PizzaPlace.Shared;
using BlazorApp.PizzaPlace.Shared.Services;

WebApplicationBuilder builder = WebApplication.CreateBuilder(args);
```

CHAPTER 10 ROUTING

```
// Add services to the container.
builder.Services.AddRazorComponents()
    .AddInteractiveServerComponents();

builder.Services
        .AddTransient<IMenuService, HardCodedMenuService>()
        .AddTransient<IOrderService, ConsoleOrderService>();

// *** Add this line ***
builder.Services.AddScoped<State>();

WebApplication app = builder.Build();

// Configure the HTTP request pipeline.
if (!app.Environment.IsDevelopment())
{
  _ = app.UseExceptionHandler("/Error",
        createScopeForErrors: true);
  _ = app.UseHsts();
}

app.UseHttpsRedirection();

app.UseStaticFiles();
app.UseAntiforgery();

app.MapRazorComponents<App>()
    .AddInteractiveServerRenderMode();

app.Run();
```

Run the application. Everything should still work! What you've done is to use the _Singleton Pattern_ to inject the State singleton into the Home component. Let's add another component that will use the same State instance.

You want to display more information about a pizza using a new component, but before you do this, you need to update the State class. Add a new property called CurrentPizza to the State class, as shown in Listing 10-34.

CHAPTER 10　ROUTING

Listing 10-34. Adding a CurrentPizza property to the State class

```
namespace BlazorApp.PizzaPlace.Shared;
public class State
{
  public Pizza[] Pizzas { get; set; } = [];
  public ShoppingBasket Basket { get; } = new();

  public Customer Customer { get; set; } = new()
  {
    Id = 0,
    Name = string.Empty,
    Street = string.Empty,
    City = string.Empty,
    ZipCode = string.Empty
  };

  public decimal TotalPrice
  => Basket.Orders.Sum(id => GetPizza(id)!.Price);

  public Pizza? GetPizza(int id)
  => Pizzas.SingleOrDefault(pizza => pizza.Id == id);

  // *** Add this line **
  public Pizza? CurrentPizza { get; set; }
}
```

Now when someone clicks a pizza on the menu, it will display the pizza's information. Update the `PizzaItem` component by wrapping the pizza name in an anchor, like in Listing 10-35. Add a new `ShowPizzaInformation` parameter, and if this is non-null, we wrap it in an anchor which invokes the `ShowPizzaInformation` action.

Listing 10-35. Adding an anchor to display the pizza's information

```
<div class="row">
  <div class="col">
    @if (ShowPizzaInformation is not null)
    {
      <a href="#" @onclick="() => ShowPizzaInformation.Invoke(Pizza)">
```

```
          @Pizza.Name
        </a>
      }
      else
      {
        @Pizza.Name
      }
    </div>
    <div class="col text-right">
      @($"{Pizza.Price:0.00}")
    </div>
    <div class="col"></div>
    <div class="col">
      <img src="@SpicinessImage(Pizza.Spiciness)"
           alt="@Pizza.Spiciness" />
    </div>
    <div class="col">
      <button class="btn btn-success pl-4 pr-4"
              @onclick=@(async () => await ButtonAction.InvokeAsync(Pizza))>
        @ButtonText
      </button>
    </div>
  </div>
</div>

@code {

    [Parameter]
    [EditorRequired]
    public required Pizza Pizza { get; set; }

    [Parameter]
    [EditorRequired]
    public required string ButtonText { get; set; }

    [Parameter]
    public EventCallback<Pizza> ButtonAction { get; set; }

    [Parameter]
```

```
public Action<Pizza>? ShowPizzaInformation { get; set; }

private string SpicinessImage(Spiciness spiciness)
 => $"images/{spiciness.ToString().ToLower()}.png";
}
```

Update the Menu component to set the PizzaItem component's ShowPizzaInformation parameter as in Listing 10-36.

When someone clicks this link, it should set the State instance's CurrentPizza property. But you don't have access to the State object. One way to solve this would be by injecting the State instance in the PizzaItem component. But you don't want to overburden this component, so you add a ShowPizzaInformation callback delegate to tell the containing Menu component that you want to display more information about the pizza. Clicking the pizza name link simply invokes this callback without knowing what should happen.

You are applying a pattern here known as "_Dumb and Smart Components_." A dumb component is a component that knows nothing about the global picture of the application. Because it doesn't know anything about the rest of the application, a dumb component is easier to reuse. A smart component knows about the other parts of the application (such as which service to use to talk to the database) and will use dumb components to display its information. In our example, the Menu and PizzaItem are dumb components because they receive all their data through data binding, while the Home component is a smart component which talks to services.

Listing 10-36. Adding a PizzaInformation callback to the Menu component

```
<ItemList>
  <Header>
    <h1>Our selection of pizzas</h1>
  </Header>
  <Row>
    @foreach (Pizza pizza in Pizzas)
    {
      <PizzaItem Pizza="@pizza"
        ButtonText="Add"
        ButtonAction="@Selected"
        ShowPizzaInformation="@ShowPizzaInformation" />
    }
```

```
    </Row>
</ItemList>

@code {
  [Parameter]
  [EditorRequired]
  public Pizza[] Pizzas { get; set; } = [];

  private string SpicinessImage(Spiciness spiciness)
    => $"images/{spiciness.ToString().ToLower()}.png";

  [Parameter]
  public EventCallback<Pizza> Selected { get; set; }

  [Parameter]
  public Action<Pizza>? ShowPizzaInformation { get; set; }
}
```

You added a ShowPizzaInformation callback to the Menu component, and you simply pass it to the PizzaItem component. The Home component will set this callback, and the Menu will pass it to the PizzaItem component.

Update the Home component to set the State instance's CurrentPizza, and navigate to the PizzaInfo component, as shown in Listing 10-37. The Home component tells the Menu component to call the ShowPizzaInformation method when someone clicks the information link from the PizzaItem component. The ShowPizzaInformation method then sets the State's CurrentPizza property (which we need in the PizzaInfo component) and navigates using the NavigationManager's NavigateTo method to the /PizzaInfo route.

> **Note** If you call NavigateTo as part of a callback, Blazor returns to the original route. That is why I use a background Task so Blazor will navigate after the callback.

Listing 10-37. The Home component navigates to the PizzaInfo component

```
@page "/"

@inject IMenuService MenuService
@inject IOrderService OrderService
@inject NavigationManager NavigationManager
```

CHAPTER 10   ROUTING

```
<PageTitle>The PizzaPlace</PageTitle>

<Menu Pizzas="@State.Pizzas"
      Selected="AddPizzaToBasket"
      ShowPizzaInformation="ShowPizzaInformation" />

<Basket @bind-State="@State"/>

<CustomerEntry Title="Please enter your details below"
   @bind-Customer="@State.Customer"
   SubmitTitle="Place Order"
   SubmitClicked="SubmitClicked"/>

<p>@State.ToJson()</p>

@code {
  [Inject]
  public required State State { get; set; }

  protected override async Task OnInitializedAsync()
  {
    State.Pizzas = await MenuService.GetMenu();
  }

  private void AddPizzaToBasket(Pizza pizza)
  {
    State.Basket.Add(pizza.Id);
  }

  private async Task SubmitClicked()
  {
    await OrderService.PlaceOrder(State.Customer, State.Basket);
  }

  private void ShowPizzaInformation(Pizza selected)
  {
    this.State.CurrentPizza = selected;
    Task.Run(() => this.NavigationManager
```

                    .NavigateTo($"/pizzainfo/{selected.Id}"));
    }
}

Right-click the Components folder, and add a new Razor component called PizzaInfo, as shown in Listing 10-38 (to save you some time and to keep things simple, you can copy most of the PizzaItem component). The PizzaInfo component shows information about the State's CurrentPizza. This works because you share the same State instance between these components. The Home component will set the CurrentPizza property in State, which is then displayed by the PizzaInfo component. Because State's CurrentPizza property can be null, I also added a helper property to the PizzaInfo component that always returns a non-nullable CurrentPizza (using the null forgiving operator) to avoid compiler warnings.

Listing 10-38. Adding a PizzaInfo component

```
@page "/pizzainfo/{Id:int}"
@rendermode InteractiveAuto

@if (CurrentPizza is not null)
{
  <h2>Pizza @CurrentPizza.Name Details</h2>

  <div class="row">
    <div class="col">
      @CurrentPizza.Name
    </div>
    <div class="col">
      @($"{CurrentPizza.Price:0.00}")
    </div>
    <div class="col">
      <img src="@SpicinessImage(CurrentPizza.Spiciness)"
           alt="@CurrentPizza.Spiciness" />
    </div>
  </div>
}
<div class="row">
  <div class="col">
```

```
    <a class="btn btn-primary" href="/">Back to Menu</a>
  </div>
</div>

@code {
  [Inject]
  public required State State { get; set; }

  [Parameter]
  public int Id { get; set; }

  private Pizza? CurrentPizza { get => State.GetPizza(Id); }

  private string SpicinessImage(Spiciness spiciness)
  => $"images/{spiciness.ToString().ToLower()}.png";
}
```

At the bottom of the markup, you add an anchor (and made it look like a button using Bootstrap styling) to return to the menu. It's an example of changing the route with anchors. Of course, in a real-life application, you would show the ingredients of the pizza, a nice picture, and nutritional information. I leave this as an exercise for you.

Summary

In this chapter, we looked at single-page applications, layouts, routing, and lazy loading components. Single-page applications avoid navigating to other URLs because the browser will wipe its memory before loading the next page. By staying on the same page, we can keep data in memory, and to update the UI, we use code to replace part of the page. Layouts allow you to avoid replicating markup in your application and help keep your application's look consistent. We also saw that layouts can be nested. Routing is an important part of building single-page applications and takes care of picking the component to show based on the browser's URI. You define route templates using the @page syntax where you use route parameters and constraints. Navigation in your single-page application can be done using anchor tags and from code using the NavigationManager class. We also saw that you can lazy-load components by moving them into a component library and then dynamically load the library just when you need it. Finally, we modified the Pizza Place application to show how to share information between different routes in a Blazor application.

CHAPTER 11

Blazor Render Modes

Blazor with .NET 8 introduces something brand new: render modes. This allows you to build Blazor websites, ranging from completely static websites (just like ASP.NET Core MVC), interactive websites running on the server, and interactive websites running completely in the browser (just like Angular and React)! You can even mix modes, using server-side rendering for pages that only need to display information, and use interactive pages running on the server or browser. There is also a new Blazor project type, the Blazor Web App, which allows you to build any of these using the same project. The older project types are still supported, but I do recommend the new project type for new websites.

Server-Side Rendering

With Blazor Server-Side Rendering (SSR), you can build websites that mainly show information, like blogs, news, etc. Great for search engine optimization too (SEO) because all the HTML rendering is done on the server. This also scales very well because all the rendering is done is in stateless fashion. It supports the same component model, meaning you can use a lot of existing components. However, this model does not support interactivity beyond the classic forms model where the user enters information, then clicks on a submit button, and then receives feedback such as validation errors. No support for events like @onclick. For this we need to enable interactivity.

Examine a SSR Project

Open Visual Studio and create a new project. Select the Blazor Web App template as in Figure 11-1 and click Next.

CHAPTER 11   BLAZOR RENDER MODES

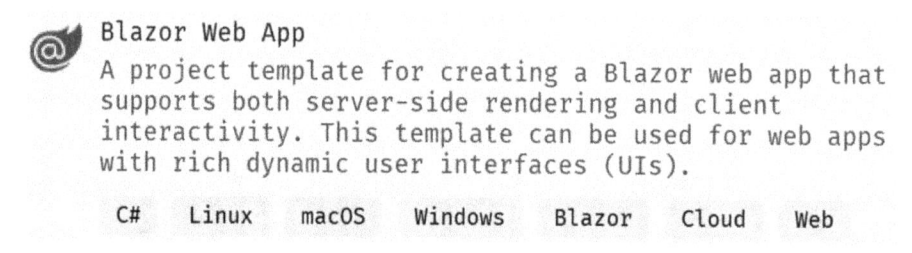

```
Blazor Web App
A project template for creating a Blazor web app that
supports both server-side rendering and client
interactivity. This template can be used for web apps
with rich dynamic user interfaces (UIs).

  C#    Linux    macOS    Windows    Blazor    Cloud    Web
```

Figure 11-1. The Blazor Web App template

Name it BlazorApp.SSR and click Next.

Select None for Interactive render mode, and leave the other settings to default as shown in Figure 11-2. Click Create.

Figure 11-2. Select Server-Side Rendering

If you like, you can also use this PowerShell script to create the project:

```
$ProjectName = "BlazorApp.SSR"
mkdir $ProjectName
cd $ProjectName
dotnet new sln -n $ProjectName
mkdir src
cd src
```

CHAPTER 11   BLAZOR RENDER MODES

```
dotnet new blazor -n $ProjectName --interactivity None
cd ..
dotnet sln add src\$ProjectName
```

Open Program as show in Listing 11-1. First look at the line where AddRazorComponents gets called. This method is used to set up the necessary infrastructure for using Razor components in a Blazor application, ensuring that all required services are available and properly configured.

Near the bottom, you see the MapRazorComponents method, which configures the endpoint routing for Razor components in an ASP.NET Core Blazor Server application. Blazor Web Apps set up routing in a similar manner to ASP.NET Core MVC does, meaning you can use both at the same time. Great for updating existing MVC applications with new Blazor pages!

Listing 11-1. Program.cs

```csharp
using BlazorApp.SSR.Components;

namespace BlazorApp.SSR;
public class Program
{
  public static void Main(string[] args)
  {
    var builder = WebApplication.CreateBuilder(args);

    // Add services to the container.
    builder.Services.AddRazorComponents();

    var app = builder.Build();

    // Configure the HTTP request pipeline.
    if (!app.Environment.IsDevelopment())
    {
      app.UseExceptionHandler("/Error");
      app.UseHsts();
    }

    app.UseHttpsRedirection();
```

CHAPTER 11 BLAZOR RENDER MODES

```
    app.UseStaticFiles();
    app.UseAntiforgery();

    app.MapRazorComponents<App>();

    app.Run();
  }
}
```

Now open the App component as shown in Listing 11-2. This just contains the `<head>` and `<body>` elements, including the HeadOutlet and Routes component. There is some JavaScript included, but you can even remove this for SSR. Leave it because we will need this for enhanced navigation and streaming rendering.

Listing 11-2. The App component

```
<!DOCTYPE html>
<html lang="en">

<head>
  <meta charset="utf-8" />
  <meta name="viewport" content="width=device-width, initial-scale=1.0" />
  <base href="/" />
  <link rel="stylesheet" href="bootstrap/bootstrap.min.css" />
  <link rel="stylesheet" href="app.css" />
  <link rel="stylesheet" href="BlazorApp.SSR.styles.css" />
  <link rel="icon" type="image/png" href="favicon.png" />
  <HeadOutlet />
</head>

<body>
  <Routes />
  <script src="_framework/blazor.web.js"></script>
</body>

</html>
```

We discussed the Routes component in the Routing chapter, nothing new here.

Open the Home component and update it to Listing 11-3. I have added some logic in this component to demonstrate that components still work with SSR (except interactivity).

Listing 11-3. The Home component

```
@page "/"

<PageTitle>Home</PageTitle>

<h1>Hello, world!</h1>

Welcome to your new app on @someDate

@code {
  public string someDate = string.Empty;

  protected override void OnInitialized()
  {
    someDate = DateTime.Now.ToLongDateString();
  }
}
```

Run. The Home component renders as expected.

Note This has full support for hot reload.

Enhanced Navigation

With the browser still running, open the browser development tools on the network tab. Hit refresh, and you will see the browser do a normal get on the home page as shown in Figure 11-3. You will see some other (web sockets) network traffic used by the debugger, so ignore these.

CHAPTER 11 BLAZOR RENDER MODES

Name	Status	Type
localhost	200	document
bootstrap.min.css	200	stylesheet
app.css	200	stylesheet
BlazorApp.SSR.styles.css	200	stylesheet
blazor.web.js	304	script

Figure 11-3. *The browser GETS the blazor home page*

Now click the Weather link in the navigation menu. Instead of doing a normal GET for the weather page, the browser performs a FETCH as shown in Figure 11-4.

Name	Status	Type
weather	200	fetch

Figure 11-4. *Blazor Runtime uses Fetch*

So instead of loading the whole page and making the browser render the whole page, the Blazor runtime uses a FETCH to download the page as a string and then updates the DOM with the differences to render the page. This makes the experience faster and smoother. It even gives you the SPA experience. And you don't have to do anything! Remember the script tag from Listing 11-2? This takes care of enhanced navigation.

Note Enhanced navigation only works when navigating between pages of the same application.

Keeping an Element's Value

Maybe you want to keep part of the page unaffected? Open the component and add a search box near the bottom as in Listing 11-4.

Listing 11-4. Adding a search box

```
<div class="top-row ps-3 navbar navbar-dark">
  <div class="container-fluid">
    <a class="navbar-brand" href="">Enhanced Navigation</a>
  </div>
</div>

<input type="checkbox" title="Navigation menu" class="navbar-toggler" />

<div class="nav-scrollable"
     onclick="document.querySelector('.navbar-toggler').click()">
  <nav class="flex-column">
    <div class="nav-item px-3">
      <NavLink class="nav-link" href="" Match="NavLinkMatch.All">
        <span class="bi bi-house-door-fill-nav-menu" aria-hidden="true">
        </span> Home
      </NavLink>
    </div>

    <div class="nav-item px-3" >
      <NavLink class="nav-link" href="about">
        <span class="bi bi-plus-square-fill-nav-menu" aria-hidden="true">
        </span> About
      </NavLink>
    </div>

    <div class="nav-item px-3">
      <form>
        <input type="search" placeholder="search" />
      </form>
    </div>

  </nav>
</div>
```

Run the application and enter some text in the search box. When you navigate to another page, you will see the search box lose its value. Now update the form element as in Listing 11-5. Try again. Now you will see the search box keep its value!

Listing 11-5. Add the data-permanent attribute

```
<div class="nav-item px-3">
  <form data-permanent>
    <input type="search" placeholder="search" />
  </form>
</div>
```

Disabling Enhanced Navigation for Links

If you like, you can disable enhanced navigation for links. Simply add the `data-enhance-nav` attribute to the `NavLink` component as in Listing 11-6.

Listing 11-6. Disabling enhanced navigation

```
<div class="nav-item px-3">
  <NavLink class="nav-link" href="weather"
           data-enhance-nav="false">
    <span class="bi bi-list-nested-nav-menu" aria-hidden="true"></span>
    Weather
  </NavLink>
</div>
```

Streaming Rendering

When you do server-side rendering like with MVC, and the server needs to fetch data that takes a while (e.g., from a database), normally the user needs to wait for the page to completely render before seeing anything (wondering where my data is!?). With streaming rendering, we can display some UI to the user (a loading UI) and render parts of the page as they become available. This again improves the experience for the user!

Examine the `Weather` component. In the `OnInitializedAsync` method it loads the data and contains a `Task.Delay` to emulate talking to the database as in Listing 11-7.

Listing 11-7. Faking a slow process

```
protected override async Task OnInitializedAsync()
{
  await Task.Delay(500);
```

Let us compare the user's experience with and without streaming rendering. First update the `Task.Delay` to 5000 milliseconds (to make it really slow). Also comment or remove the attribute on the second line.

Run the application and navigate to the Weather component. For the next 5 seconds, you will not see any movement, which of course will make the user wonder if they clicked the link in the first place! And after the delay, the page updates using enhanced navigation.

Now uncomment or add the attribute to the Weather component as in Listing 11-8.

Listing 11-8. Enabling streaming rendering

```
@page "/weather"
@attribute [StreamRendering]
```

Run (or hot reload) the application and navigate from the Home to the Weather component. Now the page loads immediately, and you will see a loading UI (in real life you would use some nice CSS animated bit of UI) while the server is busy getting the data. When that finishes, the UI will update showing the proper data, automatically!

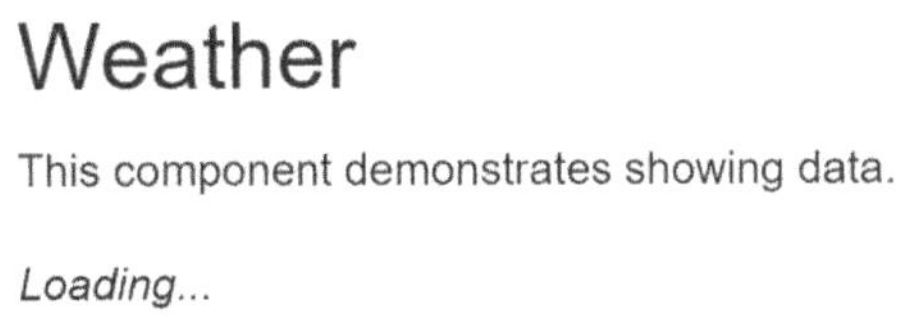

Weather

This component demonstrates showing data.

Loading...

Figure 11-5. Streaming rendering loading UI

Streaming rendering makes your screens appear as if you are using a SPA, without the effort!

SSR and Forms

What about Forms? The sources provided with this book contain a Data folder, which contains a Forms component with dependencies. Copy this to the project's folder. Before you can build it, you also need to add the Blazored.FluentValidation package to the project.

Run. Your forms now run using SSR. Open the browser debugger's network tab again. Hit the submit button, and you will see a POST back to the server, just like any regular server-side web page. Clear the name field and hit submit. You get some validation errors, and each time the page completely refreshes. But we can do better! First add the Enhance attribute to the Forms as in Listing 11-9.

Listing 11-9. Enhancing Forms

```
<EditForm FormName="member-form"
  OnValidSubmit="Submit" Model="@Member"
  Enhance>
```

This will now use FETCH, because we enabled enhanced navigation for this Forms component, again improving the user experience. Instead of reloading the whole page, enhanced navigation updates the UI with the differences, giving the SPA experience!

We are not done yet. Let us update this with some feedback when the user clicks the submit button. Add a message field and the UI to render the message as in Listing 11-10.

Listing 11-10. Adding a message

```
</EditForm>

<br/>

@if (message is { Length: > 0 })
{
  <div class="btn btn-info">@message</div>
}

@code {
  private string? message;
```

Also update the Submit method to display a message that we are saving, and when done the result. The code is Listing 11-11.

Listing 11-11. The Submit method

```
public async Task Submit()
{
  message = "Saving..."; // Streamed rendering will show this first
  await Task.Delay(TimeSpan.FromSeconds(1.5)); // Fake Save
  message = "Saved!"; // After saving will update the UI
}
```

Run. When you click submit, the message appears after a while. But you don't see the Saving... message? Well, the page waits for the Submit method to finish and then renders. Didn't we see a way to have a page render is a streamed fashion? Where it would display the Saving... message, and later the Saved message? Simply enable streaming rendering as in Listing 11-12.

Listing 11-12. Enabling streaming rendering

```
@page "/Forms"
@attribute [StreamRendering]
```

Run. Click submit. See the UI update just like with a SPA, but without breaking a sweat!

Up to this point, we have not yet touched on interactivity features from Blazor. We only used built-in improvements that require (almost) no effort on your part!

Interactive Server

What if your components need to handle click events, like the `Counter` component? In this case you need to enable interactivity. You have the choice between server, WebAssembly, or both. And you can enable this globally or choose for each component. Let us start with server interactivity. We discussed Blazor Server in the first chapter, but a quick recap. With Blazor Server, your components are running on a server, and for each user, a SignalR connection is made with the browser. SignalR allows you to create a two-way connection between the server and the browser. As components get updated, this SignalR connection is used to send component changes from the server to the browser, and events from the browser to the server, which trigger components changes, etc.

CHAPTER 11　BLAZOR RENDER MODES

Examine a Blazor Server Web App

Let us create a Blazor Server Web App using Visual Studio (or PowerShell). Start Visual Studio and create a new Blazor Web App project named BlazorApp.ServerInteractivity. When presented with the options, choose Server as the Interactive render mode, and Per Page/component for the Interactivity location, as illustrated by Figure 11-6.

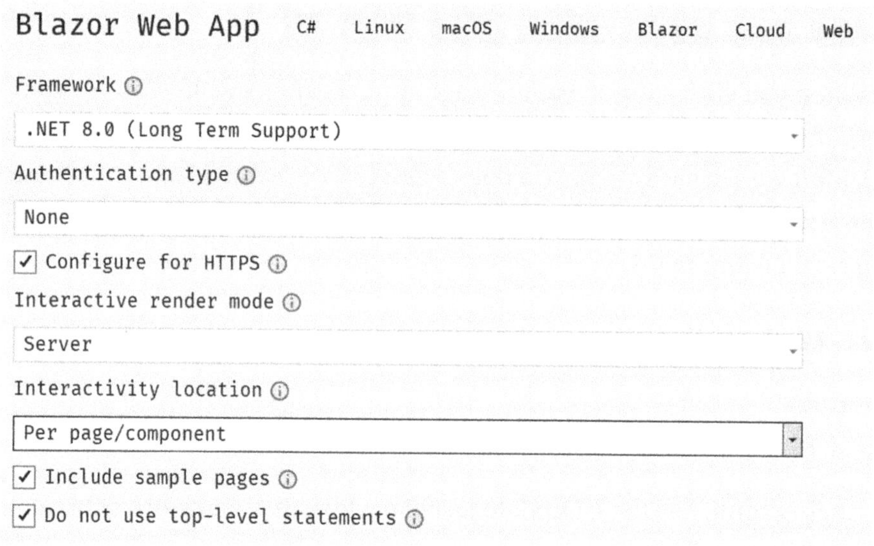

Figure 11-6. Select server interactivity

If you like, you can also use this PowerShell script to create the project:

```
$ProjectName = "BlazorApp.ServerInteractivity"
mkdir $ProjectName
cd $ProjectName
dotnet new sln -n $ProjectName
mkdir src
cd src
dotnet new blazor -n $ProjectName --all-interactive --interactivity Server
cd ..
dotnet sln add src\$ProjectName
```

Open Program.cs as in Listing 11-13, showing the important differences with SSR. To enable interactivity, you call the `AddInteractiveServerComponents` method which adds the dependencies required for server interactivity, such as SignalR. We also need to invoke the AddInteractiveServerRenderMode method, which configures routing to enable SignalR, enables prerendering of components, and of course enables the server interactivity render mode.

Listing 11-13. Program.cs

```
builder.Services.AddRazorComponents()
  .AddInteractiveServerComponents();
...
app.MapRazorComponents<App>()
  .AddInteractiveServerRenderMode();
```

The App, Routes, Home, and Weather components function just like before and are using the SSR model as before. You will see another component: Counter. This component is interactive, and that is because it enables server interactivity by adding the @rendermode directive from Listing 11-14.

Listing 11-14. Enabling server interactivity

```
@rendermode InteractiveServer
```

Note If you started with a SSR project and you want to enable interactivity, you just make the update from Listing 11-13, and you enable interactive mode on the components that require it.

When you run the project, you can interact with the counter by clicking the button. The InteractiveServer render mode will take care of handling the click event using SignalR. You can see the Blazor runtime create this SignalR connection if you like. Start by running the project. When the browser is ready, open the network tab of your browser's debugger and filter on web sockets as in Figure 11-7. Select the Home tab in the browser. Because the Home component is using SSR, there is no web socket open. When you run this as a developer Visual Studio also uses some websocket connections, so ignore these.

CHAPTER 11   BLAZOR RENDER MODES

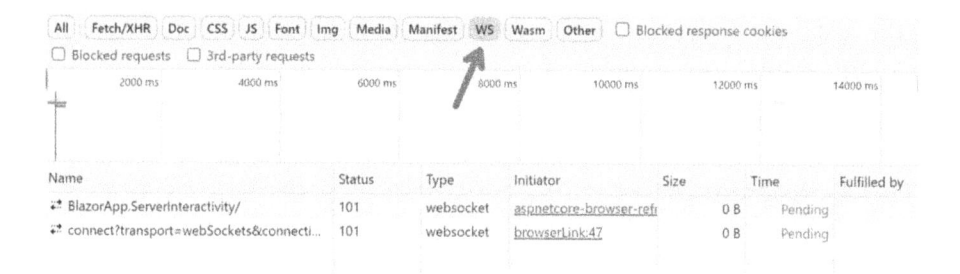

Figure 11-7. *Showing the WebSocket connections*

Now navigate to the Counter tab, and you will see a new web socket connection as in Figure 11-8.

Figure 11-8. *Showing the Counter opens a new Web Socket*

When you select this new web socket connection, you can inspect the messages as in Figure 11-9. Each time you click the button, you should see a new message.

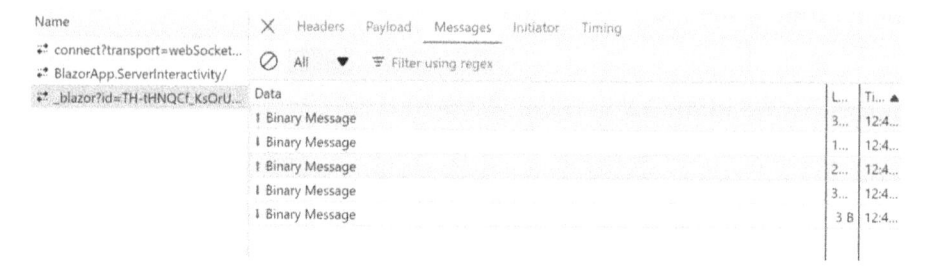

Figure 11-9. *Inspecting the Counter Web Socket messages*

Now select the Home tab. The web socket should disappear because we don't need it anymore. If the web socket is still in the list, look at the Time column. When the web socket is Pending, it means the connection is still being used. When it shows a time, it means the connection was closed.

Render Modes

A render mode is a class implementing the `IComponentRenderMode` interface, and for convenience, there exists the `RenderMode` class which has pre-constructed render modes.

- InteractiveServer
- InteractiveWebAssembly
- InteractiveAuto

The imports.razor file uses a `static using` to make these static properties available so you don't have to prefix it with the class.

`@using static Microsoft.AspNetCore.Components.Web.RenderMode`

Setting the Render Mode

Blazor allows you to choose the render mode for a component. A component can set its own render mode, for example, the `Counter` component does that in Listing 11-13. Of course, this means that this component only supports this render mode.

You can also set the render mode on a component where you use it. For example, you can use the Weather component with server interactivity on the Home component, with an example in Listing 11-15. Normally, a component that does not set its render mode inherits the render mode of the parent, and the Home component here uses SSR so the Weather component would use that too. But if you like a component to use a more specific render mode, you can use the @rendermode directive as shown in Listing 11-15.

Listing 11-15. Setting render mode using a component

```
@page "/"

<PageTitle>Home</PageTitle>

<h1>Hello, world!</h1>

Welcome to your new app.

<Weather @rendermode="InteractiveServer" />
```

CHAPTER 11 BLAZOR RENDER MODES

Can I use this to override the render mode of a component? No. For example, if you try to add the Counter component to the Home component and set its render mode as in Listing 11-16, you will get a compiler error.

```
Cannot override render mode for component 'BlazorApp.ServerInteractivity.
Components.Pages.Counter' as it explicitly declares one.
```

Listing 11-16. Overriding the render mode

```
@page "/"

<PageTitle>Home</PageTitle>

<h1>Hello, world!</h1>

Welcome to your new app.

<Weather @rendermode="InteractiveServer" />

<Counter @rendermode="InteractiveServer"/>
```

Another option is to make it global, meaning each component uses that render mode by default. Since the render mode is inherited, you set it on the highest level component. Normally that means the Routes component.

When you create a new Blazor Web App project, you are given that option as shown in Figure 11-10.

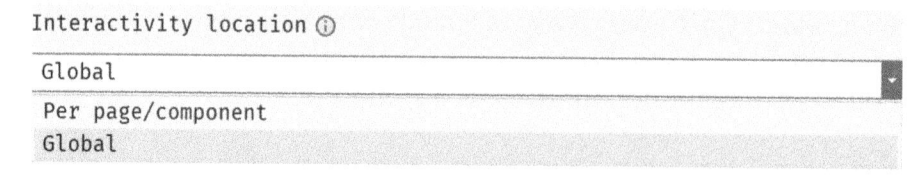

Figure 11-10. *Choosing global or per component interactivity*

This will set the render mode on the HeadOutlet and Routes component as shown in Listing 11-17. Please ensure you use the same render mode on both!

CHAPTER 11   BLAZOR RENDER MODES

Listing 11-17. Setting the render mode globally

```
<!DOCTYPE html>
<html lang="en">

<head>
    <meta charset="utf-8" />
    <meta name="viewport" content="width=device-width, initial-scale=1.0" />
    <base href="/" />
    <link rel="stylesheet" href="bootstrap/bootstrap.min.css" />
    <link rel="stylesheet" href="app.css" />
    <link rel="stylesheet" href="BlazorApp.ServerInteractivity.styles.css" />
    <link rel="icon" type="image/png" href="favicon.png" />
    <HeadOutlet @rendermode="InteractiveServer" />
</head>

<body>
    <Routes @rendermode="InteractiveServer" />
    <script src="_framework/blazor.web.js"></script>
</body>

</html>
```

You can still override the render mode with a more specific one, but you cannot have a parent and child with different interactive modes.

When the parent is a SSR rendered component, it can pass parameters to an interactive child component on the condition that the parameters need to be JSON serializable.

Interactive WebAssembly

Let us have a look at Blazor with WASM interactive render mode. With this render mode, your component will be running in the browser using WebAssembly.

CHAPTER 11   BLAZOR RENDER MODES

Examine a Blazor WASM Web App

Start Visual Studio and create a new Blazor Web App Project named BlazorApp.
WASMInteractivity. When presented with the options, choose WebAssembly as the
Interactive render mode and Per Page/component for the Interactivity location, as
illustrated by Figure 11-11.

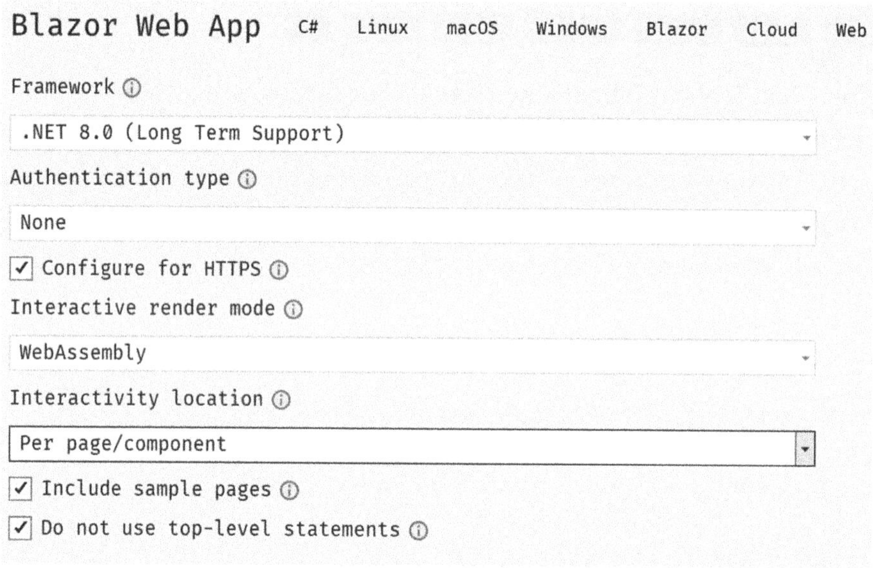

Figure 11-11. Select WebAssembly Interactivity

If you like, you can also use this PowerShell script to create the project:

```
$ProjectName = "BlazorApp.WASMInteractivity"
mkdir $ProjectName
cd $ProjectName
dotnet new sln -n $ProjectName
dotnet new nugetconfig
dotnet new globaljson
mkdir src
dotnet new blazor -n $ProjectName -o src --interactivity WebAssembly
dotnet sln add ".\src\$ProjectName\"
dotnet sln add ".\src\$ProjectName.Client\"
```

One of the big differences you will see here is that we have two projects. With Blazor WebAssembly, the browser downloads your components. Which components? Look in the BlazorApp.WASMInteractivity project's Components/Pages folder. You should find the Home and Weather component. Why? Because these can be SSR rendered, they don't need any interactivity! Now look in the BlazorApp.WASMInteractivity.Client project's Pages folder. The Counter component lives here, which requires interactivity. When you run this project, some components still get server rendered, because we don't need them in the browser!

Note The Client project is built into an assembly which gets downloaded in the browser, containing all the components and services required.

Open Program.cs from the BlazorApp.WASMInteractivity project. Listing 11-18 shows the differences again, with similar AddInteractiveWebAssemblyComponents and AddInteractiveWebAssemblyRenderMode methods.

Listing 11-18. Program for Interactive WebAssembly render mode

```
_ = builder.Services.AddRazorComponents()
    .AddInteractiveWebAssemblyComponents();
...
_ = app.MapRazorComponents<App>()
    .AddInteractiveWebAssemblyRenderMode()
    .AddAdditionalAssemblies(typeof(Client._Imports).Assembly);
```

Routing scans your assembly for @page directives. But when your components live in another assembly, you need to pass them to the router for scanning. Here the AddAdditionalAssemblies method takes care of that.

Run the project. When the browser runs, open the browser's developer tools and show the network tab. Ensure the Home page is shown, and hit refresh. The browser will download the usual files, like HTML and CSS files. But no WASM files, not DLL files. This is because the Home component is using SSR.

Now select the Counter link. You will see a series of wasm files being downloaded. These are .NET assemblies using a firewall-friendly format. Now interact with the Counter component by clicking the button. No more network traffic. The Counter component is running inside your browser. You could even go offline, and everything keeps working.

CHAPTER 11 BLAZOR RENDER MODES

Of course, you need to be online to switch back to the Home component (which uses enhanced navigation; see earlier).

Look at the Counter component as in Listing 11-19. Here the component chooses InteractiveWebAssembly.

Listing 11-19. The Counter component's render mode

```
@rendermode InteractiveWebAssembly
```

Interactive Auto

Can I have both? Please? Yes, you can! If you like, you can use the same component with SSR, Interactive Server, and Interactive WebAssembly render mode.

Examine a Blazor Server Auto Web App

Let us create a Blazor Server Web App using Visual Studio (or PowerShell). Start Visual Studio and create a new Blazor Web App project named Select BlazorApp. AutoInteractivity. When presented with the options, choose Auto (Server and WebAssembly) as the Interactive render mode and Per Page/component for the Interactivity location, as illustrated by Figure 11-12.

Figure 11-12. *Select Auto Interactivity*

CHAPTER 11   BLAZOR RENDER MODES

If you like, you can also use this PowerShell script to create the project:

```
$ProjectName = "BlazorApp.AutoInteractivity"
mkdir $ProjectName
cd $ProjectName
dotnet new sln -n $ProjectName
dotnet new globaljson
mkdir src
dotnet new blazor -n $ProjectName -o src -int Auto
dotnet sln add ".\src\$ProjectName\"
dotnet sln add ".\src\$ProjectName.Client\"
```

Open Program.cs from the BlazorApp.AutoInteractivity project. Listing 11-20 again shows the differences, or should I say commonalities? Since we need both render modes, we add support for both. And of course, WebAssembly rendered components need to live in the Client project, but we can still use them for service side rendering.

Listing 11-20. Program.cs

```
_ = builder.Services.AddRazorComponents()
    .AddInteractiveServerComponents()
    .AddInteractiveWebAssemblyComponents();
...
_ = app.MapRazorComponents<App>()
    .AddInteractiveServerRenderMode()
    .AddInteractiveWebAssemblyRenderMode()
    .AddAdditionalAssemblies(typeof(Client._Imports).Assembly);
```

Open the Counter component. Currently it is using Auto render mode. But what does that mean? Build and run this project. Let us look at the network again. The Home component still uses SSR, so there are no differences there. Now select the Counter link. The Counter is displayed and is immediately interactive using server interactivity. In Figure 11-13, you can see the WebSocket being used. But the download does not stop here.

351

CHAPTER 11   BLAZOR RENDER MODES

Name	Status	Type	Initiator	Size	Time
counter	200	fetch	blazor.web.js:1	4.9 kB	220 ms
dotnet.js	200	script	blazor.web.js:1	11.7 kB	26 ms
blazor.boot.json	200	fetch	polyfills.ts:120	9.0 kB	12 ms
dotnet.runtime.8.0.7.yhkey06b4k.js	200	script	run.ts:443	64.8 kB	81 ms
dotnet.native.8.0.7.nswtm9hxif.js	200	script	run.ts:450	36.3 kB	79 ms
initializers	200	fetch	blazor.web.js:1	65 B	88 ms
dotnet.native.wasm	200	wasm	polyfills.ts:120	1.2 MB	131 ms
negotiate?negotiateVersion=1	200	fetch	blazor.web.js:1	344 B	47 ms
_blazor?id=Elo_1B0bsJTIXzn_dquiVA	200	websocket	blazor.web.js:1	0 B	Pending
appsettings.Development.json	200	fetch	polyfills.ts:120	185 B	10 ms
appsettings.json	200	fetch	polyfills.ts:120	167 B	44 ms

Figure 11-13. Counter component using server interactivity

While the Counter component is fully interactive, the Blazor runtime downloads add the necessary files for running the Counter component in WebAssembly. But your user can still interact with your component, no delays. Figure 11-14 shows some of the files being downloaded, with emphasis on runtime assemblies and your client assembly.

System.Xml.XmlDocument.wasm	200	wasm	polyfills.ts:120	2.4 kB	5 ms
System.Xml.XmlSerializer.wasm	200	wasm	polyfills.ts:120	2.9 kB	7 ms
System.Xml.wasm	200	wasm	polyfills.ts:120	4.3 kB	5 ms
System.wasm	200	wasm	polyfills.ts:120	11.8 kB	7 ms
WindowsBase.wasm	200	wasm	polyfills.ts:120	2.6 kB	7 ms
mscorlib.wasm	200	wasm	polyfills.ts:120	14.9 kB	5 ms
netstandard.wasm	200	wasm	polyfills.ts:120	26.1 kB	6 ms
System.Private.CoreLib.wasm	200	wasm	polyfills.ts:120	1.4 MB	93 ms
BlazorApp.AutoInteractivity.Client.w...	200	wasm	polyfills.ts:120	3.8 kB	5 ms
BlazorApp.AutoInteractivity.Client.pdb	200	fetch	polyfills.ts:120	10.4 kB	8 ms

Figure 11-14. Blazor runtime and assemblies

If you keep this Counter open, it is still using the web socket; thus, server interactivity. But when you click another tab and go back, you will see that the Counter component is now using WebAssembly interactivity (no more network activity). So, with Auto render, you get best of both worlds.

Note Careful: Auto mode requires your components to handle both server and wasm.

Using a Component with Difference Render Modes

Can I use a component with different render modes? Yes, I would even say this is easy. Open the Counter component and remove its @rendermode directive as in Listing 11-21. Also remove the @page directive and other unneeded stuff taking up space.

Listing 11-21. The Counter component

```
<p role="status">Current count: @currentCount</p>

<button class="btn btn-primary" @onclick="IncrementCount">Click me</button>

@code {
  private int currentCount = 0;

  private void IncrementCount()
  {
    currentCount++;
  }
}
```

Now open the Home component, and add three Counter instances as in Listing 11-22.

Listing 11-22. Home using Counter components with different render mode

```
@page "/"
@using BlazorApp.AutoInteractivity.Client.Pages

<PageTitle>Home</PageTitle>

<h1>Hello, world!</h1>

Welcome to your new app.

<div>
  <h2>Server Interactivity</h2>
  <Counter @rendermode=InteractiveServer/>
</div>
```

CHAPTER 11   BLAZOR RENDER MODES

```
<div>
  <h2>WASM Interactivity</h2>
  <Counter @rendermode=InteractiveWebAssembly />
</div>

<div>
  <h2>Auto Interactivity</h2>
  <Counter @rendermode=InteractiveAuto />
</div>
```

When you run, you are using the same component with three different render modes. You could add another `Counter` without the `@rendermode` directive; this would then use SSR and not be interactive (the button would do nothing when clicked).

Detecting the Current Render Mode

Is there an easy way to detect which render mode a component is using? The short answer is no (but in .NET 9 this becomes yes), but with a bit of work you can turn that into a resounding yes. There are four cases we need to think about:

- Is the component running in the browser? If yes, then we are using WASM interactivity. You can use the `OperatingSystem.IsBrowser` method for that.

- Is the component running on the server? Then we still have three different cases.

- Is the component running in a circuit? If yes, then it is using server interactivity. Circuit detection is covered a little further on.

- If not, is the component using streamed rendering? We can detect that by checking for the attribute in the class metadata.

- If all questions result in no, then we are using SSR.

Let us implement all of this. Start by adding the `RenderModes` class to the client project as in Listing 11-23. This provides nice named instances for each render mode.

Listing 11-23. The RenderModes type

```
namespace BlazorApp.AutoInteractivity.Components;

public class RenderModes
{
  public const string InteractiveWebAssembly
    = nameof(InteractiveWebAssembly);
  public const string InteractiveServer
    = nameof(InteractiveServer);
  public const string ServerStaticStreamed
    = nameof(ServerStaticStreamed);
  public const string ServerStatic
    = nameof(ServerStatic);
}
```

Now to answer the question if we are running inside a circuit. What you can do is to install a circuit handler, so that the Blazor runtime notifies our application when a circuit becomes (un)available.

> **Note** A circuit handler allows you to execute logic when the circuit gets opened or closed.

We need a helper class to keep track of the current circuit, as in Listing 11-24. Add this to the client project. The `ActiveCircuitState` has a Boolean `CircuitExists` property, tracking if we are running inside a circuit (thus Blazor Server).

Listing 11-24. ActiveCircuitState

```
namespace BlazorApp.AutoInteractivity.Components;

public class ActiveCircuitState
{
  public bool CircuitExists { get; set; }
}
```

CHAPTER 11 BLAZOR RENDER MODES

Add the ActiveCircuitHandler class from Listing 11-25, which will be notified by the Blazor runtime every time a circuit gets opened/closed. Careful, this class belongs in the server project!

Listing 11-25. The ActiveCircuitHandler

```
using Microsoft.AspNetCore.Components.Server.Circuits;

namespace BlazorApp.AutoInteractivity.Components;

public class ActiveCircuitHandler(ActiveCircuitState state)
  : CircuitHandler
{
  public override Task OnCircuitOpenedAsync(Circuit circuit,
    CancellationToken cancellationToken)
  {
    state.CircuitExists = true;
    return base.OnCircuitOpenedAsync(circuit, cancellationToken);
  }

  public override Task OnCircuitClosedAsync(Circuit circuit,
    CancellationToken cancellationToken)
  {
    state.CircuitExists = false;
    return base.OnCircuitClosedAsync(circuit, cancellationToken);
  }
}
```

Open Program.cs from the main project and add the ActiveCircuitHandler as a scoped dependency as in Listing 11-26. This way the Blazor runtime can find it.

Listing 11-26. Adding the CircuitHandler

```
builder.Services.AddScoped(typeof(CircuitHandler),
                          typeof(ActiveCircuitHandler));
```

Also add a scoped instance of the ActiveCircuitState as in Listing 11-27. This way there is one instance per user/circuit. When the circuit is open the CircuitExists property will be true, and when the circuit is closed the CircuitExists property will be false.

Listing 11-27. Add the ActiveCircuitState

```
builder.Services.AddScoped<ActiveCircuitState>();
```

Let us put all of this together in the RenderModeProvider class with the GetRenderMode method from Listing 11-28. This is the implementation of the reasoning from the start of this section. It will not compile yet.

Listing 11-28. RenderModeProvider's GetRenderMode method

```
using Microsoft.AspNetCore.Components;

namespace BlazorApp.AutoInteractivity.Components;

public class RenderModeProvider(ActiveCircuitState activeCircuitState)
{
  public string GetRenderMode(ComponentBase page)
  {
    if (OperatingSystem.IsBrowser())
    {
      return RenderModes.InteractiveWebAssembly;
    }
    else if (activeCircuitState.CircuitExists)
    {
      return RenderModes.InteractiveServer;
    }
    else if (UsesStaticRendering(page))
    {
      return RenderModes.ServerStaticStreamed;
    }
    return RenderModes.ServerStatic;
  }
}
```

How do we know if a component is using streamed rendering? Well, there will be a StreamRenderingAttribute attribute on the component's type, and we can use reflection to detect it. Add the methods from Listing 11-29 to the RenderModeProvider class.

Listing 11-29. Detecting streamed rendering

```
private bool UsesStaticRendering(ComponentBase page)
=> UsesStaticRendering(page.GetType());

private bool UsesStaticRendering(Type pageType)
=> pageType.GetCustomAttribute<StreamRenderingAttribute>() is not null;
```

Finally, we need to add the RenderModeProvider as another dependency. Your Program.cs should resemble Listing 11-30.

Listing 11-30. Dependency injection in Program.cs

```
public static void Main(string[] args)
{
  WebApplicationBuilder builder =
    WebApplication.CreateBuilder(args);

  // Add services to the container.
  _ = builder.Services.AddRazorComponents()
      .AddInteractiveServerComponents()
      .AddInteractiveWebAssemblyComponents();

  builder.Services.AddScoped<ActiveCircuitState>();
  builder.Services.AddScoped(typeof(CircuitHandler),
                             typeof(ActiveCircuitHandler));
  builder.Services.AddTransient<RenderModeProvider>();

  WebApplication app = builder.Build();
  ...
```

Using RenderModeProvider

Update the Counter component as in Listing 11-31 to use the RenderModeProvider to display its render mode.

Listing 11-31. The Counter using the RenderModeProvider

```
@using BlazorApp.AutoInteractivity.Components
@inject RenderModeProvider renderModeProvider

<p role="status">Current count: @currentCount</p>
<p>@renderModeProvider.GetRenderMode(this)</p>
<button class="btn btn-primary" @onclick="IncrementCount">Click me</button>

@code {
  private int currentCount = 0;

  private void IncrementCount()
  {
    currentCount++;
  }
}
```

Do the same for the Home component, shown in Listing 11-32.

Listing 11-32. Home using the RenderModeProvider

```
@page "/"
@using BlazorApp.AutoInteractivity.Client.Pages
@inject RenderModeProvider renderModeProvider

<PageTitle>Home</PageTitle>

<h1>@renderModeProvider.GetRenderMode(this)</h1>

...
```

Because we are using the type in the client project, we also need to configure dependency injection as in Listing 11-33.

Listing 11-33. The Client DI

```
using BlazorApp.AutoInteractivity.Components;
using Microsoft.AspNetCore.Components.WebAssembly.Hosting;

namespace BlazorApp.AutoInteractivity.Client;
```

CHAPTER 11 BLAZOR RENDER MODES

```
internal class Program
{
  static async Task Main(string[] args)
  {
    var builder = WebAssemblyHostBuilder.CreateDefault(args);

    builder.Services.AddTransient<RenderModeProvider>();
    builder.Services.AddScoped<ActiveCircuitState>();

    await builder.Build().RunAsync();
  }
}
```

Run the application. After a little while, you should see the Home component using ServerStatic render mode, the top Counter using InteractiveServer, and the two other Counters InteractiveWebAssembly. If you are fast (or your computer is slow) you will also see that the components initially all render using ServerStatic render mode. Why? Because by default Blazor also uses prerendering.

Detecting RenderMode in .NET 9

With .NET 9 the team building Blazor decided that having an easy way to detect the current render mode was important enough to add a new RendererInfo property to the ComponentBase class. This has two properties, Name and IsInteractive. The Name property tells you the platform the component is running on (Static, Server, WebAssembly, or WebView). The IsInteractive property reflects if the component is currently interactive.

There is also an AssignedRenderMode property which contains the render mode the component will eventually use (after prerendering). The combination of these three properties allows your component to take different execution paths, for example, while prerendering.

Time to look at prerendering.

Prerendering

Your components will render, no matter which render mode you are using. But with Blazor WebAssembly, your component only gets rendered when the application has downloaded all the runtime files. This means that search engines might not see your component's content because they need to be rendered in the browser. Not all search engines will run your application (Google, Bing, Yandex, and Baidu do run your application before indexing its content). And that is where prerendering becomes useful. Your server will initially render your component on the server using server-side rendering, no matter which render mode it uses.

Prerendering shows the component immediately to the user, giving a better user experience, especially for web assembly components. But prerendered components will not be interactive until they are actually running in their interactive mode. You might also see another side effect; since your component renders twice, it will execute the OnInitialized(Async) life-cycle method twice, and if this calls a service, this service will run twice, sometimes with unexpected results.

> **Note** Prerendering is enabled by default to interactive components.

What can we do when our component does not work correctly with prerendering? Either disable prerendering or add support for prerendering.

Disabling Prerendering

To disable prerendering, you need to set render mode using the proper IComponentRenderMode instance. For example, look at Listing 11-34, where the Home component disables prerendering for each Counter.

Listing 11-34. Disabling prerendering

```
@page "/"
@using BlazorApp.AutoInteractivity.Client.Pages

<PageTitle>Home</PageTitle>

<h1>Home</h1>
```

CHAPTER 11 BLAZOR RENDER MODES

Welcome to your new app.

```
<div>
  <Counter @rendermode=noPreRenderInteractiveServer />
</div>

<div>
  <Counter @rendermode=noPreRenderInteractiveWebAssembly />
</div>

<div>
  <Counter @rendermode=noPreRenderInteractiveAuto />
</div>

@code {

  IComponentRenderMode noPreRenderInteractiveServer =
    new InteractiveServerRenderMode(prerender: false);
  IComponentRenderMode noPreRenderInteractiveWebAssembly =
    new InteractiveWebAssemblyRenderMode(prerender: false);
  IComponentRenderMode noPreRenderInteractiveAuto =
    new InteractiveAutoRenderMode(prerender: false);
}
```

Running the application does reveal one drawback: your components only get rendered when they are completely ready. You will probably see a slight delay between the interactive server Counter, and the WebAssembly Counter, this is because it takes longer to get the WebAssembly runtime to initialize.

Supporting Prerendering

You can also make your component do different things during prerendering. Remember the RenderModeProvider from earlier? Add the IsInteractive method from Listing 11-35 to this class.

CHAPTER 11 BLAZOR RENDER MODES

Listing 11-35. Add IsInteractive to RenderModeProvider

```
public class RenderModeProvider(ActiveCircuitState activeCircuitState)
{
  public string GetRenderMode(ComponentBase page)
  {
    ...
  }
  public bool IsInteractive(ComponentBase page)
  => GetRenderMode(page) switch
  {
    RenderModes.InteractiveWebAssembly => true,
    RenderModes.InteractiveServer => true,
    _ => false
  };

  ...
}
```

This method makes it easy for the component to detect prerendering.

Copy the Counter component, rename it PrerenderedCounter, and update it to Listing 11-36.

Listing 11-36. Supporting prerendering

```
@page "/counter"
@rendermode InteractiveServer

@using BlazorApp.AutoInteractivity.Components
@inject RenderModeProvider renderModeProvider

@if (renderModeProvider.IsInteractive(this))
{
  <p role="status">Current count: @currentCount</p>
  <button class="btn btn-primary" @onclick="IncrementCount">
    Click me
  </button>
}
```

363

```
else
{
  <p role="status">Current count: 0</p>
  <button class="btn btn-secondary" disabled="@true">
    Click me
   </button>
}
@code {
  private int currentCount = 0;

  private void IncrementCount()
  {
    currentCount++;
  }
}
```

This component uses the `renderModeProvider.IsInteractive` method to detect prerendering and in this case renders a disabled button with a different color to make it clear that it is non-functioning.

Run. You should first see the prerendered counter, with a gray button. Shortly after the component starts running with WebAssembly and turns blue.

State Persistence

Let us examine the case where we have a component that loads some data from a service in the `OnInitialized(Async)` method. With prerendering this method gets called, and it gets called again when the component renders interactively. This can result in weird behavior, the least of which is the flickering of the component. Let us look at an example.

Using PersistentComponentState

In the code provided with this book, you can find the `StatePersistance` folder, containing a solution which uses auto rendering. When you run, the Weather component will prerender and generate some random weather data. Then when it becomes interactive, it will render the component again with other random data,

CHAPTER 11 BLAZOR RENDER MODES

causing it to flicker and show different data. This could be your component that grabs data from a server.

> **Note** This project is actually the final solution for the Communication chapter.

Examine the Weather component; it uses the `InteractiveAuto` render mode as in Listing 11-37.

Listing 11-37. Change Weather's render mode

```
@page "/weather"
@rendermode InteractiveAuto
```

Again, we could disable prerendering on the Weather component; update the @rendermode with disabled prerendering as in Listing 11-38.

Listing 11-38. Disable prerendering

```
@rendermode @(new InteractiveServerRenderMode(prerender: false))
```

But there is another option. What if we save the data from the service during prerendering, and pass it to the interactive rendering? We can use a service named `PersistentComponentState`. What this allows you to do is to save any data you need after rendering and reuse that data in the next render.

Start by injecting the `PersistComponentState` service as in Listing 11-39.

Listing 11-39. Inject PersistComponentState

```
@page "/weather"
@using BlazorApp.Communication.Client.Entities
@using BlazorApp.Communication.Client.Services
@implements IDisposable
@inject IWeatherService WeatherService
@inject PersistentComponentState ApplicationState

<PageTitle>Weather</PageTitle>

...
```

365

```csharp
@code {
  private WeatherForecast[]? forecasts;

  PersistingComponentStateSubscription _sub;

  protected override async Task OnInitializedAsync()
  {
    _sub = ApplicationState.RegisterOnPersisting(PersistState);

    WeatherForecast[] state = default!;
    bool foundInState = ApplicationState
      .TryTakeFromJson<WeatherForecast[]>("WEATHER", out state);

    if (foundInState && state is not null)
    {
      forecasts = state;
    }
    else
    {
      forecasts = await WeatherService.GetForecasts();
    }
  }

  private Task PersistState()
  {
    ApplicationState.PersistAsJson("WEATHER", forecasts);
    return Task.CompletedTask;
  }

  public void Dispose()
  {
    _sub.Dispose();
  }
}
```

In the `OnInitializedAsync` method, we subscribe to the rendering engine and register a method (here named `PersistState`) to be invoked right after each render. In the `PersistState` method we save the data we used during rendering. The `PersistComponentState` service will allow us to read this saved data next time the component renders. This will be another instance of the `Weather` component because the next time the `Weather` component will be running in the browser using WebAssembly.

We are not ready in `OnInitializedAsync`. Maybe we have already rendered, and the `PersistState` method has saved the state we want. So, we call the `TryTakeFromJson` method which returns `true` when it finds state from a previous render. In that case we use the same data to render. Otherwise, we fetch the data, and the `PersistState` method will pass it to the next render.

> **Note** `PersistComponentState` only works for passing data from the prerender to the next render. Do not use it to persist data for longer periods of time.

You should also dispose of the subscription when the component is disposed, so we need to implement `IDisposable` where we dispose of the subscription.

Run. Navigate to the Weather page. It loads the data once and uses the data during the prerender, and the next render.

There are still topics I want to discuss with you about state management. We will do this in the State Management chapter.

Summary

Today you can use Blazor components almost everywhere. You can use a Blazor component to render some HTML, just like MVC uses Views to render HTML. In this case, you use Blazor Server-Side Rendering. But you can also use that same component running on the server and make it interactive using Blazor Server render mode. Since your component is running on the server, you can access databases, the server's file system, etc. Blazor also allows you to run that component interactively inside the Browser using Blazor WebAssembly render mode. However, accessing databases and other server-only resources requires you to add support for this. We will discuss this some more in the Communication chapter. Finally, you can have a component run first on the server while the browser is downloading the required runtime files, and once this is done, we can have the component run in the browser using Blazor Auto render mode. In this chapter, we also discussed prerendering. Prerendering allows you to render your WebAssembly component first on the server, which makes search engines' lives a little easier but can give you some unexpected side effects.

CHAPTER 12

JavaScript Interoperability

Sometimes, there is just no escape from using _JavaScript_. For example, Blazor itself uses JavaScript to update the browser's _DOM_ from your Blazor components. In this chapter, you will look at interoperability with JavaScript, and as an example, you will build a Blazor component library to display a map using a popular open source JavaScript library. This chapter does require you to have some basic JavaScript knowledge.

Calling JavaScript from C#

Browsers have a lot of capabilities you might want to use in your Blazor web site. For example, you might want to use the Browser's _local storage_ to keep track of some data. Thanks to Blazor's JavaScript interoperability, this is easy.

Providing a Glue Function

To call JavaScript functionality, you start by building a glue function in JavaScript. I like to call these functions glue functions (my own naming convention) because they become the glue between .NET and JavaScript.

Glue functions are regular JavaScript functions. A JavaScript glue function can take any number of arguments, on the condition that they are _JSON serializable_ (meaning that you can only use types that are convertible to JSON, including classes whose properties are JSON serializable. Blazor uses System.Text.Json serialization). This is required because the arguments and return type are sent as JSON between .NET and JavaScript runtimes.

You then add this function to the JavaScript _global scope_ object, which in the browser is the _window_ object. You will look at an example a little later, so keep reading. You can then call this JavaScript glue function from your Blazor component.

CHAPTER 12　JAVASCRIPT INTEROPERABILITY

Using IJSRuntime to Call the Glue Function

Back to .NET land. To invoke your JavaScript glue function from C#, you use the .NET _IJSRuntime_ instance provided through dependency injection. This instance has the `InvokeAsync<T>` generic method, which takes the name of the glue function and its arguments and returns a value of type T, which is the .NET return type of the glue function. If your JavaScript method returns nothing, there is also the `InvokeVoidAsync` method. If this sounds confusing, you will look at an example right away.

The `InvokeAsync` method is asynchronous to support all asynchronous scenarios, and this is the recommended way of calling JavaScript. If you need to call the glue function synchronously, you can downcast the `IJSRuntime` instance to `IJSInProcessRuntime` and call its synchronous `Invoke<T>` method. This method uses the same arguments as `InvokeAsync<T>` with the same constraints.

Using synchronous calls for JavaScript interop is not recommended! This only works for Blazor WebAssembly; Blazor Server requires the use of asynchronous calls because the calls will be serialized over SignalR to the client.

Storing Data in the Browser with Interop

It's time to look at an example, and you will start with the JavaScript glue function. Open the provided BlazorApp.JavaScriptInterop solution (or you can create a new Blazor project from scratch with the following Powershell script):

```
$ProjectName = "BlazorApp.JavaScriptInterop"
mkdir $ProjectName
cd $ProjectName
dotnet new sln -n $ProjectName
mkdir src
cd src
dotnet new blazor -n $ProjectName --all-interactive --interactivity Server
cd ..
dotnet sln add src\$ProjectName
```

Open the wwwroot folder from the BlazorApp.JavaScriptInterop project, and add a new subfolder called scripts. Add a new JavaScript file to the scripts folder called interop. js, and add the glue functions from Listing 12-1. This will add the `blazorLocalStorage` object to the global `window` object, containing three glue functions. These glue functions allow you to access the localStorage object from the browser, which allows you to store data on the client's computer so you can access it later, even after the user has restarted the browser or computer.

Listing 12-1. The blazorLocalStorage glue functions

```
window.blazorLocalStorage = {
  get: key => key in localStorage ? JSON.parse(localStorage[key]) : null,
  set: (key, value) => { localStorage[key] = JSON.stringify(value); },
  delete: key => { delete localStorage[key]; },
};
```

Your Blazor website needs to include this script, so open the App component and add a script reference after the Blazor script, as shown in Listing 12-2.

> **Note** Visual Studio Tip: You can drag and drop the interop.js file from Solution Explorer into the component, and Visual Studio will do the rest.

Listing 12-2. Including the script reference

```
<!DOCTYPE html>
<html lang="en">

<head>
  <meta charset="utf-8" />
  <meta name="viewport" content="width=device-width, initial-scale=1.0" />
  <base href="/" />
  <link rel="stylesheet" href="bootstrap/bootstrap.min.css" />
  <link rel="stylesheet" href="app.css" />
  <link rel="stylesheet" href="BlazorApp.JavaScriptInterop.styles.css" />
  <link rel="icon" type="image/png" href="favicon.png" />
  <HeadOutlet @rendermode="InteractiveServer" />
</head>

<body>
  <Routes @rendermode="InteractiveServer" />
  <script src="_framework/blazor.web.js"></script>
```

CHAPTER 12   JAVASCRIPT INTEROPERABILITY

```
  <!-- Add this -->
  <script src="scripts/interop.js"></script>
</body>

</html>
```

Now let's look at how to call these set/get/delete glue functions. Open the Counter Blazor component and modify it to look like Listing 12-3. The Counter component now will use local storage to remember the last value of the counter. Even restarting your browser will not lose the value of the counter because local storage is permanent. To do this, you use a CurrentCount property, which invokes your glue functions in the property setter to store the last value.

Note Local storage is not shared among different browsers!

The Counter component overrides the OnAfterRenderAsync method to retrieve the last stored value from local storage using the window.blazorLocalStorage.get glue function. And because the currentCount can receive a new value, we need to explicitly call StateHasChanged to make the component re-render the new value. It is possible that there is no value yet, and that is why we need to catch the exception that gets thrown in this case. I tried using a nullable int as in Listing 12-4, but the IJSRuntime throws an error when converting a JavaScript null to a value type.

Listing 12-3. Invoking the glue functions from a Blazor component

```
@page "/counter"
@inject IJSRuntime jsRuntime

<PageTitle>Counter with IJSRuntime</PageTitle>

<h1>Counter</h1>

<p role="status">Current count: @CurrentCount</p>

<button class="btn btn-primary" @onclick="IncrementCount">Click me</button>

@code {
  private int currentCount = 0;

  public int CurrentCount
```

```csharp
{
  get => currentCount;
  set
  {
    if (currentCount != value)
    {
      currentCount = value;
      jsRuntime.InvokeVoidAsync("blazorLocalStorage.set",
        nameof(CurrentCount), currentCount);
    }
  }
}
protected override async Task OnAfterRenderAsync(bool firstRender)
{
  if (firstRender)
  {
    try
    {
      currentCount = await jsRuntime
        .InvokeAsync<int>("blazorLocalStorage.get",
                    nameof(CurrentCount));
      StateHasChanged();
    }
    catch { }
  }
}
private void IncrementCount()
{
  CurrentCount++;
}
}
```

Listing 12-4. Using nullable types

```
protected override async Task OnAfterRenderAsync(bool firstRender)
{
  if (firstRender)
  {
    try
    {
      int? c = await jsRuntime
        .InvokeAsync<int?>("blazorLocalStorage.get",
                          nameof(CurrentCount));
      currentCount = c ?? 0;
      StateHasChanged();
    }
    catch { }
  }
}
```

Note Be careful that you don't create infinite loops when calling StateHasChanged. In this example, we avoid this by only calling IJSInterop when firstRender is true.

Run the solution and modify the Counter's value. Now when you refresh your browser, you will see the last value of Counter. The Counter now persists between sessions! You can exit your browser, open it again, and you will see the Counter again with the last value.

Use OnAfterRenderAsync

You should only perform JavaScript interop when you are sure the browser has rendered the component. With Blazer Server, your component can be prerendered, where there is no JavaScript interop available. Add the following method to the Counter component from Listing 12-5.

Listing 12-5. Doing Interop with OnInitializedAsync

```
protected override async Task OnInitializedAsync()
{
  currentCount = await jsRuntime
    .InvokeAsync<int>("blazorLocalStorage.get",
                     nameof(CurrentCount));
}
```

Run. When you navigate to the Counter component, you will get the following error:

```
InvalidOperationException: JavaScript interop calls cannot be issued at
this time. This is because the component is being statically rendered. When
prerendering is enabled, JavaScript interop calls can only be performed
during the OnAfterRenderAsync lifecycle method.
```

You can disable prerendering, but it might be better to simply invoke your JavaScript calls in the OnAfterRender/OnAfterRenderAsync method.

Before continuing, comment the OnInitializedAsync method.

Passing a Reference to JavaScript

Sometimes your JavaScript needs to access one of your HTML elements. You can do this by storing the element in an ElementReference and then pass this ElementReference to the glue function.

Note Never use JavaScript interop to modify the DOM because this will interfere with the Blazor rendering process! If you need to modify the browser's DOM, use a Blazor component.

You should use this ElementReference as an opaque handle, meaning you can only pass it to a JavaScript glue function, which will receive it as a JavaScript reference to the element. You cannot even pass the ElementReference to another component. This is by design, because each component gets rendered independently, and this might make the ElementReference point to a DOM element that is no longer there.

Let's look at an example by setting the focus on an `<input>` element using interop. To be honest, there is a built-in method in Blazor to do this, but I want to use this as a simple example. Keep on reading; I will show you how to focus an input element without interop.

Start by adding a property of type `ElementReference` to the `@code` area in the `Counter` component as in Listing 12-6.

Listing 12-6. Adding an ElementRef property

```
@code {
  private int currentCount = 0;

  // Add this ElementReference
  private ElementReference? inputElement;
```

Then add an `<input>` element with a `@ref` attribute to set the `inputElement` field as in Listing 12-7. We have seen this `@ref` syntax before; you can use it to get a reference to a Blazor component, but also to a HTML element.

Listing 12-7. Setting the inputElement

```
<p role="status">Current count: @CurrentCount</p>

<!-- Add this div and input element -->
<div>
  <input @ref="inputElement" @bind="@CurrentCount" />
</div>
```

Now add another JavaScript file focus.js with the glue function from Listing 12-8. Don't forget to add the script reference to index.html.

Listing 12-8. Adding the setFocus glue function

```
window.blazorFocus = {
  set: (element) => { element.focus(); }
}
```

Now comes the "tricky" part. Blazor will create your component and then call the lifecycle methods such as `OnInitializedAsync`. If you invoke the `blazorFocus.set` glue function in `OnInitializedAsync`, the DOM has not been updated with the input element, so this will result in a runtime error because the glue function will receive a null reference. You need to wait for the DOM to be updated, which means that you should only pass the `ElementReference` to your glue function in the `OnAfterRender/OnAfterRenderAsync` method!

Override the `OnAfterRenderAsync` method as in Listing 12-9. Since Rendering is complete, we can expect the `inputElement` to be set, and we call the `blazorFocus.set` glue function. But just to be on the safe side, I check if `inputElement` is not `null`.

Listing 12-9. Passing the ElementReference in OnAfterRenderAsync

```
protected override async Task OnAfterRenderAsync(bool firstRender)
{
  if (firstRender)
  {
    try
    {
      currentCount = await jsRuntime
        .InvokeAsync<int>("blazorLocalStorage.get",
                          nameof(CurrentCount));
      StateHasChanged();
    }
    catch { }

    if (inputElement is not null)
    {
      await jsRuntime
        .InvokeVoidAsync("blazorFocus.set", inputElement);
    }
  }
}
```

Add a script reference to the focus.js file as in Listing 12-10.

Listing 12-10. Add the script reference

```
<!DOCTYPE html>
<html lang="en">

<head>
```

CHAPTER 12   JAVASCRIPT INTEROPERABILITY

```html
  <meta charset="utf-8" />
  <meta name="viewport" content="width=device-width, initial-scale=1.0" />
  <base href="/" />
  <link rel="stylesheet" href="bootstrap/bootstrap.min.css" />
  <link rel="stylesheet" href="app.css" />
  <link rel="stylesheet" href="BlazorApp.JavaScriptInterop.styles.css" />
  <link rel="icon" type="image/png" href="favicon.png" />
  <HeadOutlet @rendermode="InteractiveServer" />
</head>

<body>
  <Routes @rendermode="InteractiveServer" />
  <script src="_framework/blazor.web.js"></script>
  <script src="scripts/interop.js"></script>
  <!-- Add this -->
  <script src="scripts/focus.js"></script>
</body>

</html>
```

Run your solution and you should see that the input element receives focus automatically, as in Figure 12-1.

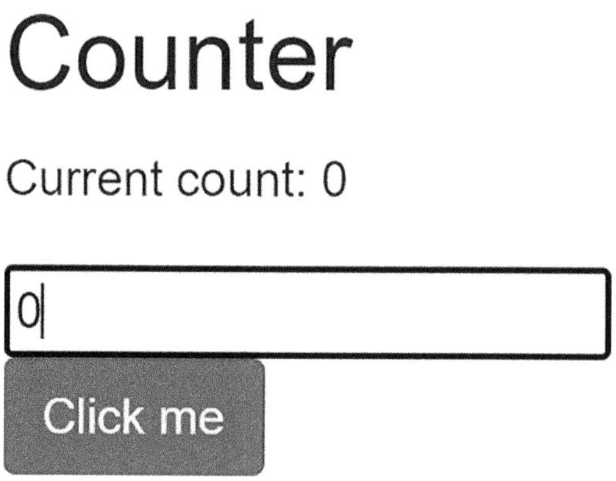

Counter

Current count: 0

[0|]

[Click me]

Figure 12-1. *The Counter input element receives focus automatically*

Calling .NET Methods from JavaScript

You can also call .NET methods from JavaScript. For example, your JavaScript might want to tell your component that something interesting has happened, like the user clicking something in the browser currently handled by the JavaScript library. Or your JavaScript might want to ask the Blazor component about some data it needs. You can call a .NET method, but with a couple of conditions. First, your .NET method's arguments and return value need to be _JSON serializable_, the method must be public, and you need to add the `JSInvokable` attribute to the method. The method can be a static or instance method.

Note Imagine that JavaScript could call any method on your component. This would be a huge security risk! That is why Blazor will only invoke methods that have the `JSInvokable` attribute.

To invoke a `static` method, you use the JavaScript `DotNet.invokeMethodAsync` or `DotNet.invokeMethod` function, passing the name of the assembly, the name of the method, and its arguments. To call an instance method, you pass the instance wrapped as a `DotNetObjectRef` to a JavaScript glue function, which can then invoke the .NET method using the `DotNetObjectRef`'s invokeMethodAsync or invokeMethod function, passing the name of the .NET method and its arguments. If you want your component to work in Blazor Server, you need to use the asynchronous functions.

Adding a Glue Function Taking a .NET Instance

Let's continue with the previous example. When you make a change to local storage, the storage triggers a JavaScript storage event, passing the old and new value (and more). This allows you to register for changes in other browser tabs or windows and use it to update the page with the latest data in `localStorage`.

Open interop.js from the previous example and add a `watch` function, as in Listing 12-11. The `watch` function takes a reference to a `DotNetObjectRef` instance and invokes the `UpdateCounter` method on this instance when storage changes. You can detect changes in storage by registering for the JavaScript storage event.

CHAPTER 12   JAVASCRIPT INTEROPERABILITY

Listing 12-11. The watch function

```
window.blazorLocalStorage = {
  get: key => key in localStorage ? JSON.parse(localStorage[key]) : null,
  set: (key, value) => { localStorage[key] = JSON.stringify(value); },
  delete: key => { delete localStorage[key]; },
  watch: async (instance) => {
    window.addEventListener('storage', (e) => {
      instance.invokeMethodAsync('UpdateCounter');
    });
  }
};
```

When anyone or anything changes the local storage for this web page, the browser will trigger the `storage` event, and our JavaScript interop will invoke the `UpdateCounter` method (which we will implement next) in our C# Blazor component.

Time to add the `UpdateCounter` method. Open Counter.razor and add the `UpdateCounter` method to the @code area, as shown in Listing 12-12.

Listing 12-12. The UpdateCounter method

```
[JSInvokable]
public async Task UpdateCounter()
{
  try
  {
    currentCount = await jsRuntime
      .InvokeAsync<int>("blazorLocalStorage.get",
        nameof(CurrentCount));
    StateHasChanged();
  }
  catch { }
}
```

This method triggers the UI to update with the latest value of `CurrentCounter`. Please note that this method follows the .NET _async pattern_ returning a `Task` instance because the JavaScript interop will call this asynchronously using the `invokeMethodAsync` function from Listing 12-11. To complete the example, update the

OnAfterRenderAsync lifecycle method shown in Listing 12-13. The OnAfterRenderAsync method wraps the Counter component's this reference in a DotNetObjectRef and passes it to the blazorLocalStorage.watch glue function.

Listing 12-13. The OnAfterRenderAsync method

```
protected override async Task OnAfterRenderAsync(bool firstRender)
{
  if (firstRender)
  {
    await UpdateCounter();

    if (inputElement is not null)
    {
      await jsRuntime.InvokeVoidAsync("blazorFocus.set",
        inputElement);
    }

    DotNetObjectReference<Counter> objRef =
      DotNetObjectReference.Create(this);
    await jsRuntime.InvokeVoidAsync("blazorLocalStorage.watch",
      objRef);
  }
}
```

To see this in action, open two browser tabs side-by-side on your website. When you change the value in one tab, you should see the other tab update to the same value automatically! You can use this to communicate between two tabs in the same browser as we do here. If this does not seem to work, make your browser do a hard refresh to update the cache.

Using Services for Interop

The previous example is not the way I would recommend doing interop with JavaScript because our components are tightly coupled to the IJSRuntime. There is a better way, and that is encapsulating the IJSRuntime code in a _service_. This will hide all the dirty details of interacting with JavaScript and allow for easier maintenance. In future generations of Blazor, some of this functionality might just be included, and then we only need to update the service implementation. Services like this can also easily be replaced during unit testing.

Building the LocalStorage Service

Add a new Services folder to the project. Add a new interface inside this folder, name it ILocalStorage, and add the three methods from Listing 12-14 to it.

Listing 12-14. Building the ILocalStorage service interface

```csharp
namespace BlazorApp.JavaScriptInterop.Services;

public interface ILocalStorage
{
  ValueTask<T> GetProperty<T>(string propName);
  ValueTask SetProperty<T>(string propName, T value);
  ValueTask WatchAsync<T>(T instance) where T : class;
}
```

These methods correspond with the glue functions from interop.js.

Now add a new class to the same Services folder, and name it LocalStorage. This class should implement the ILocalStorage interface as in Listing 12-15. See how this class hides away all the details of performing JavaScript interop? And this is a simple case!

Listing 12-15. Implementing the LocalStorage service class

```csharp
using Microsoft.JSInterop;

namespace BlazorApp.JavaScriptInterop.Services;

public class LocalStorage : ILocalStorage
{
  private readonly IJSRuntime _jsRuntime;

  public LocalStorage(IJSRuntime js) => _jsRuntime = js;

  public ValueTask<T> GetProperty<T>(string propName)
    => _jsRuntime.InvokeAsync<T>("blazorLocalStorage.get", propName);
```

```
    public ValueTask SetProperty<T>(string propName, T value)
    => _jsRuntime.InvokeVoidAsync("blazorLocalStorage.set", propName, value);

    public ValueTask WatchAsync<T>(T instance) where T : class
    => _jsRuntime.InvokeVoidAsync("blazorLocalStorage.watch",
       DotNetObjectReference.Create(instance));
}
```

Components will receive this service through _dependency injection_, so add it as a _Scoped_ service as in Listing 12-16.

Listing 12-16. Registering the LocalStorage service in dependency injection

```
using BlazorApp.JavaScriptInterop.Components;
using BlazorApp.JavaScriptInterop.Services;

WebApplicationBuilder builder = WebApplication.CreateBuilder(args);

// Add services to the container.
builder.Services
  .AddRazorComponents()
  .AddInteractiveServerComponents();

// Register LocalStorage Service
builder.Services
  .AddScoped<ILocalStorage, LocalStorage>();

WebApplication app = builder.Build();

// Configure the HTTP request pipeline.
if (!app.Environment.IsDevelopment())
{
  _ = app.UseExceptionHandler("/Error", createScopeForErrors: true);
  _ = app.UseHsts();
}

app.UseHttpsRedirection();

app.UseStaticFiles();
app.UseAntiforgery();
```

CHAPTER 12   JAVASCRIPT INTEROPERABILITY

```
app.MapRazorComponents<App>()
    .AddInteractiveServerRenderMode();

app.Run();
```

Copy the Counter.razor file as CounterWithService.razor. Change the @page directive to use the counter-service routing template as in Listing 12-17. While you are at it, replace IJSRuntime with ILocalStorage.

Listing 12-17. Adding another Counter with different route

```
@page "/counter-service"
@using BlazorApp.JavaScriptInterop.Services

@inject ILocalStorage LocalStorage

<PageTitle>Counter with Service</PageTitle>

<h1>Counter</h1>
```

Add a navigation link to the NavMenu component as shown in Listing 12-18.

Listing 12-18. Adding a NavLink to NavMenu

```
<div class="nav-item px-3">
  <NavLink class="nav-link" href="counter">
    <span class="bi bi-plus-square-fill-nav-menu" aria-
    hidden="true"></span>
      Counter
  </NavLink>
</div>

<!-- Add this -->
<div class="nav-item px-3">
  <NavLink class="nav-link" href="counter-service">
    <span class="bi bi-plus-square-fill-nav-menu" aria-
    hidden="true"></span>
      With Service
  </NavLink>
</div>
```

CHAPTER 12　JAVASCRIPT INTEROPERABILITY

Go back to the `CounterWithService` component, and replace each call of IJSRuntime using blazorLocalStorage with the LocalStorage service as in Listing 12-19.

Listing 12-19. Using the LocalStorage service

```
public int CurrentCount
{
  get => currentCount;
  set
  {
    if (currentCount != value)
    {
      currentCount = value;
      LocalStorage.SetProperty(
        nameof(CurrentCount),
        currentCount);
    }
  }
}
protected override async Task OnAfterRenderAsync(bool firstRender)
{
  if (firstRender)
  {
    await UpdateCounter();
    await LocalStorage.WatchAsync(this);
  }
}

[JSInvokable]
public async Task UpdateCounter()
{
  try
  {
    currentCount =
      await LocalStorage.GetProperty<int>(nameof(CurrentCount));
```

385

```
    StateHasChanged();
  }
  catch { }
}
```

Run the application and navigate to the new `CounterWithServices`. It should work just like the other `Counter`, but now it is using a service which gives better flexibility.

Setting Focus to an Input Element

And finally, update the `OnAfterRenderAsync` method as in Listing 12-20. This method now also uses the built-in `FocusAsync` method to set the focus on the input. No need for JavaScript interop! This method does require you to add a `@using` statement because `FocusAsync` is an extension method.

Listing 12-20. The CounterWithService's OnAfterRenderAsync method

```
// Add this @using
@using Microsoft.AspNetCore.Components

// Make this non-nullable
private ElementReference inputElement;

...

protected override async Task OnAfterRenderAsync(bool firstRender)
{
  if (firstRender)
  {
    await UpdateCounter();
    await LocalStorage.WatchAsync(this);
    await inputElement!.FocusAsync(preventScroll:false);
  }
}
```

This was not so hard, was it?

Dynamically Loading JavaScript with Modules

Our application currently includes some JavaScript code on the root page, which means it gets downloaded regardless of whether it is used (e.g., if no one clicks on the Counter or CounterWithService link). This is inefficient. Additionally, our JavaScript introduces a new identifier to the global window object, which poses a risk of name conflicts with other components. In this section, we will explore how to dynamically load JavaScript modules, ensuring they are only downloaded when needed.

Using JavaScript Modules

Early use of JavaScript was for small and straightforward functionality. Then JavaScript usage started to explode making programs complex and hard to maintain. Since then, there have been attempts at introducing "libraries" in JavaScript which could be included in your program. Today, JavaScript has a module mechanism that we can use in Blazor. You can compare a JavaScript module like a .NET library, which you can load dynamically. In the current Blazor application we have been building, copy the interop.js file, name it localstorage.js, and modify it to look like Listing 12-21. Instead of adding the get, set, and watch functions to the global window object, we export these functions (like the C# public keyword being used to make classes available outside the library) using a JavaScript module. A module also acts like a namespace, making the get, set, and watch functions relative to the module, and not contaminating the global JavaScript window object.

Listing 12-21. The LocalStorage JavaScript module

```
let get = key => key in localStorage ? JSON.parse(localStorage[key]) : null;
let set = (key, value) => { localStorage[key] = JSON.stringify(value); };
let watch = async (instance) => {
  window.addEventListener('storage', (e) => {
    instance.invokeMethodAsync('UpdateCounter');
  });
};

export { get, set, watch };
```

CHAPTER 12   JAVASCRIPT INTEROPERABILITY

Loading the Module into a Blazor Service

Once the module is ready, we can import it into a Blazor component, or a service using the IJSRuntime instance. It works just like any other JavaScript interop, by using the InvokeAsync<T> method, but now we use the IJSObjectReference type for T, calling the import function which is provided by Blazor.

Create a copy of the LocalStorage.cs service, and name it LocalStorageWithModule. cs. Modify it to look like Listing 12-22. The LocalStorageWithModule class will lazily load the localstorage JavaScript module, using a Task<IJSObjectReference>. The Lazy<T> class executes the delegate when you ask for its value, and it ensures it calls the delegate only once, making it thread safe. Here we invoke the "import" method, passing the path to the JavaScript module. Blazor dynamically loads it and returns an IJSObjectReference. Each method, like GetProperty<T> asks the lazy moduleTask for its value, an IJSObjectReference, and then uses a version of InvokeAsync to call the JavaScript function. This class also implements IAsyncDisposable to ensure we properly cleanup the IJSObjectReference.

Listing 12-22. Loading a JavaScript module

```csharp
using Microsoft.JSInterop;

namespace BlazorApp.JavaScriptInterop.Services;

public class LocalStorageWithModule : ILocalStorage, IAsyncDisposable
{
    private readonly Lazy<Task<IJSObjectReference>> moduleTask;

    public LocalStorageWithModule(IJSRuntime jsRuntime)
    {
        moduleTask = new(() => jsRuntime.InvokeAsync<IJSObjectReference>(
            "import", "./scripts/localstorage.js").AsTask());
    }

    public async ValueTask<T> GetProperty<T>(string propName)
    {
        IJSObjectReference module = await moduleTask.Value;
        return await module.InvokeAsync<T>("get", propName);
    }
```

```
public async ValueTask SetProperty<T>(string propName, T value)
{
  IJSObjectReference module = await moduleTask.Value;
  await module.InvokeVoidAsync("set", propName, value);
}

public async ValueTask WatchAsync<T>(T instance) where T : class
{
  IJSObjectReference module = await moduleTask.Value;
  await module.InvokeVoidAsync("watch",
    DotNetObjectReference.Create(instance));
}

public async ValueTask DisposeAsync() {
  if (moduleTask.IsValueCreated)
  {
    IJSObjectReference module = await moduleTask.Value;
    await module.DisposeAsync();
  }
 }
}
```

Change dependency injection to use the `LocalStorageWithModule` implementation, so update Program as in Listing 12-23.

Listing 12-23. Using the LocalStorageWithModule service

```
builder.Services
  .AddScoped<ILocalStorage, LocalStorageWithModule>();
```

Build and run, everything should still work. The big advantage is that we don't need to add JavaScript to the root page. This becomes even more interesting for component libraries!

CHAPTER 12   JAVASCRIPT INTEROPERABILITY

Adding a Map to PizzaPlace

Many physical businesses use a map to show to people where they are located. Wouldn't it be nice to embellish the PizzaPlace application with a map, showing where you are and where the PizzaPlace restaurant is? That is what we will do next.

Choosing the Map JavaScript Library

Which map library will we use? There are many JavaScript libraries to choose from, for example, Google maps, Bing maps, etc. The author's prerogative is to choose the maps library, and I have chosen the Leaflet open source library, which is lightweight, has many customization options, and is used by some of the leading companies such as GitHub, Flickr, Etsy, and Facebook. You can find the library's website at https://leafletjs.com.

Adding the Leaflet Library

Open the PizzaPlace solution, and add the Leaflet styling and JavaScript script to your App component as in Listing 12-24. The easiest way to do this is by copying this from the leaflet QuickStart page at https://leafletjs.com/examples/quick-start/. This will also ensure you use the latest version (at the risk of breaking changes).

Listing 12-24. Adding the Leaflet library

```
<!DOCTYPE html>
<html lang="en">

<head>
  <meta charset="utf-8" />
  <meta name="viewport" content="width=device-width, initial-scale=1.0" />
  <base href="/" />
  <link rel="stylesheet" href="bootstrap/bootstrap.min.css" />
  <link rel="stylesheet" href="app.css" />
  <link rel="stylesheet" href="BlazorApp.PizzaPlace.styles.css" />
  <link rel="icon" type="image/png" href="favicon.png" />
  <!-- Add Leaflet Library-->
  <link rel="stylesheet" href="https://unpkg.com/leaflet@1.9.4/dist/
  leaflet.css"
```

```
        integrity="sha256-p4NxAoJBhIIN+hmNHrzRCf9tD/miZyoHS5obTRR9BMY="
        crossorigin="" />
  <HeadOutlet @rendermode="InteractiveServer" />
</head>

<body>
  <Routes @rendermode="InteractiveServer" />
  <script src="_framework/blazor.web.js"></script>
  <!-- Add Leaflet Library-->
  <script src="https://unpkg.com/leaflet@1.9.4/dist/leaflet.js"
          integrity="sha256-20nQCchB9coOqIjJZRGuk2/Z9VM+kNiyxNV1lvTlZBo="
          crossorigin=""></script>
</body>

</html>
```

Note We use _SubResource Integrity Checking_ to download this library to ensure we are using the correct library. British Airways (BA) got hacked (`https://gbhackers.com/british-airways-hacked/`), and more than 380.000 payment cards got compromised. So how could this have happened? Imagine that BA uses some external JavaScript library. If a hacker can change this external source and add his/her own code to the library, it is a piece of cake to steal any information that the user enters on the website. So how can you avoid this hack? _SubResource Integrity (SRI) checking_ add a hash value (a checksum of the file) to the `<script>` tag, so if the external source gets modified, the browser will refuse to load and execute it.

Building the Leaflet Map Razor Library

You can use a map in many applications, so I think it makes a lot of sense to build this as a Razor Library. You can find Blazor component libraries that give you a map component (e.g., `https://github.com/fis-sst/BlazorMaps`, or `https://github.com/ichim/LeafletForBlazor-NuGet`), but here we will build one as an exercise. Add a new Razor Class Library to your solution and name it Leaflet.Map.

CHAPTER 12 JAVASCRIPT INTEROPERABILITY

Remove all the files from this project except the Imports.razor file and wwwroot folder. Add a new map.js JavaScript file as in Listing 12-25 inside wwwroot. To save on typing (and typos), I suggest you copy this from the provided sources.

Listing 12-25. The Map JavaScript module

```
let showOrUpdate = (elementId, zoom, markers) => {
  let elem = document.getElementById(elementId);
  if (!elem) {
    throw new Error('No element with ID ' + elementId);
  }

  // Initialize map if needed
  if (!elem.map) {
    elem.map = L.map(elementId).setView([50.88022, 4.29660], zoom);
    elem.map.addedMarkers = [];

    L.tileLayer('https://api.mapbox.com/styles/v1/{id}/tiles/{z}/{x}/
    {y}?access_token=pk.eyJ1IjoicGV0ZXJoaW1zY2hvb3QiLCJhIjoiY2x3c3p00HI
    yMDFscjJxc2FwZjluN20wcyJ9.w0-GDo-lI6freNpoeyXYlw', {
      attribution: 'Map data &copy; <a href="https://www.openstreetmap.org/
      copyright">OpenStreetMap</a> contributors, Imagery
      © <a href="https://www.mapbox.com/">Mapbox</a>',
      maxZoom: 18,
      id: 'mapbox/streets-v11',
      tileSize: 512,
      zoomOffset: -1,
      accessToken: 'pk.eyJ1IjoicGV0ZXJoaW1zY2hvb3QiLCJhIjoiY2x3c3p00HIyMD
      FscjJxc2FwZjluN20wcyJ9.w0-GDo-lI6freNpoeyXYlw'
    }).addTo(elem.map);
  }

  // Add markers
  let map = elem.map;
  markers = markers || [];
  if (map.addedMarkers.length !== markers.length) {
    // Markers have changed, so reset
    map.addedMarkers.forEach(marker => marker.removeFrom(map));
```

CHAPTER 12 JAVASCRIPT INTEROPERABILITY

```
    map.addedMarkers = markers.map(m => {
      return L.marker([m.y, m.x]).bindPopup(m.description).addTo(map);
    });

    // Auto-fit the view
    var markersGroup = new L.featureGroup(map.addedMarkers);
    map.fitBounds(markersGroup.getBounds().pad(0.3));

    // Show applicable popups. Can't do this until after the view was
    auto-fitted.
    markers.forEach((marker, index) => {
      if (marker.showPopup) {
        map.addedMarkers[index].openPopup();
      }
    });
  } else {
    // Same number of markers, so update positions/text without changing
    view bounds
    markers.forEach((marker, index) => {
      animateMarkerMove(
        map.addedMarkers[index].setPopupContent(marker.description),
        marker,
        4000);
    });
  }
};

let animateMarkerMove = (marker, coords, durationMs) => {
  if (marker.existingAnimation) {
    cancelAnimationFrame(marker.existingAnimation.callbackHandle);
  }

  marker.existingAnimation = {
    startTime: new Date(),
    durationMs: durationMs,
    startCoords: { x: marker.getLatLng().lng, y: marker.getLatLng().lat },
    endCoords: coords,
```

393

CHAPTER 12 JAVASCRIPT INTEROPERABILITY

```
      callbackHandle: window.requestAnimationFrame(() =>
      animateMarkerMoveFrame(marker))
  };
}

let animateMarkerMoveFrame = (marker) => {
  var anim = marker.existingAnimation;
  var proportionCompleted = (new Date().valueOf() - anim.startTime.
  valueOf()) / anim.durationMs;
  var coordsNow = {
    x: anim.startCoords.x + (anim.endCoords.x - anim.startCoords.x) *
    proportionCompleted,
    y: anim.startCoords.y + (anim.endCoords.y - anim.startCoords.y) *
    proportionCompleted
  };

  marker.setLatLng([coordsNow.y, coordsNow.x]);

  if (proportionCompleted < 1) {
    marker.existingAnimation.callbackHandle = window.requestAnimationFrame(
      () => animateMarkerMoveFrame(marker));
  }
}

export { showOrUpdate };
```

There is one more thing we need to do to complete Listing 12-25. There is the ACCESSTOKEN placeholder which you need to replace with your own token which we will do next.

Registering with the Map Provider

Leaflet will download its maps from a map provider, and here we will use _MapBox_ which you can use for free for development. You can find their site at https://www.mapbox.com/maps. You will need to sign-up with this site to get your access token. So after signing up, you should go to your account and create an access token. Copy this token and replace ACCESSTOKEN with your token in Listing 12-25 (twice!).

Creating the Map Component

Now add a new Razor component to the Leaflet.Map library project and call it Map. Implement the component as shown in Listing 12-26. This component uses a `<div>`, which leaflet will replace with the map. This `<div>` needs a unique id, which we generate using the Guid type from .NET and we set its style to fill the parent element. The JavaScript module from Listing 12-25 uses the id to retrieve the `<div>` from the DOM:

```
let elem = document.getElementById(elementId);
```

The Map component then loads the map.js module using a path to the static map.js resource from wwwroot. We only need to do this once, so we check if we have already loaded the leaflet reference.

Finally, when the map component has been rendered, we call the leaflet library using our module in the OnAfterRenderAsync method. Then we invoke the showOrUpdate JavaScript method.

Listing 12-26. The map component

```
@using Microsoft.JSInterop
@inject IJSRuntime JSRuntime

<div id="@elementId" style="height: 100%; width: 100%;"></div>

@code {
  string elementId = $"map-{Guid.NewGuid().ToString("D")}";

  [Parameter]
  [EditorRequired]
  public double Zoom { get; set; } = 17.0;

  private IJSObjectReference? leaflet;

  protected async override void OnAfterRender(bool firstRender)
  {
    if( leaflet is null)
    {
      leaflet = await JSRuntime.InvokeAsync<IJSObjectReference>
          ("import", "./_content/Leaflet.Map/map.js");
    }
```

```
    if (leaflet is not null)
    {
      await leaflet.InvokeVoidAsync(
          "showOrUpdate",
          elementId, Zoom);
    }
  }
}
```

Consuming the Map Component

In the BlazorApp.PizzaPlace project, add a project reference to the Leaflet.Map component library.

Add a `@using Leaflet.Map` to your BlazorApp.PizzaPlace project's Imports.razor file as in Listing 12-27. This will facilitate using the library.

Listing 12-27. Add a using to Imports.razor

```
@using System.Net.Http
@using System.Net.Http.Json
@using Microsoft.AspNetCore.Components.Forms
@using Microsoft.AspNetCore.Components.Routing
@using Microsoft.AspNetCore.Components.Web
@using static Microsoft.AspNetCore.Components.Web.RenderMode
@using Microsoft.AspNetCore.Components.Web.Virtualization
@using Microsoft.JSInterop
@using BlazorApp.PizzaPlace
@using BlazorApp.PizzaPlace.Components
@using BlazorApp.PizzaPlace.Shared
@using Leaflet.Map
```

Open Home.razor, and below the `CustomerEntry` component, add the `Map` component as in Listing 12-28. We also need to set the `Zoom` parameter, and I have found that Zoom 17 will show the location in sufficient detail to see roads. You can experiment with this parameter if you like.

Listing 12-28. Adding the map component

```
<CustomerEntry Title="Please enter your details below"
               @bind-Customer="@State.Customer"
               SubmitTitle="Place Order"
               SubmitClicked="SubmitClicked" />

<div class="map">
  <Map Zoom="17" />
</div>

<p>@State.ToJson()</p>
```

Add a new file called Home.razor.css to the project in the Pages folder, and add the map class as in Listing 12-29.

Listing 12-29. Styling the map container

```
.map {
  width: 550px;
  height: 550px;
}
```

Run the PizzaPlace application. You should see a map like in Figure 12-2. As you can see, the map shows the location of where I work. If you like, you can change the coordinates in Listing 12-25 to suit where you live or work.

CHAPTER 12   JAVASCRIPT INTEROPERABILITY

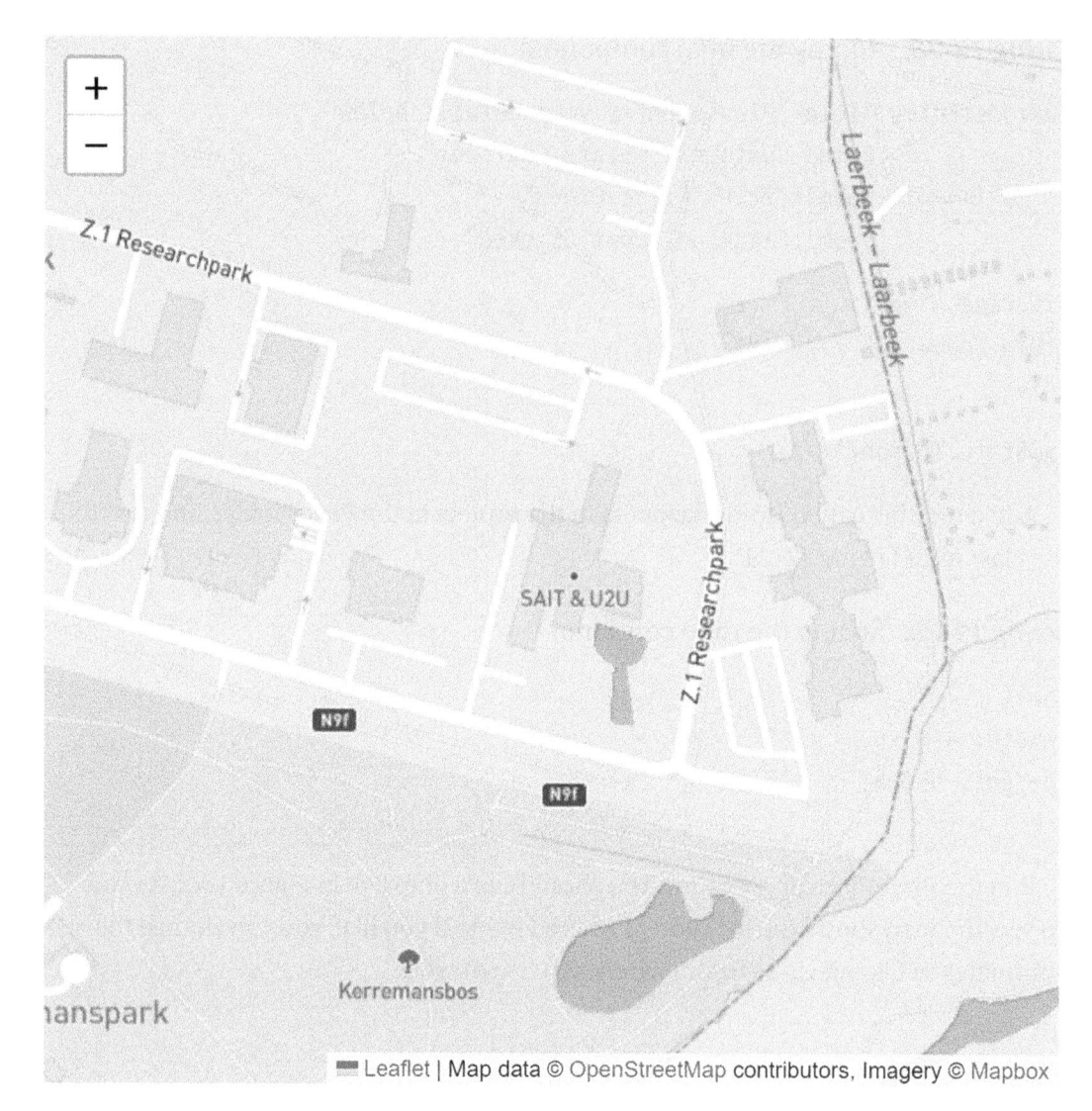

Figure 12-2. The map showing a location

Adding Markers to the Map

Showing just a map is not enough. Let us add some markers to show the PizzaPlace location and your location. First add a new class `Marker` to the Leaflet.Map project as in Listing 12-30. The class will serialize to a JavaScript object used by the Leaflet library. On the Leaflet Library website, you can find more information to add circles, polygons, and popups. We will not do that since this is very similar to markers.

CHAPTER 12   JAVASCRIPT INTEROPERABILITY

Listing 12-30. The Marker class

```
namespace Leaflet.Map;
public class Marker
{
  public required string Description { get; set; }

  public double X { get; set; }

  public double Y { get; set; }

  public bool ShowPopup { get; set; }
}
```

Add a new parameter to the Map component called Markers as in Listing 12-31.

Listing 12-31. The Map's Markers parameter

```
[Parameter]
[EditorRequired]
public double Zoom { get; set; } = 17.0;

[Parameter]
public List<Marker> Markers { get; set; } = [];

private IJSObjectReference? leaflet;
```

Update the showOrUpdate method to pass the Markers parameter as in Listing 12-32.

Listing 12-32. Passing the Markers parameter to JavaScript

```
protected async override void OnAfterRender(bool firstRender)
{
  if (leaflet is null)
  {
    leaflet = await JSRuntime.InvokeAsync<IJSObjectReference>
        ("import", "./_content/Leaflet.Map/map.js");
  }
  if (leaflet is not null)
  {
    await leaflet.InvokeVoidAsync(
```

399

```
            "showOrUpdate",
            elementId, Zoom, Markers);
    }
}
```

Our JavaScript already implements adding markers. When the markers argument is not empty, it will tell leaflet to add them.

Now let us add some markers to our PizzaPlace application. Add a new List<Marker> to the Home.razor component as in Listing 12-33. Feel free to update the coordinates to a place near you.

Listing 12-33. Adding some Markers

```
private List<Marker> Markers = [
  new Marker {
    X = 4.29660,
    Y = 50.88022,
    Description = "Pizza Place"
  },
  new Marker {
    X = 4.27638,
    Y = 50.87136,
    Description = "You",
    ShowPopup = true
  },
];
```

Databind this to the Map component's Markers parameter as in Listing 12-34.

Listing 12-34. Passing the Markers to the Map component

```
<div class="map">
  <Map Zoom="17" Markers="@Markers"/>
</div>
```

Build and run the PizzaPlace application. You should now see markers on the map as in Figure 12-3. When you click on the marker, it will show a popup.

CHAPTER 12 JAVASCRIPT INTEROPERABILITY

Figure 12-3. The Map showing Markers

Summary

In this chapter, you saw how you can call JavaScript from your Blazor components using the `IJSRuntime.InvokeAsync<T>` method. This requires you to register a JavaScript glue function by adding this function to the browser's `window` global object. Or you can expose a JavaScript module, and then load this module dynamically.

You can call your .NET static or instance method from JavaScript. Start by adding the `JSInvokable` attribute to the .NET method. If the method is `static`, you use the JavaScript `DotNet.invokeMethodAsync` function (or `DotNet.invokeMethod` if the call is synchronous), passing the name of the assembly, the name of the method, and its arguments. If the method is an instance method, you pass the .NET instance wrapped in a `DotNetObjectRef` to the glue function, which can then use the `invokeMethodAsync` function to call the method, passing the name of the method and its arguments.

Finally, you applied this knowledge by adding a map to the PizzaPlace application. You built a Blazor component library which uses a JavaScript module to call the Leaflet library and added a class to pass markers to the map.

When should we use JavaScript interop? Whenever you need to use a feature of the Browser, such as local storage or the geolocation API, which is not supported by WebAssembly, you will have to resort to JavaScript interop. There are a lot of nice people out there who already did the work and provide their implementation as a Blazor Component library, saving you a lot of time. Google around a bit first!

CHAPTER 13

Testing Components with BUnit

In previous chapters, we have been building a PizzaPlace application, which contains several components. We have tested these components by running the application and interacting with it. Here we will look at writing unit tests for Blazor components using bUnit and NSubstitute.

Where Can We Find Bugs?

When building software, what are the causes of bugs? As it turns out, in every step of building software, bugs can be introduced. Let us walk over the lifetime of a software project as shown in Figure 13-1. This figure also illustrates another obvious fact: the sooner you can find a bug, the cheaper it is to fix it.

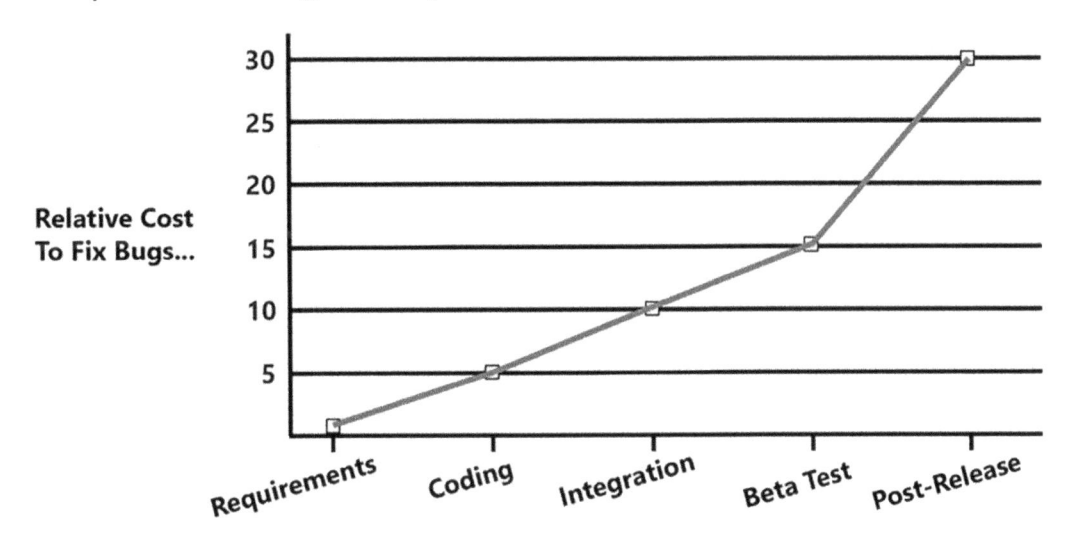

Figure 13-1. The cost of fixing bugs

Requirements

Sometimes bugs are introduced even before a single line of code is written. Writing good requirements is hard, because these need to explain business concepts to developers who are typically not well versed in this domain. The same thing counts for advanced engineering concepts, like rocket building. Let's look at an example. NASA lost its 125.000.000$ Mars Climate Orbiter because of a simple missing piece of information in the requirements: Which units to use? One team was using metric units (meters, kilogram), while another team was using imperial units (inch, pounds), and there was no conversion in place because each team thought the other team was using the same units! You can read more about it here: `https://www.latimes.com/archives/la-xpm-1999-oct-01-mn-17288-story.html`.

This bug could easily be averted! Since the specifications never mentioned the units, if someone had asked which units to use and add this to the specifications, this Mars Orbiter would probably be spinning around Mars right now! So as a developer, if you think something is confusing or ambiguous, ask! Never assume anything!

Coding

While coding, it is easy to introduce bugs. That is part of developing software. Code that was working very well can become buggy by a benign change. So how can we discover these bugs? We should automate our testing. By writing a piece of code (a unit test) that checks if another piece of code is behaving as expected, we can run this test every day and discover the bug hours after it was written. Have you ever received a bug report about some functionality you wrote three months ago? You will probably rub your head wondering what you were trying to do (and you write this code!). After studying your code for a while, understanding kicks in and you fix the bug (let us say a simple one-off bug). Now imagine the bug is discovered an hour after you made the change. Do you need to figure out what your code was doing? No, it is still fresh in your memory. That makes unit testing so efficient. And when you finish your code, and all your unit tests are green (meaning check out ok), you can go home and sleep soundly!

Same thing counts for refactoring code. I mean, cleaning up some code and keeping the same functionality. How do you know if you introduced bugs while refactoring when there are no unit tests? If there are unit tests and they all pass before refactoring, it is easy to see after refactoring if you broke something. Just run the unit tests, and if they all pass, you did not break anything that was known to be working! Again you can go home and sleep knowing you made your code more maintainable and did not introduce any new bugs!

Integration

Your code works on your machine. And your colleague's code also works on their machine. But will your code work together with your colleague's code? That is what integration is all about. A long time ago, teams would integrate code from different teams at the end of the project. Guess what!? This never went well, resulting in project overruns, sometimes by months. So, development teams started to integrate at the end of each month. Then at the end of the week. Integrations started to become automated using build systems. Now we can do continuous integration where we integrate changes to the code after each commit in source code. And when we have unit tests, we can run these after the compilation ends and use that to catch breaking changes. Again, this should illustrate the role of good unit tests. You use them to see if your code is working, and also to see if everyone's code keeps on working.

Beta-Testing

At a certain point in time, you should expose end users to your application. Why? Because developers are not normal people. End users want things to be as simple as possible. For example, look at google.com. This site only has one textbox where you type your question and a button to do the search. This simplicity made google the most used search engine (sorry Microsoft). Developers are control freaks; they want power, not simplicity! Just open the options screen in Visual Studio. You can tweak just about anything! And most end users are not as proficient using computers as developers, sometimes resulting in surprises. Let me tell you about a personal experience I once had. We had built software that runs in a factory, and on a Sunday (they work in that factory continuously), I get a call from an end user. He told me "The button does not work!". After half an hour on the phone, I decided to drive over there and see for myself. I get there and I click the button, and it works! So what was the problem? The button was small because we needed to cram a lot on the screen, and the end user has a bit of a tremor and moved the mouse when clicking, resulting in a click outside of the button. So we fixed the bug by making the button bigger. This is a nice example of a usability problem, where we as developers are not always aware of. So expose your software to your users often, and gain their feedback. We are building it for our end users, right?

Post-release

Perfect software does not exist. Have you ever written an application that is bug-free? No? I have! It is called "Hello World!". Anything beyond that is impossible. But having an end user discover a bug is bad news. It will lower the trust in the development team and in the quality of the software. So how do we stop bugs from making it into production. You can't! The only thing you can do is to test as much as possible and warn the users that they may encounter bugs, especially early after release.

Why Should We Use Unit Tests?

So how do you test your Blazor application? Hit run and interact with the UI? No problem there, except every time you make a change to your application, you should test everything again. Who has time for that? Can't someone else do it? Yes, that machine in front of you can! With _unit testing_, we automate this unit testing process.

What Makes a Good Unit Test?

When you practice unit testing, your development life cycle looks like this: Make some change to the code, build, fix compiler errors, build again, and then run all your tests. Then fix the bugs discovered by your tests. And then you start again. How long does building your application take? A couple of seconds? Now imagine that your unit tests take 5 minutes. Would you want to wait for that? Would you be tempted to disable running the unit tests? _A good unit test should be fast_, so we don't have to wait very long. What makes unit tests slow? Typically, this is caused by accessing slow resources, like databases, disks, and the network. With a unit test, we will avoid using slow resources. What if your unit tests need some setup? Every time you need to run the tests, you would have to prepare some things manually. Again, we don't have time for that. _A good unit test should also be automatic and repeatable_, meaning that the test should report on success or failure and that again we avoid things that need some manual setup. What could that be? Again databases, files on disk, and the network! Another aspect of a good unit test is _consistency_. If your unit test fails, this should be because of a bug in your code, not because someone tripped over a network cable making the database or network inaccessible! So again, we should avoid things like databases, file shares, and networks.

Tests which do not have all the aspects from above do exist. You will have to write a test to interact with the database (but don't start testing the framework used to access the database; that is the framework's author's job!). These tests are known as _integration tests_, because we will run them during the build, not during the development life cycle.

Unit Testing Blazor Components

Let us create a couple of tests for a Blazor application. In the code download for this chapter, you can find the _Testing_ solution. Open it with your favorite editor. Everything in the project should look familiar. There is the Counter component and the Weather component which uses an IWeatherService to retrieve the weather forecasts from a server.

Adding a Unit Test Project

Let us look at an example using _xUnit_, which is a popular testing library for .NET which we will also use for testing our Blazor components.

When you are using Visual Studio, right-click the test folder and select Add new project. In the Add New Project dialog, search for the _xUnit Test Project_ template. Now click Next. Set the Location to the test folder and name it BlazorApp.Testing.Tests.

If you are using Code, open the command prompt to the test folder and execute the following command:

```
dotnet new xunit -n BlazorApp.Testing.Tests
```

Now change the directory to the parent directory and execute:

```
dotnet sln add .\test\BlazorApp.Testing.Tests
```

No matter which tool you are using, add project references to the Blazor project. The test project file should look like Listing 13-1.

CHAPTER 13 TESTING COMPONENTS WITH BUNIT

Listing 13-1. The Testing.ComponentTests project

```xml
<Project Sdk="Microsoft.NET.Sdk">

  <PropertyGroup>
    <TargetFramework>net8.0</TargetFramework>
    <ImplicitUsings>enable</ImplicitUsings>
    <Nullable>enable</Nullable>

    <IsPackable>false</IsPackable>
    <IsTestProject>true</IsTestProject>
  </PropertyGroup>

  <ItemGroup>
    <PackageReference Include="coverlet.collector" Version="6.0.0" />
    <PackageReference Include="Microsoft.NET.Test.Sdk" Version="17.8.0" />
    <PackageReference Include="xunit" Version="2.5.3" />
    <PackageReference Include="xunit.runner.visualstudio" Version="2.5.3" />
  </ItemGroup>

  <ItemGroup>
    <ProjectReference Include="..\..\src\BlazorApp.Testing\BlazorApp.Testing.csproj" />
  </ItemGroup>

  <ItemGroup>
    <Using Include="Xunit" />
  </ItemGroup>

</Project>
```

Adding bUnit to the Test Project

With the current unit test project, we can test our services and other non-Blazor classes. To test Blazor components, we need to add _bUnit_. Use your favorite method to add the _bUnit_ package (choose the latest stable version).

You also need to change the SDK for your project as in Listing 13-2. We need to do this because we will use razor syntax to build unit tests for Blazor components.

Listing 13-2. bUnit projects

```
<Project Sdk="Microsoft.NET.Sdk.Razor">
```

Write Your First Unit Test

Now that we have everything in place, we can write our first unit test. We will start by writing a simple unit test and see how this works with Visual Studio and Code.

Writing Good Unit Test Methods

Every unit test will consist of three phases: _Arrange_, _Act_, and _Assert_, also known as the _triple-A of unit testing_. The Arrange phase will set up the unit test, by creating the _Subject-Under-Test_ (SUT), by which I mean the class we want to test and its dependencies. The Act phase will perform the call on the method we want to test, and the Assert will verify if the outcome is successful.

Add a new class called Utils to the Shared folder as in Listing 13-3. The Square method should return the square of a number (and it has a bug).

Listing 13-3. A simple Utils class

```
namespace BlazorApp.Testing.Shared;

public class Utils
{
  public int Square(int i)
  {
    return i;
  }
}
```

Let us write a simple unit test for this method, as in Listing 13-4. With xUnit, a unit test is a _public_ method with the [Fact] attribute on it. As this attribute says, the result of the test should be a fact! In the Arrange phase, we set up the Subject-Under-Test which I like to call sut. This way it is easy for me to identify the instance that I want to test (just a convention, name it as you like). Then in the Arrange phase, we call the Square method, storing the result in the actual variable. Next comes the Assert phase, where I

CHAPTER 13   TESTING COMPONENTS WITH BUNIT

am using the `Assert` class from xUnit, to verify if the result matches the expected result. The `Assert` class has a whole range of methods to check if the outcome of the test is the expected outcome. Here we are using the `Equals` method to see if the outcome equals 9, which should be the square of 3.

Listing 13-4. Testing the Square method

```csharp
using BlazorApp.Testing.Shared;

namespace BlazorApp.Testing.Tests;
public class SquareShould
{
  [Fact]
  public void Return9For3()
  {
    // Arrange
    Utils sut = new();
    // Act
    int result = sut.Square(3);
    // Assert
    Assert.Equal(expected: 9, actual: result);
  }
}
```

Running Your Tests

With Visual Studio, open the Test Explorer window (Test ➤ Test Explorer) as in Figure 13-2. With Visual Studio, Test Explorer is the place to run unit tests and review the results. After opening Test Explorer, it will scan your solution for unit tests and list them. Now click the left green arrow in this window to run all your tests.

CHAPTER 13 TESTING COMPONENTS WITH BUNIT

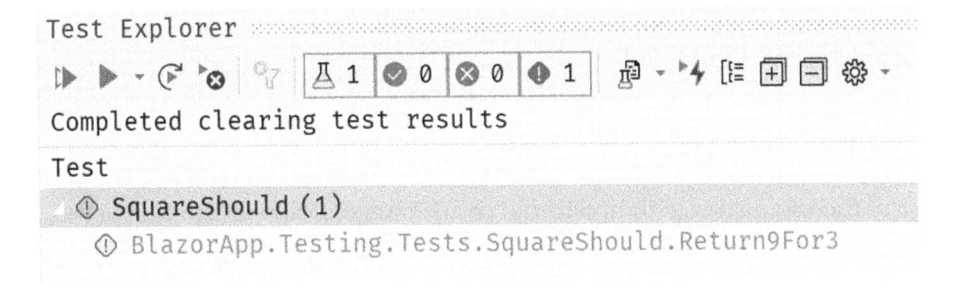

Figure 13-2. *The Test Explorer*

The test will run and fail as shown in Figure 13-3.

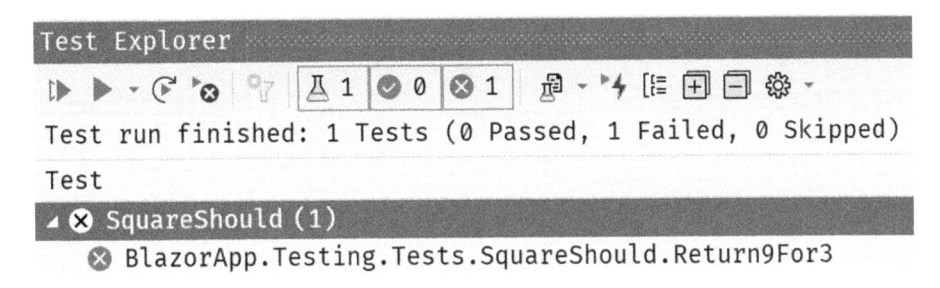

Figure 13-3. *The test fails*

Making Your Test Pass

Why did the test fail? If you put a breakpoint in the Square method and click the arrow in Test Explorer again, you will see that Visual Studio does not stop on the breakpoint. Why? Debugging needs some special setup, and this takes time. Remember that we want our tests to be completed as short as possible? With Visual Studio you can enable the debugger as follows. Right-click the test in the Test Explorer window and select Debug. Now the debugger will stop on your breakpoint. When you step in the Square method, you should see the bug (duh!). Fix it as in Listing 13-5.

Listing 13-5. *The Corrected Square method*

```
namespace BlazorApp.Testing.Shared;

public class Utils
{
  public int Square(int i)
```

```
    {
        return i*i; // Fixed it!
    }
}
```

Now run the test again (with or without the debugger). Now it should pass as in Figure 13-4.

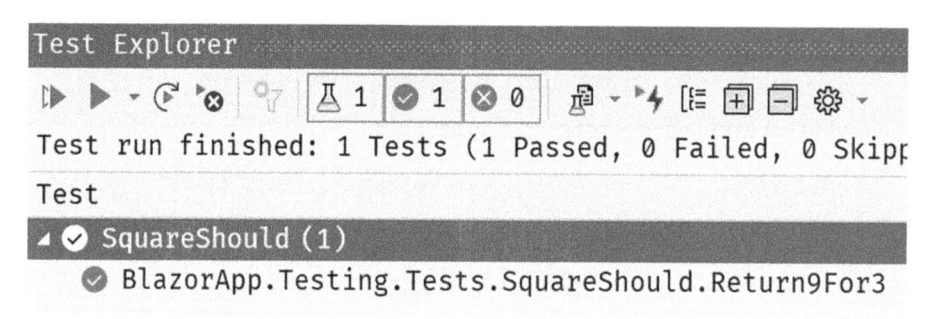

Figure 13-4. *The test passes*

Facts and Theories

But what about other values? With xUnit we can write a whole series of tests without having to copy-paste a ton of them (copy-paste to duplicate code is generally bad, also known as _Don't Repeat Yourself_ (DRY)). Add another unit test to the SquareShould class as in Listing 13-6. Here we are using the [Theory] attribute to tell xUnit to run this with different arguments. And we use the [InlineData] attribute to pass the arguments to the test method.

Listing 13-6. Using theories

```
[Theory]
[InlineData(1, 1)]
[InlineData(2, 4)]
[InlineData(-1, 1)]
public void ReturnSquareOfNumber(int number, int square)
{
    // Arrange
    Utils sut = new();
```

```
    // Act
    int result = sut.Square(number);
    // Assert
    Assert.Equal(expected: square, actual: result);
}
```

Now when we run our tests, you will see in Figure 13-5 that xUnit runs three tests, one for each [InlineData] attribute.

```
▲ ⊙ BlazorApp.Testing.Tests.SquareShould.ReturnSquareOfNumber (3)                        6 ms
    ⊙ BlazorApp.Testing.Tests.SquareShould.ReturnSquareOfNumber(number: 1, square: 1)    < 1 ms
    ⊙ BlazorApp.Testing.Tests.SquareShould.ReturnSquareOfNumber(number: -1, square: 1)   6 ms
    ⊙ BlazorApp.Testing.Tests.SquareShould.ReturnSquareOfNumber(number: 2, square: 4)    < 1 ms
```

Figure 13-5. *VS test results with theories*

Checking Your Sanity

Have you ever had a piece of code that did things differently than what you expected? Personally, I start to doubt my sanity then, like "Am I going crazy?" Or have you used someone's method that was badly documented and did not do as it should? With unit testing, you can set up checks to see if a method does what you think it should do. And if it does not, maybe you need to talk to the author and see what makes more sense. When you have a unit test, you can attach it to a bug report, making it easy for the author to reproduce the bug. Let us look at an example again. Now I want to see if the Square method throws an error when we pass a big integer to it (and not every squared integer is another integer because it is limited in range). Add another test method like in Listing 13-7. So here we call Square with the largest int possible. The result can never fit into an int, so we expect this to throw an OverflowException.

Listing 13-7. Testing exceptional cases

```
[Fact]
public void ThrowOverflowForBigNumbers()
{
    // Arrange
    Utils sut = new();
    // Act & Assert
    Assert.Throws<OverflowException>(() =>
```

413

CHAPTER 13 TESTING COMPONENTS WITH BUNIT

```
    {
      int result = sut.Square(int.MaxValue);
    });
}
```

But when we run, the test fails as in Figure 13-6.

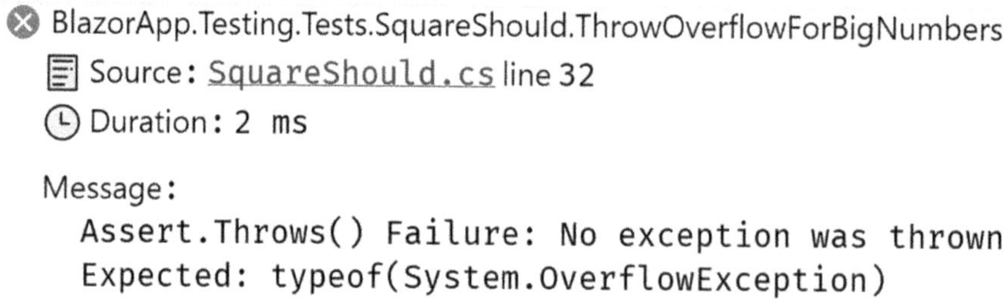

> ❌ BlazorApp.Testing.Tests.SquareShould.ThrowOverflowForBigNumbers
> 📄 Source: SquareShould.cs line 32
> 🕒 Duration: 2 ms
>
> Message:
>   Assert.Throws() Failure: No exception was thrown
>   Expected: typeof(System.OverflowException)

Figure 13-6. *Sanity check please?*

Why does this fail? Let us put a breakpoint on the Square method. Maybe we are doing something wrong here? Run the test with the debugger. When the debugger stops, look at the value of the argument: 2147483647. This is the largest signed int. Now step out of the method until after the result is set. What is its value? It is 1. Now 2147483647 times 2147483647 is not 1! So again, what is happening? It turns out that C# works like C++ and C. These programming languages do not throw exceptions by default when a calculation overflows! They even use this to create hashing and encryption algorithms. So how can we fix this? You can turn on overflow checking using the C# checked keyword as in listing 13-8.

Listing 13-8. Enabling overflow checking

```
namespace BlazorApp.Testing.Shared;

public class Utils
{
  public int Square(int i)
  {
    checked // Check for overflow
    {
      return i * i;
    }
  }
}
```

Run your test again. Now it passes. Whew! This was normal behavior.

Unit testing is great to discover these weird behaviors and allows you to catch modifications that cause bugs later.

Write bUnit Tests with C#

We have seen how we can write unit tests for .NET classes and their methods. Here we will look at how we can write tests for Blazor components on top of xUnit.

> **Note** All tests written here use xUnit, but you can also use NUnit or MSTest. All of these are test frameworks that apply the same principles. You can even mix these frameworks, so you don't have to rewrite old tests when moving to another test framework!

Understanding bUnit

bUnit is a testing library for Blazor components, written by Egil Hansen, and the sources can be found in GitHub at `https://github.com/bUnit-dev/bUnit`. With bUnit you can easily write unit tests for Blazor components. Why should we write unit tests for Blazor components? Same reason you write unit tests for regular classes: to ensure they work as expected and that they keep on working in case some dependency gets updated. Of course, most of your testing should be on the service classes that implement business logic. For example, you want to make sure your Blazor component calls a certain method on a service when the user interacts with that component. With bUnit we can automate that, so no user has to actually click a button! And we can run these tests continuously, so we will know when we break a component minutes after the change.

Part of testing a Blazor component is to render and examine the output of a component. But it goes way beyond this. You can interact with the component and see the changes, replace dependencies, etc.

Let us start with the `Counter` component, as in Listing 13-9. This now familiar component displays a `currentCount` field which is initially 0. So a very simple unit test would be to see if the component's output matches the expected output.

CHAPTER 13 TESTING COMPONENTS WITH BUNIT

Listing 13-9. The Counter component

```
@page "/counter"

<PageTitle>Counter</PageTitle>

<h1>Counter</h1>

<p role="status">Current count: @currentCount</p>

<button class="btn btn-primary" @onclick="IncrementCount">\
  Click me
</button>

@code {
  private int currentCount = 0;

  private void IncrementCount()
  {
    currentCount++;
  }
}
```

Add a new class called `CounterShould` to the unit test project. You can name this class anything you want, but I like the naming convention where I use the method or component name and then the word "Should." Derive this class from the `TestContext` base class, which will give you access to all the handy methods from bUnit. We will be using these methods as we go along, and by deriving your test class from `TestContext`, they become available through inheritance. Implement the first unit test `RenderCorrectlyWithInitialZero` as in Listing 13-10.

Listing 13-10. The CounterShould class

```
[Fact]
public void RenderCorrectlyWithInitialZero()
{
  IRenderedComponent<Counter> cut = RenderComponent<Counter>();
  Assert.Equal(@"
      <h1>Counter</h1>
      <p  role=""status"">Current count: 0</p>
```

```
    <button class=""btn btn-primary"" >
      Click me
    </button>
    ", cut.Markup);
}
```

Here we are using _xUnit_ together with bUnit, so our unit test has the `[Fact]` attribute. First, we do the Arrange phase, where we create the _Component-Under-Test_ (which I name `cut`, like `sut`) by calling the `RenderComponent<Counter>` method. This will create the component and render it in one go. This also takes care of the Act phase. Next, we do the Assert phase, where we want to see if the component generated the right kind of output.

This test will fail. Why? Just run the test and look at the test output as in Figure 13-7. Look again at the Assert statement in Listing 13-10. Here we expect the markup of our component to match the literal string. And it does match in a way, except for whitespace and newlines. We could now do the work and update our string to the real output, but this is too sensitive to little changes we might make later to our component!

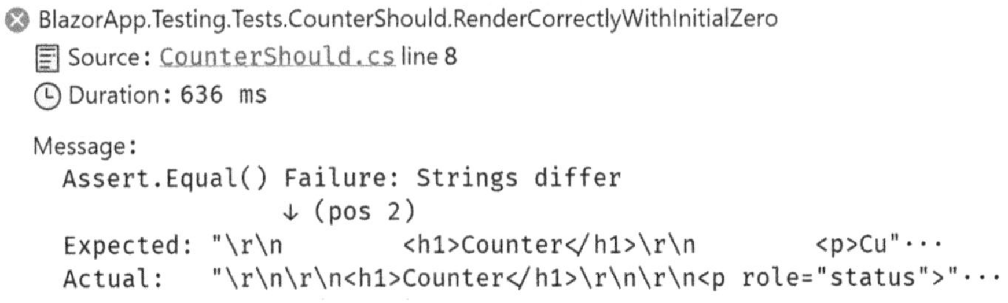

```
⊗ BlazorApp.Testing.Tests.CounterShould.RenderCorrectlyWithInitialZero
  Source: CounterShould.cs line 8
  Duration: 636 ms
Message:
  Assert.Equal() Failure: Strings differ
                  ↓ (pos 2)
  Expected: "\r\n          <h1>Counter</h1>\r\n          <p>Cu"···
  Actual:   "\r\n\r\n<h1>Counter</h1>\r\n\r\n<p role="status">"···
```

Figure 13-7. *Our test fails*

Let us improve the test as in Listing 13-11. Now we are using the `MarkupMatches` method, which will perform a _Semantic Compare_ between the component's markup and our string. This will ignore whitespace, newlines, comments, and other irrelevant things during the comparison, and now we should see the test pass! Now our test will no longer break when we add a newline or a comment in the component that changes the markup's formatting!

CHAPTER 13   TESTING COMPONENTS WITH BUNIT

Listing 13-11. Improving our unit test with symantic compare

```
[Fact]
public void RenderCorrectlyWithInitialZero()
{
    IRenderedComponent<Counter> cut = RenderComponent<Counter>();
    cut.MarkupMatches(@"
        <h1>Counter</h1>
        <p role=""status"">Current count: 0</p>
        <button class=""btn btn-primary"" >
          Click me
        </button>
        ");
}
```

We can even do better and focus on the relevant part of the component. We know that our `Counter` component uses a `<p>` element to render the `currentCount` variable, but how do we access this part of the render tree? The bUnit library has a `Find` method that takes a _CSS selector_ and returns the result of the query. Add another test method to the `ShouldRender` class as in Listing 13-12. We `Find` the `<p>` element, and we can see if it matches the expected output using the `MarkupMatches` method, which ignores whitespace.

Listing 13-12. Using the Find method

```
[Fact]
public void RenderParagraphCorrectlyWithInitialZero()
{
    IRenderedComponent<Counter> cut = RenderComponent<Counter>();
    cut.Find(cssSelector: "p")
       .MarkupMatches(@"<p role=""status"">Current count: 0</p>");
}
```

Run your tests and see if they pass, which they should.

What happens when the test fails?

In the `RenderParagraphCorrectlyWithInitialZero` method, replace the 0 with a 1. Run the test. It fails! Select the test and you should see the following output as in

Figure 13-8. This output shows us what is wrong, and now we can change the component (or the test) until the test passes. Fix the test.

```
Bunit.HtmlEqualException : HTML comparison failed.

The following errors were found:
  1: The expected text at p(0) > #text(0) and the actual

Actual HTML:
<p role="status">Current count: 0</p>

Expected HTML:
<p role="status">Current count: 1</p>
```

Figure 13-8. *Our bUnit test fails*

Testing Component Interaction

Our Counter component has a button, and when you click the button, it should increment the currentCount by 1 and render the new value. Let us look at how we can perform a test on a Blazor component by interacting with it and see if the component was updated correctly. Add a new unit test to the CounterRender class as in Listing 13-13. The second line in the test uses the Find method to retrieve the button and then uses the Click method to perform the @onclick event on it. This should have the expected side effect, which we test on the next line to see if the component rendered with the expected value. Run the test, which should pass. Hey, this was easy!

Listing 13-13. Interacting with the Counter component

```
[Fact]
public void IncrementCounterWhenButtonIsClicked()
{
  IRenderedComponent<Counter> cut = RenderComponent<Counter>();
  cut.Find(cssSelector: "button")
     .Click();
  cut.Find(cssSelector: "p")
     .MarkupMatches(@"<p role=""status"">Current count: 1</p>");
}
```

CHAPTER 13 TESTING COMPONENTS WITH BUNIT

The bUnit library comes with many dispatch methods that make it possible to trigger events on your component. Retrieve the element in the component using the Find method, and then call the appropriate dispatch method on it, for example, Click. These dispatch methods also allow you to pass event arguments. So let us look at an example.

Start by adding a new component to your Blazor project called MouseTracker with markup from Listing 13-14.

Listing 13-14. The MouseTracker component's Markupv

```
<div style="width: 300px; height: 300px;
            background: green; margin:50px"
        @onmousemove="MouseMove">
    @pos
</div>

@code {
    private string pos = "";

    private void MouseMove(MouseEventArgs e)
    => pos = $"Mouse at {e.ClientX}x{e.ClientY}";
}
```

In the unit test project, add a new class called MouseTrackerShould with a single unit test as in Listing 13-15. During the Arrange phase of the bUnit test, we create an instance of MouseEventArgs with ClientX and ClientY set to some value. We then create an instance of the MouseTracker component using the TestContext's RenderComponent method. Now we Find the div from the component and store it in the theDiv reference.

Now we can perform the Act phase of the test by triggering the MouseMove event, passing the MouseMoveEventArgs instance we created before. This will re-render the component, so we are ready for the Assert phase where we check if the theDiv has the expected content using the MarkupMatches method. Do note that we use Semantic Compare again, and here we can tell the compare to also ignore the style attribute using the style:ignore attribute. We will talk more about this in a later section of this chapter.

Listing 13-15. The MouseTrackerShould unit test

```
using BlazorApp.Testing.Components;
using Bunit;
using Microsoft.AspNetCore.Components.Web;

namespace BlazorApp.Testing.Tests;

public class MouseTrackerShould : TestContext
{
  [Fact]
  public void ShowCorrectMousePosition()
  {
    MouseEventArgs eventArgs = new()
    {
      ClientX = 100,
      ClientY = 200
    };
    IRenderedComponent<MouseTracker> cut = RenderComponent<MouseTracker>();
    AngleSharp.Dom.IElement theDiv = cut.Find(cssSelector: "div");
    theDiv.MouseMove(eventArgs);
    theDiv.MarkupMatches(
      $"<div style:ignore>Mouse at {eventArgs.ClientX}x{eventArgs.ClientY}"
    );
  }
}
```

Run the test; it should pass.

Passing Parameters to Our Component

With data binding, we can pass parameters from the parent component to a child component. How do we pass parameters with bUnit? Start by copying the Counter component in the Blazor project, rename it to TwoWayCounter, and change it to look like Listing 13-16. This TwoWayCounter component has a couple of parameters, including the CurrentCount and the Increment parameter.

CHAPTER 13 TESTING COMPONENTS WITH BUNIT

Listing 13-16. The TwoWayCounter component

```
<h1>Two Way Counter</h1>
<p  role="status">Current count: @CurrentCount</p>
<button class="btn btn-primary"
        @onclick="IncrementCount">
  Click me
</button>

@code {

  [Parameter]
  public int CurrentCount { get; set; }

  [Parameter]
  public int Increment { get; set; } = 1;

  [Parameter]
  public EventCallback<int> CurrentCountChanged { get; set; }

  [Parameter]
  public EventCallback<int> IncrementChanged { get; set; }

  private async Task IncrementCount()
  {
    CurrentCount += Increment;
    await CurrentCountChanged.InvokeAsync(CurrentCount);
  }
}
```

Add another unit test to the test project called TwoWayCounterShould and add the first bUnit test as in Listing 13-17. We want to pass two parameters to this component, and we can do this by using an overload of the RenderComponent method as shown in Listing 13-17. This takes a delegate which has a parameters argument of type ComponentParameterCollectionBuilder<TComponent>. This class has an Add method with two arguments: expression where you pass the name of the parameter and the value for the parameter.

422

CHAPTER 13   TESTING COMPONENTS WITH BUNIT

Listing 13-17. The TwoWayCounterShould test class

```
using BlazorApp.Testing.Components.Pages;
using Bunit;

namespace BlazorApp.Testing.Tests;
public class TwoWayCounterShould : TestContext
{
  [Fact]
  public void IncrementCounterWhenClicked()
  {
    IRenderedComponent<TwoWayCounter> cut =
      RenderComponent<TwoWayCounter>(
        parameters => parameters
          .Add(counter => counter.CurrentCount, 0)
          .Add(counter => counter.Increment, 1)
      );
    cut.Find("button")
       .Click();
    cut.Find("p")
       .MarkupMatches(@"<p role=""status"">Current count: 1</p>");
  }
}
```

This way of passing parameters to a component is very convenient, since we can use _intellisense_ to choose the parameter's name. There are other ways to pass the parameters, as shown in Listing 13-18. Here we use xUnit's `Theory` to pass different parameters to the component, and each parameter is passed as a `ValueTuple`, containing the name and value of each parameter (that is why these are wrapped in an opening and closing parenthesis).

However, I personally don't like this way of working, because now we are passing the argument's name as a `string`. The compiler will not check the contents of a string to see if it is the name of a parameter. What happens when you make a mistake (Or you decide later to rename the parameter)? The compiler will not complain, and you will get a failing test with the following message:

CHAPTER 13 TESTING COMPONENTS WITH BUNIT

Message:

System.InvalidOperationException : Object of type 'BlazorApp.Testing.Components.Pages.TwoWayCounter' does not have a property matching the name 'CurreentCount'.

Using hardcoded strings in code that contain names of classes, properties, and other code constructs is an anti-pattern which I call "String-based programming" and should be avoided.

Listing 13-18. Using a theory to test different cases

```
[Theory]
[InlineData(3)]
[InlineData(-3)]
public void IncrementCounterWithIncrementWhenClicked(int increment)
{
  IRenderedComponent<TwoWayCounter> cut =
  RenderComponent<TwoWayCounter>(
    ("CurrentCount", 0),
    ("Increment", increment)
  );
  cut.Find("button")
     .Click();
  cut.Find("p")
     .MarkupMatches(@$"<p role=""status"">Current count: {increment}</p>");
}
```

Of course, with modern C# we can fix this and still use this style as in Listing 13-19. Here we use the nameof operator, which takes the name of a property and returns the string representation of that property. You can also use nameof with classes, methods, and other things.

Listing 13-19. Using nameof to Pass Property Names

```
[Theory]
[InlineData(3)]
[InlineData(-3)]
```

```
public void IncrementCounterWithIncrementWhenClickedWithNameOf(int increment)
{
  IRenderedComponent<TwoWayCounter> cut =
  RenderComponent<TwoWayCounter>(
    (nameof(TwoWayCounter.CurrentCount), 0),
    (nameof(TwoWayCounter.Increment), increment)
  );
  cut.Find("button")
     .Click();
  cut.Find("p")
     .MarkupMatches(@$"<p role=""status"">Current count: {increment}</p>");
}
```

Testing Two-Way Data Binding and Events

Our TwoWayCounter has parameters to implement two-way data binding. Let us see if this component implements this correctly. We can use the same technique as before to pass handlers to the CurrentCountChanged and IncrementChanged parameters. But before we do this, add the FluentAssertions package to your test project. FluentAssertions allows you to write your assert statements in a more readable and concise way, and we will use it here (although this is not required). You can find out more about fluent assertions at https://fluentassertions.com.

Look at the bUnit test from Listing 13-21. We are adding four parameters, where two of them are of type EventCallback<int>. We assign a value to the EventCallback<int> using a delegate, and this delegate increments a local variable. This way we count the number of invocations of the CurrentCountChanged and IncrementChanged event callback.

Note You can also use this technique to test regular delegates like Action and Func.

After clicking the button, we expect the CurrentCountChanged to have been invoked, and we test this using the FluentAssertions Should().Be(1) method call. But we also want to test the Increment property's changed handler, and we can do this by accessing the component using the cut.Instance property and directly assigning a new value to Increment. The compiler will issue a warning on this statement; that is normal because you are normally not allowed to access a component's parameters directly from code. Let us fix this by adding the SetIncrement method from Listing 13-20 to the component.

Listing 13-20. Add the SetIncrement method.

```
public async Task SetIncrement(int newIncrement)
{
  Increment = newIncrement;
  await IncrementChanged.InvokeAsync(Increment);
}
```

Listing 13-21. Testing two-way changed handlers

```
[Fact]
public async Task TriggerChangedEventForCurrentCounter()
{
  int nrOfCurrentCountChanged = 0;
  int nrOfIncrementChanged = 0;
  IRenderedComponent<TwoWayCounter> cut =
  RenderComponent<TwoWayCounter>(parameters =>
  parameters.Add(counter => counter.CurrentCount, 0)
           .Add(counter => counter.Increment, 1)
           .Add(counter => counter.CurrentCountChanged,
           () => nrOfCurrentCountChanged++)
           .Add(counter => counter.IncrementChanged,
           () => nrOfIncrementChanged++)
  );

  cut.Find("button").Click();
  await cut.Instance.SetIncrement(2);
  nrOfCurrentCountChanged.Should().Be(1);
  nrOfIncrementChanged.Should().Be(1);
}
```

You can also change a parameter value after the first render of your component. Look for an example in Listing 13-22, where we use the SetParametersAndRender method to modify the value of the CurrentCount parameter. This will also re-render the component.

Listing 13-22. Modifying the value of a parameter

```
[Fact]
public void TriggerChangedEventForCurrentCounter2()
{
  IRenderedComponent<TwoWayCounter> cut =
  RenderComponent<TwoWayCounter>(parameters =>
    parameters.Add(counter => counter.CurrentCount, 0)
  );
  cut.SetParametersAndRender(parameters =>
    parameters.Add(counter => counter.CurrentCount, 2));
  cut.Find("p")
      .MarkupMatches(@$"<p role=""status"">Current count: 2</p>");
}
```

Testing Components That Use RenderFragment

What about components that use RenderFragment such as ChildContent and Templated Components? RenderFragment is a special Blazor type, so it needs some special care. Start by adding an Alert component to your Blazor project such as Listing 13-23.

Listing 13-23. The alert component

```
<div class="alert alert-secondary mt-4" role="alert">
  @ChildContent
</div>

@code {
  [Parameter]
  public required RenderFragment ChildContent { get; set; }
}
```

Now add the AlertShould class from Listing 13-24 to your test project. As you can see, the ChildContent is just another parameter, but comes with some convenience methods to make it easy to add. This example also illustrates the use of a new way of writing strings in C#: raw strings.

Raw strings allow you to copy-paste HTML, XML, C# code, and other strings containing quotes, without having to escape the quotes. Look at Listing 13-20, where we match a string containing quotes, and to tell the C# compiler we need to use double quotes ("") to tell it is a quote which is part of the string. With raw strings, you start a string with at least three quotes, and the C# compiler will see everything literally until you end the string with the same number of quotes. Look at Listing 13-24 where we use a raw string in the MarkupMatches method.

Listing 13-24. The AlertShould Test class

```
using Bunit;
using BlazorApp.Testing.Components;

namespace BlazorApp.Testing.Tests;

public class AlertShould : TestContext
{
  [Fact]
  public void RenderSimpleChildContent()
  {
    IRenderedComponent<Alert> cut =
    RenderComponent<Alert>(parameters =>
      parameters.AddChildContent("<p>Hello world!</p>"));
    cut.MarkupMatches(
      """
      <div class="alert alert-secondary mt-4" role="alert">
        <p>Hello world!</p>
      </div>
      """);
  }
}
```

Should the Alert component have additional parameters, we can pass them just like in listing 13-18.

In Listing 13-25. we pass some simple HTML as the ChildContent, but we can do more complex things. For example, in Listing 13-25, we pass the Counter as the ChildContent.

Listing 13-25. Passing a Counter as ChildContent

```
[Fact]
public void RenderCounterAsChildContent()
{
  IRenderedComponent<Alert> cut =
    RenderComponent<Alert>(parameters =>
    parameters.AddChildContent<Counter>()
  );
  cut.Find("p")
    .MarkupMatches("""<p role="status">Current count: 0</p>""");
}
```

We can even pass parameters to the ChildContent, for example, when using the TwoWayCounter as in Listing 13-26.

Listing 13-26. Passing the TwoWayCounter as ChildContent

```
[Fact]
public void RenderTwoWayCounterWithParametersAsChildContent()
{
  IRenderedComponent<Alert> cut =
  RenderComponent<Alert>(parameters =>
    parameters.AddChildContent<TwoWayCounter>(parameters =>
      parameters.Add(counter => counter.CurrentCount, 3))
  );
  cut.Find("p")
    .MarkupMatches("""<p role="status">Current count: 3</p>""");
}
```

You can even call AddChildContent multiple times to add more than one fragment. Listing 13-27 illustrates this where we add both a HTML string and a Counter. Also note the use of a const string so we don't need to sync the content used in the AddChildContent and MarkupMatches methods (_Don't Repeat Yourself Principle_ -DRY).

CHAPTER 13 TESTING COMPONENTS WITH BUNIT

Listing 13-27. Calling AddChildContent multiple times

```
[Fact]
public void RenderTitleAndCounterAsChildContent()
{
    const string header = "<h1>This is a counter</h1>";
    IRenderedComponent<Alert> cut =
    RenderComponent<Alert>(parameters =>
      parameters.AddChildContent(header)
                .AddChildContent<Counter>());
    AngleSharp.Dom.IElement h1 = cut.Find("h1");
    h1.MarkupMatches(header);
    AngleSharp.Dom.IElement p = cut.Find("p");
    p.MarkupMatches("""<p role="status">Current count: 0</p>""");
}
```

What about Templated components? Start by adding (copying from the provided code download with this book) the templated component from Listing 13-28. This templated component uses two RenderFragments and one RenderFragment<TItem>. It also has a parameter to pass a Loader which is a function that grabs the items for this component. First, we will look at the RenderFragment and then the RenderFragment<TItem>.

Listing 13-28. The TemplatedList component's markup

```
@typeparam TItem

@if (items is null)
{
    @LoadingContent
}
else if (items.Count() == 0)
{
    @EmptyContent
}
else
{
```

```razor
  <div class="list-group @ListGroupClass">
    @foreach (var item in items)
    {
      <div class="list-group-item">
        @ItemContent(item)
      </div>
    }
  </div>
}

@code {
  IEnumerable<TItem>? items;

  [Parameter]
  public Func<ValueTask<IEnumerable<TItem>>>? Loader { get; set; }

  [Parameter]
  public RenderFragment LoadingContent { get; set; } = default!;

  [Parameter]
  public RenderFragment? EmptyContent { get; set; } = default!;

  [Parameter]
  public RenderFragment<TItem> ItemContent { get; set; } = default!;

  [Parameter]
  public string ListGroupClass { get; set; } = string.Empty;

  protected override async Task OnParametersSetAsync()
  {
    if (Loader is not null)
    {
      items = await Loader();
    }
  }
}
```

Now add the `TemplatedListShould` class to your test project from Listing 13-29. Here we add two parameters, one for the `Loader` parameter and one for the `LoadingContent` template. As you can see, we can use the same Add method, just like normal parameters.

Listing 13-29. Using a RenderFragment in a test

```
using BlazorApp.Testing.Components;
using Bunit;

namespace BlazorApp.Testing.Tests;
public class TemplatedListShould : TestContext
{
  [Fact]
  public void RenderLoadingTemplateWhenItemsIsNull()
  {
    const string loading =
    "<div class=\"loader\">Loading...</div>";

    static ValueTask<IEnumerable<string>?> loader()
    => new ValueTask<IEnumerable<string>?>(result: null);

    IRenderedComponent<TemplatedList<string>> cut =
    RenderComponent<TemplatedList<string>>(parameters =>
      parameters.Add(tl => tl.Loader, loader)
            .Add(tl => tl.LoadingContent, loading)
    );
    cut.Find("div.loader")
       .MarkupMatches(loading);
  }
}
```

But what about the `ItemContent` parameter which uses the more complex `RenderFragment<TItem>`? Add a new unit test as in Listing 13-30. Here we will pass five strings using the loader `Func<ValueTask<IEnumerable<string>>>`. Do note the use of the `Enumerable.Repeat` method to create a collection of elements. We pass the loader as a parameter to the `TemplatedList<string>` component, and we also pass the `ItemContent`, which is a `RenderFragment<string>`. Since this takes an argument, we use a `Func<string, string>` delegate which will return a `RenderFragment<string>` (because the Add method takes care of this).

Now we want to check if it has used the `ItemContent` for each item from our collection (of 5 "A" strings). There is a `FindAll` method taking a CSS selector that will return all elements that match the selector. The `ItemContent` `RenderFragment` uses a `<p>`, so we use this as the CSS selector. We check if the number of paragraph matches the number of items, and then we iterate over each of these and check if the markup matches the expected output.

Listing 13-30. Passing a RenderFragment

```
[Fact]
public void RenderItemsCorrectly()
{
  const int count = 5;
  static ValueTask<IEnumerable<string>> loader()
    => new ValueTask<IEnumerable<string>>(
       Enumerable.Repeat("A", count)
    );
  IRenderedComponent<TemplatedList<string>> cut =
  RenderComponent<TemplatedList<string>>(parameters =>
    parameters.Add(tl => tl.Loader, loader)
             .Add(tl => tl.ItemContent,
                  (context) => $"<p>{context}</p>"));

  IRefreshableElementCollection<AngleSharp.Dom.IElement> ps =
    cut.FindAll("p");
  _ = ps.Should().NotBeEmpty();
  foreach (AngleSharp.Dom.IElement p in ps)
  {
    p.MarkupMatches("<p>A</p>");
  }
}
```

Run this test; it should normally pass. And if it does not, we will discuss this in the section on asynchronous re-renders, so keep reading.

One final example. Let us use another component as the ItemContent, and pass the context as a parameter. Add a new component called ListItem from Listing 13-31 (which is a copy-paste of the ItemContent from Listing 13-31.

Listing 13-31. The ListItem component

```
<p>@Item</p>

@code {
  [Parameter]
  public string Item { get; set; } = default!;
}
```

Now copy and paste the RenderItemsCorrectly method, renaming it as in Listing 13-32. The only other part of this listing that needs some modification is where we pass the ItemContent parameter. If you want to use a component to pass as a RenderFragment<TItem>, you need to use the Add<ComponentType, TItem> overload, where the first generic argument is the type of the component to use, and the second is the type of the generic argument for RenderFragment<TItem>. In this specific case, the ComponentType is ListItem, and the TItem is string (because we pass an IEnumerable<string> to the TemplateList.

Listing 13-32. Passing a component as a RenderFragment

```
[Fact]
public void RenderItemsWithListItemCorrectly()
{
  const int count = 5;
  static ValueTask<IEnumerable<string>> loader()
    => new ValueTask<IEnumerable<string>>(
      Enumerable.Repeat("A", count)
    );
  IRenderedComponent<TemplatedList<string>> cut =
  RenderComponent<TemplatedList<string>>(parameters =>
    parameters.Add(tl => tl.Loader, loader)
             .Add<ListItem, string>(tl => tl.ItemContent,
                (context) => itemParams
```

```
            => itemParams.Add(p => p.Item, context)
        ));

  IRefreshableElementCollection<AngleSharp.Dom.IElement> ps = 
    cut.FindAll("p");
  _ = ps.Should().NotBeEmpty();
  foreach (AngleSharp.Dom.IElement p in ps)
  {
    p.MarkupMatches("<p>A</p>");
  }
}
```

This `Add<ListItem, string>` overload takes two expressions, the first returns the parameter to set `ItemContent`, and the second expression needs some deeper explanation. Let us have a look at this somewhat hard to read piece of code:

```
Add<ListItem, string>(
  tl => tl.ItemContent,
  context => itemParams
        => itemParams.Add(p => p.Item, context)
));
```

So the first argument is `tl => tl.ItemContent` which returns the parameter to set. The second argument is a lambda function, which takes the value for `TItem` (so in our case a string) and returns another lambda function which takes an `ComponentParameterCollectionBuilder<TComponent>`. Does this sound familiar? Yes. It is the same type we have used to pass parameters to a component from the beginning of this section (Listing 13-18 example). Here we add parameters to the `ListItem` component by calling `Add`.

Run this test (and the others if you like). All tests should pass. Phew!

Using Cascading Parameters

Some components use one or more cascading parameters, so to test these components we will need to pass a value for the cascading parameter. Start by making a copy of the `Counter` component and rename it to `CounterWithCV`. Add an `Increment` cascading parameter as in Listing 13-33.

CHAPTER 13   TESTING COMPONENTS WITH BUNIT

Listing 13-33. The CounterWithVC component

```
@page "/counterCV"

<PageTitle>Counter</PageTitle>

<h1>Counter</h1>

<p role="status">Current count: @currentCount</p>

<button class="btn btn-primary" @onclick="IncrementCount">Click me</button>

@code {
  [CascadingParameter]
  public int Increment { get; set; }

  private int currentCount = 0;

  private void IncrementCount()
  {
    currentCount+=Increment;
  }
}
```

Add a new test class called `CounterWithCVShould` and implement the test as in Listing 13-34. As you can see, since cascading properties are identified through their type, you only need to pass the value.

Listing 13-34. Testing a component with a cascading parameter

```
using BlazorApp.Testing.Components.Pages;
using Bunit;

namespace BlazorApp.Testing.Tests;
public class CounterWithVCShould : TestContext
{
  [Fact]
  public void ShouldUseCascadingIncrement()
  {
    IRenderedComponent<CounterWithCV> cut =
    RenderComponent<CounterWithCV>(parameters =>
```

```
        parameters.AddCascadingValue(3));
    cut.Find(cssSelector: "button")
        .Click();
    cut.Find(cssSelector: "p")
        .MarkupMatches("""<p role="status">Current count: 3</p>""");
    }
}
```

You can also have named cascading values, to try this first name the `Increment` cascading parameter as in Listing 13-35 and update the test as in Listing 13-36.

Listing 13-35. Using a named cascading parameter

```
[CascadingParameter(Name = "Increment")]
```

Listing 13-36. Passing a named cascading parameter

```
RenderComponent<CounterWithCV>(parameters =>
    parameters.AddCascadingValue(name: "Increment", cascadingValue: 3));
```

Using NSubstitute to Create Fake Implementations

We have seen that components should do one thing very well (the Single Responsibility Principle) and that we should use Services to implement logic such as retrieving data using REST, or to implement business logic. We pass these services to the component using dependency injection. Here we will look at how to pass dependencies to components using bUnit and how to replace your services with fake implementations to better drive your unit tests.

Injecting Dependencies with bUnit

Let us start by reviewing the `Weather` component from Listing 13-37. This component takes one dependency, an `IWeatherService`.

Listing 13-37. The Weather component

```
@page "/weather"

@inject IWeatherService WeatherService

<PageTitle>Weather</PageTitle>

<h1>Weather</h1>

<p>This component demonstrates showing data.</p>

@if (forecasts == null)
{
  <p><em>Loading...</em></p>
}
else
{
  <table class="table">
    <thead>
      <tr>
        <th>Date</th>
        <th>Temp. (C)</th>
        <th>Temp. (F)</th>
        <th>Summary</th>
      </tr>
    </thead>
    <tbody>
      @foreach (var forecast in forecasts)
      {
        <tr>
          <td>@forecast.Date.ToShortDateString()</td>
          <td>@forecast.TemperatureC</td>
          <td>@forecast.TemperatureF</td>
          <td>@forecast.Summary</td>
        </tr>
      }
    </tbody>
```

```
    </table>
}

@code {
  private WeatherForecast[]? forecasts;

  protected override async Task OnInitializedAsync()
  {
    forecasts = await WeatherService.GetForecasts();
  }
}
```

When you use this component in a Blazor application, the Blazor runtime will take care of injecting the IWeatherService dependency. When you use the component in a bUnit test, the bUnit runtime will take care of injecting the dependency. The only thing we need to tell it which class to use to instantiate the instance.

Add a new test class to the test project, call it WeatherShould, and complete it as in Listing 13-38. To configure dependency injection in a bUnit test, you add your dependencies to the Services property, using the same methods as regular dependency injection, AddSingleton, AddTransient, and AddScoped.

Listing 13-38. Testing the Weather component

```
using BlazorApp.Testing.Components.Pages;
using BlazorApp.Testing.Services;
using Bunit;
using FluentAssertions;
using Microsoft.Extensions.DependencyInjection;

namespace BlazorApp.Testing.Tests;
public class WeatherShould : TestContext
{
  [Fact]
  public void UseWeatherService()
  {
    // Use Services for dependency injection
    _ = Services.AddSingleton<IWeatherService, WeatherService>();
    IRenderedComponent<Weather> cut = RenderComponent<Weather>();
```

```
        IRefreshableElementCollection<AngleSharp.Dom.IElement> rows =
          cut.FindAll("tbody tr");
        _ = rows.Count.Should().Be(5);
    }
}
```

Try running this test. It fails? Look at the output of the failed test. As it turns out, the WeatherService fetches the forecasts in an asynchronous way (taking seconds). We could fix this (as you will see later), but we should use a fake object for this test! Let us talk about fake objects.

Expected _ = rows.Count to be 5, but found 0 (difference of -5).

Replacing Dependencies with Fake Objects

When you are testing a component, you want full control over dependencies. This means in many cases that you cannot use the real dependency. First, remember that tests should be fast and automatic? If the real dependency uses a database, or a REST call to fetch data, this will make your test slow. Networks, disks, and databases are several factors slower than accessing data from memory. So, we want to avoid these things. Also, databases and disks have memory, so when a test makes modifications to the data, the next time the test runs it is using different data and will probably fail. We don't want to use the real dependency (we are testing the component, not the dependency!). We will use a _fake_ implementation of the dependency, and that is why it is so important to have your dependencies implement an interface. Building another class with the same interface is easy and practical.

And there are different kinds of fake objects. Let us discuss stubs and mocks as shown in Figure 13-9. As you can see, both stubs and mocks are special cases of fake objects. The terminology (stub, mock, fake) used here unfortunately is not consistent in the testing community. Some people classify fake objects using different names, and some people even use taxonomies containing seven different kinds of stubs!

CHAPTER 13   TESTING COMPONENTS WITH BUNIT

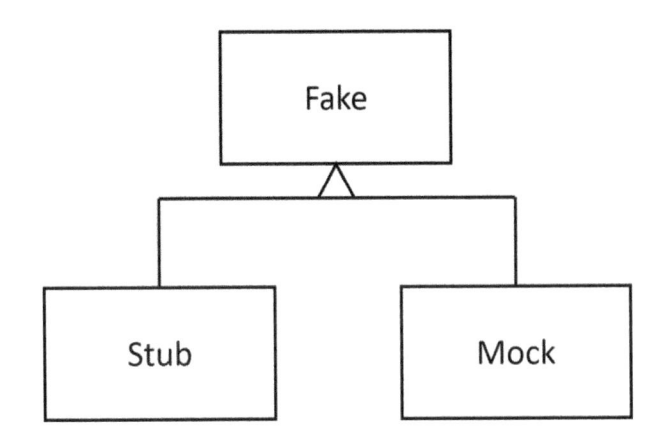

Figure 13-9. Fake, stub, and mock objects for testing

Using Stubs

Let us start with stubs. A _stub_ is a fake implementation of a dependency that is just there to assist in a test. Our Weather component will fetch a couple of forecasts from the IWeatherService dependency. But how many forecasts will this return? If we use the real service, this might depend on a bunch of things which are out of our control. So we use a stub implementation of the IWeatherService where we have full control. The stub is just there to assist in the test, and we will perform our Assert phase on the subject under test, not the stub. Let me use another example. Imagine you work for a car company, and you want to test your new type of car for safety. You want to run this car into a wall and see if it will explode (like in the movies). Will you run the car into a real wall? Someone's house? No. You will have someone build a fake wall, in a controlled environment so no one will risk getting hurt. You drive the car into the wall, and then the wall has served its purpose. You will examine the car to see the outcome of the test; the wall is no longer important. This is illustrated in Figure 13-10.

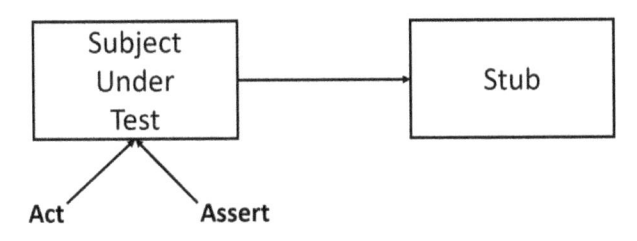

Figure 13-10. Using a stub during a test

441

Tests that use stubs are also known as _State Verification Tests_.

Let us build a stub for the IWeatherService. Start by adding a new class called WeatherServiceStub to the test project.

Implement the interface like Listing 13-39. Our stub has a property that will hold the data that we will return from the service.

Listing 13-39. Implementing a IWeatherService stub

```
using BlazorApp.Testing.Entities;
using BlazorApp.Testing.Services;

namespace BlazorApp.Testing.Tests;

internal class WeatherServiceStub : IWeatherService
{
  public required WeatherForecast[]? FakeForecasts { get; set; }

  public ValueTask<WeatherForecast[]?> GetForecasts()
    => ValueTask.FromResult(FakeForecasts);
}
```

Now update the UseWeatherService test as in Listing 13-40. We create an instance of the stub, initialize it with the data we want, and then pass it to dependency injection as a singleton. When the Weather component gets initialized with will use the stub, and we are sure that our service returns five rows of data (or a different number, that is why I use a const for easy update).

Listing 13-40. Testing the Weather component with a stub

```
[Fact]
public void UseWeatherService()
{
  const int nrOfForecasts = 5;

  WeatherServiceStub stub = new WeatherServiceStub
  {
    FakeForecasts = Enumerable.Repeat(new WeatherForecast(),
                nrOfForecasts).ToArray()
  };
```

```
    _ = Services.AddSingleton<IWeatherService>(stub);
    IRenderedComponent<Weather> cut = RenderComponent<Weather>();
    IRefreshableElementCollection<AngleSharp.Dom.IElement> rows =
      cut.FindAll("tbody tr");
    _ = rows.Count.Should().Be(nrOfForecasts);
}
```

Run the test. It should pass.

Using Mocks

What is a mock? A _mock_ is a fake implementation where we want to verify if the subject under test called certain methods and properties on the mock. A mock therefore works a little like a data recorder, remembering which methods were called, even recording the values of the arguments in the method call. It should not come as a surprise that building a mock is a lot more work! When you use a mock in a test, you will do your assert phase through the mock, with questions like did the subject under test call this method? Let us use the car example again. Now we want to see if the driver of the car gets hurt in a frontal crash into a wall. We already have a wall, but now we need a driver. Any volunteers? No? Of course not. We will mimic the driver (a mock object) using a crash test dummy. These dummies look a lot like a human (if you are Homer Simpson) and are crammed full of sensors. You let the car crash into the wall. After the crash, you are not interested in the wall, nor the car. You will ask the dummy (the mock remember) where it hurts. This is illustrated in Figure 13-11.

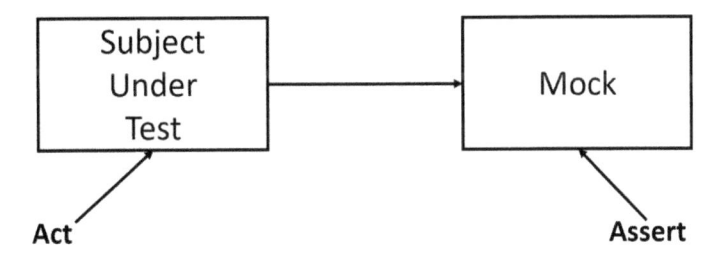

Figure 13-11. Using a mock during testing

Tests like these are known as _Object Interaction Tests_.

Let us update the Weather component to perform some logging, so add an @inject for an ILogger and use it in the OnInitializedAsync as in Listing 13-41.

CHAPTER 13 TESTING COMPONENTS WITH BUNIT

Listing 13-41. Update the Weather component to use logging

```
@page "/weather"
@using Microsoft.Extensions.Logging

@inject IWeatherService WeatherService
@inject ILogger logger

<PageTitle>Weather</PageTitle>

<h1>Weather</h1>

<p>This component demonstrates showing data.</p>

@if (forecasts == null)
{
  <p><em>Loading...</em></p>
}
else
{
  <table class="table">
    <thead>
      <tr>
        <th>Date</th>
        <th>Temp. (C)</th>
        <th>Temp. (F)</th>
        <th>Summary</th>
      </tr>
    </thead>
    <tbody>
      @foreach (var forecast in forecasts)
      {
        <tr>
          <td>@forecast.Date.ToShortDateString()</td>
          <td>@forecast.TemperatureC</td>
          <td>@forecast.TemperatureF</td>
          <td>@forecast.Summary</td>
```

```
      </tr>
    }
    </tbody>
  </table>
}
@code {
  private WeatherForecast[]? forecasts;

  protected override async Task OnInitializedAsync()
  {
    logger.LogInformation("Fetching forecasts");
    forecasts = await WeatherService.GetForecasts();
  }
}
```

We want to test if the `ILogger` is used during the `OnInitializedAsync`. We need a mock implementation because we don't want to have to parse log files. Add a new class to your test project called LoggerMock as in Listing 13-42. Implementing this class alone takes some work! We will next look at how we can make this easier. Our mock logger simply records a couple of arguments in the Journal list.

Listing 13-42. Implementing an ILogger mock

```
using Microsoft.Extensions.Logging;

namespace BlazorApp.Testing.Tests;
internal class LoggerMock : ILogger
{
  public List<(LogLevel logLevel, object? state)> Journal { get; set; }
    = []; // New C# collection initializer syntax

  public IDisposable? BeginScope<TState>(TState state)
    => throw new NotImplementedException();

  public bool IsEnabled(LogLevel logLevel)
    => true;
```

```
public void Log<TState>(LogLevel logLevel, EventId eventId,
    TState state, Exception? exception,
    Func<TState, Exception?, string> formatter)
    => Journal.Add((logLevel, state));
}
```

Add a new unit test to the WeatherShould class like in Listing 13-43.

Listing 13-43. Testing the Weather component using a mock

```
[Fact]
public void UseProperLogging()
{
    const int nrOfForecasts = 5;
    WeatherServiceStub stub = new()
    {
        FakeForecasts = Enumerable.Repeat(new WeatherForecast(), nrOfForecasts)
                        .ToArray()
    };
    _ = Services.AddSingleton<IWeatherService>(stub);
    LoggerMock logger = new();
    _ = Services.AddSingleton<ILogger>(logger);
    _ = RenderComponent<Weather>();
    _ = logger.Journal.Count.Should().Be(1);
    _ = logger.Journal.First().state.Should().NotBeNull();
    _ = logger.Journal.First().state!.ToString()
                    .Should().Contain("Fetching forecasts");
}
```

We create a stub for the IWeatherService, a mock for the ILogger, and then we render the component. Now we want to check the Journal of the LoggerMock. There should be one call to the logger, so we check the length of the Journal. Then we check the entry's state to see if it contains the message. All straightforward but a lot of work!

Run all your tests. The UseWeatherService test breaks! Why? Because we introduced another dependency, we need to dependency inject a logger in this test too. I will leave the fixing in your capable hands.

Building Stubs and Mocks with NSubstitute

How can we implement stubs and mocks with a lot less work? Other people have been asking the same question, and some of them have built libraries that make this possible. Generally, these libraries are known as _Isolation Frameworks_. Isolation Frameworks allow you to quickly generate stubs and mocks for classes and interfaces, where you implement just the methods you need for the test and verify if the subject under test invoked methods with certain arguments a certain number of times. Here we will look at _NSubstitute_ which is currently one of the most popular in the testing community. We will cover a lot of features of NSubstitute here, but if you want to learn more you can visit `https://nsubstitute.github.io/`.

Start by adding the NSubstitute Nuget package to the test project. Now copy the `UseWeatherServices` test method and rename it to `UseWeatherServiceWithNSubstitute`. Change its implementation like Listing 13-44. First we create the forecasts data we want the `IWeatherService` to return.

Next we create an instance of `IWeatherService` using the `Substitute.For<IWeatherService>()` which is a static factory method and class from NSubstitute. This class allows us to set up methods from the interface and returns a certain result. It is that simple to provide a stub implementation. But NSubstitute allows you to go further, and make the method return different results, depending on the arguments, for example.

Next, we configure bUnit's dependency injection to inject a singleton instance, passing the stub, which is an instance implementing the `IWeatherService` interface. No need to build our own class to create a stub.

Our `Weather` component also needs a logger, but here we are not interested in the interaction between the component and the logger, so we create another stub. The rest of the test remains unchanged.

Listing 13-44. Implementing a stub with NSubstitute

```
[Fact]
public void UseWeatherServiceWithNSubstitute()
{
  const int nrOfForecasts = 5;

  WeatherForecast[]? fakeForecasts =
    Enumerable.Repeat(new WeatherForecast(), nrOfForecasts)
            .ToArray();
```

CHAPTER 13 TESTING COMPONENTS WITH BUNIT

```
    IWeatherService stub = Substitute.For<IWeatherService>();
    stub.GetForecasts().Returns(fakeForecasts);
    _ = Services.AddSingleton<IWeatherService>(stub);
    ILogger logger = Substitute.For<ILogger>();
    _ = Services.AddSingleton<ILogger>(logger);
    IRenderedComponent<Weather> cut = RenderComponent<Weather>();
    IRefreshableElementCollection<AngleSharp.Dom.IElement> rows =
      cut.FindAll("tbody tr");
    _ = rows.Count.Should().Be(nrOfForecasts);
}
```

Run the test; it should pass.

Now it is time to implement a mock, where we want to see if the Weather component will invoke the logger. Copy the UseProperLogging test method and name it UseProperLoggingWithNSubstitute as in Listing 13-45. Here you should focus on the Received method. Here we verify if the Log method got called. The Log method takes a bunch of arguments, and the way this Log method works is somewhat awkward. The first argument is of type LogLevel, which we check if the LogLevel.Information value was used.

Each argument is represented with a check of the argument's value. You can pass a real value, or you can also ignore the value of the argument with Arg.Any<T>, specifying the type of the argument.

For example:

```
logger.Received().Log(LogLevel.Information, message: Arg.Any<string>());
```

This type of argument is needed to disambiguate overloading. Other arguments work in a similar way, even generic arguments. For example, if an argument is of type List<T>, and you cannot know T, you use Arg.Any<List<Arg.AnyType>>().

Listing 13-45. Implementing a mock using NSubstitute

```
[Fact]
public void UseProperLoggingWithNSubstitute()
{
  const int nrOfForecasts = 5;
  WeatherServiceStub stub = new()
  {
```

CHAPTER 13 TESTING COMPONENTS WITH BUNIT

```
        FakeForecasts = Enumerable.Repeat(new WeatherForecast(), nrOfForecasts)
                            .ToArray()
    };
    _ = Services.AddSingleton<IWeatherService>(stub);
    // Create an ILogger mock
    ILogger logger = Substitute.For<ILogger>();
    _ = Services.AddSingleton<ILogger>(logger);
    _ = RenderComponent<Weather>();
    // Did the Log method get called?
    logger.Received()
          .Log(LogLevel.Information, message: "Fetching forecasts");
}
```

Run the test. It should pass.

Writing bUnit Tests in Razor

When you build unit tests with bUnit, you sometimes end up with long tests because of all the markup that gets generated. Also, the `MarkupMatches` method takes a string, and if your markup uses HTML attributes, you need to escape your quotes with \", or use raw strings. For these kinds of tests, we can also use razor to author tests. Writing unit tests with razor requires two things: The project needs to reference the razor SDK, meaning your test project should set the SDK type to razor:

```
<Project Sdk="Microsoft.NET.Sdk.Razor">
```

Second, you should add an _Imports.razor file to the test project for easy reference, as in Listing 13-46.

Listing 13-46. *The _Imports.razor file for test projects*

```
@using System.Net.Http
@using System.Net.Http.Json
@using Microsoft.AspNetCore.Components.Forms
@using Microsoft.AspNetCore.Components.Routing
@using Microsoft.AspNetCore.Components.Web
@using static Microsoft.AspNetCore.Components.Web.RenderMode
```

CHAPTER 13   TESTING COMPONENTS WITH BUNIT

```
@using Microsoft.AspNetCore.Components.Web.Virtualization
@using Microsoft.JSInterop
@using BlazorApp.Testing
@using BlazorApp.Testing.Components
@using BlazorApp.Testing.Components.Pages
@using BlazorApp.Testing.Entities
@using BlazorApp.Testing.Services
@using Bunit
@using FluentAssertions
```

I do advise to add your project's namespaces here too.

The First Razor Test

In your test project, add a new razor component called `RCounterShould` as in Listing 13-47. Here I will prefix the razor unit tests with an R, so we don't get a name conflict with our other `CounterShould` test class. We will make the test inherit from `TestContext`, just like our test classes written in C#. Then we add a `@code` section and put our xUnit test method in there. Because this is a razor file, we can write the test's markup using razor inside the `Render` method.

And inside the `MarkupMatches` method, we can also write the markup using plain razor. This makes writing tests like these simpler and agreeable.

Listing 13-47. Writing a simple unit test with Razor

```
@inherits Bunit.TestContext

@code {
  [Fact]
  public void RenderCorrectlyWithInitialZero()
  {
    var cut = Render(@<Counter />);
    cut.Find("p")
      .MarkupMatches(@<p role="status">Current count: 0</p>);
  }

  [Fact]
  public void IncrementCounterWhenButtonIsClicked()
```

```
{
    var cut = RenderComponent<Counter>();
    cut.Find(cssSelector: "button")
        .Click();
    cut.Find(cssSelector: "p")
        .MarkupMatches(@<p role="status">Current count: 1</p>);
  }
}
```

What about passing parameters? Add a new component called RTwoWayCounterShould like in Listing 13-48. Since we can render our component using plain razor, we can pass parameters inside the razor syntax as shown in the first test method! The second test method illustrates how we can test two-way data binding, again using the same familiar razor syntax.

Listing 13-48. Passing parameters in a razor test

```
@inherits Bunit.TestContext

@code {
  [Fact]
  public void IncrementCounterWhenButtonIsClicked()
  {
    var cut = Render(@<TwoWayCounter CurrentCount="1" Increment="2"/>);
    cut.Find("button").Click();
    cut.Find("p")
        .MarkupMatches(@<p role="status">Current count: 3</p>
    );
  }

  [Fact]
  public void TriggerChangedEventForCurrentCounter2()
  {
    int currentCount = 1;
    var cut = Render(@<TwoWayCounter
                        @bind-CurrentCount="currentCount"
                        Increment="2"/>
    );
```

CHAPTER 13　TESTING COMPONENTS WITH BUNIT

```
    cut.Find(cssSelector: "button")
      .Click();
    currentCount.Should().Be(3);
  }
}
```

Let us look at an example that uses `ChildContent`. Add a new razor component called RAlertShould to the test project as in Listing 13-49. The Alert component uses ChildContent, and we can pass this by nesting the child content inside the Alert markup. And to see if the component gets rendered as expected, we can use simple HTML markup inside the MarkupMatches method.

Listing 13-49. Testing a component with ChildContent

```
@inherits Bunit.TestContext

@code {
  [Fact]
  public void RenderSimpleChildContent()
  {
    var cut = Render(
      @<Alert>
        <h1>Hello world!</h1>
      </Alert>
    );
    cut.MarkupMatches(
      @<div class="alert alert-secondary mt-4" role="alert">
        <h1>Hello world!</h1>
      </div>
    );
  }
}
```

Add another razor component, called RTemplatedListShould from Listing 13-50. Again, we want to see if the component displays the loading RenderFragment when the items are null. Passing a RenderFragment is again done using razor.

452

CHAPTER 13 TESTING COMPONENTS WITH BUNIT

Listing 13-50. Using a razor test for a templated component

```
@inherits Bunit.TestContext

@code {
  [Fact]
  public void RenderLoadingTemplateWhenItemsIsNull()
  {
    RenderFragment loading =
  @<div class="loader">Loading...</div>;

    Func<ValueTask<IEnumerable<string>?>> loader =
    () => new ValueTask<IEnumerable<string>?>(
    result: null);

    var cut = Render(

  @<TemplatedList Loader="@loader">
    <LoadingContent>
      <div class="loader">Loading...</div>
    </LoadingContent>
  </TemplatedList>
    );

    cut.Find("div.loader")

    .MarkupMatches(loading);
  }
}
```

Handling Asynchronous Re-renders

When you build a component that overrides `OnInitializedAsync` or `OnParametersSetAsync`, your component will at least render itself twice. First, when the component gets created, and after completion of the `OnInitializedAsync` and again after completion of each `OnParametersSetAsync`.

Inside a bUnit test, this can give you issues. Let us look at an example.

Add the following unit test from Listing 13-51 to the RTemplatedListShould class. In this test we make the loader really asynchronous using the TaskCompletionSource<T> class. Instances of this class have a Task<T> which will continue execution by calling the SetResult method. Until then the Task will block any awaiter. This allows us to render the component, see the loading UI, then make the Task complete by calling SetResult, and then see if the items get rendered.

> **Note** This test will fail, so keep on reading.

Listing 13-51. Testing asynchronous re-renders

```
[Fact]
public void RenderItemsAftersItemsLoadedAsyncCorrectly()
{
  const int count = 5;
  var tcs = new TaskCompletionSource<IEnumerable<string>?>();
  Func<ValueTask<IEnumerable<string>?>> loader =
    () => new ValueTask<IEnumerable<string>?>(tcs.Task);
  var cut = Render(
@<TemplatedList Loader="@loader">
  <LoadingContent>
    <div class="loader">Loading...</div>
  </LoadingContent>
  <ItemContent Context="item">
    <ListItem Item="@item" />
  </ItemContent>
</TemplatedList>
);

  cut.Find("div.loader")
     .MarkupMatches(@<div class="loader">Loading...</div>);

  // Complete the loader task,
  // this should rerender the component asynchronously
  tcs.SetResult(Enumerable.Repeat("A", count));
```

```
    var ps = cut.FindAll("p");
    ps.Should().NotBeEmpty();
    foreach (var p in ps)
    {
        p.MarkupMatches(@<p>A</p>);
    }
}
```

Run the test. It will fail! Why? Because our component will render the UI on another thread, and the test will check the UI before rendering completes. We need to wait a bit till the UI rendering completes. How can we do this? Add this line of code after the `SetResult` call, with the complete method in Listing 13-52.

```
cut.WaitForState(() => cut.FindAll("p").Any());
```

The `WaitForState` method will wait till the condition returns `true`. We know that the UI will render a bunch of paragraphs, so we wait till we see them. The `WaitForState` also has a parameter (not shown here) to set the timeout, which has a default value of 1 second. If the cut does not pass the condition within the timeout, the test will fail with the `WaitForFailedException`.

Listing 13-52. Testing asynchronous re-renders

```
[Fact]
public void RenderItemsAftersItemsLoadedAsyncCorrectly()
{
    const int count = 5;
    var tcs = new TaskCompletionSource<IEnumerable<string>?>();
    Func<ValueTask<IEnumerable<string>?>> loader =
        () => new ValueTask<IEnumerable<string>?>(tcs.Task);
    var cut = Render(
@<TemplatedList Loader="@loader">
    <LoadingContent>
        <div class="loader">Loading...</div>
    </LoadingContent>
    <ItemContent Context="item">
        <ListItem Item="@item" />
    </ItemContent>
```

```
</TemplatedList>
);

  cut.Find("div.loader")
    .MarkupMatches(@<div class="loader">Loading...</div>);

  // Complete the loader task,
  // this should rerender the component asynchronously
  tcs.SetResult(Enumerable.Repeat("A", count));
  // Wait for rendering to complete
  cut.WaitForState(() => cut.FindAll("p").Any());
  var ps = cut.FindAll("p");
  ps.Should().NotBeEmpty();
  foreach (var p in ps)
  {
    p.MarkupMatches(@<p>A</p>);
  }
}
```

Configuring Semantic Compare

The bUnit testing library uses the _AngleSharp Diffing library_ to compare the generated markup with the expected markup in the MarkupMatches method. You can find AngleSharp on github at https://github.com/AngleSharp/AngleSharp.Diffing. To make your tests more robust, you can configure how the semantic comparison works, for example, we can tell it to ignore certain HTML attributes and elements.

Why Do We Need Semantic Compare?

Using strings to compare markup is too sensitive to small changes in the markup. For example, formatting your code might add some whitespace, and since string comparison will compare each character, a working test will suddenly fail. And there are many more innocent changes that will break a test, for example, changing the order of attributes, or reordering the classes in the class attribute, or adding comments. Semantic Comparison will ignore all these changes, resulting in tests that will not break because of a simple change.

CHAPTER 13   TESTING COMPONENTS WITH BUNIT

Customizing Semantic Compare

Remember one of our previous tests, where we told the `MarkupMatches` method to ignore the attribute (Listing 13-15). The AngleSharp Diffing library allows us to use special attributes to ignore certain elements and attributes, for example, `<div style:ignore>` will ignore the style attribute's contents. We can also make it ignore certain HTML elements, for example, add the test from Listing 13-53 to the `AlertShould` class.

Listing 13-53. Ignoring an element with semantic compare

```
[Fact]
public void RenderCorrectly()
{
  IRenderedComponent<Alert> cut =
  RenderComponent<Alert>(parameters =>
    parameters.AddChildContent("<p>Hello world!</p>"));
  cut.MarkupMatches(
  """
  <div class="alert alert-secondary mt-4" role="alert">
          <p diff:ignore></p>
  </div>
  """);
}
```

We can do the same with razor tests, for example, Listing 13-54 which should be added to the `RAlertShould` razor file.

Listing 13-54. Ignoring an element with a razor test

```
[Fact]
public void RenderCorrectly()
{
  var cut = Render(
@<Alert>
  <h1>Hello world!</h1>
</Alert>
);
```

457

```
  cut.MarkupMatches(
@<div class="alert alert-secondary mt-4" role="alert">
  <h1 diff:ignore></h1>
</div>
  );
}
```

By default, semantic compare will ignore whitespace, but in some cases you want to verify if the component actually renders some whitespace. Do this with `diff:whitespace="preserve"`.

You can also tell semantic compare to ignore case, or use a regular expression for your comparison.

Let us test the simple Card component from Listing 13-55.

Listing 13-55. A simple Card component

```
<h3 id="card-@Id">Card @Id</h3>

@code {
  [Parameter]
  public int Id { get; set; }
}
```

A unit test that will check if the `id` attribute matches `card-` followed by one to four digits, and the contents matches `Card` with one to four digits looks like Listing 13-56. We also want the test to ignore the casing on the card's contents.

Listing 13-56. Ignore casing and using regular expressions

```
using BlazorApp.Testing.Components;
using Bunit;
using System.Text.RegularExpressions;

namespace BlazorApp.Testing.Tests;
public class CardShould : TestContext
{
  [Fact]
  public void RenderCorrectlyWithProperId()
  {
```

```
    IRenderedComponent<Card> cut =
      RenderComponent<Card>();
    cut.MarkupMatches(
    """
    <h3 diff:ignorecase diff:regex id:regex="card-\d{1,4}">
      card \d{1,4}
    </h3>
    """);
  }
}
```

Summary

In this chapter, we had a look at unit testing. With unit testing, you can see if your code and components behave as expected and allows you to test if they continue behaving, so small changes that cause bugs are found as fast as possible. Good unit tests are fast, consistent, repeatable, and automatic. We have seen that with bUnit testing Blazor components becomes very practical, and we can author tests using C# or Razor. And with NSubstitute, we can quickly generate stubs and mocks to replace dependencies in our tests.

CHAPTER 14

Communication

In the services chapter, you built a service using ASP.NET Core to retrieve the menu of pizzas. Retrieving data from a database with Blazor Server is easy, since your server can directly talk to the database. But with Blazor WebAssembly, and especially auto rendering, your application can also run in the browser, with no direct access to the database. In this chapter, you will add support to the Blazor client to talk to that service over the network using REST.

Examining the Server Project

The sources that come with this book have a starter project named BlazorApp. Communication you can use to follow along with the material presented in this book. This project uses auto rendering, and everything works for components running on the server. But when the Weather component starts running in Blazor WebAssembly, there is a problem.

The Server Project

Look at the BlazorApp.Communication server project and look for the WeatherService class, which is in Listing 14-1.

Listing 14-1. The WeatherService class

```
using BlazorApp.Communication.Client.Entities;
using BlazorApp.Communication.Client.Services;

namespace BlazorApp.Communication.Services;
```

CHAPTER 14 COMMUNICATION

```csharp
public class WeatherService : IWeatherService
{
  public async ValueTask<WeatherForecast[]> GetForecasts()
  {
    // Simulate asynchronous loading from database
    await Task.Delay(500);

    DateOnly startDate = DateOnly.FromDateTime(DateTime.Now);
    string[] summaries = [
      "Freezing", "Bracing", "Chilly",
      "Cool", "Mild", "Warm", "Balmy",
      "Hot", "Sweltering", "Scorching"
      ];
    WeatherForecast[] forecasts =
    Enumerable.Range(1, 5)
              .Select(index => new WeatherForecast
    {
      Date = startDate.AddDays(index),
      TemperatureC = Random.Shared.Next(-20, 55),
      Summary = summaries[Random.Shared.Next(summaries.Length)]
    }).ToArray();

    return forecasts;
  }
}
```

Does this look somewhat familiar? Of course it does; this is a service that simulates loading weather forecasts from a database.

This service is used by the Weather component to load its WeatherForecast data, and it receives the service through dependency injection as shown in Listing 14-2.

Listing 14-2. The Weather component

```razor
@page "/weather"
@using BlazorApp.Communication.Client.Entities
@using BlazorApp.Communication.Client.Services

@inject IWeatherService WeatherService

...
```

CHAPTER 14　COMMUNICATION

When you run the project and you navigate to the Weather link, you should normally see the random forecasts, and after a short while, you will see an error. Why? Because the Weather component first runs on the server, and then starts to run on the browser using WASM (we are using auto rendering), and there is no IWeatherService service registered for WebAssembly.

Maybe you just copy the service to the BlazorApp.Communication.Client project? Sorry, this will not work since the service retrieves the data from a database (well, just pretend). We need to implement the IWeatherService to retrieve the data using the network from the server.

Adding a WebAPI Endpoint

Blazor projects are just another kind of ASP.NET project, meaning you can still return other functionality, such as MVC web pages and APIs. Here we will add an API to the server project which reuses the WeatherService and allows clients to retrieve this using a HTTP request.

Note Learning to build Web APIs using ASP.NET Core is material enough to fill another book (and there are books aplenty!).

Open the Program class from the server project and near the bottom add Listing 14-3. The app.MapGet method adds an API endpoint, and when the server receives a GET method for the /forecasts URL (first argument), it will execute the lambda function passed as the second argument. This lambda function receives the server's IWeatherService through dependency injection, and we simply return the result of the GetForecasts method from the WeatherService. It is that simple! Both the Weather component and the Web API running on the server use the same service and implementation.

Listing 14-3. Adding an API endpoint

```
app.MapRazorComponents<App>()
    .AddInteractiveServerRenderMode()
    .AddInteractiveWebAssemblyRenderMode()
    .AddAdditionalAssemblies(
      typeof(BlazorApp.Communication.Client._Imports).Assembly);
```

```
// Add the API endpoint
app.MapGet("/forecasts",
  async (IWeatherService weatherService) =>
  {
    WeatherForecast[] forecasts =
      await weatherService.GetForecasts();
    return forecasts;
  });
app.Run();
```

You can test this by running the project, and when the browser opens, navigate to the /forecasts URL, and you should see some JSON serialized forecasts.

The Client Project

A Blazor WebApp that uses auto rendering will have two projects, the server and the client project. The server project hosts pages which render on the server, and the client project contains the Blazor components that can run on both server and browser. The App component always runs on the server, and that is why you will find it in the server project, but the other components can be found in the client project, together with any other types used on both server and client. For example, in the client's Services folder, you will find the IWeatherService interface and WeatherForecast class, while the server implementation sits in the Services folder in the Server project since this class needs to talk to a database. The Client project is referenced by the server project as a class library, and this means any public type in the Client project can also be used on the Server.

The WeatherForecast Class

The WeatherForecast class from Listing 14-4 is straightforward, containing the Date of the forecast, the temperature in Celsius and Fahrenheit, and a Summary, but I want to draw your attention to the fact that this class lives in the Client project. This project is used both by the server and the client project.

Listing 14-4. The WeatherForecast class

```
namespace BlazorApp.Communication.Client.Entities;

public class WeatherForecast
{
  public required  DateOnly Date { get; set; }
  public required int TemperatureC { get; set; }
  public required string? Summary { get; set; }
  public int TemperatureF
    => 32 + (int)(TemperatureC / 0.5556);
}
```

If you ever created a web app with JavaScript, you should be familiar with the experience of building a data exchange class for the server project, for example, in C#, and building another class in JavaScript (or Typescript) for the client. You must make sure that both classes serialize to the same JSON format; otherwise, you will get runtime errors, or even worse, lose data! If the model grows, you must update both classes again. This is a HUGE maintenance problem in these kinds of projects, because you run the risk of updating only one side on a busy workday.

With Blazor, you don't suffer from this because both server and client use C#. And that is why there is a Client project. You put your classes here, and they are shared between the server and client, and then you use them by simply adding a reference to the Client project. Adding another piece of data means updating a shared class, which works easily! No longer must you update two pieces of code.

The Weather Component

Now look at the BlazorApp.Communication.Client project. Inside the Pages folder, you will find the Weather component. This component uses an IWeatherService, and when it is running on the server, it can simply use the server's WeatherService. But when this runs in the browser using WebAssembly, we need to pass it another implementation of IWeatherService.

The Weather component uses the IWeatherService service, provided by dependency injection. The OnInitializedAsync method uses this service to grab the weather forecasts as shown in Listing 14-5.

Listing 14-5. Weather's OnInitializedAsync method

```
@code {
  private WeatherForecast[]? forecasts;

  protected override async Task OnInitializedAsync()
  {
    forecasts = await WeatherService.GetForecasts();
  }
}
```

The OnInitializedAsync method will make the component render twice. The first time the forecasts field will not be initialized yet, and the second time after completion of the GetForecasts method (and the forecasts field has a value).

That is why you should test the data used during rendering, and if it has not yet been initialized to render some placeholder, for example, like Listing 14-6.

Listing 14-6. Test data used during rendering

```
@if (forecasts == null)
{
  <p><em>Loading...</em></p>
}
else
{
  <table class="table">
    ...
  </table>
}
```

Retrieving Data from the Server

When the Weather component runs in the browser, how does it retrieve data from the server? We need to make a GET request to the /forecasts URL. How can we do this? Blazor comes with a built-in class named HttpClient.

Understanding the HttpClient Class

All communication between the client and server passes through the `HttpClient` class. This is the same class other applications in .NET use, and its role is to make the HTTP request to the server and to expose the result from the server. It also allows you to exchange binary or other formatted data, but in Blazor we normally use JSON. With Blazor WASM, the `HttpClient` class uses the Browser's network stack to talk on the network.

Add a new class named `WeatherServiceProxy` to the Services folder in the Client project. Refer to Listing 14-7 for its implementation.

Listing 14-7. The WeatherServiceProxy class

```
using BlazorApp.Communication.Client.Entities;
using System.Net.Http.Json;

namespace BlazorApp.Communication.Client.Services;

public class WeatherServiceProxy : IWeatherService
{
  private readonly HttpClient _httpClient;

  public WeatherServiceProxy(HttpClient httpClient)
  => _httpClient = httpClient;

  public async ValueTask<WeatherForecast[]> GetForecasts()
  {
    WeatherForecast[]? forecasts =
      await _httpClient
        .GetFromJsonAsync<WeatherForecast[]>("/forecasts");
    return forecasts!;
  }
}
```

The `WeatherServiceProxy` uses dependency injection to get an instance of the `HttpClient` class and stores it in the `_httpClient` field. The `GetForecasts` method then uses the `_httpClient` to create the HTTP GET request for the /forecasts URL, and the `GetFromJsonAsync` method deserializes the result in a `WeatherForecast[]`.

CHAPTER 14   COMMUNICATION

To complete the implementation, you need to add the Microsoft.Extensions.Http NuGet package, and configure dependency injection as shown in Listing 14-8.

Listing 14-8. Configuring dependency injection

```
WebAssemblyHostBuilder builder = WebAssemblyHostBuilder.CreateDefault(args);
builder.Services.AddScoped(sp => new HttpClient {
  BaseAddress = new Uri(builder.HostEnvironment.BaseAddress)
});
builder.Services.AddScoped<IWeatherService,
                          WeatherServiceProxy>();
await builder.Build().RunAsync();
```

Two things happen here. When a service requests dependency injection to inject a `HttpClient` instance, we can configure this instance. This code sets the `HttpClient`'s `BaseAddress` to the server's base address. And we also tell Blazor WebAssembly, that when the Weather component needs a `IWeatherService` to inject a `WeatherServiceProxy` instance.

Note You should never instantiate an instance of the `HttpClient` class yourself. Blazor sets up the `HttpClient` class in a special way, and if you create an instance yourself, it simply will not work as expected! Another reason not to create an instance yourself is that this is a dependency of the component, and we learned in the chapter on dependency injection that classes and components should never create dependencies themselves!

Run. First time you visit the Weather link, the server will render the forecasts using `WeatherService`, but as soon as all WebAssembly dependencies have been downloaded in the browser, it will use the `WeatherServiceProxy`.

CHAPTER 14 COMMUNICATION

Emulating a Slow Network in Chrome or Edge

When you run a project on your laptop, the network is fast, and you might want to see what the loading UI looks like on slow networks. Most browsers allow you to emulate a slow network, and here we will look at Edge (and Chrome).

Start your Blazor project so the browser opens the Home page. Now open the debugger tools from the browser (on Windows with Edge or Chrome, you do this by pressing F12), and select the Network tab as in Figure 14-1. On the right side, you should see a drop-down list that allows you to select which kind of network to emulate. Select Slow 3G.

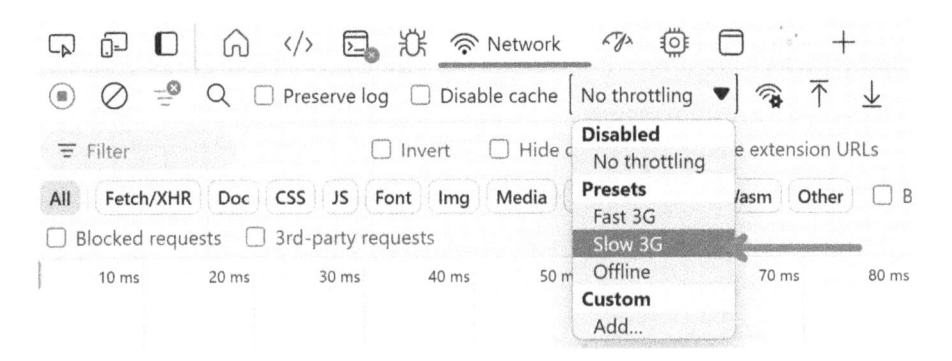

Figure 14-1. Using the Chrome browser debugger to emulate a slow network

Next, select the Weather tab on your Blazor site (should you already be on this tab, refresh your browser). Because you now are using a slow network, the Loading... feedback will appear, as shown in Figure 14-2.

Figure 14-2. The Loading... feedback with a slow network

After testing your Blazor website with a slow network, don't forget to select No throttling from the drop-down from Figure 14-1 to restore your network to its normal speed.

469

CHAPTER 14   COMMUNICATION

The HttpClientJsonExtensions Methods

To make it a lot easier to talk to JSON microservices, .NET provides you with a bunch of handy extension methods that take care of converting between .NET objects and JSON, which you can find in the `HttpClientJsonExtensions` class. This class lives in the `System.Net.Http.Json` namespace. I advise you to use these methods, so you don't have to worry about serializing and deserializing JSON.

GetFromJsonAsync

The `GetFromJsonAsync` extension method makes an asynchronous GET request to the specified URI. Its signature is in Listing 14-9. There are a couple of overloads available too.

Listing 14-9. The GetFromJsonAsync extension method signature

```
public static Task<TValue?> GetFromJsonAsync<TValue>(
  this HttpClient client,
  string? requestUri,
  JsonSerializerOptions? options,
  CancellationToken cancellationToken = default);
```

Because it is an extension method, you call it as a normal instance method on the `HttpClient` class, as shown in Listing 14-10.

This is also true for the other extension methods.

Listing 14-10. Using the GetJsonAsync extension method

```
forecasts = await Http.GetFromJsonAsync<WeatherForecast[]>
  ("WeatherForecast");
```

`GetFromJsonAsync<T>` will expect the response to contain JSON as specified by the generic argument. For example, in Listing 14-10, it expects an array of `WeatherForecast` instances. You normally invoke the `GetFromJsonAsync` method by prefixing it with the `await` keyword. Don't forget that you can only use the `await` keyword in methods and lambda functions that are `async`.

As you can see in Listing 14-9, there are additional arguments which we discuss later in this section.

470

CHAPTER 14   COMMUNICATION

You can always inspect the request and response using your browser's debugger. Run your Blazor project and open the browser's debugger on the Network tab. Now select the Weather tab in your Blazor website to make it load the data and look at the browser's Network tab as in Figure 14-3.

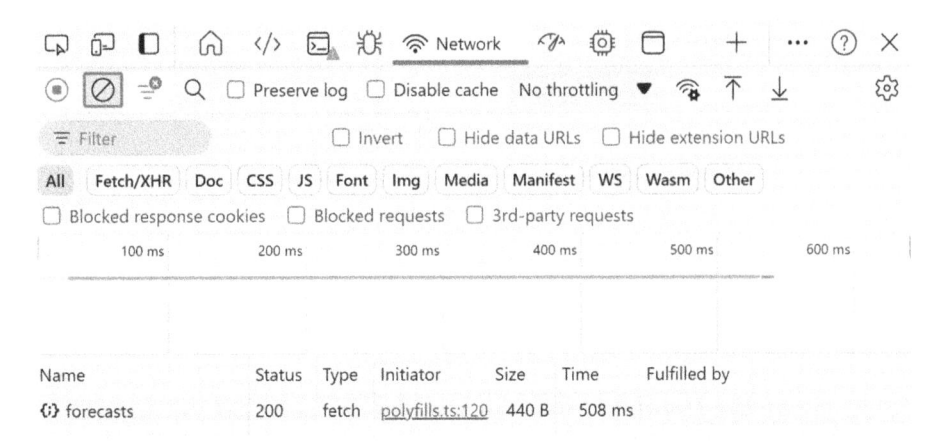

Figure 14-3. Inspecting the network using the browser's debugger

You can always clear the Network tab from previous requests before making the request using the clear button, which in Edge looks like a circle with a slash through it (the forbidden sign).

See the forecasts entry in Figure 14-3? Now you can click that entry to look at the request and response. Let's start with the request preview shown in Figure 14-4. Using the Preview tab, you can see the server's response.

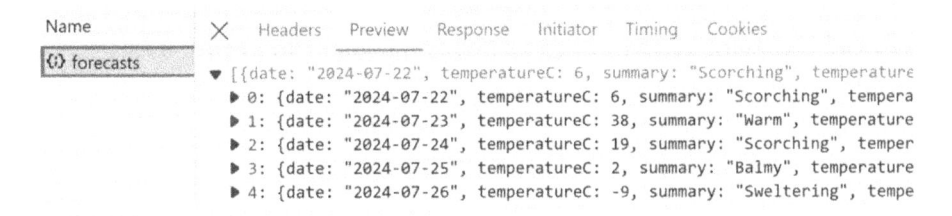

Figure 14-4. Using the Preview tab to look at the response

If you want to look at the request and response headers, you can click the Headers tab, as shown in Figure 14-5.

471

CHAPTER 14   COMMUNICATION

Name							
{} forecasts	×	Headers	Preview	Response	Initiator	Timing	Cookies

▼ General

Request URL: https://localhost:7287/forecasts
Request Method: GET
Status Code: ● 200 OK
Remote Address: [::1]:7287
Referrer Policy: strict-origin-when-cross-origin

▶ Response Headers (3)

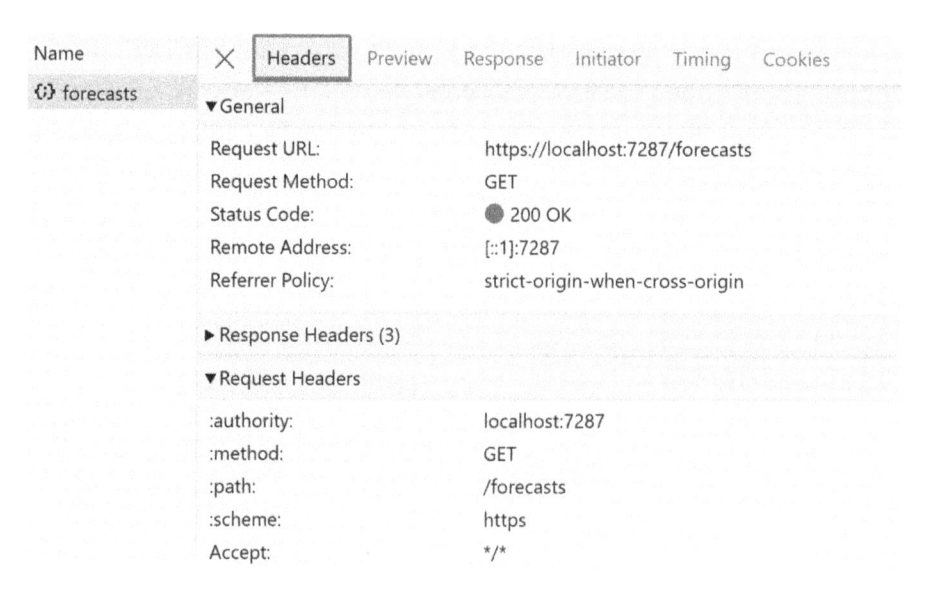

▼ Request Headers

:authority: localhost:7287
:method: GET
:path: /forecasts
:scheme: https
Accept: */*

Figure 14-5. *Using the Headers tab to look at the request and the request/response headers*

Here you can see the request's URL and GET method (the request method). It also shows the HTTP status code 200 OK. Scroll down to look at the headers. One of the response headers is Content-Type with a value of application/json, which was set by the server telling the client to expect JSON.

PostAsJsonAsync and PutAsJsonAsync

The `PostAsJsonAsync` extension method makes a POST request with the content argument serialized in the request body as JSON to the specified URI. Its signature is in Listing 14-11.

Listing 14-11. *The PostAsJsonAsync method's signature*

```
public static Task<HttpResponseMessage> PostAsJsonAsync<TValue>(
  this HttpClient client,
  string? requestUri,
  TValue value,
  JsonSerializerOptions? options = null,
  CancellationToken cancellationToken = default);
```

The `PutAsJsonAsync` extension method makes a PUT request with the content argument serialized as JSON in the request body to the specified URI. Its signature is in Listing 14-12. Its usage is very similar to `PostJsonAsync`; the only difference is that it uses the PUT verb.

Listing 14-12. The PutAsJsonAsync method's signature

```
public static Task<HttpResponseMessage> PutAsJsonAsync<TValue>(
  this HttpClient client,
  string? requestUri,
  TValue value,
  JsonSerializerOptions? options = null,
  CancellationToken cancellationToken = default);
```

Customizing Serialization with JsonSerializerOptions

Each of these methods takes an optional `JsonSerializerOptions` argument which allows you to control how JSON serialization works. For example, the default options will serialize the property names with the casing of the property name. However, there are services that require camel-casing for properties. Let us see how we can control this with Listing 14-13. To change the casing, you can set the `PropertyNamingPolicy` property. Here we set it to `JsonNamingPolicy.CamelCase`. This example also shows how you can control the serialization of enumerations. Normally enumerations get serialized with their int value. For example, `Spiciness.Spicy` will get serialized as 1. But if you like, you can also use the name of the enumeration value, so `Spiciness.Spicy` will get serialized as "Spicy". Do this by using the `JsonStringEnumConverter` as in Listing 14-13. Don't forget you will have to pass the `JsonSerializerOptions` as an extra argument using `GetFromJsonAsync` and similar methods.

Listing 14-13. Controlling casing with JsonSerializerOptions

```
protected readonly JsonSerializerOptions options =
  new JsonSerializerOptions
  {
    PropertyNamingPolicy = JsonNamingPolicy.CamelCase,
```

```
    Converters =
    {
        new JsonStringEnumConverter()
    }
};
```

Using IHttpClientFactory

In the `WeatherServiceProxy` class from Listing 14-7, we use the `HttpClient` class, and dependency injection provides the instance. But what if we need different `HttpClient` instances, for example, to talk to another service that uses a different base address?! Microsoft provides the IHttpClientFactory service, which creates for you the proper `HttpClient`, and you can configure it to provide different `HttpClient` instances depending on API requirements, such as headers.

Why Use IHttpClientFactory?

Your service requires a `HttpClient`, so you could create an instance of `HttpClient` in code, as shown in Listing 14-14.

Listing 14-14. Using HttpClient directly

```
public async ValueTask<WeatherForecast[]> GetForecasts()
{
  HttpClient httpClient = new();
  WeatherForecast[]? forcasts =
    await httpClient
      .GetFromJsonAsync<WeatherForecast[]>("/forecasts");
  return forcasts ?? [];
}
```

Simple, right? But as your application starts to grow, and more and more requests are made, you will start to get some weird issues. And that is because this code is not optimal.

Every time you create a new instance of `HttpClient`, it occupies a socket. And you should release said socket by disposing of `HttpClient`. So, you change your implementation by adding a `using` as in Listing 14-15.

Listing 14-15. Disposing HttpClient

```
public async ValueTask<WeatherForecast[]> GetForecasts()
{
  using HttpClient httpClient = new();
  WeatherForecast[]? forcasts =
    await httpClient
      .GetFromJsonAsync<WeatherForecast[]>("/forecasts");
  return forcasts ?? [];
}
```

Disposing the `HttpClient` instance does not immediately free the socket due to the `TIME_WAIT` state (more in https://github.com/dotnet/runtime/issues/28842). With high loads, this can lead to socket exhaustion. And there is more. Every time you make the call, you create a new `HttpClient` instance, while you could also reuse the same instance. But reusing the same instance also has issues, because the `HttpClient` instance could become corrupt, and then it is your responsibility to create a new instance. More in https://learn.microsoft.com/dotnet/architecture/microservices/implement-resilient-applications/use-httpclientfactory-to-implement-resilient-http-requests.

And each different service will have to configure the `HttpClient` instance, things like `BaseAddress`, and headers. This complicates your code and make it harder to maintain.

Use `IHttpClientFactory`. It solves the socket exhaustion and instantiation problem for you. And it is quite easy to use. With `IHttpClientFactory`, you configure the `HttpClient` instance in a central location (`Program` class), and you can configure it differently for different services.

Let us configure it for our `WeatherServiceProxy`. First add the Microsoft.Extensions.Http package to the Client project (the WebAssembly project). Open Program.cs from the Client project and change it to reflect Listing 14-16.

Listing 14-16. Configuring a typed HttpClient with IHttpClientFactory

```
using BlazorApp.Communication.Client.Services;
using Microsoft.AspNetCore.Components.WebAssembly.Hosting;

WebAssemblyHostBuilder builder = WebAssemblyHostBuilder.
CreateDefault(args);

//builder.Services.AddScoped(sp => new HttpClient {
//    BaseAddress =
//        new Uri(builder.HostEnvironment.BaseAddress)
//});

builder.Services.AddHttpClient<WeatherServiceProxy>(
  httpClient =>
  {
    httpClient.BaseAddress =
        new Uri(builder.HostEnvironment.BaseAddress);
  }
);

builder.Services
       .AddScoped<IWeatherService, WeatherServiceProxy>();

await builder.Build().RunAsync();
```

What is the difference?

The AddHttpClient registers the IHttpClientFactory with dependency injection. Simply calling this method without arguments allows you to grab the IHttpClientFactory in your service and use it to create an instance of HttpClient. Listing 14-17 shows how you would do this.

Listing 14-17. Basic IHttpClientFactory usage

```
public class HttpClientFactoryBasicUsage : IWeatherService
{
  private readonly IHttpClientFactory _httpClientFactory;

  public HttpClientFactoryBasicUsage(IHttpClientFactory httpClientFactory)
  {
```

```
    _httpClientFactory = httpClientFactory;
  }
  public async ValueTask<WeatherForecast[]> GetForecasts()
  {
    HttpClient httpClient = _httpClientFactory.CreateClient();
    httpClient.BaseAddress = ...
    WeatherForecast[]? forcasts =
      await httpClient.GetFromJsonAsync<WeatherForecast[]>("/forecasts");
    return forcasts ?? [];
  }
}
```

You can also tell the IHttpClientFactory to configure a HttpClient for you. With this technique, you can configure different HttpClient instances. During registration you configure the HttpClient, passing a unique name, as in Listing 14-18.

Listing 14-18. Configuring a named HttpClient

```
builder.Services.AddHttpClient("NamedClient", httpClient =>
{
  httpClient.BaseAddress =
    new Uri(builder.HostEnvironment.BaseAddress);
});
```

Then you pass the name of the configured client during creation as in Listing 14-19.

Listing 14-19. Creating a named HttpClient

```
public class HttpClientFactoryNamedClient : IWeatherService
{
  private readonly IHttpClientFactory _httpClientFactory;

  public HttpClientFactoryNamedClient(
    IHttpClientFactory httpClientFactory)
  {
    _httpClientFactory = httpClientFactory;
  }
```

```
public async ValueTask<WeatherForecast[]> GetForecasts()
{
  HttpClient httpClient =
    _httpClientFactory.CreateClient("NamedClient");
  WeatherForecast[]? forcasts =
    await httpClient
      .GetFromJsonAsync<WeatherForecast[]>("/forecasts");
  return forcasts ?? [];
}
}
```

Each time you invoke `CreateClient("NamedClient")`, a new instance of `HttpClient` is created, and the configuration logic from Listing 14-18 is called.

Using a named client requires a string, but you can also use the type of the service as the key. Listing 14-16 and Listing 14-7 use this typed client technique. In Listing 14-16 we configure the service (e.g., setting the `BaseAddress` property). Then in Listing 14-7 dependency injection will create an instance of the `HttpClient` class, configure its `BaseAddress`, and then pass it to the service.

Enhancing PizzaPlace

Currently the PizzaPlace application is a Blazor Server application. First, we will enable Blazor WebAssembly for this project, and then we will make PizzaPlace run inside the browser.

Enabling Blazor WebAssembly

This chapter comes with sources, and you can find there the PizzaPlace application in the chapter's Starter folder (this is a copy of the JavaScript Interop chapter). We will use this one in this exercise. Open the solution.

Update Server Project

Add the Microsoft.AspNetCore.Components.WebAssembly.Server package to the server project. We need this for the following code change. Open Program.cs from the server project, and add two changes as shown in Listing 14-20.

Listing 14-20. Enabling Blazor WebAssembly

```
// Add services to the container.
builder.Services.AddRazorComponents()
    .AddInteractiveServerComponents()
    .AddInteractiveWebAssemblyComponents();

app.MapRazorComponents<App>()
  .AddInteractiveServerRenderMode()
  .AddInteractiveWebAssemblyRenderMode()
  .AddAdditionalAssemblies(typeof(Pizza).Assembly);
```

The AddInteractiveWebAssemblyComponents method adds the dependencies for Blazor WebAssembly, and the AddInteractiveWebAssemblyRenderMode method enables the WebAssembly render mode. Finally, the AddAdditionalAssemblies looks for additional routes in the client project. If this is not clear, you might need to read the chapters on Routing and Render Modes first.

Update the Shared Project

Add the Microsoft.AspNetCore.Components.WebAssembly NuGet package to the shared project and change the Sdk as in Listing 14-21.

Listing 14-21. The shared project

```
<Project Sdk="Microsoft.NET.Sdk.BlazorWebAssembly">
```

Add a new Program class from Listing 14-22

Listing 14-22. The shared project's program class

```
using Microsoft.AspNetCore.Components.WebAssembly.Hosting;

namespace BlazorApp.PizzaPlace.Shared;
internal class Program
{
  private static async Task Main(string[] args)
  {
```

CHAPTER 14 COMMUNICATION

```
    WebAssemblyHostBuilder builder =
      WebAssemblyHostBuilder.CreateDefault(args);

    await builder.Build().RunAsync();
  }
}
```

This `Program` class allows us to set up dependency injection for the Shared project, which will be running inside your browser using WASM.

Copy the _Imports.razor into this project. Without the _Imports.razor file, the project will not be correctly built!

Now add a new Components folder to the Shared project, and move the following components from the server to the shared project.

- Layout/MainLayout
- Layout/NavMenu
- Basket
- Counter
- CustomerEntry
- Home
- ItemList
- Menu
- PizzaInfo
- PizzaItem
- Routes
- Weather

Your Shared project should now build! You can run it if you like, but you are still using Blazor Server.

To run everything with Blazor WebAssembly, update the `rendermode` of the `Routing` and `HeadOutlet` in the `Home` component to Listing 14-23.

Listing 14-23. Updating the App component

```
@using BlazorApp.PizzaPlace.Shared.Components

<!DOCTYPE html>
<html lang="en">

<head>
  ...
  <HeadOutlet @rendermode="InteractiveWebAssembly" />
</head>

<body>
  <Routes @rendermode="InteractiveWebAssembly" />
  <script src="_framework/blazor.web.js"></script>
  ...
</body>

</html>
```

We also need to support some dependencies, so update Program.cs from the Shared project as in Listing 14-24.

Listing 14-24. Configure dependency injection

```
WebAssemblyHostBuilder builder =
  WebAssemblyHostBuilder.CreateDefault(args);

builder.Services
 .AddTransient<IMenuService, HardCodedMenuService>()
 .AddTransient<IOrderService, ConsoleOrderService>();

builder.Services.AddScoped<State>();

await builder.Build().RunAsync();
```

CHAPTER 14　COMMUNICATION

Talking to the Server

Time to add some server services so our WASM client can invoke them. First the service to retrieve the menu. We already have the `HardCodedMenuService`, but we will again pretend that this service only works on the server. To make this more explicit, move the Services folder from the Shared project to the server project.

Retrieving the Menu

Now add a GET method to Program on the server to retrieve the menu from the /pizzas endpoint, as shown in Listing 14-25.

Listing 14-25. Add the menu REST endpoint

```
app.MapRazorComponents<App>()
   .AddInteractiveServerRenderMode()
   .AddInteractiveWebAssemblyRenderMode()
   .AddAdditionalAssemblies(typeof(Pizza).Assembly);

app.MapGet("/pizzas", async Task<Pizza[]> (
   IMenuService menuService) =>
{
   return await menuService.GetMenu();
});
app.Run();
```

Time to implement the client for this. Start by adding the Microsoft.Extensions.Http package to the Shared project. Also add a new Services folder to the Shared project (you just moved it to the server project) and add the new `MenuServiceProxy` class from Listing 14-26. You will complete this class later.

Listing 14-26. The MenuServiceProxy class

```
namespace BlazorApp.PizzaPlace.Shared.Services;

public class MenuServiceProxy : IMenuService
{
   public ValueTask<Pizza[]> GetMenu()
      => throw new NotImplementedException();
}
```

CHAPTER 14 COMMUNICATION

To get our application to compile (because we moved the services to the server project), add another class `OrderMenuProxy` from Listing 14-27.

Listing 14-27. The OrderMenuProxy class

```
namespace BlazorApp.PizzaPlace.Shared.Services;

public class OrderMenuProxy : IOrderService
{
  public async ValueTask PlaceOrder(
    Customer customer, ShoppingBasket basket)
  => throw new NotImplementedException();
}
```

Back to Program. Add the code from Listing 14-28 to configure the `HttpClient` for the `MenuServiceProxy`.

Listing 14-28. Configuring HttpClient for MenuServiceProxy

```
using BlazorApp.PizzaPlace.Shared.Services;
using Microsoft.AspNetCore.Components.WebAssembly.Hosting;

namespace BlazorApp.PizzaPlace.Shared;

internal class Program
{
  private static async Task Main(string[] args)
  {
    WebAssemblyHostBuilder builder =
      WebAssemblyHostBuilder.CreateDefault(args);

    builder.Services.AddScoped<State>();

    // ADD HttpClient configuration
    builder.Services.AddHttpClient(nameof(MenuServiceProxy),
    httpClient =>
    {
      httpClient.BaseAddress =
        new Uri(builder.HostEnvironment.BaseAddress);
    });
```

483

CHAPTER 14 COMMUNICATION

```
    builder.Services.AddHttpClient<OrderMenuProxy>(
    httpClient =>
    {
      httpClient.BaseAddress =
        new Uri(builder.HostEnvironment.BaseAddress);
    });

    builder.Services
      .AddScoped<IMenuService, MenuServiceProxy>()
      .AddScoped<IOrderService, OrderMenuProxy>();

    await builder.Build().RunAsync();
  }
}
```

Now we can implement the MenuServiceProxy class. We will ask dependency injection for an IHttpClientFactory instance using the constructor and use to the make a GET request to the server. Look at Listing 14-29 for the implementation.

Listing 14-29. Implement MenuServiceProxy

```
using System.Net.Http.Json;

namespace BlazorApp.PizzaPlace.Shared.Services;

public class MenuServiceProxy : IMenuService
{
  private readonly IHttpClientFactory _httpClientFactory;

  public MenuServiceProxy(IHttpClientFactory httpClientFactory)
  {
    _httpClientFactory = httpClientFactory;
  }

  public async ValueTask<Pizza[]> GetMenu()
  {
    using HttpClient _httpClient =
      _httpClientFactory
        .CreateClient(nameof(MenuServiceProxy));
```

```
    return await _httpClient.GetFromJsonAsync<Pizza[]>("pizzas")
            ?? [];
  }
}
```

Placing the Order

Placing the order is slightly harder; this is because the PlaceOrder method takes two arguments.

```
ValueTask PlaceOrder(Customer customer, ShoppingBasket basket);
```

If we want to make this a REST Api, we need a single request message, so add the Order class from Listing 14-30 to the client project. This class is the contract for the JSON message, also known as a Data Transfer Object (DTO).

Listing 14-30. Add the Order DTO class

```
namespace BlazorApp.PizzaPlace.Shared;

public class Order
{
  public required Customer Customer { get; set; }
  public required ShoppingBasket Basket { get; set; }
}
```

We can now add a REST endpoint to the server, just like the MenuService. Listing 14-31 shows an implementation. Note that we receive an Order DTO instance, which contains the Customer and ShoppingBasket.

Listing 14-31. Implement the REST service

```
app.MapGet("/pizzas", async Task<Pizza[]> (
  IMenuService menuService) =>
{
  return await menuService.GetMenu();
});
```

Chapter 14 Communication

```csharp
app.MapPost("/order", async ValueTask (
  IOrderService orderService, [FromBody] Order order) =>
{
  await orderService.PlaceOrder(order.Customer, order.Basket);
});

app.Run();
```

Now for the OrderMenuProxy service. This will take a Customer and ShoppingBasket, wrap it into an Order DTO instance, and make the REST call as implemented in Listing 14-32.

Listing 14-32. The OrderMenuProxy class

```csharp
using System.Net.Http.Json;

namespace BlazorApp.PizzaPlace.Shared.Services;

public class OrderMenuProxy : IOrderService
{
  private readonly IHttpClientFactory _httpClientFactory;

  public OrderMenuProxy(IHttpClientFactory httpClientFactory)
  {
    _httpClientFactory = httpClientFactory;
  }

  public async ValueTask PlaceOrder(Customer customer,
                                    ShoppingBasket basket)
  {
    Order order = new()
    {
      Customer = customer,
      Basket = basket
    };
    HttpClient httpClient =
      _httpClientFactory.CreateClient(nameof(OrderMenuProxy));
    await httpClient.PostAsJsonAsync("order", order);
  }
}
```

Build and run. Everything should work, except now the application is running in the browser and uses REST to communicate with the server.

> **Note** In the previous edition, I would have made you store the menu and orders in a real database, but I decided not to do this in this edition because that is a different topic.

There is one more thing. When the application starts, it shows the menu and such, but after a short while it refreshes, causing this annoying flicker. This is caused by prerendering, so we opt to disable this.

Disable Prerendering

With Blazor WebAssembly, the App component uses the `InteractiveWebAssembly` render mode, which enables prerendering by default. To disable prerendering, we need to set a different render mode instance, so add the code section from Listing 14-33 to the App component (in the server project).

Listing 14-33. Change RenderMode

```
@code{
  IComponentRenderMode noPreRenderInteractiveWebAssembly
    = new InteractiveWebAssemblyRenderMode(prerender: false);
}
```

Update the `HeadOutlet` and `Routes`'s rendermode of the `App` component as in Listing 14-34.

Listing 14-34. Update the global render mode

```
  <HeadOutlet @rendermode="noPreRenderInteractiveWebAssembly" />
</head>

<body>
  <Routes @rendermode="noPreRenderInteractiveWebAssembly" />
```

CHAPTER 14   COMMUNICATION

This disables the prerendering of the PizzaPlace application, but does create a new one. On a slow network, it takes some time for the application to download, so maybe you want to show a loading screen?

Showing a Loading Screen

You will probably first see an empty white screen, especially on a slow network. This might confuse some customers so let's add some UI to tell the customer to wait a bit. It is important we add this HTML to a server rendered component, and in our case that is the App component.

Add the following HTML from Listing 14-35 to the App component.

Listing 14-35. The Loading UI

```
<body>

  <!-- Loading screen -->
  <div id="loading-screen">
    <div class="spinner"></div>
    <p>Loading...</p>
  </div>

  <Routes @rendermode="noPreRenderInteractiveWebAssembly" />
```

This also requires some CSS, so add a new App.razor.css file with content from Listing 14-36.

Listing 14-36. The CSS for the Loading UI

```
/* App.razor.css */

#loading-screen {
  position: fixed;
  top: 0;
  left: 0;
  width: 100%;
  height: 100%;
  display: flex;
  justify-content: center;
```

```
  align-items: center;
  background-color: white;
  z-index: 9999; /* Make sure it's above everything else */
}

.spinner {
  border: 16px solid #f3f3f3;
  border-top: 16px solid #3498db;
  border-radius: 50%;
  width: 120px;
  height: 120px;
  animation: spin 2s linear infinite;
}

@keyframes spin {
  0% {
    transform: rotate(0deg);
  }

  100% {
    transform: rotate(360deg);
  }
}
```

When our WebAssembly components start to run, we need to hide this Loading UI. Add the following script from Listing 14-37 to the App component.

Listing 14-37. Hide the Loading UI

```
<script>
  window.hideLoadingScreen = function () {
    var loadingScreen =
      document.getElementById('loading-screen');
    if (loadingScreen) {
      loadingScreen.style.display = 'none';
    }
  };
</script>
```

CHAPTER 14   COMMUNICATION

Where should we invoke this function? From a component which will run in WebAssembly, I have chosen the Routes component. Add a code section to the Routes component from Listing 14-38.

Listing 14-38. The Routes component hides the Loading UI.

```
@code {
  [Inject]
  public required IJSRuntime JSRuntime { get; set; }

  protected override async Task OnInitializedAsync()
  {
    await JSRuntime.InvokeVoidAsync("hideLoadingScreen");
  }
}
```

Run. You will first see a loading UI as in Figure 14-6, and when the application has been downloaded in the browser, the loading UI will hide and your application becomes available.

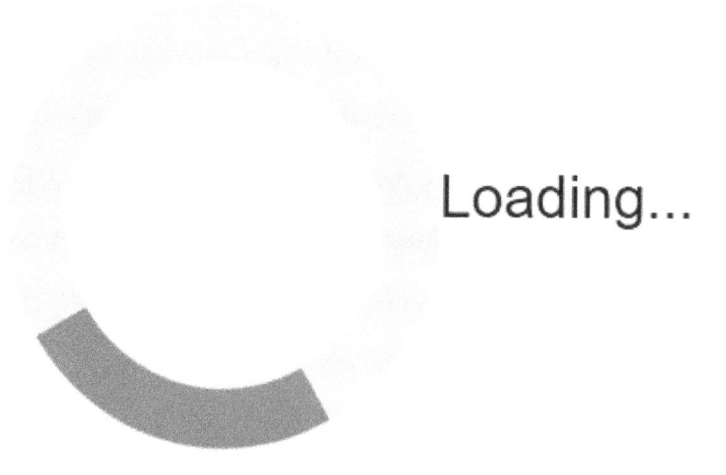

Figure 14-6. *The Loading UI*

Summary

In this chapter, you learned that in Blazor you talk to the server using the `HttpClient` class, calling the `GetFromJsonAsync` and `PostAsJsonAsync` extension methods. You also learned that you should encapsulate calling the server using a client-side service class so you can easily change the implementation by switching the service type using dependency injection.

Where we were at it, we also converted a Blazor Server application into a Blazor WebAssembly application and added a loading screen.

CHAPTER 15

Building Real-Time Applications with Blazor and SignalR

What if your application needs some real-time communication between client and server, and even between clients? In this case, you can use SignalR. In this chapter, we will explore how we can use SignalR in Blazor to build real-time applications.

What Is SignalR?

SignalR is a library that allows you to build real-time applications and allows the server and clients to send messages to each other. You can use SignalR in desktop applications, mobile applications, and of course websites. There is an implementation for .NET, and one for JavaScript. A typical application that should use SignalR is a chat application, where clients communicate with each other over a server. When the server receives a chat message from the client, it can send this message back to the other clients. SignalR is especially useful for applications that need high-frequency updates, such as multi-player games, social networks, auctions, etc.

How Does SignalR Work?

SignalR uses WebSockets, which, unlike HTTP, uses a full-duplex connection between client and server, meaning that clients and server keep the TCP connection open and thus can send messages to each other without the classic model where the client has to start the conversation. To implement this, WebSockets sets up a TCP connection between client and server over the existing HTTP connection, which is way more efficient to send small messages. All modern browsers support WebSockets, as shown on `https://caniuse.com/?search=websockets` and Figure 15-1.

SignalR takes care of the connection and allows you to send messages to all clients simultaneously, or to specific groups of clients, or even to a single specific client.

Building a WhiteBoard Application

Let us build a whiteboard application, in which you will have a whiteboard (such as you can find in many offices) on which you can draw. After this we will add SignalR so all users can interact with the white board and can see what others are drawing in real time.

Creating the WhiteBoard Solution

Start by creating a new Blazor WebApp solution using WebAssembly interactivity, and name it BlazorApp.SignalR. You can use the following PowerShell script if you like.

```
$ProjectName = "BlazorApp.SignalR"
mkdir $ProjectName
cd $ProjectName
dotnet new sln -n $ProjectName
dotnet new nugetconfig
dotnet new globaljson
mkdir src
dotnet new blazor -n $ProjectName -o src --all-interactive --interactivity WebAssembly
dotnet sln add ".\src\$ProjectName\"
dotnet sln add ".\src\$ProjectName.Client\"
```

Remove all Blazor Components from the Pages and Shared folder. We don't need these. Also remove all contents of the App component. Finally remove the `@using WhiteBoard.Client` statement from _Imports.razor.

Start by adding a new C# `struct` called `LineSegment` from Listing 15-1 to the Client project. We will use this `struct` in both the server and the client to represent the drawing, segment by segment.

CHAPTER 15 BUILDING REAL-TIME APPLICATIONS WITH BLAZOR AND SIGNALR

Listing 15-1. The LineSegment class

```cs
using System.Drawing;

namespace BlazorApp.SignalR.Client;

public struct LineSegment
{
    public required PointF Start { get; set; }

    public required PointF End { get; set; }
}
```

Figure 15-1. Supporting browsers

Add a new component to the Client project and name it `Board`. Complete the markup as in Listing 15-2. Our board component will use a HTML `<canvas>` element to show the drawing and handle the user interaction with the board.

Listing 15-2. The Board component

```
<canvas width="600" height="600"
        @onmousedown="MouseDown"
        @onmouseup="MouseUp"
        @onmousemove="MouseMove"
```

CHAPTER 15 BUILDING REAL-TIME APPLICATIONS WITH BLAZOR AND SIGNALR

```
        @ref="board">
</canvas>

@code {
  [Parameter]
  public required List<LineSegment> LineSegments { get; set; }

  [Parameter]
  public required Func<LineSegment, Task> AddSegment { get; set; }

  public ElementReference board = default!;

  private void MouseDown(MouseEventArgs e)
  {
  }

  private void MouseUp(MouseEventArgs e)
  {
  }

  private void MouseMove(MouseEventArgs e)
  {
  }
}
```

For the moment this class does not do a lot of useful stuff, except making the project compile, but we will get to this next.

Add another component, name it `WhiteBoard`, and implement it as per Listing 15-3. The `WhiteBoard` component will keep track of the line segments, so it passes the segments as an argument and passes the `AddLineSegment` callback to the board.

Listing 15-3. The WhiteBoard component

```
<h1>White Board</h1>

<Board LineSegments="@LineSegments"
       AddSegment="AddLineSegment" />

@code {
  private List<LineSegment> LineSegments = [];
```

CHAPTER 15　BUILDING REAL-TIME APPLICATIONS WITH BLAZOR AND SIGNALR

```
  private Task AddLineSegment(LineSegment segment)
  {
    List<LineSegment> segments = [segment];
    this.LineSegments.AddRange(segments);
    return Task.CompletedTask;
  }
}
```

Now update the App component's markup (from the server project) to Listing 15-4. The App component explicitly renders the WhiteBoard component as Blazor WebAssembly.

Listing 15-4. The App component

```
<!DOCTYPE html>
<html lang="en">

<head>
  <meta charset="utf-8" />
  <meta name="viewport" content="width=device-width, initial-scale=1.0" />
  <base href="/" />
  <link rel="stylesheet" href="bootstrap/bootstrap.min.css" />
  <link rel="stylesheet" href="app.css" />
  <link rel="stylesheet" href="BlazorApp.SignalR.styles.css" />
  <link rel="icon" type="image/png" href="favicon.png" />
  <HeadOutlet @rendermode="InteractiveWebAssembly" />
</head>

<body>
  <WhiteBoard @rendermode="InteractiveWebAssembly" />
  <script src="_framework/blazor.web.js"></script>
</body>

</html>
```

CHAPTER 15   BUILDING REAL-TIME APPLICATIONS WITH BLAZOR AND SIGNALR

Implementing the Mouse Handling Logic

Now we can implement the Board component's mouse handling logic. When the user clicks and drags the mouse, we will add a new segment. Start by adding the MouseButton enumeration from Listing 15-5 next to the Board component. This abstracts the numbers used for mouse buttons by the mouse events (I hate using "mystery" numbers in code).

Listing 15-5. The MouseButton enumeration

```
namespace BlazorApp.SignalR.Client;

public enum MouseButton
{
  Left, Middle, Right
}
```

Now update the Board's mouse handling methods as in Listing 15-6. The trackMouse field is used to track whether the left mouse button is down. It is set to true in the MouseDown event handling method, and back to false in the MouseUp event handling method.

The MouseMove event handling method calls the AddSegment callback when the trackMouse field is true. But we need another thing. Mouse events can easily trigger tens of times per second, so we need to throttle these events. That is why the lastEvent field tracks the difference between the mouse moves and will only call the AddSegment callback with at least 200 milliseconds between them. Of course, we need to know the mouse position and for that this implementation uses the lastPos field. We initialize this to the current mouse position in the MouseDown method when the left mouse button is pressed. We then use this field to invoke the AddSegment callback with lastPos and currentPos. Finally, we reset the lastPos to the current mouse position because this will become the starting point for the next segment.

Listing 15-6. Implementing mouse tracking

```
private PointF lastPos = new PointF(0, 0);
private DateTime lastEvent;
private bool trackMouse = false;
private IJSObjectReference? canvas = default;

private void MouseDown(MouseEventArgs e)
```

498

```csharp
{
    if (e.Button == (int)MouseButton.Left)
    {
        this.trackMouse = true;
        this.lastPos = new ((float)e.OffsetX, (float)e.OffsetY);
    }
}

private void MouseUp(MouseEventArgs e)
 => this.trackMouse = false;

private void MouseMove(MouseEventArgs e)
{
    PointF currentPos = new((float)e.OffsetX, (float)e.OffsetY);
    DateTime currentEvent = DateTime.Now;
    TimeSpan time = currentEvent - this.lastEvent;
    if (this.trackMouse && time.TotalMilliseconds > 200)
    {
        AddSegment.Invoke(new LineSegment
          { Start = this.lastPos, End = currentPos });
        this.lastEvent = currentEvent;
        this.lastPos = currentPos;
    }
}
```

Painting the Segments on the Board

Running the application will not yield the proper result. We need to paint the segments. And since we are using a `<canvas>` element, we need some JavaScript to paint on it.

Add a new scripts folder below the wwwroot folder, and add a new JavaScript file called canvas.js as in Listing 15-7. This JavaScript module exports a single `drawLines` function, which draws each line segment on the canvas.

To draw on a canvas, we need a reference to it, so we pass the `ElementReference` as the first argument, and the segments as the second argument. Next, we ask the canvas element to give us a 2D context by calling the `getContext` method. Then we iterate over each segment, calling the `drawLine` method. This method then uses the 2D context to draw the line.

CHAPTER 15 BUILDING REAL-TIME APPLICATIONS WITH BLAZOR AND SIGNALR

Listing 15-7. JavaScript to draw on canvas

```
let drawLine = (context, x1, y1, x2, y2, strokeStyle) => {
  context.beginPath();
  context.moveTo(x1, y1);
  context.lineTo(x2, y2);
  context.strokeStyle = strokeStyle || "black";
  context.stroke();
  context.closePath();
}

let drawLines = (board, segments) => {
  let context = board.getContext('2d');
  for (let i = 0; i < segments.length; i += 1) {
    let segment = segments[i];
    drawLine(context, segment.start.x, segment.start.y,
      segment.end.x, segment.end.y);
  }
}

export { drawLines };
```

We now should import this module in our `Board` component. Use dependency injection to get a reference to the `IJSRuntime` instance as in Listing 15-8.

Listing 15-8. Use the inject attribute to inject the JSRuntime

```
@code {
  [Inject]
  public required IJSRuntime JSRuntime { get; set; }
```
...

Where should we call the JavaScript module? We can only do this after the Blazor runtime has updated the browser's DOM, so we should override the `OnAfterRenderAsync` method as described in the JavaScript interop chapter. Override the `OnAfterRenderAsync` method as in Listing 15-9. This code should be familiar from the chapter on JavaScript Interop, and it loads a JavaScript module into an `IJSObjectReference`.

500

CHAPTER 15 BUILDING REAL-TIME APPLICATIONS WITH BLAZOR AND SIGNALR

After loading the module, we invoke the drawLines JavaScript method, passing the board and serializable LineSegments.

Listing 15-9. Importing the JavaScript module

```
protected override async Task OnAfterRenderAsync(bool firstRender)
{
  if( this.canvas is null)
  {
    this.canvas = await JSRuntime.InvokeAsync<IJSObjectReference>
      ("import", "./scripts/canvas.js");
  }
  if (this.canvas is not null)
  {
    await this.canvas
    .InvokeVoidAsync("drawLines", this.board, LineSegments);
  }
}
```

Finally, let us set some style to make the board stand out. Create a Board.razor.css file and add the CSS from Listing 15-10 to it. Feel free to improvise!

Listing 15-10. The Board components style

```
canvas {
  background-color: lightgray;
  border: dashed red;
}
```

Build and run. Now you can make some abstract art like I did in Figure 15-2.

CHAPTER 15   BUILDING REAL-TIME APPLICATIONS WITH BLAZOR AND SIGNALR

Figure 15-2. *The WhiteBoard application in action*

Adding a SignalR Hub on the Server

Our WhiteBoard application currently supports a single user. Let us make this an application where everyone can draw on the same white board using SignalR.

With SignalR we need to create a Hub on the server, which will have methods we can call from the clients. On the client we will implement methods that we will invoke from the hub. A hub sits at the heart of SignalR and runs on the server. The clients will send messages to the central hub, which can then notify the other clients.

Implementing the BoardHub Class

In the server project, add a new Hubs folder, and add the BoardHub class from Listing 15-11. We need to derive this class from the Hub base class (or strongly typed Hub<T> class). Currently it has the allSegments list, containing the segments of the Board.

Listing 15-11. The BoardHub class

```
using BlazorApp.SignalR.Client;
using Microsoft.AspNetCore.SignalR;

namespace BlazorApp.SignalR.Hubs;

public class BoardHub : Hub
{
    private static readonly List<LineSegment> allSegments = [];
```

```
private readonly ILogger<BoardHub> _logger;

public BoardHub(ILogger<BoardHub> logger)
  => this._logger = logger;
}
```

Our BoardHub needs two methods, GetAllSegments and SendSegments. The GetAllSegments method from Listing 15-12 is used by a new client to retrieve the already present segments from other clients. So how does the server know who the clients are? The Hub base class has a Clients property of type IHubCallerClients. This interface has three properties: All, Caller, and Others. The All property gives you access to all the clients connected to the Hub, the Caller property returns the client calling the BoardHub, and the Others returns all clients except the caller. Since the GetAllSegments method needs to return its allSegments collection to the client, we use Clients.Caller and call the client's InitSegments method. This method also performs some server-side logging using the ILogger.

Listing 15-12. The BoardHub's GetAllSegments method

```
public async Task GetAllSegments()
{
  _logger.LogInformation(
    $"{nameof(GetAllSegments)} - {allSegments.Count}");
  await Clients.Caller.SendAsync("InitSegments", allSegments);
}
```

The SendSegments method from Listing 15-13 is used by a client to notify the other clients. Here the server adds the client's segments to its collection and notifies the other clients by calling their AddSegments method.

Listing 15-13. The SendSegments method

```
public async Task SendSegments(IEnumerable<LineSegment> segments)
{
  _logger.LogInformation(nameof(SendSegments));
  allSegments.AddRange(segments);
  await Clients.Others.SendAsync("AddSegments", segments);
}
```

Configuring the Server

Open Program.cs on the server project and configure dependency injection to Listing 15-14 for SignalR. To really make the SignalR messages as small as possible, we also add the response compression middleware dependencies.

Listing 15-14. Adding the required SignalR dependencies

```
builder.Services.AddRazorComponents()
    .AddInteractiveWebAssemblyComponents();

// Add the following
builder.Services.AddSignalR();
builder.Services.AddResponseCompression(opts =>
{
  opts.MimeTypes = ResponseCompressionDefaults.MimeTypes
   .Concat(new[] { "application/octet-stream" });
});

var app = builder.Build();
```

Configure the server's request pipeline as in Listing 15-15. The response compression middleware should come first, and we need to add our BoardHub to the server's endpoints. Our BoardHub can now receive messages from clients using the /board URL.

Listing 15-15. Adding SignalR middleware

```
if (app.Environment.IsDevelopment())
{
  app.UseWebAssemblyDebugging();
}
else
{
  app.UseExceptionHandler("/Error", createScopeForErrors: true);
  app.UseHsts();
}
app.UseResponseCompression(); // Add this
app.UseHttpsRedirection();
```

```
app.UseStaticFiles();
app.UseAntiforgery();
app.MapHub<BoardHub>("/board"); // Add this
app.MapRazorComponents<App>()
   .AddInteractiveWebAssemblyRenderMode()
   .AddAdditionalAssemblies(typeof(BlazorApp.SignalR.Client._Imports).
   Assembly);

app.Run();
```

Implementing the SignalR Client

Start by adding the Microsoft.AspNetCore.SignalR.Client package to the client project.

Our Board component does not need to know we are using SignalR, so we will add the SignalR logic to the WhiteBoard component which will communicate with BoardHub.

Making the SignalR Hub Connection

Start by adding the NavigationManager to the WhiteBoard component through dependency injection and a HubConnection field as in Listing 15-16.

Listing 15-16. Adding some dependencies

```
[Inject]
public required NavigationManager navigationManager { get; set; }

private HubConnection? hubConnection;
```

We need to create the HubConnection in the OnInitializedAsync method as in Listing 15-17. First, we use the HubConnectionBuilder to create the HubConnection, passing the URL of our server's SignalR endpoint. To retrieve the SignalR server's URL, we use the navigationManager.ToAbsoluteUri method.

Then we define the AddSegments method (which the server will call) which simply adds the segments to the WhiteBoard component's segments. Since this call is asynchronous, we need to call StateHasChanged so the WhiteBoard component will perform change detection and render itself.

We also add the InitSegments method, which by some weird coincidence does the same as the AddSegments method (but this may change in the future).

Now our hubConnection is ready, so we call StartAsync, and when this returns the connection has been made and we ask the server to send its segments (which could have been modified by other clients) using the GetAllSegments method.

Listing 15-17. Creating the HubConnection

```
protected override async Task OnInitializedAsync()
{
  this.hubConnection = new HubConnectionBuilder()
  .WithUrl(navigationManager.ToAbsoluteUri("/board"))
  .Build();

  this.hubConnection.On<IEnumerable<LineSegment>>("AddSegments",
  segments =>
  {
    LineSegments.AddRange(segments);
    StateHasChanged();
  });

  this.hubConnection.On<List<LineSegment>>("InitSegments",
  allSegments =>
  {
    LineSegments.AddRange(allSegments);
    StateHasChanged();
  });
  await hubConnection.StartAsync();
  await hubConnection.SendAsync("GetAllSegments");
}
```

Notifying the Hub From the Client

Our WhiteBoard component should notify the server when the user added a segment, so we call the hubConnection's SendSegments method, passing the extra segment. This will update any other client out there. Add the AddLineSegment method from Listing 15-18.

Listing 15-18. Updated AddLineSegment method

```
private async Task AddLineSegment(LineSegment segment)
{
  List<LineSegment> segments = [segment];
  // Add this line
  await hubConnection!.SendAsync("SendSegments", segments);
  LineSegments.AddRange(segments);
}
```

Cleaning Up the Hub Connection

Finally, we should not forget to notify the server that we are not interested in other messages.

Start by declaring the IAsyncDisposable interface on the WhiteBoard component as in Listing 15-19.

Listing 15-19. Declaring the IAsyncDisposable interface

```
@using Microsoft.AspNetCore.SignalR.Client

@implements IAsyncDisposable

<h1>White Board</h1>
```

Implement the DisposeAsync method in the WhiteBoard component as in Listing 15-20. Here we call DisposeAsync on the hubConnection, which will unregister this client with the server's hub.

Listing 15-20. Implementing IAsyncDisposable

```
public async ValueTask DisposeAsync()
{
  if (hubConnection is not null)
  {
    await hubConnection.DisposeAsync();
  }
}
```

Build and run. Open another browser tab on the same URL (or another browser). Drawing in one tab will automatically draw in another tab. Again, open another tab or browser; the current drawing should be shown as in Figure 15-3 (Using Edge and Chrome).

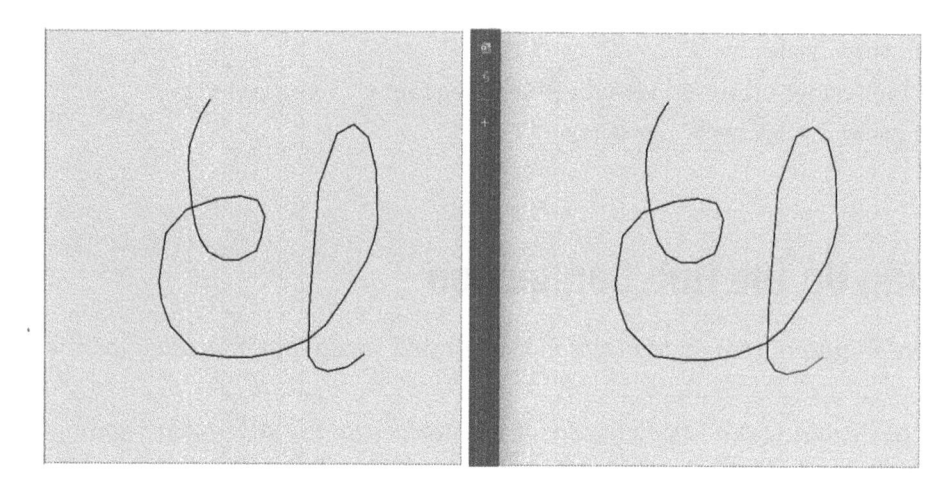

Figure 15-3. The WhiteBoard application in action

Summary

In this chapter, we looked at using SignalR for building real-time applications. Who is using SignalR out there? First of all, Blazor Server uses SignalR to set up the two-way communication between the server and the browser. Microsoft Azure also uses SignalR. It is also used by lots of companies. Any time you need real-time communication, SignalR is the choice to make. We could integrate SignalR in our PizzaPlace application to notify the customers when their pizza enters the oven, then when it is put in the pizza box, and when delivery is estimated to arrive. They could even see where the delivery is in traffic!

You start by adding a Hub to the server, and then you make clients connected to this hub using a HubConnection. Once this connection has been established, both client and server can send messages to each other. We only scratched the surface of what is possible with SignalR, but as we have seen, using SignalR is easy!

CHAPTER 16

Efficient Communication with gRPC

Blazor WebAssembly applications that have the need to exchange large amounts of data will probably run into communication overhead when using REST. With _gRPC_ you can use a more efficient way to exchange data with the backend.

What Is gRPC?

Before we were using SOAP and REST, developers were using _Remote Procedure Calls_ (_RPC_) to invoke methods in another process. We've seen how to communicate with REST APIs between two applications, but the serialization to and from JSON causes some overhead. This is mostly done to make messages human readable. If the communication only needs to happen between applications and there is no need to have a human readable form, we can use gRPC. Because the serialized data does not have to be readable by humans, it can be more compact and efficient and thus more performant.

Pros and Cons of RPC

With RPC you can expose a method in another process and call it just like a normal method, using the same syntax. Behind the scenes, the client method serializes the method call itself with its arguments and sends it to another process, for example, using a network stack. The other process would then call the actual server method and return the return value back over the network, after which the client method deserializes the return value and returns it. With RPC, developers at the client end do not see the difference between a normal method call and a remote call. This is of course quite convenient but comes at a price. Imagine you are talking to some other person directly, or you would have to talk to someone using a fax-machine (remember?) or good old mail. Talking directly to another person allows for a chatty interface where small messages get exchanged, like "How are you?" and "Good, and you?". While using a letter over mail or fax would use a chunky interface, where you would write down everything at once because you know the answer will take a long time. Just ask your parents 😉. The dream of RPC was that you would not be able to see the difference. But making calls over a network for a computer has the same efficiency as using a fax-machine or (snail) mail for us. So, designing RPC calls requires some thought and should use chunky interfaces.

Understanding gRPC

What is gRPC? This framework gives us a modern and highly efficient way to communicate with the same principles of RPC. It works for languages such as C#, Java, JavaScript, Go, Swift, C++, Python, NodeJS, and other languages. It provides interoperability between different languages through the use of an _Interface Definition Language_ (_IDL_) described in _.proto_ files. These files are then used to generate the necessary code used by both server and client.

Using gRPC is highly performant and very lightweight. A gRPC call can be up to 8 times faster than the equivalent REST call. Because it uses binary serialization, messages can be 60 to 80 percent smaller than JSON. Some of you might be familiar with _Windows Communication Foundation_ (WCF). In that case think of gRPC as the equivalent of using the `NetTcpBinding` in WCF.

Protocol Buffers

The gRPC framework uses an open source technology called _Protocol Buffers_ which was created by Google. With protocol buffers, we use an IDL specified in a text-based .proto file to allow us to communicate with other languages. With this IDL you create service contracts, each containing one or more RPC methods, and each method takes a request and a response message.

Describing Your Network Interchange with Proto Files

Let us update an existing application that currently uses REST to use gRPC. The source code that comes with this book contains a starter solution (in the Starter folder) called

BlazorApp.UsinggRPC. Open this solution. You can run it if you like, but to keep things simple and familiar, it uses the same components as before. Here the "Weather" component uses a "WeatherService" to request a list of "WeatherForecast" instances using REST. We also serialize images (sun, cloud, rain) from the server, and because these are large, it makes sense to use a more efficient protocol, so we will make this use gRPC.

Let us now describe the contract between the server and client. Since we are using Blazor, we can use the Client project to generate the code for both.

Installing the gRPC Tooling

First thing that we should do to use gRPC is to add a couple of packages to the Client project (take the latest stable version of each):

- Google.Protobuf
- Grpc.Net.Client
- Grpc.Net.Client.Web
- Grpc.Tools

Now add a new text file called WeatherForecast.proto. When you are using Visual Studio, you should set the Build Action to Protobuf compiler as in Figure 16-1.

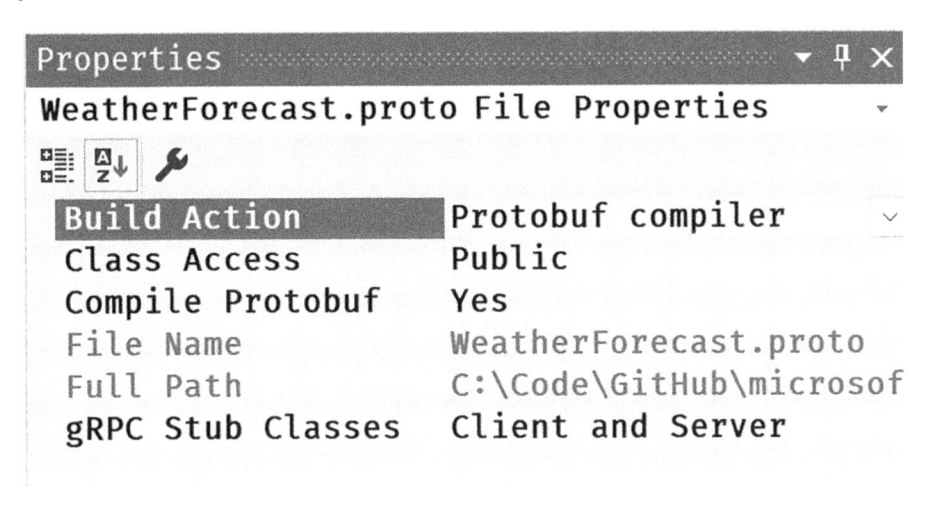

Figure 16-1. Proto file settings

When you are using another tool like Visual Studio Code, you can directly set the build action in the project file as in Listing 16-1.

CHAPTER 16   EFFICIENT COMMUNICATION WITH GRPC

Listing 16-1. Setting the build action in the project file

```
<Project Sdk="Microsoft.NET.Sdk.BlazorWebAssembly">

  <PropertyGroup>
    <TargetFramework>net8.0</TargetFramework>
    <ImplicitUsings>enable</ImplicitUsings>
    <Nullable>enable</Nullable>
    <NoDefaultLaunchSettingsFile>true</NoDefaultLaunchSettingsFile>
    <StaticWebAssetProjectMode>Default</StaticWebAssetProjectMode>
  </PropertyGroup>

  <ItemGroup>
    <None Remove="Proto\WeatherForecast.proto" />
  </ItemGroup>

  <ItemGroup>
    <PackageReference Include="Google.Protobuf" Version="3.27.2" />
    <PackageReference Include="Grpc.Net.Client" Version="2.63.0" />
    <PackageReference Include="Grpc.Net.Client.Web" Version="2.63.0" />
    <PackageReference Include="Grpc.Tools" Version="2.64.0">
      <PrivateAssets>all</PrivateAssets>
      <IncludeAssets>runtime; build; native; contentfiles; analyzers;
      buildtransitive</IncludeAssets>
    </PackageReference>
    <PackageReference Include="Microsoft.AspNetCore.Components.WebAssembly"
    Version="8.0.7" />
    <PackageReference Include="Microsoft.Extensions.Http" Version="8.0.0" />
  </ItemGroup>

  <ItemGroup>
    <Protobuf Include="Proto\WeatherForecast.proto" />
  </ItemGroup>

</Project>
```

When you build the .proto file, it will generate C# code for the service contract.

CHAPTER 16 EFFICIENT COMMUNICATION WITH GRPC

Adding the Service Contract

Update the .proto file as in Listing 16-2. First, we choose the syntax to be "proto3" syntax. Then we tell it which C# namespace we want the generated code to use.

Listing 16-2. The initial proto file

```
syntax = "proto3";

option csharp_namespace = "BlazorApp.UsinggRPC.Protos";
```

What should the service contract look like? A service contract consists of at least one method, a mandatory request message and mandatory response message. When declaring a contract, you should focus on the messages first, so let us think about the request message. We don't have any arguments for the "GetForecasts" method, but we still need to declare the request message with zero parts as in Listing 16-3. Should we decide later that we need an extra argument, we can easily add it to this message.

Listing 16-3. Declaring the request message

```
// The request message
message getForecastsRequest {
  // empty
}
```

The response message does contain data: a list of "weatherForecast" instances. First, we declare the "weatherForecast" message as in Listing 16-4. This message has four fields: the "date" using the "google.protobuf.Timestamp" type – kind of like "DateTime", the "temperatureC" using the "int32" type, a "summary" of "string" type, and finally the "image" which is of "bytes" type, representing a collection of "byte". As you can see, the types used in the proto IDL kind of match with .NET types (but other language mappings such as Java exist too).

Listing 16-4. The WeatherForecast message IDL

```
message weatherForecast {
  google.protobuf.Timestamp date = 1;
  int32 temperatureC = 2;
```

513

```
    string summary = 3;
    bytes image = 4;
}
```

To use the "google.protobuf.Timestamp" type, we do need to import this as in Listing 16-5.

Listing 16-5. Using the Timestamp type

```
option csharp_namespace = "BlazorApp.UsinggRPC.Protos";

// Support for google.protobuf.Timestamp
import "google/protobuf/timestamp.proto";
```

As Listing 16-4 illustrates, each field also has a unique number which is used to identify the field during serialization and deserialization. With JSON and REST, each field is identified through its name; with protobuf, the unique number is used which results in faster and more compact serialization.

The "getForecastResponse" message from Listing 16-6 is declared as a list of "weatherForecast" instances, using the repeated keyword. In C# this will generate a "Google.Protobuf.Collections.RepeatedField<T>" type which implements "IList<T>".

Listing 16-6. The GetForecastResponse message

```
// The response message
message getForecastsResponse {
    repeated weatherForecast forecasts = 1;
}
```

Now that we have the request and response message, we can create the service contract as in Listing 16-7. Here we define the "protoWeatherForecasts" service with just one "getForecasts" method. Of course, you can add more than one RPC method here.

Listing 16-7. The service contract

```
service protoWeatherForecasts {
    rpc getForecasts(getForecastsRequest) returns (getForecastsResponse);
}
```

CHAPTER 16   EFFICIENT COMMUNICATION WITH GRPC

Listing 16-8 contains the whole .proto file just to allow you to check the order of each statement.

Listing 16-8. The whole proto file

```
syntax = "proto3";

option csharp_namespace = "BlazorApp.UsinggRPC.Protos";

// Support for google.protobuf.Timestamp
import "google/protobuf/timestamp.proto";

// The request message
message getForecastsRequest {
  // empty
}

message weatherForecast {
  google.protobuf.Timestamp date = 1;
  int32 temperatureC = 2;
  string summary = 3;
  bytes image = 4;
}

// The response message
message getForecastsResponse {
  repeated weatherForecast forecasts = 1;
}

service protoWeatherForecasts {
  rpc getForecasts(getForecastsRequest) returns (getForecastsResponse);
}
```

Build the Client project; this should compile without errors.

If you are interested, you can look at the generated C# code inside the obj/Debug/net8.0/Proto folder. Especially look for the "protoWeatherForecastsBase" and "protoWeatherForecastsClient" classes inside the WeatherForecastGrpc.cs file.

515

CHAPTER 16 EFFICIENT COMMUNICATION WITH GRPC

Implementing gRPC on the Server

With the Client project ready, we can implement the server side of the gRPC service. Start by adding the following packages to the BlazorApp.UsinggRPC project (take the last stable version for each):

- Grpc.AspNetCore
- Grpc.AspNetCore.Web

Implementing the Service

Inside the Services folder, add a new `WeatherForecastProtoService` class as in Listing 16-9 which inherits from the generated `protoWeatherForecasts.protoWeatherForecastsBase` class.

Listing 16-9. Inheriting from the generated base class

```
using BlazorApp.UsinggRPC.Protos;
using Google.Protobuf.WellKnownTypes;
using Google.Protobuf;
using Grpc.Core;

namespace BlazorApp.UsinggRPC.Services;

public class WeatherForecastProtoService
  : protoWeatherForecasts.protoWeatherForecastsBase
{
}
```

Our service needs the "ImageService" through dependency injection so add a constructor as in Listing 16-10.

Listing 16-10. Adding dependencies

```
public class WeatherForecastProtoService
  : protoWeatherForecasts.protoWeatherForecastsBase
{
```

CHAPTER 16   EFFICIENT COMMUNICATION WITH GRPC

```
private readonly ImageService imageService;

public WeatherForecastProtoService(ImageService imageService)
  => this.imageService = imageService;
```

We also need to implement the service; this is done by overriding the "getForecasts" method from the base class as in Listing 16-11. This implementation will generate a couple of random forecasts. We also need some Summaries.

Listing 16-11. Implementing the getForecasts service method

```
private static readonly string[] Summaries = new[]
{
  "Freezing", "Cool", "Warm", "Hot", "Sweltering", "Scorching"
};

public override Task<getForecastsResponse> getForecasts(
  getForecastsRequest request,
  ServerCallContext context)
{
  IEnumerable<weatherForecast>? forecasts =
  Enumerable.Range(1, 5).Select(index => new weatherForecast
  {
    Date = Timestamp.FromDateTime(
      DateTime.UtcNow.AddDays(index)),
    TemperatureC = Random.Shared.Next(-20, 55),
    Summary = Summaries[Random.Shared.Next(Summaries.Length)],
    Image = ByteString.CopyFrom(this.imageService.RandomImage())
  });
  var response = new getForecastsResponse();
  response.Forecasts.AddRange(forecasts);
  return Task.FromResult(response);
}
```

A couple of remarks about this implementation. Protobuf uses the "Timestamp" type, so we need to convert our "DateTime" using the "FromDateTime" method. The "Timestamp" type is provided through the Google.Protobuf.WellKnownTypes namespace from the Google.Protobuf NuGet package. The "Image" property is of type "ByteString", and we can use the "ByteString.CopyFrom" method to convert from a "byte[]". The base class's "getForecasts" method is asynchronous so we need to return the result as a "Task" using the "Task.FromResult" method. In real life, this service would read the data from a database, so it makes a lot of sense that this method is asynchronous.

Adding gRPC

With the service implemented, all that rests (some pun here!) is to add gRPC support to the server. Start by configuring dependency injection as in Listing 16-12.

Listing 16-12. Configuring dependency injection in program

```
// Add services to the container.
builder.Services.AddRazorComponents()
    .AddInteractiveWebAssemblyComponents();

builder.Services.AddScoped<IWeatherService, WeatherService>();
builder.Services.AddSingleton<ImageService>();
builder.Services.AddGrpc();

var app = builder.Build();
```

Then add the gRPC middleware to Program as in Listing 16-13. Because Blazor uses the JavaScript library for gRPC, we need to use GrpcWeb implementation instead of regular gRPC. Because gRPC uses the HTTP/2 stack in a way that is not supported by browsers, we need to use a proxy to take care of the proper message format, and that is what gRPC Web does. Regular gRPC clients (e.g., desktop applications) can still talk to our service so using gRPC Web does not break regular gRPC.

Listing 16-13. Adding the gRPC middleware

```
// Configure the HTTP request pipeline.
if (app.Environment.IsDevelopment())
{
  app.UseWebAssemblyDebugging();
}
```

```
else
{
  app.UseExceptionHandler("/Error", createScopeForErrors: true);
  app.UseHsts();
}

app.UseHttpsRedirection();

app.UseStaticFiles();
app.UseAntiforgery();

app.UseGrpcWeb();

app.MapGrpcService<WeatherForecastProtoService>()
   .EnableGrpcWeb();

app.MapRazorComponents<App>()
   .AddInteractiveWebAssemblyRenderMode()
   .AddAdditionalAssemblies(typeof(BlazorApp.UsinggRPC.Client._Imports).
   Assembly);

app.MapGet("/forecasts", async (IWeatherService weatherService) =>
{
  WeatherForecast[] forecasts = await weatherService.GetForecasts();
  return forecasts;
});

app.Run();
```

Build the Server project.

Think about this. What you had to do was quite simple: inherit from a base class, override the base method, and use protobuf types with some conversions. No need to think about headers, deserialization, etc.

Building a gRPC Client in Blazor

Now we can add gRPC support to the client project.

CHAPTER 16   EFFICIENT COMMUNICATION WITH GRPC

Creating the ForecastGrpcService

Inside the Client project, add a new class called "ForecastGrpcService" to the "Services" folder as in Listing 16-14. To use gRPC, we first need a "GrpcChannel" which we request through dependency injection. Inside the "getForecasts" method, we create the gRPC "protoWeatherForecastsClient" client (generated from the .proto file) passing it the "GrpcChannel" instance. Then we create the request message and invoke the "getForecastsAsync" method. This returns a "getForecastsResponse" instance containing a "RepeatedField<weatherForecast>". Now we need to convert these to the regular "WeatherForecast" instances our "Weather" component uses which we do using a LINQ "Select".

Listing 16-14. The ForecastGrpcService class

```
using BlazorApp.UsinggRPC.Client.Entities;
using BlazorApp.UsinggRPC.Protos;
using Grpc.Net.Client;

namespace BlazorApp.UsinggRPC.Client.Services;

public class ForecastGrpcService
{
  private readonly GrpcChannel grpcChannel;

  public ForecastGrpcService(GrpcChannel grpcChannel)
  => this.grpcChannel = grpcChannel;

  public async Task<WeatherForecast[]> GetForecasts()
  {
    var client =
      new protoWeatherForecasts.protoWeatherForecastsClient(this.
      grpcChannel);
    var request = new getForecastsRequest();
    getForecastsResponse? response =
      await client.getForecastsAsync(request);
    return response.Forecasts.Select(f =>
      new WeatherForecast
```

```
    {
      Date = DateOnly.FromDateTime(f.Date.ToDateTime()),
      TemperatureC = f.TemperatureC,
      Summary = f.Summary,
      Image = f.Image.ToByteArray()
    }).ToArray();
  }
}
```

Enabling gRPC on the Client

Now we need to configure dependency injection for the "GrpcChannel" instance. This instance requires a URL to talk to the server, and we will put this in configuration. Update the appsettings.json file to the client project's wwwroot folder and complete it as in Listing 16-15. Update the port number to the port number your server project uses. You can find this by running the server project and look for the port number in the URL.

Listing 16-15. The GrpcChannel configuration

```
{
  "Logging": {
    "LogLevel": {
      "Default": "Information",
      "Microsoft.AspNetCore": "Warning"
    }
  },
  "gRPC": {
    "weatherServices": "https://localhost:7295"
  }
}
```

Update the Client's "Program" so we can read configuration while instructing dependency injection how to create a valid "GrpcChannel" as in Listing 16-16. First, we add a scoped "ForecastGrpcService". Then we add a scoped "GrpcChannel" using a lambda function which reads the configuration and creates a "GrpcChannel" using the "ForAddress" method. Because we are using gRPC Web, we need to tell the "GrpcChannel" to use the "GrpcWebHandler".

Listing 16-16. Configuring dependency injection

```
using BlazorApp.UsinggRPC.Client.Services;
using Grpc.Net.Client.Web;
using Grpc.Net.Client;
using Microsoft.AspNetCore.Components.WebAssembly.Hosting;

var builder = WebAssemblyHostBuilder.CreateDefault(args);

builder.Services.AddHttpClient(nameof(IWeatherService), httpClient =>
  httpClient.BaseAddress = new Uri(builder.HostEnvironment.BaseAddress));

// builder.Services.AddScoped<IWeatherService, WeatherServiceProxy>();

builder.Services.AddScoped<IWeatherService, ForecastGrpcService>();

builder.Services.AddScoped(services =>
 {
   IConfiguration config =
   services.GetRequiredService<IConfiguration>();
   string backEndUrl = config["gRPC:weatherServices"]!;
   var httpHandler =
   new GrpcWebHandler(GrpcWebMode.GrpcWebText,
   new HttpClientHandler());
   return GrpcChannel.ForAddress(backEndUrl,
   new GrpcChannelOptions { HttpHandler = httpHandler });
 });
await builder.Build().RunAsync();
```

Build and run. Choose the Weather data link. You should get forecasts like in Figure 16-2.

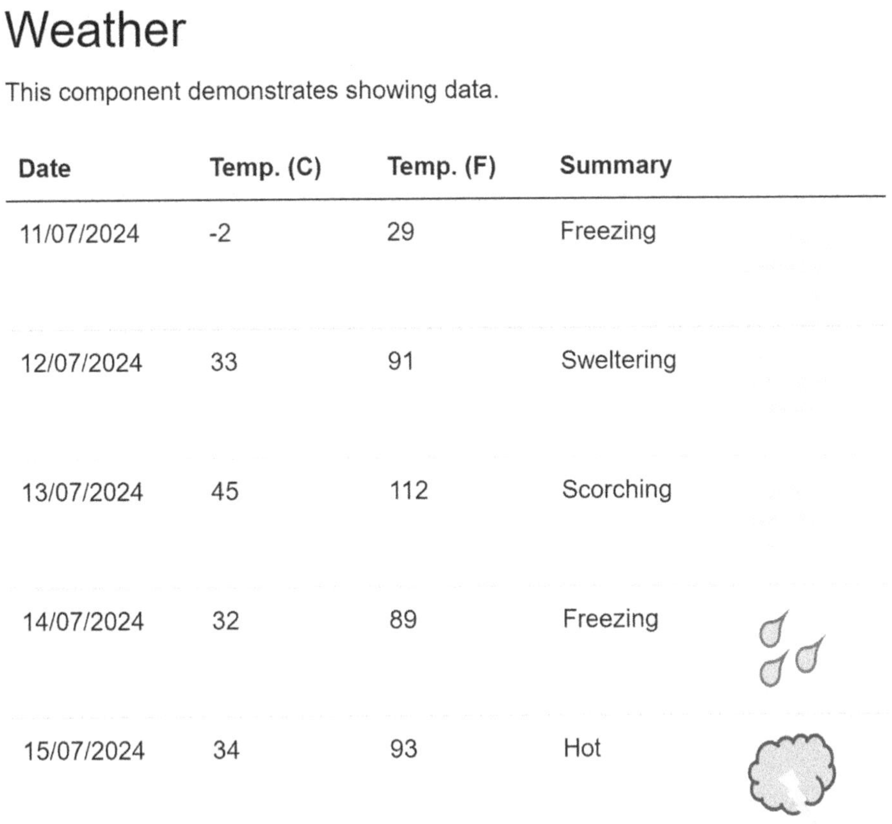

Weather

This component demonstrates showing data.

Date	Temp. (C)	Temp. (F)	Summary
11/07/2024	-2	29	Freezing
12/07/2024	33	91	Sweltering
13/07/2024	45	112	Scorching
14/07/2024	32	89	Freezing
15/07/2024	34	93	Hot

Figure 16-2. Displaying forecasts

Comparing REST with gRPC

Let us see how REST compares to gRPC. Let us try REST first, so restore the "WeatherService" in the "Program" class as in Listing 16-17.

Listing 16-17. Updating the FetchData component

```
builder.Services.AddScoped<IWeatherService, WeatherServiceProxy>();
```

Note This sample serializes a lot of images from a limited pool of images. In this case you could serialize each image once and use a placeholder for each copy of the image. Let us pretend that each image is unique for the sake of this example.

CHAPTER 16   EFFICIENT COMMUNICATION WITH GRPC

In the server project, update the "WeatherService" as in Listing 16-18 to return 250 rows instead of 5.

Listing 16-18. Returning 250 forecasts

```
WeatherForecast[] forecasts = Enumerable.Range(1, 250).Select(...
```

Run the application and open the browser's debugger on the Network tab. Now select the Weather link. This will make the REST call and the network tab should display the amount of data sent and how long this took. Figure 16-3 displays what I got.

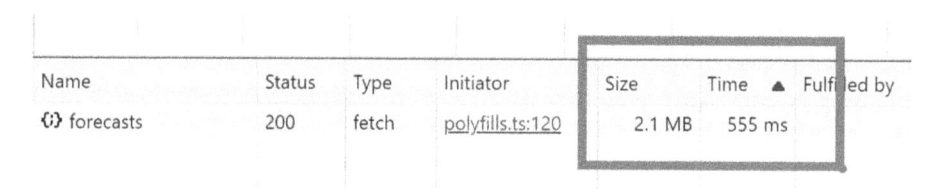

Figure 16-3. *Using a REST call*

You can click on the request row to see what the serialized data looks like, for example, Figure 16-4.

Figure 16-4. *REST using JSON*

Restore Listing 16-17 and update the "WeatherForecastProtoService" to also return 250 rows as in Listing 16-19.

524

CHAPTER 16   EFFICIENT COMMUNICATION WITH GRPC

Listing 16-19. Returning 250 rows using gRPC

```
Enumerable.Range(1, 250).Select(...
```

Run again and use the browser's debugger to capture the network traffic when visiting the Weather link. Figure 16-5 shows what I got.

Name	Status	Type	Initiator	Size	Time	Fulfilled by
getForecasts	200	fetch	polyfills.ts:120	2.0 MB	102 ms	

Figure 16-5. *Using gRPC with text encoding*

Not the expected result. Response time is faster, but the payload is about as big. Why? Let us look at the response of the "getForecasts" request as in Figure 16-6. This is clearly not using binary encoding.

	Headers	Payload	Preview	Response	Initiator	Timing	Cookie
1	AAAYE7sKyEMKDAjZ2b+0BhCgrP+cAhA2GglTY29yY2hpbmciqkOJUE5HDQo						

Figure 16-6. *The Base-64 encoded response*

Ok. Time to fix this. We need to use gRPC Web with binary encoding. Modify the client's Program to use `GrpcWebMode.GrpcWeb` as in Listing 16-20.

Listing 16-20. Using binary encoding

```
builder.Services.AddScoped(services =>
{
  IConfiguration config =
  services.GetRequiredService<IConfiguration>();
  string backEndUrl = config["gRPC:weatherServices"]!;
  var httpHandler =
  new GrpcWebHandler(GrpcWebMode.GrpcWeb/*Text*/,
  new HttpClientHandler());
```

525

CHAPTER 16   EFFICIENT COMMUNICATION WITH GRPC

```
    return GrpcChannel.ForAddress(backEndUrl,
    new GrpcChannelOptions { HttpHandler = httpHandler });
});
await builder.Build().RunAsync();
```

Run the application again. Now we can see a nice decrease in network traffic size and time as in Figure 16-7. Compare this to Figure 16-3.

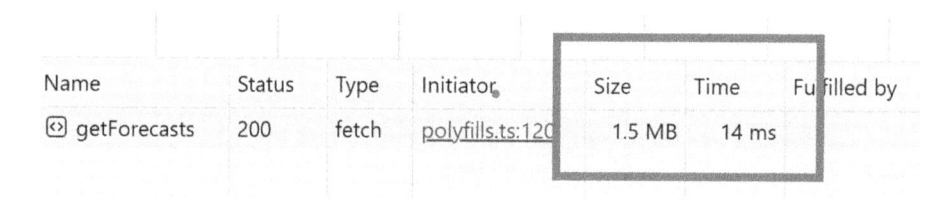

Figure 16-7. Using gRPC with binary encoding

We can also see that we are using binary encoding as in Figure 16-8.

Figure 16-8. The binary encoded response

Summary

In this chapter, we looked at using gRPC with Blazor. We started with a discussion about what RPC means, and that gRPC is a modern implementation of RPC. We then created our service contract using a .proto file and generated the code for the messages and service contract. Implementation of the server is easy because we can derive from the generated server base class and override the service contract method. The client side allows us to call the server using again the generated code; we only need to supply the configured "gRpcChannel". We then verified if performance was actually better, and we changed encoding to use binary encoding getting the promised performance increase.

CHAPTER 17

Deploying Your Blazor Application

At a certain point in time, your Blazor application will be ready for the big public. Yeah! But the work is not yet done. We need to take our application and copy it to a server connected to the network so other people can use their browser to admire your work! Let us look at how we can deploy our Blazor application. We will start by deploying a standalone Blazor application, and then we will look at deploying Blazor Web Apps which require a server that supports ASP.NET Core.

Deploy Standalone Blazor WebAssembly

When your Blazor Application does not require any server support, you can host the application just like any other static website. In this case, the host just needs to serve the files to the browser since everything is executed on the browser.

Hosting on GitHub

GitHub is a free service that allows you to collaborate with others on a development project. It has support for git source control, builds automation, and allows you to host static websites, all free of charge.

Note If you are not familiar with git source control, there is an excellent book available for free digitally at `https://git-scm.com/book/en/v2`.

CHAPTER 17   DEPLOYING YOUR BLAZOR APPLICATION

Here we will host our Blazor application on GitHub, and the process is similar for other static hosting platforms. There are many other excellent hosting solutions out there, but I had to pick one, and GitHub is widely known in the developer community.

Using GitHub requires some knowledge about git. If all of this is familiar, great. If not, the walkthrough gives you the git commands you need to execute.

If you don't have a GitHub account, you will need to create one on https://github.com/. Because modern websites have the tendency to change how they look, I won't be using screenshots here, but the process should explain itself.

Once you have an account, you should create an organization at https://github.com/settings/organizations. GitHub allows you to have multiple organizations, and each can host a static website. Select a unique name for your organization; here I will use the MicrosoftBlazorBook organization. After creating the organization, select it. Your browser will show the organization's page, for example, https://github.com/MicrosoftBlazorBook.

Here you can find a list or repositories. A repository will host all your sources and their history as you make changes to files using git source control. Since you have just created the organization, you will have to create a new repository. Click the New button; give your repository a nice name and description. You should also choose if you want the repository to be public (anyone can see your code) or private. The deployment process is the same for either, so pick one. Complete creating the repository, but don't add any files like README.

After completion, GitHub will show you a page that displays the command line commands you can use to create the repository locally.

Note   I will be using Windows Terminal here, which has built-in support for PowerShell commands. All commands should work well with Linux and OSX command line.

On your local machine, create a folder where you want your project to go, open a command line on that folder, and execute the commands shown in github (just use copy-paste). For example, my organization is called MicrosoftBlazorBook and the repository is StandAloneWASM:

```
echo "# StandAloneWASM" >> README.md
git init
git add README.md
git commit -m "first commit"
```

```
git branch -M main
git remote add origin https://github.com/MicrosoftBlazorBook/
StandAloneWASM.git
git push -u origin main
```

First this will create a README.md file in the current folder, and then this will create a git repository in the current folder. Next this adds the README.md file to the repository, creates a new commit with a comment, and finally pushes the repository to the GitHub server. Now we are ready to deploy a static website.

Creating a Simple Website

Add a new index.html file in your folder with some simple content like Listing 17-1.

Listing 17-1. A basic HTML file

```
<!DOCTYPE html>
<html lang="en">
<head>
  <meta charset="UTF-8">
  <meta http-equiv="X-UA-Compatible" content="IE=edge">
  <meta name="viewport" content="width=device-width, initial-scale=1.0">
  <title>Document</title>
</head>
<body>
  <h1>Hello world!</h1>
</body>
</html>
```

Since we made a change to your site, we will upload these changes into GitHub using git in the command line.

First you need to add the modifications to git by executing the `git add .` command. Don't forget the `.` which will make git add all changes in the current folder and subfolders to the commit when we create it, so make sure you are in the project's folder where the README.md file is.

```
git add .
```

Now we need to take all these changes and group them into a commit with:

`git commit -m "Simple"`

A git commit is all the changes grouped with metadata, including a mandatory message which we set using the `-m` parameter. And finally, we can send our changes to the GitHub repository using

`git push`

When you refresh the GitHub repository page, you should see index.html.

Deploying a Simple Site in GitHub

To host your simple website in GitHub, we need to select a specific branch it should host. Think of a branch as a separate copy of your files with its own history. Branches are normally used so developers can work on new features without bothering other developers. When the feature is complete, we can take the changes and apply it to the main branch where everyone will merge their changes. You can select the branch using the `https://github.com/MicrosoftBlazorBook/StandAloneWASM/settings/pages` page, but there is another way. If the branch is named gh-pages, then GitHub picks that branch automatically. Run the following commands to create a gh-pages branch locally, choose the gh-pages as the current branch using the checkout command, and push it to the GitHub repository on the server.

```
git branch gh-pages
git switch gh-pages
git push --set-upstream origin gh-pages
```

After executing these commands, the deployment process will start, and by refreshing the pages page (URL above), you can see the status. Refresh until GitHub tells you it is ready.

Click the link (e.g., `https://microsoftblazorbook.github.io/StandAloneWASM/`), and you should see your static website in action!

Deploying a Blazor WASM Project

Let us create and deploy a standalone Blazor WASM project now. First, we need to use the main branch:

`git switch main`

Using the command line, create a new Blazor WASM project:

`dotnet new blazorwasm`

When we compile our Blazor project, two new folders will be created: obj and bin. We don't need to keep these folders in source control, and an easy way to do this is by telling git to ignore these. Since this is a common scenario, we can use

`dotnet new gitignore`

Finally, we don't need the index.html file from the previous part:

`rm index.html`

Now we can commit all our changes to GitHub with:

```
git add .
git commit -m "Created"
git push
```

Fix the Base Tag

Before we can deploy, we need to fix the `<base>` element in the index.html page (since this is a Blazor Standalone WebAssembly project, the `<base>` element can be found in index.html). This element is used to create the path to download our CSS and JavaScript and is also used by routing. Set the path to your repository's name, and don't forget the leading and trailing slash (/) as in Listing 17-2. Now the browser will download static files by prefixing the URL with the `<base>` element.

Listing 17-2. Fixing the `<base>` element

```
<head>
  <meta charset="utf-8" />
  <meta name="viewport" content="width=device-width, initial-scale=1.0" />
```

```
<title>StandAloneWASM</title>
<base href="/StandAloneWASM/" />
<link rel="stylesheet" href="css/bootstrap/bootstrap.min.css" />
<link rel="stylesheet" href="css/app.css" />
<link rel="icon" type="image/png" href="favicon.png" />
<link href="StandAloneWASM.styles.css" rel="stylesheet" />
</head>
```

Now we can push our change to GitHub with the following commands:

```
git add .
git commit -m "Fix base tag"
git push
```

Wait for the deployment to complete and refresh your site's page. You can review the deployment process at `https://github.com/MicrosoftBlazorBook/StandAloneWASM/actions`, replacing your organization and repository name in the URL.

Publish the Project

Now we are ready to publish our project. You can choose between using Visual Studio, or command line.

Using Visual Studio

Using Visual Studio, right-click your project and select Publish. This will display the Publish wizard from Figure 17-1.

CHAPTER 17 DEPLOYING YOUR BLAZOR APPLICATION

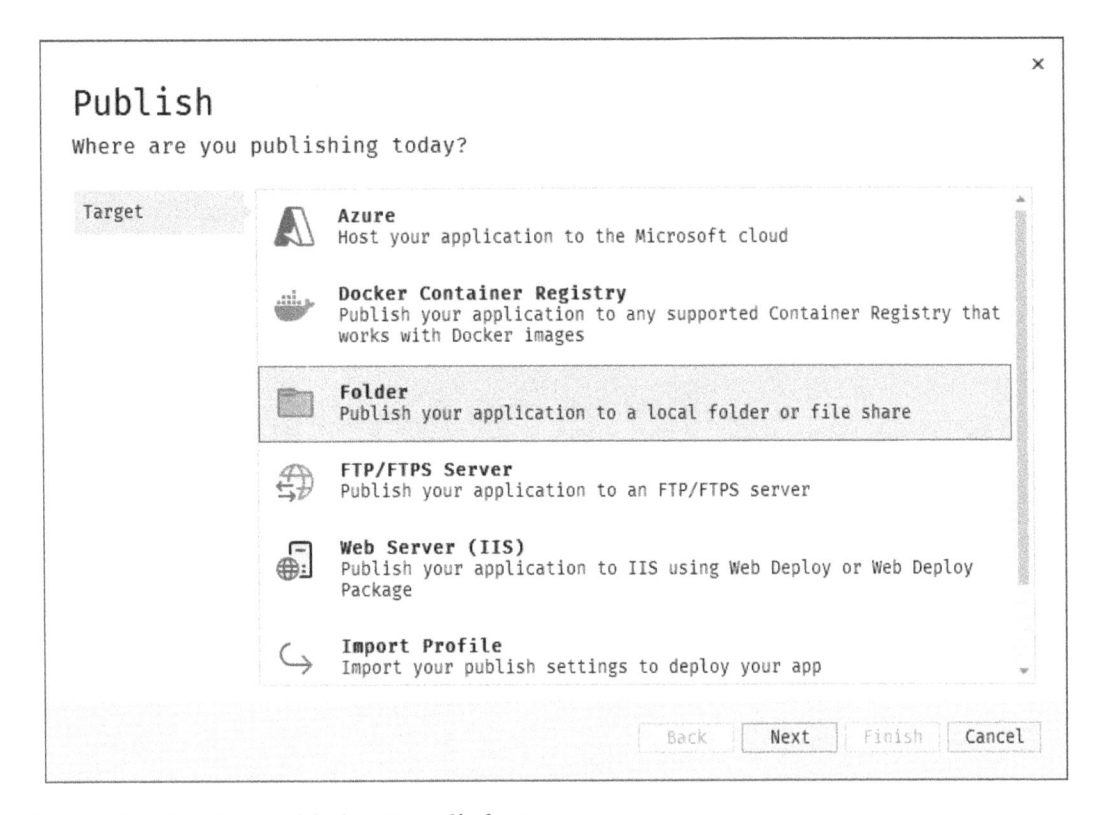

```
Publish                                                              ×
Where are you publishing today?

  Target          Azure
                  Host your application to the Microsoft cloud

                  Docker Container Registry
                  Publish your application to any supported Container Registry that
                  works with Docker images

                ┌─────────────────────────────────────────────────────────────┐
                │ Folder                                                      │
                │ Publish your application to a local folder or file share    │
                └─────────────────────────────────────────────────────────────┘

                  FTP/FTPS Server
                  Publish your application to an FTP/FTPS server

                  Web Server (IIS)
                  Publish your application to IIS using Web Deploy or Web Deploy
                  Package

                  Import Profile
                  Import your publish settings to deploy your app

                                        Back    Next    Finish    Cancel
```

Figure 17-1. *The Publish wizard's first step*

Select Folder, and then Next.

You can now select where you want your project published as in Figure 17-2. I will leave this set to the default value. Then click Finish, and then Close.

533

CHAPTER 17   DEPLOYING YOUR BLAZOR APPLICATION

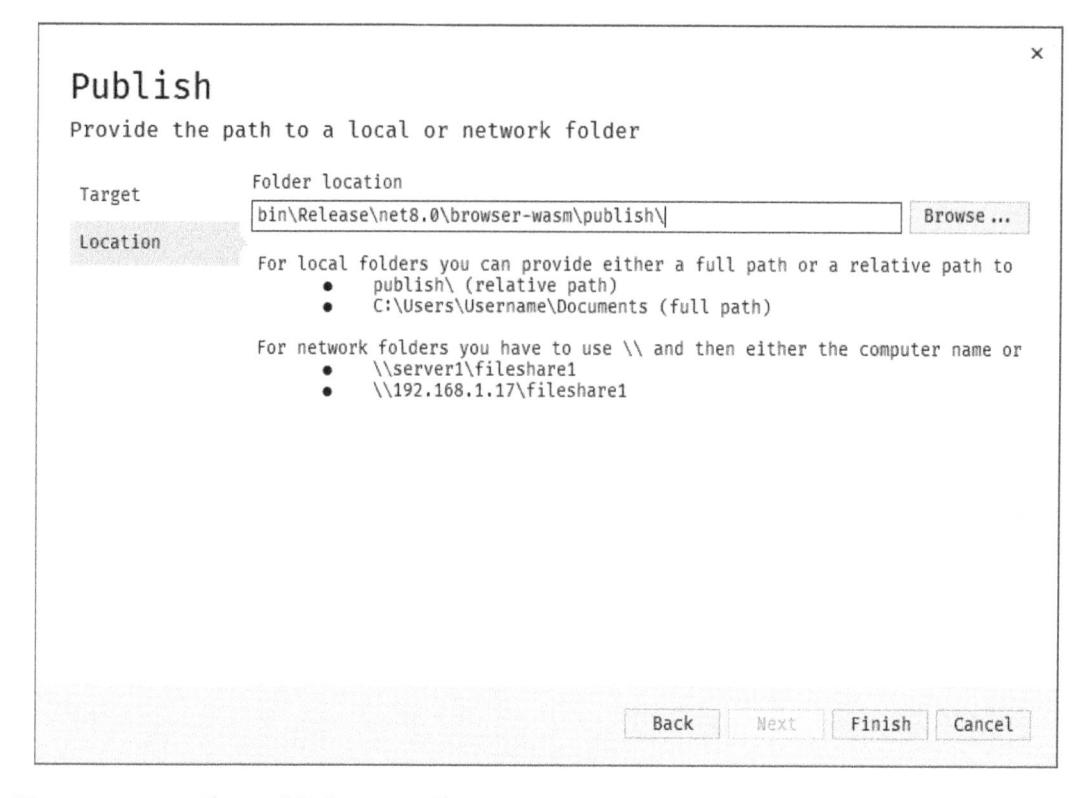

Figure 17-2. The Publish wizard's second step

You can now click the Publish button from Figure 17-3 every time you want to publish a new version.

Figure 17-3. The Publish profile

Click Publish to create your first deployment.

Using the Command Line

We will tell `dotnet` to create a release version using the `-c` option and put it into a release folder using the `-o` option. Publishing will optimize our Blazor WASM project by removing all unneeded code and assemblies, making the initial download smaller. This will take longer to build and shorter to load the Blazor site in the browser.

```
dotnet publish -c Release -o release
```

Copying to the GitHub Branch

When publishing finishes, we will copy the release folder into the gh-pages branch. Start by moving the release folder to a temporary folder outside our local repository because when we switch branch, this will be removed.

Now checkout the gh-pages branch:

```
git switch gh-pages
```

You will find some unneeded folders left behind. Remove these folders:

```
rm -r bin
rm -r obj
```

Now examine the publish folder. The web.config file is used for Internet Information Services (IIS) deployments, but we don't need it for GitHub. We only need the files from the `wwwroot` folder so copy the wwwroot folder's contents in our `gh-pages` branch:

Git works for both Windows- and Unix-based operating systems. However, these use different file endings, and we don't want git to change these. Why? Because the Blazor runtime will check using a hash if our files have been changed after deployment, and it will refuse to load these files (a good security measure). We can tell git not to make changes using a .gitattributes file, so add one using the following command:

```
"* binary" >> .gitattributes
```

CHAPTER 17   DEPLOYING YOUR BLAZOR APPLICATION

This tells git to treat all our files as binary, so it will not try to fix file endings. Commit these files and push them to the git repository on GitHub:

```
git add .
git commit -m "Deploy"
git push
```

Now you can reload the site (which will not work yet), for example, in my case, this would be `https://microsoftblazorbook.github.io/StandAloneWASM/`.

Disabling Jekyll

Still not working. Let us look at the browser debugger's console as shown in Figure 17-4. It is loading the JavaScript and css files, but it cannot find the _framework files.

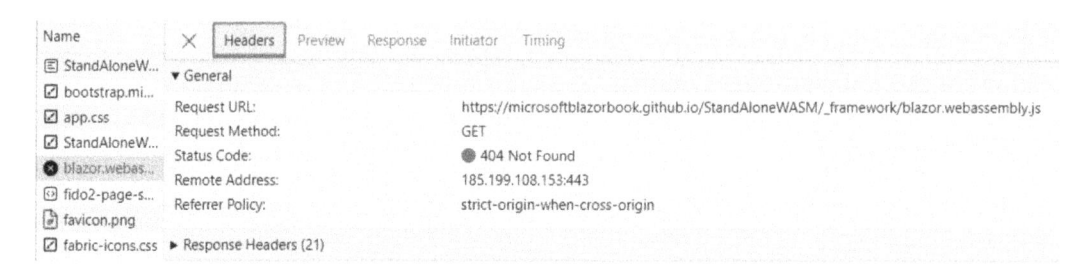

Figure 17-4. Blazor does not find the _framework files

Why? GitHub uses Jekyll (`https://github.com/jekyll`) which is a static site generator. Jekyll stores its files in folders that start with an underscore, and GitHub will not host files inside folders that start with an underscore. We can disable Jekyll by adding an empty `.nojekyll` file in the root folder. Use your favorite editor again to add this file, and use the following commands to send this to GitHub:

```
git add .
git commit -m "Fix Jekyll"
git push
```

Wait for the deployment to complete and refresh your site's page. Your Blazor site should work! Great!

CHAPTER 17 DEPLOYING YOUR BLAZOR APPLICATION

Fixing GitHub 404s

There is still one problem we need to fix. Navigate in your Blazor site to the Counter route and make the browser refresh by hitting F5. It will display a 404 page! This is because GitHub will try to load the Counter file from the URL. We can fix this by copying our root index.html file to a 404.html file, which GitHub will then send back to the browser.

First copy index.html to 404.html using this command:

```
cp index.html 404.html
```

Now we need to push this change back the GitHub with these commands:

```
git add .
git commit -m "Fix 404 page"
git push
```

Now refreshing the counter route will work.

Note Here we have been deploying our standalone Blazor WebAssembly application by pushing changes in source control to GitHub. Some other hosts also allow you to do this too, for example, you can deploy your application using Azure DevOps. If you want to host your Blazor application on a host that does not have source control integration, you will have to upload the publish folder using the host its own tools; this might even be with FTP!

Production Download Size

Let us have a quick peek at the download size of our published Blazor WebAssembly application. Since we have one running in GitHub, open the site in your browser. Open the debugging tools and open the Application tab and clear the site data (contains the cached runtime) as shown in Figure 17-5.

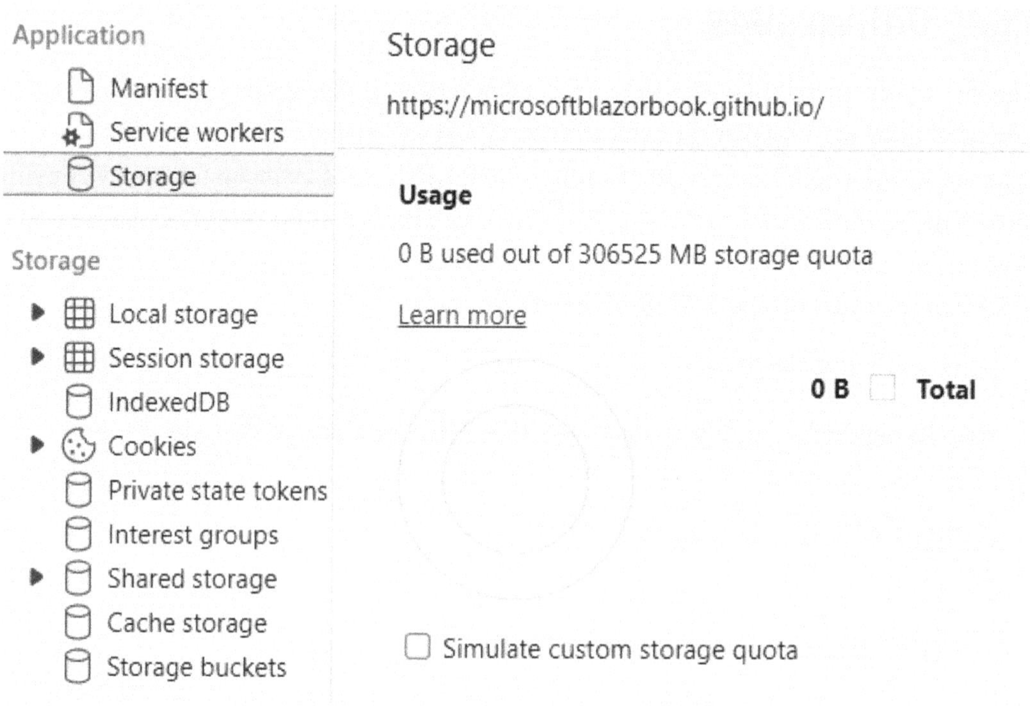

CHAPTER 17   DEPLOYING YOUR BLAZOR APPLICATION

Figure 17-5.   Clear site data

Open the network tab and hit Ctrl-R to force a reload of the website. This will be downloaded as a first-time user. Look near the bottom of the logs. The download is around 3.0 MB! A lot smaller than the 10MB we got during development (Figure 17-6).

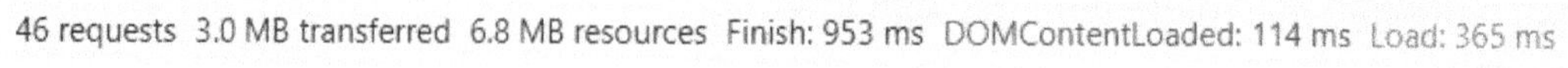

46 requests   3.0 MB transferred   6.8 MB resources   Finish: 953 ms   DOMContentLoaded: 114 ms   Load: 365 ms

Figure 17-6.   The initial first download

Hit Ctrl-R again. This will use the cache now, resulting in a download of 192 kB (Figure 17-7)!

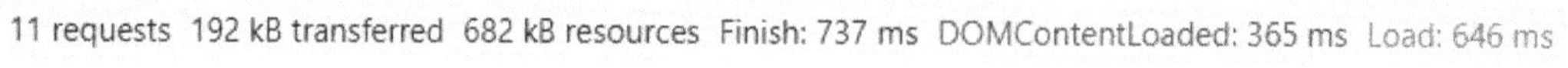

11 requests   192 kB transferred   682 kB resources   Finish: 737 ms   DOMContentLoaded: 365 ms   Load: 646 ms

Figure 17-7.   The next download

Alternatives for GitHub

There are many alternatives to deploy your Blazor Standalone WebAssembly project, each will have its own little quirks to make it work, but everyone will require you to set the base tag in index.html correctly. For example, you could also deploy your project as an *Azure Static Web Site*. For more information about deploying your project as an Azure Static Web Site, visit `https://docs.microsoft.com/azure/static-web-apps/deploy-blazor`. With Azure you can also deploy a Standalone Blazor WebAssembly together with an Azure Function which will provide data as a REST service. You can find more information at `https://learn.microsoft.com/en-us/azure/static-web-apps/deploy-blazor`

Ahead-of-Time Compilation

With .NET 6+ we can now compile our complete solution as a WASM file, and run everything as WebAssembly. By default, you will run .NET assemblies in the Browser where the WASM .NET runtime will interpret IL instructions. By compiling everything into WASM, you can get significant performance improvements! However, the WASM file is larger than the .NET assembly equivalent, so compiling everything as WASM will come at the cost of a longer initial download. This is also known as *Ahead-of-Time compilation* (*AOT*). AOT mainly benefits applications that are CPU intensive, so you might not even need this for your application.

To enable AOT compilation, you should add the `RunAOTCompilation` flag to your project as shown in Listing 17-3.

Listing 17-3. Enabling AOT compilation

```
PropertyGroup>
 <TargetFramework>net8.0</TargetFramework>
 <Nullable>enable</Nullable>
 <ImplicitUsings>enable</ImplicitUsings>
 <RunAOTCompilation>true</RunAOTCompilation>
/PropertyGroup>
```

Now you can publish your application just like before with the publish command:

```
dotnet publish -c Release -o release
```

CHAPTER 17   DEPLOYING YOUR BLAZOR APPLICATION

This will take some time, so grab something to drink. While you are developing, AOT is not used because compiling takes so much longer.

Once deployment is ready, look inside the release/_framework folder and search for dotnet.native.wasm. This file on my machine is around 11 MB! Without OAT this file is around 2MB. Do note that the actual download is a lot smaller due to the compression used by Blazor.

We can now deploy our AOT compiled release just like before.

Deploying Hosted Applications

For both the Hosted Blazor WebAssembly and Blazor Server applications, you will need to deploy to a host that supports executing .NET on the server. You can deploy this to Windows Internet Information Services (IIS), or to Linux Apache.

Understanding the Deployment Models

With ASP.NET Core hosted applications, we have several choices for deploying our application.

One option is to use a *framework-dependent deployment*. In this case, the deployment files only contain your application files with their dependencies. No runtime is deployed, so this will only work on a server where the .NET runtime has been deployed before. One advantage of using framework-dependent deployment is that your deployment will work everywhere since portable .NET assemblies are used.

The other option is to use a *self-contained deployment*. In this case the deployment contains all the files that are needed to run the application, including the runtime. Because of this, you need to specify which platform you want to target, for example, 64-bit windows, and it will only deploy to that platform. The main advantage of this is that there is no dependency on what has been installed on the server, except for the platform of course. Another advantage is that you can use any version of .NET, even previews. Most commercial hosts will only give you long-term support versions of the .NET runtime.

To create a deployment, you use the `dotnet publish` command. For example, to create a self-contained deployment for 64bit Linux, you use:

```
dotnet publish -c Release -o release --self-contained --runtime linux-x64
```

CHAPTER 17 DEPLOYING YOUR BLAZOR APPLICATION

And if you want to create a portable framework-dependent deployment:

```
dotnet publish -c Release -o release –no-self-contained
```

Deploying to Microsoft Azure

Most of us don't have a server lying around to deploy to, so here we will deploy to an Azure WebApp. If you don't have an Azure account, you can get one for free. Open your browser and visit https://azure.microsoft.com/. Here you can create a free account, and you even get $200 credit.

An Azure WebApp is a hosting service that makes it very easy to deploy and run your Blazor application.

We will use Visual Studio to create a release and deploy it into Azure. Create a new WebApp Server project (or another render mode, your choice). Before we can deploy to Azure, we need to add our Azure account to Visual Studio. So open File ➤ Account Settings. Click Add as in Figure 17-8 to add your Azure account.

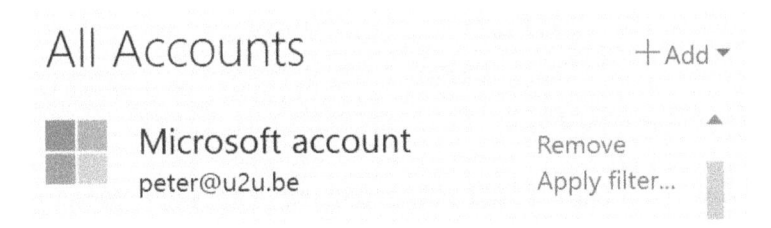

Figure 17-8. Add your Azure account

Creating the Publishing Profile

Right-click the server project and select Publish from the drop-down menu. The publish wizard will open which gives you a choice between deployment targets. Choose Azure as in Figure 17-9.

541

CHAPTER 17   DEPLOYING YOUR BLAZOR APPLICATION

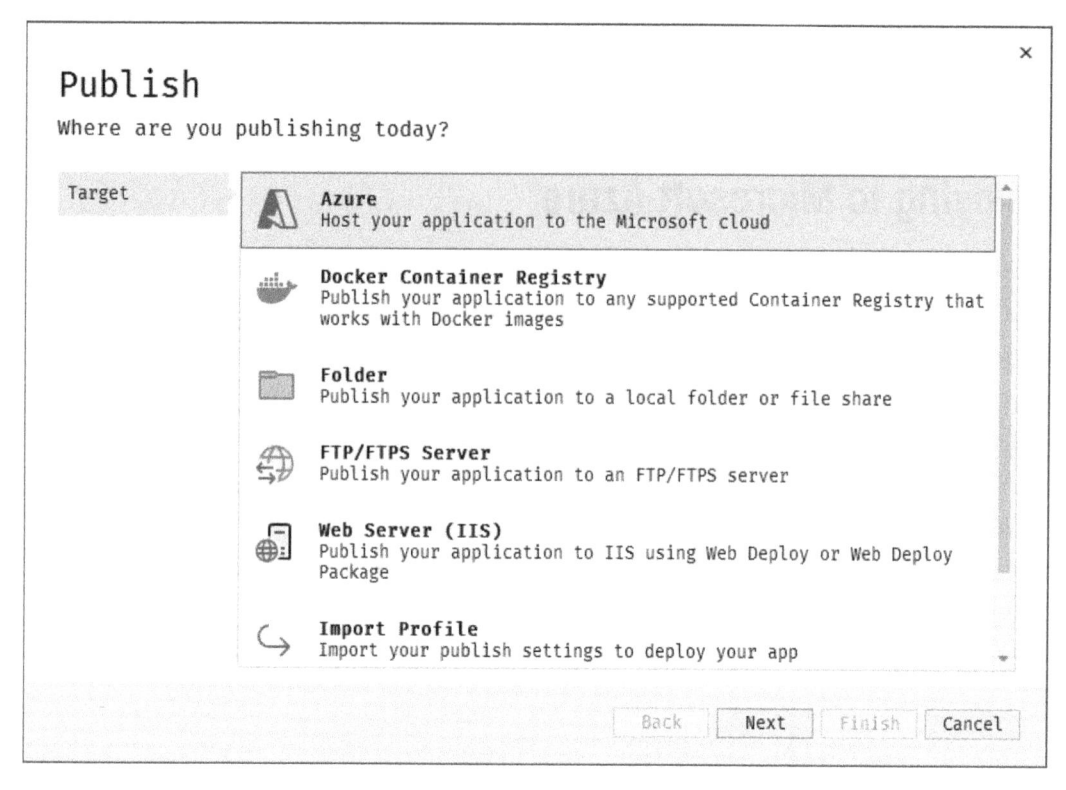

Figure 17-9. Deploy to Azure

Click Next. Now you are presented with deploying to an Azure Web App, a container or a virtual machine as shown in Figure 17-10.

CHAPTER 17 DEPLOYING YOUR BLAZOR APPLICATION

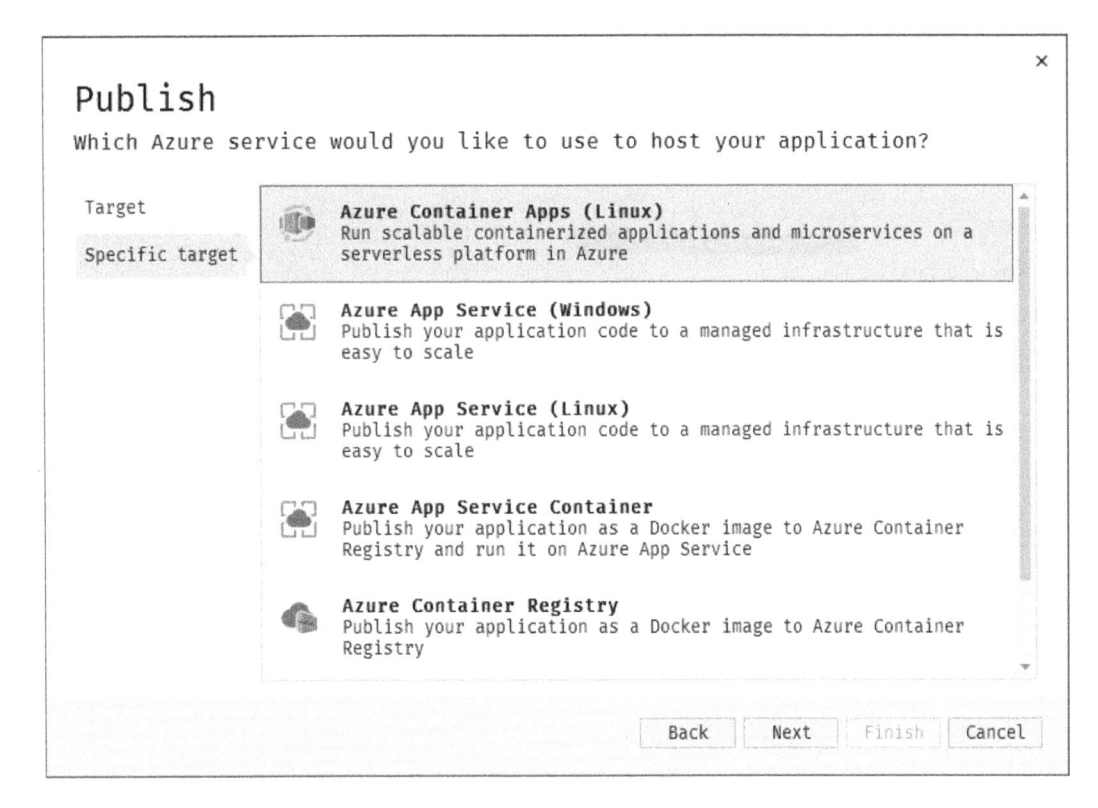

```
Publish
Which Azure service would you like to use to host your application?

Target              Azure Container Apps (Linux)
Specific target     Run scalable containerized applications and microservices on a
                    serverless platform in Azure

                    Azure App Service (Windows)
                    Publish your application code to a managed infrastructure that is
                    easy to scale

                    Azure App Service (Linux)
                    Publish your application code to a managed infrastructure that is
                    easy to scale

                    Azure App Service Container
                    Publish your application as a Docker image to Azure Container
                    Registry and run it on Azure App Service

                    Azure Container Registry
                    Publish your application as a Docker image to Azure Container
                    Registry

                                            Back    Next    Finish    Cancel
```

Figure 17-10. Azure deployment choices

Select Azure App Service (Windows) and click Next. Now the Select an Azure App Service dialog from Figure 17-11 appears. You can either select an existing App Service or create a new one.

543

CHAPTER 17   DEPLOYING YOUR BLAZOR APPLICATION

Figure 17-11. Select Azure App Service

Click the + button to add a new Azure App Service. Enter a unique name, select your azure subscription if you have more than one, and create a new resource group and hosting plan.

A resource group groups together a bunch of Azure resources, such as a Web App and its database, and allows you to manage and delete all of them as one. To create a new resource group, click New, and enter a new resource group name.

A hosting plan will select what kind of hardware your site will run on, and the data center where the hardware resides. Click New and enter a name, select a datacenter near you, and select the Free size. You can have up to 10 free hosting plans per region for your subscription.

Click Next again, and select the Publish option as in Figure 17-12. The other option will set up for you a Continuous Integration and Deployment using *GitHub Actions* which is a better option. With GitHub actions, you can have your site deployed automatically every time you push new features into your repository. If you would like to learn more about GitHub Actions, visit https://github.com/features/actions, or if you prefer a book, read https://www.apress.com/gp/book/9781484264638.

CHAPTER 17   DEPLOYING YOUR BLAZOR APPLICATION

```
Publish                                                    ×
How would you like to deploy your application?

Target              Publish (generates pubxml file)
Specific target     Deploys application to target on click of Publish button.

App Service         CI/CD using GitHub Actions workflows (generates yml file)
                    Deploys application to target automatically on code push to GitHub
Deployment type     repo.




                                            Back    Next    Finish    Cancel
```

Figure 17-12. Publish or use CI/CD

Select Finish.

Selecting Publishing Options

VS will now display the publish profile as in Figure 17-13, and you can change some of the deployment options before proceeding.

545

CHAPTER 17   DEPLOYING YOUR BLAZOR APPLICATION

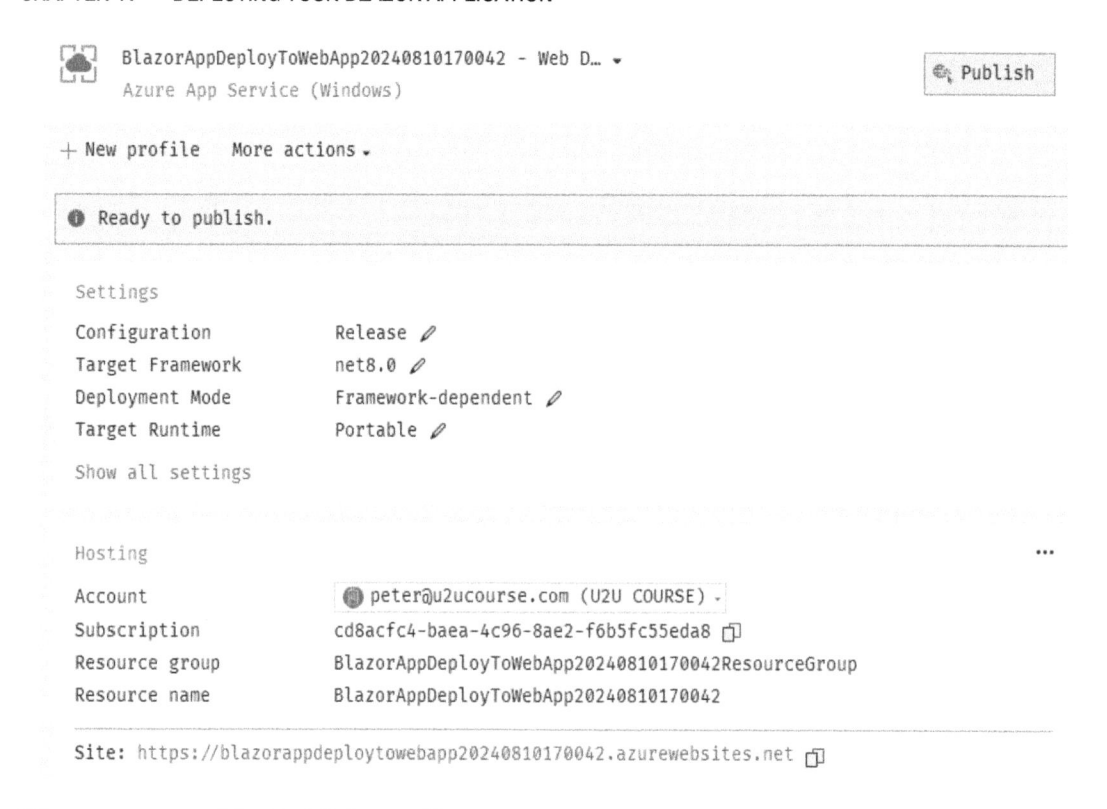

Figure 17-13. The Publish profile

Click the Show all settings link, which will display the publish options as in Figure 17-14. With the Deployment Mode dropdown, you can choose between Framework-dependent or Self-Contained as discussed previously in this chapter. Please select Self-Contained and win-x64 as the target runtime and Save.

CHAPTER 17   DEPLOYING YOUR BLAZOR APPLICATION

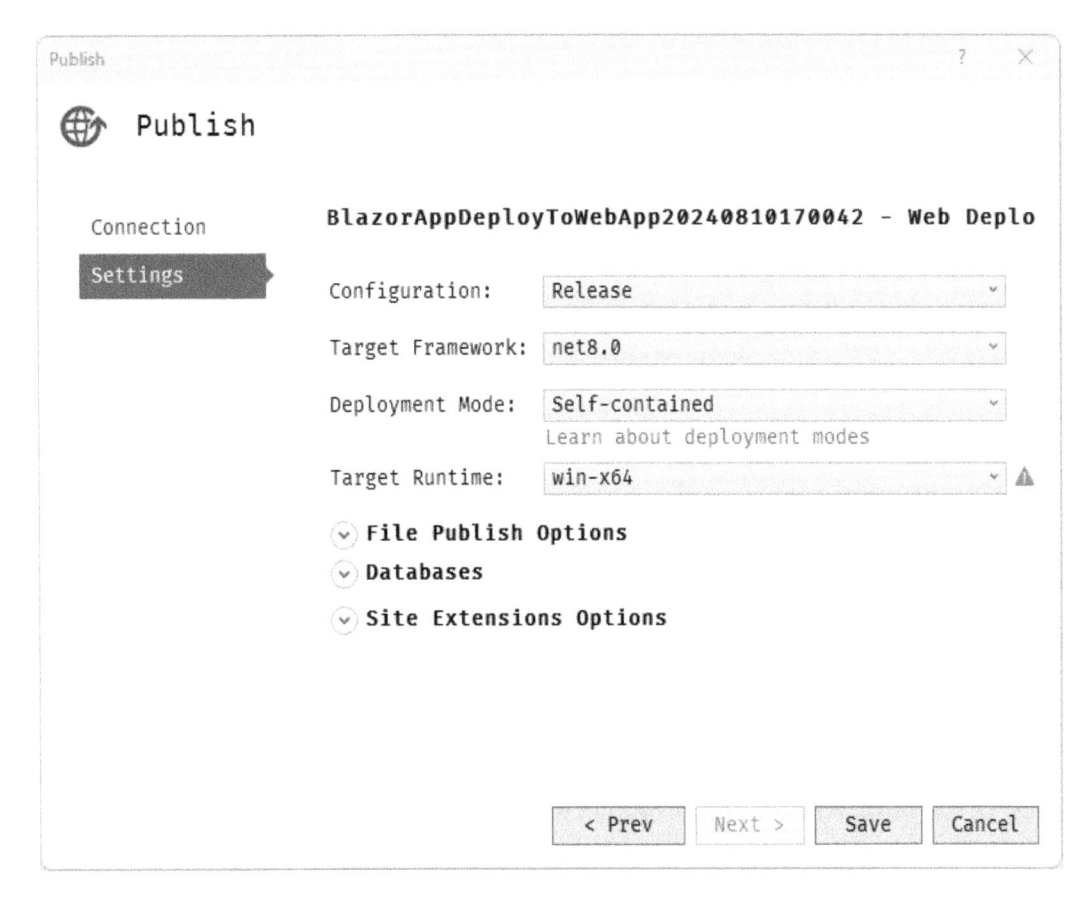

Figure 17-14. Publish options

Publishing the Application

Now you can click the Publish button as shown in the top-right corner of Figure 17-13. Visual Studio will build a release version and deploy it to Azure.

When publishing completes, an alert as in Figure 17-15 will be shown. Click the Navigate link to look at the result of the publish. Now everyone with an Internet connection can admire your work!

CHAPTER 17 DEPLOYING YOUR BLAZOR APPLICATION

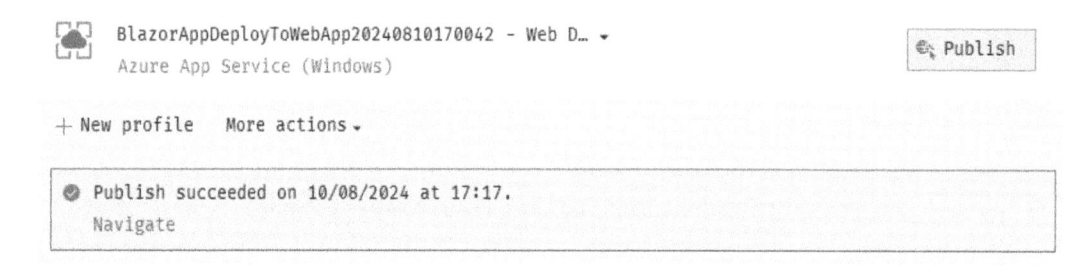

```
BlazorAppDeployToWebApp202408101700042 - Web D... ▾        Publish
Azure App Service (Windows)

+ New profile    More actions ▾

  ● Publish succeeded on 10/08/2024 at 17:17.
    Navigate
```

Figure 17-15. Publish complete

Summary

In this chapter, we looked at deploying a Blazor application. With a standalone Blazor WebAssembly application, all we need is a file server so the browser can download the HTML, CSS, JavaScript, and DLL files. As an example, we used GitHub to deploy to. Remember to set the `<base>` tag in the HTML page to match the location where the files are downloaded from.

Deploying a Blazor Web App project is just like deploying an ASP.NET Core site. As an example, we deployed our application to Azure as a WebApp. Visual Studio takes care of most of the work. Without Visual Studio, we can still create a deployment using the command line, and then we would need to upload the files onto the server. Each hosting provider has their own specific way of doing this.

CHAPTER 18

Security with OpenId Connect

Many web applications need some way to identity the user, also known as *authentication*. Sometimes this is only to show the user what they were looking at before, so we need an identity to retrieve the user's state from the server. Sometimes we need to protect certain resources, also known as *authorization*, which can be personal information, or contents that the user has paid for, or because of some legal requirement. In this chapter, we will look at *OpenId Connect*, and how we can use this to identify the user and decide what the current user can do.

Representing the User

Let us first discuss how we can represent users. You might think that we just need to know the user's name, but this is not true. We will represent the user as a collection of properties about the user, which can include the user's name, but also information like age and which department the user works for. We call this *claims-based security*. Some claims can represent things the user can do, these are known as roles. For example, one claim could state that the user has the admin role, allowing for our software to check the role instead of the name. Users can move around in an organization, and then you simply change the role-claims to give users permission to do things with the software.

Using Claims-Based Security

Claims-based security uses a *token* to represent the user, and this token is a collection of *claims* about the user. Claims represent statements about the user, for example, one claim could be that the user's first name is Peter. In real life we also have tokens, for example, your passport is a nice example of a token, containing claims such as your nationality, name, date of birth, etc. If this was all there was about a token, they would be worthless because anyone could create a token. Why does the airport security trust your passport? Because it was issued by a *trusted party*, also known as an *identity provider*. In my case the airport security trusts the claims on my passport because it was issued by the Belgian government. Passports use all kinds of nifty protections such as holograms to make it hard to create a passable fake passport. Tokens used by computers work in the same manner; they are issued by a trusted party, which uses a digital signature so that the *relying party* (the application) can verify to see if the token was issued by a trusted party known to the application. Of course, the identity provider will need a way to verify who the user is. They can use any means they want, a user and password combination, or some smart card you need to insert in a card reader. This whole process is illustrated in Figure 18-1.

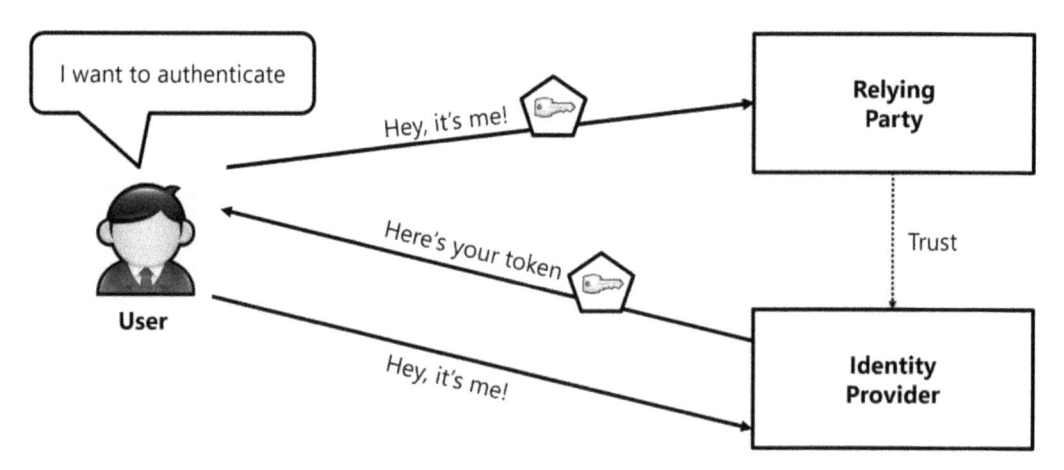

Figure 18-1. The authentication process

One more aspect about tokens is that once a user has received a token, the user can use it again and again without the need to go back to the identity provider. Of course, there needs to be a limit to this, and that is why tokens have a valid period, and after this period the user will need to get a new token. My passport was issued to me a couple of years ago, but I can still use it until it expires. Then I will have to go back to city hall and get a new one. Software tokens do not last that long, because it is easy to get a new one over the network.

Understanding Token Serialization

How are tokens serialized over a network? Modern applications using REST use the *JSON Web Token* (*JWT*) open standard. This allows us to transmit tokens in a secure way in the form of a JSON object.

JWT tokens are serialized as a base-64 encoded string, and each token consists of three parts, a header, a payload containing the claims, and a signature. Listing 18-1 shows an example of a serialized token. Each part of the token is separated with a dot (.).

Listing 18-1. A serialized token

```
eyJhbGciOiJSUzI1NiIsImtpZCI6InVibTdLa1BjQXZ5Z0NXYlR1djRVQWciLCJ0eXAiO
iJKV1QifQ.eyJuYmYiOjE2MjY5NTIzMDAsImV4cCI6MTYyNjk1MjYwMCwiaXNzIjoiaH-
R0cHM6Ly9sb2NhbGhvc3Q6NTAwMCIsImF1ZCI6ImJsYXpvciIsImlhdCI6MTYyNjk1M-
jMwMCwiYXRfaGFzaCI6Ik9oMFRJdXExZVh6S2pDaXExdVpKdGciLCJzX2hhc2giOiJOaWwwcml-
lZzUwdlBTdU45TVNnTzl3Iiwic2lkIjoibXBqODR0WkdNa0lORGtXUWgwROFNQSIsIn-
N1YiI6IjZkOTY4NjIxLTI3ZTAtNDZkYS1iNzNiLTlkNWNjODc4ZGIwYSIsImF1dGhfdG-
ltZSI6MTYyNjk1MjI5OSwiaWRwIjoibG9jYWwiLCJhbXIiOlsicHdkIl19.f0Rm_sVF
lwc2PnJwFmufrDLY9h1HJ6VnejdouMKhMY0wfyKLukUa6D3Zum5gRw-4jJQvevaBQe5d
GFmZzN24nS8bzT0C3UxSLUTtdNIajiQ5SpH0dkuM5HD09A0mdKygy5MizAsXTiClOymXF
Xun-gS1YfM2mezrvjJbhgY-gRAxCyOnnPaIDs1M6gQ_zMuyblwznj5ovo-Hh_tWD3qHE_
ttEsDJe6KR9aM1-Qyz87sKn-wL_oo6DKiyCimG_y6qe27hjmuSg-B5BD0eOUEaHEpSHXwrdJCTu
YAY88Jx2k5W_fDnqwWPFx9Yvtkycp-nrBoOlbsOEzByj8QHOCoTBg
```

This token is not human readable, but using a tool like `https://jwt.io`, you can easily inspect the token's content. Doing this reveals that this token contains following header with the type of the token (JWT) and the signing algorithm:

```
{
  "alg": "RS256",
  "kid": "ubm7KkPcAvygCWbTuv4UAg",
  "typ": "JWT"
}
```

CHAPTER 18   SECURITY WITH OPENID CONNECT

Generally, you should ignore the header, but the payload contains the following claims:

```
{
  "nbf": 1626952300,
  "exp": 1626952600,
  "iss": "https://localhost:5000",
  "aud": "blazor",
  "iat": 1626952300,
  "at_hash": "OhoTIuq1eXzKjCiq1uZJtg",
  "s_hash": "Nil0rieg50vPSuN9MSgO9w",
  "sid": "mpj84NZGMkINDkWQhOGAMA",
  "sub": "6d968621-27e0-46da-b73b-9d5cc878db0a",
  "auth_time": 1626952299,
  "idp": "local",
  "amr": [
    "pwd"
  ]
}
```

The **issuer** claim (iss) states that this token was issued by my development identity provider with URL https://localhost:5000, and the **not before** claim (nbf) together with the **expiry** claim (exp) gives this token a validity period. The **audience** claim (aud) states that this token is intended for the application called blazor. Finally, the **subject** claim (sub) contains a unique identifier for the current user. There are a lot of other official claims you can find in a token, and you can find their meaning on the IANA JSON Web Token Registry's site at https://www.iana.org/assignments/jwt/jwt.xhtml.

Note   The payload of the token is not encrypted, so never include sensitive information in here!

The signature allows our software to check if the token has been modified, and again you should ignore this (but not our software!).

Representing Claims In .NET

So how are claims represented on .NET? From the start, Microsoft has provided us with two interfaces to represent the user, `IPrincipal` and `IIdentity`.

The `IPrincipal` interface represents the security context for the current user, including the user's identity (the `IIdentity` interface) and roles. It is implemented by the `ClaimsPrincipal` class which holds a collection of `Claim` instances in its `Claims` property. Our code will use the `ClaimsPrincipal` instance to see if a user holds a certain claim. For example, we can retrieve the user's name using the implementation from Listing 18-2.

Listing 18-2. Retrieving the name of the user from ClaimsPrincipal

```
Claim givenNameClaim =
  authState.User.FindFirst(ClaimTypes.GivenName);
```

Here we use the `AuthenticationState` class (more details later) with the `User` property of type `ClaimsPrincipal`. The `ClaimsPrincipal` class has the `FindFirst` method which will search the collection of `Claims` and returns the claim with given key or returns a `null` if there is no claim with the given key. The key can be anything you like, but there are many predefined standard keys to represent common things about users, such as the name, email, etc. Here I use the `ClaimTypes` class which holds the name of most standard claims.

OpenId Connect

OpenId Connect is a standard protocol that allows us to secure our applications, including websites, mobile applications, and server and desktop applications. Because of differences in application types, OpenId Connect describes several flows, such as Resource Owner Password Credentials, Client Credentials, Implicit, Authorization Code, and Hybrid flow. With Blazor we will use the Hybrid and Authorization Code flows. Now let us have a look at some flows.

CHAPTER 18   SECURITY WITH OPENID CONNECT

Understanding OpenId Connect Hybrid Flow

In Blazor Server, we will use the *Hybrid flow*, so let us review how this flow works as illustrated in Figure 18-2.

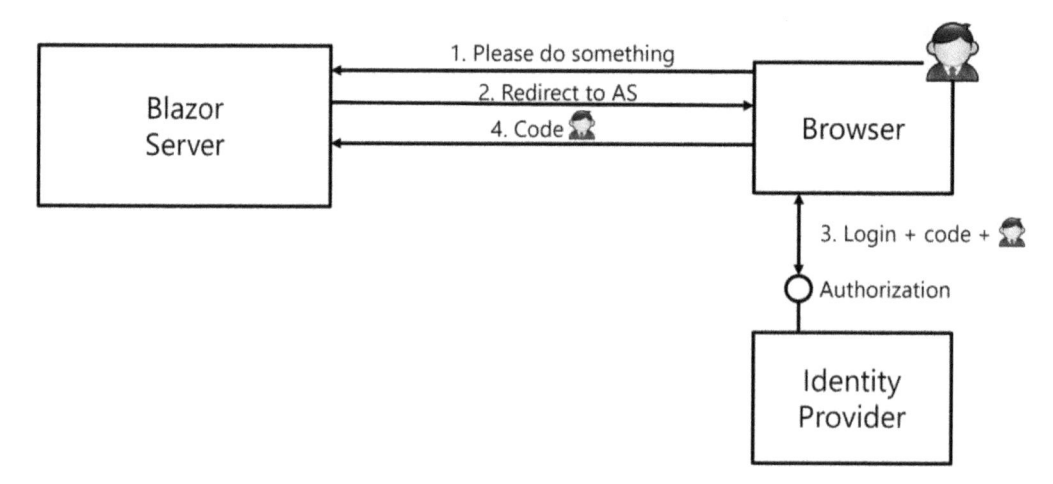

Figure 18-2. *The OpenId Connect hybrid flow*

This figure shows the Identity Provider, our Blazor Server application, and the user using a browser. When we look at Blazor WebAssembly, we will review Authorization Code flow.

When the not yet authenticated user visits a protected resource (step 1), the Blazor Server will return a HTTP redirect result (step 2) which will make the browser visit the identity provider, also known as an authorization server (AS). The URL contains credential information about the client (the ClientId) together with a redirect URI. The identity provider identifies the client application through its ClientId and verifies if the redirect URL matches its list of registered client redirect URLs. The Identity Provider will then present the user with some kind of login UI (step 3), for example, to enter the username and password. The identity provider is free how this login process works, and after a successful login, the identity provider will return a HTTP redirect to the browser (step 4) so the browser will visit the redirect URL (the Blazor Server application) with the request containing a code and identity token. The redirect URL is then processed by the Blazor application, the identity token is turned into a `ClaimsPrincipal,` and the user has been authenticated. The Blazor application is also responsible for storing the `ClaimsPrincipal`, and with Blazor Server, this is done by storing the `ClaimsPrincipal` in a cookie, so the next request containing that cookie can deserialize it again. For the moment, we don't need the code, but we will use it later.

CHAPTER 18 SECURITY WITH OPENID CONNECT

A couple of remarks: An Identity Provider will only send tokens to known redirect URLs, so these must be registered with the identity provider. This prevents unknown parties (hackers!) from hijacking requests. When you deploy your application, you should not forget to register the new redirect URL in the Identity Provider. There can be several registered redirect URLs, so you can keep developing locally and run the application in production using the same identity provider.

Identity Providers

There are many identity providers out there. For example, there is Microsoft Entra, Google, Facebook, etc. Each of these identity providers comes with their own UI, but if they use OpenID Connect, the implementation works on the same principles.

Here I want to use Duende IdentityServer (https://github.com/DuendeSoftware/IdentityServer) which allows you to build your own identity provider for free (however, Identity Server is not free for commercial use). These people need to eat too!

Implementing the Identity Provider with IdentityServer

Let us start by creating the project that we will use as our identity provider, using IdentityServer. Create a new ASPNET Core Empty project and name it IdentityProvider.

Modify the ports in Properties/launchSettings.json as in Listing 18-3. Our identity provider needs to run on another URL, and changing the port is the easiest way. Here we will use HTTPS port 5011.

Listing 18-3. Changing the port

```
"profiles": {
  "http": {
    ...
  },
  "https": {
    "commandName": "Project",
    "dotnetRunMessages": true,
    "launchBrowser": true,
    "applicationUrl": "https://localhost:5011;http://localhost:5209",
    "environmentVariables": {
```

CHAPTER 18 SECURITY WITH OPENID CONNECT

```
      "ASPNETCORE_ENVIRONMENT": "Development"
    }
  },
  "IIS Express": {
    ...
  }
}
```

Use NuGet to add the latest stable version of *Duende.IdentityServer* or modify your project directly as in Listing 18-4.

Listing 18-4. Use NuGet to add IdentityServer

```
<Project Sdk="Microsoft.NET.Sdk.Web">

  <PropertyGroup>
    <TargetFramework>net8.0</TargetFramework>
    <Nullable>enable</Nullable>
    <ImplicitUsings>enable</ImplicitUsings>
  </PropertyGroup>

  <ItemGroup>
    <PackageReference Include="Duende.IdentityServer" Version="7.0.6" />
  </ItemGroup>

</Project>
```

Configure dependency injection for IdentityServer by modifying the `Program` class as in Listing 18-5.

Listing 18-5. Configuring dependency injection

```
using IdentityProvider;

internal class Program
{
  private static void Main(string[] args)
  {
```

CHAPTER 18 SECURITY WITH OPENID CONNECT

```
    var builder = WebApplication.CreateBuilder(args);

    builder.Services
      .AddIdentityServer()
    ;
```

And use IdentityServer in the ASP.NET Pipeline as in Listing 18-6.

Listing 18-6. Adding IdentityServer to the pipeline

```
var app = builder.Build();
app.UseIdentityServer();
app.Run();
```

IdentityServer can be configured using a database or an in-memory configuration. We will use the latter because it is easier for learning and experimentation. Add a new class called `Config` to the project next to Program.cs. This `Config` class will contain the configuration for IdentityServer.

First, we need a couple of users, so add the `GetUsers` method from Listing 18-7.

Listing 18-7. Adding users to IdentityServer

```
public static List<TestUser> GetUsers()
=> [
  new TestUser
  {
    SubjectId = "{223C9865-03BE-4951-8911-740A438FCF9D}",
    Username = "peter@u2u.be",
    Password = "u2u-secret",
    Claims = new List<Claim>
    {
      new Claim("given_name", "Peter"),
      new Claim(JwtClaimTypes.Name, "Peter Himschoot"),
      new Claim("family_name", "Himschoot"),
    }
  },
  new TestUser
  {
```

557

```
    SubjectId = "{34119795-78A6-44C2-B128-30BFBC29139D}",
    Username = "student@u2u.be",
    Password = "u2u-secret",
    Claims = new List<Claim>
    {
      new Claim("given_name", "Student"),
      new Claim(JwtClaimTypes.Name, "Student Blazor"),
      new Claim("family_name", "Blazor"),
    }
  }
];
```

We use IdentityServer's `TestUser` class which allows us to set the `SubjectId` unique key, `Username`, `Password`, and `Claims`. We also add a couple of standard identifying claims which belong to the *Profile* scope. *Scopes* are used to group a number of claims and can be requested during the authentication process.

Next, we need to add a couple of identity resources with the `GetIdentityResources` method from Listing 18-8.

Listing 18-8. Adding identity resources

```
public static IEnumerable<IdentityResource>
  GetIdentityResources()
=> [
  new IdentityResources.OpenId(),
  new IdentityResources.Profile(),
];
```

These map to scopes that will give us access to certain claims from configuration. Scopes are used to group claims and provide an easy way to request claims. The `OpenId` method will give us access to the subject id (`sid`) with is a unique identifier of the current user, and the `Profile` method gives us access to claims about the user such as given_name and family_name.

We will also need to add the client applications that our identity provider will support. For the moment we will only have one client, so implement the `GetClients` method as in Listing 18-9.

CHAPTER 18　SECURITY WITH OPENID CONNECT

Listing 18-9. Adding clients

```
public static IEnumerable<Client> GetClients()
=> [
  new Client
  {
    ClientName = "Blazor Server",
    ClientId = "BlazorServer",
    AllowedGrantTypes = GrantTypes.Hybrid,
    RedirectUris = new List<string>{
      "https://localhost:5002/signin-oidc"
    },
    RequirePkce = false,
    AllowedScopes = {
      IdentityServerConstants.StandardScopes.OpenId,
      IdentityServerConstants.StandardScopes.Profile
    },
    ClientSecrets = { new Secret("u2u-secret".Sha512()) },
    RequireConsent = true
  }
];
```

Here we added the `ClientId` and `ClientSecrets` which the client will use to prove itself. We will use the *Hybrid* flow as described before, and we set the `RedirectUris` to include the client's URL. We also need to configure which scopes our client application will get. The Profile and OpenId scopes are provided by default, but we will add more scopes later, and it does not hurt to be explicit.

Now we are ready to complete the configuration as in Listing 18-10.

Listing 18-10. Adding users, identity resources, and clients

```
builder.Services
  .AddIdentityServer(options =>
  {
    options.EmitStaticAudienceClaim = true;
  })
  .AddInMemoryIdentityResources(
```

CHAPTER 18   SECURITY WITH OPENID CONNECT

```
    Config.GetIdentityResources())
  .AddTestUsers(Config.GetUsers())
  .AddInMemoryClients(Config.GetClients())
  .AddDeveloperSigningCredential()
;
```

Here we are adding our users, identity resources, and clients. We also need a valid certificate for signing, and when developing, we can use the `AddDeveloperSigningCredentials`. When you move to production, you will have to get a valid certificate and use the `AddSigningCredentials` method.

You can now run your identity provider if you like. However, you will not get any UI until we complete the next step. IdentityServer will emit logging in the console, for example:

```
info: Duende.IdentityServer.Startup[0]
      Starting Duende IdentityServer version
7.0.6+765116a2d4fb0671b6eba015e698533900c61c8e (.NET 8.0.7)
warn: Duende.IdentityServer.License[0]
      You do not have a valid license key for the Duende software. This
is allowed for development and testing scenarios. If you are running in
production you are required to have a licensed version. Please start a
conversation with us: https://duendesoftware.com/contact
warn: Duende.IdentityServer.License[0]
      You have automatic key management enabled, but you do not have a
license. This feature requires the Business or Enterprise Edition tier of
license. Alternatively you can disable automatic key management by setting
the KeyManagement.Enabled property to false on the IdentityServerOptions.
info: Duende.IdentityServer.Startup[0]
      **You are using the in-memory version of the persisted grant store.
This will store consent decisions, authorization codes, refresh and
reference tokens in memory only. If you are using any of those features in
production, you want to switch to a different store implementation.**
info: Duende.IdentityServer.Startup[0]
      Using the default authentication scheme idsrv for IdentityServer
info: Microsoft.Hosting.Lifetime[14]
      Now listening on: https://localhost:5011
```

```
info: Microsoft.Hosting.Lifetime[14]
      Now listening on: http://localhost:5209
info: Microsoft.Hosting.Lifetime[0]
      Application started. Press Ctrl+C to shut down.
info: Microsoft.Hosting.Lifetime[0]
      Hosting environment: Development
info: Microsoft.Hosting.Lifetime[0]
      Content root path: C:\Code\GitHub\microsoft-blazor-book-4\Ch18\
OpenIdConnect\BlazorWithOpenIdConnect\src\IdentityProvider
```

Adding the Login UI to our Identity Provider

When our users want to login to the identity provider, the identity provider will present a login screen to the user. IdentityServer comes with a built in UI, so here we will add this to the IdentityProvider project.

Getting everything installed is easy with dotnet CLI.

You can get all files installed using dotnet CLI using the following command from your IdentityProvider project's folder:

```
dotnet new install Duende.IdentityServer.Templates
dotnet new isui
```

This will install two new folders called Pages and keys and will also install some css and scripts in the wwwroot folder.

Of course, we need to add support for Razor Pages in the IdentityProvider project so it can render the login and consent pages. Configure dependency injection as in Listing 18-11.

Listing 18-11. Configure services for MVC

```
var builder = WebApplication.CreateBuilder(args);
```

builder.Services.AddRazorPages();

And use the middleware from Listing 18-12 in the pipeline.

CHAPTER 18   SECURITY WITH OPENID CONNECT

Listing 18-12. Adding MVC middleware

```
var app = builder.Build();
app.UseStaticFiles();
app.UseRouting();
app.UseIdentityServer();
app.UseAuthorization();
app.MapRazorPages().RequireAuthorization();

app.Run();
```

Running the application will show the UI like Figure 18-3.

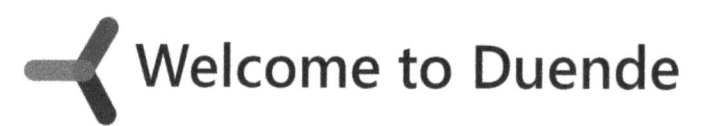

Welcome to Duende IdentityServer (version 7.0.6)

IdentityServer publishes a discovery document where you can find metadata and links to all the endpoints, key material, etc.

Click here to see the claims for your current session.

Click here to manage your stored grants.

Click here to view the server side sessions.

Click here to view your pending CIBA login requests.

Here are links to the source code repository, and ready to use samples.

Figure 18-3. The identity server home page

Click the second link (see the claims), and you will be asked to login (with one of our users from Listing 18-7) after which it will display the claims just like Figure 18-4.

CHAPTER 18   SECURITY WITH OPENID CONNECT

Authentication Cookie

Claims

sub
{223C9865-03BE-4951-8911-740A438FCF9D}

name
peter@u2u.be

idp
local

amr
pwd

auth_time
1723387264

Properties

session_id
3E0177FD3A9D83CFBF5B8C162310727A

.issued
Sun, 11 Aug 2024 14:41:04 GMT

.expires
Mon, 12 Aug 2024 00:41:04 GMT

Figure 18-4. Displaying the user's claims

Understanding User Consent

OpenId Connect is used to authenticate users, but it is also used to allow an application to access another application's resources. Facebook, for example, uses this to allow third-party applications to use Facebook's identity provider as an authentication mechanism and then to post things on your Facebook page. When the user logs in for the first time, an identity provider should tell the user which claims will be used by the application, and a user can then decide which claims it will allow. IdentityServer's default UI will look somewhat like Figure 18-5. This will list the personal information that the application will be able to access and any APIs that the application can access on the user's behalf. Users can then click the "Yes, allow" button after optionally unchecking any claims they don't want to share. Next time the identity provider will not ask this question again because this information is stored by the identity provider. Because we are running IdentityServer in memory, every time we re-run the IdentityProvider project, you will be asked for consent. Listing 18-9 has enabled this user consent, and while developing you can use this to temporarily test stuff by unchecking claims and see how your application reacts to this missing claim. Feel free to disable user consent during development if you find it annoying.

563

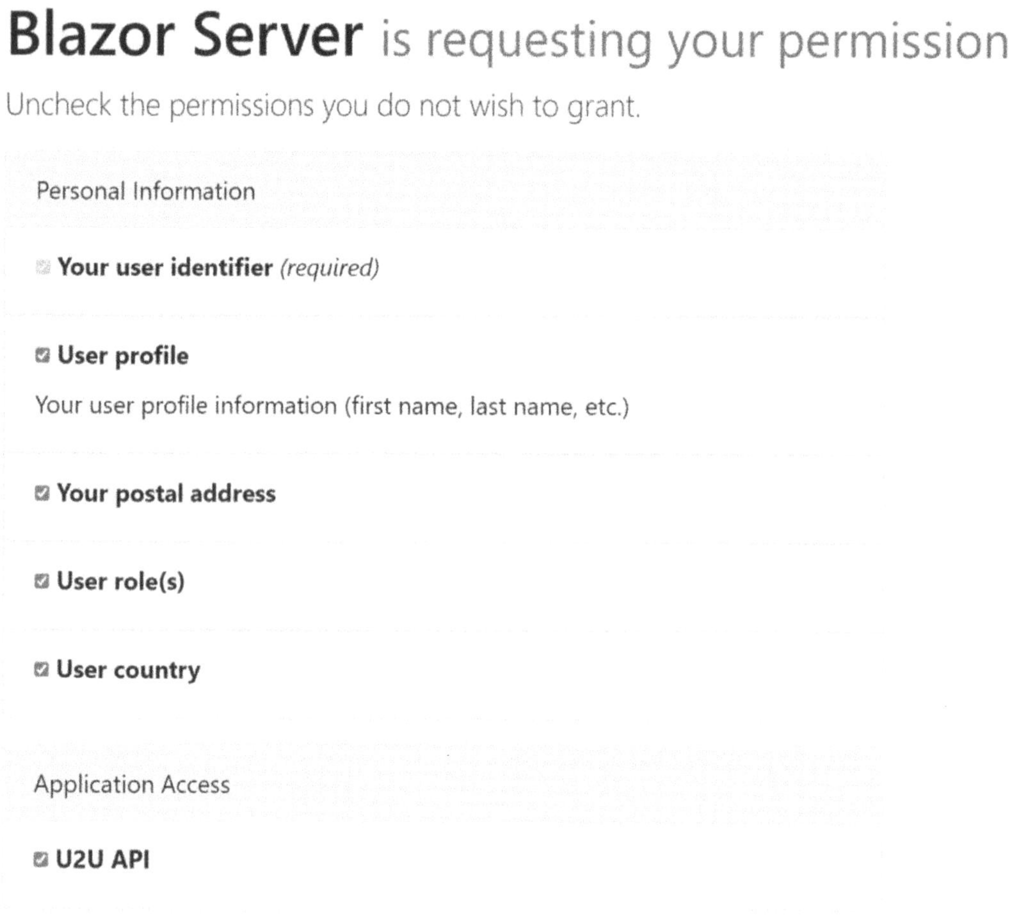

CHAPTER 18   SECURITY WITH OPENID CONNECT

Blazor Server is requesting your permission

Uncheck the permissions you do not wish to grant.

Personal Information

☑ **Your user identifier** *(required)*

☑ **User profile**
Your user profile information (first name, last name, etc.)

☑ **Your postal address**

☑ **User role(s)**

☑ **User country**

Application Access

☑ **U2U API**

Figure 18-5. The user consent screen

Protecting a Blazor Server Application with Hybrid Flow

Now that we have our own identity provider, we can build a Blazor Server application and secure it. Later we will do the same for Blazor WebAssembly and Blazor Web Apps.

Add a new Blazor WebApp application, with global Server interactive render mode to the existing solution and name it BlazorApp.Server.WithOpenIdConnect. This will generate the project without any authentication components. In the next chapter on using OpenId Connect with Blazor WebAssembly, you will use a more practical approach that will generate the authentication components for you using the Authentication Type set to Individual Accounts.

Also modify the port of the Blazor server application to use port 5002, mimicking the port for this client in Listing 18-9.

Adding OpenId Connect to Blazor Server

Add the `Microsoft.AspNetCore.Authentication.OpenIdConnect` package to the BlazorApp.Server.WithOpenIdConnect project.

Now add Listing 18-13 to the `Program` class of your Blazor Server project.

Listing 18-13. Configuring authentication

```
var builder = WebApplication.CreateBuilder(args);

builder.Services.AddAuthentication(options =>
{
  options.DefaultScheme =
    CookieAuthenticationDefaults.AuthenticationScheme;
  options.DefaultChallengeScheme =
    OpenIdConnectDefaults.AuthenticationScheme;
})
.AddCookie(CookieAuthenticationDefaults.AuthenticationScheme);
```

This tells authentication to retrieve and store the `ClaimsPrincipal` in a cookie and use it as the `DefaultScheme`. You can also configure the cookie's name and expiry period here, but we will go with the defaults. We are also telling the middleware that when the user is not yet authenticated that it should use OpenId Connect through the `DefaultChallengeScheme` property.

Next, we should add the authentication/authorization middleware in the `Program` class as shown in Listing 18-14.

Listing 18-14. Add authentication middleware

```
app.UseHttpsRedirection();

app.UseStaticFiles();
app.UseAntiforgery();
```

CHAPTER 18　SECURITY WITH OPENID CONNECT

```
app.UseAuthentication();
app.UseAuthorization();

app.MapRazorComponents<App>()
    .AddInteractiveServerRenderMode();
```

We still need to tell the OpenIdConnect middleware where it should go if there is no valid cookie containing the `ClaimsPrincipal`. Add Listing 18-15 to the `Program` class right after the `AddCookie` method.

Listing 18-15. Configuring OpenId Connect

```
.AddCookie(CookieAuthenticationDefaults.AuthenticationScheme)
.AddOpenIdConnect(OpenIdConnectDefaults.AuthenticationScheme,
  options =>
  {
    options.SignInScheme =
      CookieAuthenticationDefaults.AuthenticationScheme;
    options.Authority = "https://localhost:5011";
    options.ClientId = "BlazorServer";
    options.ClientSecret = "u2u-secret";
    options.ResponseType = "code id_token";
    // It's recommended to always get claims from the
    // UserInfoEndpoint during the flow.
    options.GetClaimsFromUserInfoEndpoint = true;
  });

builder.Services.AddRazorComponents()
    .AddInteractiveServerComponents();
```

Here we set the `Authority` property to the URL of the Identity Provider (which runs on localhost port 5011), and we pass the `ClientId` and `ClientSecret` of the Client we configured in Listing 18-9. We also tell it to use the hybrid flow (`code id_token`) and that it should get the profile claims such as given_name from the userinfo endpoint which will result in a smaller initial id token.

Implementing Authorization in Blazor Server

Before running the application, we should also protect one of our resources; otherwise, there is no need to authenticate using the identity provider. But first we need to understand how authentication works in Blazor using the `AuthenticationState` and `AuthenticationStateProvider` classes.

AuthenticationState

The `AuthenticationState` class allows access to the current user's claims with the User property of type `ClaimsPrincipal`, and the `AuthenticationStateProvider` abstracts away how we retrieve the current `AuthenticationState`, because the process is different in Blazor Server and Blazor WebAssembly. You should always use the `AuthenticationStateProvider` in your Blazor components if you want these to work in both Blazor Server and Blazor WebAssembly. Update the Home component's as in Listing 18-16 which contains a nice example of how you do this.

Listing 18-16. Using the AuthenticationState in a component

```
@page "/"
@using Microsoft.AspNetCore.Authorization
@using Microsoft.AspNetCore.Components.Authorization
@using System.Security.Claims
@attribute [Authorize]

<PageTitle>Home</PageTitle>

<h1>Welcome @UserName</h1>

@if (Claims is not null)
{
  foreach (Claim claim in Claims)
  {
    <p>@claim.Type - @claim.Value</p>
  }
}
```

```
@code {

  [Inject]
  public required AuthenticationStateProvider
    AuthenticationStateProvider { get; set; }

  private IEnumerable<Claim>? Claims { get; set; }

  public string UserName { get; set; } = "Unknown";

  protected override async Task OnInitializedAsync()
  {
    AuthenticationState authState =
      await AuthenticationStateProvider
            .GetAuthenticationStateAsync();

    if (authState is not null)
    {
      Claims = authState.User.Claims;
      Claim? givenNameClaim =
        authState.User.FindFirst("given_name");
      if (givenNameClaim is not null)
      {
        UserName = givenNameClaim.Value;
      }
    }
  }
}
```

Here we use the `AuthenticationStateProvider` received through dependency injection and call its `GetAuthenticationStateAsync` asynchronous method. In Blazor Server, the user's `ClaimsPrincipal` is stored in the `HttpContext.User` property so `AuthenticationStateProvider` retrieves it there.

When we receive a non-null `AuthenticationState` instance, we set the `Claims` and `UserName` properties for use in the component, which we use to display the `UserName` property and iterate over each `Claim` and display it. We also protect the Home link using the `Authorize` attribute so only authenticated users can see it.

CHAPTER 18   SECURITY WITH OPENID CONNECT

Explicit Login and Logout

Let us see how we can redirect the user to the identity provider and back. Add a new component called LogInOrOut with contents from Listing 18-17.

Listing 18-17. The LogInOrOut component

```
@using Microsoft.AspNetCore.Components.Authorization
@implements IDisposable

@inject NavigationManager NavigationManager

<div class="nav-item px-3">
  <AuthorizeView>
    <Authorized>
      <form action="authentication/logout" method="post">
        <AntiforgeryToken />
        <input type="hidden" name="ReturnUrl" value="@currentUrl" />
        <button type="submit" class="nav-link">
          <span class="bi bi-arrow-bar-left-nav-menu" aria-hidden="true">
          </span> Logout @context.User.Identity?.Name
        </button>
      </form>
    </Authorized>
    <NotAuthorized>
      <a class="nav-link" href="@LoginUrl">
        <span class="bi bi-person-badge-nav-menu" aria-hidden="true"></span> Login
      </a>
    </NotAuthorized>
  </AuthorizeView>
</div>

@code {
  private string? currentUrl;

  protected override void OnInitialized()
```

CHAPTER 18 SECURITY WITH OPENID CONNECT

```
  {
    currentUrl = NavigationManager.ToBaseRelativePath(NavigationManager.Uri);
    NavigationManager.LocationChanged += OnLocationChanged;
  }

  private void OnLocationChanged(object? sender,
  LocationChangedEventArgs e)
  {
    currentUrl = NavigationManager.ToBaseRelativePath(e.Location);
    StateHasChanged();
  }

  public void Dispose()
  {
    NavigationManager.LocationChanged -= OnLocationChanged;
  }

  private string LoginUrl => "authentication/login?returnUrl=" + currentUrl;
}
```

This Blazor component uses the built-in `AuthorizeView` component to either display a Login or a Logout button, based whether the user is already logged in. We will discuss this component in the next section. When you click the login link, it will redirect to the authentication/login URL and in a similar manner to the authentication/logout URL. This component will also provide the Login URL with the page to redirect to after the login. When you are on the /counter page, after the login, you will be redirected back to the /counter page. How does that work? This `LogInOrOut` component tracks the current URL using the `NavigationManager`. Each time the user clicks on another route, the `LocationChanged` event triggers which updates the `currentUrl`. This `currentUrl` is then used to set the `href` of the login and logout links.

Now we need to react to the login and logout URL, so add the `LoginLogoutEndpointRouteBuilderExtensions` class from Listing 18-18.

Listing 18-18. Handling Login and Logout

```
using Microsoft.AspNetCore.Authentication;
using Microsoft.AspNetCore.Authentication.Cookies;
using Microsoft.AspNetCore.Authentication.OpenIdConnect;
```

CHAPTER 18 SECURITY WITH OPENID CONNECT

```
namespace Microsoft.AspNetCore.Routing;

internal static class LoginLogoutEndpointRouteBuilderExtensions
{
  internal static IEndpointConventionBuilder MapLoginAndLogout(this
  IEndpointRouteBuilder endpoints)
  {
    RouteGroupBuilder group = endpoints.MapGroup("");

    group.MapGet("/login", (string? returnUrl) => TypedResults.Challenge(Ge
    tAuthProperties(returnUrl)))
        .AllowAnonymous();

    // Sign out of the Cookie and OIDC handlers. If you do not sign out
    with the OIDC handler,
    // the user will automatically be signed back in the next time they
    visit a page that requires authentication
    // without being able to choose another account.
    group.MapPost("/logout", (string? returnUrl) => TypedResults.SignOut(Ge
    tAuthProperties(returnUrl),
        [CookieAuthenticationDefaults.AuthenticationScheme,
        OpenIdConnectDefaults.AuthenticationScheme]));

    return group;
  }

  private static AuthenticationProperties GetAuthProperties(string?
returnUrl)
  {
    // TODO: Use HttpContext.Request.PathBase instead.
    const string pathBase = "/";

    // Prevent open redirects.
    if (string.IsNullOrEmpty(returnUrl))
    {
      returnUrl = pathBase;
    }
    else if (!Uri.IsWellFormedUriString(returnUrl, UriKind.Relative))
```

```
    {
      returnUrl = new Uri(returnUrl, UriKind.Absolute).PathAndQuery;
    }
    else if (returnUrl[0] != '/')
    {
      returnUrl = $"{pathBase}{returnUrl}";
    }

    return new AuthenticationProperties { RedirectUri = returnUrl };
  }
}
```

This method adds two endpoints to our server application. The /login endpoint returns a `Challenge` result, which triggers the authentication middleware to perform authentication by redirecting to the login page from our IdentityProvider project. The /logout endpoint returns a `SignOut` result, which tells the Authentication middleware to logout and redirects to the IdentityProvider project to notify it about the logout. Do note that here you list all the authentication providers (you could let the user choose between different providers, such as Google, Facebook, GitHub, etc. In this case you would list all of them).

We also need to call the `MapLoginAndLogout` method in the Program class as listed in Listing 18-19.

Listing 18-19. Invoking MapLoginAndLogout

```
app.MapRazorComponents<App>()
    .AddInteractiveServerRenderMode();

app.MapGroup("/authentication").MapLoginAndLogout();

app.Run();
```

Now we can use the LogInOrOut component. Open the NavMenu component, and add it to the end as in Listing 18-20.

Listing 18-20. Using the LogInOrOut component

```
<div class="nav-scrollable" onclick="document.querySelector('.navbar-
toggler').click()">
  <nav class="flex-column">
    <div class="nav-item px-3">
      ...

    <div class="nav-item px-3">
      <NavLink class="nav-link" href="weather">
        <span class="bi bi-list-nested-nav-menu"
              aria-hidden="true"></span> Weather
      </NavLink>
    </div>

    <LogInOrOut />
  </nav>
</div>
```

You might want to copy the NavMenu.razor.css and LogInOrOut.razor.css files from the provided sources and copy them next to their component.

One more thing. The `AuthorizeView` requires access to the `AuthenticationState` using a cascading property. Add Listing 18-21 to the program class to take care of that.

Listing 18-21. Adding the Cascading AuthenticationState

```
builder.Services.AddCascadingAuthenticationState();

// Add services to the container.
builder.Services.AddRazorComponents()
    .AddInteractiveServerComponents();
```

This method gives any component access to the current `AuthenticationState`. For example, modify the `Counter` component as in Listing 18-22.

573

CHAPTER 18   SECURITY WITH OPENID CONNECT

Listing 18-22. Using Cascading AuthenticationState in your component

```
@page "/counter"
@using Microsoft.AspNetCore.Components.Authorization
@using System.Security.Claims

<PageTitle>Counter</PageTitle>

<h1>Counter @UserName</h1>

<p role="status">Current count: @currentCount</p>

<button class="btn btn-primary" @onclick="IncrementCount">Click me</button>

@code {

  [CascadingParameter]
  public required Task<AuthenticationState>? AuthenticationStateTask { get; set; }

  public string UserName { get; set; } = "Unknown";

  protected override async Task OnInitializedAsync()
  {
    if( AuthenticationStateTask is null)
    {
      return;
    }

    AuthenticationState auth = await AuthenticationStateTask;

    Claim? givenNameClaim =
      auth?.User.FindFirst("given_name");
    if (givenNameClaim is not null)
    {
      UserName = givenNameClaim.Value;
    }
  }

  private int currentCount = 0;
```

```
    private void IncrementCount()
    {
      currentCount++;
    }
}
```

Walkthrough

Let us walk through the authentication process step by step. First start the IdentityProvider project; next start the Blazor.Server.OpenIdConnect project.

Note Please do not forget to always start the IdentityProvider project; the easiest way with Visual Studio is to set up multiple startup projects. The latest version of Visual Studio even allows you to create multiple configurations!

On the Browser tab for the localhost:5002 URL, open the browser debugger on the Network tab and now click on the Login link in your Blazor application. You should see Figure 18-6.

Name	Status
login?returnUrl=	302
authorize?client_id=BlazorServer&redirect_uri=http...REpUG&x-client-SKU=ID_...	302
Login?ReturnUrl=%2Fconnect%2Fauthorize%2Fcallback%...x-client-SKU%3DID...	200
bootstrap.min.css	200
bootstrap-glyphicons.min.css	200
site.css	200
duende-logo.svg	200
jquery.slim.min.js	200
bootstrap.bundle.min.js	200

Figure 18-6. Redirecting to the Identity Provider

This shows that clicking the Login link or visiting any protected page (first line) will redirect (Status 302) to the IdentityServer's authorize endpoint (second line), which will then cause the middleware to redirect (Status 302 again) to the identity provider (third line) which will show its login page. Should your browser immediately show the Home component, you need to clear your cookies and try again.

CHAPTER 18   SECURITY WITH OPENID CONNECT

After completing the Login process, you will be redirected to the Blazor server's signin-oidc URL which will be handled by the OpenId Connect middleware. This middleware will convert the identity token into a `ClaimsPrincipal` and redirect to the original URI that initiated the login process. The Cookie middleware will serialize the `ClaimsPrincipal` into a cookie (it might use multiple cookies because of the limited length of cookies). The browser then will process the original URI, convert the cookie into ClaimsPrincipal, and because now the user is authenticated will give access to the Home component.

Select the signin-oidc URL in the browser's debugger, and open the Payload tab. You will see that this will return the code and the identity token as in Figure 18-7.

Figure 18-7.   Receiving the code and id token

You can inspect the id token by copying its value; open another browser tab on `https://jwt.io` and pasting the value as shown in Figure 18-8.

CHAPTER 18 SECURITY WITH OPENID CONNECT

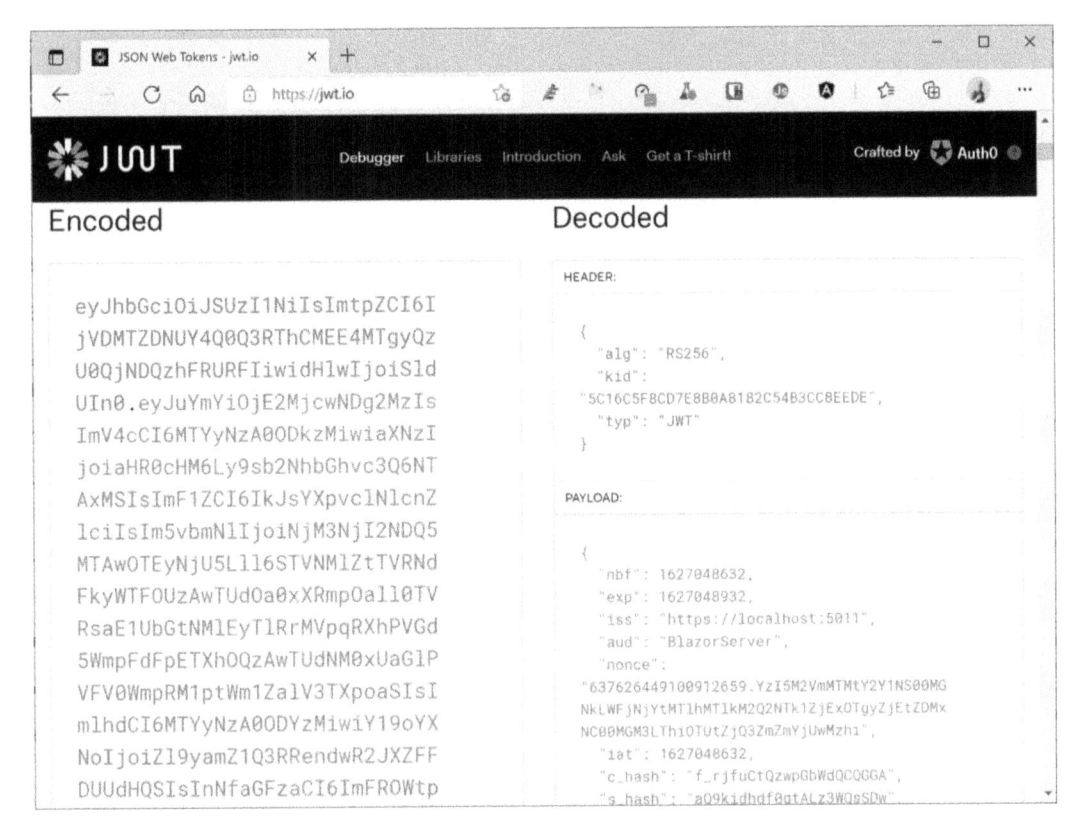

Figure 18-8. Using jwt.io to inspect a token

Congratulations. You have just added authentication to your Blazor Server application!

Using AuthorizeView

How can we show different things to the user depending on if that user is logged in or not? Blazor comes with the `AuthorizeView` templated component, which has three properties `Authorized`, `NotAuthorized`, and `Authorizing` which will render a UI when the user is authorized, not authorized, and in the process of authorizing. We used this to modify our navigation menu to either show a Login link, or a Logout link as in Listing 18-17. Do note that the `AuthorizeView` requires a `CascadingAuthenticationState`, which we added earlier.

Run the application, and login. Then click the logout link which will take you to the identity server logout page as shown in Figure 18-9.

CHAPTER 18   SECURITY WITH OPENID CONNECT

Duende IdentityServer

Logout You are now logged out

Figure 18-9. *The Logout page*

The problem here is that this page will stay put; now the user must manually navigate to the site to login back again. There are solutions for this, but that is outside the scope of this chapter. Please consult Duende IdentityServer's documentation on this.

Adding and Removing Claims

Let us add another claim for our users; let's say we need to know the country of the user. We will need to add a scope to the identity provider, and then we will need to request this scope from the client. Start by adding the country claim to each user as in Listing 18-23.

Listing 18-23. Adding an additional claim to the users

```
public static List<TestUser> GetUsers()
=> [
  new TestUser
  {
    SubjectId = "{223C9865-03BE-4951-8911-740A438FCF9D}",
    Username = "peter@u2u.be",
    Password = "u2u-secret",
    Claims = new List<Claim>
    {
      new Claim("given_name", "Peter"),
      new Claim(JwtClaimTypes.Name, "Peter Himschoot"),
      new Claim("family_name", "Himschoot"),
```

```
          new Claim("country", "BE")
        }
    },
    new TestUser
    {
        SubjectId = "{34119795-78A6-44C2-B128-30BFBC29139D}",
        Username = "student@u2u.be",
        Password = "u2u-secret",
        Claims = new List<Claim>
        {
            new Claim("given_name", "Student"),
            new Claim(JwtClaimTypes.Name, "Student Blazor"),
            new Claim("family_name", "Blazor"),
            new Claim("country", "UK")
        }
    }
];
```

Now we need to add a new scope (using an IdentityResource) for address to the GetIdentityResources method as in Listing 18-24.

Listing 18-24. Adding an IdentityResource for country

```
public static IEnumerable<IdentityResource>
    GetIdentityResources() => [
        new IdentityResources.OpenId(),
        new IdentityResources.Profile(),
        new IdentityResource(name: "country",
            displayName: "User country",
            userClaims: [ "country" ])
    ];
```

And we should allow this scope for our client application as in Listing 18-25.

CHAPTER 18 SECURITY WITH OPENID CONNECT

Listing 18-25. Allowing the country scope for a client

```
new Client
{
  ClientName = "Blazor Server",
  ClientId = "BlazorServer",
  AllowedGrantTypes = GrantTypes.Hybrid,
  RedirectUris = ["https://localhost:5002/signin-oidc"],
  PostLogoutRedirectUris = [ "https://localhost:5002/" ],
  RequirePkce = false,
  AllowedScopes = {
    IdentityServerConstants.StandardScopes.OpenId,
    IdentityServerConstants.StandardScopes.Profile,
    "country"
  },
  ClientSecrets = { new Secret("u2u-secret".Sha512()) },
  RequireConsent = true
},
```

Now we can request this claim in our client application by adding the country scope as in Listing 18-26.

Listing 18-26. Requesting the country scope

```
.AddOpenIdConnect(OpenIdConnectDefaults.AuthenticationScheme,
  options =>
  {
    ...
    options.GetClaimsFromUserInfoEndpoint = true;
    options.Scope.Add("country");
    options.ClaimActions.MapUniqueJsonKey("country", "country");
  });
```

The `MapUniqueJsonKey` will retrieve the address from the JWT and create the country claim.

Running the application and logging in again (!) will show the country claim.

580

Enabling Role-Based Security

Currently we have claims that allow us to identify the user. We have the user's name and country. But what if we would like to protect certain parts of our application so only certain users can access it? Should we check a long list of usernames? No, in this case we will define several roles, assign these roles to some of our users, and only allow access when the user has a specific role. This is known as *role-based access control* (*RBAC*).

Start by adding some role claims to each user as in Listing 18-27. Here Peter will have the admin role, while Student will have the tester role.

Listing 18-27. Adding user roles

```
public static List<TestUser> GetUsers()
=> [
  new TestUser
  {
    SubjectId = "{223C9865-03BE-4951-8911-740A438FCF9D}",
    Username = "peter@u2u.be",
    Password = "u2u-secret",
    Claims = new List<Claim>
    {
      new Claim("given_name", "Peter"),
      new Claim(JwtClaimTypes.Name, "Peter Himschoot"),
      new Claim("family_name", "Himschoot"),
      new Claim("country", "BE"),
      new Claim("role","admin")
    }
  },
  new TestUser
  {
    SubjectId = "{34119795-78A6-44C2-B128-30BFBC29139D}",
    Username = "student@u2u.be",
    Password = "u2u-secret",
    Claims = new List<Claim>
    {
      new Claim("given_name", "Student"),
```

```
    new Claim(JwtClaimTypes.Name, "Student Blazor"),
    new Claim("family_name", "Blazor"),
    new Claim("country", "UK"),
    new Claim("role","tester")
      }
    }
];
```

This also means we need to add a roles scope, so update the `GetIdentityResources` method as in Listing 18-28. This also illustrates how we can add a custom `IdentityResource`. The `displayName` property is used during user consent.

Listing 18-28. Adding a roles scope

```
public static IEnumerable<IdentityResource>
GetIdentityResources() => [
  new IdentityResources.OpenId(),
  new IdentityResources.Profile(),
  new IdentityResource(name: "country",
    displayName: "User country", userClaims: [ "country" ]),
  new IdentityResource(name: "roles",
    displayName: "User role(s)",
    userClaims: [ "role" ]),
];
```

And in our client's configuration, we add the roles scope as in Listing 18-29.

Listing 18-29. Adding the roles scope

```
new Client
{
  ClientName = "Blazor Server",
  ClientId = "BlazorServer",
  AllowedGrantTypes = GrantTypes.Hybrid,
  RedirectUris = ["https://localhost:5002/signin-oidc"],
  PostLogoutRedirectUris = [ "https://localhost:5002/" ],
  RequirePkce = false,
  AllowedScopes = {
```

```
    IdentityServerConstants.StandardScopes.OpenId,
    IdentityServerConstants.StandardScopes.Profile,
    "country",
    "roles"
  },
  ClientSecrets = { new Secret("u2u-secret".Sha512()) },
  RequireConsent = true
}
```

All like adding the country scope. Guess what we need to do in our Blazor application? Same steps as for country, but with one additional piece of code as in Listing 18-30 that declares the "role" claim to be used for RBAC.

Listing 18-30. Declaring the roles scope and role claim

```
options.Scope.Add("roles");
options.ClaimActions.MapUniqueJsonKey("roles", "roles");
options.TokenValidationParameters = new()
{
  RoleClaimType = "role"
};
```

Run the application, login again, and the user's role should be shown.

Now we can protect one of our routes. Add the `Authorize` attribute to the Counter component as in Listing 18-31. With the `Authorize` attribute, we can verify if the user has a certain role.

Listing 18-31. Using the Authorize attribute for RBAC

```
@page "/counter"
@using Microsoft.AspNetCore.Authorization
@using Microsoft.AspNetCore.Components.Authorization
@using System.Security.Claims

@attribute [Authorize(Roles = "admin")]
```

We can also use the `AuthorizeView` component to show certain content based on a user's role, for example, add Listing 18-32 to the Home component.

Listing 18-32. Using AuthorizeView to show additional content

```
<AuthorizeView Roles="admin">
  <Authorized>
    Hey, you're an admin!
  </Authorized>
</AuthorizeView>
```

We can do the same in the NavMenu component as in Listing 18-33 to hide the Counter component when the user does not have the proper role.

Listing 18-33. Hiding NavLinks in the NavMenu

```
<AuthorizeView Roles="admin">
  <Authorized>
    <div class="nav-item px-3">
      <NavLink class="nav-link" href="counter">
        <span class="bi bi-plus-square-fill-nav-menu"
              aria-hidden="true"></span> Counter
      </NavLink>
    </div>
  </Authorized>
</AuthorizeView>
```

Run and login with a user who has the admin role, you should see the counter link in the navigation bar, and it should appear when you click it. Do the same for a user without the admin role, now there should be no counter link in the navigation bar, and even manually modifying the browser's URL to `/counter` will redirect to the login screen.

Accessing a Secured API

Where are we? We can use OpenId Connect to implement the authentication for our Blazor Server site, and we can use roles to protect certain sections of our application, either by writing code using the `AuthenticationState` or declaratively using the `Authorize` and `AuthorizeView` classes. This is enough when your Blazor Server accesses data itself. There is one more thing. Your Blazor Application might need to access a protected API running in another application. How do we do this? The answer is of course more claims!

CHAPTER 18   SECURITY WITH OPENID CONNECT

Using an Access Token

Access tokens are just ordinary tokens, but they don't contain information about the user; they contain information about the client application and what the current user can do with the API. Because the API is yet another application, both should use the same identity provider. The client application (Blazor) can then use an OpenId Connect flow to request an access token from the identity provider and use it to access the API. Let us look at this process using the OpenId Connect hybrid flow as shown in Figure 18-10.

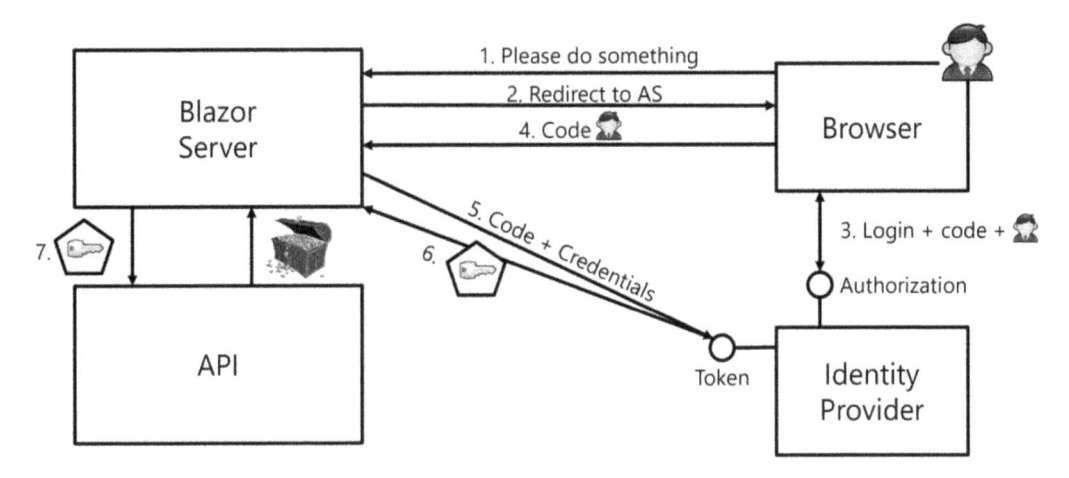

Figure 18-10. *API authorization with OpenId Connect hybrid flow*

Steps 1 through 4 as the same as before, and our Blazor Server application receives an identity token and a code (which we ignored until now). This code can then be used together with the Blazor Server application's identifying information to retrieve an access token (step 5) from the identity provider. The identity provider will then use the code to verify which claims it should give to the Blazor server application (step 6). Once our application has an access token, it can send it along with the API request (step 7) using a header to the API application, which can then use the claims in the access token to determine how it should behave.

Let us create an API application and register it with our identity provider. Add a new ASP.NET Core Web API project and name it WeatherAPI. Change its launchSettings to run HTTPS at port 5005 as in Listing 18-34.

585

CHAPTER 18 SECURITY WITH OPENID CONNECT

Listing 18-34. Change the API project's port

```
https": {
 "commandName": "Project",
 "dotnetRunMessages": true,
 "launchBrowser": true,
 "launchUrl": "swagger",
 "applicationUrl": "https://localhost:5005;http://localhost:5148",
 "environmentVariables": {
    "ASPNETCORE_ENVIRONMENT": "Development"
 }
```

Run the API project. By default, it will open the browser and show the *Swagger* UI as in Figure 18-11. This will allow you to test the API (which is currently unprotected).

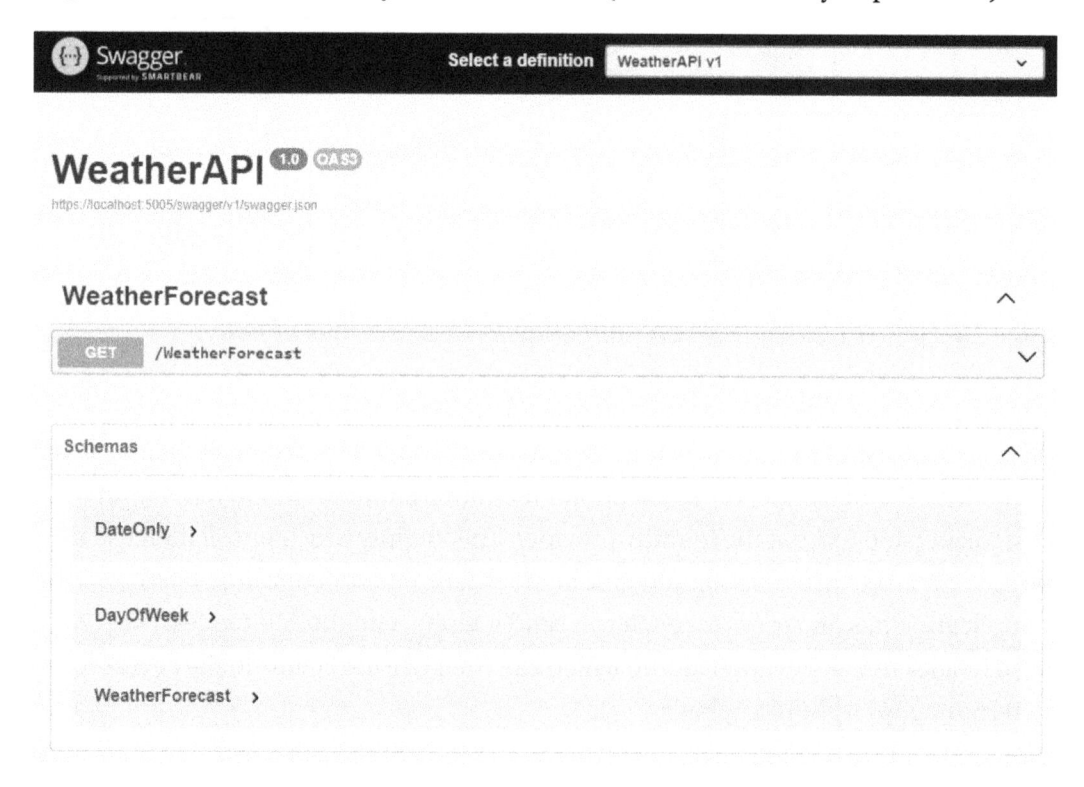

Figure 18-11. *The Swagger UI*

Click the GET button, and then click Try It Out and then Execute. You should see some forecasts.

CHAPTER 18　SECURITY WITH OPENID CONNECT

Since our client will come from another origin, we also need to enable CORS. Add Listing 18-35 to the API's Program class. Here we allow any origin because we will use an access token to protect our services.

Listing 18-35. Creating the CORS policy

```
internal class Program
{
  private static void Main(string[] args)
  {
    var builder = WebApplication.CreateBuilder(args);

    // Add services to the container.

    builder.Services.AddControllers();
    // Learn more about configuring Swagger/OpenAPI at https://aka.ms/
        aspnetcore/swashbuckle
    builder.Services.AddEndpointsApiExplorer();
    builder.Services.AddSwaggerGen();

    builder.Services.AddCors(options =>
    {
      options.AddPolicy("CorsPolicy",
        builder =>
                builder.AllowAnyOrigin()
                .AllowAnyMethod()
                .AllowAnyHeader());
    });

    var app = builder.Build();

    // Configure the HTTP request pipeline.
    if (app.Environment.IsDevelopment())
    {
      app.UseSwagger();
      app.UseSwaggerUI();
    }
```

CHAPTER 18 SECURITY WITH OPENID CONNECT

```
    app.UseHttpsRedirection();
    app.UseCors("CorsPolicy");

    app.UseAuthorization();

    app.MapControllers();

    app.Run();
  }
}
```

Register the API Project with the Identity Provider

Now we are ready to register the WeatherAPI client with our identity provider. To do this we create an APIScope, so add Listing 18-36. Add this after the GetClients method in the identity provider's Config class. This APIScope will be included in the scope claim and is used to verify if the client has access.

Listing 18-36. Adding an APIScope

```
public static IEnumerable<ApiScope> GetApiScopes()
=> [
  new ApiScope("u2uApi", "U2U API")
];
```

We also need to create an APIResource so add Listing 18-37 below the GetApiScopes method.

Listing 18-37. Creating an ApiResource

```
public static IEnumerable<ApiResource> GetApiResources()
=> [
  new ApiResource("u2uApi", "U2U API")
  {
      Scopes = [ "u2uApi" ]
  }
];
```

CHAPTER 18 SECURITY WITH OPENID CONNECT

We can now grant our Blazor Server application access to this API resource by adding the API scope to the client's `AllowedScopes` as in Listing 18-38.

Listing 18-38. Allowing the client to access an API

```
new Client
{
  ClientName = "Blazor Server",
  ...
  AllowedScopes = {
    IdentityServerConstants.StandardScopes.OpenId,
    IdentityServerConstants.StandardScopes.Profile,
    "country",
    "roles",
    "u2uApi"
  },
  ClientSecrets = { new Secret("u2u-secret".Sha512()) },
  RequireConsent = true
},
```

Finally, we should invoke the `Config.GetApiScopes` and `Config.GetApiResources` methods as in Listing 18-39.

Listing 18-39. Registering the Api scopes and Api resources

```
builder.Services
  .AddIdentityServer(options =>
  {
    options.EmitStaticAudienceClaim = true;
  })
  .AddInMemoryIdentityResources(Config.GetIdentityResources())
  .AddTestUsers(Config.GetUsers())
  .AddInMemoryClients(Config.GetClients())
  .AddDeveloperSigningCredential()
  .AddInMemoryApiScopes(Config.GetApiScopes())
  .AddInMemoryApiResources(Config.GetApiResources())
;
```

589

CHAPTER 18 SECURITY WITH OPENID CONNECT

Adding JWT Bearer Token Middleware

A client application will send the access token using a HTTP Authorization Bearer header, and we need our API project to look for this header and install the `ClaimsPrincipal` from the access token. Use NuGet to install the `Microsoft.AspNetCore.Authentication.JwtBearer` package in the WeatherAPI project.

Now we can register this JWT handling using dependency injection, so add Listing 18-40 to the WeatherAPI project's `Program` class.

Listing 18-40. Adding JWT authentication

```
builder.Services
  .AddAuthentication("Bearer")
  .AddJwtBearer("Bearer", opt =>
  {
    // for development purposes, disable in production!
    opt.RequireHttpsMetadata = false;
    opt.Authority = "https://localhost:5011";
    opt.Audience = "u2uApi";
  });
```

Authentication will look for the Bearer header, convert the JWT access token into a `ClaimsPrincipal`, and then process the request. We need to set the `Authority` property to the trusted identity provider's URL (which in our case uses port 5011), and we use the `Audience` property so set the u2uApi scope to use. Do note that we are hardcoding everything here; for a real production application, we should read this from configuration because these settings will change going into production.

And don't forget to add the Authentication and Authorization middleware as in Listing 18-41.

Listing 18-41. Adding the Authentication middleware

```
app.UseCors("CorsPolicy");

app.UseAuthentication();
app.UseAuthorization();

app.MapControllers();

app.Run();
```

That's all for the moment for our WeatherAPI.

Enabling the Bearer Token in the Client

Our client application should now use the received code to request an access token from the identity provider and use it in its API requests.

Update the Blazor Server WeatherForecastService as in Listing 18-42. This class uses the IHttpClientFactory interface to create an HttpClient instance. We do this so we can configure it to automatically use the access token.

Listing 18-42. The WeatherForecastService

```
using System;
using System.Net.Http;
using System.Net.Http.Json;
using System.Threading.Tasks;

namespace Blazor.Server.OpenIdConnect.Data
{
  public class WeatherForecastService
  {
    private readonly IHttpClientFactory httpClientFactory;

    public WeatherForecastService(
      IHttpClientFactory httpClientFactory)
    => this.httpClientFactory = httpClientFactory;

    public async ValueTask<WeatherForecast[]> GetForecastAsync(
      DateTime startDate)
```

CHAPTER 18 SECURITY WITH OPENID CONNECT

```
    {
      HttpClient httpClient =
        this.httpClientFactory
            .CreateClient(nameof(WeatherForecastService));
      var result =
        await httpClient
          .GetFromJsonAsync<WeatherForecast[]>("weatherforecast");
      return result;
    }
  }
}
```

We also need to configure dependency injection in the Blazor Server project to give us an instance of the IHttpClientFactory. The IHttpClientFactory will give us a HttpClient that will be configured for us to include the access token, and which will send it as a Bearer token to the API.

Proceed by adding the new API scope to our list of scopes as in Listing 18-43.

Listing 18-43. Adding the API scope to the client

```
// Save the tokens we receive from the IDP
options.SaveTokens = true;

options.Scope.Add("u2uApi");
```

We should also enable persistence for our tokens. When you set the SaveTokens option to true, the tokens received from the identity provider (IDP) are stored in the authentication properties. These properties are accessible via the HttpContext in your application. This can be useful in scenarios where you need to use these tokens later in the application, for example, to call other APIs on behalf of the user or to perform token-based actions.

Now to exchange the code for an access token, add the IdentityModel.AspNetCore package to the client project. This package will take care of things like exchanging the code for an access token and attaching it to the HttpClient request. Now we can add this to dependency injection, so add Listing 18-44 to the Program class of the client project. Now when the WeatherService creates the HttpClient instance through the IHttpClientFactory, it will be configured with the access token.

Listing 18-44. Add token management

```
builder.Services.AddAccessTokenManagement();
builder.Services.AddUserAccessTokenHttpClient(
  nameof(WeatherService), null,
  client =>
  {
    client.BaseAddress = new Uri("https://localhost:5005");
  });
builder.Services.AddScoped<WeatherService>();
```

Start the IdentityProvider project, next the WeatherServices project, and finally the Blazor.Server.OpenIdConnect project. Logout (if you're still logged in) and Login again. This will refresh our tokens.

Now we can use the debugger to inspect the `ClaimsPrincipal` in the WeatherServices project. Put a breakpoint on the `Get` method, and now use the client to fetch the forecasts. Debugging should stop on the breakpoint, and now we can use the watch window to inspect the `this.User` property as in Figure 18-12.

CHAPTER 18   SECURITY WITH OPENID CONNECT

```
Watch 1
Search (Ctrl+E)                              Search Depth: 3
Name                                Value
▲ ⚙ this.User                       {System.Security.Claims.ClaimsPrincipal}
  ▲ ⚙ Claims                        {System.Security.Claims.ClaimsPrincipal.<get_Claims>d__22}
    ▷ Non-Public members
    ▲ Results View                  Expanding the Results View will enumerate the IEnumerable
      ▷ [0]                         {nbf: 1627567401}
      ▷ [1]                         {exp: 1627571001}
      ▷ [2]                         {iss: https://localhost:5011}
      ▷ [3]                         {aud: u2uApi}
      ▷ [4]                         {client_id: BlazorServer}
      ▷ [5]                         {http://schemas.xmlsoap.org/ws/2005/05/identity/claims/nameiden...
      ▷ [6]                         {auth_time: 1627567399}
      ▷ [7]                         {http://schemas.microsoft.com/identity/claims/identityprovider: local}
      ▷ [8]                         {jti: 8111B26C3B2028A1181135014B1CCFCD}
      ▷ [9]                         {sid: 414DD47CD67FF29DA51F811B0837984A}
      ▷ [10]                        {iat: 1627567401}
      ▷ [11]                        {scope: openid}
      ▷ [12]                        {scope: profile}
      ▷ [13]                        {scope: address}
      ▷ [14]                        {scope: roles}
      ▷ [15]                        {scope: u2uApi}
      ▷ [16]                        {http://schemas.microsoft.com/claims/authnmethodsreferences: pwd}
```

Figure 18-12. The WeatherServices ClaimsPrincipal

If the results view is empty, you will need to review your code because you forgot something. You should see the `scope: u2uApi` claim.

Now we can protect our `WeatherForecastController`'s `Get` method by adding the `Authorize` attribute as in Listing 18-45.

Listing 18-45. Protecting the WeatherForecastController

```
using Microsoft.AspNetCore.Authorization;
using Microsoft.AspNetCore.Mvc;

namespace WeatherAPI.Controllers;
[ApiController]
[Route("[controller]")]
public class WeatherForecastController : ControllerBase
{
    ...

    [Authorize]
```

594

CHAPTER 18 SECURITY WITH OPENID CONNECT

```
[HttpGet(Name = "GetWeatherForecast")]
public IEnumerable<WeatherForecast> Get()
{
  ...
}
}
```

Run everything again; you should be able to retrieve the weather forecasts using the Blazor Server application where you logged in first, but when you use the Swagger UI, you will get a `401 Unauthorized` as in Figure 18-13.

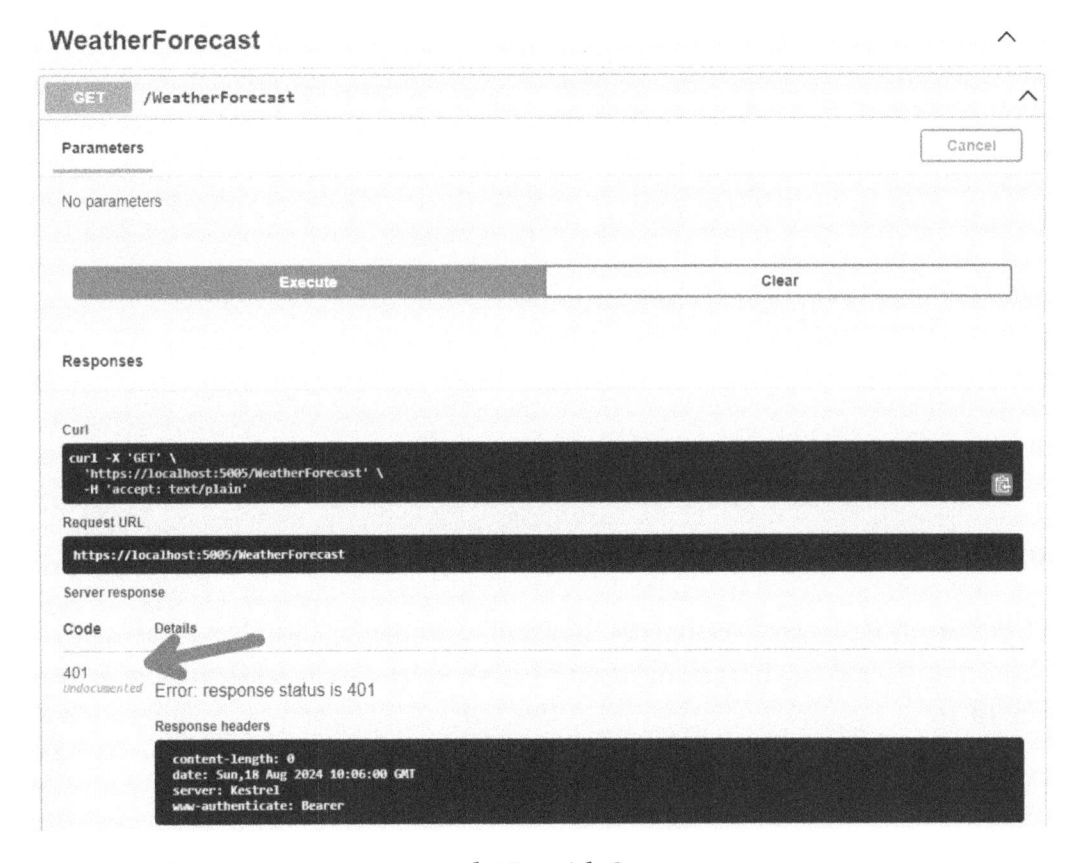

Figure 18-13. Accessing a protected API with Swagger

Let us examine the Authorization header being sent. Since this is a request emanating from the server, we cannot use the browser's debugger to look at the request. However, we can use the debugger itself. Put a breakpoint inside the WeatherForecastController's Get method. Navigate to the Weather component in

595

CHAPTER 18 SECURITY WITH OPENID CONNECT

your client application to hit the Get method. Use the watch windows to look at the controller's HttpContext.Request.Headers. You should see the Authorization header and expand it to look at its value as shown in Figure 18-14.

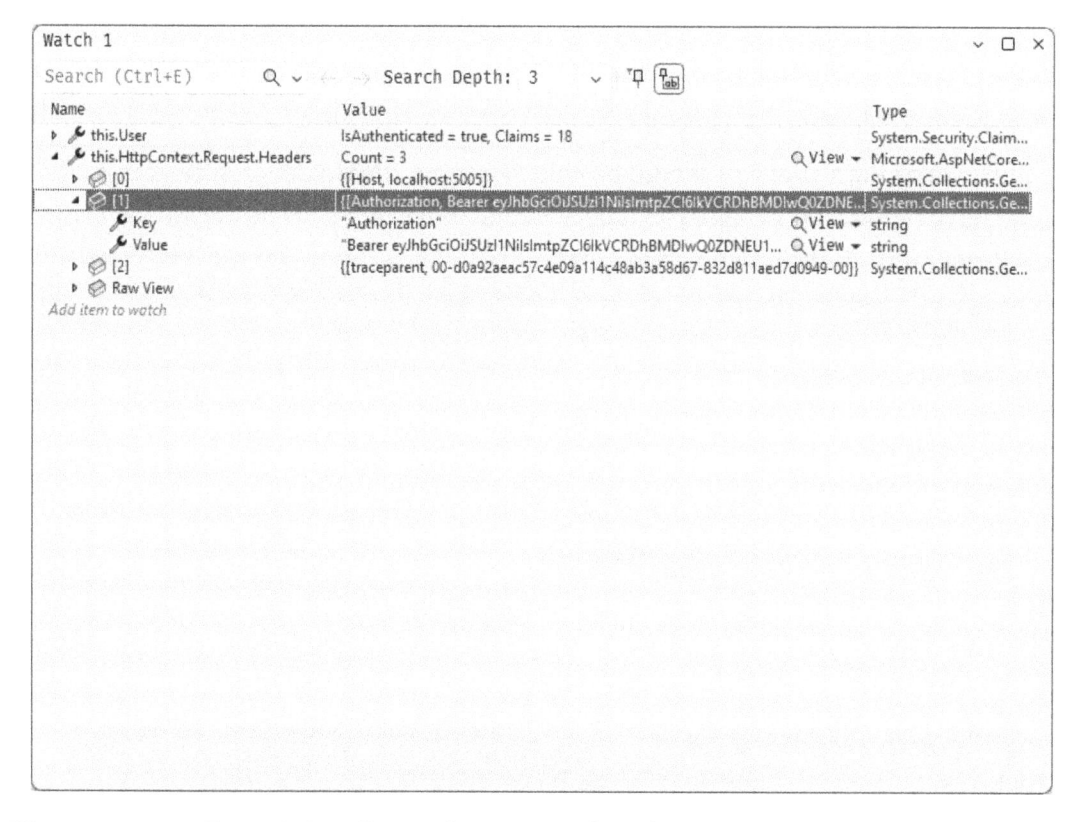

Figure 18-14. Examining the Authorization header

If you are using a recent version of Visual Studio examining the token is easy, click the magnifying class next to the header's value which should show the screen in Figure 18-15.

596

CHAPTER 18 SECURITY WITH OPENID CONNECT

```
Text Visualizer                                                      ˅ ☐ ×
Expression:   (new Microsoft.AspNetCore.Server.Kestrel.Core.Internal.Http.HttpHeaders.HttpHeadersDebugView(this.Htt|↻
String manipulation:   JWT Decode
Header:
{
  "alg": "RS256",
  "kid": "EBD8A020CFC4E55CBED35E1B7711E61E",
  "typ": "at+jwt"
}
Payload:
    "u2uApi",
    "https://localhost:5011/resources"
  ],
  "scope": [
    "openid",
    "profile",
    "country",
    "roles",
    "u2uApi"
  ],
  "amr": [
    "pwd"
  ],
Signature:
AfLdjFXJgFMFnNLgVQj5O6LoYeBsQoMy7-eQ074qRp-TZQNeF1JM7sWmqT9gqmKsLLJQRNgdS0yxBkGWKFpCkoyrDyI6Gvx601gKVsV-
BVKJbXquLN_XsuItb0zWnqTzAj1jeJkXIa4EWFbpDm6f1P2gGkKJ9xqb4P_8nswcPoI1FzG0zjrrwg-4XuLk5xaR5Pov95fpJ1Qb6odn_kF2j220vq6WBFT
O1tP9wzL7ds0gf58YP7p3hkUhY9z3S6FQ1LHEo3xT184v2DU7ayZAunWSgHXJyvvVLGmw8OPYmEv1_yHCEVhYawMxO7fim93fG9F7LdAvGpx6PgHQIc3PzQ

☑ Word Wrap
```

Figure 18-15. Examining the Authorization header's value

You should see the scope claim with value u2uApi.

Using Policy-Based Access Control

What if we want to use one or more claims to determine if the user can access a certain resource? For example, we might only want to allow authenticated users that live in Belgium to access the forecasts. In that case, we can use *Policy-Based Access Control* (*PBAC*).

Policies allow us to combine claims to determine if the user can access a certain component or API resource. You can even build complex policies that can, for example, check the age of a user by using the birthdate claim. We could accomplish the same just with roles, but this requires a lot more maintenance of the user's roles. And we don't like maintenance, do we? With PBAC we need to create a policy instance and then apply this policy to the protected resource using the `Authorize` attribute. Let us enhance our application with this as an example.

Remember where we added the country claim to our users? We will check this claim in the WeatherAPI service using a Policy. First, we need to configure the identity provider to include the "country" claim into the access token when we ask for it. Update the `GetApiResources` method in the `Config` class of our IdentityProvider project as in Listing 18-46.

Listing 18-46. Including the country claim

```
public static IEnumerable<ApiResource> GetApiResources()
=> [
  new ApiResource("u2uApi", "U2U API")
  {
      Scopes = [ "u2uApi" ],
      UserClaims = [ "country" ]
  }
];
```

Next, we should add the policy configuration to the end of the client's `Program` class as in Listing 18-47. Here we add a policy named `FromBelgium`, requiring the user to be authenticated and having the country claim set to BE (which the peter@u2u.be user has).

Listing 18-47. Adding the FromBelgium policy

```
// Policies
builder.Services.AddAuthorization(options =>
{
  options.AddPolicy("FromBelgium", policyBuilder =>
  {
    policyBuilder.RequireAuthenticatedUser();
    policyBuilder.RequireClaim("country", "BE");
  });
});

// Add services to the container.
builder.Services.AddRazorComponents()
    .AddInteractiveServerComponents();
```

We also need to hide the navigation menu to not show the fetch link. How can we do this? We have seen the `AuthorizeView` component which allows us to show content when the user has been authenticated, or when the user has a certain role. We can also use this to show content when a user passes a certain policy. Modify the NavMenu component as in Listing 18-48 (just wrap the Weather NavLink into an `AuthorizeView`).

Listing 18-48. Using policies with the AuthorizeView

```
<AuthorizeView Roles="admin">
  <Authorized>
    <div class="nav-item px-3">
      <NavLink class="nav-link" href="counter">
        <span class="bi bi-plus-square-fill-nav-menu"
              aria-hidden="true"></span> Counter
      </NavLink>
    </div>
  </Authorized>
</AuthorizeView>

<AuthorizeView Policy="FromBelgium">
  <Authorized>
    <div class="nav-item px-3">
      <NavLink class="nav-link" href="weather">
        <span class="bi bi-list-nested-nav-menu"
              aria-hidden="true"></span> Weather
      </NavLink>
    </div>
  </Authorized>
</AuthorizeView>

<LogInOrOut />
```

Running the application and logging in as student@u2u.be will not show the link because this user is from France, while logging in as peter@u2u.be will show the link since the `FromBelgium` policy passed. This completes the client.

CHAPTER 18　SECURITY WITH OPENID CONNECT

But protecting the client is not enough. We want to use this policy with the WeatherAPI project as well, so we could copy this code. Let us do the proper thing and move the policy into a library project so we can use the same policy in our Blazor and API projects.

Start by adding a new library project to the solution called BlazorApp.Policies. Add the Microsoft.AspNetCore.Authorization package. Now add the Policies class from Listing 18-49. This class will create a new AuthorizationPolicy which will check if the user has been authenticated and is from Belgium.

Listing 18-49. The Policies class

```
using Microsoft.AspNetCore.Authorization;

namespace BlazorApp.Policies;

public class Policies
{
  public const string FromBelgium = "FromBelgium";

  public static AuthorizationPolicy FromBelgiumPolicy()
     => new AuthorizationPolicyBuilder()
       .RequireAuthenticatedUser()
       .RequireClaim("country", "BE")
       .Build();
}
```

Add the BlazorApp.Policies project as a project reference to WeatherAPI project. Now we can add this as an authorization policy in the WeatherAPI project's Program class as in Listing 18-50.

Listing 18-50. Enabling the FromBelgium policy in the API project

```
builder.Services.AddAuthorization(options =>
{
  options.AddPolicy(Policies.FromBelgium,
    Policies.FromBelgiumPolicy());
});
```

Now do the same instead of Listing 18-50 for the Client project. This way both projects use the same policy as the library project. Now we can update everything by updating the policy (less maintenance).

In the WeatherAPI project, modify the `Authorize` attribute on the `WeatherForecastController`'s `Get` method to use this policy as in Listing 18-51.

Listing 18-51. Using a policy to protect the WeatherAPI

```
[Authorize(Policy =Policies.FromBelgium)]
[HttpGet(Name = "GetWeatherForecast")]
public IEnumerable<WeatherForecast> Get()
...
```

Run all three projects, and login with peter@u2u.be as the user, the Weather link should be shown, and when you click the link, you should get a list of forecasts.

Congratulations. You just completed authentication and authorization for Blazor Server applications! Now let us look at Blazor WebAssembly in the next chapter.

Summary

In this chapter, we looked at protecting a Blazor Server application using OpenId Connect. In our modern world, applications use claims to allow applications to identify the current user and to protect resources. We then learned about the OpenId Connect Hybrid flow and used it for authentication, getting an identity token containing user's claims. We then used the `AuthenticationState` class to access these claims. We updated routing to check the `Authorize` attribute and used the `AuthorizeView` component to conditionally render an UI according to the user's claims. After this we looked at retrieving an access token and using it to protect an API. This allows us to use different applications with the same Web API, each given different levels of access to our API. All this using Duende IdentityServer as the identity provider.

CHAPTER 19

Securing Blazor WebAssembly

In the previous chapter, we looked at securing a Blazor Server application using OpenId Connect with identity and access tokens. Here we will do the same but for Blazor WebAssembly (standalone). This time we will use another OpenId Connect Flow: *Authorization Code flow* with PKCE (which stands for Proof Key for Code Exchange, pronounced Pixie).

I do recommend that you read the previous chapter before this one because it builds on top of some of the topics we saw there, and it continues with the code example from that chapter.

Authorization Code Flow with PKCE

When comparing the Authorization Code flow from Figure 19-1 and Hybrid flow, you will see a lot of similarities.

CHAPTER 19 SECURING BLAZOR WEBASSEMBLY

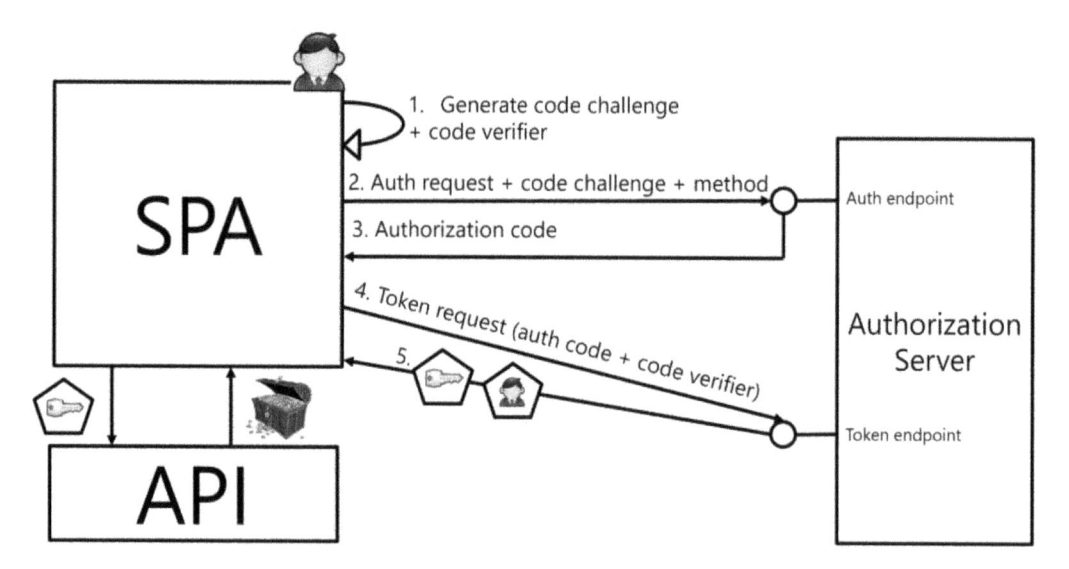

Figure 19-1. Authorization code flow with PKCE

The big difference is that the identity token is only returned when the client application sends the code to the identity provider. Since the code is sent using the browser, there is a chance of this code being intercepted by a malicious user using a "Authorization Code Interception Attack," so to protect this code, we will use *Proof Key for Code Exchange* (*PCKE*). This is to prevent another party from using the code to gain an access token.

Understanding PKCE

How does PKCE work? It is all about *proving ownership*. Imagine the user wants to login. The browser will generate a cryptographically random **code verifier**, and then uses a **code challenge method** to turn the code verifier into a **code challenge** (step 1). The code verifier is a block of random generated bytes, and the code challenge is the hash (the code challenge method) of that block of random generated bytes. The code challenge is then sent to the identity provider together with the code challenge method (step 2). The identity provider will then make the user login (with optional consent), save the code challenge (the hash) with code challenge method, and return the code that allows the token retrieval back to the application (step 3). The application can then use the code with the code verifier (step 4) to prove that it was the client requesting the code (assuming a third party is unable to retrieve the code verifier from the code challenge – that is why generally a cryptographic hash method is used because it is practically impossible to retrieve reverse a hash). After the identity provider checks that the code verifier and code challenge match by applying the code challenge method to the code verifier and then comparing the results it returns the requested tokens. Of course, this only works over HTTPS; otherwise, figuring out the code verifier is a piece of cake.

Registering the WASM Client Application

Let's start by adding authentication to a Blazor WebAssembly Standalone application. Start with the solution from the previous chapter (which you can find in the provided sources should you want).

Creating and Examining the Application

Add a new Blazor WebAssembly Standalone App project called BlazorApp.WASM. WithOpenIdConnect. You need to choose the *Individual Accounts* option as in Figure 19-2.

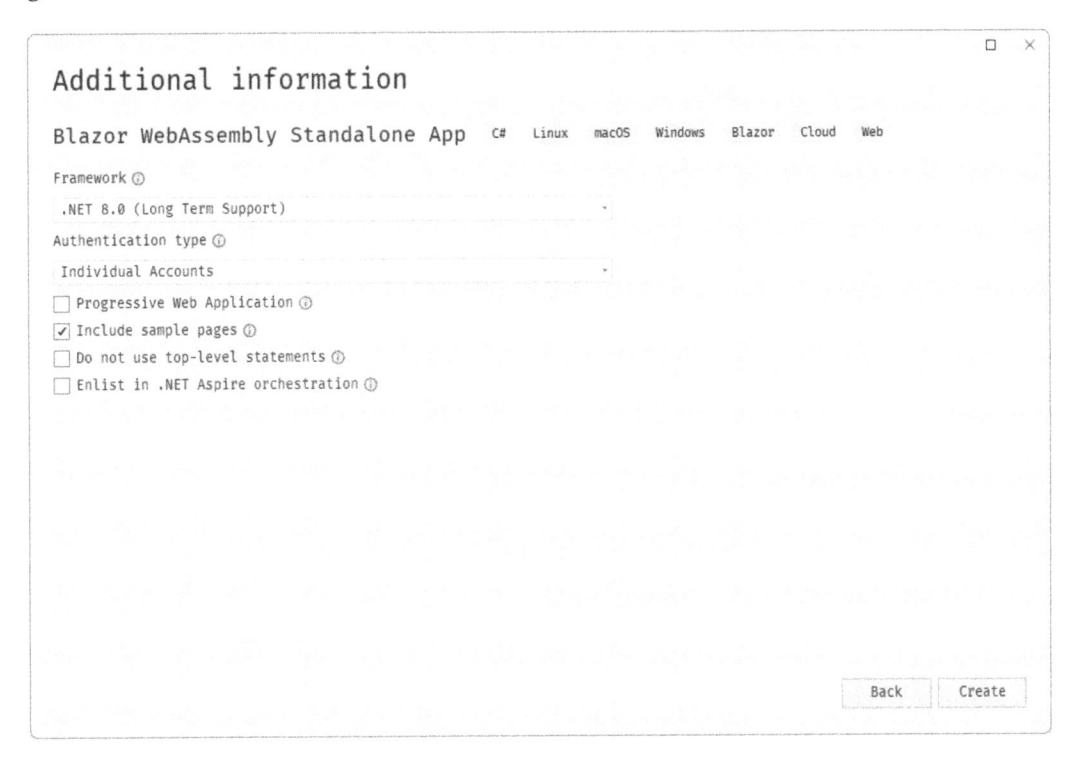

Figure 19-2. Creating the Blazor WebAssembly standalone project

CHAPTER 19   SECURING BLAZOR WEBASSEMBLY

Using the dotnet CLI, you can use the following command:

```
dotnet new blazorwasm -au Individual -o BlazorApp.Wasm.WithOpenIdConnect
```

The Individual Accounts option will automatically add the Microsoft.AspNetCore.Components.WebAssembly.Authentication package to your project and will also register a javascript library in wwwroot/index.html as in Listing 19-1. This library is used by Blazor to take care of talking to the identity provider.

Listing 19-1. The Authentication JavaScript library

```
<script src="_content/Microsoft.AspNetCore.Components.WebAssembly.
Authentication/AuthenticationService.js"></script>
```

In the Pages folder, you will also find the Authentication component as in Listing 19-2 which handles the /authentication/{action} URL. This component delegates the action to the RemoteAuthenticatorView which takes care of the OpenIdConnect authentication process.

Listing 19-2. The Authentication component

```
@page "/authentication/{action}"
@using Microsoft.AspNetCore.Components.WebAssembly.Authentication
<RemoteAuthenticatorView Action="@Action" />

@code{
  [Parameter] public string Action { get; set; }}
```

To allow the user to login, there is also the LoginDisplay component from Listing 19-3.

Listing 19-3. The LoginDisplay component

```
@using Microsoft.AspNetCore.Components.WebAssembly.Authentication
@inject NavigationManager Navigation

<AuthorizeView>
    <Authorized>
        Hello, @context.User.Identity?.Name!
        <button class="nav-link btn btn-link"
```

```
            @onclick="BeginLogOut">Log out</button>
    </Authorized>
    <NotAuthorized>
        <a href="authentication/login">Log in</a>
    </NotAuthorized>
</AuthorizeView>

@code{
    public void BeginLogOut()
    {
        Navigation.NavigateToLogout("authentication/logout");
    }
}
```

When the user has been authorized, this will display a logout button, and when clicked, it will redirect with the logout action to the Authentication component. When the user is not authorized, this component displays a login link which will take us to the login action. Using the AuthorizeView component makes this easy.

The App component is similar to the one in the Blazor Server component which will redirect us to the login page when the user is not yet authenticated.

Update the applicationUrl in the Properties/launchSettings.json file as in Listing 19-4 to change the port number to 5003 for HTTPS.

Listing 19-4. LaunchSettings for Blazor.Wasm.OpenIdConnect

```
{
  "$schema": "http://json.schemastore.org/launchsettings.json",
  "iisSettings": {
    ...
  },
  "profiles": {
    "https": {
      "commandName": "Project",
      "dotnetRunMessages": true,
      "launchBrowser": true,
      "inspectUri": "{wsProtocol}://{url.hostname}:{url.port}/_framework/debug/ws-proxy?browser={browserInspectUri}",
```

```
      "applicationUrl": "https://localhost:5003;http://localhost:5099",
      "environmentVariables": {
        "ASPNETCORE_ENVIRONMENT": "Development"
      }
    },
    "IIS Express": {
      ...
    }
  }
}
```

Now we are ready to register this Blazor WASM application in our identity provider.

Registering the Client Application

Add a new client called BlazorWasm to the Config class in the IdentityProvider project as shown in Listing 19-5.

Listing 19-5. Registering the Blazor WASM client

```
new Client
{
  ClientName = "BlazorWasm",
  ClientId = "BlazorWasm",
  AllowedGrantTypes = GrantTypes.Code,
  RequirePkce = true,
  RequireClientSecret = false,
  RedirectUris = new List<string>{
    "https://localhost:5003/authentication/login-callback"
  },
  PostLogoutRedirectUris = new List<string> {
    "https://localhost:5003/authentication/logout-callback"
  },
  AllowedCorsOrigins = {
    "https://localhost:5003"
  },
```

```
  AllowedScopes = {
    IdentityServerConstants.StandardScopes.OpenId,
    IdentityServerConstants.StandardScopes.Profile,
  }
  // RequireConsent = true
}
```

Here we specify the client's name and Id, we choose the Authorization Code flow with PKCE, and we pass it the `redirectUris` for our client application. Finally, we also list the required scopes. Since we first will implement authentication, we only need the OpenId and Profile scopes. Optionally you can also enable client consent, but I left this out for practicality. You should enable this before going to production.

Implementing Authentication

In the Blazor Server application, we hard-coded all the options for OpenId Connect; here we will use configuration. Look for appsettings.json in the wwwroot folder, and replace it as in Listing 19-6. Here we specify the identity provider's URL in the Authority property, and we set the remaining properties to the same values as in Listing 19-5.

Listing 19-6. The application settings

```
{
  "oidc": {
    "Authority": "https://localhost:5011/",
    "ClientId": "BlazorWasm",
    "ResponseType": "code",
    "DefaultScopes": [
      "openid",
      "profile"
    ],
    "PostLogoutRedirectUri": "authentication/logout-callback",
    "RedirectUri": "authentication/login-callback"
  }
}
```

CHAPTER 19 SECURING BLAZOR WEBASSEMBLY

Open the BlazorApp.WASM.WithOpenIdConnect project's `Program` class and replace the configuration section name as in Listing 19-7. This will read all options from configuration.

Listing 19-7. Binding to the OIDC configuration

```
using BlazorApp.WASM.WithOpenIdConnect;
using Microsoft.AspNetCore.Components.Web;
using Microsoft.AspNetCore.Components.WebAssembly.Hosting;

internal class Program
{
  private static async global::System.Threading.Tasks.Task
  Main(string[] args)
  {
    var builder = WebAssemblyHostBuilder.CreateDefault(args);
    builder.RootComponents.Add<App>("#app");
    builder.RootComponents.Add<HeadOutlet>("head::after");

    builder.Services.AddScoped(sp => new HttpClient {
      BaseAddress = new Uri(builder.HostEnvironment.BaseAddress)
    });

    builder.Services.AddOidcAuthentication(options =>
    {
      builder.Configuration.Bind("oidc",
        options.ProviderOptions);
    });

    await builder.Build().RunAsync();
  }
}
```

Now we are ready to test our solution. Start the IdentityProvider project and then your Blazor WASM application. After a little while your browser should show the Blazor application as shown in Figure 19-3 with a login link in the top-right corner. You can ignore the alert, or even better, remove it.

CHAPTER 19   SECURING BLAZOR WEBASSEMBLY

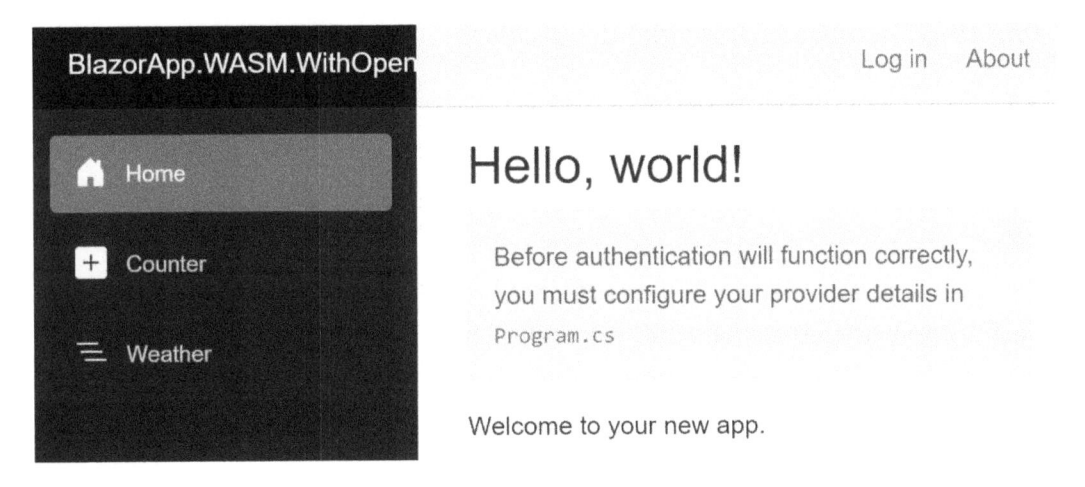

Figure 19-3. The Blazor application before log in

Click the login link and then complete the login procedure with a registered user, for example, peter@u2u.be and password u2u-secret. After this the Blazor application will display the user's name as in Figure 19-4.

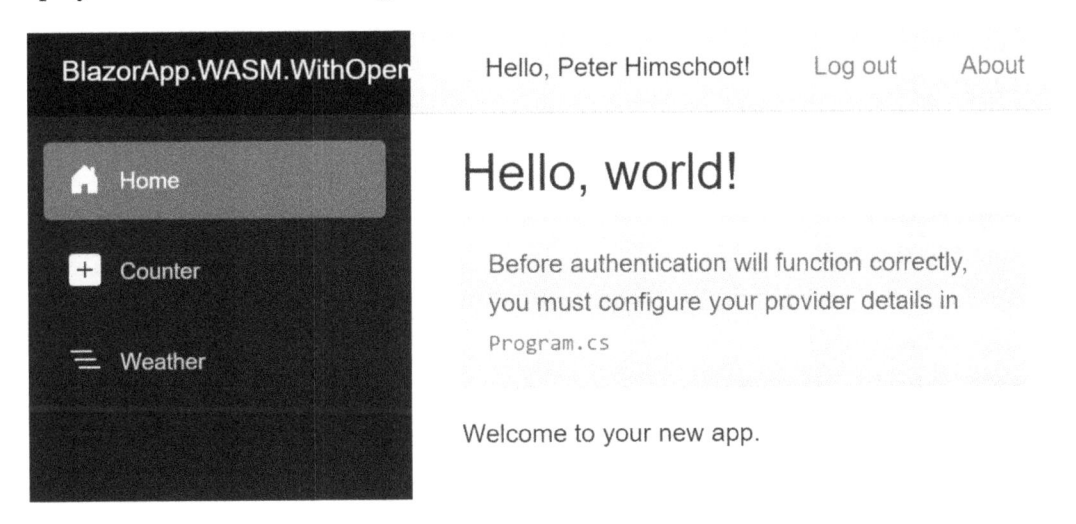

Figure 19-4. The Blazor application after log in

Customizing the Login Experience

There are still a couple of things we can do. Let us first remove the alert in Listing 19-8 from the Home component warning us about the need to configure our provider details. Since authentication works, we don't need this anymore.

611

CHAPTER 19 SECURING BLAZOR WEBASSEMBLY

Listing 19-8. Remove the provider details alert

```
<div class="alert alert-warning" role="alert">
    Before authentication will function correctly, you must configure your
    provider details in <code>Program.cs</code>
</div>
```

Next, we can customize the RemoteAuthenticatorView. This has a series of RenderFragment properties that allow you to display a UI during the process of logging in and out. Listing 19-9 shows a couple of simple examples. Make these changes to the Pages/Authentication.razor file.

Listing 19-9. Customizing the login and logout process

```
@page "/authentication/{action}"
@using Microsoft.AspNetCore.Components.WebAssembly.Authentication
<RemoteAuthenticatorView Action="@Action">
  <LoggingIn>
    <p>Logging in...</p>
  </LoggingIn>
  <LogInFailed>
    <p>Login failed.</p>
  </LogInFailed>
  <LogOutSucceeded>
    <p>You have successfully logged out.</p>
  </LogOutSucceeded>
</RemoteAuthenticatorView>

@code {
  [Parameter] public string? Action { get; set; }
}
```

Congratulations! You have just completed the process of authentication with Blazor WASM. Here most of the code was generated by the application's template so this was not a lot of work!

CHAPTER 19　SECURING BLAZOR WEBASSEMBLY

Understanding the Login Process

What happens when you press the login link from Figure 19-3? This will redirect to the Authentication component, passing the *login* action. The RemoteAuthenticatorView will use this to talk to the JavaScript from Listing 19-1. This JavaScript library then takes care of talking to the Identity Provider, which allows us to login. Start the application again, open the browser's developer tools, and open the network tab. Click the login link in the application. You will see the browser redirecting to the identity provider, passing the client Id, redirecting URI, and coding challenge as shown in Figure 19-5.

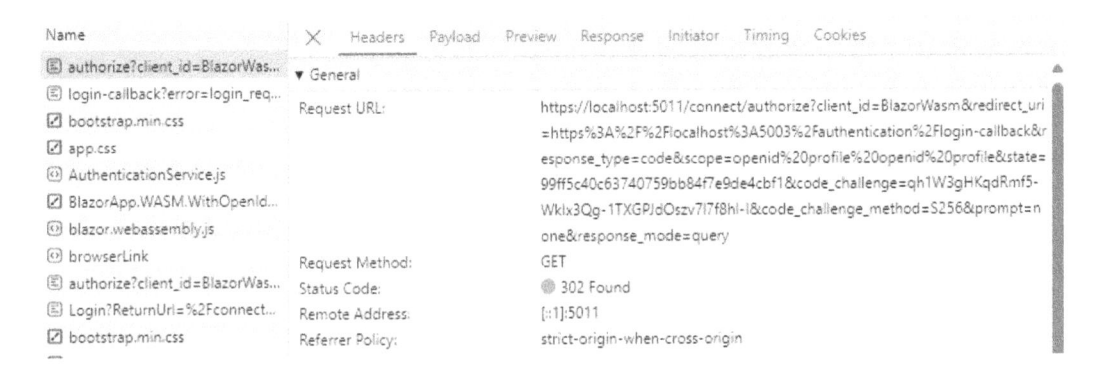

Figure 19-5.　Redirecting to the Identity Provider using PKCE

The browser will now allow you to login. Once you have been logged in, the identity provider sends the code back to the browser as shown in Figure 19-6.

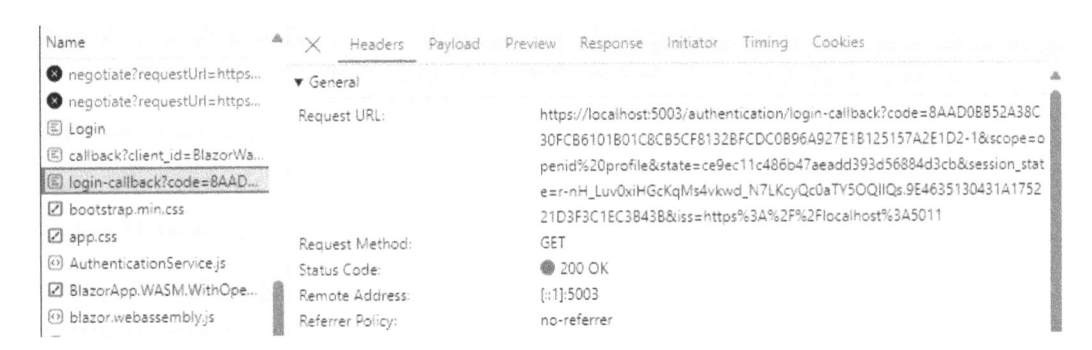

Figure 19-6.　The browser receives the code

613

CHAPTER 19 SECURING BLAZOR WEBASSEMBLY

This executes the `RemoteAuthenticatorView` using the *login-callback* action when it can store the code from the identity provider. We have not received the identity of the user yet, so `RemoteAuthenticatorView` uses the code it received to retrieve information from the token endpoint. Search lower in the network history for the *token* URL, and look at the payload, as shown in Figure 19-7.

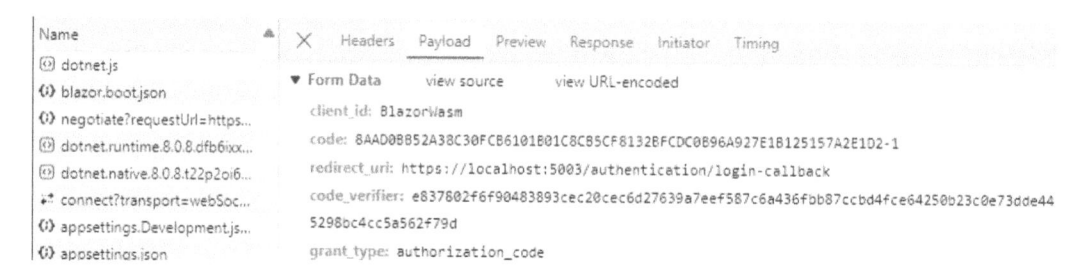

Figure 19-7. *Using the code to retrieve*

The payload contains the code and the code_verifier for PKCE. The response contains an *id_token* and an *access_token*. We still need more information about the current user, so the `RemoteAuthenticatorView` uses the *access_token* to retrieve user information. You can see this for yourself by looking for the *userinfo* URL, as shown in Figure 19-8.

Figure 19-8. *Retrieving user information*

When all of this is done the `RemoteAuthenticatorView` has the user's identity, which we can now retrieve using the `AuthenticationState`.

The `RemoteAuthenticatorView` also handles logout and error handling.

Accessing a Protected API

Time to implement the Weather link. Currently this uses some sample data, and of course we want to access this data from the WeatherAPI just like in the previous chapter.

CHAPTER 19 SECURING BLAZOR WEBASSEMBLY

Fetching Forecasts from WeatherAPI

Start by installing the Microsoft.Extensions.Http package in the Blazor WASM project. Add a new folder called Services to the BlazorApp.WASM.WithOpenIdConnect project, and inside it, add a new WeatherForcastService class as in Listing 19-10. Just like with Blazor Server, this uses an IHttpClientFactory instance to create the configured HttpClient.

Listing 19-10. The WeatherForecastService class

```
using System;
using System.Net.Http;
using System.Net.Http.Json;
using System.Threading.Tasks;
using static Blazor.Wasm.OpenIdConnect.Pages.FetchData;

namespace Blazor.Wasm.OpenIdConnect.Services
{
  public class WeatherForecastService
  {
    private readonly IHttpClientFactory httpClientFactory;

    public WeatherForecastService(
      IHttpClientFactory httpClientFactory)
      => this.httpClientFactory = httpClientFactory;

    public async ValueTask<WeatherForecast[]>
      GetForecastAsync(DateTime startDate)
    {
      HttpClient httpClient =
        this.httpClientFactory
            .CreateClient(nameof(WeatherForecastService));
      WeatherForecast[] result =
        await httpClient
          .GetFromJsonAsync<WeatherForecast[]>("weatherforecast");
      return result;
    }
  }
}
```

CHAPTER 19 SECURING BLAZOR WEBASSEMBLY

Copy the WeatherForecast class next to this service.

Now we are ready to configure dependency injection, so add Listing 19-11 to the Blazor WASM project's Program class.

Listing 19-11. Configuring dependency injection

```
builder.Services.AddHttpClient<WeatherForecastService>(
client =>
  client.BaseAddress = new Uri("https://localhost:5005")
);

builder.Services.AddSingleton<WeatherForecastService>();
```

Append Listing 19-12 to your _imports.razor.

Listing 19-12. Adding the Services namespace

```
@using BlazorApp.WASM.WithOpenIdConnect.Services
```

Update the Weather component as in Listing 19-13 to use the WeatherForecaseService.

Listing 19-13. The FetchData component using the WeatherForecastService

```
@page "/weather"
@inject WeatherForecastService WeatherService

...

@code {
  private WeatherForecast[]? forecasts;

  protected override async Task OnInitializedAsync()
  {
    forecasts = await WeatherService.GetForecastsAsync();
  }
}
```

First let us see if all this works by first removing the Authorize attribute from the WeatherForecastController.Get method. Run the IdentityProvider, WeatherAPI, and BlazorApp.WASM.WithOpenIdConnect projects. Click the Weather link, and you should get the forecasts from the WeatherAPI. Nice!

616

Using the AuthorizationMessageHandler

Add the Authorize attribute again, now without a policy like in Listing 19-14. Later we will enable the policy.

Listing 19-14. Protecting the WeatherService API

```
[Authorize]
//[Authorize(Policy =Policies.FromBelgium)]
[HttpGet(Name = "GetWeatherForecast")]
public IEnumerable<WeatherForecast> Get()
```

However, clicking the Weather link will not work! We need to retrieve an access token and pass it using a Bearer header to the WeatherAPI which requires the u2uApi scope. So first we need to tell IdentityService to grant access to this scope by adding it to the list of AllowedScopes as in Listing 19-15.

Listing 19-15. Adding the scope to the client configuration

```
AllowedScopes = {
  IdentityServerConstants.StandardScopes.OpenId,
  IdentityServerConstants.StandardScopes.Profile,
  "u2uApi",
}
```

We should also add this to the client configuration as in Listing 19-16.

Listing 19-16. Requesting the u2uApi scope in configuration

```
{
  "oidc": {
    "Authority": "https://localhost:5011/",
    "ClientId": "BlazorWasm",
    "ResponseType": "code",
    "DefaultScopes": [
      "openid",
      "profile",
      "u2uApi"
    ],
```

CHAPTER 19   SECURING BLAZOR WEBASSEMBLY

```
      "PostLogoutRedirectUri": "authentication/logout-callback",
      "RedirectUri": "authentication/login-callback"
   }
}
```

When accessing the API, we will need to attach the proper access token. For this we need to use the AuthorizationMessageHandler, a special kind of HttpMessageHandler. With HttpMessageHandler you can configure the request, so here we retrieve the AuthorizationMessageHandler, and make it attach the access token for the u2uApi scope. Update dependency injection by adding an HttpMessageHandler as in Listing 19-17 which will do just that. We do need to pass the base URI to which access tokens need to be attached by setting the authorizedUrls property.

Listing 19-17. Adding the AuthorizationMessageHandler

```
builder.Services.AddHttpClient<WeatherForecastService>(
client =>
  client.BaseAddress = new Uri("https://localhost:5005")
)
.AddHttpMessageHandler(handlerConfig =>
{
  AuthorizationMessageHandler handler =
  handlerConfig.GetRequiredService<AuthorizationMessageHandler>()
  .ConfigureHandler(
    authorizedUrls: ["https://localhost:5005"],
    scopes: ["u2uApi"]
    );
  return handler;
})
;
```

Run your solution again. Now you should be able to access the WeatherAPI. Whohoo!

Adding Client-Side Authorization

Should the user be able to click on the Weather link when they're not authorized? Of course not. We should protect the Weather component. Add the Microsoft.AspNetCore.Authorization namespace to your _Imports.razor file as in Listing 19-18.

Listing 19-18. Using Microsoft.AspNetCore.Authorization

```
@using Microsoft.AspNetCore.Authorization
```

Now apply the `Authorize` attribute to the Weather component as in Listing 19-19.

Listing 19-19. Protecting the Weather component

```
@page "/weather"
@inject WeatherForecastService WeatherService
@attribute [Authorize]
```

Any unauthorized user will now be redirected to the login page when they click the Weather link in the navigation menu. I do think it is better to hide the link using the `AuthorizeView` in the NavMenu component as in Listing 19-20.

Listing 19-20. Hiding the Weather link

```
<AuthorizeView>
  <Authorized>
    <div class="nav-item px-3">
      <NavLink class="nav-link" href="weather">
        <span class="bi bi-list-nested-nav-menu"
              aria-hidden="true"></span> Weather
      </NavLink>
    </div>
  </Authorized>
</AuthorizeView>
```

Run the solution again. When you're not logged in, the Weather link should be hidden, and then you login it will show.

Again, congratulations are in order. You added support for calling a protected API. Next thing we will do is to use roles to protect our API even further.

CHAPTER 19   SECURING BLAZOR WEBASSEMBLY

Using Role-Based Security

Time to add some role-based access control. We can assign role claims to users and then use a role to give certain users access to components and resources, and other others will be denied access although they have been authenticated. Here we will add a component to review the user's claims and then we will use the user's role to protect it.

Creating the Claims Component

Let us start by adding a route to view the user's claims. Add Listing 19-21 to the _Imports. razor file. This will give us access to the Claim type.

Listing 19-21. Using System.Security.Claims

```
@using System.Security.Claims
```

Now add a new Blazor component called Claims, and modify it to match Listing 19-22. Here we inject the AuthenticationStateProvider which allows us to access the AuthenticationState. In the OnInitializedAsync method, we call the GetAuthenticationStateAsync method and use it to fill the UserName and UserClaims properties (just like in the previous chapter).

Listing 19-22. Listing the user's claims

```
@page "/claims"

@inject AuthenticationStateProvider AuthenticationStateProvider

@attribute [Authorize]

<h3>Claims</h3>

<h2>Hi @UserName</h2>

@foreach (var claim in UserClaims)
{
  <p>@claim.Type - @claim.Value</p>
}
```

```
@code {
  public required IEnumerable<Claim> UserClaims { get; set; }
  private string UserName { get; set; } = "Unknown";

  protected override async Task OnInitializedAsync()
  {
    AuthenticationState authState =
      await AuthenticationStateProvider.GetAuthenticationStateAsync();
    if (authState is not null)
    {
      UserName = authState.User.Identity!.Name!;
      UserClaims = authState.User.Claims;
    }
  }
}
```

Now add a new navigation link to the NavMenu component as in Listing 19-23. We only give access to users that have been authenticated so we wrap this inside a AuthorizeView.

Listing 19-23. Adding the claims link to the NavMenu

```
<!-- Put this below the Weather link -->
<AuthorizeView>
  <Authorized>
    <div class="nav-item px-3">
      <NavLink class="nav-link" href="claims">
        <span class="bi bi-list-nested-nav-menu"
              aria-hidden="true"></span> Claims
      </NavLink>
    </div>
  </Authorized>
</AuthorizeView>
```

Run your solution (IdentityProvider, WeatherAPI, and BlazorApp.WASM. WithOpenIdConnect). After logging in with peter@u2u.be, you should see the user's claims as in Figure 19-9.

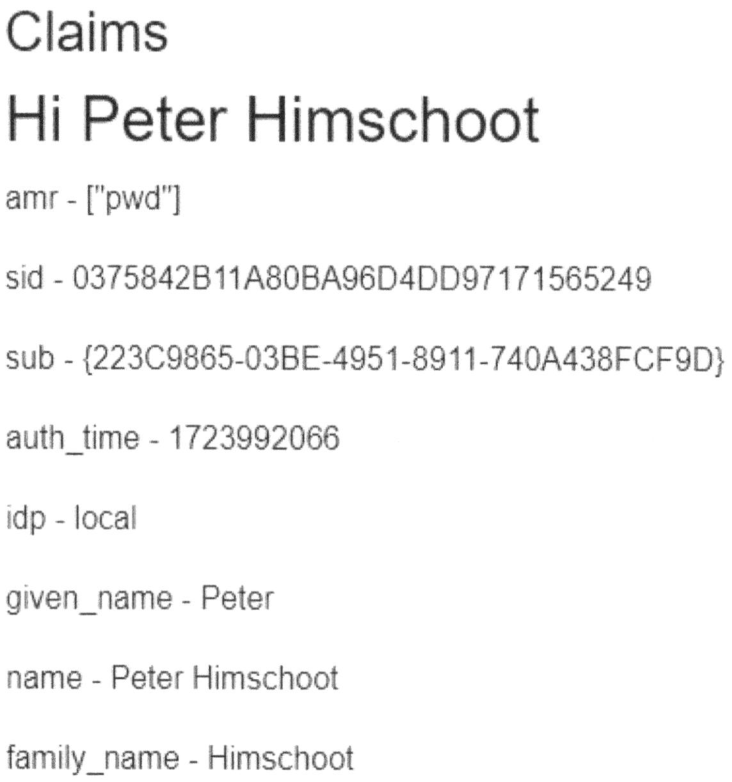

CHAPTER 19   SECURING BLAZOR WEBASSEMBLY

Claims

Hi Peter Himschoot

amr - ["pwd"]

sid - 0375842B11A80BA96D4DD97171565249

sub - {223C9865-03BE-4951-8911-740A438FCF9D}

auth_time - 1723992066

idp - local

given_name - Peter

name - Peter Himschoot

family_name - Himschoot

Figure 19-9. *The user's claims*

Hmm. No roles claim. Let us fix this.

Enabling RBAC

Let us first look at the IdentityProvider project's `Config.GetClients` method. As you can see, this client does not have the roles scope in the `AllowedScopes` property. Add it as in Listing 19-24.

Listing 19-24. Adding the roles scopes to the client

```
new Client
{
  ClientName = "BlazorWasm",
  ...
  AllowedScopes = {
    IdentityServerConstants.StandardScopes.OpenId,
```

```
    IdentityServerConstants.StandardScopes.Profile,
    "u2uApi",
    "roles",
  }
  // RequireConsent = true
}
```

Our client should also require the roles scope, so update the appsettings.json from the Blazor.Wasm.OpenIdConnect project as in Listing 19-25.

Listing 19-25. Updating the appsettings.json File

```
{
  "oidc": {
    "Authority": "https://localhost:5011/",
    "ClientId": "BlazorWasm",
    "ResponseType": "code",
    "DefaultScopes": [
      "openid",
      "profile",
      "u2uApi",
      "roles"
    ],
    "PostLogoutRedirectUri": "authentication/logout-callback",
    "RedirectUri": "authentication/login-callback"
  }
}
```

Run again. Now you should see the role claim (if not, try logging out and then log in again since the claims are stored in a cookie and you need to refresh that cookie).

Viewing a user's claims should only be possible for people who have sufficient rights to do so, so let us protect the Claims route so only users with an admin role can see it. This is quite simple: update the `Authorize` attribute to include the admin role as in Listing 19-26.

CHAPTER 19   SECURING BLAZOR WEBASSEMBLY

Listing 19-26. Requiring the Admin role

```
@attribute [Authorize(Roles = "admin")]
```

Run again. However, you will not be allowed to access the Claims component as shown in Figure 19-10. Why?

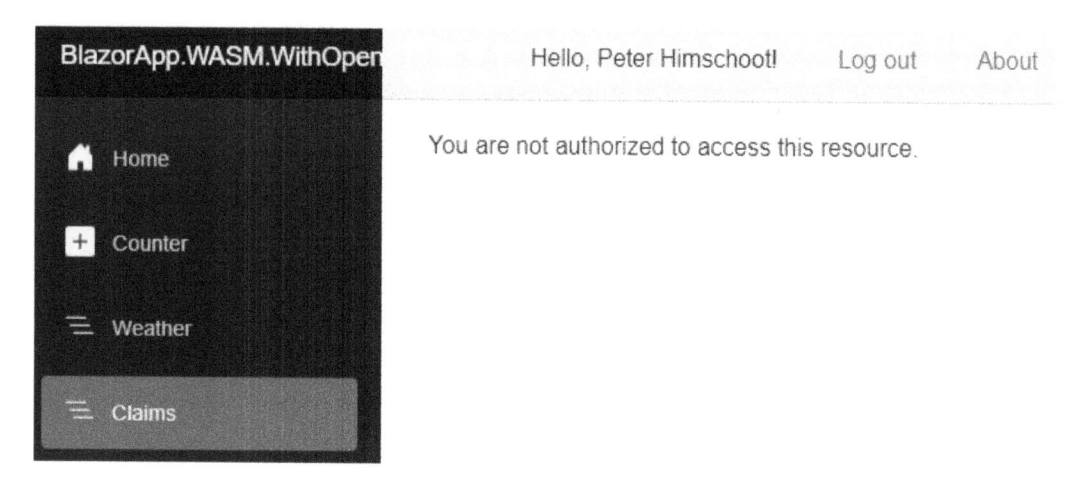

Figure 19-10.   Unauthorized user

Promoting the Role Claim

Which claim represents the user's role? Using claims is very flexible, so you could use any claim. That is why we need to tell the OIDC middleware which claim represents the role, so in the Blazor project we need to set the userOptions.RoleClaim property as in Listing 19-27.

Listing 19-27. Specifying the role claim

```
builder.Services.AddOidcAuthentication(options =>
{
  builder.Configuration.Bind("oidc", options.ProviderOptions);
  // Explain which claim contains the roles of the user
  options.UserOptions.RoleClaim = "role";
});
```

Run again. Log in with peter@u2u.be who has the admin role. You should be able to see the Claims route. Login again as student@u2u.be and you will see the unauthorized message. Maybe we should hide the Claims link when the user is not an admin? Update the NavMenu component by wrapping the claims NavLink with a <AuthorizeView Roles="admin"> as in Listing 19-28 which should take care of that.

Listing 19-28. Using AuthorizeView with roles

```
<div class="@NavMenuCssClass" @onclick="ToggleNavMenu">
  <nav class="flex-column">
    <div class="nav-item px-3">
      <NavLink class="nav-link" href="" Match="NavLinkMatch.All">
        <span class="oi oi-home"
              aria-hidden="true"></span> Home
      </NavLink>
    </div>
    <div class="nav-item px-3">
      <NavLink class="nav-link" href="counter">
        <span class="oi oi-plus"
              aria-hidden="true"></span> Counter
      </NavLink>
    </div>
    <AuthorizeView>
      <Authorized>
        <div class="nav-item px-3">
          <NavLink class="nav-link" href="fetchdata">
            <span class="oi oi-list-rich"
                  aria-hidden="true"></span> Fetch data
          </NavLink>
        </div>
      </Authorized>
    </AuthorizeView>
    <AuthorizeView Roles="admin">
      <Authorized>
        <div class="nav-item px-3">
          <NavLink class="nav-link" href="claims">
```

```
            <span class="oi oi-list-rich"
                    aria-hidden="true"></span> Claims
        </NavLink>
      </div>
    </Authorized>
  </AuthorizeView>
 </nav>
</div>
```

Using Policy-Based Access Control

Let us change our mind a little and decide that forecasts can only be seen by users with the country claim set to Belgium. For this we will re-use the `FromBelgium` policy we created in the previous chapter. First, we need to enable the country scope in both the identity provider project and the Blazor project.

Updating Scopes

Update the `GetClients` method in the IdentityProvider project by adding an additional scope to the `AllowedScopes` property as in Listing 19-29.

Listing 19-29. Adding the country scope to the Identity Provider

```
AllowedScopes = {
  IdentityServerConstants.StandardScopes.OpenId,
  IdentityServerConstants.StandardScopes.Profile,
  "u2uApi",
  "roles",
  "country"
}
```

Update the Blazor project's appsettings.json as in Listing 19-30.

Listing 19-30. Adding the country scope to the Blazor client

```
{
  "oidc": {
    "Authority": "https://localhost:5011/",
    "ClientId": "BlazorWasm",
    "ResponseType": "code",
    "DefaultScopes": [
      "openid",
      "profile",
      "u2uApi",
      "roles",
      "country"
    ],
    "PostLogoutRedirectUri": "authentication/logout-callback",
    "RedirectUri": "authentication/login-callback",
  }
}
```

If you like, you can run the solution again to verify that you got the country claim.

Adding Policies

Time to add the `FromBelgium` policy to your BlazorApp.WASM.WithOpenIdConnect project. Add the BlazorApp.Policies project as a project reference to the BlazorApp.WASM.WithOpenIdConnect project. Then add Listing 19-31 to `Program`, before `await builder.Build().RunAsync();`. This will enable the `FromBelgium` policy in our client project.

Listing 19-31. Enabling policy authorization

```
builder.Services.AddAuthorizationCore(options =>
{
    options.AddPolicy(Policies.FromBelgium,
                     Policies.FromBelgiumPolicy());
});
```

CHAPTER 19   SECURING BLAZOR WEBASSEMBLY

Now enable this policy in the WeatherAPI. We did most of the work in the previous chapter, so we only need to protect the `WeatherForecastController.Get` method using the `FromBelgium` policy as in Listing 19-32.

Listing 19-32. Using a policy to protect an API

```
[Authorize(Policy = Policies.FromBelgium)]
public IEnumerable<WeatherForecast> Get()
```

Run your project and login as peter@u2u.be. You should be able to access the forecasts because this user has the country claim with value Belgium. Now try again with user student@u2u.be whose country claim has a different value. You will get an error. You can review this error by opening the browser's debugger, and on the browser's Console tab just like in Figure 19-11, you should see status code 403 (Forbidden).

```
crit: Microsoft.AspNetCore.Components.WebAssembly.Rendering.WebAssemblyRenderer[100]    blazor.webassembly.js:1
      Unhandled exception rendering component: Response status code does not indicate
success: 403 (Forbidden).
System.Net.Http.HttpRequestException: Response status code does not indicate success: 403 (Forbidden).
   at System.Net.Http.HttpResponseMessage.EnsureSuccessStatusCode()
   at System.Net.Http.Json.HttpClientJsonExtensions.
<<FromJsonAsyncCore>g__Core|12_0>d`2[[BlazorApp.WASM.WithOpenIdConnect.Services.WeatherForecast[],
BlazorApp.WASM.WithOpenIdConnect, Version=1.0.0.0, Culture=neutral, PublicKeyToken=null],
[System.Text.Json.JsonSerializerOptions, System.Text.Json, Version=8.0.0.0, Culture=neutral,
PublicKeyToken=cc7b13ffcd2ddd51]].MoveNext()
   at BlazorApp.WASM.WithOpenIdConnect.Services.WeatherForecastService.GetForecastsAsync() in
C:\Code\GitHub\microsoft-blazor-book-
4\Ch18\OpenIdConnect\BlazorWithOpenIdConnect\src\BlazorApp.WASM.WithOpenIdConnect\Services\WeatherForecastService.
cs:line 18
   at BlazorApp.WASM.WithOpenIdConnect.Pages.Weather.OnInitializedAsync() in C:\Code\GitHub\microsoft-blazor-book-
4\Ch18\OpenIdConnect\BlazorWithOpenIdConnect\src\BlazorApp.WASM.WithOpenIdConnect\Pages\Weather.razor:line 45
   at Microsoft.AspNetCore.Components.ComponentBase.RunInitAndSetParametersAsync()
   at Microsoft.AspNetCore.Components.RenderTree.Renderer.GetErrorHandledTask(Task taskToHandle, ComponentState
owningComponentState)
```

Figure 19-11. *Accessing the API with the wrong claims*

We can prevent users from accessing this resource by hiding the Weather link in the NavMenu as in Listing 19-33.

Listing 19-33. Hiding the NavLink

```
<AuthorizeView Policy="FromBelgium">
  <Authorized>
    <div class="nav-item px-3">
      <NavLink class="nav-link" href="fetchdata">
        <span class="oi oi-list-rich"
```

```
                aria-hidden="true"></span> Fetch data
        </NavLink>
      </div>
    </Authorized>
</AuthorizeView>
```

Summary

In this chapter, we used OpenId Connect to protect a Blazor WebAssembly project. We configured our identity provider for this application and then went on to use authentication. Then we used the `AuthorizationMessageHandler` to attach an access token so we can invoke a protected API. We also used role-based access control and policy-based access control to protect some of our components and resources.

CHAPTER 20

Securing Blazor Auto

Now we know how we can add authentication and authorization to a Blazor Server and Blazor WASM application; we need to look at the new Blazor auto render mode model. With Blazor Auto, your components can transition from Blazor Server to Blazor WebAssembly, and this gives us some challenges to implement authentication and authorization.

The Challenge

How do we implement authentication that works for both Blazor Server and WASM? We learned from the previous chapters that each requires a different approach. The solution to our problem is having the Server project do all the authentication, and then provide the credentials to the auto render mode components so they can use the `AuthorizeView` and `AuthtenticationState` to protect their resources.

This chapter comes with starter files for your convenience. So here you can look at the provided code, saving you lots of typing! You can find the solution in the code folder for Chapter 18.

The Blazor Server Project

Open the BlazorApp.Auto.WithOpenIdConnect project. Here you will find the usual files, including the `WeatherService`. But there is also the `PersistingAuthenticationStateProvider` class. What does this class do?

PersistingAuthenticationStateProvider

We have seen that the `AuthenticationState` contains the `ClaimsPrincipal`, and with Blazor we use an `AuthenticationStateProvider` to retrieve the current `AuthenticationState` with the provider abstracting where the `ClaimsPrincipal` is currently stored.

In this project we override the default `AuthenticationStateProvider` with one that can serialize the current `ClaimsPrincipal` from Blazor Server to Blazor WASM using the `PersistentComponentState` service. But first we need to examine the `UserInfo` class from Listing 20-1.

Listing 20-1. The UserInfo class

```
public sealed class UserInfo
{
  public required string UserId { get; init; }
  public required string Name { get; init; }
  public required string GivenName { get; init; }
  public required string Country { get; init; }

  public const string UserIdClaimType = "sid";
  public const string NameClaimType = "name";
  public const string GivenNameClaimType = "given_name";
  public const string CountryClaimType = "country";

  public static UserInfo FromClaimsPrincipal
    (ClaimsPrincipal principal) =>
    new()
    {
      UserId =
        GetRequiredClaim(principal, UserIdClaimType),
      Name =
        GetRequiredClaim(principal, NameClaimType),
      GivenName =
        GetRequiredClaim(principal, GivenNameClaimType),
      Country =
        GetRequiredClaim(principal, CountryClaimType)
    };
```

```
  public ClaimsPrincipal ToClaimsPrincipal() =>
    new(new ClaimsIdentity(
      [
        new(UserIdClaimType, UserId),
        new(NameClaimType, Name),
        new(GivenNameClaimType, GivenName),
        new(CountryClaimType, Country),
      ],
      authenticationType: nameof(UserInfo),
      nameType: NameClaimType,
      roleType: null));

  private static string GetRequiredClaim
    (ClaimsPrincipal principal, string claimType) =>
    principal.FindFirst(claimType)?.Value
    ?? throw new InvalidOperationException($"Could not find required '{claimType}' claim.");
}
```

This class is used to serialize claims required by Blazor WASM components. It has two methods, the FromClaimsPrincipal which copies claims from the ClaimsPrincipal into a new instance of UserInfo. This allows the PersistingAuthenticationStateProvider to serialize these claims to WASM. The ToClaimsPrincipal turns the current instance back into a ClaimsPrincipal.

This implementation of UserInfo serializes four claims; if you require other claims, you should enhance the UserInfo class to include them. Look at the Country claim for an example.

Note The UserInfo class is used to serialize and deserialize claims.

Now let us look at an excerpt of the PersistingAuthenticationStateProvider from Listing 20-2.

Listing 20-2. The PersistingAuthenticationStateProvider class

```
internal sealed class PersistingAuthenticationStateProvider
  : AuthenticationStateProvider
  , IHostEnvironmentAuthenticationStateProvider
  , IDisposable
{
  private readonly PersistentComponentState persistentComponentState;
  private readonly PersistingComponentStateSubscription subscription;
  private Task<AuthenticationState>? authenticationStateTask;

  public PersistingAuthenticationStateProvider(
    PersistentComponentState state)
  {
    persistentComponentState = state;
    subscription = state.RegisterOnPersisting(OnPersistingAsync,
                   RenderMode.InteractiveWebAssembly);
  }

  private async Task OnPersistingAsync()
  {
    var authenticationState = await GetAuthenticationStateAsync();
    var principal = authenticationState.User;

    if (principal.Identity?.IsAuthenticated == true)
    {
      persistentComponentState.PersistAsJson(nameof(UserInfo),
        UserInfo.FromClaimsPrincipal(principal));
    }
  }

  public void Dispose()
  {
    subscription.Dispose();
  }
}
```

The `PersistingAuthenticationStateProvider` class receives the `PersistentComponentState` service in its constructor where it subscribes to the Persisting event. The `OnPersistingAsync` method then retrieves the current `ClaimsPrincipal` and uses the `UserInfo` to serialize the claims.

If you are wondering where the `ClaimsPrincipal` get set: The `PersistingAuthenticationStateProvider` implements the `IHostEnvironmentAuthenticationStateProvider` interface which allows the runtime to pass a `AuthenticationState` Task using the `SetAuthenticationState` to this instance, which contains the actual `ClaimsPrincipal`.

The only thing required to install the `PersistingAuthenticationStateProvider` is to tell dependency injection to use this type, as shown in Listing 20-3.

Listing 20-3. Installing the PersistingAuthenticationStateProvider

```
builder.Services.AddScoped<AuthenticationStateProvider,
  PersistingAuthenticationStateProvider>();
```

Note Ensure you register the PersistingAuthenticationStateProvider as scoped; this way in Blazor Server, each circuit has its own instance.

The Blazor WASM Project

In the BlazorApp.Auto.WithOpenIdConnect.Client project, you will also find a `PersistentAuthenticationStateProvider` class. This implements the receiving side of our story. Look at its implementation in Listing 20-4.

Listing 20-4. The WASM PersistentAuthenticationStateProvider

```
internal sealed class PersistentAuthenticationStateProvider
  : AuthenticationStateProvider
{
  private static readonly
    Task<AuthenticationState> defaultUnauthenticatedTask =
      Task.FromResult(
        new AuthenticationState(
```

```
          new ClaimsPrincipal(
            new ClaimsIdentity())));

  private readonly Task<AuthenticationState> authenticationStateTask
    = defaultUnauthenticatedTask;

  public PersistentAuthenticationStateProvider(
    PersistentComponentState state)
  {
    if (!state.TryTakeFromJson<UserInfo>(nameof(UserInfo), out var
    userInfo)
      || userInfo is null)
    {
      return;
    }

    authenticationStateTask =
      Task.FromResult(
        new AuthenticationState(userInfo.ToClaimsPrincipal()));
  }
  public override Task<AuthenticationState> GetAuthenticationStateAsync()
    => authenticationStateTask;
}
```

When the WASM PersistentAuthenticationStateProvider receives the PersistentComponentState service, it deserializes the UserInfo instance and converts it into a ClaimsPrincipal which is then returned through the AuthenticationState.

This takes care of authentication. The client application now has a ClaimsPrincipal, and we can use the AuthorizeView to protect our resources.

Invoking Services with Auto

How do we secure APIs with auto render mode? Again, our component can be running server or client side. Let us start by considering two options. The service we need it running inside the server project (an internal service), or we want to invoke an external service running in another domain, protected by OpenId Connect.

Using an Internal Service

The BlazorApp.Auto.WithOpenIdConnect project has the WeatherService, running on the server. When our component is running on the server, we can simply pass it the WeatherService. But what when our component starts running in the browser?

The solution is that we expose the WeatherService as an API endpoint in the same domain, and we use the cookie we already have (after authentication) to protect this API endpoint.

Look at the Program class where we add an API endpoint as in Listing 20-5.

Listing 20-5. Exposing a service as an API endpoint

```
app.UseAntiforgery();

app.MapGet("/forecasts-internal",
  async ValueTask<IEnumerable<WeatherForecast>>
  (IWeatherService weatherService) =>
  {
    return await weatherService.GetForecastsAsync();
  })
  .RequireAuthorization(Policies.FromBelgium);

app.MapRazorComponents<App>()
    .AddInteractiveServerRenderMode()
    .AddInteractiveWebAssemblyRenderMode()
    .AddAdditionalAssemblies(typeof(_Imports).Assembly);
```

When the WASM client invokes this API endpoint, the cookie already set by authentication will be passed to the server project, which sets the ClaimsPrincipal. WebAPI will then verify if we should be able to invoke this service, for example, by evaluating any policies set. This endpoint then invokes the original WeatherService and returns the result.

Note You will also see that the server project has the CookieOidcRefresher class. This takes care of refreshing the cookie in case the access token expires. The implementation of this is a security topic, and a bit outside the scope of this book.

Using an External Service

What if I need to invoke a REST API which is in another domain? We have seen in the previous chapter that we can request an access token using OpenId Connect and use it to secure (and gain access) to a REST API. But now the access token sits in the server, and how can we use this access token from the WASM side?

We will invoke the same WeatherAPI from previous chapters. But how can we invoke this from Blazor WASM? We need an access token. Invoking the WeatherAPI from Blazor Server and passing the access token was discussed previously. How do we gain access to the access token in the Blazor WASM project?

We could pass the access token from Blazor Server to Blazor WASM but think about this. Storing the access token on the server is secure, but passing the access token to the WASM application lowers the security of the access token! This opens a lot of ways in which someone could steal the access token. So, we should not do this. What is the alternative?

Backend for Frontend

What we can also do is to invoke an internal API from our Blazor WASM application (as seen in the previous section), which will then invoke the external API, passing the access token. This is known as the Backend for Frontend (BFF) pattern as illustrated by Figure 20-1.

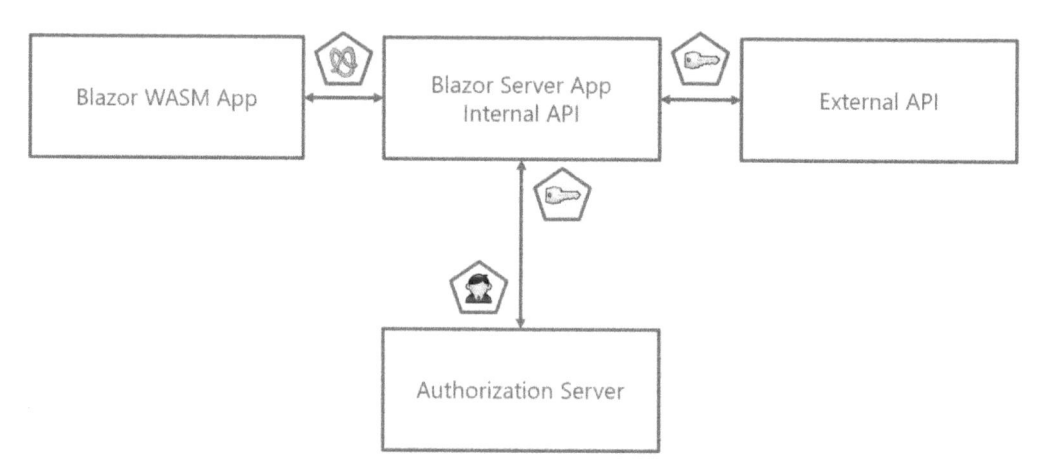

Figure 20-1. Backend for Frontend

When the Blazor WebAssembly project wants to invoke the external service, it invokes an endpoint from the Blazor Server app, which runs in the same domain, so we can use the already set authentication cookie for authentication. The Server API then calls the external API, passing an access token, and returns the result back to WASM.

BFF on the Server

First, we add to the server the internal service which will invoke the external service as in Listing 20-6.

Listing 20-6. Implementing the forwarder service

```
app.MapRazorComponents<App>()
    .AddInteractiveServerRenderMode()
    .AddInteractiveWebAssemblyRenderMode()
    .AddAdditionalAssemblies(typeof(_Imports).Assembly);

app.MapGet("forecasts-forwarder",
  async ([FromServices] ExternalWeatherService weatherService) =>
{
  return await weatherService.GetForecastsAsync();
})
.RequireAuthorization(Policies.FromBelgium);
```

We also need to implement the `ExternalWeatherService` to invoke the external endpoint as shown in Listing 20-7.

Listing 20-7. The ExternalWeatherService

```
public class ExternalWeatherService : IExternalWeatherService
{
  private readonly HttpClient _httpClient;
  private readonly IHttpContextAccessor _httpContextAccessor;

  public ExternalWeatherService(HttpClient httpClient
    , IHttpContextAccessor httpContextAccessor)
  {
    _httpClient = httpClient;
```

```
    _httpContextAccessor = httpContextAccessor;
  }

  public async ValueTask<IEnumerable<WeatherForecast>>
    GetForecastsAsync()
  {
    HttpContext? httpContext =
      _httpContextAccessor.HttpContext
      ?? throw new InvalidOperationException(
        "No HttpContext available");
    string accessToken =
      await httpContext.GetTokenAsync("access_token")
      ?? throw new InvalidOperationException(
        "No access_token was saved.");

    _httpClient.DefaultRequestHeaders.Authorization =
      new("Bearer", accessToken);

    return await _httpClient.GetFromJsonAsync<WeatherForecast[]>
      ("/WeatherForecast") ?? [];
  }
}
```

The ExternalWeatherService first retrieves the access token it already has (ASP. NET Core stores the access token in HttpContext, and you can retrieve it using the GetTokenAsync extension method) and passes it as the Bearer Authorization header to the external service.

Now we need to configure dependency injection in the server project.

We provide the dependencies in case the Weather component is running on the server. In Listing 20-8, we provide two interfaces because there are two weather components.

Listing 20-8. Providing dependencies for server side

```
// Services for Weather component when running server side

builder.Services.AddScoped<IWeatherService, WeatherService>();
builder.Services.AddScoped<IExternalWeatherService, WeatherService>();
```

In Listing 20-7, we require an `ExternalWeatherService`, which requires an `HttpClient`, so we register the `HttpClient` as in Listing 20-9.

Listing 20-9. Registering the HttpClient

```
// Service required for the BFF

builder.Services.AddHttpClient<ExternalWeatherService>(
  client =>
  {
    client.BaseAddress = new Uri("https://localhost:5005");
  });
```

BFF on the WASM Side

Our `ExternalWeather` component requires an `IExternalWeatherService`. The server implements this using the server's `WeatherService` (see Listing 20-8). For WASM, we need to implement this as in Listing 20-10.

Listing 20-10. ExternalWeatherService

```
public class ExternalWeatherServiceProxy :
  IExternalWeatherService
{
  private readonly HttpClient _httpClient;

  public ExternalWeatherServiceProxy(HttpClient httpClient)
  {
    _httpClient = httpClient;
  }

  public async ValueTask<IEnumerable<WeatherForecast>>
    GetForecastsAsync()
  => await _httpClient.GetFromJsonAsync<WeatherForecast[]>
    ("/forecasts-forwarder") ?? [];
}
```

So, this invokes the internal forwarder service. The WASM cookie will be passed automatically to the server, that is all we need to do.

Run the application (run IdentityProvider, then WeatherApi, then BlazorApp.Auto. WithOpenIdConnect, or use the BlazorAuto launchprofile provided with this solution). Login. Select one of the Weather components, and you should see weather forecasts. If you like you can use the browser's debugger and examine the network tab to see the requests being made.

Summary

In this chapter, we looked at how we can build components that use the auto render mode and that require REST services. When using an internal service running on the server project, we can simply rely on the cookie set during authentication. But when we need to invoke an external API, we make the server do all the work and expose an internal API to make the call to the external API. This is known as the Backend for Frontend pattern.

CHAPTER 21

Blazor State Management

Blazor is used to build single-page applications and has a stateful programming model, meaning that a Blazor application keeps its state in memory, as long as the user does not refresh the browser. Refreshing the browser will restart your Blazor application, losing all state in memory. How can you keep the application's state? In this chapter, we will look at how your application can manage its state and pass data between pages, browser tabs, and even different browsers. Some of these techniques we have been using before, and we will also look at building complex Blazor applications using the Redux pattern.

Examining Component State

This chapter comes with a prepared demo, because it reviews some of the techniques we have seen before. So, start Visual Studio and open the StateManagement demo solution. Now start the BlazorApp.StateManagement.WASM project. Your browser should open. Navigate to the Counter page by clicking the Counter link in the navigation column of the application. A familiar component should render.

Click the button a couple of times and then refresh your browser. The Counter goes back to 0! The same thing happens when you click another link in the navigation menu. Imagine that this is your application, and the user just spent a couple of minutes entering their data. Your user clicks on another page, maybe to look at some references the user needs, the user comes back, and all the painstakingly entered data is gone! Should I encounter an application like this, I will most likely vow to never use this application again!

In a Blazor WebAssembly application, your component is running in the browser, and data gets stored in the memory of the browser. With Blazor Server, all the work is done on the server with a SignalR connection to update the DOM. The application's data gets stored in a circuit, which is the way Blazor server differentiates between data of different users. Data in a circuit gets stored in the server's memory. But when the browser is refreshed, the Blazor runtime creates a new circuit, losing all data stored in the original circuit.

All of this means that you should do some extra things to keep your user's data. What kind of data does Blazor store in the browser's memory/circuit?

- Render Tree: Each time Blazor renders your components, it stores this in the Render Tree, which is an in-memory representation of all the HTML markup. This allows Blazor to calculate the difference between the previous render tree, so it only updates the DOM with the changes.

- Component's fields and properties.

- Dependency injection instances.

- JavaScript interop data.

Where can we store data, so it does not get lost, even after a browser refresh? Options are not to store the data, use local storage, use a server, or use the URL.

What Not to Store

First, I would like to note that you only need to save the data that is being created by the user. All other data can easily be reconstructed, for example, it is useless to store the render tree yourself. Blazor can always recreate this from scratch, provided your component's still have their state. Data retrieved using a service, for example, the weather forecasts, can also be retrieved by revisiting the server. You only need to store changes made by the application user, for example, shopping carts, registration information for new users, etc.

Local Storage

All modern browsers allow you to persist data in the browser. You can choose between local storage and session storage, and their use is similar. The main difference is that local storage is kept even when you shut down your machine, while session storage will be lost when you close the application's browser tab or the browser. Another advantage of local storage is that you can easily share data between browser tabs.

CHAPTER 21 BLAZOR STATE MANAGEMENT

With the BlazorApp.StateManagement.WASM application running, click the Local Storage link in the navigation menu. Click the button to increment the counter. Now navigate to the Counter page, and back to the Local Storage page. Your counter keeps its value! Refresh your browser. Again, the counter keeps its value. You can even restart the browser.

How does this work? In the JavaScript interop chapter, we built a local storage service which uses JavaScript interop to store values in local storage. Let us review this again.

Start with the service, which you can find in Listing 21-1. Here we use IJSRuntime to load the JavaScript module from Listing 21-2. It has methods to store values in local storage.

Listing 21-1. The LocalStorage service

```
using Microsoft.JSInterop;

namespace BlazorApp.StateManagement.WASM.Client.Services;

public class LocalStorage : IAsyncDisposable
{
  private readonly Lazy<Task<IJSObjectReference>> moduleTask;

  public LocalStorage(IJSRuntime jsRuntime)
  {
    moduleTask = new(() =>
      jsRuntime.InvokeAsync<IJSObjectReference>(
        "import", "./scripts/localstorage.js").AsTask());
  }

  public async ValueTask<T> GetProperty<T>(string propName)
  {
    IJSObjectReference module = await moduleTask.Value;
    return await module.InvokeAsync<T>("get", propName);
  }

  public async ValueTask SetProperty<T>(string propName, T value)
  {
    IJSObjectReference module = await moduleTask.Value;
    await module.InvokeVoidAsync("set", propName, value);
  }
```

645

CHAPTER 21 BLAZOR STATE MANAGEMENT

```
  public async ValueTask WatchAsync<T>(T instance)
    where T : class
  {
    IJSObjectReference module = await moduleTask.Value;
    await module.InvokeVoidAsync("watch",
      DotNetObjectReference.Create(instance));
  }

  public async ValueTask DisposeAsync()
  {
    if (moduleTask.IsValueCreated)
    {
      IJSObjectReference module = await moduleTask.Value;
      await module.DisposeAsync();
    }
  }
}
```

Listing 21-2. The JavaScript LocalStorage module

```
let get = key => key in localStorage ? JSON.
parse(localStorage[key]) : null;
let set = (key, value) => { localStorage[key] = JSON.stringify(value); };
let watch = async (instance) => {
  window.addEventListener('storage', (e) => {
    instance.invokeMethodAsync('UpdateCounter');
  });
};

export { get, set, watch };
```

The PersistantCounter component from Listing 21-3 uses the local storage service to get the value when it initializes, and again to store the value whenever the user changes it by clicking the button.

Listing 21-3. The PersistantCounter component

```
@page "/persistant-counter"
@using BlazorApp.StateManagement.WASM.Client.Services

<PageTitle>Counter</PageTitle>

<h1>Counter</h1>

<p role="status">Current count: @CurrentCount</p>

<button class="btn btn-primary" @onclick="IncrementCount">Click me</button>

@code {
  private int currentCount = 0;

  [Inject]
  public required LocalStorage LocalStorage { get; set; }

  public int CurrentCount
  {
    get => currentCount;
    set
    {
      if (currentCount != value)
      {
        currentCount = value;
        LocalStorage.SetProperty(nameof(CurrentCount),
          currentCount);
      }
    }
  }

  protected override async Task OnAfterRenderAsync(
    bool firstRender)
  {
    if (firstRender)
    {
```

```
      await UpdateCounter();
      await LocalStorage.WatchAsync(this);
    }
  }

  [JSInvokable]
  public async Task UpdateCounter()
  {
    try
    {
      currentCount = await LocalStorage.GetProperty<int>(
        nameof(CurrentCount));
      StateHasChanged();
    }
    catch { }
  }

  private void IncrementCount()
  {
    CurrentCount++;
  }
}
```

You do need to be careful with the value retrieved from local storage. When this value gets corrupted, it might crash the component, and since this value persisted, the user cannot simply restart the application to fix the problem. That is why there is a try-catch block around this code. Worst case the counter will start from 0 again. In some cases, using session storage is a better alternative, because this will clear once the user closes the tab in the browser.

You can use the browser's debugger to examine data stored in local and session storage. Open the browser's debugger and open the debugger's application tab. Select Local Storage and click the application's URL (e.g., https://localhost:5001). This will display all the local storage keys and values as in Figure 21-1. You might have other keys here, especially when developing because other applications you are building might have data stored here.

CHAPTER 21   BLAZOR STATE MANAGEMENT

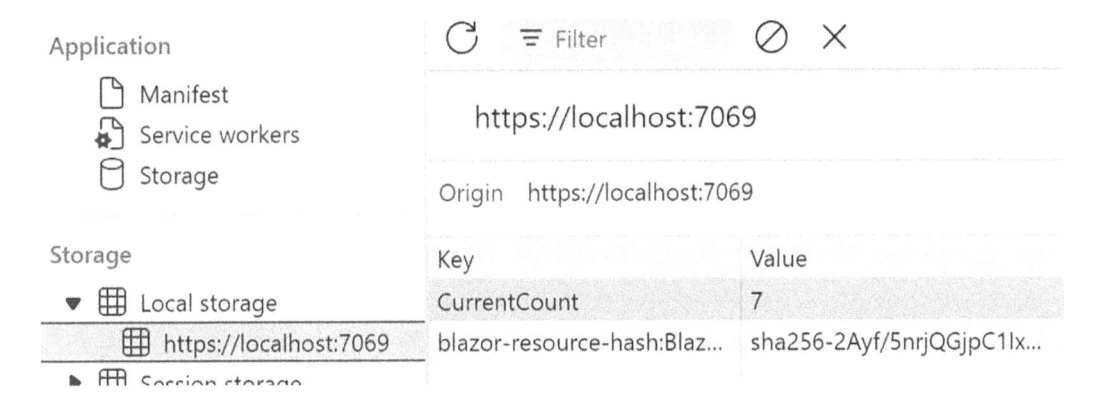

Figure 21-1. The Browser's local storage

One disadvantage of this is that tech savvy users can open local storage in the browser debugger and see or modify the value. So do not store secrets here! With Blazor Server, you can use Protected Storage, which we will discuss later in this chapter.

Local Storage can also be used to communicate between two or more tabs in your browser. With the Local Storage page open, copy the URL and open a new tab to it. Select the Local Storage page and increment the counter. You will see the counter update in the other tab! Every time a value in local storage is modified, the browser will trigger the `storage` event, and you can register for this using the `WatchAsync` method from the local storage service. This will invoke the `UpdateCounter` method from the component, as in Listing 21-3.

URL

In some cases, it might make a lot of sense to store your navigation data, for example, the step count in a wizard, or the product ID being shown, in the URL of the page. This has the advantage that users can add this page to their favorites, and data stored in the URL will survive a browser refresh and work across different browsers. Let us look at an example.

Using the StateManagementWASM demo, click the URL link in the navigation column. This will show the URLCounter component. Now increment the counter using the button and look at the URL. This is where we store the current value of the counter.

Look at the URLCounter component in Listing 21-3. Here we use routing to put the value of the `CurrentCount` in the parameter with the same name. I have also used the `int?` constraint to make this parameter an optional integer. When the button gets clicked, we use the `NavigationManager` to navigate to the same URL, but with an incremented value. That's it.

Listing 21-4. The CounterURL component

```
@page "/url-counter/{CurrentCount:int?}"
@inject NavigationManager navigationManager

<PageTitle>Counter</PageTitle>

<h1>Counter</h1>

<p role="status">Current count: @CurrentCount</p>

<button class="btn btn-primary" @onclick="IncrementCount">Click me</button>
@code {
  [Parameter]
  public int CurrentCount { get; set; }

  private void IncrementCount()
  {
    navigationManager.NavigateTo
      ($"/url-counter/{CurrentCount + 1}");
  }
}
```

Note In a real-life example, you would override OnParametersSet to fetch any data you need for the current URL.

Using Protected Browser Storage

You can use the same techniques to store your state with Blazor Server, but there is one more possibility. We can have our data stored in local or session storage, but now using encryption. This uses the ASP.NET Core Data Protection API which will encrypt your data on the server which will then store the encrypted data in the browser's local storage (or session storage). This only works with Blazor Server because the data protection API requires the server to provide encryption.

In the demo solution, you can find the BlazorApp.StateManagement.Server project. Run this project and click the Local Storage navigation link. Increment the counter and now open the browser's debugger. Choose the application tab and click the application's URL in Local Storage. Look at the counter key (again, other keys might show up from other projects). The counter key is clearly encrypted here (containing some integer value).

Let us look at the ProtectedStorageCounter component as in Listing 21-5.

Listing 21-5. The CounterProtectedStorage component

```
@page "/protected-counter"
@using Microsoft.AspNetCore.Components.Server.ProtectedBrowserStorage

<PageTitle>Counter</PageTitle>

<h1>Counter</h1>

<p role="status">Current count: @currentCount</p>

<button class="btn btn-primary" @onclick="IncrementCount">
  Click me
</button>

@code {

  [Inject]
  public required ProtectedLocalStorage localStorage
  { get; set; }

  private int currentCount = 0;

  private async Task IncrementCount()
  {
    currentCount++;
    await localStorage.SetAsync("counter", currentCount);
  }

  protected override async Task OnInitializedAsync()
  {
    var state = await localStorage.GetAsync<int>("counter");
    if (state.Success)
```

```
    {
      currentCount = state.Value;
    }
  }
}
```

To use protected storage, you use the `ProtectedLocalStorage` (or `ProtectedSessionStorage`) instance which you request using dependency injection. This instance allows you to get, set, and delete a key asynchronously.

In the `OnInitializedAsync` method, use the `GetAsync` method to retrieve the value. This might not succeed so this method returns a `ProtectedBrowserStorageResult`, which has a `Success` property. When this property is `true`, you can access the value using the `Value` property.

When the button gets clicked, use the `SetAsync` method to update the value.

The Redux Pattern

Building complex applications with Blazor can become challenging. Single-page applications must manage a lot more states than traditional web pages because some of this state is shared among different pages. Sometimes customers might also want advanced features such as Undo/Redo functionality. *Redux* is a pattern used to reduce an application's complexity. With redux we will apply a couple of principles which are based on a minimal API and giving us predictable behavior using immutability. With redux, state mutability becomes predictable. Let us start with a couple of building blocks in redux.

The Big Picture

With redux we have an application store which we modify through actions and reducers. When the user interacts with the application, we *dispatch* an action which holds the changes we need to apply. Then the *reducer* applies these changes to the *store*, resulting in a new store instance. Our components (the *view*) will then update themselves from the store. This process then repeats itself, as illustrated in Figure 21-2. Note the *unidirectional flow of changes*.

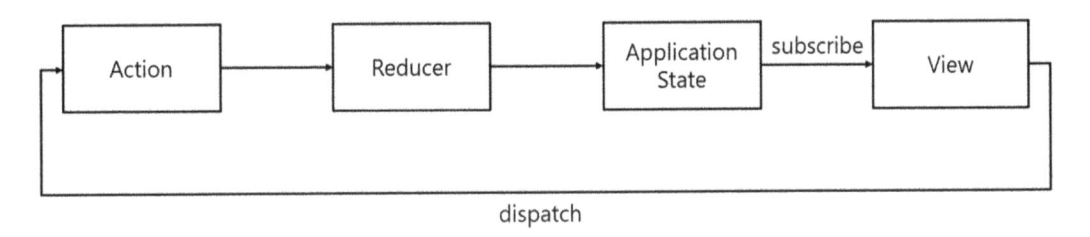

Figure 21-2. Redux overview

The Application Store

With redux we will store all our state in a single object hierarchy, known as the application store. We will consider this store to be the "Single Source of Truth." To keep things manageable, the store is immutable, meaning that every change to the store will result in a new instance. Please realize that this does not mean that we will create a deep clone of the store instance after every change, no; a single object in the hierarchy will be replaced with a new instance when it needs a change. For example, with the PizzaPlace application, the store would contain three pieces of data, the menu, the shopping basket, and the customer information. When we add something to the shopping basket, we will get a new store instance, with the same menu and customer; only the shopping basket will be replaced with a new instance. Note that this allows us to keep track of each state change and easily undo this, opening features like undo/redo. To undo a change, we simply restore the previous state from our tracked states! The application store allows the views (Blazor Components) to access its data and uses reducers to modify it (by creating new immutable fragments).

There is another pattern called *flux*; the only difference between these two is that with flux we have multiple stores, and redux chooses to put everything in a single store.

Actions

Whenever the application wants to trigger a state change, for example, because of the user clicking a button, a timer expiring, etc., we dispatch an action. The action contains the data needed so the dispatcher knows what to do. For example, with the Counter component, we can have an IncrementCounterAction class, which does not contain any data because the Type of the instance is enough for the dispatcher to handle it. Should we want to set the Counter to a specific value, we can have the UpdateCounterAction which would contain the desired value. Actions describe what happened in the application and are used by the dispatcher to apply the desired change.

Reducers

The responsibility of a reducer is to apply an action to the store. Reducers must be pure functions. A *pure function* is a function that always returns the same result for its parameters. For example, adding two numbers together is a pure function; calling add on 2 and 3 will always return 5. Getting the time is not, since calling this function returns a different value at different points in time.

Views

Views (in our case Blazor components) access the store to render the data and subscribe for changes in the store so they can update themselves when the data has been changed through a reducer.

Using Fluxor

Time to look at an actual implementation using the redux pattern. We will use *Fluxor*, which was written by Peter Morris and the GitHub community and which is an amazing implementation of the flux pattern (of which redux is a special case).

Start by creating a new Blazor Server Web App project; call it BlazorApp.WithRedux.

Let us first implement the Counter component using the Fluxor library, so add the Fluxor.Blazor.Web NuGet package to the project.

Creating the Store

Add a new folder called Stores to the project.

Add a new class called `AppStore` as in Listing 21-6.

CHAPTER 21   BLAZOR STATE MANAGEMENT

Listing 21-6. Our application's store

```
using BlazorApp.WithRedux.Entities;

namespace BlazorApp.WithRedux.Stores;

public record AppStore(
    int ClickCounter,
    bool IsLoading,
    WeatherForecast[]? Forecasts
    );
```

Here I am using the new C# `record` type, which is a very practical way to build an immutable reference type. With its convenient syntax, we can create the `AppStore` type and add three immutable properties. Because of that, the parameters of the `AppStore` type use *pascal casing*. These parameters will get compiled into public read-only properties on the `AppStore` type, so we should use the naming convention for properties. You can learn more about record types at https://docs.microsoft.com/dotnet/csharp/whats-new/tutorials/records. The `ClickCounter` property holds the Counter's data, and the `IsLoading` and `Forecasts` properties hold the data used by the Weather component.

The `AppStore` instance will be initialized using the generic `Feature<T>` type that comes with the Fluxor library. Add a new folder called Features to the project and add the `AppFeature` class as in Listing 21-7.

Listing 21-7. The AppFeature class

```
using BlazorApp.WithRedux.Stores;
using Fluxor;

namespace BlazorApp.WithRedux.Features;
public class AppFeature : Feature<AppStore>
{
    public override string GetName()
    => nameof(AppStore);

    protected override AppStore GetInitialState()
    => new(
        ClickCounter: 0,
```

655

```
        IsLoading: false,
        Forecasts: []
        );
}
```

The `AppFeature` will initialize our `AppStore` instance, since Fluxor will call the `GetInitialState` method and use the result as the initial store's value.

Using the Store in Our Blazor Application

Open Program.cs and add support for Fluxor by configuring dependency injection as in Listing 21-8. Fluxor uses dependency injection to find our redux classes such as the reducers. Since these are defined in the project, we use the `AppStore` class to retrieve the appropriate assembly.

Listing 21-8. Enabling Fluxor in Blazor

```
builder.Services.AddRazorComponents()
    .AddInteractiveServerComponents();

builder.Services.AddFluxor(options =>
{
  options.ScanAssemblies(typeof(AppStore).Assembly);
});

builder.Services.AddScoped<WeatherService>();
```

Open the App.razor class and add the `StoreInitializer` component to the top as in Listing 21-9. This component will initialize the store for the current user using the `AppFeature` class.

Listing 21-9. Adding the store initializer

```
<Fluxor.Blazor.Web.StoreInitializer />

<Router AppAssembly="typeof(Program).Assembly">
  <Found Context="routeData">
    <RouteView RouteData="routeData" DefaultLayout="typeof(Layout.
    MainLayout)" />
```

```
    <FocusOnNavigate RouteData="routeData" Selector="h1" />
  </Found>
</Router>
```

Let us implement the Counter and Weather component using the redux pattern. We will put each component in its own folder, because each will require a couple of classes, and this makes this better organized (in my humble opinion).

Create a new Counter folder in the Pages folder, and move the Counter component inside it. Our counter allows the user to increment the counter, so we need an action. Add the IncrementCounterAction from Listing 21-10 to the Counter folder.

Listing 21-10. The IncrementCounterAction

```
namespace BlazorApp.WithRedux.Components.Pages.Counter;

public record IncrementCounterAction()
{ }
```

Again, I use a record type, since the action should not be mutable (and I like the conciseness). This action does not need any data, since the type of the action is enough to allow the reducer to do its work.

Implement the Counter component as in Listing 21-11.

Listing 21-11. The counter's code

```
@page "/counter"
@inherits Fluxor.Blazor.Web.Components.FluxorComponent

<PageTitle>Counter</PageTitle>

<h1>Counter</h1>

<p role="status">Current count: @AppStore.ClickCounter</p>

<button class="btn btn-primary" @onclick="IncrementCount">Click me</button>

@code {
  [Inject]
  public required IState<AppStore> State { get; set; }

  [Inject]
```

```
  public required IDispatcher Dispatcher { get; set; }

  public AppStore AppStore => State.Value;

  private readonly IncrementCounterAction _incrementCounterAction = new();

  private void IncrementCount()
  {
    Dispatcher.Dispatch(_incrementCounterAction);
  }
}
```

Each component that uses the store should subscribe to changes in the store. The `FluxorComponent` takes care of that, so we need to derive our component from this base class.

Our counter needs access to the store, so we use dependency injection to retrieve an instance of `IState<AppStore>`. This interface wraps our `AppState` and can be retrieved using the `Value` property. To simplify access, I have also added a helper property `AppStore`. Our counter needs to display a counter which is in the store, so we use the `@AppStore.ClickCounter` to display its value.

When you click the increment button, we dispatch the `IncrementCounterAction` instance to the Dispatcher, which we also get using dependency injection.

Build and run the application. Select the Counter link. You get a Counter with initial value 0, but the button does not do anything yet. Time to add a reducer.

Implementing the Reducer

Add a new class called `CounterReducer` to the Counter folder and implement it as in Listing 21-12.

Listing 21-12. The CounterReducer static class

```
using BlazorApp.WithRedux.Stores;
using Fluxor;

namespace BlazorApp.WithRedux.Components.Pages.Counter;

public static class CounterReducer
{
```

```
    [ReducerMethod]
    public static AppStore ReduceIncrementCounterAction(
        AppStore state, IncrementCounterAction action)
        => state with { ClickCounter = state.ClickCounter + 1 };
}
```

This static class can have reducer methods, taking the current state and an action, and returning a new state. Reducer methods should be pure functions, so calling a reducer with the same arguments should result in the same result. I know I am repeating myself, but this is very important. Since reducers should be pure, they normally do not require any data except what they can find in the AppStore and Action class. So not to be tempted, I advise you make reducer methods `static`, and you add it to a `static` class. This should not limit the testability of your reducers.

Fluxor also requires you to add the `[ReducerMethod]` attribute to the method, enabling it to detect reducers with reflection. In general, using reflection is slow, but if you just do reflection once, especially during the initialization of your application, this is no problem. So don't worry about this. This reducer should return a new AppStore instance, with the ClickCounter incremented by 1. Again, C# records are very practical for this because we can make a full copy (a shallow clone) of the AppStore using the *with syntax*, and listing the properties that need to change. This syntax will return a new instance of the store, with new values for the listed properties. With redux your component knows the action, but not how this will be implemented by a reducer, again keeping this logic out of your component!

Run the application and click the button on the Counter component. It should increase! Nice!

Redux Effects

What if we need to call an asynchronous method? Do we call it from within the reducer? No! Since reducers are synchronous, calling the asynchronous method would either block the reducer or return without the required result. To solve this, redux uses *effects*, which are asynchronous and function through use of actions and reducers. With effects we will use two actions, one to start the effect asynchronously, and when the effect is done, it uses another action to dispatch the result. The best way to understand effects is with an example, so let us implement the Weather component with redux. Create a Weather folder and move the Weather component inside.

CHAPTER 21   BLAZOR STATE MANAGEMENT

Adding the First Action

Start by adding a `FetchWeatherAction` action from Listing 21-13 to the Weather folder which will initiate the asynchronous call to fetch the weather forecasts.

Listing 21-13. The FetchWeatherAction record

```
namespace BlazorApp.WithRedux.Components.Pages.Weather;

public record FetchWeatherAction
{}
```

Implement the Weather component as in Listing 21-14.

Listing 21-14. The Weather component's code

```
@code {
  [Inject]
  public required IState<AppStore> State { get; set; }

  [Inject]
  public required IDispatcher Dispatcher { get; set; }

  public AppStore AppStore => State.Value;

  private WeatherForecast[]? forecasts;

  private readonly FetchWeatherAction _fetchDataAction = new();

  protected override async Task OnInitializedAsync()
  {
    Dispatcher.Dispatch(_fetchDataAction);

    // Simulate asynchronous loading to demonstrate a loading indicator
  }
}
```

Update the Weather component as in Listing 21-15 to inherit from `FluxorComponent`. Again, we inject the store and dispatcher, and we dispatch the `FetchWeatherAction` in the `OnInitialized` life-cycle method.

CHAPTER 21 BLAZOR STATE MANAGEMENT

We also check the Store's `IsLoading` property to show the loading UI while we are fetching the data. Finally, we will iterate over the `Forecasts` property to show the weather forecasts.

Listing 21-15. The Weather component's markup

```
@page "/weather"
@inherits Fluxor.Blazor.Web.Components.FluxorComponent

@using BlazorApp.WithRedux.Entities

<PageTitle>Weather</PageTitle>

<h1>Weather</h1>

<p>This component demonstrates showing data.</p>

@if (AppStore.IsLoading && AppStore.Forecasts is not null)
{
  <p><em>Loading...</em></p>
}
else
{
  <table class="table">
    <thead>
      <tr>
        <th>Date</th>
        <th>Temp. (C)</th>
        <th>Temp. (F)</th>
        <th>Summary</th>
      </tr>
    </thead>
    <tbody>
      @foreach (var forecast in AppStore.Forecasts!)
      {
        <tr>
          <td>@forecast.Date.ToShortDateString()</td>
          <td>@forecast.TemperatureC</td>
```

661

CHAPTER 21 BLAZOR STATE MANAGEMENT

```
            <td>@forecast.TemperatureF</td>
            <td>@forecast.Summary</td>
        </tr>
      }
    </tbody>
  </table>
}
```

We also need to add a reducer for this action, so add the FetchWeatherReducer class to the Weather folder from Listing 21-16. This will simply set the IsLoading property on our store, so the Weather component will show the loading UI.

Listing 21-16. The ReduceFetchDataAction reducer method

```
using BlazorApp.WithRedux.Stores;
using Fluxor;

namespace BlazorApp.WithRedux.Components.Pages.Weather;

public class FetchWeatherReducer
{
  [ReducerMethod]
  public static AppStore ReduceFetchWeatherAction(
    AppStore state, FetchWeatherAction action)
    => state with { IsLoading = true };
}
```

Implement the WeatherService

Add the WeatherService to the Weather folder from Listing 21-17.

Listing 21-17. The WeatherService

```
using BlazorApp.WithRedux.Entities;

namespace BlazorApp.WithRedux.Components.Pages.Weather;

public class WeatherService
{
```

CHAPTER 21 BLAZOR STATE MANAGEMENT

```
  static string[] summaries = ["Freezing", "Bracing", "Chilly", "Cool",
"Mild", "Warm", "Balmy", "Hot", "Sweltering", "Scorching"];

  public async Task<WeatherForecast[]> GetForecastsAsync()
  {
    // Simulate asynchronous loading to demonstrate a loading indicator
    await Task.Delay(5000);

    var startDate = DateOnly.FromDateTime(DateTime.Now);
    return Enumerable.Range(1, 5).Select(index => new WeatherForecast
    {
      Date = startDate.AddDays(index),
      TemperatureC = Random.Shared.Next(-20, 55),
      Summary = summaries[Random.Shared.Next(summaries.Length)]
    }).ToArray();
  }
}
```

Add the Second Action and Effect

Add another action called FetchWeatherResultAction to the Weather folder as in Listing 21-18. This type has one property holding the forecasts which we will use in the reducer.

Listing 21-18. The FetchWeatherResultAction record

```
using BlazorApp.WithRedux.Entities;

namespace BlazorApp.WithRedux.Components.Pages.Weather;

public record FetchWeatherResultAction(WeatherForecast[]? Forecasts);
```

Add a new FetchWeatherEffect class to the Weather folder. Now implement the effect as in Listing 21-19.

Listing 21-19. The FetchWeatherActionEffect class

```
using BlazorApp.WithRedux.Entities;
using Fluxor;

namespace BlazorApp.WithRedux.Components.Pages.Weather;
```

```
public class FetchWeatherEffect : Effect<FetchWeatherAction>
{
  private readonly WeatherService _weatherService;
  public FetchWeatherEffect(WeatherService weatherService)
  {
    _weatherService = weatherService;
  }
  public override async Task HandleAsync
    (FetchWeatherAction action, IDispatcher dispatcher)
  {
    WeatherForecast[]? forecasts =
      await _weatherService.GetForecastsAsync();
    dispatcher.Dispatch(new FetchWeatherResultAction(forecasts));
  }
}
```

Our effect needs to inherit from the Effect<T> base class, where T is the action that will trigger the effect. When the Weather component dispatches the FetchWeatherAction, this effect gets instantiated, and the HandleAsync method will be invoked by Fluxor. When your effect needs some dependency, it can just ask using the effect's constructor. Dependency Injection will provide! Inside the HandleAsync method, we call the asynchronous method, in this case the GetForecastsAsync, and when that returns, we dispatch the result using the FetchWeatherResultAction.

Now we need another reducer, so add the method to the FetchWeatherReducer class as in Listing 21-20. This will set the store's IsLoading to false and set our Forecasts store property to the Forecasts that were fetched by the effect.

Listing 21-20. The ReduceFetchWeatherResultAction reducer

```
[ReducerMethod]
public static AppStore ReduceFetchWeatherResultAction(
  AppStore state, FetchWeatherResultAction action)
  => state with { IsLoading = false, Forecasts = action.Forecasts };
```

Build and run. You should be able to fetch the forecasts now!

Think of effects as an interception mechanism that gets triggered by dispatching a certain action, resulting in another action to complete the deal.

Summary

In this chapter, we looked at state management, so how do we keep state around even when the user refreshes the browser? We can store our application state in local storage, the server and the URL. Then we looked at the Redux pattern, which is used to build complex applications. Redux makes this easier by applying a couple of principles. Components data bind to the Store object, which you mutate by dispatching actions that contain the required change. Then a reducer applies this change to the store which will trigger an update of your components, completing the circle. Redux and flux have the advantage that you end up with a lot of little classes which are easier to maintain, applying the single responsibility principle.

Index

A

ACCESSTOKEN placeholder, 394
Access tokens, 585–588, 638, 640
Actions, 652-654, 657, 659, 660, 662–665
ActiveCircuitHandler, 356
AddAdditionalAssemblies, 349, 351
AddHttpClient, 476
AddInteractiveServerComponents, 22, 342, 343, 351, 358
AddInteractiveServerRenderMode, 343, 351
AddInteractiveWebAssemblyComponents, 349, 351, 358, 479
AddInteractiveWebAssemblyRenderMode, 349, 351
AddKeyed methods, 171
AddLineSegment, 496, 506, 507
AddPizzaToBasket method, 104
AddRazorComponents, 22, 333, 343, 349, 351, 358
AddSegments method, 505
AddSigningCredentials method, 560
AddSingleton extension method, 158
Ahead-Of-Time compilation (AOT), 539, 540
Ajax, 2
Alert component, 51–53, 427, 452
AllowedScopes, 617, 622, 626
AngleSharp Diffing library, 456, 457
Angular, 9, 65
AnimalKind enumeration, 258, 259
Ant Blazor, 254

APIScope, 588
App component, 23, 58, 254, 312, 334, 371, 390, 464, 481, 487, 488, 497, 607
applicationUrl, 607
app.MapGet method, 463
appsettings.json file, 609, 623, 626
AS, *see* Authorization server (AS), 554
ASP.NET Blazor, 277
   See also QuickGrid
ASP.NET Core, 7, 11, 13, 16, 18, 22, 463
ASP.NET MVC, 7, 43
ASP.NET project, 463
Asynchronous operations, 81
Asynchronous re-renders
   SetResult, 454
   TaskCompletionSource<T> class, 454
   testing, 454–456
   WaitForState method, 455
Attribute splatting, 231, 232
aud, 552
Authentication, 549, 550, 567, 590, 609–611, 631
Authentication component, 606, 607
AuthenticationState, 553, 567, 568, 573, 574, 584, 601, 620
AuthenticationStateProvider class, 567, 568, 620, 632
Authorization, 549
Authorization Code flow, 554, 603, 609
AuthorizationMessageHandler, 618
Authorization server (AS), 554
Authorize, 616, 617, 619, 620, 623, 624, 628

INDEX

AuthorizeView, 569, 570, 573, 577, 583, 584, 599, 601, 606, 607, 619, 621, 625, 626, 628, 629, 631, 636
AuthtenticationState, 631
Auto, 350–354
AutoIncrement method, 81

B

Backend for Frontend (BFF) pattern, 638–642
Base-64 encoded response, 525
Bearer, 590–592
Beta-testing, 405–406
BFF pattern, *see* Backend for Frontend (BFF) pattern
Binary encoding, 525, 526
@bind-value, 73, 74
Blazor
    App component, 23
    auto rendering, 12
    bootstrap process, 31–35
    debugging, 26–29
    dependency injection, 22
    hot reload, 29–31
    JavaScript, 23
    layout component, 24–26
    middleware, 22
    nullable reference, 36–42
    project's structure, 24
    RTM version, 12
    Server, 9–11
    in SignalR (*see* SignalR)
    static website, 7
    WASM, 7, 9
BlazorApp.Auto.WithOpenIdConnect project, 637, 642

BlazorApp.Components. ComponentLibraries.csproj file, 243
BlazorApp.Components. MyComponentLibrary, 242, 243
BlazorApp.DependencyInjection. Comparison project, 162, 165
BlazorApp.JavaScriptInterop project, 370
Blazor application, 10–12, 28, 34, 60, 159, 186, 275, 313, 387
BlazorApp.PetHotel, 258
BlazorApp.PizzaPlace project, 396
    ConsoleOrderService, 178
    HardCodedMenuService class, 175
    Home component, 172
    IMenuService, 173, 174
    IOrderService, 178, 179
    IOrderService abstraction as C# interface, 177
    MenuService, 176
    PlaceOrder method, 178, 179
    State property, 173
BlazorApp.PizzaPlace.Shared project, 142
BlazorApp.Policies, 627
BlazorApp.ServerInteractivity, 342
BlazorApp.UsinggRPC, 511, 516
BlazorApp.WASMInteractivity, 348
BlazorApp.WASM.WithOpenIdConnect, 605, 610, 615, 617, 621, 627
Blazor auto render mode
    BFF pattern, 638
        on server, 639–641
        on WASM, 641–642
    Blazor WASM project, 635–636
    challenges, 631
    invoke services with auto
        use external service, 638
        use internal service, 637

INDEX

PersistingAuthenticationStateProvider class, 633–636
Blazor Bootstrap, 252, 253
Blazor component, 43, 376, 402
    Add New Item, 50
    alert component, 51-53
    @code section, 46
    ComponentBase, 46
    Counter component, 47
    EditorRequired, 53, 54
    generated code, 47-50
    and HTML markup, 46
    life cycle (*see* Life cycle hooks)
    logging, 60-64
    and MVC applications, 46
    and namespaces, 54, 55
    new component with code, 51
    PowerShell command, 46
    source generator, 47
    styling, 58-60
    view and view model, 56-57
    with Visual Studio, 50
Blazor dependency lifetime
    Blazor Server Experiment, 165, 166
    Blazor Wasm, 161
    Blazor WebAssembly Experiment, 162, 164
    experiment result, 169, 170
    OwningComponentBase class, 167–169
    SRUsingServices, 162
    WASMUsingServices, 162
Blazor error boundaries, 217-220
Blazor forms
    add Radio Buttons, 118, 119
    Countries class, 114
    DebuggingExtensions, 115
    enter details, member, 119, 120
    genders, 114
    InputCheckbox, 118
    InputSelect, 117, 118
    InputText, 116
        Email, 116
        Password, 117
    InputTextArea, 117
    Member class, 114
    MemberForm, 115, 116
    PowerShell script, 113
blazorLocalStorage glue functions, 371
Blazor project
    Counter screen, 20, 21
    fetch data screen, 21
    Home component, 20
    install prerequisites
        .NET CLR, 13
        PowerShell, 16
        Visual Studio (VS), 13, 14
        VSC, 15
    Kestrel, 22
    SPA, 20
    templates
        ASP.NET Core, 16
        description, 16
        .NET CLI, 18, 19
        SignalR, 17
        Visual Studio, 17, 18
        VSC, 16, 20
        WASM, 16
    VS, 20
    Weather link, 21
Blazor routing
    browser's URI, 303
    Counter component, 304
    Found template, 304
    Open Routes.razor, 303
    Router component, 304

INDEX

Blazor runtime, 13, 69, 79, 195, 245, 336, 352, 439, 535
blazorserver template, 17
Blazor Server, 9, 159, 160, 162, 312, 341, 370, 461, 631, 632, 638, 639
    JavaScript, 10
    render tree, 10
    running, 12
    runtime model, 10
    SignalR, 10
    vs. WASM, 11
    Web App, 342
Blazor templates, 52
Blazor validation
    custom validation feedback, 126
        CSS validation rules, 125, 126
        custom CSS rules, change validation feedback, 126
        invalid input, invalid class, 125
        add modified class, 125
        validation messages, validation-message CSS class, 125
        valid class, 124, 125
    DataAnnotations, 120–122
    ValidationMessage, 122, 124
    ValidationsSummary, 122, 124
Blazor WASM, 160
Blazor.Wasm.OpenIdConnect, 607
blazorwasm template, 16
Blazor Web App, 17, 464
    ASP.NET Core, 18
    Blazor Server, 18
    template, 17, 20, 23
    URL, 19
Blazor WebAssembly, 16, 43, 61–63, 159, 164, 312, 315, 361, 461, 468, 487
BlazorWebAssemblyLazyLoad element, 315

Blazor website, 371
BoardHub class, 502, 503
Boolean expression, 69
Bootstrap process
    Blazor Server
        browser's debugger, 34
        project and solution, 34
        server-side Blazor network activity, 35
        SignalR, 35
        VSC, 34
    Blazor WASM
        clear browser's storage, 32
        download size with empty cache, 33, 34
        download size with filled cache, 33, 34
        F12, 31
        free download, 31
        .NET libraries, 33
        network log, 32, 33
Browser war, 1–3
Bugs
    beta-testing, 405
    coding, 404
    integration, 405
    post-release sofrware, 406
    requirements, 404
    software project, 403
builder.Build().RunAsync(), 627
BuildRenderTree method, 49
Built-in components
    component libraries (*see* Public component libraries)
    DynamicComponent (*see* DynamicComponent component)
    HeadContent component, 257
    HeadOutlet component, 257

PageTitle component, 256, 257
uploading files with InputFile (*see*
　　InputFile component)
Built-in virtualization, 222
bUnit tests, razor
　ChildContent, 452
　Imports.razor file, 449
　MarkupMatches method, 450
　passing parameters, 451, 452
　RAlertShould, 452
　RCounterShould, 450
　RTemplatedListShould, 452
　RTwoWayCounterShould, 451
　sample test, 450
　templated component, 453

C

C#
　compiler, 56
　editor, 57
　lambda function, 71
　nullable reference, 36–38
　for VSC, 15
Claims-based security, 549
canvas.js, 499
CascadingAuthenticationState, 577
CascadingParameter attribute, 199, 204
CascadingValue component, 198, 201
　fixed cascading value, 203
　named cascading value, 201
　root-level cascading value, 204
　SomeComponent component, 202
Chakra, 3
Change detection
　AutoIncrement method, 80
　Counter.razor, 79
　DOM, 79
　lambda function, 80
　StateHasChanged, 81, 82
　SynchronizationContext, 80
Child components, 60, 95–96
ChildContent, 48, 51–54, 56, 57, 64
Circuit, 643, 644
Claims, 549, 551–553, 558, 562, 563, 566,
　　567, 581, 584, 585, 597, 601
Claims based security, 549
ClaimsPrincipal, 553, 554, 565–568, 576,
　　590, 593, 594, 632, 633, 635–637
CLI, *see* Command Line Interface (CLI)
ClientId, 554, 559, 566, 580, 582
ClientSecret, 554, 566
cloud.png file, 245
Code challenge, 604–605
Code verifier, 604, 605
Coding, 404–405
Command Line Interface (CLI), 6, 16, 18, 30
ComponentBase, 46, 64, 84, 260, 295, 360
Component library
　add new component library
　　project, 241
　BlazorApp.Components.
　　MyComponentLibrary, 242
　build, 241
　create, 241
　dotnet new command, 242
　"ListView" and "PWListView"
　　components, 242
　NuGet package, 243
　static resource, 245–246
　@using statements, 244
　using library components, 244–245
Components, 43, 46, 47, 51, 53–55, 64
Conditional attributes, 68, 69
Config.GetClients method, 622
ConsoleOrderService class, 178

INDEX

Constant-based routing, 312
    string constants, 312
Constructor dependency injection, 154, 155
Counter component, 47, 59, 249, 256, 308, 309, 313, 315, 316, 349, 351–353, 374, 375
CounterData class, 197
Counter.razor, 49
Counter Route's NavLink, 302
Counter styles, 78
CounterWithService component, 385, 386
CounterWithShouldRender component, 190, 192
Count property, 197, 198
Cryptographic hash method, 604
CSS isolation, 58–60
CurrentCount parameter property, 305
Customer class, 138
CustomerEntry component, 139, 140, 145, 396
CustomerFluentValidator, 142–144
Custom validation
    CustomValidator<T> class, 130
    dataAnnotations, 135
    EditContext, 126, 127
    EditForm component, 128, 130
    GetFieldValidator method, 132
    MemberCustomValidatior, 130
    MemberCustomValidator, 128, 132
    OnFieldChanged event, 130
    OnInitialized method, 128
    OnValidationRequested event, 130
    ValidateEmail method, 132

D

DataAnnotations, 120–122, 135
DataAnnotationsValidator, 122

Data binding
    asynchronous method, 92, 93
    @bind-value:{event}, 74, 75
    change detection, 79–82
    child component, 95–96
    C# lambda function, 71
    and event handling, 69–79
    home component, 94
    one-way, 65–69
    parent–child communication, 82–92
    PizzaPlace single-page application, 96–110
    two-way, 65, 71–74
Data Protection API, 650
Data Transfer Object (DTO), 485, 486
Debugging, 26, 105, 106
Debugging Blazor
    VS, 26, 28
    VSC, 26, 28, 29
DebuggingExtensions, 105
DefaultScheme, 565
Delay component, 84–87, 90–92
Delay to the Components folder, 84
DepartmentSelector component, 185
Dependencies
    inject bUnit, 437, 439, 440
    replace fake objects, 440
Dependency Injection
    constructor, 154, 155
    IoCC, 154, 156, 157
    .NET 8 keyed services
        AddKeyed methods, 171
        IGreeter implementations, 171
        IGreeter interface with implementations, 170
    .NET 9 constructor injection, 172
    ProductsService, 153
    Program class, 157

INDEX

properties, 155, 156
scoped dependency, 160
Singleton dependencies, 158, 159
transient dependencies, 159, 160
Dependency inversion
    component, ProductsService, 150
    ProductList component, 150
    ProductsService, 150
    Service object, 149
    as _tight-coupling_, 150
Dependency inversion principle, 153
    IProductsService interface
        abstraction, 151
            ProductList component, 151, 152
        testing, 152
Deploying Blazor Web Apps
    alternatives, 539
    create simple website, 529, 530
    download size, 537, 538
    fix base tag, 531, 532
    fixing GitHub 404s, 537
    gh-pages, 530
    GitHub, 527, 528
    Publish
        Command Line, 535
        disabling Jekyll, 536
        GitHub Branch, 535, 536
        Visual Studio, 532–534
    WASM project, 531
DevExpression Blazor Components, 254
Disabled attribute, 68, 69
discards, 80
DismissibleAlert, 56–57, 82–84, 86, 87, 91, 95
Dismissible.razor
    code, 57
    markup, 56
Dispatcher, 658, 660
Dispose method, 194, 195

DisposeAsync method, 195
Don't Repeat Yourself_ (DRY), 412
DTO, *see* Data Transfer Object (DTO)
Duende IdentityServer, 555, 560, 578, 601
Dumb and Smart Components, 326
DynamicComponent component, 258
    AnimalComponent, 260
    AnimalKind, 258, 259
    AnimalMetaData, 264
    AnimalSelector, 262, 263, 265–267
    BlazorApp.PetHotel, 258
    CatComponent, 260, 263
    ComponentMetadata, 264
    DogComponent, 261

E

ECMAScript, 2
EditContext, 137
EditorRequired, 53, 54
Electron, 9
ElementReference, 499
EmitCompilerGeneratedFiles, 47
EmployeeList component, 185
Enhance, 340
ErrorBoundary component, 217, 218, 220
Error-prone process, 65
EventCallback, 91, 92
Event handling
    default actions, 75–76
    event arguments, 70
    event binding syntax, 69, 70
    event propagation, 77–79
    formatting dates, 79
    IncrementCount method, 69
Event propagation, 77–79
{EVENT}:stopPropagation attribute, 78
exp, 552

INDEX

ExternalWeather component, 641
ExternalWeatherService, 639-641

F

F12, 31
FetchData component, 523
FilteredEmployees, 287, 289
FluentMemberValidator, 133, 134
FluentUI components, 249, 250
FluentValidation, 133-135, 142-144
FluentValidationValidator, 134, 144
Flux, 653
Fluxor, 654
FocusOnNavigate component, 304
ForecastGrpcService, 520-521
Forms, 340, 341
    Blazor, 113-119
    component, 340
    HTML, 111-113
Framework-dependent deployment, 540
FromBelgium policy, 626, 627
FromClaimsPrincipal, 633

G

GetAllSegments method, 506
GetAuthenticationStateAsync method, 620
GetClients method, 626
GetFieldValidator method, 132
GetForecastResponse, 514
GetForecasts method, 463, 467, 513
getForecasts service method, 517
GetFromJsonAsync, 467, 470-473, 491
GetMeasurementPage method, 229
GetMeasurements method, 223
GetMeasurementsPage method, 227
GetMenu method, 174

GetTokenAsync extension method, 640
GetUsers method, 557
GitHub, 12, 527
Glue functions, 369, 382
Google Earth, 4
Google Maps, 2
Google's Gmail, 294
GrandChild component, 199, 200
GrandMother component, 198, 200
Grid component, 207
Grid templated component, 207-209, 211
Grid<TITem> component, 206
gRPC
    BlazorApp.UsinggRPC, 511
    client
        ForecastGrpcService, 520-521
        GrpcChannel
            configuration, 521-523
    configure dependency injection, 518
    framework, 510
    middleware, 518
    principles, 510
    protocol buffers, 510
    vs. REST, 523-526
    REST call, 510
    on server, 516
    service contract, 513-515
    services, 516-518
    with text encoding, 525
    tool installation, 511, 512
GrpcChannel configuration, 521-523
GrpcWebHandler, 521
Gutter, 28, 29

H

HardCodedMenuService class, 175
HeadContent component, 257

HeadOutlet
    component, 256, 257
Home component, 146, 172, 191, 234, 343
Hosted Blazor WebAssembly
    Azure account, 541
    deployment, 540
    publish complete, 547, 548
    publish profile, 545–547
    publish wizard, 541–545
Hot reload, 29
    .NET CLI, 30
    VS, 30, 31
HTML5, 2
HTML forms
    example form, 111
    <form>, 111, 112
    <input type="checkbox">, 113
    <input type="email">, 113
    <input type="password">, 113
    <input type="radio">, 113
    <input type="submit">, 113
    <input type="text">, 112
    <select>, 113
    <textarea> input, 113
HttpClient, 466–468, 470, 472, 474, 491
HttpClientJsonExtensions methods
    GetFromJsonAsync, 470–472
    IHttpClientFactory, 474
    JsonSerializerOptions, 473
    PostAsJsonAsync, 472, 473
HttpContext, 640
HubConnection, 505, 506
Hub on the server, SignalR
    BoardHub class, 502, 503
    cleaning up, 507, 508
    client, 506, 507
    configuring, 504, 505
Hybrid flow, 554

I

IAsyncDisposable interface, 507
IAsyncEnumerable interface, 195
Identity provider (IDP), 550, 555, 592
IdentityServer, 555, 556
IDisposable interface, 184, 194, 195, 211
IHttpClientFactory, 474–478, 615
IIdentity, 553
IJSRuntime, 500, 645
ImageService, 516
IMenuService, 173, 174
Immutable reference type, 655
@implements syntax, 194
Imports.razor file, 244, 620
IncrementCount method, 9, 28, 29, 69–71
InitSegments method, 506
INotifyPropertyChanged interface, 200
InputFileChangeEventArgs, 272
InputFile component
    add UploadFiles razor
        component, 268–270
    implement Server
        UploadService, 272–274
    implement WASM
        UploadService, 275–277
    OnChange event triggers, 268
Integration tests, 407
InteractiveServer render mode, 343
Interactivity, 331, 333, 335, 341–343, 345, 348, 349, 352, 354
Interface Definition Language
    (_IDL_), 510
Internet Information Services (IIS), 535, 540
Inversion-of-Control Container
    (IoCC), 154–157
InvokeAsync method, 91
IOrderService, 178, 179

675

INDEX

IPrincipal, 553
IQuerable<TGridItem>, 279
IReadOnlyList<TItem> interface, 207
Isolation Frameworks, 447
iss, 552
ItemList templated component, 237–240
ItemsProvider, 229
IUploadService interface, 268, 272
IWeatherService, 319, 463
IWeatherServiceFactory, 321

J

JavaScript, 1–3, 5, 8–11, 23, 24, 42, 75, 369, 376, 392, 402
    Blazor component, 388
    components, 381
    Counter component, 376
    ElementReference, 375
    function, 369
    functionality, 369
    HTML elements, 375
    IJSRuntime, 381
    ILocalStorage, 382
    interoperability, 369
    map provider, 394
    module mechanism, 387
    modules, 387
    .NET methods, 379
    static method, 379
    use, 387
    watch function, 379
JavaScript glue function
    Blazor project, 370
    Counter component, 372
    Counter's value, 374
    IJSRuntime, 372
    InvokeAsync method, 370

JavaScript libraries, 390, 391
JavaScript module, 388, 500, 501
JavaScript object, 398
jQuery, 65
JSInvokable attribute, 401
JsonNamingPolicy.CamelCase, 473
JsonSerializerOptions, 473
JSON Web Token (JWT), 551, 580, 590

K

Kestrel, 22

L

Lambda function, 71, 80, 107, 212, 213, 463, 521
Layout components, 24–26, 295, 296
    BlazorApp., 295
    Body parameter, 296
    Counter component, 298
    Home and Counter, 298
    _Imports.razor file, 299
    @layout component, 299
    @layout razor directive, 297
    MainLayout component, 296
    MainLayoutRight, 297
    NavMenu component, 300
    nested layout, 299, 300
    RouteView component, 296, 297
Lazy loading, 313, 315–316
LifeCycleDemo component, 181
Life cycle hooks, 181, 183
    asynchronous methods, 195
    component's constructor, 184
    IDisposable/IAsyncDisposable interface, 194–195
    IDisposable interface, 184

INDEX

@implements syntax, 181
LifeCycleDemo, 181–183
OnAfterRender and
    OnAfterRenderAsync
    methods, 193–194
OnInitialized and OnInitializedAsync
    methods, 189–190
OnParametersSet or
    OnParametersSetAsync, 185–189
SetParametersAsync method, 184
ShouldRender method, 190–193
LineSegments, 494, 501
ListView component, 212, 213
Loading component, 281
Local storage, 644–646, 648–651, 665
LocalStorage.cs service, 388
LocalStorageWithModule, 389
Logging for components
    Blazor Server, 61, 62
    Blazor Web application, 60
    Blazor WebAssembly, 61–63
    framework, 60
    home component, 61
    in Program.cs, 64
LoginDisplay component, 606
Long-term release (LTS) version, 13
<blink> and <marquee> elements, 1
<body> element, 254
<canvas> element, 249
<head> element, 254

M

Map component, 395, 400
Map JavaScript module, 392
MapLoginAndLogout method, 572
MapRazorComponents, 333, 334, 343,
    349, 351

Map's Markers parameter, 399
MarkupMatches method, 449
MeasurementService class, 223
Member class, 120, 121, 130
MemberForm component, 307
Menu component
    @code area, 103
    @code section, 101, 102
    converter function, 103
    converting a value with a converter
        function, 103
    @foreach loop, 102
    home component with, 104
    images folder, 103
    parameters, 104
    PizzaPlace application, 104
    Pizzas parameter, 101
    selected callback parameter, 103
    SpicinessImage method, 103
MenuServiceProxy class, 482
Message component, 233, 234
Microsoft.AspNetCore.Authorization, 619
Microsoft.AspNetCore.Components.
    WebAssembly.Authentication
    package, 606
Microsoft Fluent UI, 249
Middleware, 22
Mocha, 2
Mocks, 443
    car test, 443
    ILogger, 445, 446
    implementation, 448
    IWeatherService, 446
    UseWeatherService, 446
    Weather component, logging, 443, 445
    WeatherShould class, 446
Mono, 6–7
MouseButton enumeration, 498

677

INDEX

Mouse handling logic, 498–499
MouseMove event handling, 498
Mouse tracking, 498
MouseUp event handling method, 498
MudBlazor, 251, 252

N

Navigation interception
    ConfirmExternalNavigation, 310
    demo application, 310
    editContext.IsModified(), 311
    NavigationLock component, 310
    OnBeforeInternalNavigation, 310
NavigationManager class, 330, 569, 570
NavigationManager.BaseUri property, 312
NavLink class, 625, 628
NavLink components, 302, 303, 308, 338
NavMenu component, 300, 301, 384, 619, 621, 625, 628
    Layout folder, 300
nbf, 552
NestedLayout component, 299, 300
.NET 8 keyed services, 170, 171
.NET 9 constructor injection, 172
.NET APIs, 11
.NET CLI, 6, 18, 19
    hot reload, 30
.NET CLR, 13
.NET libraries, 33, 41–42, 387
.NET MAUI (Xamarin), 6
.NET methods, 379
NonVirtualizedMeasurements component, 224, 226
NonVirtualizedMeasurements.razor file, 226
NSubstitute
    arguments, 448

bUnit's dependency injection, 447
IWeatherService, 447
Log method, 448
mocks, 448
Nuget package, 447
Received method, 448
stubs, 447, 448
Nullable flag, 38, 40
Nullable reference
    apology, 36
    C#, 36–38
    null forgiving operator, 40
    NullReferenceException, 36
    required properties, 41
    types and .NET libraries, 41, 42
    using references, 39, 40
Null forgiving operator, 40
NullReferenceException, 38

O

Object Interaction Tests, 443
OnAfterRenderAsync method, 193–195, 381, 386, 500
OnAfterRender method, 193, 194
OnAfterRender/OnAfterRenderAsync method, 377
@on{EVENT} syntax, 69
One-way data binding, 65, 68
    attribute binding, 67–68
    component to DOM, 67
    conditional attributes, 68, 69
    counter page, 66, 67
    with Counter.razor, 66
    DOM, 65
    parent–child communication, 82–84
    syntax, 66–67
OnInitialized method, 189

OnInitializedAsync method, 174, 189, 190, 195, 366, 375, 376, 620
OnNavigateAsync, 316
OnParametersSetAsync method, 185-189, 195
OnParametersSet method, 185
OpenId Connect, 549, 553, 554, 563-566, 576, 584, 585, 601, 603, 609, 617, 622, 626, 629
Order DTO, 486
OrderMenuProxy class, 483, 486
Outlook Web Access (OWA), 2
OwningComponentBase class, 167-170

P

Page components, 307
@page directive, 49
PagedVirtualizedMeasurements, 230
PagedVirtualMeasurements, 228
PageTitle component, 256, 257
Parent-child communication
    delay component, 84-87, 90-92
    one-way data binding, 82-84
    two-way data binding, 87-90
Pascal casing, 655
PBAC, *see* Policy-based access control (PBAC)
PersistentAuthenticationStateProvider class, 635, 636
PersistentComponentState, 364, 365, 632, 635, 636
PersistingAuthenticationStateProvider class, 631-636
Pig-wig syntax, 215
PizzaInfo component, 327, 329
PizzaItem
    component, 235, 236, 327

PizzaPlace application, 234, 240, 321, 390, 397, 400
    add FluentValidation, 142-144
    add menu REST endpoint, 482
    add two-way data binding, 144, 145
    Blazor WebAssembly
        AddInteractiveWebAssembly Components method, 479
        update server project, 478
    CurrentPizza, 323
    Customer class, 138
    CustomerEntry component, 139, 140
    Customer property, State class, 138
    disable prerendering, 487, 488
    EditForm, CustomerEntry component, 140, 141
    Home component, 322
    HttpClient, MenuServiceProxy, 483
    implement MenuServiceProxy class, 484
    Loading UI, 488, 490
        CSS, 488
        hide, 489
        routes component hides, 490
    Menu and PizzaItem, 326
    MenuServiceProxy class, 482
    OrderMenuProxy class, 483
    parent component, 145-147
    PizzaItem component, 324
    placing the order, 485-487
    routing, 322
    shared project, 479-481
    ShowPizzaInformation, 326
    Singleton Pattern., 322
PizzaPlace single-page application
    classes represention, 97-99
    creation, 96, 97
    debugging, 105, 106

INDEX

PizzaPlace single-page application (*cont.*)
    features, 96
    menu component, 101–104
    ShoppingBasket, 98, 106–110
    State class, 98
    UI to shows the menu, 99–101
    @using statement, 100
    VS debugger, 99
PizzaPlace solution, 390
PKCE, *see* Proof Key for Code Exchange (PKCE)
PlaceOrder method, 178
Policy, 587, 597–601
Policy-based access control (PBAC), 597, 626–628
    add policy, 627–628
    update scopes, 626–627
PostAsJsonAsync, 472, 491
PowerShell command, 16, 31, 46
Prerendering, 361
    detecting, 363
    disable, 361
    supporting, 362, 363
preventDefault() method, 75
ProductService class, 158
ProductsService constructor, 155
Profile, 558, 559, 579, 580, 582, 583, 589, 609, 617, 623, 626
Program class, 22, 64, 157, 463, 479, 480, 556, 565, 587, 590, 592, 598, 600, 610, 616
Proof Key for Code Exchange (PKCE), 603–605, 609, 613, 614
PropertyColumn, 280
Property dependency injection, 155, 156
Protected Browser Storage, 650
ProtectedLocalStorage, 651, 652
ProtectedSessionStorage, 652

proto3 syntax, 513
Protocol buffers, 510
Proto files, 511–520
protoWeatherForecasts, 514
Public component libraries
    Ant Blazor, 254
    Blazor Bootstrap, 252, 253
    Blazorise, 253
    common styles, 249
    DevExpression Blazor, 254
    FluentUI components, 249, 250
    MudBlazor, 251, 252
    Radzen Blazor, 254
    SyncFusion Blazor UI, 254
    Telerik Blazor, 254
Pure function, 654
PutAsJsonAsync, 472, 473
PWListView component, 214, 215

Q

QuickGrid, 277
    add Filtered columns, 286–289
    add simple QuickGrid, 279–281
    add PaginationState, 290–291
    fix layout, 289–290
    Sort columns, 281–282
    Starter project, 277–279
    use TemplateColumn, 282–286
    Virtualize component, 291

R

Radzen Blazor Components, 254
Razor
    ASP.NET MVC, 43
    comments, 45
    component, 329, 395

INDEX

control structures, 44
directive attributes, 45, 46
directives, 45
HTML, 43
language, 43
library, 391
@ symbol, 44
Razor Pages, 561
Razor Template, 212
RBAC, *see* Role-based access control (RBAC)
Record, 655, 657, 660, 663
Reducer, 652, 654, 657–659, 662–665
Redux, 643, 652, 653, 659, 665
Reference type, 36, 37
Relying party, 550
RemoteAuthenticatorView, 606, 612–614
Remote Procedure Calls (_RPC_), 509, 510
    principles, 510
RemoveFromBasket method, 109
RenderComponent<Counter> method, 417
RenderFragment, 212, 213
@rendermode, 343–347, 350, 353, 354
RenderModeProvider
    AssignedRenderMode property, 360
    Home component, 359
    InteractiveServer, 360
    .NET 9, 360
    ServerStatic, 360
renderModeProvider.IsInteractive method, 364
Render modes, 331, 345, 351, 353–355
    AddRazorComponents, 333
    data-permanent attribute, 338
    Home component, 335
    MapRazorComponent, 333
    navigation and streaming, 334

    NavLink component, 338
    search box, 338
    SSR, 331
    streaming, 338, 339
    Weather component, 339
Render tree, 9, 10, 644
REST
    vs. gRPC, 523–526
Role-based access control (RBAC), 581, 620, 622–624, 629
    create claim component, 620–621
    enable RBAC, 622–624
    promote role claim, 624–625
Root-level cascading value, 204
RouteAttribute, 49
Route constraints
    corresponding .NET type, 306
    parameters, 306
Router component, 314, 316, 490
RouteView component, 304

S

Scoped CSS file, 58
_scoped_dependency, 160
Scoped lifetime, 170
Scoped objects, 179
Scope identifier, 59, 60
Search engine optimization (SEO), 331
Select server interactivity, 342
Self-contained deployment, 540
Semantic compare
    customization
        Card component, 458
        casing, regular expressions, 458, 459
        ignoring elements, 457
        razor tests, 457, 458
    formatting code, 456

INDEX

SendSegments method, 503, 506
SEO, *see* Search engine optimization (SEO)
Server project
   Client project, 464
   retrieve data
      emulate slow network, 469
      HttpClient, 466–468
   test data use during rendering, 466
   Weather component, 462, 463, 465, 466
   WeatherForecast class, 464, 465
   WeatherService class, 461
   WebAPI Endpoint, 463, 464
Server scalability, 11
Server Side Rendering (SSR), 308, 331, 351, 367
   and Forms, 340
Service contract, 513–515
Service object, 149
Session storage, 644, 648, 650
SetParametersAsync method, 184
Shared project, 479–481
ShoppingBasket class, 98
Shopping basket component
   @code section, 106
   Home component, 109, 110
   markup, 107, 108
   order, 110
   LINQ's Select, 107
   RemoveFromBasket method, 109
   StateChanged EventCallback<State> property, 109
   TotalPrice method, 109
   tuples, 106
   two-way data binding, 109
   ValueTuples, 107, 108
Shorter notation, 76
ShouldRender method, 190, 192, 193
ShowAlert, 83, 87

SignalR, 1, 10, 11, 17, 35, 341–343
   applications, 493
   dependencies, 504
   in desktop applications, 493
   HubConnection, 505, 506
   Hub on the Server, 502–505
   middleware, 504
   real-time applications, 493
   supporting browsers, 495
   WebSockets, 493
   whiteboard application, 494–502
   WhiteBoard component, 505
Single-page applications (SPAs), 1, 20, 293, 303, 336, 339–341
   advantages, 294
   dynamic pages, 293
   HTML file, 293
   JavaScript, 294
   web application, 294
   web page, 293, 294
Single Responsibility Principle, 43, 437
Singleton classes, 158
Singleton dependencies, 158, 159
Singleton lifetime, 170
Singleton objects, 179
Socket exhaustion, 475
SomeComponent component, 200, 202
Source generator, 47
SPAs, *see* Single-page applications (SPAs)
Spiciness class, 97
Spiciness.Spicy, 473
SSR, *see* Server Side Rendering (SSR)
Stack-based virtual machine, 5
StateHasChanged, 81, 82, 87, 90
State Verification Tests, 442
Static resources, 245–247
Store, 644–646, 649, 650, 652–656, 658–662, 664, 665

INDEX

Streamed rendering, 354, 357, 358
Streaming rendering, 338–339, 341
Stubs, 441
    car test, 441
    implementation, 447, 448
    IWeatherService, 441
    UseWeatherService, 442, 443
    WeatherServiceStub class, 442
Styling components
    App.razor file, 58
    and child components, 60
    CSS isolation, 58–60
sub, 552
SubmitClicked EventCallback, 146
Submit method, 116, 340
Swagger, 586
SyncFusion Blazor UI Components, 254
SynchronizationContext, 80
System.ComponentModel.DataAnnotations, 120
System.Security.Claims, 620
System.Threading.Timer, 86

T

Token, 549–552
Telerik Blazor, 254
TemplateColumn, 280, 282, 283
Templated components, 205
    BlazorApp.Components.Templated, 205
    generic type constraints, 211–212
    Grid<TITem> component, 206
    Grid templated component, 207–211
    RenderFragment, 212–213
    Row parameter, 207
    templated grid component, 206
    TItem type parameter, 211
tight-coupling, 150

Timestamp type, 514
TItem type parameter, 211
ToClaimsPrincipal, 633
ToggleAlert method, 53, 85–87
ToJson method, 106
Transient, 159
Transient dependencies, 159, 160
Transient lifetime, 170
Transient objects, 179
Trusted party, 550
TryTakeFromJson method, 367
tuples, 106
Two-way data binding, 65, 71, 73, 74, 87, 88, 92, 109, 110
    @bind-{NameOfProperty} syntax, 87
    component to component, 87
    DismissibleAlert class, 88
    explicit binding, 73, 74
    parameters, 88
    Show parameter, 87
    Show property, 89
    syntax, 71–73
    UpdateShow, 89, 90
Two-way explicit binding, 73, 74

U

Unit tests, 406
    bUnit, 415
        Counter component, 415, 416
        CounterShould class, 416, 417
        Find method, 418
        MarkupMatches method, 417
        phases, 420
        projects, 408
        RenderCorrectlyWithInitialZero, 416
        RenderParagraphCorrectlyWithInitialZero method, 418

INDEX

Unit tests (cont.)
    Semantic Compare, 417, 418
    TestContext class, 416
    test output, 417, 418
  cascading parameters, 435, 437
  command, 407
  component interaction
    Counter component, 419
    Find method, 420
    MouseTracker project, 420
    MouseTrackerShould class, 420, 421
  debugger, 414
  debugging, 411
  directory, 407
  expectional cases, 413, 414
  failure, 414
  methods, 409, 410
  overflow checking, 414
  pass parameters to component
    failiure test message, 424
    nameof operator, 424, 425
    RenderComponent method, 422
    string argument, 423
    xUnit's Theory, 423
    TwoWayCounter component, 421, 422
    TwoWayCounterShould class, 422, 423
    xUnit's Theory, 424
  phases, 409
  razor, 449
  RenderFragment
    AddChildContent, 429, 430
    Add<ListItem, string>, 435
    Alert component, 427
    AlertShould class, 427–429
    arguments, 435
    C# compiler, 428
    ChildContent, 428, 429
    Enumerable.passing, 433
    Enumerable.Repeat method, 432
    ItemContent parameter, 432, 433
    ListItem parameter, 434
    parameters, 432
    raw strings, 427
    RenderItemsCorrectly method, 434, 435
    templated components, 430, 431
    testing, 432
    TwoWayCounter, 429
  run, 410–412
  setup, 406
  Square method, 411
  test project file, 407, 408
  theories, 412, 413
  two-way data binding and events, 425–427
  xUnit, 407
UpdateCounter method, 380
UploadFiles component, 268–270
UploadFiles.razor.css file, 270
URL, 644, 649–651, 665
User Consent, 563, 564
UserInfo class, 632, 633, 635, 636
UseStaticFiles method, 22
@using, 54, 55
Utils class, 409

V

V8, 3
ValidateEmail method, 132
Validation
  Blazor (see Blazor validation)
  custom (see Custom validation)
  disable the Submit button

disabled attribute, 136
  EditContext class, 136, 137
  explicit validation, 137
  MemberFormFluen, 136
 FluentValidation, 133–135
ValueTuples, 107, 108
Value types, 36, 37
View and view model, 56–57
View model, 56
Virtualization, 222
  add paging to
    MeasurementsService, 227–231
  NonVirtualizedMeasurements
    component, 224, 226
Virtualize component, 226, 227, 291
VirtualizedMeasurements component,
    227, 230
VirtualMeasurements component, 228
Visual Studio Code (VSC), 9, 13, 15, 16, 20,
    26, 31, 34, 511
  debugging, 28, 29
Visual Studio (VS), 13, 14, 16–20, 26, 28,
    31, 37, 38
  debugging, 26, 28
  hot reload, 30, 31

W, X, Y, Z

WASM client application
  create and examine
    application, 606–609
  customize login and logout
    process, 612–613
  implement authentication, 609–611
  login process, 613–614
  register, 608–609
WASM PersistentAuthenticationState
    Provider, 635

WASMSingletonService, 163
WASMTransientService, 163
WASMUploadService, 275
WASMUsingServices, 163
WeatherAPI
  add Client-Side Authorization, 619
  AuthorizationMessageHandler,
    618–619
  fetch forecasts, 615–617
Weather component, 195, 208, 318, 320,
    338, 339, 345, 462, 465, 466, 511
WeatherForcastService class, 615, 616
WeatherForecast class, 464, 465, 513, 616
WeatherForecastController's Get method,
    594, 595, 601, 616, 628
WeatherForecast.proto, 511
Weather link, 336
WeatherService class, 461, 468, 523, 524,
    631, 637, 641
WeatherServiceProxy class, 467, 474, 475
WebAPI Endpoint, 463, 464
WebAssembly (WASM), 1, 6, 10, 11, 16, 22,
    23, 26, 31–33, 42
  application's code, 5
  binary format, 5
  Blazor, 7, 9, 11
  browser supports, 6
  to C++ applications, 5
  execution process, 3, 4
  Google Earth, 4
  Just-In-Time compiled, 3
  and Mono, 6, 7
  official site, 5
  runtime, 12
  Windows 2000 operating
    system, 5
Web development, 14
WebSockets, 35, 344, 493

INDEX

Whiteboard application
    in action, 508
    App component, 497
    board component, 495, 496
    LineSegment, 494, 495
    mouse handling logic, 498–499
    paint segments, 499–502
    PowerShell script, 494
    WebAssembly, 494
Wig-pig syntax, 215–216
Windows Communication Foundation (WCF), 510
    NetTcpBinding in, 510
wwwroot folder, 245